SECURITY ARRANGEMENTS IN THE PERSIAN GULF

SECURITY ARRANGEMENTS IN THE PERSIAN GULF

With Special Reference to Iran's Foreign Policy

MAHBOUBEH F. SADEGHINIA

SECURITY ARRANGEMENTS IN THE PERSIAN GULF
With Special Reference to Iran's Foreign Policy

Published by
Ithaca Press
8 Southern Court
South Street
Reading
RG1 4QS
UK

www.ithacapress.co.uk
www.twitter.com/Garnetpub
www.facebook.com/Garnetpub
www.garnetpub.wordpress.com
www.thelevant.wordpress.com

Ithaca Press is an imprint of Garnet Publishing Ltd.

Copyright © Mahboubeh F. Sadeghinia 2011

All rights reserved.
No part of this book may be reproduced in any form or by any electronic or mechanical means, including information storage and retrieval systems, without permission in writing from the publisher, except by a reviewer who may quote brief passages in a review.

First Edition 2011

ISBN-13: 978-0-86372-369-8

British Library Cataloguing-in-Publication Data
A catalogue record for this book is available from the British Library

Jacket design by Garnet Publishing
Typeset by Samantha Barden

Printed in Great Britain by the
MPG Books Group, Bodmin and King's Lynn

To my children, Sadegh, Abbas and Zeinab

Contents

List of Tables, Figures and Maps	ix
List of Abbreviations	xi
Definitions	xiii
Foreword	xv
Introduction	xvii

PART I
GEOPOLITICS OF THE PERSIAN GULF

1	Geography and resources of the Persian Gulf	3
2	The European Union and Persian Gulf energy security	15
3	Asian-Pacific Region and Persian Gulf energy security	29
4	Threats to Persian Gulf energy security	45

PART II
SECURITY IN THE PERSIAN GULF: TYPES AND NATURES OF INSECURITY FACTORS

5	Territorial, boundary and maritime disputes in the Persian Gulf	65
6	The Arabian Peninsula states of the Persian Gulf: The GCC	95
7	Iraq	123
8	Iran's security threats and challenges	157
9	Final conclusion: shape of security arrangements in the Persian Gulf	217

Selected bibliography	273
Index	277

Map of the Middle East and its sub-region of the Persian Gulf

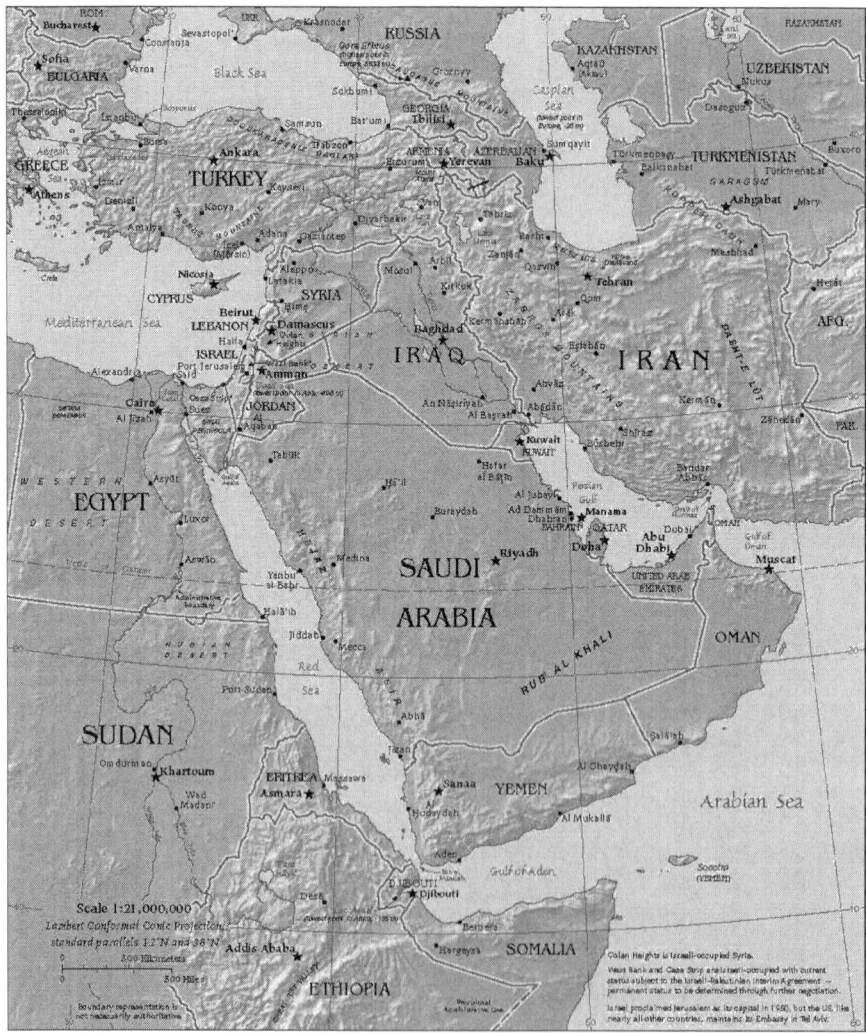

Source: University of Texas Libraries

Tables, Figures and Maps

TABLES
2.1	Energy supply indicators, EU and accession countries	18
2.2	Total primary energy consumption by energy type (per cent of total consumption), 2002	19
2.3	Caspian Sea region oil and natural gas reserves	24
4.1	Share of Iranian imports by source traditional suppliers	57
4.2	Iran's export product array product	57
9.1	Security models	220
9.2	The balance of power between the three regional powers	249
9.3	Possible stabilisation measures (–2003)	250

FIGURES
A	Geopolitical views of the world: Mackinder, Spykman and Cohen	xxvi
B	Persian Gulf's oil and gas as a percentage of world (2006)	xxvi
C	World crude oil reserves, 1980–2006	xxvii
D	PG oil exports by route, 2002	xxvii
E	Flow map of world crude oil, regarding the Strait of Hormuz, 2010	xxviii
F	The Pyramid Security Model	xxxvii
1.1	The oil corridor	10
1.2	Major oil fields of the Middle East	10
2.1	US crude oil imports by source	16
2.2	World energy consumption, 2001	18
2.3	Net oil imports from the PG as a percentage of total net oil imports	23

3.1	China's oil production and consumption, 1980–2003	30
3.2	India's oil production and consumption, 1990–2006	34
5.1	Evolution of territorial limits and claims in southern and south-eastern Arabia, 1903–1955	74
5.2	Evolution of delimited state territory in northern Arabia, 1913 to the present day	75
5.3	The contemporary framework in southern Arabia	76
5.4	a: Ancient Iran, 728 BCE–CE 640; Medes (Mâdhâ) Dynasty, 728–550 BCE	81
	b: Achaemenid (Hakhâmaneshiyân) Dynasty, 550–330 BCE	81
	c: Parthian (Ashkâniân) Dynasty, 247 BCE–CE 224	82
	d: Sasanid (Sâsâniân) Dynasty, CE 224–640	82
	e: Safavid Empire AD 1501–1722	83
	f: Afsharid Dynasty AD 1736–1802	83
5.5	Iran today	84
6.1	Cumulative Saudi Arabian arms imports relative to those of the other Persian Gulf states: 1986–1999	107
6.2	Comparative military expenditures of the PG powers as a percentage of GNP: 1989–1999	108
6.3	Saudi Arabia's oil production and consumption, 1980–2006	110
6.4	Share of OPEC net oil export revenues for selected countries, 1972–2006	110
7.1	Kurdish- and Shiite-dominated areas in Iraqi oil resources and facilities	128
7.2	Iraq's land-locked location	133
8.1	Islamic Republic of Iran's power chart	165
9.1	The Pyramid Security Model	258

MAP
Map of the Middle East and its sub-region of the Persian Gulf   viii

Abbreviations

AP	Asian-Pacific
APEC	Asia-Pacific Economic Cooperation
bbl/d	Barrels per day
CBM	Confidence-building Measures
CIA	Central Intelligence Agency
EIA	Energy Information Administration
EU	European Union
GCC	Gulf Cooperation Council
GDP	Gross Domestic Product
GME	Greater Middle East
ICJ	International Court of Justice
IAEA	International Atomic Energy Agency
IEA	International Energy Agency
IMF	International Monetary Fund
IR	International Relations
IRGC	Islamic Revolutionary Guard Corps
IRI	Islamic Republic of Iran
IRP	Islamic Republic Party
mb/d	Million barrels per day
ME	Middle East
MENA	Middle East and North Africa
MODAFL	Ministry of Defence and Armed Forces Logistics
MOU	Memorandum Of Understanding
NATO	North Atlantic Treaty Organisation
OECD	Organisation for Economic Cooperation and Development
OPEC	Organisation of Petroleum Exporting Countries
PG	Persian Gulf
RDF	Rapid Development Force (US)
RRF	Rapid Reaction Force (EU)
SANG	Saudi Arabia National Guard
SAVAK	National Security and Information Organisation (Iran)

SIS (Britain)	Secret Intelligence Service
TCF	Trillion Cubic Feet
UAE	United Arab Emirates
UN	United Nations
US	United States of America
USSR	Union of Soviet Socialist Republics
WMDs	Weapons of mass destructions
WTO	World Trade Organisation
WWI	First World War
WWII	Second World War

Definitions

1) The **Persian Gulf**, a semi-enclosed sea in the Southwest Asian region, is in the inferior folds of the southern Zagros Mountains and is an extension of the Indian Ocean that is situated between Iran and the Arabian Peninsula. Eight countries with a coastline on the PG are Iran, Iraq, Kuwait, Saudi Arabia, Bahrain, Qatar, United Arab Emirates and Oman.

2) **Security system** has been defined, as Michael Kraig expresses it, "to create a stable and peaceful structure of relationships that allows every state to meet its minimum security needs and develop its economy and political institutions without at the same time increasing the level of threat toward its neighbours".[1]

3) Regularly, terms such as **international system, international political system, international politics, international affairs**, and **world politics**, have been used as synonyms for **international relations (IR)**.

4) **Geostrategy** has been defined as a subfield of geopolitics which refers to foreign policy based on geographical factors and a desire for the control of foreign geographic resources. As Zbigniew Brzezinski explains, "Geostrategy is the geographic direction of a state's foreign policy. More precisely, geostrategy describes where a state concentrates its efforts by projecting military power and directing diplomatic activity."[2] Therefore, geostrategic region has been used to define those geographical locations with such features.

5) **Hegemony** is defined as power, control or influence exercised by a leading state over other states.[3] It is a concept that has been used as

a strategy of the US, based on: an imbalance of power and interests, the use of both offensive and defensive threats, and a network of friends and allies who greatly share the US' foreign policy goals.

6) **Geopolitics** in a simple way means studying the role of geography in politics, or as Pirouz Mojtahed-Zadeh notes, it "deals with the geographical dispersion of power in the world and the study of structural relations among them". Therefore, geopolitical region refers to those geographical locations with such affect. See Pirouz Mojtahed-Zadeh, *Security and territoriality in the Persian Gulf* (Richmond, Surrey: Curzon Press, 1999), 3.

7) In general a **balance of power** signifies parity or stability between competing forces; as a term in international law it also expresses intention to prevent any one nation from becoming strong enough to compel the others to obey its political agenda.

8) **Grand strategy** is military strategy at the level of movement and use of an entire nation-state or empire's resources.

Foreword

The intention of this book is to provide a conceptual and analytical foundation for a discussion about the future shape of security arrangements in the Persian Gulf. The Persian Gulf is a region whose strategic and economic characteristics have strengthened its vital significance to all littoral states as well as the entire world's economy and political life. Its significant geopolitical situation, in addition to its dominant position as an energy source and gateway for global energy, has caused this region to be a worthy rival to outside powers, particularly the West, while also being the most unstable and chaotic of any world region.

Therefore the objective of this study has been to provide a security model for the Persian Gulf that addresses the need for a stable and peaceful structure of relationships which will provide security for all individual littoral states, as well as assuring the interests of the external powers.

The study's hypothesis of cooperation as the only possible basis for a comprehensive strategy for peace and stability in this region has been substantiated by employing a variety of conceptual and analytical tools to understand the reasons for the failure of security models in the Persian Gulf and to confront the huge obstacles to a security system for this region. The relevance of this model is supported by the modern global political landscape, most especially the events that have occurred since the end of the Cold War, in addition to various successful cooperation models that are to be found in other regions of the globe, e.g. the European Union (EU). This is assisted by the unprecedented opportunity for regional cooperation and the conditions for the creation of new security arrangements in the Persian Gulf and beyond that have been created since the downfall of Saddam Hussein's regime in 2003, which was one of the major elements of insecurity in this region.

To this end, this study has analysed various security models in this significant geopolitical region of the world since 1962, with special reference to Iran's foreign policy. Particular reference has been made to Iran because of its geostrategic and geopolitical situation and because, as the hegemonic power in the Persian Gulf, regardless of its political regimes, it has great national and security concerns and plays a determinant role in the peace and security of the region.

With emphasis on dialogue as the best solution to the regional security problems in the Persian Gulf, this study has come up with the Pyramid Security Model on the basis of the region's geopolitical realities which emphasise the need for domestic reforms as well as interaction and cooperation and a balance of interests between all regional and non-regional players.

The bulk of the research for this monograph was completed in late 2007. To the extent practicable, the author has updated descriptions of major events and conditions described throughout the monograph through early 2009.

NOTES

1 Michael Kraig (Fall 2004), "Assessing Alternative Security Frameworks for the Persian Gulf", *Middle East Policy*, Washington: vol. 11, issue 3, cited in the site of *Gulf 2000* of Columbia University, NY, USA.
2 Zbigniew Brzezinski, *The Grand Chessboard: American Primacy and Its Geostrategic Imperatives*. (New York: Basic Books, 1997), 40, cited in *Wikipedia*, http://en.wikipedia.org/wiki/Geostrategic#_note-1 (3 November 2007).
3 Oxford University Press, www.oup.com/uk/orc/bin/9780199281954/01student/flashcards/glossary.htm (accessed 11 June 2008).

Introduction

The Persian Gulf (PG) is one of the most significant geopolitical regions in the world as well as the main dominant energy source and gateway for global energy. This region is of vital significance to all littoral states as well as the entire world economy and political life. Considering such significance – which has caused the PG to be a worthy rival to outside powers, particularly the West, as well being the most unstable and chaotic of any world region – requires close scrutiny of the important geopolitical elements and security concerns and systems in this region.

Persian Gulf Security Arrangements, With Special Reference to Iran's Foreign Policy has employed a variety of conceptual and analytical tools to understand the reasons for the failure of security models in the PG and to confront the huge obstacles to a security system for this region. The perceptions of what constitutes a threat to regional security varies among the Arabs, Iranians and the ultra-regional powers, and all accordingly have different solutions to what they perceive as the problem. Nevertheless, regardless of the relevant parties' differences of opinion, all the consequent issues along with three decades of crises in the PG illustrate how urgent it is for the problem regarding regional security to be resolved.

The approach in this book chosen to provide a foundation for a discussion about the future shape of security arrangements in the PG focuses on historical analysis and is theoretical. It aims to address the need for a stable and peaceful structure of relationships that provides security for all individual littoral states, as well as assuring the interests of the external powers. The methodology adopted to conduct this research uses theories of geopolitics and of security, and draws upon the level of analysis framework in international relations to the foreign policies of select PG states and the forces that affected them. As it will be explained in the following chapters, it presents a conceptual framework of important works of literature related to the security issues of the PG.

The issue of security will be studied from a combination of different perspectives – political, social, military, economic, geopolitical and international – all of which affect security in this region. This is the reason this research tries to study relations between these factors as different variables relevant to modelling security in the region.

The context of the discussion is the period 1962–1997, but some analysis is given of geopolitical and security developments since 1997 in order to support the analysis of the period of primary focus and to provide a warning about the impact of further policies of regional and non-regional players on the security of the region. The reason for focusing on this period of time is that it highlights the following points that are relevant to the study.

1) The fundamental and significant role of Iran in any security approach in this region: Iran's significant role in regional political evolutions and Tehran's national and security concerns, regardless of the nature of its political regime in the country at any one time. For this reason, throughout the entire study Iran's role in various events is given close attention. Following an empirical analysis of external threats and Iran's recent trends in its foreign relations, especially concerning the security of the PG in relation to key countries including the Great Powers and its PG neighbours, 1962 marks the beginning of Tehran's increasing interest in regional issues of the PG. The failures and successes in the period leading up to 1997 of Iran's policy towards the PG will be divided into three different phases of the pre- and post-revolution era and within both the bipolar and unipolar system of international system.

2) The prevailing application of the traditional policy is that "to dominate a region it is necessary to weaken regional powers": the crucial position of the PG in world politics, and the geostrategic situation of Iran, encouraged Britain and later the US to establish domination over Iran and the PG. For this reason Iran's efforts to establish power in the PG were totally unacceptable to and annulled by Britain. It severely vetoed every action, measure, or proposal by Iran to establish a navy for security in the PG. Moreover, the US only accepted Iran's superiority in the region when Tehran was acting as a US proxy. Instead, during their dominance these two major ultra-regional powers continued their military superiority in the region in order to prevent any other countries gaining control over the region and its mass energy resources, and

also to maintain their military access to the geostrategic region of the PG, thereby allowing them to control events in many other significant regions of the world. In addition, the old excuse given by Britain for preventing Iran from gaining power in the PG, i.e. its uncertainty about "what Iran's intentions might be" – e.g. when Nasereddin Shah Qajar tried in 1865 to form a navy and his request for British help was rejected – was also used by the US, especially regarding Iran's nuclear plans since 2003. This important historical political fact is highly suggestive of the strategy of the major powers in the region.

3) The increased militarisation in the region, together with the belief that for political survival or to ensure strategic interest, a back-up military power is a necessity. The US' direct military involvement in the PG has resulted in competing reactions from emerging powers with interests in this region viz., China, the EU and Russia. This is to secure their strategic interests by gaining extensive access to PG security and adopting a greater geopolitical role in this waterway, and also because of their deep concerns over US permanent hegemony in the ME/PG. The US military presence has also stimulated popular discontent in the host countries, particularly against Arab regimes. This situation has resulted in increasing militarism, whether in the form of extending the military presence and power of different regional and non-regional parties, directly or indirectly, or in the form of terrorist attacks.

4) The importance of a proper relationship between the US and Iran for any durable security approach in this region. The study argues that establishing peace and security would be impossible without such a relationship between these two major players. In addition to the need to construct comprehensive multilateral coalitions, the argument is made that it is important to recognise the significance of the relationship between major regional and non-regional powers in order to achieve a durable and long-term security situation in any region. In this regard the study focuses particularly on the major regional and ultra-regional powers with the most influence over any security approaches; the major topic of analysis is the behaviour of Iran and the US. This study is necessary owing to the failure of all security models in the PG during the time period of this study. Also, the vast and extended regional and global consequences of

regional crises combined with the increasing complexity of methods of competition, specifically the more frequent resort to military solutions with more sophisticated weapons rather than to diplomacy or socio-economic cooperation. Hence, under such circumstances, achieving even remotely stable security is increasingly difficult.

5) The noticeable double standards of the international system due to the huge influence of the Great Powers, particularly the US, to protect their own interests, had a great influence on the security of this region during the period covered by this study. Such an international political system which applies different criteria could coerce some states into pursuing a dangerous policy to achieve their foreign policy goals. In studying Iraq's behaviour it is possible to show a complete turnabout of attitudes from the international countries: from offering aid to open hostility.

This study has taken advantage of a great variety of secondary sources of historical, analytical data, as well as some primary documents such as interviews and also various Iranian Foreign Ministry documents. Moreover, detailed primary source material accumulated from the author's experiences during 1980–2003 as a journalist and also political researcher in Iran has been followed up through discussion with the key actors. In addition to advice, comments and the assistance of prominent scholars in the field of PG issues such as Anoush Ehteshamin, Keith McLachlan, Richard Schofield and Mahmood Sariolghalam, I had the opportunity to take advantage of honest and friendly talks, discussions and interviews with different high-ranking Iranian authorities as well as many elites and scholars in the Arabian Peninsula who assisted me, these being an important factor in helping me to gain a better and deeper understanding of various issues and concerns in the PG. I also had the opportunity to travel to most of the region's countries and to live from 1985 to 1987 in Bandar Abbas, capital of Hormozgan Province on the southern coast of Iran, which occupies a strategic position on the narrow Strait of Hormuz and is the location of the main base of the Iranian Navy. Having the opportunity to visit and study various areas, and talk and socialise with the inhabitants of Hormozgan in my several visits to different cities and villages, as well as to the islands – including Abu Musa, Hormuz, Larak, Qeshm and Hengam – helped me to better understand the lifestyles and original and natural interrelations between the inhabitants of the southern and northern side of the PG. It also assisted me to gain a clearer comprehension about the geographical dimensions of various islands in respect to their significant location regarding security issues in such a geostrategic waterway.

Geopolitical approach

This study focuses on debates surrounding geopolitics to provide a more comprehensive understanding of the significance of the PG as a sub-system of the ME and its impact on the politics of the region. The intention is not to discuss different kinds of geopolitical schools of thought as power knowledge but rather to highlight the effect of the natural geographical location of the PG on power struggles in international politics. A further aim is to examine the foreign policy goals of the Great Powers and to be able to predict more accurately political developments in the region. One of the outcomes of this study is to emphasise the necessity of having a geopolitical vision of the regional states in the PG to be able to understand their significant situation in balance-of-power politics and to be able to take advantage of various opportunities resulting from geopolitical developments in their best interests as well as that of the region's security and stability. Geopolitical discourse typically provides us with an explanation of relationships between geography, power and international relations. Here, the idea of geopolitics as a key to develop a security model in this region is drawn from many geopoliticians' definitions, such as those of the two prominent scholars referred to below.

Gearóid Ó Tuathail
The conventional understanding today is that geopolitics is discourse about world politics, with a particular emphasis on state competition and the geographical dimensions of power.[1]

Ezzatolah Ezzati
Geopolitics means understanding the realities of geographical environment to achieve power, through being able to involve in great level of global games and to secure national and vital interests. In other words, geopolitics

means knowledge about relationships within a geographical environment and discerning their effect on the political fate of nations.²

Non-regional states' geopolitical intention
Emphasis on debates enclosing geopolitics is to be found throughout the whole study to support the discussion about the rivalries and foreign policy goals of the Great Powers in the region, in particular the US in regard to the significance of Iran's geopolitical situation. What is obvious is that, despite various concepts of geopolitics in different historical periods and structures of world order in the twentieth and twenty-first centuries (viz. imperialist geopolitics, Cold War geopolitics, new world order geopolitics, environmental geopolitics, and anti-geopolitics; including definitions ranging from geopolitics as an unproblematic description of the world political map to a culturally and politically varied way of describing, representing and writing about geography and international politics – critical geopolitics), as Ó Tuathail notes, geopolitics as a shape of "power/knowledge", which was obviously responsible for many chauvinist, racist and imperialist ideologies in the first half of the twentieth century, and which supported oppressive European colonial empires that assumed a white supremacy hypothesis and imperialist interventionism (a process which resulted in WWII), did not disappear after WWII. Geopolitics is still a very popular discourse, especially in respect of the later years of the Cold War, where it has been used to explain the global rivalry between the US and the USSR for control over the states and strategic resources and wealth of the world, and the basic and dynamic theoretical role of geopoliticians to politicians to extend such power/knowledge.³

An important point is that geopolitical debates are still being used as both theory and practice, just as they were during the Cold War. Compared to the imperialist geopolitics of the beginning of the twentieth century when physical geography had a determining influence on foreign policy and global strategy, in Cold War geopolitics geography was entwined closely with ideology in descriptions of US–Soviet antagonism. So, as Ó Tuathail notes, "The very geographical terminology used to describe the world map was also a description of ideological identity and difference." During the Cold War, the West was more than a geographical region and US leaders viewed their state as leading the "free world" with democratic regimes and the highest standards of civilisation and development, in a crusade against "evil". The USSR was never simply a territory, but was represented by the West as a constantly expanding threat. The continuity of this geopolitical debate and how US statesmen conceptualised the role of their state in world affairs, which intensified after 11 September 2001 (9/11), can be seen through the US terminology used. Instead of "the evil empire" used by Ronald Reagan to describe the USSR, George W. Bush's terminology for the official enemies of the US in 2002 was the "axis of evil", an axis which includes Iraq, Iran and North Korea. As Ó Tuathail notes,

> Hostility to collective action against the long term degradation of the planet by the occupants of the White House is not new (…). What is new, from their point of view, is the global war against terrorism that began when terrorists attacked the World Trade Center and Pentagon (…) a new post-September 11 era that marked the end of the post-Cold War era. The US president declared the United States at war and the phrase "global war on terror" became so ubiquitous within the US government that it earned a bureaucratic acronym: GWOT. (…) [The] illegal action [of invading Iraq in 2003] and the general unilateralism of the Bush administration produced a significant rift in transatlantic relations. (…) But GWOT and the Iraq war has been good for certain groups within the United States. The US Department of Defense budget is at a record level and it remains the most powerful bureaucracy within the US state. US defense contractors, some with strong ties to the White House, are cashing in on the swelling appropriations. And, despite dangerously low popularity ratings, George W. Bush was able to use his self-appointed status as a "wartime president" to win a close re-election battle in November 2004. Bush's Republican Party also made electoral gains, leaving it in control of both the Congress and White House. GWOT, in short, has been very good for the GOP (the Grand Old Party, the nickname for the US Republican Party).[4]

In the context of this geopolitical discourse, it is not unlikely that Washington has a plan invade Iran, as the other "axis of evil" state. In this respect, the work of geopoliticians such as Mahan (1890), Mackinder (1904) or Spykman (1944) about geopolitical significance of the ME/PG region and, particularly, the great influence of their theme of imperial expansionism in a variety of ways on the Great Powers' geopolitical expansion, have been briefly presented to enrich the subject of study.

Their views, which have been used by US politicians, were all focused on the containment of the USSR to prevent it from dominating the Eurasian marginal crescent. Halford Mackinder, restating the importance of land power as a response to the sea power doctrine of Alfred Mahan being the first necessary condition for global power, described part of the Russian land mass as the "heartland", a geographical and territorial region. In Mackinder's view, competing for authority in a marginal crescent to which the maritime powers have approachability, the Mediterranean and Middle East were key regions in the conflict.

Nicholas John Spykman's great influence on US policy since WWII advocated that the US should adopt policies that would promote American influence in the marginal crescent, which he called "the rimland", or at least try to keep the USSR away from controlling or seizing them. He believed the rimland is more important than Mackinder's heartland and also argued that the balance of power in Eurasia directly affected US security. The rimland's defining characteristic is that it is an intermediate region, lying between the heartland and the marginal sea powers. It includes the European Continent (except the USSR) and Central Asia, Iran, Iraq, Saudi Arabia, Afghanistan, India, the southeast of Asia, China, Korea and Siberia. He noted that all these lands as the amphibious buffer zone between the land powers and sea powers must defend themselves from both sides, and therein lie their fundamental security problems. Spykman believed that whoever controls the rimland rules Eurasia, and whoever rules Eurasia commands the world. Evidence of the vital geographical location of the rimland for Washington is seen in the US military strategy at the end of the twentieth century. As Ezzati notes, the US has three defence positions in the world: first the USA, second Western Europe and third the PG.[5]

However, Drysdale and Blake's opinion in 1985 regarding lack of validity in the ideas of the heartland (Mackinder) and rimland (Spykman), and the struggle between land power and sea power to secure control of the marginal states in the modern world for different reasons – including more developed military technology – except for the ME rimland, is still credible, as the ME still has a key strategic role in the global power struggle, besides concerns over access to its energy resources.[6]

The view of Saul Bernard Cohen, who suggested a more dynamic and less controversial scheme of world geostrategic regions, will also be drawn upon. The general view of the geopolitical world that Cohen provides is more dynamic than the previous model of a bipolarised world because of his concerns about the emergence of "second order" powers in the world political hierarchy system, e.g. Europe, China and Japan, and also regional powers such as Iran, Nigeria and India with the potential for regional authority and infiltration. In contrast to Mackinder, who surveys the globe as a "closed" political space,[7] Cohen believes that the space is not united strategically, but a fundamentally divided world is a composition of a number of separate areas and so the overall picture of the geopolitical world is a multiple power-node world with many overlapping areas with influence. Similar to the others, in his theory the ME is defined as a crucial contact zone between Eurasia and the maritime world.

Interestingly, Iran's situation in various geopolitical theories as shown in Figure A is very significant. This situation arises because of the country's connection to free seas through the PG and Oman Sea. In addition to Iran's passage situation, its northern parts are embedded in the heartland in addition to Iran's plateau, which is positioned in the rimland's heartland.

In addition to the fact that the PG contains 55 per cent of proven world oil reserves (see Figures B and C), about 93 per cent of the PG oil exported travels through the Strait of Hormuz, with Iran controlling it (see Figures D and E). This is besides the fact that Iran is the second largest OPEC (Organisation of the Petroleum Exporting Countries) oil producer and has the second highest natural gas reserves in the world.

A recent model of the emerging world order has been discussed by the American neoconservative political scientist Samuel Huntington (1993), namely the "clash of civilizations" as a dominant factor in future global politics. While emphasising the continuation of nation-states' position as the most powerful actors in world politics, he also claimed that culture will be the dominant source of conflict and an element in divisions between nations and groups of different civilisations in the future. In his opinion the most fundamental of such clashes is the conflict between the West and the Rest of the World.[8]

Emphasising the importance of democratic organisations and institutions of authority, especially the military, he believes that organisation was the path to political power, and so notes that "in the modernizing world he controls the future who organises its politics", criticising *détente*

FIGURE A
Geopolitical views of the world: Mackinder, Spykman and Cohen

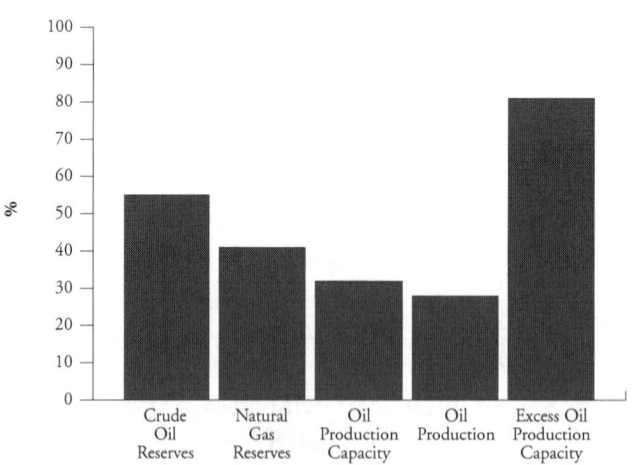

Source: Drysdale and Blake[9], by permission of *Oxford University Press, Inc.*

FIGURE B
Persian Gulf's oil and gas as a percentage of world (2006)

Sources: *Oil and Gas Journal* and *EIA* Short Term Energy Outlook

INTRODUCTION

FIGURE C
World crude oil reserves, 1980–2006

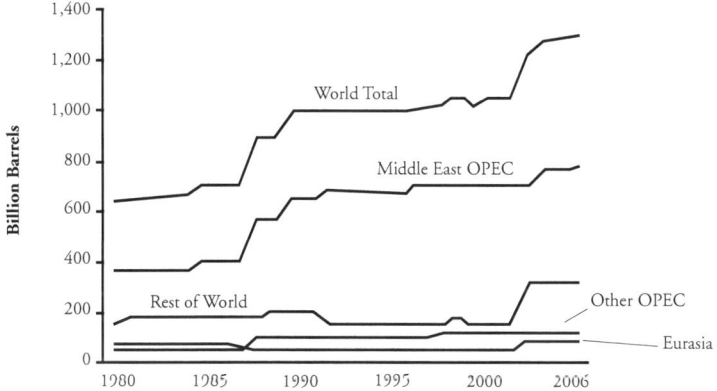

Source: 1980–1993: "Worldwide Oil and Gas at a Glance", *International Petroleum Encyclopedia* (Tulsa, OK: PennWell Publishing, various issues); 1994–2006: *Oil & Gas Journal* (various issues)

FIGURE D
Persian Gulf oil exports by route, 2002

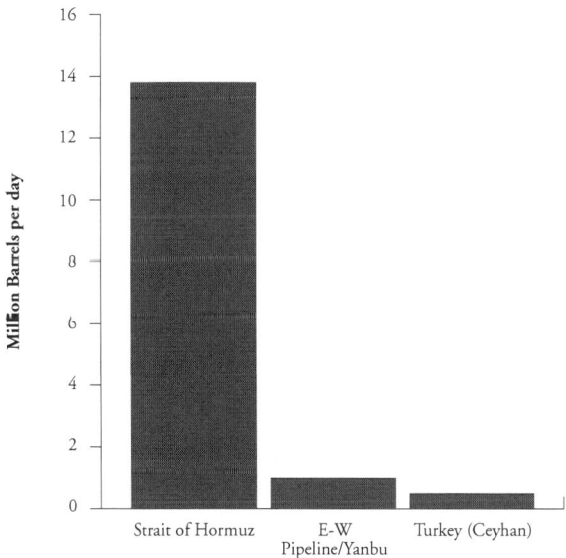

Source: EIA Fact Sheet in http://www.eia.doe.gov/cabs/pgulf2.html

Figure E
Flow map of world crude oil, regarding the Strait of Hormuz, 2010

Source: Kemp and Harkavy, *Strategic Geography and the Changing Middle East* & EIA (Energy Information Administration)[10]

Note: This flow map of world crude oil illustrates well the global importance of the PG region for petroleum. It also shows the strategic importance of the Strait of Hormuz as a chokepoint.

policy and supporting US military build-up since President Carter, Huntington's imperial and militarism vision, despite the end of the Cold War, was not changed and so he remarked that the emerging world "is likely to lack the clarity and stability of the Cold War and to be a more jungle-like world of multiple dangers, hidden traps, unpleasant surprises and moral ambiguities".[11]

According to the new post-Cold War geopolitical world picture of Huntington, three principal American strategic interests were: perpetuating the primacy of the US as the global power, which meant watching carefully Japan's goal of attaining economic dominance and their strategy of reaching such ambition; impeding the emergence of any political and military hegemonic power in Eurasia; and asserting substantial US interests in the PG and ME. Despite vast disagreement with his theory as a remarkably simplistic thesis, Ó Tuathail notes,

> It is significant, nevertheless, as an example of how neoconservative intellectuals of statecraft are endeavoring to chart global space after the Cold War. What is most interesting about this act of geopower is how it uses the assumptions, goals and methods of Cold War strategic culture to re-territorialize the global scene in a way which perpetuates the society of security and politics as *Kulturkampf*.[12]

Huntington's post-Cold War strategic debate, as Ó Tuathail also notes, due to its aim of maintaining the US as the premier global power, should be based on "renewing its Western civilization from within and actively containing, dividing and playing off other civilizations against each other". The other point that Ó Tuathail remarks on is that Huntington's model describes a world of potential and actual Cold War threats against the US. However in his new debate concerning the "clash of civilizations", his major concerns regarding the necessity of renewal of the society of security within the "West" instead of Japan focuses more on a new danger, which is:

> a "Confucian–Islamic connection" which features a militaristic Chinese economy exporting arms to Islamic states who are determined to seek nuclear, chemical and biological weapons capabilities. "A Confucian–Islamic military connection has … come into being, designed to promote acquisition by its members of the weapons and weapons technologies needed to counter the military power of the West. (…) A new form of arms competition is thus occurring between Islamic–Confucian states and the West." (…) Huntington's response, amongst other things, is to call for a moderation in (…) [military] reduction of Western military capabilities and for the West to "maintain military superiority in East and Southeast Asia".[13]

Therefore, Ó Tuathail concludes that "Huntington's thesis is not about the clash of civilizations. It is about making global politics a clash of civilizations."[14]

Regarding Huntington's perception of the potentially rough conflict between Western and Islamic civilisations as a defining feature of an evolving world order, as Kemp and Harkavy note, "[T]he Middle East (including the Caspian Basin region) has now assumed the role of the strategic high ground, a key strategic prize in the emerging global system at the juncture between the twentieth and twenty-first centuries."[15]

In general, this study agrees with Huntington when he downplays the continuing major power of the nation-states in the future of global politics. The specific point of agreement is not his point of view that employs 'cultures' of people as the dominant source of conflicts in the future global politics, but from the point of view that people (individuals and groups) will gain much more power and will play a greater role in international political affairs in the future. The modern world's wider and more complex set of interactions, in addition to the growing capacity and importance of and emphasis on reforms, will encourage nations and groups to have more influence on world affairs. Nevertheless the orientation of future global politics is important as to whether they serve the interest of a premier global power or the benefit of a world that appreciates diversity and contains different nations and civilisations. This is where the study has stressed the need to consider more seriously President Khatami's theory of dialogue among civilisations in international relations. This theory, which was mainly provided in response to Huntington's, emphasises the importance of dialogue, despite cultural diversities, in a time where all nations and the globe itself need the most cooperation and harmony possible; some major examples are global warming, environmental degradation and resource depletion.

Regional states' geopolitical perspectives
As there is a basic place for power in geopolitical discourses this domain of knowledge and expertise can provide power for whoever applies it. In addition, the advantage of this knowledge is that it predicts the future direction of international affairs with all its conflict and cooperation possibilities.

However, as long as the ME/PG is a disparate region lacking a single geopolitical perspective, the intention of this study is to gather all PG states' attention towards this important element in their strategies. Lack of attention to their geographical location will cause more geopolitical problems. The topography of this part of the world has affected its peoples' regional and not global geopolitical perceptions; also long-standing divisions and traditional contentions between regional states have caused them to focus on regional rather than global dangers. Hence, as long as the ME/PG political regimes do not support geographical integration or recognise the existence of a mosaic of related and imbricated geopolitical spheres in this region, there will not be any possibility of security and stability there. But, as Ezzati notes, if the countries in the Fertile Crescent, from east of the Mediterranean through the PG and sea of Oman (Jordan, Iraq, Syria, Lebanon, Arabian Peninsula and Iran) – which, owing to their significant geopolitical situation, have for centuries comprised a region of rivalries and so been a cause of insecurity – were able to take advantage of their geographical contiguity and establish free movement within this region, then stability and security would return to these territories. Therefore, besides external threats and interferences, other reasons which involve their domestic and regional threats and problems are major reasons why the PG states have regional geopolitical perspectives rather than global views. Because of this significance, three chapters of this study (Chapters 6–8) are dedicated to the foreign policy approach of littoral states. In addition, the borders between these states have been left as *de facto* boundaries in a way each state looks at its neighbouring states as its own complementary.

Chapter 5 is dedicated to territorial and boundary disputes between the littoral states as a major source of instability in the PG. However, only if such a fragile region were able to take advantage of a single geopolitical perspective would it be able to sort out most of its political, social, economic and military problems. For the PG states it is a necessity to look at this region as a whole, not as divided states and groups of individuals ranged against the other states or groups. Having a geopolitical perspective would provide better understanding and recognise the geopolitical significance of this region from the non-regional players' views too.

This study fills some of the gaps left by global geostrategic models with respect to geopolitical visions in this region. First, it aims to show how it is possible to change the geopolitical significance of the PG, which has been a disruptive element in the region's security due to its being a subject of rivalries, into a convergent element that encourages cooperation among all beneficiary parties.

Second, all the models not based on the major geopolitical realities of this region were so preoccupied with superpower rivalry that they ignored the role of humans in their equations. Such ignorance, as Drysdale and Blake note, was present whether regarding the deeply complex and relevant regional geopolitical relationships or the geopolitical perspectives of the people.¹⁶ This study's security model appreciates the role of peoples' communication.

Third, it has an inclusive vision which considers the interests of all regional and ultra-regional parties whose security and interests are somehow related to this region. The theories outlined above, in contrast, had different expansionist visions deriving from their own countries' political interests, regardless of the regional states' security concerns and national interests. In this regard, as Ó Tuathail also notes:

> Geopolitical experts are never detached but embedded in economic, political, racial and sexual relations of power (as Mackinder certainly was). They do not see objectively but within the structures of meaning provided by their socialization into certain (usually privileged) backgrounds, intellectual contexts, political beliefs and culture. They do not see "the real" but see that which their culture *interprets* and *constructs* as "the real." Their so-called "laws" of strategy are often no more than self-justifications for their own political ideology and that of those in power within their state. Their production of knowledge about international politics, in other words, is a form of power which they wield to serve their own political ends.¹⁷

Considering this significant geopolitical position of the PG required close scrutiny of the important geopolitical elements and security concerns and systems in this region. Therefore, the geopolitical elements, especially oil and gas, and their impact on the ultra-regional powers' politics has been studied (through Chapters 1 and 2 to 4) to yield a clearer understanding of different security models in the region with respect to all regional and ultra-regional players' interests and security concerns.

Foreign policy approach

In order to be able to analyse the determinant factors of a security system this study has drawn upon the level of analysis framework in international relations. This has examined the issues involved in creating a regional security model so as to turn threats into opportunities for regional cooperation and sustainability, especially through being able to identify casual factors of international politics. Taking advantage of arguments of scholars such as Steven Spiegel (UCLA political science professor and author), Theodore Couloumbis and James Wolfe about the significance of finding links between the insights derived at the various levels and from different actors and units of analysis to be able to identify what Couloumbis and Wolfe note as, "different pieces of a multidimensional puzzle" which at the end could be able to "put these pieces together into a general theory of interaction, a theory that has both descriptive and predictive powers",[18] this study discusses all three levels of the PG states' foreign policies and the forces that have affected them, including the systemic level (the interaction between states) and the debate that occurs at the domestic and individual levels (see Chapters 6 to 8). These chapters also draw upon social analysis, to provide an analysis of the situation in PG states with regard to their social backgrounds and belief systems. They also draw upon elite theory to provide an analysis of power relationships or policy-planning networks in PG states' societies, as well as their different definitions of security and national interests.

Besides issues of particular importance to other countries, this study makes especial effort to evoke the perspective from which the PG states themselves view their problems and choose their domestic and foreign policy priorities in respect to their legitimate strategic concerns which arise from their geographic, social, and historical context. This is a fundamental factor which motivates states' political behaviour to ensure each state's security, territorial integrity, national cohesion and approach to the sources of wealth essential to develop its economy and political institutions effectively and independently. What is usually missing from many analyses in the West, specifically in Washington, is that security in the PG will be very heavily influenced by how they understand the regional states' perceptions of threat as well as their national security issues. Therefore, Chapters 6–8 focus on the PG littoral states using the following framework: 1) political history; 2) political system; 3) internal threat; 4) external threat to stability of PG states. Although non-Western scholars including Iranians, such as Rouhollah Ramazani, Shahram Chubin, Sepehr Zabih, etc., have paid more attention to the regional states' concerns and their role in any security arrangements in the region their studies left a gap, filled by the present study, with respect to the vital role of the two strongest regional and global powers with some interest in the region in establishing a long-term multilateral security approach and ensure peace and security in that region, as a principal. The study has emphasised the need for an appropriate relationship between these two regional and non-regional powers (in this study, Iran and the US) to assure a more stable region and security for all players.

Security approach

To lay the groundwork for developing a better and more comprehensive future security arrangement, this study appeals to empirical data and observation, as well as to theoretical framework and critical analysis, to articulate the reasons for the failure of security models in the PG. The arguments are supported by detailed evidence for each model, during the time period 1962–1997. Regional security is examined in order to explain the major strategic choices available to both the PG and the external powers' decision-makers in a different international atmosphere in this regard. This analysis is conducted through the prism of three fundamental schools of thought in international relations – realism, neo-liberalism or the cooperative-security school – and the hegemonic or counterproliferation. The present aim in this study is to investigate a comprehensive strategy for peace and stability in the PG. In order to do this the relative strengths and weaknesses of the three theories by studying their differences and similarities as well as the various historical challenges in applying the frameworks to the PG security environment will be assessed in much detail in the final conclusion.

The differences and similarities between these security theories are indicated in this study by referring Kraig as follows: proponents of traditional realpolitik consider international security to be a balance of interests based on a rough balance of power, whereas the more recent US strategic model is based on an imbalance of power and interests (hegemony) and on the use of both offensive and defensive threats. According to neo-liberals, the cooperative model can be considered as a balance of interests based upon mutual reassurance. However, despite the similarity of realpolitik and cooperative in that both strategies advocate the importance of brokering a balance of interests, they differ in their preferred model of guaranteeing this balance. The realpolitik theory relies to a great extent on implicit military and economic threats (and temporary alliances to build up power), while the cooperative theory relies on promises and reassurances as firm and impenetrable factors.

Nevertheless, both of these schools are quite different to the evolving US hegemony strategy, which is increasingly focused on establishing a unitary and dominant value system based on a network of friends and allies in keeping with US foreign policy objectives. The hegemonic approach assumes no possibility for competitors with different goals and values, while the realpolitik and cooperative security models believe that each nation-states' national interests should be guaranteed at some minimal level. In addition, the cooperative school of thought shares some of its theoretical assumptions with realism, e.g. requiring a set of geopolitical circumstances. For instance, both assume that the primary actor is the sovereign state and that such states will be domestically stable, immune from the sort of domestic turmoil evident in Iran's 1979 revolution, and therefore the mutual agreements ordering relations would remain stable.[19]

This study will show how the policies of selective multilateralism, bilateralism and unilateralism have been unsuccessful in bringing about security in the PG. It will be shown that this is because the most prominent states favour inextricably exclusionary types of coalition. All of the above policies result in the systematic exclusion, economically or militarily, of a major state and of non-state actors in the security order. Regarding strategic properties of the PG which affect how successful a security system in it will be and the fragility of temporary alignments of the classical kind of two against the third pillar, there is an emphasis on a combination of two synergistic components of balance of power between the three key regional players, Iran, Iraq and Saudi Arabia, and meaningful reform in the littoral states for the future PG security system; where the region lacks both. Therefore, analysts and scholars, as well as policy-makers, have drawn similar conclusions concerning the two dominant contending frameworks for PG security: US hegemony and its dominant military presence and principled multilateralism. These conclusions are viewed as even more valid in the post-Saddam era. Accordingly, by studying the analysis of Michael Kraig, Steven Spiegel, Richard Russell, Rathmell and Bjørn Møller, who all, with regard to strategic properties of the PG, emphasise the need for a new approach and policy options for security in the PG regional and external powers' security policies towards the region – from various angles and different solutions – this study has tried to come up with a more practicable approach to the security of this region.

A number of key research gaps have been highlighted regarding security in the final conclusion, which has resulted in an alternative security model in the PG. The Pyramid Security Model could be a solution to the highly volatile situation in the PG, because in addressing major security issues this model is based on the geopolitical realities, as well as the political and economic concerns, of all regional and ultra-regional parties. It is also able to avoid the typical problems that arise for models based on a competition for power between states with conflicting national interests and agendas, like Russell's,[20] as it does not base a balance of power on such confrontational foundations.

Building on international experiences and successes and failures of previous models, this study has created a model on the basis of the mixed approaches of a cooperative-security (liberalism) framework and realpolitik (realism) which would be able to manage relations between states and create a regulation of power, which would mean the rule of "law" and not "the powers". To achieve such a goal, analysts have suggested multiple different approaches. For instance, Kraig has suggested a "principled multilateral" approach which includes a rules-based system in which international law is applicable to all actors in the PG, including the US.

Pyramid is a model of developing security through the feelings of attachment and interdependency which should occur when the littoral states have a single geopolitical vision. It is designed (see Figure F) with three sides consisting of: a) the policies of the littoral Arab states; b) the policies of ultra-regional powers; c) Iran's policies – Iran being the most powerful regional player in the PG. The base of the pyramid, which interacts with all three sides, is the geopolitics of the PG.

Choosing geopolitics as the base of the new model stems from the need to emphasise a convergent element among the PG states for ensuring the long-term functionality of a security model, as an element which can assure and remove the fear of bigger states by smaller states. This is due to the fact that geopolitics is the most fixed and firm feature of the region, with an impact on every single nation-state's interests and national security. Emphasising the region's geopolitics shows that every state, as a part of this geopolitical region, like pieces of a puzzle, has a unique and non-ignorable place in the security system. Irrespective of their size, all states have a similar, though unequal, weight.

FIGURE F
The Pyramid Security Model

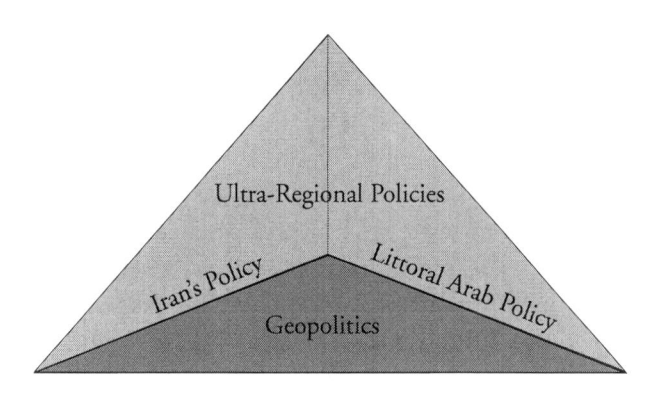

Ultra-Regional Policies
Iran's Policy
Littoral Arab Policy
Geopolitics

In the Pyramid model regional states have been urged to have global and not merely regional geopolitical perspectives. This would result in a single geopolitical vision as a power/knowledge for all the regional states in the PG, which would enable them to play a major role in balance of power politics. They would thus be able to take advantage of various opportunities resulting from geopolitical developments, to their best interests as well as to the region's security and stability. Only by addressing this fragile region as a whole, not as divided states and groups of individuals ranged against the other states or groups, would it be possible to prevent further geopolitical problems in this region and change the traditional disruptive role of geopolitical significance of the PG in the region's security to enable it to become a convergent element. Under such circumstances, geopolitics would work as an element that encourages cooperation among all beneficiary parties instead of being an expansion lever of the external powers.

Hence, by increasing the geopolitical position of the region, every member state will benefit. By emphasising geopolitical elements, especially socio-political and economic power, rather than military power, it is possible to minimise the significance of smaller states' fear of bigger states. This would in turn lessen the possibility of any states withdrawing from the model because of any sudden ideological or political changes. Therefore, the pyramid is immune to any significant internal changes to the littoral states. In addition, this model connects the issues of legitimacy and authority closely with the issue of sustainability. A major cause of the potential success of the model is the way it construes the gains it aims to achieve: the gains are mutual gains for all participants, not gains for one particular actor, or set of actors. It can thereby more plausibly make the assurance that remaining in the system will be in the interests of all the relevant parties.

This study has come up with two new mechanisms for the pyramid, which differentiates it from previous security models. First, is the necessity of a proper and positive relationship between the strongest regional actor and the major non-regional player (with great influence and interest in that region), as a general and certain principle to attain regional security in any region. The lesson to be learned from the experience of the most geopolitical region in the world, the PG, is that no other alternative strategy would be able to fulfil regional and ultra-regional interests and meet security concerns in any region, including the PG. Hence, it is argued that, in addition to the need to construct comprehensive multilateral coalitions, the key issue for achieving a durable collective security approach in the PG region will remain Iran–US relations. This is in marked contrast to the other analysts' approaches, whereby all the key players in the region – namely, Iraq, Iran and Saudi Arabia – are given the same weight.

Besides the regional perception of the importance of cooperation models and the significance of the US–Iran relationship, this study emphasises the significance of the role of other ultra-regional players, especially emerging powers like the EU and some key states in the AP (viz. China, India and Japan) to construct a more sustainable PG security system. Through their strategic interest in the PG, especially their growing dependency on PG energy supplies which exceeds that of the US, their close ties with the region by a network of economic and political linkages and their deep concerns over US permanent hegemony in the ME/PG, which have resulted in their recognition of a need to adopt a greater geopolitical role independently of Washington, it is possible to create a counterbalance to the US hegemony in the PG in benefit of developing a multilateral security regime (mainly explained in Chapters 2 and 3).

The second mechanism the Pyramid model introduces is a fourth element to previous categories of the important, interlocking elements needed to establish a workable, legitimate and authoritative security model in the PG. An appropriate international political environment with a proper international security system's structure is added to a further three elements: an inclusive and multilateral approach; a balance of power, preferably through arms control negotiations among all three regional key players; and domestic developments and reforms in the littoral states. Such stress is also important because many scholars, such as Kraig; perceive an external contribution to improve the security situation within the region as important, owing to the fragility of domestic politics and interregional relations in the PG.[21]

The importance of this model stems not only from the role that states have in its architecture and their effect on its functionality, but also that some consideration is given to the role of people (even sub-national groups), their interactions, as well as their satisfaction. Its emphasis on reforms will encourage positive competition among all littoral states to upgrade their weight in this security framework via greater civil development, rather than military power or territorial size. This is true for ultra-regional players too; in particular, by contributing towards the regions' development they can upgrade their role in this region.

Notes

1. Gearóid Ó Tuathail, "General introduction; thinking critically about geopolitics". In Gearóid Ó Tuathail, Simon Dalby, and Paul Routledge (eds), *The geopolitics reader* (US and Canada: Routledge, 2006), 1.
2. Ezzatolah Ezzati, *Geopolitic dar Gharn-e Bist-o Yekom* [Geopolitics in the Twenty-first Century] (Tehran: SAMT, 1380 Solar Calendar [2001]), 7.
3. Ó Tuathail (edition: 1998), op. cit., 1, 24.
4. Ó Tuathail (2006), op. cit., 3.
5. Ezzati, op. cit., 18–19.
6. Alasdair Drysdale and Gerald Blake, *The Middle East and North Africa: A political geography* (New York: Oxford Press, 1985), 27.
7. Ó Tuathail (1998), op. cit., 16.
8. Samuel Huntington (summer 1993), "The clash of civilizations?", *Foreign Affairs*, 22–49.
9. Drysdale and Blake, op. cit., 26.
10. Figure cited from Geoffrey Kemp and Robert Harkavy, *Strategic geography and the changing Middle East* (Washington, D. C.: Brookings Institution Press, 1997), 118.

11 Gearóid Ó Tuathail, "Samuel Huntington and the 'civilizing' of global space". In Ó Tuathail (et al) (1998), op. cit., 170–171, cited from Samuel Huntington, *Political Order in Changing Societies* (New Haven: Yale University Press, 1968), 8.
12 Ibid., 171, 173.
13 Ibid., 174.
14 Ibid., 175.
15 Kemp and Harkavy, op. cit., 7–8.
16 Drysdale and Blake, op. cit., 28.
17 Ó Tuathail (1998), "Introduction: thinking critically about geopolitics", op. cit., 17.
18 Theodore Couloumbis and James Wolfe, *Introduction to international relations: Power and justice* (New Jersey: Prentice-Hall, Inc. 1990), 19–31.
19 Ibid.
20 Richard Russell (winter 2005) "The Persian Gulf's collective-security mirage", *Middle East Policy Council*, vol. XII, no. 4, 81.
21 Michael Kraig (Fall 2004), "Assessing Alternative Security Frameworks for the Persian Gulf", *Middle East Policy*, Washington: vol. 11, issue 3, cited in the site of *Gulf2000* of Columbia University, NY, USA.

PART I

GEOPOLITICS OF THE PERSIAN GULF

1

Geography and resources of the Persian Gulf

The significant geographical location of the Persian Gulf

Introduction
Throughout history the PG has had the richest and longest-running seafaring tradition of any world region and has connected the continents of Asia, Europe and Africa. However, its ancient and traditional role as an important crossroads for trade and communication has become less significant compared to its geopolitical character that has given this waterway a strategic importance. These two elements, economic and strategic, which strengthened the region's vital significance to all littoral states as well as the entire world economy and political life, have caused the PG to be a worthy rival to outside powers, particularly the West, while also being the most unstable and chaotic of any world region.

Initially the importance of the PG lay in the trade of merchandise such as pearls, spices and silks. Later, from the end of the fifteenth century to the eighteenth century, different European trading companies belonging to the Portuguese, British, French, Dutch and Russians, who realised that the domination of this region was critical to their colonial policies in the East, sought to establish footholds and trading monopolies in this waterway. Since earliest times, the geographical location of the PG as the sub-system of the ME, which was recognised as the centre of the old world, has given this waterway its importance as the heart of the old world, as the great trade routes of the old world had to pass through this region. The region was considered a vital passage between Asia and Europe, despite the link that had been provided by the Suez Canal between the Red Sea and the Mediterranean.

Since then, this international trade waterway has altered to become an important strategic region of the world, especially after the discovery in the early twentieth century of the largest oil reserves in the world on its shores. This created large industries connected to the extracting and refining of oil and also led to the appearance of large and sophisticated oil tankers in this waterway.

The geopolitical importance of the PG will remain unchallenged in an international context not only because of its high proportion of the world's hydrocarbon resources, but also due to the importance of the location of the littoral areas of this waterway, which combined form the heart of the world centre. The competition for oil and gas reserves has had a great impact on intra-regional relations and border arrangements since the British military withdrew from its territorial base in the PG in 1971, an impact that will be examined in the next chapters.

The Persian Gulf from global geopolitical perspectives
There have been various attempts amongst geopoliticians to provide the most comprehensive geopolitical models of inter-state relationships in the global hierarchy system. Their efforts have enabled politicians to tilt the geopolitical weight of power in favour of their own interests by gaining access to the new geographical locations and by enhancing their power and influence relative to their rivals. Following the ideas of the American historian A. T. Mahan about sea power in international strategy and its importance for controlling waterways and straits due to a scansorial process of trade and business between states, the US strengthened its maritime forces. Controlling the seas was the first necessary condition for global power. The British geographer Halford Mackinder, who started almost all discussions of global geopolitical perspectives, restated the importance of land power as a response to Mahan's views. As Drysdale and Blake explain,

> Mackinder's basic thesis was that the inner area of Eurasia is the pivot region of world politics. With its abundant resources, it is also beyond the reach of the maritime powers (...) this pivotal area was surrounded by a marginal crescent, which encircled the Middle East [including the Persian Gulf]. If the pivot state should ever gain control of the marginal lands, thus gaining access to the sea, "the empire of the world would then be in sight".[1]

Mackinder expressed his views in his 1904 thesis "The geographical pivot of history". According to Hans Morgenthau, Mackinder was the first person who expressed space as the basic conception of geopolitics and emphasised geography as an absolute factor that determines the power, and hence the fate of nations. Morgenthau adds: "According to geopolitics, it is a law of history that peoples must expand by 'conquering space' or perish, and that the relative power of nations is determined by the mutual relation of the conquered spaces."[2] Mackinder, who believed that the 'World-Island' was organised of three continents of Europe, Asia, and Africa, around which the lesser lands of the world were grouped, concluded that, "Who rules East Europe commands the Heartland: Who rules the Heartland commands the World-Island: Who rules the World-Island commands the World."[3] On the basis of this analysis, Mackinder predicted the emergence of Russia, or some other nation, which would control this territory as the dominating world power. In Mackinder's view, with the land-based power competing for authority in a marginal crescent to which the maritime powers have approachability, the Mediterranean and the ME were key regions in the conflict. Drysdale and Blake point out that, "The U.S. policy of post-World War II containment [of Communism], according to which alliances and bases were established within the Eurasian marginal crescent, was designed to prevent the outward expansion of this heartland power, the U.S.S.R."[4]

According to this view, the pivot region, which in 1919 was named the Heartland, comprised a great part of Russia, Iran, and the western part of China and Mongolia, all of which extended to near maritime boundaries. In 1943 Mackinder emphasised the importance of having links to free seas as well. Most criticism of Mackinder's thought was concentrated on the Heartland concept and the effects of new technology upon strategy, such as a land power's access to an ocean-going fleet, intercontinental ballistic missiles and developed strategic air forces. Other criticisms of the Heartland concept came about because of his underestimation of the resistant power of peninsular states, particularly those in alliance with the US, and upon the details of the Soviet Union's strength within the Heartland. However, his thesis was true regarding the ME, at least until the collapse of the USSR. In this region, as Drysdale and Blake noted in 1985, the US was concerned about any territorial expansion by the Heartland power, whereas the USSR deeply feared US influence in borderland states regarded as vital to Soviet security.[5]

Nicholas John Spykman, who named the marginal crescent "the rimland", believed that whoever controlled the rimland ruled Eurasia, and whoever ruled Eurasia commanded the world. His basic thesis focused attention on the possibility of connection between land and sea due to the maritime situation of the rimland states. Since oceans and the navy were important to him, marginal states (rimland) were more consequential in his mind. Chronological studies gave him the idea of competition between Britain and the USSR over the marginal crescent during WWII, so he advocated that the US adopt policies that would promote American influence in the marginal crescent, "the rimland", or at least try to prevent the USSR from controlling or seizing marginal states.

Saul Bernard Cohen, an American geopolitician, moved away from Mackinder's Heartland-Rimland theory and suggested a rather less controversial scheme of world geostrategic regions in which the ME, along with Egypt, Sudan, and part of Libya, are characterised as "the Middle East shatter belt". Cohen defined a shatter belt as "a large, strategically located region that is occupied by a number of conflicting states and is caught between the conflicting interests of the Great Powers". He recognised only two such regions: the ME and Southeast Asia.

Cohen looked at the world in terms of being "geostrategic" and "geopolitical" regions, and believed that the space is not united strategically, but is fundamentally divided between a number of separate areas. His framework for geopolitical analysis is distinguished between divisions with global extent known as geostrategic regions, and divisions of a regional extent, which were called geopolitical regions. Cohen (1963) in his *Geography and politics in a world divided* explains that, "The geostrategic region is the expression of the interrelationship of a large part of the world in terms of location, movement, trade orientation, and cultural or ideological bonds." According to this definition, he goes on to say, "control of strategic passageways on land and sea is frequently crucial to the unity of geostrategic regions". The geopolitical regions were subdivisions of each "geostrategic region" and had a tendency to be relatively contiguous in terms of some norms of politics, economy, and culture. According to his definition "the geostrategic region has a strategic role to play and the geopolitical region has a tactical one".[6]

Cohen believes in only two geostrategic regions, each dominated by two of the Great Powers. He calls them "the Trade-Dependent Maritime World": the Maritime Ring of the USA; and "the Eurasian Continental World": the Russian Industrialised Triangle. He subdivides geostrategic regions into various geopolitical regions, and between the two geostrategic regions he introduces two distinct geopolitical regions as shatter belts

– the ME and Southeast Asia. According to Cohen, these two geopolitical regions are politically fragmented, with both geostrategic regions having "footholds" there. "Shatter belts evolve from both internal fragmentation and external pressures."[7] Drysdale and Blake also note that the ME is a definite contact zone between Eurasia and the Maritime World in Cohen's scheme of world geostrategic regions. According to them, Cohen's theory has two infirmities with respect to its application to the Middle East and North Africa (MENA), namely:

> First, the global perspective tends to obscure the infinitely complex and pertinent geopolitical relationships within the region itself. In reality a mosaic of related and overlapping geopolitical spheres exists. Second, global geostrategic models are so preoccupied with superpower rivalry that the geopolitical perspectives of the people of the region are distorted or ignored altogether. A better grasp of these perspectives might cause external powers, particularly the United States, to rethink their policies in the region.[8]

The general view of the geopolitical world that Cohen provides seems more dynamic than the previous model of a bipolarised world, due to his concerns about the emergence of "second order" powers[9] in the world hierarchy system. This is one of the advantages of his model for a world political hierarchy system.

The ME as a highly divided area of almost no strategic, political, cultural or economic homogeneity, in Cohen's consideration, is mentioned as a shatter belt where great variations lead to great diversities in its character as a geopolitical region.

Although the ME is a contact zone between Eurasia and the Maritime World, it is not a unit geopolitical region and it includes a variety of geopolitical regions with different basic geopolitical objectives. As a sub-region of the ME, the PG represents a congruent perimeter in itself. The PG includes nations varying in some cultural aspects, but with similarities in economic, political and strategic interests. Although, according to Drysdale and Blake, there has not been a similar and singular view of geopolitical perspective of the ME states, including the PG, but a variety of views conditioned by history, political ideology and geographic location. In other words, people's real geopolitical preoccupations are mostly regional and not global, since their long-standing political differences and traditional rivalries dominate relationships between states.

They give an example of the Arab states' fear of the USSR or the US, which is only half as strong as their fear of Iranian military and ideological expansionism. The Iran–Iraq War served to concentrate minds on regional dangers, and the Gulf Cooperation Council (GCC) was formed as a regional response.[10]

In sum: geographical location put the PG at the heart of the old world; its political environment was created by each power that came to dominate it, especially during most of the nineteenth and twentieth centuries by Britain and since that time by the US.

This, together with the economic shift from fishing and trade to the oil industry that has occurred since the first half of the twentieth century, has shaped the distinctive environment that is the geopolitical region of the PG. Therefore, it is obvious that any regional or non-regional crises and chaos in this region would affect all continents of the world, especially Asia and Europe. On the other hand, according to the impact of major evolutions in international relations on the geopolitical position of different regions, the geopolitics of the PG also has been changed during previous centuries. Pervasive wars, the collapse of empires, the expansion of capitalism and state socialism, the establishment of international organisations, great revolutions and the transition of balance to a bipolar system and its later tailspin, have all had considerable impact on the importance of the geopolitical position of the PG.

Considering this, the significant geopolitical position of the PG requires close examination of the important geopolitical elements and security concerns of all regional and ultra-regional players. Hence, in the following section and next three chapters, the geopolitical elements of the PG particularly, geographical locations of the energy resources, as well as the massive oil and gas reserves available, and also their impact on the ultra-regional powers' politics especially, will be studied in order to gain a clearer understanding of different security models in this region.

Persian Gulf oil and gas

Introduction

> If you want to rule the world you need to control the oil. All the oil, anywhere.
>
> Michel Collon (2001)[11]

The PG is of vital significance to all littoral states as well as to the entire world economy and political life. Oil and gas, as the major elements of the modern industrial age, have also given this waterway a new and invaluable global paramountcy.

Since early twentieth-century exploration for oil in the PG, this waterway has occupied a special place in the political strategies of international powers, and its major regional players have entered the highly complex equation of oil and global power.

In the global structure and function of the twenty-first century, oil will still emerge as an effective variable and will determine the nature of relations and rivalries, i.e. divergence or integration among international personages. Valid evaluations and analyses emphasise that oil will account for the main portion of global consumption and its role in the global economy will remain of greatest concern. Therefore oil will remain an independent and effective variable in the arena of global equations.

The political geography and geopolitics of oil and gas

Oil has been the cause of many political geography issues in the PG as well as in the entire oil-rich region of the ME. In fact, oil has transformed the political and strategic map as much as the economic one: it is the reason for the existence of some Middle Eastern boundaries and countries, particularly in the PG. The ownership of oil fields and the control of oil transit routes continue to be a significant factor influencing the geographic distribution of wealth and balance of power within this region. Competition between the Great Powers to access them continually increases. Moreover, oil-related boundary and hydrocarbon exploitation issues increasingly complicate contemporary inter-state links.[12]

The oil deposits in the world are geographically very concentrated, and the PG as a sub-system of the ME contains the single most important oil region in the world (see Figures 1.1 and 1.2). The existence of much of the ME's oil within a few large fields has a bearing on two issues: the distribution of wealth and power; and the emergence of regional and international policies. As Drysdale and Blake note, this is because of the following points.

1) The ME's main oil reserves lie in the PG in the area between Iran and the Arab zone. Saudi Arabia, Kuwait, Iran and Iraq together

have about 80 per cent of the ME's oil reserves, which is two-thirds of the world's reserves – in other words, more proven reserves under their soil than in the rest of the world combined.
2) Low costs of oil exploration as well as easy oil transition to the global market from the PG has very much attracted the world's attention, and especially that of the Great Powers, to this geopolitical region.[13]

For these reasons the security of oil supplies from the PG is very significant for the developed world.

During the twentieth century the importance of oil caused many political, social and economic cataclysms in both oil-producing and oil-consuming countries. The dependence of oil-producing countries on oil income, as well as the economic development of industrial and developing countries, made the oil market extremely political. The oil

FIGURE 1.1
The oil corridor

FIGURE 1.2
Major oil fields of the Middle East

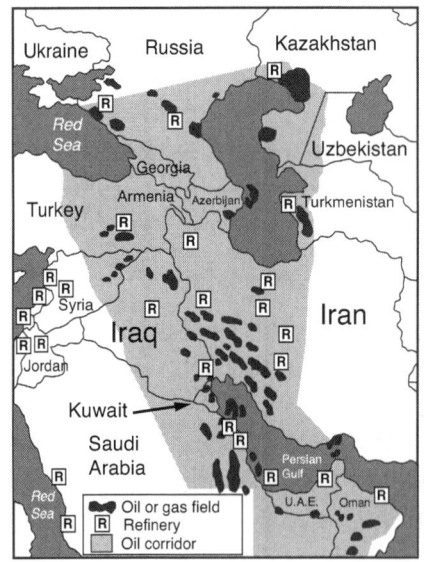

Source: *Asian Times Online*

Source: *Middle East Map Gallery* (2000), http://maps.unomaha.edu/Peterson/funda/ MapLinks/SWAsia/gallery.html. Courtesy of Encyclopaedia Britannica

market has been the most complex and involved market effecting political events and changes in the whole world, as it has been impossible to make accurate economic decisions in the oil market without regard for political factors and similarly impossible to take political strategic decisions without attention to the oil market. Any fluctuation in oil prices has caused heavy damage to finance, economy, employment and social stability in the oil-producing countries. Indeed, the high speed with which crude oil prices soared has threatened people's daily lives in oil-consuming countries and thus brought social unrest and turmoil in some countries. Consequently, it has affected the basis of sustainable growth of the global economy.

The significance of the PG's huge natural gas reserves, which equate to about 41 per cent of total proven world natural gas reserves, has increased the geopolitical importance of the PG. Enumerating the reserves of the Caspian Basin, which raises the figure, as well as the exploitation of new technologies to reduce the high costs associated with gas transportation, would further increase the world desirability of the region's natural gas.

The strategic position of oil

Since the early twentieth century, oil, because of its significance as a major element of energy in industry and transportation, has increasingly played a strategic role in ties and relations between different nations throughout the world. This strategic position of oil has had a basic impact on the geopolitical importance of the ME and caused severe and increasing competition among the Great Powers to secure the principal production areas and transportation routes of oil via various military or diplomacy manners.

During the twentieth century, oil has caused a rapid technological change with regard to transportation, and changed both military and commercial significance regarding types of war and weaponry. Consequently it has had a radical impact on the rise and fall of the political powers. As Kemp and Harkavy observe:

> Because of the rapidity of the shift from coal to oil to fuel ships, this period of the early twentieth century provides a particularly good example of how the power of an empire can be eroded by lack

of access to a vital resource. Britain became increasingly dependent upon one of its major industrial rivals, the United States. Equally important it demonstrates how quickly a hitherto backward region such as Mesopotamia can assume great strategic importance in a relatively short time.[14]

From the end of WWII and since the emergence of the bipolar system, oil has become involved in superpower rivalries, because the most important objectives of the West in the PG have been to contain Soviet influence and protect a stable access to oil. At the same time, the Soviet Union has attempted to increase its political and security influence in this region, specifically through unaligned and anti-West countries.

In the global structure and function of the twentieth century, oil emerged as an effective variable and the main portion of global consumption; hence its role in the global economy, especially in the Western economy, remained of greatest concern and an effective variable in the political equations of Western countries.

In addition, the tension over the Iranian government's decision to nationalise oil demonstrated the vulnerable position of individual Middle Eastern governments confronting a united front of giant companies which had exclusive control of all stages of oil operations, including an optional setting of the oil price. The establishment of the Organisation of the Petroleum Exporting Countries (OPEC) in 1960 by five countries – Iran, Iraq, Saudi Arabia, Kuwait and Venezuela – was one device that responded to the attempts of oil-importing countries that also affected the global oil market.

The location of more than 75 per cent of the proven reserves of oil in the world away from the main industrial countries' territories has made this element not only a fundamental economic product but also a product with political aspects. The failure to discover new major oil reserves in its main domains, and the approaching maximum production levels in existing oil reserves – e.g. Alaska and the North Sea, which decrease the proven reserves of the US both absolutely and proportionately – together with the failure of innovative policies in the 1970s to develop alternatives and reduce dependence on the PG in order to diminish the dependence of the West on PG oil, have had a significant impact on world demand for energy. Kemp and Harkavy point out that, "In more recent times access to Persian Gulf oil has been the prize and that factor has profoundly influenced strategic planning by the major powers. (…)

Similarly, advances in military technology have had a most significant impact upon strategic access problems."[15]

Consequently, since the 1970s energy issues have become a security matter for Western countries. The security aspects of this issue are related to the control and domination of the oil resources and the contrast with oil-producing countries' interests. Additionally, most of the oil-consumer countries take their vulnerable need to import oil as a threat to their national securities. The potential for any interruption of oil imports could affect their economic security in particular and their political-social security in general – a matter that will be studied throughout the remainder of Part I of this book.

NOTES

1 Alasdair Drysdale and Gerald Blake, *The Middle East and North Africa: A political geography* (New York: Oxford Press, 1985), 23.
2 Hans Morgenthau, *Politics among nations: The struggle for power and peace*. Revised by Kenneth Thompson (New York: Alfred A. Knopf Inc., 1985), 178.
3 Halford Mackinder, *Democratic ideal and reality* (New York: Henry Holt and Co. 1919), 150.
4 Drysdale and Blake, op. cit., 23–27.
5 Ibid., 27.
6 Saul Cohen, *Geography and politics in a world divided* (New York: Random House, 1963), 62, 229.
7 Ibid., 231.
8 Drysdale and Blake, op. cit., 27–28.
9 The emergence of new world powers such as Europe, China and Japan, and also regional powers such as Iran, Nigeria and India, with potentiality for regional authority and infiltration.
10 Drysdale and Blake, op. cit., 28.
11 Michel Collon (2001) Monopoly-US-British Imperialism. *The Four Winds*, http://www.fourwinds10.com/news/05-government/C-fraud/04-US-gov/2003/05C4-12-07-03-monopoly-us-british-imperialism.html (18 April 2004; can no longer be accessed).
12 Keith McLachlan, "Hydrocarbons and Iranian policies towards the Gulf States". In Richard Schofield (ed.), *Territorial foundations of the Gulf states* (London: UCL Press, 1994), 236; also Drysdale and Blake, op. cit., 313.
13 Drysdale and Blake, op. cit., 313–318.
14 Geoffrey Kemp and Robert Harkavy, *Strategic geography and the changing Middle East* (Washington, D. C.: Brookings Institution Press, 1997), 37.
15 Ibid., 25.

2

The European Union and Persian Gulf energy security[1]

Introduction

The European Union (EU), as the world's second-largest energy consumer after the US, considers energy a political priority. Most of its oil needs have historically been supplied by the ME, especially the PG.

The EU, which faces the geopolitical effects of its growing dependence on external energy, specifically gas as a preferred energy source, coming mainly from Russia and North Africa, does not yet have all the means necessary to change the international energy market.

The international strategic importance of PG energy, specifically its huge natural gas resources that amount to 41 per cent of the total proven world gas reserves, its geopolitical consequences together with the EU's energy supply policy has encouraged this union to consider an extensive access to PG security and to adopt a greater geopolitical role in this waterway. Besides the EU's vulnerability to the volatility of oil prices and also its growing dependence on imported energy, it faces US and Asian-Pacific (AP) energy, political, economic and military policies in the PG. Consequently, the EU as an emerging global power needs to consider every possible means of ensuring the success of its energy security policy in the PG region.

The European Union challenges

In 2003 the PG, as the main dominant energy source and gateway for global energy in the future, had about 27 per cent of the world's oil production, while holding 57 per cent (715 billion barrels) of the world's crude oil reserves. Besides oil, the PG region also has huge reserves (2,462 trillion cubic feet – TCF) of natural gas, accounting for 41 per cent of total proven world gas reserves.[2]

The 1970s' oil shocks developed the concept of "energy security", and with the Soviet withdrawal from Afghanistan, *glasnost*, the end of the Cold War, and also the crisis of the Iraqi invasion of Kuwait in 1990, US security policy found a great opportunity to be stabilised in the region.

Such great geopolitical changes of regional security, along with the "Desert Storm" operation in 1990–1991, paved the way for the "Bush doctrine" and his "new world order" on the basis of US hegemony and provided the possibility of US control and access to oil reserves of the southern littoral states of the PG; extended to Iraq since its occupation in 2003. Although the US has formed its importing energy strategy on decreasing dependency on the PG and has safeguarded almost 58 per cent of its total oil demand from supplies in Canada, Venezuela, Nigeria and Mexico, Washington has increased its presence in the region and its efforts to control the area's oil vent pipe. The US, by its military superiority and by applying a unipolar security system in the region, could also impart the geopolitical consequences of growing demand for the abundant and low-priced oil and natural gas of the PG as a critical prerequisite for Japanese and EU growth, and increasingly for the industrial growth of Asia and much of the developing world. In addition, with domestic production in decline the US will become ever more dependent on imports from the PG[3] (see Figure 2.1).

FIGURE 2.1
US crude oil imports by source

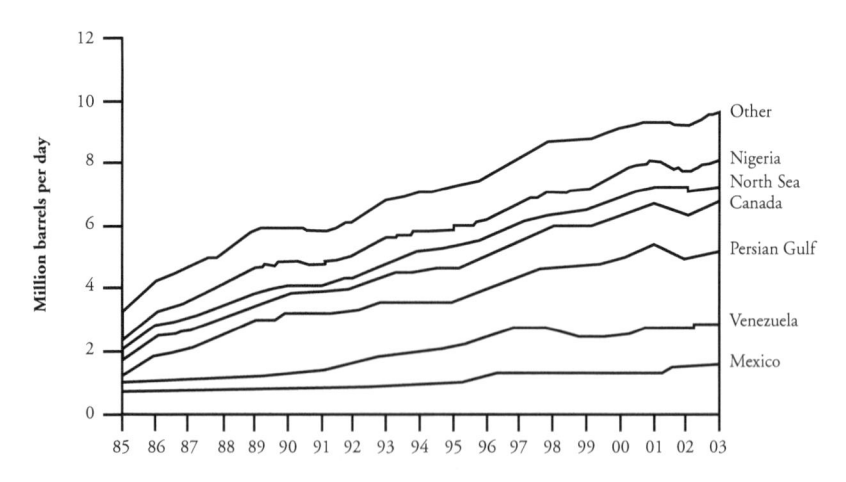

Source: Energy Information Administration, (EIA), http://www.eia.doe.gov/emeu/cabs/usa.html

Furthermore, the EU – like the US – faces the steady increase of AP demand for oil and gas from the PG, which is already more than that of Europe and the US merged together. This is, according to Kemp and Harkavy, "a most significant statistic and one that will have a profound impact on the geopolitics of the region". Certainly it will have a major impact on EU and US energy security policies.[4] The vital interest of the AP regarding a sufficient and safe energy supply from the ME/PG, which will be studied in the next chapter, has increased the concerns of Western countries, including the EU, dependent on this region's energy.

Energy supply policy

The EU was shaped as the European Economic Community (EEC) to improve economic and political integration within Europe. Its foundation was based on compacts about energy matters – the European Coal and Steel Community – established after WWII. Hence energy, as a political priority for this union since its inception, has played a major role in its existence and plans for the future. Western Europe shifted from native coal to cheaper imported oil after WWII. According to the Energy Information Administration (EIA), EU members possess only about 0.6 per cent of the world's proven reserves of oil and 2 per cent of the world's natural gas reserves. However, the EU holds 7.3 per cent of proven coal reserves. In 2001, the EU produced 4.1 per cent of the world's crude oil, 9 per cent of the world's natural gas, and 11 per cent of the world's coal (see Table 2.1 for further details and source).

According to the EIA, in 2001 the EU consumed 16 per cent of the world's total energy consumption whilst the US consumed 24 per cent (see Figure 2.2).

The EU, which consumes 18 per cent of total world oil consumption, is responsible for less than (about) 4 per cent of world production[5] and also consumes 16 per cent of the world's natural gas. "Under current patterns of energy production and energy use, the European Union is consuming limited reserves at a rate that compromises the availability of energy to future generations and threatens the local and global environment."[6] (See Table 2.2.)

TABLE 2.1
Energy supply indicators, EU and accession countries

	Fossil Fuels Proved Reserves			Fossil Fuel Production, 2001				
	Crude Oil 1/1/03 (Million barrels)	Natural Gas 1/1/03 (Trillion cubic feet)	Coal 2001 (Million short tons)	Total Oil Production (Thousand barrels per day)	Dry Natural Gas (Trillion cubic feet)	Coal (Million short tons)	Electric Generation Capacity 2001 (Million kilowatts)	Crude Refining Capacity, 1/1/03 (Thousand barrels per day)
Austria	86	0.8	28	21	0.1	6.5	14	209
Belgium	0	0.0	0	0	0.0	13.8	14	791
Denmark	1,347	3.0	0	346	0.3	7.6	13	176
Finland	0	0.0	0	0	0.0	7.3	16	252
France	148	0.5	40	35	0.1	20.9	111	1,903
Germany	342	11.3	72,753	86	0.8	265.1	114	2,267
Greece	9	0.0	3,168	6	0.0	75.9	10	407
Ireland	0	0.7	15	0	0.0	3.2	4	71
Italy	622	8.0	37	79	0.5	22.1	69	2,300
Luxembourg	0	0.0	0	0	0.0	0.2	0	0
Netherlands	106	62.0	548	46	2.7	23.4	21	1,207
Portugal	0	0.0	40	0	0.0	5.2	10	304
Spain	158	0.1	728	7	0.0	45.2	48	1,322
Sweden	0	0.0	1	0	0.0	3.7	33	424
United Kingdom	4,715	24.6	1,653	2,541	3.7	70.8	76	1,789
Sub-total	7,533	111.0	79,010	3,167	8.3	570.7	554	13,422
Accession - 10	235	7.7	32,388	76	0.3	276.1	76	1,128
Total EU + 10	7,768	118.7	111,398	3,243	8.6	846.8	630	14,550
United States	22,446	183.5	273,656	8,957	19.4	1,121	813	16,623

Sources: *Energy Information Administration (EIA)* and *Oil & Gas Journal*

FIGURE 2.2
World energy consumption, 2001

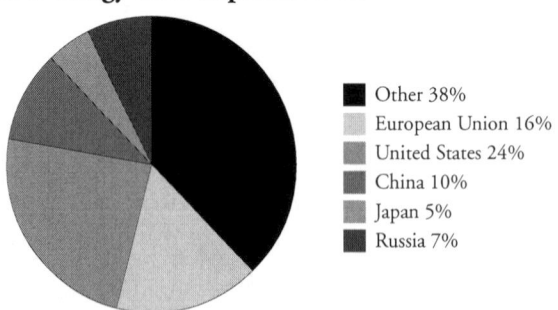

- Other 38%
- European Union 16%
- United States 24%
- China 10%
- Japan 5%
- Russia 7%

Source: EIA

TABLE 2.2
Total primary energy consumption by energy type
(percentage of total consumption), 2002

	OECD Europe	EU-15	EU-25*
Petroleum	40.7	43.1	38.4
Natural gas	22.7	23.5	22.6
Coal	16.3	13.5	18.5
Net nuclear electric power	12.6	13.9	14.4
Net hydroelectric power	6.4	4.4	5.8**
Other	1.4	1.5	0.3

Source: *EU's Parliamentary Assembly*, http://assembly.coe.int/Documents/WorkingDocs/Doc05/EDOC10458.htm

Note: 'Other' includes net geothermal, solar, wind, and biomass (wood and waste) electric power; *in 2000 (Eurostat data); **all renewable.

The EU's dependence on energy imports has been increasing constantly, while European oil production, especially from the North Sea fields, is dropping. The EU imports 50 per cent of its energy requirements,[7] and with central and eastern European countries joining the Union, imports will become more significant. According to a report published by the European Commission, two-thirds of the EU's total energy requirements will be imported by 2020.[8] The former EU Commissioner for Energy, Loyola de Palacio, anticipated that the EU will import 90 per cent of its oil and 70 per cent of its natural gas by that year.[9]

Most of the EU's oil needs have historically been supplied by the ME. In 1992 almost 4 mb/d – more than 25 per cent of total ME oil production were exported to the European continent.[10] In 1999, OPEC countries supplied 43 per cent of EU oil, 30 per cent of this coming from the PG.[11] The Energy Commission's Green Paper of 2000 expects OPEC to cover as much as half of the EU's energy needs by 2020, compared to about 40 per cent at present.[12]

A similar dependence has developed with regard to gas. In the next decades, gas use will increase most rapidly due to environmental concerns and the phasing out of much of the EU's nuclear energy capacity.[13] Europe uses natural gas for 22 per cent of its energy needs, with over 90 per cent of its total gas imports coming from just three sources – Russia, Norway and Algeria, Russia contributing 25 per cent of Europe's natural gas imports.[14]

Russia's increasing geopolitical importance as a source of different energies – oil, natural gas and electricity – and its position as the largest energy supplier outside of OPEC has encouraged Moscow to ensure its position as a major energy exporter to Europe and dominant force in Europe's markets, as well as to support its domestic and foreign policy objectives. Hence, the geopolitical dimension of the EU's growing dependence on gas and oil imports is considerable. According to an EU official report,

> Future imports of fossil fuels will tend to come from increasingly distant places with obvious price consequences (…) Such a situation [especially for those countries which are completely dependent on a single gas pipeline linking them to a single supplier country] naturally makes many European countries vulnerable to supply shocks, price oscillation, transport costs and other risks.[15]

In such a situation, as indicated earlier, "The EU does not yet have all the means possible to change the international market. This weakness was clearly highlighted at the end of 2000 by the strong increase in oil prices."[16] The oil shocks of the 1970s demonstrated the largely negative impact on Europe's economy and society that interruptions to supplies and fickle energy prices can have. The determinant impact of high oil prices on economic growth and inflation as well as unemployment in the EU also affected Europe's economic competitiveness. Although such circumstances caused changes in energy markets aimed at reducing dependence on oil, it did not affect the rise in fossil fuel demand over previous decades and is not expected to act in this way for the foreseeable future.

Strategy for security of energy supply

To tackle the two major challenges facing the EU, i.e. volatility of oil prices and its growing dependence on imported energy, the Energy Commission's White Paper in 1995 emphasised the importance of a secure energy supply as a prerequisite for the EU's successful economy. The White Paper also identified environmental protection and improving the competitiveness of European businesses as two more of its three main objectives. It stressed the significance of proper economic and political ties with oil- and gas-producing countries. So, in the geopolitical sense, the EU was seen as needing to variegate its energy supplies and suppliers as well as its energy resources.

At present, it seems that the EU is employing the same policy as the US used during President Carter's term when the 1979 oil crisis occurred. Its intention is to implement a more active role in the security of its structural interests in the PG: to link oil market security to geopolitical conditions and a more committed and apparent EU policy by establishing a military force to react in conflicts, with a focus on crisis-management.

To achieve the aims of the White Paper, the EU's need to develop a strategy aimed at enhancing its energy security in the mid and long term was highlighted (emphasised later in the Green Paper of 2000) by means of:

- the progressive substitution of oil by alternative sources of energy and their technological tools
- an effective demand policy to decrease the energy intensity of EU economies and disconnect the relation between energy consumption and economic growth with respect to a more prominent integration of energy policy among the EU members
- maximising environmental protection, including energy efficiency, energy saving and climate protection, specifically in domestic activities with respect to the Kyoto Protocol aims of reducing greenhouse gases
- to stabilise the needs of energy supply policy with the EU's economic, political and environmental goals, via intervention in the internal market and proper ties with oil- and gas-producer countries for greater market diversification, better market transparency and adequate supply pacts, and also the greater possibility of affecting the international market
- power to control any challenges to energy supply policy before they emerge as a crisis. The EU Brussels agreement of 22 November 2004 to create a rapid reaction force (RRF) of a number of units each made up of 1,500 troops, to be deployed at short notice in conflicts around the world with a focus on crisis-management, humanitarian relief and peace-keeping tasks independently of NATO is apposite in this regard.

The European Union and Persian Gulf security

The European Union energy supply policy has encouraged the EU to consider an extensive access to PG security and adopt a greater geopolitical role in this waterway. The EU's major concerns in this regard are:

- the necessity of continued access to oil and gas at predictable and controllable prices, also profitable markets in the PG oil-producer states
- the security of European investments in the PG
- the constant dominance of the PG oil fields coinciding with the reduction in production of older oil fields in Europe and North America
- uncertainty about the accessibility of oil from other major sources in the Caspian Basin, Central Asia, Russia, the South China Sea and China
- increasing global demand for oil and gas because of economic growth anticipation
- more significant trends of oil use in transportation sectors.

The EU has common concerns in the PG with the US and has played a supportive role in contributing to the coalition that liberated Kuwait from Iraqi occupation and later toppled Saddam's regime; such relations are likely to be continued in long-term policy. Nonetheless, due to some diverging interests from Washington, the EU has been keen to form its own relations with the energy-producer states in the PG.

There is no consensus on foreign policy among the members of the EU and each member pursues its own national interests, although "there is still a lingering fear in Europe that the United States will embroil European countries in conflicts that do not involve threats to their vital interests".[17] In addition, the EU, which is even more dependent on the PG's energy than the US, will continue over the next decade to use the PG as its dominant source of energy supplies, the source to which the AP region will also turn to fill its burgeoning energy demands (see Figure 2.3). Consequently, the perception is likely to arise that a serious interruption of PG oil supplies would cause severe economic and financial dislocation as well as political and social instability in the developing world, and this in turn could generate pressure for Western military action.[18] This will mean more US military presence and control over energy routes.

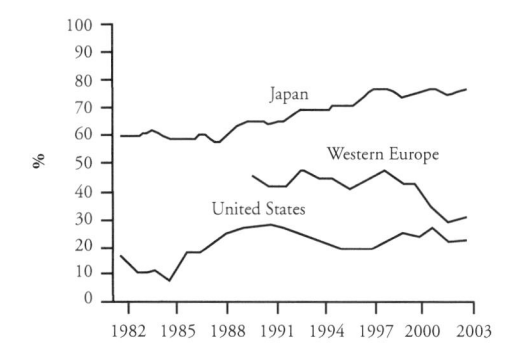

FIGURE 2.3
Net oil imports from the PG as a percentage of total net oil imports

```
100
 90
 80                    Japan
 70
 60
%50                          Western Europe
 40
 30   United States
 20
 10
  0
    1982 1985 1988 1991 1994 1997 2000 2003
```

Source: Energy Information Administration (EIA), http://www.eia.doe.gov/cabs/pgulf2.html

The significance of the PG's huge natural gas reserves at 41 per cent of total proven world gas reserves has increased the geopolitical importance of the PG. Enumerating the reserves of the Caspian Basin (about 340 TCF), which raises the figure to nearly 55 per cent, would further satisfy EU security perspectives (see Table 2.3).

Natural gas, which is regarded as the preferred fuel for electricity production in the EU, is becoming an increasingly important source of energy. The EU has more problems with its gas needs than oil. Europe's growing preference for natural gas, along with the reducing reserves in the North Sea, will give an added encouragement to political efforts already under way to strengthen ties with other major suppliers. Russia and North Africa are the main gas suppliers of the EU but studies of the European Commission predict that the Union's share of energy from foreign sources will rise from about half in 2000 to two-thirds by 2020, confirming the significance of the diversity of gas suppliers for the EU.[19]

Other EU concerns regarding its diversity of gas suppliers, besides the geopolitical advantages of Russia over the EU's markets and the EU's deep dependency on Russia's energy, is uncertainty concerning the unstable political, economic and social situation in North Africa. Preventing any disruption in gas supplies caused by, or the cause of, any possible turmoil or conflict in this area would require increasing European preparation and military planning (especially among NATO's southern European members) "to assemble a European-led force and to request NATO support for an emergency response".[20]

TABLE 2.3
Caspian Sea region oil and natural gas reserves

Country	Proven* oil reserves	Possible** oil reserves	Total oil reserves	Proven* natural gas reserves	Possible** natural gas reserves	Total natural gas reserves
Azerbaijan	1.2 BBL	32 BBL	33.2 BBL	4.4 TCF	35 TCF	39.4 TCF
Iran***	0.1 BBL	15 BBL	15.1 BBL	0 TCF	11 TCF	11 TCF
Kazakhstan	5.4 BBL	92 BBL	97.4 BBL	65 TCF	88 TCF	153 TCF
Russia***	2.7 BBL	14 BBL	16.7 BBL	N/A	N/A	N/A
Turkmenistan	0.6 BBL	80 BBL	80.6 BBL	101 TCF	159 TCF	260 TCF
Total	**10 BBL**	**233 BBL**	**243 BBL**	**170.4 TCF**	**293 TCF**	**463.4 TCF**

Sources: *Oil and Gas Journal, Energy Information Administration,* http://www.angelfire.com/dragon/asif/Caspian_Sea_Region.htm
Notes: *proven reserves are defined as oil and natural gas deposits that are considered 90 per cent probable; **possible reserves are defined as oil and natural gas deposits that are considered 50 per cent probable; ***only the regions near the Caspian are included // BBL = billion barrels, TCF = trillion cubic feet

Consequently, the EU has strengthened economic and political ties with all littoral states of the PG to ensure the continuation of its oil and gas supplies. Since the 1980s, bilateral trade relations between EU and GCC countries have changed from a negative trade balance to a positive one in favour of the EU. The GCC is the EU's fifth largest export market, while the GCC is the fourteenth biggest source of imports for the EU.[21]

The EU also benefited from Washington's absence in forming its own independent relations with Iran and Iraq (Iraq until the US invasion in 2003) to develop its business and secure its own energy deals outside of US control.

Iran, which contains the world's second largest natural gas reserves and around 10 per cent of the world's total oil resources, and with its geostrategic location as an entrance to the ME and Central Asian energy suppliers, has great potential to satisfy the political and economic needs of the emerging global powers, including the EU.

In spite of the EU's cooperation with the US in its PG security arrangements, to counterbalance the combined strength of Iran and Iraq (during Saddam Hussein's regime), in defence of the GCC states the EU did not follow the US policy of "Dual Containment" and tried to effect a more flexible policy in this region. Differences, especially over Iran, caused tension between the US and its European allies and weakened Washington's efforts to isolate Iran. The EU's disagreement with "Dual Containment" also undermined the effort to maintain international support for US policy towards Iraq during Saddam's regime. At the same time, EU flexibility modified the hostile sentiments of the region's people towards the West and provided suitable economic and political opportunities from which the EU benefits.

Hence, the bilateral trade of the EU with Iraq that was interrupted from 1991 to 1996 was once again cultivated following the start of the UN oil-for-food programme in 1997. The EU became the second main trading partner of Iraq with 33 per cent of Iraq's foreign trade, after the US with 42 per cent. According to the European Commission, in 2001 the EU, accounting for 55 per cent of Iraq's imports to its market, imported mainly energy products from Iraq, which accounted for 99.9 per cent of its imports from that country. This figure contained 2.5 per cent of the EU's total energy imports, with Iraq being its ninth highest energy supplier.[22]

Concerning Iran, Europeans, as Hollis affirms, "see this country as such a significant and powerful player in the Gulf that to attempt to exclude it from a say in regional affairs is to court antagonism".[23] The EU has successfully mediated Washington–Tehran disputes, preventing these from emerging as crises, e.g. Iran's nuclear activities – even since 2005 when such activities have become a serious international matter.

EU investments in Iranian projects like the development of South Pars (which, ranking as the world's largest offshore gas field, is Iran's largest energy project, and already has absorbed approximately US$20 billion in investment) have confronted a series of unacceptable choices for the US: whether to impose sanctions on these firms and face big risks in its relations with its allies or to ignore their activities and face weakening international support for Washington's efforts to isolate Iran. According to the European Commission, despite the ongoing question of Iran's nuclear programme having a serious negative impact on bilateral trade relations, the EU is still Iran's largest trading partner, accounting for almost a third of its exports. In 2007, EU exports to Iran were 10 billion, and its imports from Iran were 13.8 billion. According to the European Commission, close to 90 per cent of EU imports from Iran are energy related whereas this rate was about 80 per cent in 2005 (mainly oil products), representing 3.8 per cent of total EU imports of energy products. Iran ranks as the sixth highest supplier of energy products for the EU, having held seventh position in 2005.[24]

The European Commission's advice for securing the EU's gas supply by new long-term contracts for imports from third countries and, as mentioned in documents of the Parliamentary Assembly of the Council of Europe, to diversify its energy supplies and suppliers in the geopolitical sense, is for the EU to:

> [expand] the energy mix in individual countries, [develop] a closer energy partnership with the Caspian Sea region (…) and [strengthen] its long-term energy co-operation with Russia. To support an eastbound partnership (primarily in natural gas but also in oil), major investments in network and interconnection infrastructure, as well as in new transit facilities, are needed for transport from, for example, the Caspian Sea to other parts of Europe.[25]

Iran's significance in the EU energy security policy, especially the security of gas supplies, is conceivable in the EU disagreement with the US' hostile policy towards Iran, e.g. "Dual Containment". The earlier success of a British company in counselling the very important gas pipeline of "peace pipe" from Iran to India via Pakistan, which was originally opposed by Washington, is noticeable.

However, since 2005 Iran has found itself entangled with both the EU and the US over its nuclear programme, due to consistency in Western policy in respect of their red lines as well as in seeking to avoid upsetting the wider international Euro–American axis in world politics.

Conclusion

The EU, which faces the geopolitical effects of its growing dependence on external energy, specifically gas as a preferred energy source, has tried to variegate its fossil fuels supplies and suppliers. While the PG will remain the main source of EU energy supplies in coming decades, the EU, in order to reduce its dependency on energy supplies – especially natural gas from Russia and North Africa – has developed its economic and political ties with all littoral states of the PG to ensure future oil and gas supplies. In addition, the EU as an emerging global superpower is "deeply concerned about the US 'new order' in the ME",[26] and is not interested in the US plan of "The Greater ME" (GME), which is designed for US permanent hegemony in this region. The EU's difference with the US in dealing with the ME countries, which is rooted in their hidden rivalry to control the strategic region of the ME with its major energy reserves, has become particularly obvious with regard to Iran.

The EU, which is seeking to originate its own policy in the region, especially with regards to securing its energy supply, also faces the steady increase of AP demand for oil and gas from the PG. Further, Washington's intense political and military presence in the ME/AP regions, and China and India's political, economic and military activities working to assure the security of their energy supplies, will have a profound impact on the geopolitics of the PG region as well as an effective impact on EU energy security policy. Under these circumstances, which will be studied in the next chapter, the EU decision to create a rapid reaction force independently of NATO, in spite of its small and limited forces, seems a starting point for the EU to adopt a more significant geopolitical role in the strategic waterway of the PG.

Notes

1 This chapter was first published in *Journal of Middle Eastern Geopolitics*, vol. 1, no. 2, 2005, 59–73. It has subsequently been amended and updated.
2 Energy Information Administration (EIA), http://www.eia.doe.gov/emeu/cabs/pgulf.html (24 October 2005; can no longer be accessed).
3 Michael Klare (2003), "The Bush/Cheney energy strategy: implications for U.S. foreign and military policy", Information Clearing House, http://www.informationclearinghouse.info/article4458.htm (accessed 2 October 2004).
4 Geoffrey Kemp and Robert Harkavy, *Strategic geography and the changing Middle East* (Washington, D. C.: Brookings Institution Press, 1997), 120.
5 Ibid., 119.
6 *INTUSER*, "EU energy supply policy", http://www.intuser.net/ufes34.php (8 November 2004).
7 *EUROPA*, http://europa.eu.int/scadplus/leg/en/lvb/l27037.htm (17 November 2004), http://europa.eu.int/comm/energy/library/commen.pdf (7 November 2004; can no longer be accessed).

8 *EIA*, http://www.eia.doe.gov/emeu/cabs/euro.html#Table2 (can no longer be accessed).
9 *Metering International, Newsletter 1* (4 September 2002). EU energy policy focuses on reducing consumption (Europe), http://www.metering.com/bits/newsletter1_4Sep2002.htm (17 November 2004; can no longer be accessed).
10 *EIA*, http://www.eia.doe.gov/emeu/cabs/euro.html#Table2 (can no longer be accessed); also Kemp and Harkavy, op. cit., 119.
11 *EUROPA*, http://europa.eu.int/comm/energy/library/commen.pdf (can no longer be accessed).
12 *The Report of the Committee on Economic Affairs and Development of Parliamentary Assembly*, Doc. 10458 (22 February 2005) Europe's growing energy vulnerability, http://assembly.coe.int/Documents/WorkingDocs/Doc05/EDOC10458.htm (accessed 24 October 2005).
13 For details see (among many) http://www.eu-energy.com/eurosaf-fin.pdf (accessed 20 May 2008).
14 Ibid.
15 Ibid.
16 *EUROPA*, http://europa.eu.int/scadplus/leg/en/lvb/l27037.htm (can no longer be accessed).
17 Richard Sokolsky, Stuart Johnson, and Stephen Larrabee, "Persian Gulf security: Improving allied military contributions", *RAND*, http://66.218.69.11/search/cache?p=europe+gulf+security+challenges&ei=UTF-8&fl=0&u=www.rand.org/congress/terrorism/phase2/persiangulf.html&w=europe+gulf+security+challenges&d=K6o4VGFULnZP&icp=1&.intl=us (24 October 2005; can no longer be accessed).
18 Ibid.
19 Ibid.
20 Sokolsky, Johnson, and Larrabee, op. cit.
21 Statistical information from *EUROPA*, http://europa.eu.int/comm/trade/issues/bilateral/regions/gcc/index_en.htm (7 December 2004; can no longer be accessed).
22 Ibid.
23 Rosemary Hollis, "Europe and Gulf security: a competitive business". In David Long and Christian Koch (eds), *Gulf security in the twenty-first century* (Abu Dhabi: The Emirates Center for Strategic Studies and Research, 1997), 75.
24 *EUROPA* http://europa.eu.int/comm/trade/issues/bilateral/countries/iran/index_en.htm (20 November 2005 and 15 December 2008; can no longer be accessed).
25 Also, *EUROPA*, http://europa.eu.int/scadplus/leg/en/lvb/l27047.htm (can no longer be accessed).
26 Paul Rogers (20 January 2005), "A Bush administration buoyed by electoral success is extending its military ambitions to Iran and Syria", *Opendemocracy*, http://www.opendemocracy.net/themes/article.jsp?id=2&articleId=2316# (21 January 2005; can no longer be accessed).

3

Asian-Pacific region and Persian Gulf energy security[1]

Introduction

The Asian-Pacific (AP) region is the world's fastest-growing energy consumer that imports its major energy needs from the ME.

The AP's vital need to maintain a safe and sufficient energy supply, from the volatile region of the ME/PG, has increased the concerns of Western countries that are also dependent on this region's energy. The competitive attitudes of both the AP and the West, particularly the US, combined with their political trends and geostrategic interests, threaten not only PG stability but also global security.

Furthermore, the AP's growing dependence on the volatile region of the ME/PG is an increasing concern for Asian governments, seen as a matter of economy and of fundamental national security confronting them with serious economic, political and security challenges.

Energy policy and security

The AP region, according to the data of 1999, imported some 60 per cent of its oil from the ME, compared with just 13 per cent imported by the US and 21 per cent by Western Europe. In the next two decades it is expected to become the biggest world energy consumer at 27 per cent of total world energy consumption, while the US is predicted to consume 25 per cent, Western Europe 18 per cent and Japan 5 per cent.

The PG, as the main dominant energy source and gateway for global energy in the future, together with the AP region's rapid economic development reflecting its great growth of population, has paved the way for a closer relationship with and mutual reliance between East and West Asia. This entrenched interdependency between the AP and the PG in the energy sector also leads to the potential for creating a new, or at least disturbing the current, regional and international balance of power.

The growing Asian demand for energy from the PG has increased the geopolitical importance of this waterway. Although the strategic significance of these new energy linkages has not yet been outlined, the potential for significant geopolitical evolutions in this region via the interdependency of the two poles of East and West Asia is substantial.

However, for some scholars questions still remain, with no certain answers. For example, Calder asks, "Is this principally a benign commercial relationship, or could it fundamentally challenge the prevailing Western dominated political order?"[2] Manning looks at other dimensions, asking, "What are [the] geopolitical implications for PG security, for Asian security, and for the US role in both South-West and East Asia?"[3]

China, as the world's most populous country and the second largest energy consumer after the US, is expected to keep its position as the largest oil consumer in Asia, its economy having increased twofold in size during the 1990s. China, as an oil exporter until 1993, now produces only for domestic use and according to some estimates its proven oil reserves could be depleted in fourteen years. "China's oil demand is projected by EIA [July 2004] to reach 12.8 million bbl/d by 2025, with net imports of 9.4 million bbl/d [see Figure 3.1]. As the source of around 40% of world's oil demand growth over the past four years, Chinese oil demand already is a very significant factor in world oil markets."[4] India, Japan and South Korea as well will continue to be major oil consumers in the AP in the next decades.

FIGURE 3.1
China's oil production and consumption, 1980–2003

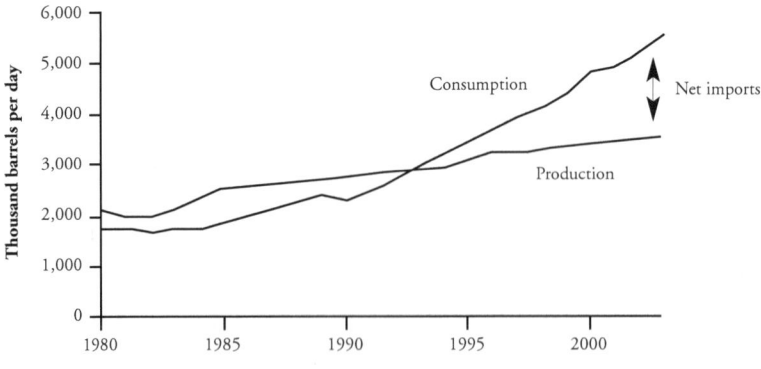

Source: Energy Information Administration

Although oil will remain the main energy source in the world, natural gas is expected to experience a faster rate growth. South Korea, Taiwan, China and India are expected to triple their demand for natural gas over the next decade. Therefore, it would not be suppositious to accept the various expectations that the AP region by 2010 will be the world's largest consumer of primary energy and will receive approximately 95 per cent of its energy needs from the ME.

As Manning observes, Asia's growing dependence on the volatile region of the ME is "a growing concern for Asian governments that have viewed energy largely in strategic terms, as one of the 'commanding heights' of the economy and a matter of fundamental national security".[5] Such a geostrategic disposition has confronted the AP region with serious challenges, as outlined below.

Economic challenges: The economic growth of the AP region, which has contributed towards regional stability and development since the end of WWII, has been facing the threat of reduction for two main reasons: 1) the rising levels of oil consumption and demand for energy at a greater rate than economic growth; and 2) the effect of oil-market volatility on the region, especially due to growing oil prices and its effect on the currencies.

The links between energy prices and financial markets confirmed in a July 2004 *Financial Times* article have profound implications for both energy security and the economics of the region.[6] The Asian financial crisis of 1997–1999 came as a shock to both the economics profession and the international policy community. Besides its impact on Asian countries' economic growth rates and on their energy demand, it raised fears of a worldwide financial contagion. Analysis of the further link between price rises for oil and other commodities revealed the AP developing countries' greater vulnerability regarding the economic aspect of energy security. Although the danger of oil shocks is not the most urgent element of energy security, it could affect economic growth, regional currency markets and domestic purchasing power, which is where the danger for these economies lies. Social unrest and political instability has even threatened some AP energy-dependent states with significant economies. The forecast these factors suggest for energy security and economics in the AP looks disturbing.[7]

Political and security challenges: The AP's high desire for oil and its external dependence on energy from a problematic region, the ME, could increase the danger of tension due to an oil shortage within the AP region itself. Any tension among specifically major regional players and key economic countries – viz. China, Japan and India – might cause some regional or global destabilisation and even new confrontation.

China's quiet shift to net oil importer status since 1993 has made Beijing an important actor in the increasingly competitive global oil and gas markets. AP energy security is closely connected to China's energy security.[8] How China satisfies its huge energy needs will be one of the most important challenges over the next decade from regional and global perspectives.

The energy security concerns and challenges within the AP, especially all those relating to the ME/PG, could have a profound impact on the geopolitics of the latter region, while, as was explained in the previous chapter, Western and particularly US dependence on oil imports from this region is also growing.

Geopolitical aspects of Asian-Pacific energy needs from the Persian Gulf

The vital interest of the AP regarding sufficient and safe energy supplies from the ME/PG has increased the concerns of Western countries dependent on this region's energy, as Kemp and Harkavy explain:

> [T]he growing needs of Asia pose a new problem, and the economic dimensions of the energy equation will have a very important security component. If the estimates of Asian energy requirements are of the right order of magnitude, it is clear that this Asian energy gap will have profound consequences for the global economy and the geopolitics of the Middle East.[9]

The energy competitive views of the AP and the West, specifically the US, and their political trends and interests in the geostrategic region of the PG threaten not just the stability of the PG but also global security.

To ensure energy supply security from the PG, the AP, like the EU, prefers to retain an independent geopolitical role from the US in PG security. Geo-economic factors have assisted proper political relations between the AP and the energy producer states in the PG, and so wider strategic interdependency has been created.

Because of the high Asian energy demand from the PG, a very wide relationship as well as a more mutual reliance has been formed within these two regions. Asia's specific attention to hydrocarbon investments in the PG region has increased the interest of the western part of Asia in trading with eastern countries in this continent. Such a relationship, along with the political support of AP countries – particularly the key economic states – could replace the cooperation axis of PG–West with PG–AP.

As Anoushiravan Ehteshami expresses it, "These trade and investment ties have given each of the two sides of the energy equation a large and equal stake in the economic stability and security of the other."[10]

China is one of these key economic states that, since the end of the Cold War, has established closer economic, political, military and security ties with many ME and Asian countries, including the regional powers. So, Beijing's strategy in this region is an amalgamation of different concerns, but on a geo-economic rather than geostrategic base. Economic profit – i.e. trade and energy – are China's strategic interests in the ME/PG and oil is "the key to the geopolitical linkage between China and the Middle East".[11] Hence, regional stability of the ME/PG is a vital political concern of Beijing. One of China's political achievements in this regard is the development of proper relations with major Middle Eastern adversaries in order to assure regional stability – e.g. Iran, Arab World and Israel – while at the same time cautiously acknowledging the US attitude in this arena to prevent any damage to its relations with Washington.

China's associations in the ME are, according to Rubin, driven by "economic goals rather than political ambitions". In 1994 President Jiang Zemin stated that China should aid dissident countries like Iran, creating profitable relationships, and oppose the US "hegemony" on the ME as "there may be no room there for any Chinese economic foothold".[12]

China, as a net oil-importer, has common interests with those of the oil-dependent West, and during the last two crises of Iraq in 1990 and 2003 has proved that "international stability furthering China's development is more important".[13] However, as a major importer of ME/PG energy it could face some clashes between its interests and its orientations with the West in the event of a further crisis, e.g. the Iranian nuclear programme. As Kemp and Harkavy note:

Unlike 1990, the key Asian countries might be less willing to accept American leadership in crisis management. (...) Similarly, if China and India become major importers of Middle East energy, they will likely have their own, more independent and possibly more confrontational, policies toward the region. There have been suggestions that China's embryonic blue water navy may eventually be deployed in the Indian Ocean in part to assure the security of oil supplies from the Gulf. (...) More speculative, but potentially very important, is the possible link between China's growing needs for Persian Gulf oil and its plans to develop a blue water navy with the capability of protecting its sea-lanes in the Indian Ocean and South China Sea and thereby posing a putative challenge to other maritime powers in the region, especially India and the United States. (...) It is impossible to imagine Chinese naval deployment in the Indian Ocean not soliciting a response from India.[14]

India has moved into sixth place in world energy consumption as one of three major powers in Asia, along with Russia and China, and is searching for a greater regional and international role. Although the Indian energy sector is mainly dependent on coal and oil accounts for about 30 per cent of India's total energy consumption, oil and gas as alternatives to the less efficient, more polluting coal energy are strategically important (see Figure 3.2).

FIGURE 3.2
India's oil production and consumption, 1990–2006*
(*2006 is an estimate)

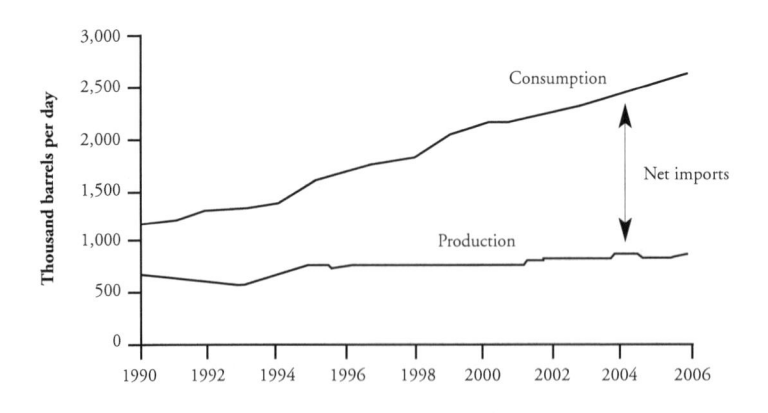

Source: *BA International Energy Annual,* 2004; *Short-term Energy Outlook,* January 2007

While India is facing declining oil production at home, approximately 75 per cent of its total oil-consumption requirements in 2006 were supposed to come from the volatile region of the ME.[15] Therefore, secure energy supplies would be significant for the continuation of its recent economic proliferation and rise as an economic power.

In this regard India's growing blue water navy has been a proper response to its increasing dependence on routes of oil tankers from the ME/PG. The expansion of India's navy, like China's, has raised some challenges to American influence in the Indian Ocean and South China Sea.[16]

From an economic point of view, India and China – besides some of their different policies and interests with Washington – appreciate their relations with the US, while the US as the most significant global and external power within Asia could assist securing the region's security as a vital factor to the economies of India and China. Washington, as well as its economic interests in these two populous developing markets that account for 37 per cent of the world's population, has various common strategic interests with each of them.[17] Interaction between these three internal and external Asian powers could affect the future stability and equilibrium of the AP region but there are some other issues that, for smooth interaction, must also be taken into consideration.

From a political perspective an objective harmonious interaction between the emerging powers of India and China with the third major regional power, Russia, would not please Washington because it would threaten US superiority and its world leadership and could lead to a multipolar world. Also, Chinese and Indian relations with Iran as an energy supplier and regional power in the PG increase Washington's unease. This is one of the most important strategic relationships since the end of the Cold War, which Ehteshami mentions as the growing military links between Asia's big three countries, China, India and Iran especially via Russia. "The growth of such relationships has also helped deepen Asian strategic interdependencies and create new opportunities for both cooperation and competition between the major continental Asian powers."[18]

US concerns about India, according to Guihong, are at the top of Washington's South Asia policy and come mostly from New Delhi's different strategy to match the emergence of China as a key world power and to cooperate, not compete, with it – especially in oil markets. The

US integrated military strategy for the Europe-Atlantic and Asian-Pacific regions perceives India in a geostrategic position in the Indian Ocean, he remarks. He also adds,

> The United States is especially concerned about China's challenge to its world leadership, while India is especially concerned about China's future relationship with Pakistan. For India [as a developing country, whose priority is economic development], creating or joining an alliance against China does not suit its national interests.[19]

Japan, with poor domestic energy resources, has been significantly dependent on the PG for its crude-oil imports. Its extreme dependence on foreign oil was the result of a massive switch from coal after WWII. The PG's portion of total Japanese crude-oil imports was 82.1 per cent during the 1969–1973 period. After that, with Tokyo's efforts to diversify geographically the sources of supply of its imported oil, especially since the first oil crisis of 1973–1974, it decreased significantly, but during the 1984–1988 period it still needed 68.9 per cent.[20] Before 1973 Iran was the biggest oil exporter of the PG to Japan, followed by Saudi Arabia. But later the Iranian position was replaced by other littoral states of the PG, viz. Saudi Arabia and the UAE.

Japan is the other AP key economic state with heavy dependence on PG energy that prefers its independent security role from the US, though is harmonious with it. Political convergence has assured Japan of US military support, but since the end of the Cold War Tokyo has realised that reliance only on Washington is not enough. Economic goals are Japan's main interest in the PG, so Tokyo will not have a challenging role in the geopolitical evolution of this region. What Japan is looking for, as Simon asserts, is an independent security role, an appropriate AP regional role and an international political role.[21] Under such circumstances energy is vital to the continuation of the economic growth of Japan.

Japan has been trying its best to reduce its dependency on the PG for its imported oil supply, but because of oils indispensability and the country's long-term needs it has sought to establish relations of interdependence with the PG states rather than total trading. According to Ishida, while the Iran–Iraq war damaged the development of Japan–PG interdependence, peace in this region from Tokyo's point of view is an absolutely necessary precondition to achieving bilateral economic and cultural relations. Consequently as he states:

Japan has always refrained from providing the Gulf with weapons in exchange for oil: in other words, Japan has sought to implement its oil strategy in the Gulf without arms deals. Japan is confident that this policy will be very helpful in keeping the Gulf peaceful.[22]

Besides concerns regarding Japan's military revival, the growing fear of US military superiority in the AP region has paved the way for China, India and Russia to enter into wide military agreements with many Asian and ME/PG countries since the end of the Cold War.

Iran and emerging Asian Great Powers' interdependency

Iran has turned away its traditional main energy interaction with the West mainly as a response to US political and economic sanctions since the victory of the Islamic Revolution.

Iran, which contains the world's second largest natural gas reserves and around 10 per cent of the world total oil resources, perceives its geostrategic location to be an entrance to the ME and Central Asian energy suppliers. Iran's great potential to satisfy political and economic needs of the emerging global powers, viz. China, India, Russia and the EU, and simultaneously its awareness of their strategic concerns, has established relations of interdependency with them, rather than one-sided trading. The US' hostile policy of Iran's containment has multiply resulted in creating natural allies in the region against US superiority as well as providing the opportunity of forming a multipolar system in the world.

The US' attempt to dominate the world's energy sectors and the growing influence of Western powers in those regions, especially in the ME/PG (with two recent wars in the PG) and Central Asia during the last decade, along with NATO's eastern expansions, have caused larger developing countries such as China and India as well as Russia economic and political concerns. Consequently, the Asian key power countries have tried to establish strategic and long-term ties with key energy producer countries in the region, especially Iran. Iran, in return, has succeeded in weakening the various US embargos and strengthening its regional position in the power balance. As Ehteshami remarks:

> [T]he spreading of American influence to this region [Central Asia], on the doorstep of so many of its competitors in Asia, could be a

costly venture. Any real gains by the United States will more than likely accelerate the pace of security cooperation between China, Russia and Iran.[23]

In this respect *China* signed a significant energy agreement with Iran, named the "Agreement of the Century" in 2004, worth an estimated US$200 billion over 25 years, during which China will purchase Iranian oil and gas and help to develop Iran's Yadavaran oil field in the western border of the country. According to *The Washington Post*, "Economic ties between two of Asia's oldest civilizations (…) have broad political implications. Holding a veto at the UN Security Council, China has become the key obstacle to putting international pressure on Iran." From a political and economic perspective the two countries also share concerns over the growing presence of US and other Western troops in Central and South Asia; hence they have considered cooperation in Central Asia in the energy sector. As *The Washington Post* cites (quoted from Ali Sabzevari who wrote in the Iranian newspaper *Keyhan International*), "Politically, the two countries share a common interest in checking the inroads being made by NATO in Asia. (…) The presence of outsiders does not bode well for peace and security."[24]

India, by signing a similar but smaller agreement with Iran in January 2005, also joined the Iran–China "Agreement of the Century". According to this agreement, which was worth US$20 billion and will reach US$40 billion over a 25-year period, Iran will export 7.5 million metric tonnes of liquified natural gas annually, starting in 2009. India will also invest in the development of Iran's biggest onshore oil field, Yadavaran, along with the Chinese company Sinopec as the operator of the field with a 50 per cent share and the National Iranian Oil Company with a 30 per cent share. Indian participation in Yadavaran, where estimates suggest up to 3 million barrels of crude oil, will be about 20 per cent (or 60,000–100,000 barrels per day). Jufeir oil field is the other area where India will invest in Iran's soil.[25]

The Indian gas-imported supplies will go through a US$4.5 billion pipeline from Iran via Pakistan. The agreement for starting technical estimates to establish the 2,775 kilometre pipeline was achieved after 12 years of political tension between India and Pakistan despite, according to some Western presses, US efforts to isolate Iran regionally by pressuring Islamabad not to enter into an energy deal with Tehran at this juncture.

The Iran–India energy agreement is part of Iran's successful policy to improve its relations with Pakistan and India, and has geostrategic importance for the region and for the US; hence it was expressed by former Iranian Foreign Minister Kamal Kharrazi as "the most significant outcome of the strategic agreements reached upon by the two countries so far". He affirmed the Iran–Pakistan–India pipeline as the best and most desirable step towards enhancing cooperation between Tehran and New Delhi in the field of energy which "no doubt, would have positive impact on the regional convergence".

Kharrazi also emphasised that the "conclusion of an agreement amongst Russia, India and Iran regarding the construction of [the] International North-South Transport Corridor is a major example of close regional cooperation (…) [and the] creation of [an] East Corridor connecting Uzbekistan, Iran, Afghanistan, is an indication of cooperation between New Delhi and Tehran".[26]

Furthermore India, in its long-term energy scheme, has made it clear that it views Iran and Russia as two significant partners for its importing of energy.

Russia, as an important Eurasian power that has strategic motives for a much wider relationship with Iran in the post-Cold War, and like Tehran, having regional geopolitical concerns and desire for a multipolar international order to challenge the hegemonic influence of the US, appreciates Iran's position in Asia's security. Therefore, Russia has ignored the US policy of Iran's containment since the 1980s, and along with China and India has strengthened its military cooperation with Tehran, Iran being very keen to build up its defence potential with their help. Moreover as Kemp and Harkavy state:

> Iran plays an important role vis-à-vis its neighbors in all directions. Its relations with Russia have political, military, and economic overtones and, indeed, Russian-Iranian decisions on the future of the Caspian Sea may be determinative for many of the oil agreements that will be worked out with Azerbaijan, Turkmenistan, and Kazakhstan in the future.[27]

Russia, despite US objections, is the only Iranian foreign partner assisting in the construction of its nuclear power stations.

Iran's astute strategic policy in the region has even caused concern among some other regional countries, especially those with energy-importing needs. According to a Turkish analyst, Ertan, Iran's significant agreements with China and India have increased Tehran's power and influence in Asia, which should be a matter of concern to all countries, including Turkey. He also stresses that these agreements have had an enormous impact on shaping the energy policy of Beijing and New Delhi and "will definitely influence the global energy-politics as well, even before the details have been examined".[28]

Furthermore, Rogers, in a 2005 article affirming the successful policy of Iran in response to US embargoes, looks at the US administration's current difficulties and thought process regarding the ME, especially the chance of military action against Iran or Syria. He asserts that the next two to three years are crucial for the neo-conservatives of the US administration, "who see an opportunity to implant their own worldview even further into US politics (…) to ensure that US security policy follows the vision of a New American Century in a manner which makes it difficult for a future administration to reverse". He adds, "For this to happen, the success of current US policy in the middle east will be pivotal"; any plan for further military strikes in the ME faces serious problems, e.g. damage to energy infrastructures and a further increase in antagonism to the US across the region. The huge range of difficulties facing any US military action against the regime in Tehran, he continues, makes these judgements especially significant:

> These difficulties are highlighted by the impressive way that Iran is rapidly forging links with other major global players. (…) These agreements [with China and India] supplement existing close cooperation between Iran and Russia. They demonstrate how Iran's political leadership is systematically developing long-term links with key states. The economic benefits are evident but the political implications, given Iran's current tense relationship with the US, may be even more important. These benefits make it well nigh impossible for the US to organise effective economic sanctions against Iran, should it try to do so.[29]

Japan, as well, has been increasing its investments in Iran under its policy of seeking overseas equity in oil projects. Japanese consortiums have signed different multi-billion dollars agreements with Iran for oil and gas development projects, viz. the huge onshore Azadegan oil field, two major oil fields of Soroush/Nowrooz located offshore, about 50 miles west of Kharg Island, the operational refinery of Arak, and the onshore natural gas of South Pars.

Japan, as the third largest oil consumer (after the US and China), and apart from its interests in the PG, has also been seeking equity stakes in the Caspian Sea region and the Russian Far East as alternatives to Japan's strategic goal of reducing its dependence on ME oil imports. Despite the feasibility of accessing other major reserve regions, including Siberia and western China, political difficulties and economic costs for developing these regions continue to reduce the possibilities of choice. In addition, the Caspian Sea region, with its potential for becoming a major oil and natural gas exporter over the next decade, could save the importing energy states from total dependence on ME/PG energy. However, besides its reserves, which are much smaller than the PG's energy resources, a number of obstacles threaten the Caspian Sea region's energy capability, e.g. a shortage of suitable export infrastructure, disparity about new export routes, and sea-bordering disagreements between its five littoral states. Consequently, the geopolitical importance of the PG stays unique and, even in a scenario of Caspian states' success in solving their political and economic problems, Iran will remain a key regional player in further power relations in Asia. Finally, the geostrategic status of the PG and the state of Iran as a key player will increase under the circumstances of:

- the growing needs of the AP region for PG oil and gas even without collective security cooperation agreements within member states
- increasing EU dependence on PG energy and its new rapid reaction force (RRF) for a more active role in the security of its structural interests in this region independently of NATO
- the US attempt to dominate the world's energy sectors and its desire for a permanent hegemony in the ME/PG and its military presence all over the Asian continent
- pursuing each side's own policy to secure its energy supply from the PG, by developing ties with the littoral states or strengthening its military forces.

Simultaneously, there would be the potential for some political and economic contradictions, which could lead to tension in both regions of the AP and the PG despite their global dimensions in relation to energy prices and security supplies. To avoid such potential conflicts, or even the occurrence of some kind of Energy Cold War between the East and the West, some analysts suggest that all parties should concentrate more on geo-economic parameters rather than geostrategic values. Salameh, a technical expert of the United Nations Industrial Development Organisation (UNIDO) in Vienna, believes that "potential conflicts can be resolved not by force but through markets and investment and also through the diversification of energy sources and the promotion of alternative energy development and use across the region".[30] In addition, Edward Luttwak, emphasising the inefficacious traditional role of military forces, affirms that, in the absence of a bipolar world order armed forces only perform a residual role while geo-economics has become the essential, fundamental factor of the world order.[31]

Conclusion

The strategic importance of the PG has increased mainly because of the development of strategic interdependency between the AP and ME regions, which has influenced the international balance of power and also the increasing dependence of the West, particularly the US, on the PG region for energy imports.

In this respect the PG states, especially Iran, are working with all parties according to their national interests. AP energy security cooperation could also reduce regional energy tensions and promote cooperative regional security. However, the military attitude in the region will provoke conflicts as the littoral states of the PG have been forced to join the process under the current situation. Hence, as Kemp and Harkavy remark, "[W]hatever happens, the many sources of conflict in the Persian Gulf region will mean that security concerns and military planning will continue to go hand in hand with economic development and efforts at conflict resolution."[32] Under current geopolitical evolutions via the interdependency of East and West Asia, the formation of a new regional and international balance of power, the PG states, by recognising their significant regional position, should emphasise their energy policies more consistently and be more active rather than objective.

However, energy security in the PG will be very heavily influenced by how the regional and ultra-regional powers understand each others' perceptions of threat as well as their national security issues, an important matter which will be studied in the next chapter.

NOTES

1. This chapter was first presented at the 16th International Conference on the Persian Gulf (18–19 September 2006). The conference was entitled "The Persian Gulf: An Emerging Security Structure" and was held in the Centre for Graduate Studies of the Faculty of Law and Political Science, University of Tehran. It has subsequently had some minor amendments.
2. Kent Calder (March–April 1996), "Asia's empty gas tank", *Foreign Affairs*, vol. 75, no. 2, cited in Robert Manning (spring 2000), "The Asian energy predicament", *Survival*, vol. 42, no. 3, 73–88, http://www.cfr.org/content/publications/attachments/Manning_Energy_Article.pdf#search='Robert%20A.%20Manning%20asian%20energy%20predicament' (accessed 29 September 2006).
3. Manning, ibid.
4. From Energy Information Administration (EIA), Country analysis Briefs, China, http://www.cfr.org/content/publications/attachments/Manning_Energy_Article.pdf#search='Robert%20A.%20Manning%20asian%20energy%20predicament (4 February 2005; can no longer be accessed).
5. Manning, op. cit.
6. Cited in Richard Giragosian (24 August 2004), "East Asia tackles energy security", *Asia Times on line*, http://www.atimes.com/atimes/Asian_Economy/FH24Dk01.html (accessed 7 November 2004).
7. Ibid.
8. Details in Ji, GX (winter 1998), "China versus Asian Pacific energy security", *Korean Journal of Defense Analysis*, vol. 10, issue 2, 109.
9. Geoffrey Kemp and Robert Harkavy, *Strategic geography and the changing Middle East* (Washington, D. C.: Brookings Institution Press, 1997), 129.
10. Anoushiravan Ehteshami, "Asian geostrategic realities and their impact on Middle East-Asia relations". In H. Carter and A. Ehteshami (eds), *The Middle East's relations with Asia and Russia* (London, USA and Canada: Routledge Curzon, 2004), 14.
11. Kemp and Harkavy, op. cit., 130.
12. Barry Rubin (March 1999), "China's Middle East strategy", *Middle East Review of International Affairs (MERIA)*, vol. 3, no. 1, http://meria.idc.ac.il/journal/1999/issue1/jv3n1a4.html (accessed 20 April 2004).
13. Ibid.
14. Kemp and Harkavy, op. cit., 130.
15. *Asia Times Online*, http://www.atimes.com/atimes/China/FB07Ad05.html (accessed 7 February 2004).
16. Keith Brasher (18 February 2005) "2 big appetites take seats at the oil table", *The New York Times* [Newspaper online], http://www.nytimes.com/2005/02/18/business/worldbusiness/18energy.html?pagewanted=1&adxnnl=0&adxnnlx=1108824803-E3sesbMYjrmP/x1qcNx82A (accessed 19 February 2005).

17 For details see Zhang Guihong (2003), "U.S.–India security relations implications for China", *Faultlines: writings on conflict and resolution*, vol. 14, article 2, http://www.satp.org/satporgtp/publication/faultlines/volume14/Article2.htm (accessed February 2005).
18 Ehteshami, op. cit., 5.
19 Guihong, op. cit.
20 Statistical information are drawn out from Sekyu Renmei (The Petroleum Association of Japan), cited in Susumu Ishida, "Japan's oil strategy in the Gulf without arms deals". In Charles Davies (ed.), *Global Interests in the Arab Gulf* (UK: University of Exeter Press, 1992), 194.
21 Among many, see S. W. Simon (winter 1999), "Multilateralism and Japan's security policy", *Korean Journal of Defense Analysis*, vol. 11, issue 2, 79–96.
22 Ishida, op. cit., 189–190.
23 Ehteshami, op. cit., 17–18.
24 Robin Wright (17 November 2004), "Iran's new alliance with China could cost US leverage", *The Washington Post*, http://www.washingtonpost.com/wp-dyn/articles/A55414-2004Nov16.html (accessed 22 February 2005).
25 http://www.atimes.com/atimes/South_Asia/GA11Df07.html.
26 *IRNA*, 21 February 2005 in New Delhi.
27 Kemp and Harkavy, op. cit., 75.
28 Among many, see Fikret Ertan (25 January 2005), "Iran–India Energy Agreement", Istanbul, *Freepublic*, http://www.freerepublic.com/focus/f-news/1331738/posts (accessed 21 February 2005).
29 Paul Rogers (20 January 2005), "A Bush administration buoyed by electoral success is extending its military ambitions to Iran and Syria", *Opendemocracy*, http://www.opendemocracy.net/themes/article.jsp?id=2&articleId=2316# (21 January 2005; can no longer be accessed).
30 Mamdouh Salameh (September 2003), "Quest for Middle East oil: the US versus the Asia-Pacific region", *Energy Policy*, vol. 31, issue 11, 1085–1091, http://www.sciencedirect.com/science?_ob=ArticleURL&_udi=B6V2W-482X5WJ-1&_coverDate=09%2F30%2F2003&_alid=252767344&_rdoc=1&_fmt=&_orig=search&_qd=1&_cdi=5713&_sort=d&view=c&_acct=C000050221&_version=1&_urlVersion=0&_userid=10&md5=0fcb9669654c01128e9b91dcd7797618 (accessed 3 March 2005).
31 See, Edward Luttwak, (Summer 1990) "From Geopolitics to Geo-Economics: Logic of Conflict, Grammar of Commerce," *National Interest*, no. 20, 17–23. Also E. Luttwak, *The Endangered American Dream: How to Stop the United States from Becoming a Third-World Country and How to Win the Geo-Economic Struggle for Industrial Supremacy* (New York: Simon and Schuster, 1993), and V. F. Dorogin (May–June 2003), "Maritime activity and Russia's geo-economic revival", *Find Articles*, http://www.findarticles.com/p/articles/mi_m0JAP/is_3_12/ai_110620091/pg_1 (accessed 14 February 2005).
32 Kemp and Harkavy, op. cit., 131.

4

Threats to Persian Gulf energy security[1]

Introduction

Across the world, demand for oil and gas is growing. The PG alone is capable of meeting much of the growing demand for energy in the industrial world, and at the same time is able to guarantee the lifeline of a single-product economic system for oil-exporting states of this waterway.

Consequently, the stability of the PG, as a geopolitical region graced with unrivalled oil reserves, has been an important focus of the littoral states as well as of major oil-importing powers and countries' strategies; so any threat to the long-term supply of oil is likely to have backlashes within the region and beyond it. However, there are different definitions and expressions of threats among the littoral states as energy producers, and the ultra-regional powers as energy importers, which must be considered in order to achieve energy security in the PG.

Energy security

Energy security in general is defined by three factors – viz. resource, traffic path and price. To achieve energy security, countries importing energy make preparations for more control over each one of these three factors for a longer time while simultaneously trying to reduce their vulnerability to threats of energy supply and dependable access with suitable prices. New security consideration for natural gas as the most favourable energy resource in the future on the one hand, and trends towards liberalisation of energy sectors and markets on the other, threaten the reliable market of energy-importing countries and cause concerns about the ability to supply them with a resource deemed vital to national security.

Although the regional oil producers have common concerns about energy security, they face different types of threats. On the one hand there are international economic sanctions on some littoral states, and on the other there is the possibility of energy terrorism and attacks on the littoral states' energy infrastructures. Also, from some states' point of view, the presence of foreign forces in the region, as well as any domestic, regional or international crises, could threaten energy supplies. The collective impact these threats could have on regional and global economies may cause a comparatively slight disruption to energy production on a global scale but could dramatically increase world energy prices.

Ultra-regional perspective
For energy-importing countries, especially the Asian-Pacific states, greater dependence on the turbulent ME for energy and consequently a greater reliance on open access to sea lanes and to secure new long-distance gas pipelines are sources of threat, while their shifting strategic relationships with PG energy producers could raise new confrontations with Washington, which may have an impact on their energy securities.

For the US, energy security is a priority with domestic and international components, as Alan Larson, Under Secretary for Economic, Business, and Agricultural Affairs of the US House International Relations Committee expresses it:

> [Our] energy security policy has two main goals. First, to ensure that our economy has access to energy on terms and conditions that support economic growth and prosperity. Second, to ensure that the United States and its foreign policy can never be held hostage by foreign oil suppliers.[2]

Hence, the stability of the PG as the most significant energy-supplying region remains certain and significant for the West's, and specifically the US', strategy. Besides its efforts to decrease dependency on PG oil, the great strategic interest of the US is the heavy dependence of its allies – viz. the EU and Japan – on energy imports from this region (as explained in the previous chapter); additionally, the impact of huge amounts of energy exports from the PG and Saudi Arabia swing production on remaining world oil prices comparatively low. Washington, by its military superiority and by applying a unipolar security system in the region, could also impart the geopolitical consequence of growing demand for the abundant and low-priced oil and natural gas of the PG as a critical prerequisite for Japanese and EU growth, and increasingly for the industrial growth of Asia and much of the developing world. In Western analysis, threats to PG energy security are attributed to, e.g. as Kemp alleges, "the overt use of force by regional hegemons armed with weapons of mass destruction; domestic instability and terrorism within the Gulf states themselves; and conflict over the Caspian Basin's promising energy reserves".[3]

Since 1980, following the Soviet invasion of Afghanistan and the overthrow of the Shah in Iran, any threat to the long-term supply of oil from the PG has been responded to with any means, including military force. This doctrine was initiated by President Jimmy Carter and has remained US policy since then. After the US military intervention in 1987–1988 to protect Kuwaiti oil tankers during the Iran–Iraq war, Washington used its forces in 1990–1991 to drive Iraqi forces out of Kuwait. This was to prevent Iraq expanding its possession of oil reserves in Kuwait and as a response to the Iraqi threat on the Eastern Province of Saudi Arabia, which holds one-quarter of the world's known oil reserves. The necessity of using military force against Iraq was explained by Secretary of Defence Dick Cheney, who stressed to the Senate Armed Services Committee on 11 September 1990 the importance of PG oil for the stability and prosperity of the American economy. He also emphasised the need to prevent Saddam Hussein from dictating the future of worldwide energy policy.[4]

US security relationships with the GCC states were simultaneously developed, and as Joseph Moynihan confirmed in 1997, it

> serves three important and interrelated interests: the uninterrupted access to the petroleum resources of the Gulf; a potential military base of operations should a regional opponent of the Middle East peace process initiate hostilities against a peace process partner; and, third, the prevention of either Iran or Iraq from attaining regional political-military dominance in a strategically important area of the world.[5]

As Klare affirms, in early 2001 George W. Bush's first priority in his foreign policy was not to prevent terrorism or to restrain the spread of weapons of mass destruction or any other purpose he has mentioned since 9/11, but to increase the flow of petroleum from foreign suppliers to US markets.[6] To assure the continuance of oil imports to the energy market from other parts of the world, especially the PG, the Bush administration's strategy was formed on the basis of increasing Washington's role by sending military power into areas of tumult, facing any risk of war or civil turbulence. Hence, despite the policy of "containment" of Iraq, by increasing its military forces in the PG region Washington paved the way for further US attacks in order to assure US domination on this significant energy-supplier region.

The US military invasion of Iraq in March 2003 relieved Washington of two main threats: first, by undermining one of the main regional powers in the PG, with 9 per cent of the world's proven oil reserves (after Saudi Arabia with 20 per cent and Iran with 10 per cent), and attempting to establish a pro-West regime to assure the West's long-term energy security; and second, by opening Iraqi territories to foreign investment, privileging American and European investors. In this respect, as Klare affirms, this invasion is also facilitating the US' interference "ever more assertively into the internal affairs of the oil-supplying nations and, in the process, exposing itself to an ever-increasing risk of involvement in local and regional conflict situations".[7]

The West's challenges for energy security in the PG
Since the 1980s, the West, specifically the US, has faced a number of challenges regarding its long-term energy security in general, and in the PG in particular, as outlined below.

1) Concerns about the region falling under the domination of anti-Western regimes that could use their control over PG oil production to damage Western interests. For example, preventing revolutionary Iran emerging as a regional power, and concerns about the military attacks of Iraq during Saddam's regime, which caused some border changes as well as disruption to oil operations.
2) Regard to the fact that US forces are perceived as a threat by some major energy producers in this region, viz. Iran and Iraq (until 2003). Their presence is seen as a significant threat to domestic security as well as to energy security in the whole region.
3) International sanctions against some oil-producing states, viz. Iran and Iraq (until 2003) as an obstacle to developing and modernising their energy infrastructures as a vital response to the growing

global energy demand and economic growth, as well as their own economic plans.

    Lack of sufficient investment in OPEC countries, especially in the PG. Looking at an IMF report dated April 2005, the insufficient investment in OPEC countries, especially in the PG, impacts on the volatility of world oil prices and an inability to saturate growing global demand of energy by the next decade could be very significant. This report suggested that, to respond, the global market for OPEC production should increase twofold in the next 25 years.[8]

4) Lack of relations or even direct contact between Iran and the US as the two major regional and non-regional players in the PG.
5) Lack of effective confidence-building measures between Iran and the GCC states, and also Iraq until 2003; a matter of creating stable and good relations among the littoral states for solid cooperation and stability in the PG.
6) Internal conflicts and domestic unrest affect high oil prices, resulting in uncertainties in the international oil market, making fragile states even more fragile. This also has an impact on the rapidly industrialising states – e.g. China, which could create unexpected security challenges for other states, including the US, by looking for stable partners such as Russia, Iran and the Caspian littoral states for its long-term energy needs.
7) Concerns about terrorist attacks on the world's energy infrastructure, including regional states, which have potentially economic implications, especially post-9/11 and the turmoil after the 2003 invasion of Iraq. For instance, in a session of the 109th Hearing of Congress on "Terrorist Threats to Energy Security" (27 July 2005), it was noted that the events in Iraq would pose a lingering risk to US energy security as well as to the global economy. This was evidenced by pipeline sabotage, attacks on shipping and the expansion of terrorist attacks, which show that insurgents have gained a measure of expertise that could be transferred elsewhere. It was also mentioned that until a stable Iraqi civilian government is secured, the risk of instability throughout the PG will remain quite high.

The West's alternative solutions

With 97 per cent of transportation in the US fuelled by oil, the US oil system is vulnerable to attacks on key energy infrastructure both overseas and domestically as well as to any oil shock waves. Washington, as was recommended in the hearing of 109th Hearing of Congress, should focus on reducing its oil demands by finding alternatives to diversify its fuel sources; emphasis was placed on the "Strategic Petroleum Reserve", or the emergency supply of federally owned crude oil, and the need to encourage other energy-consuming nations, whether within their borders or elsewhere, to do the same. The Strategic Petroleum Reserve was emphasised as a resource that could provide some protection against a major supply disruption in the US and provide the possibility to act in agreement to hold the price of oil at an appropriate level.

The fact that about 90 per cent of PG oil supplies make a passage through the Hormuz Strait, combined with US concerns about terrorist attacks and recommended alternative solutions for the West, should be enough to convince the GCC states to find other routes to supply the region's oil to the world markets. Also, by the same recommendation in the 109th Congress meeting, Saudi Arabia, as the largest producer, exporter and reserve in the world, must be treated carefully despite its "funding jihadists". As was pointed out, the US must tread softly or at least feel it has to tread softly when criticising Saudi actions, particularly when it is known to fund those ideologically committed to terrorism.

What is usually missing from many analyses in the West, specifically in Washington, is that energy security in the PG will be very heavily influenced by how they understand the regional states' perceptions of threat as well as their national security issues. Establishing good relations with all littoral states and not increasing hostility among them can assure more effective energy security, since the current "divide and rule" policy has not been successful and has, in fact, resulted in three decades of conflict and unrest in this region. Economic interdependency, especially in relation to energy between the West and all PG states, and more specifically between the US and Iran, can assure a more stable region and thus the benefit of long-term energy security for all regional and non-regional states.

Regional perspective
As mentioned earlier, regional oil-producing states, besides their common concerns about energy security with ultra-regional powers, each face different internal and external problems. The major common problems of the littoral states are as follows.

Domestically: There is the danger of political instability and terrorist attacks on their energy infrastructures. This is added to the uncertain investment environments in major oil producers, which contribute to the socio-political turmoil and, for some states, the international sanctions which affect their income.

Regionally: Concerns about their neighbours' threats and also the lack of assurance of the regions' energy security that may be caused mainly by the lack of any collective energy cooperation among the littoral states, which would create the assurance of a commitment to a common interest. This idea seems very much unwelcome to non-regional powers because their long-term interests would be in contrast with the existence of a single voice of a powerful regional energy organisation in the PG.

Externally: All PG states are suffering from the intervention of non-regional powers in their affairs, though in different ways, directly or indirectly through invasions, imposing sanctions and in some states the presence of foreign forces. Regional crisis, besides local rivalries and fears, is partly the result of such an intervention policy, which in turn threatens energy security for all.

The growing presence of foreign forces in the region since the 1980s was felt as a great threat by Iran and Iraq, causing political subversion within US political and military positions in the GCC countries as well as social and religious problems for the GCC governments. US policies, especially regarding the issue of Palestine – particularly after 11 September 2001 (9/11) – and its long-term security relationship with the GCC states, have provoked residents' indignation on the Arabian Peninsula, especially in Saudi Arabia. Such anger, along with the rise in US military presence, has been increasing since the US invasion of Iraq in 2003. This has caused internal unrest, particularly in these two countries, and could lead to serious instability and thus disruption of oil supplies from the region.

From the viewpoint of the Iranian and Iraqi governments, threats to PG instability were mostly attributed to the presence of foreign troops. Although GCC governments changed their position in this regard after the "Desert Storm" operation in 1990–1991, their people have shown more anti-American sentiments regarding the presence of foreign forces in their countries. In this regard it was stated in *The Washington Post-Kuwait* in October 2002[9] that, despite the feelings of gratitude and welcome for

Washington's protection against any external threats to the GCC countries, there are rising anti-American attitudes across these US allies. Such resentment presents complex new challenges for the region's leaders as well as for the US. Also regarding Washington's interests in the PG, Sokolsky in 2002 remarked:

> For the United States, there is no escaping the role of security guarantor of the Gulf for the foreseeable future. But trying to guarantee that security through a large-scale, visible, and permanent-looking U.S. presence will erode security, undermine security relationships with key Gulf States, impede needed political reforms, stir domestic opposition within Saudi Arabia and other Gulf States, and feed anti-American Islamic extremism.[10]

In such a situation, as Klare states, "finding a way to eradicate this opposition while at the same time persuading Riyadh to increase its oil deliveries to the United States will be one of the most difficult challenges facing American policymakers in the years ahead". On the one hand, according to him, expanding Saudi Arabia oil capacity will require hundreds of billions of dollars and cause significant technical challenges, and hence the Bush administration prefers to achieve this increase by persuading Saudi Arabia to permit more significant US oil-company investment in its territory. On the other hand "any effort by Washington to apply pressure on Riyadh to allow greater American oil investment in the kingdom is likely to meet with significant resistance from the royal family, which nationalised U.S. oil holdings in the 1970s and is fearful of being seen as overly subservient to American bidding".[11]

War on Terror in the Persian Gulf context
The vulnerability of Saudi Arabia as the world's most important oil-producing country to energy terrorism is a significant concern. Currently the possibility of attacks on the infrastructure of the Saudi energy industry, and on Western expatriate workers who are running the state-owned national oil company Saudi Aramco, has been high in order to pressurise them into changing Saudi policy towards the US. These attacks have disrupted oil markets and driven up insurance premiums. According to Peter Zeihan, Al Qaeda, in its new tactic of assassinations instead of bombings, "is trying to gain control of oil wells in order to strangle [the] Western economy. In order to achieve this goal, terrorists must de-legitimize

the Saud family and gain the support of the population."[12] Under such circumstances the House of Saud could face serious social, political and economic crises, and Washington would face common disadvantages like more anti-America sentiments in the region, lack of Saudi swing production, and higher and more volatile oil prices, all of which threaten the global energy market.

However the US, as Riyadh's main arms supplier and its major protector from external threats, sees the stability of Saudi Arabia as in its own national interest and thus faces two major challenges. First, it only has a limited ability to control its internal security problems. Second is the American public's view concerning the paradox of Washington's desire to become a long-term ally of an undemocratic and status quo regime, especially since 9/11. This has led to some extreme outlooks regarding Saudi's future in the US. The Declaration of War on Wahhabism – Saudi Arabia's political ideology based on an ultra-conservative interpretation of Islam – has been openly discussed in American society by many intellectuals such as Ray Pierce, who considers Wahhabism a threat to American and other people's civilisations. He claims that, "by declaring war on Wahhabism, all of the world's peoples and religions currently under threat will benefit, and our war will become an honest fight against evil".[13]

These kinds of extreme anti-Saudi views, according to a *Washington Post* article, "appear especially popular [among] the staff of Vice President Cheney and in the Pentagon's civilian leadership – and among neo-conservative writers and thinkers closely allied with [Bush] administration policymakers".[14] Before the US decision to invade Iraq, on 10 July 2002 there was a briefing given by Laurent Murawiec to the Defence Policy Board, a top Pentagon advisory board, which described "Saudi Arabia as an enemy of the United States, and recommended that US officials give it an ultimatum to stop backing terrorism or face invasion of the country, seizure of its oil fields (the old fields are defended by US forces, and located in a mostly Shiite area) and its financial assets invested in the United States". The report concludes by linking regime change in Iraq to altering Saudi behaviour and emphasises that "the road to the entire Middle East goes through Baghdad (…) once you have a democratic regime in Iraq, like the ones we helped establish in Germany and Japan after World War II, there are a lot of possibilities".[15]

Iran's role in Persian Gulf energy security

> No matter who rules in Iran, the Iranian nation possesses vast economic stakes in the Persian Gulf and is inspired by an ancient memory of deeply felt aspirations to play a continuously leading role in the region (Rouhollah Ramazani).[16]

The economy of Iran relies heavily on oil export revenues. Therefore, the oil factor as an element in its national security is very influential on Iranian domestic and foreign policy. Additionally, since the early 1960s Iran has been trying to strengthen its presence in the PG as a strategic priority. From Iran's point of view, energy and security are inseparable, and the security system in the PG is the exclusive responsibility of littoral states, to be achieved through their cooperation. Such a concept excludes non-littoral states from any PG security arrangements.

Hence, after the announcement of Britain about its decision to withdraw its forces from the PG in 1971, Iran's security policy in the PG was apparent: opposing displacement of the power vacuum by either of the superpowers and believing in the littoral states' responsibility for PG security, while being ready to rely on its own strength to maintain the security of this region if no security system can be developed with the other littoral states.

The Nixon regional security system of the "Twin Pillars" provided the opportunity for Iran's powerful presence in the PG on behalf of the US. However, after the occurrence of the Islamic Revolution in 1979, which ended the "Twin Pillar's" balance of power in the region, Washington barred Iran from having any part in PG regional security arrangements. Since then, US administrations have implemented a more aggressive policy towards the PG: increasing US military presence in the PG and providing a regional balance of power by supporting Saudi Arabia. At the same time, it continued to follow a dual containment policy aimed at Iran and Iraq as the two regional powers. These events show that oil was at the core of US strategy but against Iran's national and regional interests.

Iran, as a regional power with its growing security and interests, attempted to deter any foreign military presence in the region and continued to extend its influence in the PG. It perceived foreign navies in the PG as a major threat, calling for strong Iranian forces and stressing the necessity of having collective defence-security arrangements to enable

PG nations to defend themselves without relying on foreign forces. This was Iran's policy towards the establishment of lasting security in the region, which was in sharp contrast with the GCC's perceptions of security.

Despite GCC members perceiving a threat from each other, sometimes more than from their other neighbours in the PG, the GCC saw Iran and its revolutionary regime, along with Iraq, as potential threats. The littoral states were too weak to displace external powers or shoulder the responsibility of PG security themselves. More importantly, though, the conservative Arab states believed American involvement was vital to any scheme for PG security. The US was a trustworthy friend and had undertaken to protect the GCC states from all internal and external threats to their security. After the Iran–Iraq war, the need to revive the economy forced Iran to bring its foreign policy into line with its economic needs. Tehran realised it was essential to restore relations with the GCC and specifically with Saudi Arabia. This was so they could influence the limiting of output within OPEC in order to raise oil prices. Although Iranian foreign policy has become more pragmatic since the end of the Iran–Iraq war, there are still no signs of a significant shift in the GCC's stance towards a regional security arrangement.

In Western analysis the Islamic Republic of Iran (IRI) was introduced, like Saddam Hussein's regime in Iraq, as a threat to PG states on the Arabian Peninsula and thus a source of danger to energy security. Despite the revolutionary anti-status-quo rhetoric of Iranian leaders in the first decade of the revolution, which presented an ideological threat to its neighbouring conservative governments and thus the perception of a threat to their national security, IRI has not pursued any territorial ambitions against its neighbours. In addition, Iraq's invasion of Kuwait, which developed throughout the 1980s, was the consequence of the eight-year war of Iraq against Iran, and was achieved with massive political and financial support from the Arab Sheikhdoms of the PG.[17] This collective support was implemented regardless of Iraq's old and long-exhausted inter-Arab geopolitical ambitions.

Moynihan, referring (in 1997) to the goals of US security relationships with the GCC states, mentions the prevention of both Iran and Iraq from attaining regional political–military dominance. He also remarks on some factors about the US and Iran remaining adversaries for the foreseeable future. He further notes Iran's continuing economic crisis as an obstacle to any possible military adventurism. Thus, he concludes that "there are many reasons to believe that a major regional crisis is not the most likely form of conflict either the USA or the GCC can expect from Iran in the years ahead". He goes on to say that, "In seeking to prevent such a crisis, therefore, both the USA and the GCC states should ensure that the US military presence in the Gulf maintains as low a profile as possible while at the same time being aware of the cultural sensitivities and national pride of the local populations."[18]

Of course, Moynihan's perspective could still be considered persuasive. Besides the impact of the Iranian nuclear crisis, this situation has resulted in increasing oil prices and also the possibility of US/international sanctions on Tehran, which all pose a threat to energy security in the PG; therefore, Moynihan's ideas still stand. Decreasing foreign troops in the PG, respecting Iranian national pride and concentrating on direct negotiations between Tehran and Washington are still considered the most effective elements in preventing regional conflicts with Iran. Washington's humiliating behaviour towards Iran combined with efforts to prevent the natural development of a regional power have led to regional insecurity and instability. This has created a situation where the re-emergence of Iran has become a necessity, despite US sanctions. The impact of the economic instability of the PG states could cause political instability. Under these circumstances energy security is sufficiently threatened to encourage the US to rebuild normal relations with Iran.

Another reason for advising Washington to normalise its relations with Iran is that the US containment policy that massively targeted Iran's energy industry to prevent the economic development of a post-revolutionary state has failed. As Estelami demonstrates in his statistical study of 1999, "The resulting economic sanctions have historically encouraged Iran to develop strategies for diversifying trade routes, finding new economic partners [see Table 4.1] and reducing dependence on oil export revenues [see Table 4.2]."

As he explains, "In 1974, seven countries accounted for 70% of Iran's imports and exports. Twenty years later – by 1994 – a total of fourteen countries accounted for 70% of Iran's international trade, and Iran's top seven trading partners accounted for only half of its total imports."[19]

TABLE 4.1
Share of Iranian imports by source traditional suppliers

Time period	United States	Western Europe	Japan	Other
Pre-revolution (1975–1978)	18.5	48.7	15.8	17.0
Revolution and Iraq war (1979–1988)	1.8	47.8	13.0	37.4
Postwar reconstruction (1989–1992)	2.1	52.1	11.4	34.4
Dual containment (1993–1996)	3.3	45.8	8.3	42.6
Iran–Libya sanctions (1996–1999)	0.0	44.9	6.4	48.6

TABLE 4.2
Iran's export product array product

Products	1979–1988	1989–1992	1993–1994
Oil and gas	94.9%	89.2%	82.3%
Carpets	1.8	3.9	6.6
Fresh and dry fruits	1.0	2.3	3.3
Leather	0.4	0.4	0.5
Copper and metals	0.2	0.3	0.7
Caviar	0.2	0.2	0.2
Textiles	0.1	0.1	0.2
Chemicals	0.1	0.2	0.1

Source of Tables 4.1 and 4.2: Country Report – Iran, *Economist Intelligence Unit*, London; years 1980–1997

Extensive reports from the international entities and others emanating from Iranian official sources indicate that, despite the prevailing sanctions, the economy has been only marginally affected and the sanctions, despite their extreme nature, have in practice been unable to achieve their primary objective of halting international involvement in Iran's oil industry. Certainly, the impact of US sanctions is not small in terms of Iran's access to Western foreign credit, technology and markets, and its contribution to economic hardships of descending per capita income, high inflation and unemployment rates along with a rapid devaluation of Iranian currency. The effects of the trade and investment sanctions have, however, been felt more by American companies than non-American firms.[20]

However, the unstable economies of the PG countries – especially Iran, Iraq and Saudi Arabia as three regional political powers – could have a serious impact on their political and social processes as well as pose a major threat to oil supplies as a cause of domestic or regional instability. Such a situation, which could particularly develop as a result of low oil prices and a lack of investments for modernising their energy refineries and exploring new fields, would affect the US economy too.

The US and Iran have many shared interests in the region. Therefore, Washington has been advised to develop its relations with Iran to be "more nuanced and sophisticated". As Bruce Riedel, special assistant to the president and senior director for Near East and South Asian Affairs, National Security Council in the Baker Institute, emphasises:

> The US administration should formulate its policy toward Iran in a coherent regional framework that takes into consideration US interests in the Middle East, Central Asia, China and Russia. Iran's national security interests in its regional setting must be acknowledged as part of this process to promote a meaningful and constructive exchange and eventual resolution of differences.[21]

"Unrestricted flow of energy from the Persian Gulf, peace in Afghanistan, the containment of Saddam Hussein of Iraq, and the promotion and maintenance of political stability in Central Asia and the Caucasus" are some major interests in common that he notes.

Another reason for Iran and the US to solve their problems and normalise their relations to the benefit of PG energy security is the energy supplies from the Caspian region. Despite some warnings, e.g. Ehteshami, about the danger of the direct competition of the new Trans Caspian energy exporters joining the international markets with OPEC and its implications for OPEC members' future economic security, Iran is helping the Trans Caspian states to develop their energy supplies and their access to Western markets.[22] From Iran's perspective, as Ramazani remarks:

> Iran is interested in the economic and political development of its northern neighbors, not only because of its interests in the stability of these neighbors, but also because it is conceivable that the region could provide a large market in the future for Iran's non-oil exports.[23]

From the US perspective, stable and assured energy supplies from the Caspian region will increase and diversify world energy reserves and reduce its vulnerability to disruptions of oil exports through the Strait of Hormuz. Of course, Washington's goal is to build multiple pipelines from the Caspian region, but not through Iran. However, all countries and companies, both regional and international, desire control of the access lanes that will allow for the export of Caspian oil and natural gas. Washington, though, is going to have to take into account Iran's great role and interests in both the PG and Caspian Sea regions. The US will also have to take into consideration the geopolitical competition in the Caspian Basin which has significant implications for the security of the PG, as Kemp and Harkavy explain:

> As long as the United States and Iran are bitter enemies, no progress can be made in developing southern routes for oil and gas. (…) [But] it is very much in the interests of all the parties to work out cooperative arrangements to develop these resources, otherwise Caspian Basin oil and gas simply will not reach market and there will be greater pressures than ever on the Persian Gulf and the entire oil market.[24]

Conclusion

Along with the growing global energy demand, and the importance of the PG as the most significant energy-supplying region in the world, energy security in the PG will be very heavily influenced by how the regional and ultra-regional powers understand each other's perceptions of threat, as well as their national security issues. It is very much in the interest of all parties to find a cooperative arrangement to assure energy security in this region.

PG energy security comprises multi-variable components requiring regional and international community responsibility and cooperation. However, it is the policies of Iran and the US towards each other that will remain the most important factors in the security system of the PG.

On the one hand, since the end of the twin-pillar policy it has been necessary for the West that its interests be acknowledged by the regional states to establish any successful security arrangements. Iranian leaders have formally acknowledged these interests but they have been unable to reconcile their differences and assure the West of its vital interests in the PG.

On the other hand, the growing presence of American troops in the region has increased the militarism process, e.g. the attempts of the EU and the countries in the Asian and Pacific region to create their own military forces to protect energy security from the ME/PG, and also Iran's expansion of its military capabilities, particularly in the PG. Such a process, along with Washington's great efforts to limit Iran's energy production via sanctions or preventing Tehran from expanding its control over oil and gas routes, could encourage Tehran to develop its military abilities and also put Washington under pressure by its ME effective playing cards, e.g. in Iraq and Afghanistan.

The dispute has been expanded to nuclear technology. For the era after oil, control of the most likely energy source would be a significant element in the US energy security policy. Since nuclear energy seems to be the best replacement for oil in the next century and economic development and power will belong to energy producers, the West prefers to have its exclusivity. US opposition to the obtaining of nuclear technology, including mastering the fuel cycle, especially by hostile countries and those who are antipathetic to US unilateralism (e.g. Iran), this reflects too.

The ME and North Africa, especially the PG region, will have oil and gas for the next 100 years, with other regions having a maximum of 30 years supplies remaining. Despite this, the geo-strategic situation of the PG will remain, and so focus will still be on improving the relationship between the two major regional and non-regional powers, Iran and the US, and the need for a regional security arrangement even after the depletion of oil and gas.

Energy security can be assured more effectively by establishing good relations, particularly through economic interdependency. Emphasis should be placed on relations between the West and all PG states, and more specifically between the US and Iran.

It can start with regional cooperation in the fields of energy investment and trade, which is aimed at supporting the mutual interests of energy producers and consumers. Together these will promote energy production and supply within the region and enhance energy security in the PG. In this respect, financial assistance from international institutions, e.g. the World Bank and other international development banks, is vital, as is the possibility of free access of foreign companies to put capital investment into developing and modernising the existing resources and exploring and exploiting the new oil resources with modern technology, especially in Iraq and Iran, which currently have old facilities. This will provide a greater opportunity for stabilising global oil markets too.

Therefore, regional and international investment and trade in the short-term, combined with the acknowledgement of the interests of ultra-regional powers, could pave the way for a long-term strategy of regional collective defence-security arrangements, which includes all littoral states. This could be a way of safeguarding the long-term security of oil demand and supply from the PG.

Energy security in the PG will also be very heavily influenced by various sources of internal and external insecurity, which threaten the stability of the area. Learning these sources of insecurity will allow discussion about the future shape of security arrangements in the PG. Hence, the next part of this book is dedicated to studying these sources of insecurity from regional and non-regional countries' points of views.

NOTES

1. This chapter was presented under the title of "Threats to Persian Gulf Energy Security; the US Challenges", at the American Politics Group Annual Conference (4–6 January 2007), at University of Leicester, UK, and was subsequently published under the title of "Threats to Persian Gulf energy security; impacts of the US and Iran relations" in *Journal of Middle Eastern Geopolitics*, year I, no. 2 (July–September 2008).
2. Alan Larson (20 June 2002), "The international aspects of US energy security", *US Department of State*, http://216.109.117.135/search/cache?p=energy+security+oil+producing+countries&toggle=1&ei=UTF-8&u=www.state.gov/e/rls/rm/2002/11311.htm&w=energy+security+oil+producing+countries&d=9259DCD386&icp=1&.intl=us (10 April 2005; can no longer be accessed).
3. Geoffrey Kemp (2000, April), "The new (and old) geopolitics of the Persian Gulf", *Footnotes (The Newsletter of FPRI's Marvin Wachman Fund for International Education)*, vol. 6, no. 1.
4. Michael Klare (2003), "The Bush/Cheney energy strategy: implications for US foreign and military policy", *Information Clearing House*, http://www.informationclearinghouse.info/article4458.htm (accessed 2 October 2004).
5. Joseph Moynihan, "The Gulf Cooperation Council and the United States: common and uncommon security interests". In David Long and Christian Koch (eds), *Gulf security in the twenty-first century* (Abu Dhabi: The Emirates Center for Strategic Studies and Research, 1997), 72.
6. Klare, op. cit.
7. Ibid.

8. International Monetary Fund (IMF), "World economic outlook: chapter IV-Will the oil market continue to be tight?" April 2005, 18. http://www.imf.org/external/pubs/ft/weo/2005/01/pdf/chapter4.pdf (accessed 6 May 2005).
9. Rajiv Chandrasekaran (11 October 2002) "Anti-American sentiment expands in Persian Gulf, two marines shot", *The Washington Post-Kuwait*, http://www-tech.mit.edu/V122/N47/Long_4_47.47w.html (accessed 15 October 2006).
10. Richard Sokolsky (September 2002) "Beyond containment: defending US interests in the Persian Gulf", INSS (Institute for National Strategic Studies-National Defense University) *Special Report*, http://www.ndu.edu/inss/strforum/SR_03/SR_03.htm (20 October 2006; can no longer be accessed).
11. Klare, op. cit.
12. Peter Zeihan, "Al Qaeda adopts new tactics: assassinations will replace bombings", *Asianews.it*, 18 June 2004, http://www.asianews.it/view.php?l=en&art=1000 (accessed 25 April 2005).
13. Ray Pierce (5 December 2002), "Declare war on Wahhabism", http://www.newsmax.com/archives/articles/2002/12/4/210025.shtml (accessed 15 June 2004).
14. Thomas Ricks (6 August 2002), "Briefing depicted Saudis as enemies", *Washington Post*, http://www.washingtonpost.com/ac2/wp-dyn/A47913-2002Aug5?language=printer (accessed 16 June 2004).
15. Ibid.
16. Rouhollah Ramazani, *The Persian Gulf, Iran's role* (Virginia: The University Press of Virginia, 1972), 88.
17. Suroosh Irfani, "The Persian Gulf crisis: regional context and the UN response", *Strategic Studies*, vol. XIV, nos 1 and 2, autumn and winter 1990–1991, 31–32.
18. Moynihan, op. cit., 72–74.
19. Hooman Estelami (1999, September), "A study of Iran's responses to US economic sanctions", *MERIA (Middle East Review of International Affairs)* [Journal] vol. 45, no. 3.
20. Ibid., also Jahangir Amuzegar (spring 1997), "Iran's economy and the US sanctions", *The Middle East Journal*, vol. 51, issue 2, 185–199, http://web.nps.navy.mil/~relooney/Sanct_46.htm (accessed 30 April 2005).
21. *Baker Institute Study* (1998, June), no. 7, http://www.bakerinstitute.org/Pubs/study_7.pdf#search='iran%20only%20power%20security%20persian%20gulf%20%20khatami (accessed 29 April 2005).
22. Anoushiravan Ehteshami, "Iran and central Asia: responding to regional change". In Mehdi Mozaffari, *Security politics in the Commonwealth of Independent States: The southern belt* (UK: Macmillan Press Ltd, 1997), 99–100.
23. *Baker Institute Study*, op. cit.
24. Geoffrey Kemp and Robert Harkavy, *Strategic geography and the changing Middle East* (Washington, D. C.: Brookings Institution Press, 1997), 334, 131.

Part II

Security in the Persian Gulf: Types and natures of insecurity factors

5

Territorial, boundary and maritime disputes in the Persian Gulf

Introduction

Territorial and boundary disputes between the littoral states have been a major source of instability in the PG, threatening regional security for centuries. Such disputes, along with the expansionist policies of some of these states, have violated peace and security in the region, specifically since 1980, and have played a significant role in forming political and economic relations among them.

In order to understand these elements of insecurity, the source and reason of disputes, founded in disagreements about the exact location of territories and boundaries in this region, should be studied. Showing the reasons and outcomes of these kinds of disputes with their local, regional and international impacts will affirm the significance of urgent action of littoral states aimed at solving their territorial and boundary conflicts before they change into a serious crisis.

Border disputes in the Persian Gulf

Events in the 1960s encouraged regional states to seek cooperation and quickly solve their border disputes. The most important of these were: the discovery and development of offshore hydrocarbons and the need for fixed boundaries; the British Government's announcement in January 1968 of the end of Pax-Britannica in the PG; and the oil companies' reluctance to spend substantial amounts of money on the exploration and development of unsettled and controversial borders. Therefore, during this period many bilateral delimitation agreements were signed by the PG states. This process accelerated because there was a sense of necessity among the littoral states to settle their territorial and boundary differences before the departure of the main creator and arbiter of Arabian boundaries. However, Britain seemed reluctant to do this. On the one hand, as Julian Walker, a prominent British boundary-maker in the southern region of the PG, affirms:

> One problem faced over frontier settlement was that posed by the British official who believed that if a frontier was causing no problem it should be left well alone (...) The last thing to be done was to create work and friction, and sleeping dogs should be left to lie.[1]

On the other hand, according to other scholars (e.g. Amirahmadi and Mojtahed-Zadeh), Britain's reluctance to settle territorial and boundary differences before its departure was related to the British divide-and-conquer policy. By maintaining disputes between neighbours, Britain's influence in the region was guaranteed. It was further influenced by high military expenditures on Western arms of the littoral states funded by their massive oil revenues. Any military presence and Great Power geopolitical considerations in the PG were also justified, regardless of whether such speculations seem consistent, as Wilkinson explains:

> When Britain withdrew from its formal protecting role in the region during the ten-year period from 1961 to 1971, it left a heritage of *de facto* boundaries. To some extent the countries concerned have tried to resolve this frontier heritage in recent years, but even when they appeared to have reached understanding they are reluctant to finalize their agreements according to those international rules that entitle them to consider that their arrangements constituted an inviolable and permanent feature of the political map.[2]

In recent years, the major territorial disputes among littoral states of the PG have included the following.

- Territorial disputes between Iraq and Kuwait – which, by demarcation of their boundary by the United Nations, seem to be resolved.
- Disputes between Kuwait and Saudi Arabia over Qaruh and Umm al-Maradim islands.
- Saudi Arabia and Qatar conflicting over their border areas.
- Qatar and Bahrain in conflict over the Hawar islands, ended by a judgement of the International Court of Justice (ICJ) in the Hague in 2005.

- Saudi Arabia and the UAE (Abu Dhabi) struggling over Buraimi and the Liwa regions.
- The UAE's unsolved territorial issue with Oman regarding areas in the Diba region.
- Iran–Iraq border disputes over Arvand Roud (Shatt al-Arab).
- The UAE's claims to the Iranian islands of Abu Musa (under the 1971 Memorandum of Understanding – MOU – with Sharjah) and the Greater and Lesser Tunb.

In general, as Prescott classifies them, there are four kinds of border dispute, all of which can be recognised in the MENA today: positional disputes, territorial disputes, functional disputes and trans-boundary resource disputes. The most common boundary disputes in this region take place when offshore oil and gas fields straddle an international boundary. Although there are some onshore cases, such as the oil field below the Iraq–Kuwait boundary, more offshore than onshore problems confront the countries in the PG.[3]

Oil and border disputes

Besides geopolitical importance, hydrocarbon resources have given the PG territories extra value. Hence, contest for ownership of oil and gas sources has affected not just economic considerations but also the littoral states' mutual relations and boundary arrangements.

Like most of the Arabian Peninsula disputes, tribal rivalry has been overlaid with the struggle over geographical and legal conflicts, as well as the prospect of oil and, in the case of Iranian-Arabs, legal and historical rights.

Drysdale and Blake emphasise the importance of oil as the reason for some ME countries' existence, together with its permanent impact on the delimitation of political borders on land and offshore. This is because oil has not only had a great role in determining the geographic distribution of wealth but has also deeply affected the balance of power within the region. It has also been an element in provoking disputes between neighbours and in encouraging regional cooperation.[4]

Border disputes are assumed to be an essential part of inter-state politics in the PG, especially regarding the geopolitical importance of oil. Tribal competition and dynastic rivalry have traditionally been the major reasons for territorial disputes, particularly those with neighbouring states. Such disputes – in addition to those concerning oil-related boundary and hydrocarbon exploitation issues, the ownership of oil fields and the control of oil transit routes – will remain a decisive factor influencing the politics of the region.

Cross-border hydrocarbon reserves are a global issue. However, in the rich hydrocarbon region of the PG with many small states and numerous boundary disputes, cross-border resources are much more likely to occur.[5] Stevens further underlines the connection between territorial disputes and hydrocarbon exploration and development activities as a "circular relationship", which requires urgent delimitations between neighbour states. According to his explanation, what encourages such disputes is the existence of subsurface hydrocarbon deposits, which could convert a barren region into a precious one. Also, the physical characteristic of oil and gas as fluids has no respect for international boundaries, thereby creating problems. Since oil and gas discoveries in the shared borders lead inevitably to maximum output, if one side does not exploit them they will be produced by its neighbour. In this case the presence of oil or gas deposits suddenly makes border delimitation an urgent matter of national importance.

Cross-border oil and gas field exploration and development can have various impacts on inter-state relationships, from provoking disagreement to military conflict; however, it is not believed to be the exclusive cause of any regional border dispute. Some scholars, like Pike, assume that these kinds of borders have a major role but go along with some political differences or other sources of resentments. In other cases, hydrocarbon resources are used basically as a weapon in political disputes. In this regard, Iraq excused the invasion of Kuwait by claiming that Kuwait was over-pumping oil from Rumailah (the most controversial cross-border oil field in the PG during recent times). The border dispute between Saudi Arabia and Yemen in 1992, as Pike mentions, was more clearly about oil exploration along two neighbours' unsettled border, although political issues were also pertinent:

> Notably pretensions to tribal loyalties in frontier regions, Saudi opposition to the unification of Yemen and its plans for elections, Riyadh's distrust of San'a since it supported Iraq in the Gulf crisis,

and political posturing in advance of negotiations on the renewal of a border accord.⁶

Moreover, cross-border gas fields on the continental shelf of the PG, such as that between Iran and Qatar, which – despite their 1969 agreement that specified clear maritime borders – was unclear about reserve-sharing policies, became established by political means. At the beginning of 1990, Qatar ignored Iran's right to gas reserves in this area (the South Pars field in Iran and the North Dome field in Qatar) in order to decrease some of its difficulties with its neighbours and partners in the GCC, i.e. Bahrain and Saudi Arabia. Qatar then chose closer alignment with Iran as a political lever. Forced to deal with the thorny Qatar–Bahrain maritime territorial dispute over the sovereignty of the Hawar islands and the nearby shoals on the one hand, and Saudi Arabian unilateral action in building a road to detour territory of the Qatar peninsula on its south-eastern rim border with the Saudis on the other, Doha decided to look for a new alignment outside the GCC. In addition, from Qatar's economic point of view, solving a border dispute with Iran and assuring foreign investors of the benefits of long-term investment in a field without an international boundary dispute was a priority. Maritime territorial disputes, as McLachlan remarks,

> often affecting ownership of oil resources, continue to encompass both land areas, in the form of islands, and also parts of the shallow continental shelf of the Gulf. The impetus to finalize land boundary delimitations, especially where they terminate on a sea coast, has often been the discovery of substantial hydrocarbon deposits in the offshore area.⁷

In this respect, ownership of oil reserves has been disputed, for example the Iraq–Kuwait land boundary. Even the liberation of Kuwait and the United Nations' action of making controversial decisions in this regard in 1992 has not put an end to the issue. Exploration of Rumailah–Ratgah continues to bear the seeds of disputes, while Iraq's geopolitical disadvantages over its narrow coastal border in the PG will continue to exist.

In other cases, disputes take the form of silent antagonism – for instance, the Qatar–Saudi crisis following the Khafus border post incident in September 1992. This had a political rather than territorial cause, but with a connection to economic imperatives and oil production which made the two neighbours finalise land boundary delimitations. In spite of the two countries' agreeing to demarcate their boundary at the end of 1992, (after a short suspension of diplomatic relations), the border remained un-demarcated; this is a sign of the stubborn character of Saudi–Qatar relations.[8]

Other disputes can find a political and more stable solution, such as the Iran–Qatar "political accommodation" for "joint exploration", according to Iranian authorities, from their cross-border gas field; or peacefully shared oil reserves in border regions of Saudi Arabia with Bahrain (the Bu Saafah offshore field) and Kuwait (in the Divided Zone), because of their warm political ties.

The Qatar–Bahrain dispute was restrained rather than solved by the failure of Saudi Arabia to mediate the issue. Their case was finally ended in 2005 by the judgement of the ICJ, based on strict agreements defining precise territorial borders.

With the exception of the Qatar–Bahrain dispute, there are a few cases of successful long-term cooperation in developing cross-border reserves that took place as a reason for continued good bilateral relations. In these cases the agreements were not based on complicated pacts explaining the exact details of each side's exploration and production rights, but on a split of ownership or revenues.[9] The most significant example is in the Divided (formerly Neutral) Zone of 5,790 square kilometres between Saudi Arabia and Kuwait. The two countries reached an agreement in 1965 that divided the zone, which contained recoverable reserves estimated at 5 billion barrels, geographically into two equal parts. Equal rights were also agreed upon for the exploitation of hydrocarbon resources, and the rights were assured of the citizens of both countries to work in either part of the partitioned zone. In 1969, the final Saudi–Kuwait boundary was delimited in great detail on the basis of the July 1965 Partition Agreement of the two countries.

In addition, cross-border reserves not only convert borders into valued assets and make border-compromise much harder, but also compel neighbours to solve their boundary dispute as quickly as possible. This is a significant element in the improvement of political relations, and provides support for economic development or compensation for maturation of older hydrocarbons fields. As Schofield observes, the process of finalising the political map, especially in the Arabian Peninsula, accelerated during the 1990s when the total cases of minor disputes over the limits of state territory in 1997 were greatly decreased compared to the previous decade. Schofield sees that decade as the busiest among modern ME states in terms of territorial definitions and the defence of their national territories.[10]

These processes are a clear indication of the importance of interaction between political relations and border conflict management. The examples of successful long-term cooperation in developing cross-border reserves because of political ties, versus those accompanied with military activities, suggest that besides the hostile states' benefits in solving their disputes by political means, security of oil supplies and the stability of the region will be more assured. Alongside the global process of decreasing hydrocarbons reserves, including in the PG, joint cooperation of states will also pave the way for exploring and developing new reserves in dispute borders.

Political, geographical and legal disputes over borders

There are also some legal concerns for states regarding the roots of territorial disputes that cause inter-state conflicts or instability in their relations. As mentioned, sovereignty definitions from the littoral states' point of view, together with the vague legal entity of the PG as a result of being involved in the colonial powers' rivalries and struggles over the centuries, have caused various legal problems. This means that neighbouring states have been unable to prove their sovereignty and solve their territorial and maritime disputes. With regard to the many border disputes and potential border disputes in the PG, Schofield underlines that:

> This is partly explained by the origins of the region's boundaries themselves, which are surprisingly diverse, essentially the product of Britain's deliberations over the past century with the major regional powers in these parts – Persia, the Ottoman Empire and Saudi Arabia. Their unresolved legacy was certainly responsible to a large degree for the re-emergence of the classic, cyclical Irano–Arab dispute over the sovereignty of Abu Musa and Tunb islands in 1992 and the outbreak of a violent incident at Khafus on the undemarcated Saudi/Qatar border later the same year.[11]

While sovereignty dominion in the south coast of the PG was determined by "*Frontières de Convenance*", boundary delimitations in the northern part, as Kazemi explains, were more advanced. Iran's sovereignty, and territorial and maritime boundaries, were controlled by the ruling Western legal–political regulations. Kazemi suggests that this was possibly because of the significant strategic situation of Iran in the ME and the long and continued competition and wars between Iran and the Ottoman Empires. Therefore, there was a need for peace contracts and demarcation in order to end the antagonism of two neighbours.[12]

In general, in order to delimit areas in the PG, the primary necessity is to find a solution to the fundamental questions of sovereignty. In spite of PG states' enthusiasm to come to an agreement on principles of delimitation to finalise their borders, the problem is that sovereignty over territory that could affect the delimitation is disputed. This represents a critical obstacle to a final agreement. The disputed areas in the PG can be listed as:

- the north-west between Iran and Iraq (over the Arvand Roud waterway)
- between Iraq and Kuwait (the resolution of the Iraq boundary in the light of United Nations' ultimate demarcation efforts) and the resolution of the offshore boundary between Saudi Arabia and Kuwait
- the central section between Qatar and Bahrain (concerning sovereignty over the Hawar islands and nearby shoals), and
- the east around Abu Musa and the Tunb Islands.

Such problems have been due mainly to (as mentioned earlier) the reluctance of states to finalise their agreements according to those international rules that oblige them to accept their approved arrangements. For instance, regarding maritime boundaries, the Law of the Sea of the United Nations Convention states that maritime nations have a right to a 200-nautical-mile incompatible economic zone and not less than a 200-nautical-mile continental shell. However, as Bundy mentions:

> not only are the mainland coasts of Iran and the Arab littoral states separated by much less than 400 nautical miles, but the presence

of islands further complicates the picture and prevents any state from enjoying its full complement of continental shelf or exclusive economic zone. Every state abutting the Gulf, in fact, faces a dual delimitation situation: first with its adjacent neighbours and, second, with states lying apposite.[13]

Also, all of the states of the Arabian Peninsula would have difficulty presenting a watertight case at the ICJ to retain the territory they practically occupy. Despite some bilateral boundary agreements between neighbours there is a possibility that such agreements could be challenged by a third party in this waterway.[14] Nevertheless, with the exception of the North Sea and some parts of the Caribbean, there are many more maritime delimited areas in the PG than in any other similar area of the world. Despite the complicated problem of sovereignty and delimitation, some scholars, such as Bundy, suggest that the existing precedents may provide a practical guide for solving these problems[15] (see Figures 5.1 to 5.3).[16]

When considering the political map of the PG, Blake mentions some of its remarkable geopolitical features, such as the existence of some of the world's smallest states; the state of Iraq with its geographical disadvantages; the UAE's most complex territorial divisions within its seven component sheikhdoms as a federal state; those temporary attempts to resolve problems of maritime and territorial competition in the framework of state sovereignty modification rather than absolute sovereignty; and the establishment of different types of non-state sovereignty, most of which remain in operation today.[17] Hence, as Blake believes, to reduce the likelihood of conflict between neighbouring states in the region requires proper recognition of international boundaries and clear delimitations. The present shared territorial arrangements and alternative territorial strategies (such as shared zones and zones of restricted activity) still could successfully provide "temporary relief to potential flashpoints and perhaps deserve to be evaluated far more thoroughly than hitherto".[18]

Meanwhile, Schofield offers a thesis about the role of boundaries as a root cause of instability between states. He considers the ongoing debate among some social scientists, e.g. Jacques Ancel, over the existence of a "good or bad boundary" or any "dissatisfaction with boundaries *per se*" as a root of instability. Ancel emphasises the importance of "no problems

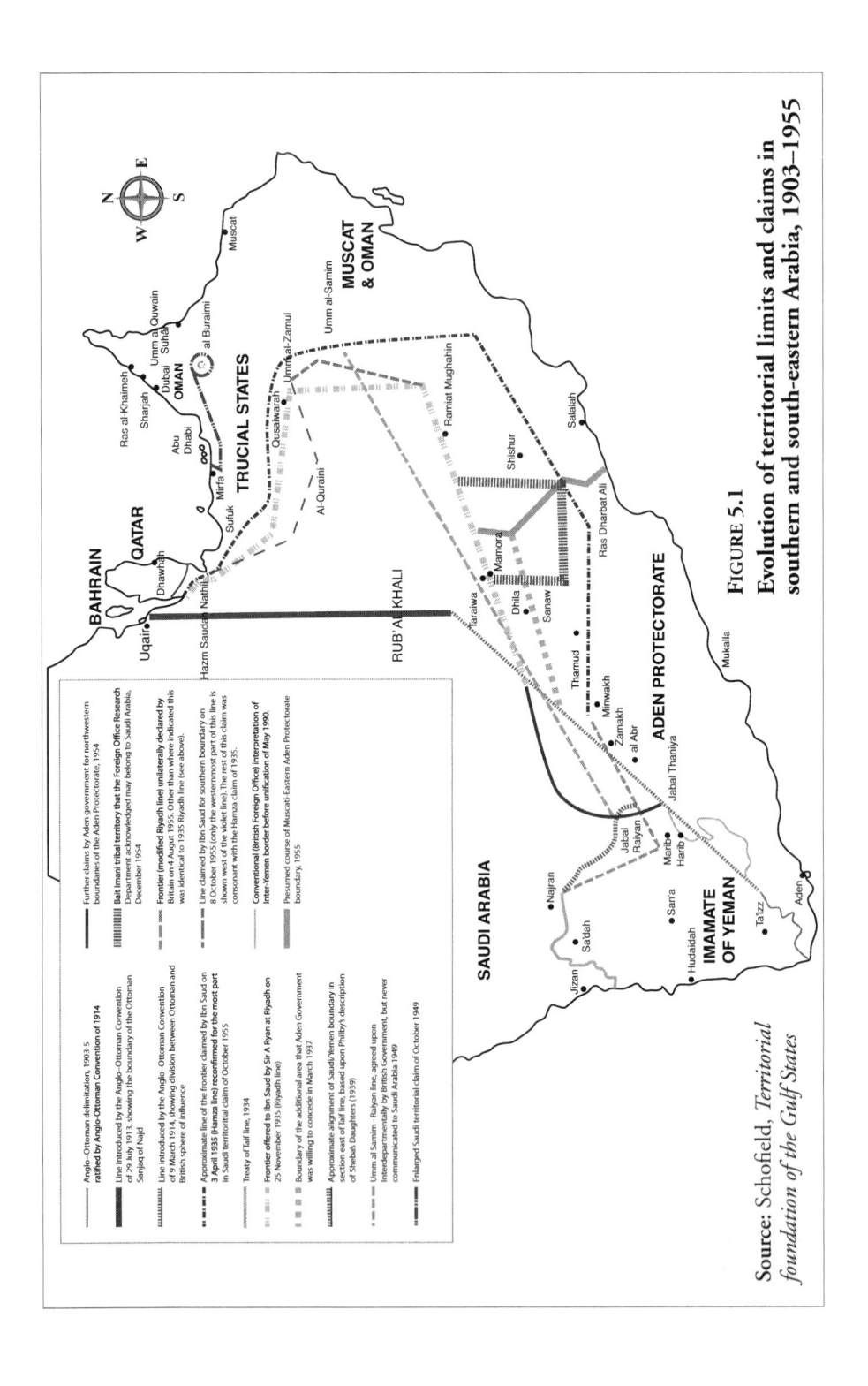

FIGURE 5.1 Evolution of territorial limits and claims in southern and south-eastern Arabia, 1903–1955

Source: Schofield, *Territorial foundation of the Gulf States*

of boundaries, only problems of nations". Looking at another geographical view, Schofield concludes that the extent of a state, including its shape and size restrained by its international boundaries, can cause original geopolitical and strategic problems, particularly problems of access and communications. He argues that the recent history of the northern PG region supports both contentions.[19] A third factor, which according to him is applicable to this area, is the difficulties of the states in accepting the very presence of an international boundary, particularly those boundaries in whose creation external powers have played a great role.[20]

FIGURE 5.2
Evolution of delimited state territory in northern Arabia, 1913 to the present day

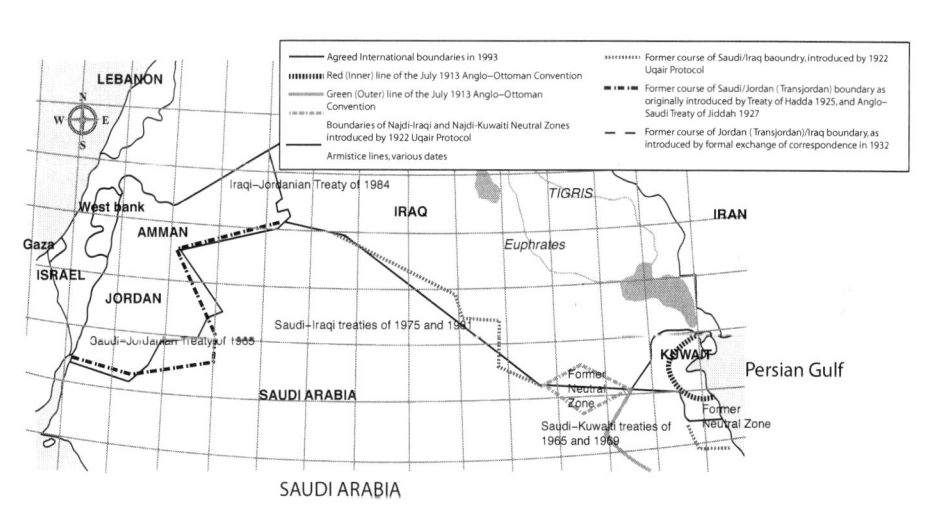

Source: Schofield, *Territorial foundation of the Gulf States*

FIGURE 5.3
The contemporary framework in southern Arabia

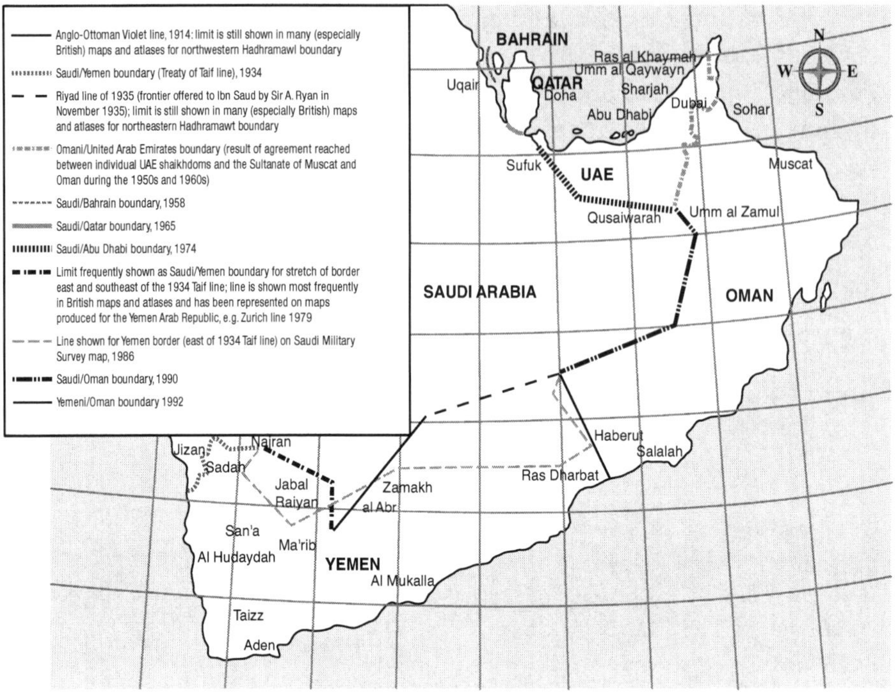
Anglo-Ottoman Violet line, 1914: limit is still shown in many (especially British) maps and atlases for northwestern Hadhramawl boundary
Saudi/Yemen boundary (Treaty of Taif line), 1934
Riyad line of 1935 (frontier offered to Ibn Saud by Sir A. Ryan in November 1935); limit is still shown in many (especially British) maps and atlases for northeastern Hadhramawt boundary
Omani/United Arab Emirates boundary (result of agreement reached between individual UAE shaikhdoms and the Sultanate of Muscat and Oman during the 1950s and 1960s)
Saudi/Bahrain boundary, 1958
Saudi/Qatar boundary, 1965
Saudi/Abu Dhabi boundary, 1974
Limit frequently shown as Saudi/Yemen boundary for stretch of border east and southeast of the 1934 Taif line; line is shown most frequently in British maps and atlases and has been represented on maps produced for the Yemen Arab Republic, e.g. Zurich line 1979
Line shown for Yemen border (east of 1934 Taif line) on Saudi Military Survey map, 1986
Saudi/Oman boundary, 1990
Yemeni/Oman boundary 1992
BAHRAIN
Ras al Khaymah
Umm al Qaywayn
QATAR
Doha
Sharjah
Uqair
Abu Dhabi
Dubai
Sohar
N
W
E
S
Sufuk
UAE
Muscat
Qusaiwarah
Umm al Zamul
SAUDI ARABIA
OMAN
Haberut
Salalah
Najran
Jizan
Sadah
Jabal
Raiyan
Zamakh
al Abr
Ras Dharbat
San'a
Ma'rib
Al Hudaydah
YEMEN
Al Mukalla
Taizz
Aden

Source: Schofield, *Territorial foundation of the Gulf States*

Iraq's behaviour regarding its southern boundaries with Iran and Kuwait is an exact example applicable to all these three theories. The long-standing dispute of Iran–Iraq about Arvand Roud and Iraq's dissatisfaction with the 1975 Algeria Accord with Iran in order to recognise a *thalweg* delimitation along this river is an example of this. So too is Iraq's disagreement over its border with Kuwait and Warbah and the Bubiyan Islands, despite the agreement of October 1963 in which Baghdad recognised an independent Kuwait and its boundaries. The geographic location of Iraq, with only a 19-kilometre coastline of the Faw peninsula on the PG, has given it a geographical disadvantage. It therefore perceives itself as "squeezed out" of the PG. Schofield concludes that, "Traditionally, over the last half century or so, Iraq has pressed Kuwait on the islands question when its relationship with Iran has seriously deteriorated over the status of the Shatt al-Arab. Successive Baghdad regimes have continually expected Kuwait to compensate Iraq for its geographic and strategic misfortune." This geographical disadvantage of Iraq was one of Saddam Hussein's reasons for aggression against Iran in 1980 and Kuwait in 1991. Iraq's attempt to solve its geopolitical and strategic problems in this manner is perceived by some analysts as a backlash against Lord Curzon and the Government of India nine decades ago, when he supported the Ruler of Kuwait's claim to Bubiyan and encouraged him to claim Warbah. This was mainly motivated by a desire to restrict the Ottoman Empire's role in the PG.[21]

The Khafus incident on the Saudi–Qatar border in 1992 and the border agreement between Oman and Yemen in 1982 clearly clarify Ancel's theory that there are no problems of boundaries, only problems of nations. In other words, by focusing on the importance of poor political relations, boundary disputes become serious.

The Oman–Yemen border agreement, which was settled with the help of the Kuwaitis, gave Yemen more territory and ended a controversial phase of relations between two neighbouring states. It was observed that the major factors behind achieving this agreement were the internal political changes in Aden's previous dogmatic politics and regional developments preferring greater cooperation rather than confrontational inter-state relations.[22] Yet the Qatar–Saudi border dispute, which had political rather than territorial causes, ended the Khafus incident and remained unsolved.

From the GCC's point of view, some of their territorial disputes have prevented them from real and effective cooperation. The GCC's mechanism meant a failure to solve its own members' border disputes – for example, the Qatar Saudi Arabian border clashes of 1992 and disputes between Bahrain and Qatar, which eventually ended at the ICJ. These have proved the GCC's inability to face even internal problems effectually.

Consequently, it can be assumed that boundaries are principally political subjects that are greatly influenced by the prevailing political conditions in inter-state relations and, even sometimes, by regional and international considerations. In this regard, issues like modern nationalism would be a serious obstacle to the rational solution of disputes (such as those between Arabs and Persians), signed but not respected present border agreements (e.g. the 1975 Algeria agreement between Iraq and Iran; the 1971 MOU over Abu Musa), and one party's continuous feeling of unjustness regarding an earlier agreement (the feeling of the UAE about the 1974 agreement with Riyadh), as factors contributing to the remaining tension in the region. Hence, an improvement in political conditions is essential to solve many of the border issues. In this respect, according to the successful precedents that already exist, it can be concluded that bilateral negotiations (even detailed and protracted) with the assistance of a third party and certain criteria are very necessary and useful. An appropriate political situation and warm relations between parties are an important and essential element for obtaining an agreement. Scholars like Gargash believe that negotiations should take place at the same time as an improvement in political conditions, because on many occasions stalled border disputes work seriously against the improvement of political ties.[23]

Ultra-regional powers' interest in border disputes

Border and territorial claims and disputes in the PG, whether apparent or concealed, are a major source of inter-state conflicts, which on some occasions have led to war. Also, such situations have, on one hand, caused a general arms build-up in the region, with high levels of military expenditure – an example of an arms race – and, on the other, have opened the region to the direct presence of external powers and even intervention, which of course are themselves major sources of insecurity and concern for the region.

Boundary disputes have a significant role in the regional geopolitics of the PG. The growing dependency of Asian-Pacific economies upon PG energy supplies, along with the West, has caused changes in the geopolitics of oil. Consequently, these inter-state conflicts take on a greater significance. Hence, the ultra regional powers' concerns about controlling the region's politics and the long-term security of oil supplies from the PG have increased. Moreover, relationships and tough competition between Iran, Iraq and Saudi Arabia, which all seek to enforce their own order in the region, will continue to have a significant role in shaping the politics of this region. Changes in the status of any of these three regional powers, other than those arising from events affecting the whole region, will have important consequences for the other two. In this respect – for instance, as Gargash notes – Saudi Arabia enjoyed greater regional influence after the Iran–Iraq war, and similarly, Tehran benefited the most from Iraq's defeat in the "Desert Storm" operation in 1990–1991. The defeat of Iraq's enormous ground forces by the US-led coalition, in addition to the immediate effect of securing Iran's long and mountainous border, significantly changed the geo-strategic balance in the region in Iran's favour.[24] Furthermore, the regional geopolitics of the PG has been greatly changed in Iran's favour as a result of the coalition forces' invasion of Iraq in 2003 – a significant factor in the more recent pressure exerted by the West on Tehran concerning Iran's nuclear activity.

Boundary disputes, as a major divergent element of regional stability and security, have contributed other divergent factors preventing the littoral states from creating a collective regional security arrangement. Therefore, the security arrangements of the region have been imposed by ultra-regional powers with their own national interests. Also, some collective security structures that were defective and unpractical – such as the GCC and the Damascus Declaration of the 6 March 1991 (6+2) – were unable to guarantee regional and even members' security, and yet resulted in the direct presence of yet more foreign troops.

With the Kuwait crisis of 1990–1991, the idea of a security system in the PG that could avert another threat to GCC territories was accelerated in Washington. Introducing the two major regional powers, Iran and Iraq, as the sources of the region's insecurity by excluding them from the system, instead of asking for the participation of two non-regional countries, Syria and Egypt, with different political purposes rather than PG security, made this system deficient and unsuccessful.

In general, territorial and boundary disputes have played a significant role in disordering the regional balance of power in favour of the major external powers, viz. Britain and the US. In this regard, Iran, as the main victim of this policy, will be considered in the following pages.

Iran and ultra regional powers' interest in border disputes

Britain

Over the centuries, control of the PG was taken away from Iran by Arabs, Turks and Western Europeans. According to Arab and Islamic historians and geographers of the early Islamic centuries such as Mas'sudi, Tabari, Yaqubi and Maqdasi, along with various European documents of later periods and different maps, "all areas of the PG belonged to Iran".[25] These sources indicate that, except for an interrupted period of Arab conquest after the advent of Islam, Iran had sovereignty over the lower Gulf (that is, Oman, Bahrain and different islands including Abu Musa, Greater and Lesser Tunbs) until the arrival of the Portuguese in the region, and was revived by the Safavids from 1501 to 1720 and later by Shah Nadir the Great until 1747 (see Figure 5.4, A–F).[26] Iranian evidence of ownership of some parts of the lower Gulf which relies strongly on historical assertion, has been challenged since the nineteenth century by the British Government and Arabs in the PG. Iran's claim has been dismissed on the basis of the historical precedent of the protectorate-style treaties signed between the Arabs and Britain during 1870 and 1880, and the lengthy uninterrupted possession of the areas by the current ruling families. Regardless of each side's assertions, the peaceful life and trade of people within the two sides of the PG before the encroachment of European powers since the end of the fifteenth century indicates that because no threats to Iran, as the only nation-state in the Gulf, emerged until the arrival of Europeans, the different governments of Iran did not need to extend their control over this waterway. After European entrance to the region, countries like Britain prevented Iran from taking necessary action in the PG.[27]

TERRITORIAL, BOUNDARY AND MARITIME DISPUTES

FIGURE 5.4A
Ancient Iran, 728 BCE–CE 640; Medes (Mâdhâ) Dynasty, 728–550 BCE

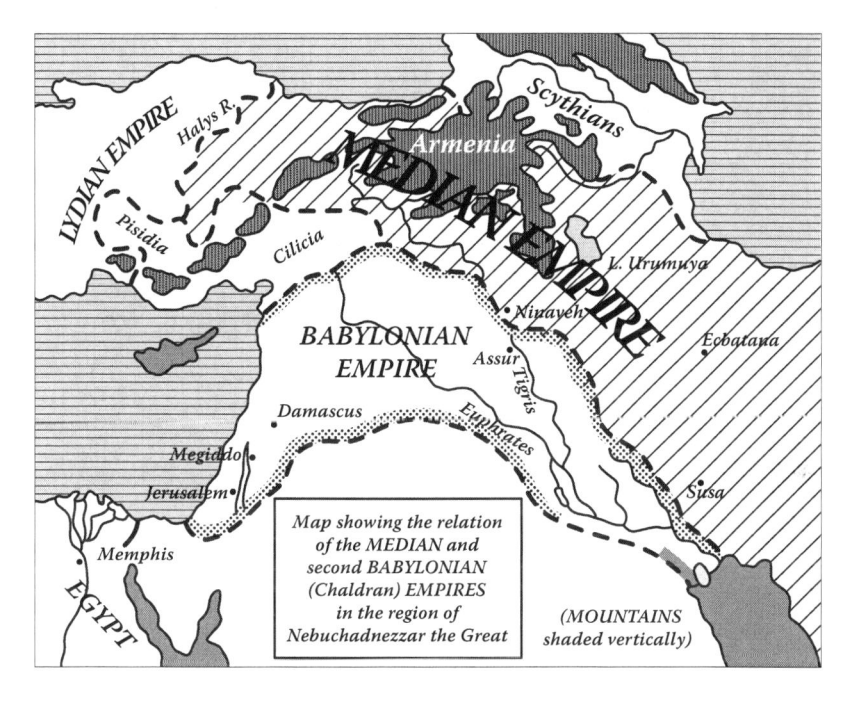

FIGURE 5.4B
Achaemenid (Hakhâmaneshiyân) Dynasty, 550–330 BCE

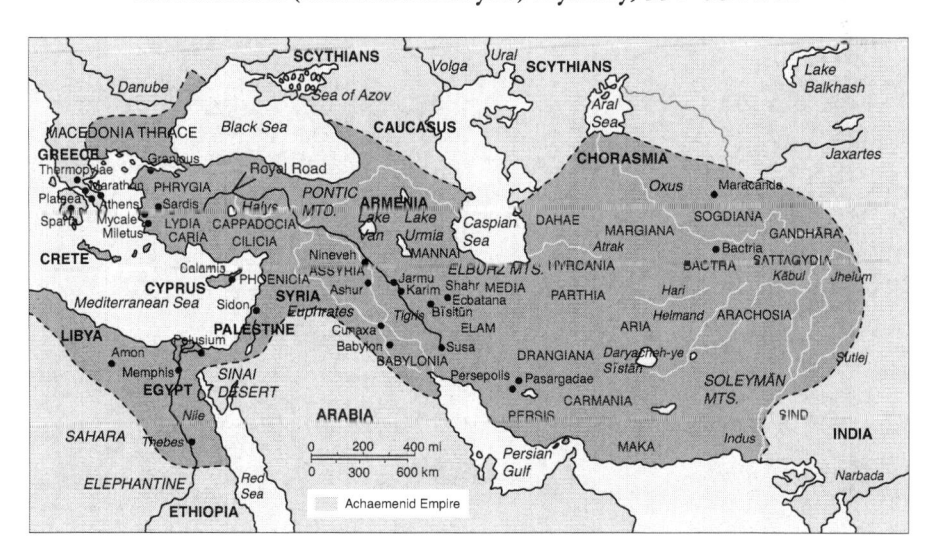

[81]

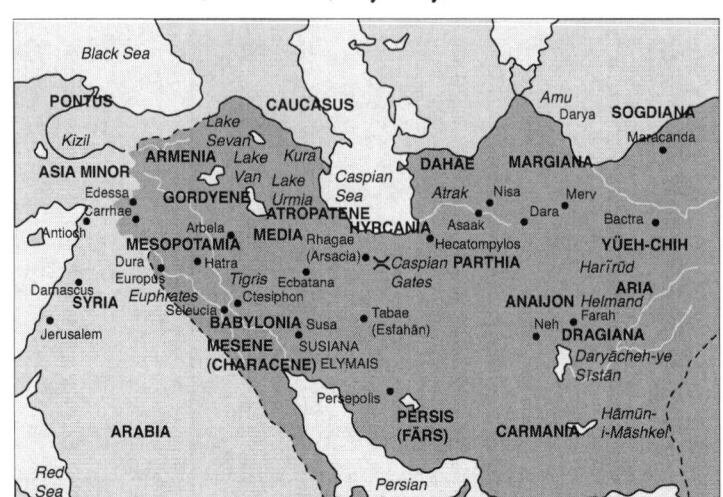

Figure 5.4C
Parthian (Ashkâniân) Dynasty, 247 BCE–CE 224

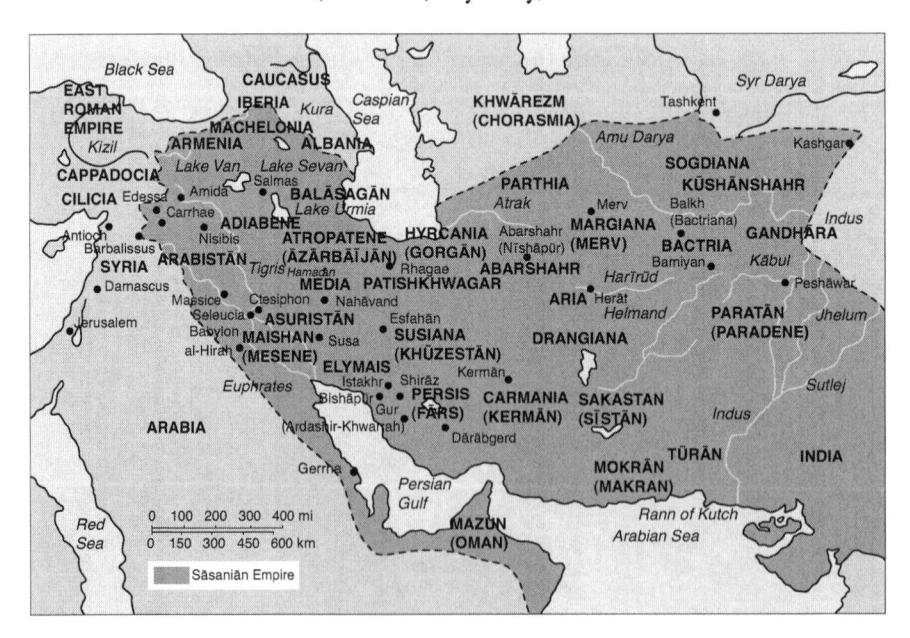

Figure 5.4D
Sasanid (Sâsâniân) Dynasty, CE 224–640

FIGURE 5.4E
Safavid Empire AD 1501–1722

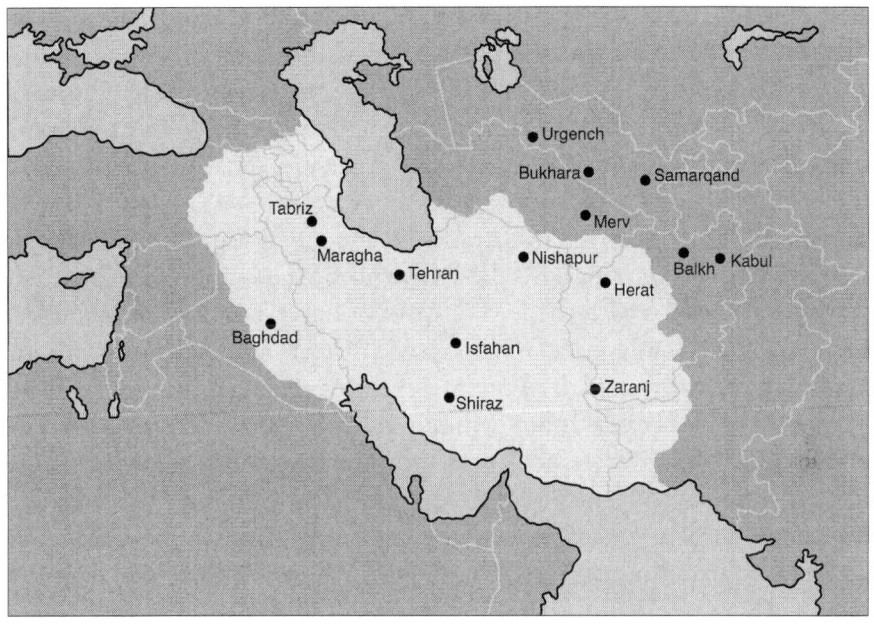

FIGURE 5.4F
Afsharid Dynasty AD 1736–1802

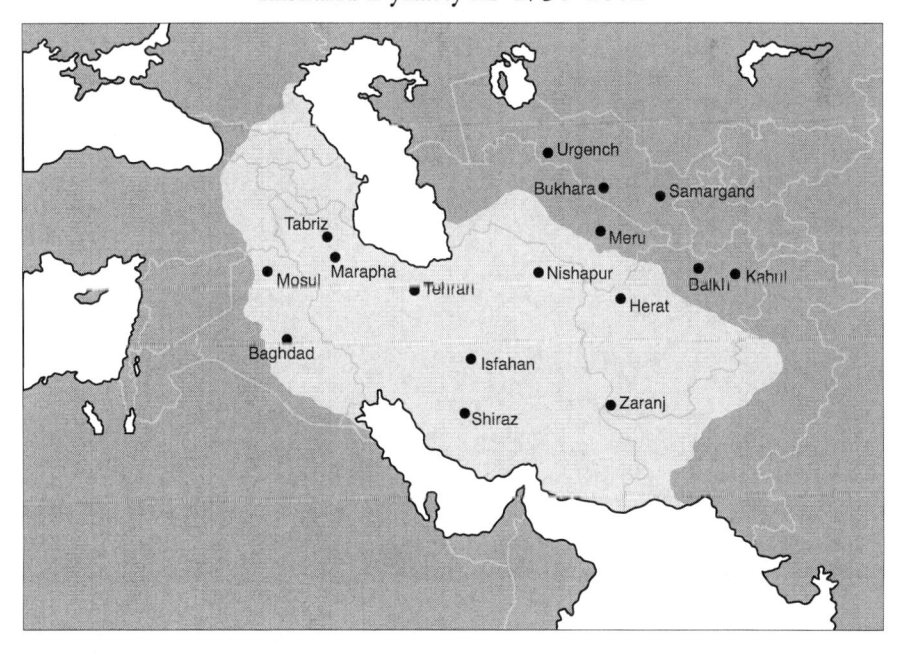

One of the elements of Britain's policy to dominate the region was to weaken Iran, the regional power, and reduce its influence in the PG by disconnecting Iran's traditional ties in the region and separating as many islands and coastal districts as possible from this country. Among these were the islands of Abu Musa and Greater and Lesser Tunb.[28] Britain's occupation of these three islands in the 1820s, and the UAE's and Iran's continuous dispute over the ownership of these islands, are still sensitive issues in regional as well as international relations.

In addition, the British introduced modern European concepts of territoriality and boundary to the PG region, where none of the littoral states were familiar with the legal impact of delimiting such boundaries. Iran's weak and imprecise relations with rulers and governors in its outermost territory and its general infirmity and defectiveness during previous centuries caused the shrinking of its borders and territories (see Figure 5.5). Moreover, besides protecting its long-term influence in the region, Britain's reluctance to settle territorial and boundary differences before its departure contributed to deepening disputes between Iran and its Arab neighbours in the PG, and to widening the divide between them.

FIGURE 5.5
Iran today

The United States of America

The US has taken advantage of Iran–Arab territorial and boundary disputes in the PG as a tool to access its interests in this region. By considering US policy concerning pre- and post-revolutionary Iran, this can be confirmed.

In the 1970s and after Britain's departure from the region, the US – which was following a twin-pillar policy to dominate the region via strong local allies, the Shah of Iran and the Saudi Arabian monarchy – did not make a big deal out of Iran's action in reasserting its sovereignty over the islands of Abu Musa and Greater and Lesser Tunb. As Iran's allies, the US and Israel saw this as a natural demonstration of Iran's role as the new regional power in the PG.

However, in the 1980s, following the failure of this strategy due to the Iranian revolution in 1979 which ended the country's pro-Western orientation and changed the strategic balance in the PG via overthrowing the Shah from power, Washington examined another security framework in the PG by taking advantage of the border claims of Iraq against Iran.

In September 1980, Iraq invaded Iran hoping to reverse the 1975 border settlement of Arvand Roud and to seize the rich, oil-producing Iranian province of Khuzestan. However, by mid-1982, Iraqi troops were cleared from most of Iran, the Iraqi army had suffered serious failure, and the general situation in the PG generated huge global concerns regarding the security of oil supplies. Therefore, the US tried to form its proper security framework of a weak balance of power between the two major local actors through intelligence and financial aid to Iraq, and thereby immediate security was arranged for neighbouring Arab regimes.

Moreover, since the 1990s Washington's support of the UAE's claims over the islands of Abu Musa and the Tunbs has contributed to the US' dual containment policy against Iran. As Amirahmadi states,

> Indeed, isolating Iran from other Persian Gulf states is the cornerstone of the US administration's dual containment policy. Thus, the island dispute is about much more than the islands; it is the most recent manifestation of the continuing ideological and political rivalry between post-revolutionary Iran and its Arab neighbors and their Western-power supporters.[29]

The anti-Western rhetoric of revolutionary Iran was seen by the West, along with pro-Western conservative governments of PG Arab monarchs, as a source of instability, Iran no longer being perceived as the cornerstone of the region's status quo. Iran's unstable foreign and regional policy aroused much scepticism among its Arab neighbours. In addition, the GCC has weaknesses in providing security for its own members and its deep dependency on the West, especially the US, in this regard. This has an impact on GCC security concerns along with its political positions regarding Iran.

Hence, the 1992 crisis involving Iran and Sharjah, which began with Iran's opposition to the entrance to Abu Musa of foreigners working for the UAE government, and to the residence of other groups on this island (for not having Iranian visas), became a broader issue in the PG region and the Arab world. Although Iran's then foreign minister Ali Akbar Velayati played down these incidents as the isolated actions of junior Iranian officials, and emphasised non-interference in the affairs of Arab residents and visitors in Abu Musa, the dispute spread to become one between Iran and the UAE. It eventually led to a resuscitation of claims by the Ras al-Khaimah to the two islands of Greater and Lesser Tunb.

In addition, concurrent with Iran's claims that suspicious traffic of individuals and ships around Abu Musa caused the 1992 crisis, reports were spread of new Iranian military measures on the island, an increase in the garrison and even the deployment of surface-to-air missiles in Abu Musa; other reports suggested the presence of anti-shipping missiles on the island. These reports, although never acknowledged by Iran, paved the way for politicising and internationalising the question of UAE claims over the islands, and meant that the US gave more attention to this issue. Without openly supporting the UAE claim, Washington – with its concern over the strategic location of Abu Musa, near the Hormuz Strait, located between the main tanker channels and close to US naval elements in the Arabian Peninsula – has supported a peaceful resolution of the dispute. Meanwhile, any strengthening of the Iranian military presence in Abu Musa has been perceived by Washington as a factor increasing Iran's influence in the region, especially in the PG, as well as a potential threat to US naval forces stationed there. Iran, while emphasising its responsibility for the security of the whole island, according to the 1971 MOU, persists in the insistence of full sovereignty over the island, its right to deploy any defensive armament to this part of its territory and its right to demand that others apply for Iranian permission to reside on the island.

Besides Iran and Sharjah's different explanations of the 1992 crisis, the impact of political situations in the PG after the "Desert Storm" operation was significant in the formation of such a problem. The GCC's action in signing the Damascus Declaration with Syria and Egypt in March 1991, aimed at defending the Arabian peninsula, although it was never really implemented, and subsequently the GCC's preferred security option of signing bilateral agreements with the US, resulted in enhancing the US military position in the PG.

In the summer of 1992 Iran performed some amphibious manoeuvres in the PG, which were perceived to signal Tehran's disagreement with the new security arrangement under US hegemony, and to represent the building up of its defences on Abu Musa.

Furthermore, the Sheikhdoms' territorial disputes with Iran have been a functional voucher for requesting the support of Western powers in their regional manoeuvring. As Ezzati remarks, Washington's welcoming of such requests was motivated by its desire to fuel Iran–Arab enmity. As he explains, while Abu Musa and the Tunbs have lost their strategic value in the post-Cold War era for Iran, Arabs and the US, intimidating Arabs with the threat of Islamic fundamentalism on the one hand, and with Iran's efforts to extend its influential domain in the region on the other, caused the US arms market among Arabs to flourish.[30] The leading role of the West, especially the US and Israel, in orchestrating Iran–Arab disputes has also paved the way for Washington to achieve its foreign policy goals in the region – that is, protecting Israel's security, preserving US allies in the region, changing the regimes and borders of certain countries, and assuring the flow of oil at a reasonable price.

To ensure such interests, only security arrangements in agreement with Washington's policy of US hegemony in the region will be acceptable to the US. However, the US' power balance policies of the 1980s and dual containment strategy of the 1990s failed to change the brittle security structure of the PG. These failures, coupled with the prevailing global atmosphere of cooperation rather than confrontation, most especially since the end of the Cold War, means that the necessity for a regional security system that includes all littoral states has become even more significant.

As Schofield argues, given Iraq's situation after the Kuwait crisis, Iran's reluctance to harbour any territorial plans in relation to its Arab neighbours, and the role of the GCC in regulating the Arabian territorial structure on a region-wide basis, the further absence of Tehran and Baghdad from any regional grouping would not be wise. Such a regional grouping can provide an opportunity to effectively air all issues, especially territorial grievances; otherwise the most serious and historically entrenched disputes in the region will become harder to settle.[31] The absence of such an inclusive group has resulted in the regional isolation of Iran as well as a missed opportunity for Iran and its Arab neighbours' to finalise their agreements concerning two main territorial disputes over Arvand Roud and Abu Musa/the Tunbs.[32]

Iran's alternatives in future Persian Gulf peace and security

As the greatest local power, Iran faces different alternatives in securing peace and security in this region. All of the insecurity elements in the region mentioned earlier underline the significance of urgent action within the littoral states – Iran more so than others – to solve territorial and boundary disputes before they become a serious crisis, and as a matter of goodwill and a step towards confidence-building to achieve regional cooperation and collective security. Under the current political situation of the PG,

- every crisis over the last three decades caused by territorial disputes has resulted in an increased presence of foreign forces in the region, seen as an insecurity element from Iran's perspective
- any future PG security solution will depend very much on US actions, particularly Washington's bilateral security agreements with the GCC members, which are based on preparation for massive military confrontation
- Washington is suspicious of any independent and multilateral local cooperation, not only between Iran and its Arab neighbours, but also among GCC members, which could result in more economic and political powers for the region
- the regional arms race is increasing, particularly within the GCC states, with the aim of balancing and deterring each other, even to the same degree as to external enemies, or its usage as a negotiating tool within the organisation.

The littoral states must find an alternative strategy to ensure regional peace and security, one that emphasises collaborative rather than confrontational relationships among the PG states. This strongly reinforces the importance of improving relations between Iran and the Arab world, which depends on improving relations between Tehran and Washington. The latter issue is largely influenced by Iranian–Israeli antagonism.

Meanwhile, Iran, by applying a more stable foreign and regional policy and avoiding positions that could raise its neighbours' mistrust and suspicion, should try to achieve some agreements over its boundary and territorial claims. For instance, regarding UAE claims over Abu Musa and the Tunbs, Salari, Iran's former ambassador to the UAE (2000–2004), believes that with a more flexible and centralised policy this issue could be solved and many cooperative opportunities in favour of Iran and other PG states would be granted.[33] In an interview with the author, Salari stated that "besides all political reasons to impasse the territorial dispute between Iran and the UAE, the current dilemma of Iran and the UAE is mostly because of the lack of an individual decision-making system in Iran, unlike the sheikhdom democracy in the UAE". He remarked that "in Iran all decisions [are] taken by a consensus of different authorities and no one has the courage to decide individually". According to him, "the islands dispute should be solved within three dimensions: 1) the Abu Musa island dispute by Iran–Sharjah; 2) the Tunbs islands dispute by Iran–Ras al-Kamiah; 3) general foreign relations by Iran–Abu Dhabi; while there is no solution for these steps in Iran regarding its present political system". Salari, who assumes the islands have lost their geostrategic and geopolitical value due to the developed technology of missiles and navies to destabilise or stabilise the PG waterway, urges Iran more than the UAE to achieve a rapid or even temporary peaceful solution to the disputes over islands in order to prevent any further possible political leverage being misused by the US against Iran in the current regional and global situation.

Other scholars, such as Amirahmadi, estimate the strategic value of the islands as entrances to the Strait of Hormuz only to be significant for security purposes during wartime, otherwise they are of little benefit to either country. In this respect, it is assumed that even if the islands were in the control of the UAE, the latter would not have the capability to defend them in a possible attack from Iran. Hence, as Amirahmadi suggests, the greatest possibility of a lasting solution to the islands' dispute, particularly with respect to the UAE's interests, is supporting the status quo and achieving a cooperative regional approach. By achieving a collective security arrangement that ensures all littoral states' territorial integrity, domestic stability and national interest, these three islands will lose their strategic value.[34]

Subsidiary to this view is Salari's observation that the major problem of the UAE is not Iran but Oman and Saudi Arabia. As he explains, the UAE, which has had territorial disputes with Oman, Saudi Arabia, Qatar and Iran, lost its entire boundary with Qatar after the 1982 confidential agreement with Riyadh. Under these circumstances Saudi Arabia has been able to exploit 500,000 barrels of oil per day from the Sheibeh reserve with a capacity of 14 billion barrels; a serious threat to UAE stability. Although the UAE did not officially approve this agreement, which caused it to lose its entire border with Qatar, Qatar nonetheless became completely surrounded by Saudi Arabia.

Abu Musa has large oil reserves, which fuel the economies of both Iran and the UAE. According to the agreement between Iran and the UAE, the two countries equally share income from the oil field. The strategic position of the island, which lies at the entrance of the narrow Strait of Hormuz, could allow the security of the shipping lane to be influenced. As Sharjah's economy depends heavily on its oil income, it is very interested in the island. Currently, the only oil that Sharjah has any claim to is the Mubarak field, which is located six miles off Abu Musa and has been producing oil and associated natural gas, shared with Iran, since 1974.

Iran's entire oil tanker traffic must cross this area, making the security of this territory very important. Therefore, recent Iranian military deployments in Abu Musa have raised concerns among PG energy producers and consumers, especially in the West, of a potential threat to shipping by blocking the strategic Strait of Hormuz. However, some scholars, such as Harold Hough, note that "the military build-up [is] part of a greater move by Iran to spread its influence in the Persian Gulf rather than an attempt to solidify its hold on the Strait". According to Hough, Abu Musa provides Iran with a base for projecting its power and influence towards the GCC, and also produces extra protection for Bandar Abbas, an Iranian port important for its oil industry and military base. Hough goes on to explain that, "If Iran wanted to deny the waterway to the US Navy, missile sites near Bandar Abbas would be more valuable since they are on the Iranian mainland and the US would be less willing to attack them for both political and military reasons."[35]

Conclusion

Boundary disputes, as a significant divergent element of regional stability and security, have contributed to other divergent factors to prevent the littoral states from creating a collective regional security arrangement. As can be seen from this chapter, diplomatic means and regional solutions are the most lasting and practical solution to the various territorial and boundary disputes in this region. The prerequisite for such solutions is the improvement of political conditions – with all regional actors including the US, in the case of Iran, honouring previous agreements and avoiding any expansionist ideas, respecting the sovereign existence and independence of all actors, together with states' comprehension of the significance of collaborative relationships in favour of all littoral members, efforts for extending CBM, and finally achieving a collective security arrangement, the components of which will be studied in the final chapter of this book.

Cooperation within the region would result in greater economic power (like the EU in Europe), and energy reserves, which have been the major element behind the continuing struggle for hegemony in this region, could transform the PG into the most powerful energy group in the world. Greater economic interaction and cooperation would also provide the basis for stronger security interactions among the littoral states of the PG. Therefore, there would be no reason for a US military presence or a flourishing US arms market in the region; a very dangerous and concerning fact in US foreign policy concerns. To help study the future shape of collective security arrangements in the region, the next three chapters will investigate other insecurity components: the littoral states' incongruity of political systems, and their different internal and external security concerns.

Notes

1 Julian Walker, "Practical problems of boundary delimitation in Arabia: the case of the United Arab Emirates". In Richard Schofield (ed.), *Territorial foundations of the Gulf states* (London: UCL Press, 1994), 112–113.
2 John Wilkinson, "Britain's role in boundary drawing in Arabia: a synopsis". In Schofield (ed.), op. cit., 96.
3 J. Prescott, *The geography of frontiers and boundaries* (London: Hutchinson, 1965), 34–40, cited in Alasdair Drysdale and Gerald Blake, *The Middle East and North Africa, a political geography* (New York and Oxford: Oxford University Press, 1985), 85.
4 Drysdale and Blake, op. cit., 313.
5 David Pike, "Cross-border hydrocarbon reserves". In Schofield (ed.), op. cit., 187.
6 Pike, op. cit., 187, 191, 193.
7 Keith McLachlan, "Hydrocarbons and Iranian policies towards the Gulf states". In Schofield (ed.), op. cit., 223, 234–236.
8 Richard Schofield, "Border disputes in the Gulf: past, present, and future". In Gary Sick and Lawrence Potter (eds), *The Persian Gulf at the millennium: Essays in politics, economy, security, and religion* (New York: St. Martin's Press, 1997), 132–133.
9 Pike, op. cit., 189.
10 Schofield, "Border disputes in the Gulf", op. cit., 156–157.
11 Schofield, "Borders and territoriality in the Gulf", op. cit., 2.
12 Ali Asghar Kazemi, *Aba'd-e hoghoghi-e hakemiat-e Iran dar Khalij-e Fars* [Legal dimensions of Iran authority in the Persian Gulf] (Tehran: Institute for Political and International Studies (IPIS), 1368 Solar Calendar [1989]), 3.
13 Rodman Bundy, "Maritime delimitation in the Gulf", in Schofield (ed.), 184, 176.
14 Wilkinson, op. cit., 94.
15 Bundy, op. cit., 185.
16 Richard Schofield (ed.), *Territorial foundation of the Gulf states* (London: UCL Press, 1994), pp. 22–23, 46 and 58.
17 Gerald Blake, "Shared zones as a solution to problems of territorial sovereignty in the Gulf states". In Schofield (ed.), op. cit., 200–201.
18 Ibid., 209.
19 Schofield, "Borders and territoriality in the Gulf", op. cit., 3.
20 Schofield, "Border disputes in the Gulf", op. cit., 132.
21 Schofield, "Borders and territoriality in the Gulf", op. cit., 4, 5, 14.
22 Anwar Gargash, "Prospects for conflict and cooperation: the Gulf toward the year 2000". In Sick and Potter (eds), op. cit., 329.
23 Details in ibid., 328, 330.
24 Ibid., 321.
25 Pirouz Mojtahed-Zadeh, *Security and territoriality in the Persian Gulf* (Richmond, Surrey: Curzon Press, 1999), 64.
26 Source of the maps: *The Circle of Ancient Iranian Studies (CAIS)*, http://www.cais-soas.com/CAIS/Iran/territorial_challenges.htm (December 2007).

27 Among many, see Graham Fuller, *The "Center of the Universe": The geopolitics of Iran* (Boulder, San Francisco and Oxford: Westview Press, 1991), 60–62.
28 One important document in Iran's Foreign Ministry, dated 1968, confirmed Britain's underplot to obtain, by theft or bribery, a very important report about different records of Iran's sovereignty over the PG islands and even some areas in the southern shore. In a "very confidential and important" letter of Mohammad Reza Amir Teimour [from the Iranian Embassy in London] to Ardeshir Zahedi, Foreign Minister on 30 Shahrivar 1347 (21 September 1968) it is mentioned that,

> This report which was written more than 80 years ago by Brigadier Haji Ahmad Khan Kababi, the then ruler of Lengah Port (Bandar Lengah) is very significant because there was documentary evidence signed by Arab sheikhs confirming Iran sovereignty right over the four islands. (…) while these sorts of documents were against Britain's policy and interest, is very likely that the originals and appendixes were stolen.

In the letter of Amir Teimour it is also mentioned that "Documents in [the] British Foreign Ministry show that the authorities in the British Embassy in Tehran, by different tricks have stolen or obtained the report by bribery then sent it to London. But this report is not among released documents in the British archive (it seems they have hidden the report)."
29 Hooshang Amirahmadi, "The colonial-political dimension of the Iran–UAE dispute". In Hooshang Amirahmadi (ed.), *Small islands, big politics: The Tonbs and Abu Musa in the Persian Gulf* (New York: St. Martin's Press, 1996), 14.
30 See, Ezzatollah Ezzati, *Tahlili bar Geopolitic-e Iran va Eragh* [An Analysis of the Geopolitics of Iran and Iraq] (Tehran: Foreign Ministry Press Centre, Institute for Political and International Studies (IPIS), 1381 Solar Calendar [2002]), 11–12.
31 Schofield, "Boundaries, territorial disputes", op. cit., 167–168.
32 Schofield, "Border disputes in the Gulf", op. cit., 158.
33 Alireza Salari, Ambassador of Iran to UAE during 2000–2004, in my exclusive interview in Abu Dhabi on 3 August 2004.
34 Amirahmadi, op. cit., 24, 13.
35 Harold Hough, "Iranian intentions: the Strait of Hormuz or beyond?" *Jane's Intelligence Review* (1 October 1995), vol. 7, no. 10, 454. Cited from http://www.american.edu/ted/abumusa.htm (accessed 2 July 2008).

6

The Arabian Peninsula States of the Persian Gulf: The GCC

Introduction

The different political position of the PG states (e.g. political structure, political history, interaction with the world's powers, national interests, etc.) has significantly affected regional security. Security, as the most important issue in the PG region, has been influenced by interaction between the eight littoral states.

Certainly, PG regional security has been the direct consequence of the superpowers' intense rivalry and, since the 1990s, of the US' hegemony policy along with other external powers' interests in this region – all of which have affected the littoral states' domestic and foreign policies. However, the domestic, regional and international politics of each of the PG states have been influenced by their perception of national interests along with their various capabilities, such as their political, economic and military power. In addition, by the end of the Cold War era and due to critical changes in international politics, the littoral states' definition of security and national interests had changed dramatically. Regional actors lost their roles and political manoeuvring ability in the bipolar international system, and while some became even more dependent than before, others faced embargos and sanctions from the dominant actor of the unipolar system.

Consequently, for the future shape of collective security arrangements in the region (besides the geopolitical importance of the PG which has already been studied), the greatest factor to consider is the national security of each nation-state. In this regard, the domestic dimension of stability and social peace and wealth as the major indicators of legitimacy and authority of the states will be considered. Hence, besides the incongruity of the political systems of the littoral states, the internal socio-economic and political developments in each country should be studied as a major element influencing regional security. In addition, from the perspective of the littoral states' different security concerns, the external challenges and threats facing them, especially from the other regional actors, will be examined.

The purpose of this section is, by considering the insecurity components in the region, to identify convergence elements among littoral states so as to turn threats into opportunities for regional cooperation and sustainability. To be able to analyse the determinant factors of a security system, this chapter, regarding Saudi Arabia (the GCC), and the two following, regarding Iraq and Iran, draw upon a level of analysis framework in international relations. In order to find links between insights derived at various levels from different actors and units of analysis, and hence to be able to identify a general theory of interaction, a theory that has both descriptive and predictive powers, this study also discusses all three levels of the PG states' foreign policies and the forces affecting them – including the systemic level and the debate that occurs at the domestic and individual levels (see Chapters 6 to 8). These chapters also draw upon social analysis, to provide an analysis of the situation in PG states with regard to their social backgrounds and belief systems. They also draw upon elite theory to provide an analysis of power relationships or policy-planning networks in the PG states' societies, as well as their different definitions of security and national interests. Applying these components in a suitable security theory can help to construct a regional security arrangement, which will be studied in the final chapter.

Political institutions: the leadership tradition in the GCC

Despite changes in economic and social features of the Arab states in the PG from oil revenues, their traditional political systems have remained fundamentally intact. Since Bedouin times a single ruler or sheikh and his ruling family – likewise, the elite classes of other clan or tribes – have determined the entire social, economic and political policies of the nation-states and mass public destiny. Family members or elites close to them dominate all important positions regarding budget, internal security, foreign policy and military issues.

It is not only decision-making in the GCC states that is dominated by this small group, which, according to Byman and Green, are "privileged by birth, not by merit";[1] they also "own the countries".[2] The ruler, chosen by a tribal council or self-appointed family member following an internal struggle, is usually the wealthiest, most powerful and influential head of a clan.

So, as Chubin suggests, "money and other forms of fortune (...) play an important part in achieving and maintaining rule. The classical tribal sheikh has to be rich enough to offer lavish hospitality to his followers and to outside dignitaries."[3] Also, as Byman and Green affirm, "All [Arab] Gulf governments are remarkably skilled at using economic control to ensure their hold on power (...) they are experts at using largesse to silence critical voices [and] oil wealth allows the state to dominate the economy."[4] The traditional autocratic tribal family government system has stayed unchanged; in the event of a ruler's failure in his obligations, not just the head of state but his ruling family would lose the leadership, thus presenting an opportunity for his rivals from another family or even other tribes to replace him.[5]

The flexibility and adaptability of the traditional system of tribal rule in this regard has ensured that ruling families attain power for decades. According to this system if the ruler is unable to adapt to any new situations that threatened to put the entire system in crisis, he could be discharged by other family members or elites through violence (on the one hand) or in a suave and respectful manner (on the other). For instance, the Amir of Qatar was replaced in 1972 by a more "modern" relative, and in 1995 Sheikh Hamad bin Khalifa Al Thani deposed his father in a bloodless coup. Such replacements take place by consultation with other leading Qatari families when they decide that the old Amir no longer meets the needs of the day. Therefore, such "ideological flexibility", as Byman and Green explain, can serve to offset outside meddling as well as opposition groups' demands, which potentially pose a great threat to the Arab regime.

This flexibility, demonstrated by certain cases of rulers being deposed in the interest of foreign powers, illustrates the heavy dependency of the political power pyramid, legitimacy and sovereignty in the southern peninsula states on the outside powers. In this regard, some analysts go further, suggesting that any power displacement and changes in conditions and policies in these countries occur as a function of the international powers' interests. As Sariolghalam states,

> The wide international dominance exerted over the PG region has a direct relation to the internal weakness of its member states and

the collapse of political thought among their elites. (...) Among the Third World regions, the Middle East (...) is the only region in the world that besides its internal potential capabilities has remained under the influence of international policy and economic control. The problem is that these regimes have no internal institutions to be able to interact reasonably, functionally and independently with the outside world and at the same time have national consensus for making interdependent decisions. The security and legitimacy of the PG authorities, where their regime security is the most important matter to them, is very much dependent to the world outside their borders. Therefore any power displacement and changes of essences and policies in these countries occur as a function of international interests. (...) Their internal security is also very much dependent on international coalitions.[6]

However, regardless of whether these speculations seem consistent regarding the geopolitical significance of the PG in recent years, the major powers have brought increased pressure to bear upon traditional rulers to carry out reforms; these might be executed either through voluntary replacement by their modern younger successors or by the actual adoption and implementation of the modern reforms themselves.

Reform dilemmas of the GCC

Implementing modern reform from the point of view of the GCC and the West, especially the US, is the only choice of the Arabian Peninsula's traditional political systems in a modern world. However, while the GCC states are aware of the need for domestic reform to make their regimes more stable and their economies more vibrant, the dilemma for them is that, due to the very traditional and conservative political systems of their regimes, especially in Saudi Arabia, serious structural and political internal reform remains off the agenda. This issue adds to the impact of the whole political situation in the region upon internal issues, which, when compounded with their domestic socio-economic and political problems, confront the GCC states with rigorous restrictions in their attempts to carry out reforms. Among various challenges to their security and stability, internal problems are the major factor. This is due to the fact that the probability of foreign military attacks is low, especially after the reduction of the two PG major powers' (Iran and Iraq) military capabilities during the last three wars in the PG, while the GCC regimes also enjoy US military protection. But as Turki Al-Hamad remarks, despite the lack of major external threats against them, they confront significant internal problems.[7]

While history and tradition are recognised as the main legitimate sources of the ruling families of the GCC, they resist major political and economic reforms that can affect their political power, wealth and fortune. In addition, their legitimacy, which derives from rentier or cradle-to-grave welfare systems, may also decline as a result of economic reforms, the GCC population's growth and the possibility of shrinking government revenue sources.

However, according to the principle of "flexibility and adaptability", along with the importance of regime security more than state security, there are few choices for ruling families who wish to keep the status quo, except for adopting significant reforms. Such reforms contain at least a limited recognition of the need for political and economic reforms, albeit with a wide and undetermined range of timing, method and degree of changes. Domestic and structural factors, along with regional and international political evolutions, are the main internal and external factors persuading GCC regimes to adopt or offer some reform measures.

Threats and external factors relating to the GCC

Despite it being a tumultuous region of the ME since the 1950s, the Arabian Peninsula has survived unchanged with regard to traditional political systems, despite its wars and revolutions. ME security strategies have been able to solve not just foreign interference and threats but the considerable domestic problems in maintaining social peace.

Regarding external threat, there are very different visions among the GCC states. Although the US military initially came to the PG to protect southern littoral monarchies from Iran and Iraq, many of these countries were mainly afraid of each other. To face external threats, they traditionally prefer diplomatic methods and political influence, whether via adaptable diplomacy or generous aid.

However, fear of the Iran–Iraq war spreading to the region and its insecurity consequences for the GCC encouraged them to invite external powers to support them, by declaring, during the "Tanker War" of 1987, that the responsibility for protecting freedom of navigation in the PG was an international duty.[8]

In general, the GCC states do not face any serious or urgent foreign invasion. While they have benefited from the US' commitment to provide military support, Iran and Iraq, the two major regional powers over the last three decades, have become weak, certainly in terms of their conventional military power. Currently, Iran is the only regional military power that, by developing its military capabilities, is perceived as a potential threat to the GCC, although it is a far less modern military power in comparative terms than it was before the eight-year war with Iraq.

Since its defeat in the 1990–1991 Kuwait crisis and the later collapse of Saddam's regime in 2003, Iraq also needs a long-term recovery period to become a regional power once more. However, some other dangers – mainly terrorist attacks from groups based in Iraq – may threaten GCC security in Iraq, as may the US' failure to establish there a stable and secure new government and improve the society's security. Yemen, which has recently been involved in its own civil war and subject to attack by Islamist extremist elements, cannot be assumed to be a serious military threat to its neighbours.

So, since the mid-1990s, as Sick, Gause and others observe, according to the conventional definition of security – i.e. shelter from foreign military invasion – the small states of the GCC seem more secure and stable than at any time in their independent history, and even more secure than the two large states of Iran and Iraq.[9]

GCC states, like all other countries, have faced outside meddling as well as domestic opposition groups' demands, both of which can pose a significant threat to the security of regimes. During the 1950s and 60s, the Arab regimes of the PG faced the efforts of opposition groups using the idea of Arab nationalism, introduced by Egyptian President Jamal Nasser, to achieve Arab unity – a message that was accompanied by the condemnation of the Arab regimes of the PG, specifically Saudi Arabia, and that supported Saudi opposition groups in their attempts to bring about the downfall of monarchies such as those in Iraq, Syria and Libya.

The peak point of such problems was in the 1980s during the Iran–Iraq war. Iran, in various ways – including inviting GCC people to overthrow their governments – tried, as Byman and Green note, to dissuade GCC governments from supporting Baghdad in its imposed war against Iran.[10]

Nevertheless, by improving the relationship between Iran and the GCC and establishing a new regime in Iraq, these kinds of threats have decreased – albeit that a continuation of US military presence on the Arabian Peninsula can always be a motive for destabilising relations between Iran and the GCC states and may even contribute to the dynamics of threat escalation. This might be especially true in the light of recent American plans for a possible attack on Iran's nuclear sites, which can only take place through US bases in the Arabian Peninsula – a situation where necessary military tools have been provided through the most recent Washington ME strategy of containment against Iran, via the arming of US Arab allies.

However, despite GCC leaders' concerns regarding Iran's growing influence in the ME and its military potential, which could be seen by the GCC as a long-term threat, neither side welcomes any threat escalation; rather, they seek to build confidence-building measures and improve relations. In this regard, for example, an Al-Jazeera broadcast, citing a senior Saudi diplomatic source concerning a possible US attack on Iran's nuclear sites, suggested that, "A lot of Saudis fear that the US will come and make mischief, then go away, but we have to live here afterwards."[11]

Most likely, unrest and internal instability, which are seen as very real potential threats, may increase in the GCC as governments' resources decrease in the future, alongside the rapid growth of their population rate. Preventing external threats and preserving the security of the regimes require the solving of internal problems.

Domestic and structural factors in the GCC

GCC governments face serious domestic and structural security threats, which, in the main, includes the problem of governments' political legitimacy, social structure and economic structure.

The problem of governments' political legitimacy

The threats faced are mainly the result of political exclusion resulting in the lack of people's political participation and the absence of the governments' accountability and transparency; the impact of the fall of oil revenues per capita as a threat to cradle-to-grave welfare or the rentier system (to provide free services to all citizens since the early 1970s of the oil bloom) which highlights the fact that the government cannot fulfil its expected role; and a firm criticism of the government's excessive dependency upon the US, which is the major reason for their internal security problems, in turn leading to religious militancy, particularly in Saudi Arabia.

Social structure
Problems here include very rapid population growth with a large and restless youthful population and high expectations; the social system's vulnerability to fluctuations in oil prices; a wide gap between rich and poor; growing unemployment; the population ratio of foreigners to locals because of manpower shortages; and the impact of rapid modernisation and Westernisation on social stability, especially the crises of citizens' identity.

Economic structure
Problems here are related to a high dependency on oil revenue and the international oil market as the main source of governments' income; economic stagnation; financial crisis and high budget deficits due to low oil prices, corruption, mismanagement and high defence spending.

According to Turki Al-Hamad, the GCC social problems are due to the combination of serious economic difficulties (as a result of the decline in oil prices such as in the mid-1980s, costly and irrational governmental spending – especially on defence and security – weak and unhealthy economic arrangements and growing indebtedness) and the high rate of foreign employment. Under such circumstances, he observes the rise of social problems such as "growing unemployment, escalating crime, and emerging terrorism" which may have political consequences, e.g. "more claims for political participation; and growing pressure for drastic reforms".[12]

In addition, as Byman and Green note, the dominant belief of GCC citizens is that their political systems are exclusive, and that peaceful political activities are not capable of influencing their country's leadership. Consequently, they observe, "[T]his opposition could have dangerous repercussions: throughout the world, rather moderate political groups have often become violent after years of repeated failures in proposing compromise."[13] They also perceive the alienation of social and economic elites as being very dangerous, especially as oil wealth has allowed the ruling families to control state finances and politics, while traditional tribal and family elites have lost influence.

The unconditional pledge of loyalty in return for free social services agreed between the rulers and the ruled in the GCC states has been shaken. This is the consequence of major corruption and uncountable government spending levels, especially the unreported annual billion-dollar revenue from petroleum exports in budgets of the GCC governments,[14] along with the economic slump – as a result of high levels of social spending, supporting Iraq's eight-year war against Iran in the 1980s, and paying for the "Desert Storm" operation in the 1990s. Moreover, the wider involvement of the royal families, particularly in Saudi Arabia and Bahrain, in business and even private sectors, traders' dissatisfaction over the circulation of money, the rapid increase in population along with a rise in expectations for a higher standard of living, adding to the shrinking revenues and growing unemployment – all have reduced citizens' loyalty, previously reinforced by money. Economic stagnation has resulted in a widespread feeling of indignation about corruption and wealth disparity, widening the gap between the rich and the poor and thus rendering it more critical.

In addition, the sudden transformation of the GCC' traditional societies and their moral and religious values as they changed from a poor economy to being wealthy oil-producer states with new norms and social organisation derived from modernisation and Westernisation, has enlarged their social crisis. More importantly, the prevailing notion that "modernisation brings secularity", or that "modernisation is a fundamental break from spirituality", has caused the rise of militant religious, social and ethnic movements in these countries. In this regard, two other major threats have confronted GCC regimes. These are the traditionally discriminated and oppressed Shiites, who form a large segment of several GCC states' populations, especially in Saudi Arabia and Bahrain, and growing anti-government religious militancy, specifically Sunni radical Muslims in several GCC states.

Discrimination against Shiite citizens – including political exclusion, limitations of their religious practice and literature, employment and financial discrimination,[15] restriction in joining the army,[16] using some laws against Shiites,[17] introducing them as heretic and causing them to be "stigmatized socially (both the government and much of the Sunni majority sees them as tantamount to apostates"),[18] as well as suffering routine harassment and imprisonment by the security services, etc. – has, in turn, been a source of turmoil.

Also, analysts consider religious militancy to be perhaps the most dangerous threat to stability in some GCC states, especially Saudi Arabia, originating mainly from Sunni radicals. Sunni religious radicals, who were encouraged and supported by GCC regimes, later began to challenge them. These radicals were reinforced from the 1960s to the 1980s regarding two basic policies of GCC regimes: divide-and-rule, and lessening the influence of Arab nationalism as an anti-monarchist political thought as well as creating a rival to the Shiite thought of Iran's Islamic revolution. As Byman and Green have remarked concerning the policy of divide-and-rule, GCC governments are not only skilful in making divisions within communities and fragmenting any political opposition, but are also very masterful in using Sunni distrust of the Shiites and even creating division within the Shiite communities themselves.[19] Regarding the Islamic Revolution of Iran, according to Esposito,

> Iran captured the headlines and imaginations of many throughout the Muslim world and the West (...). For a secular-oriented West the specter of the spread of revolutionary Islam seemed both retrogressive and a threat to Western allies and interests (oil and trade). The reality was in fact far more complex. Iran proved far more effective as a source of inspiration rather than emulation. For rulers in the Gulf, response to the strength and threat of Islamic political activism was complicated by the fact that many of them were Sunni rulers with significant Shiite populations.[20]

Consequently, common resentment of oppositions, due to the regimes' domestic policy of repression as the preferred response to all political opposition in the majority of GCC countries, and political exclusion systems, together with the radicals' objection to their governments' over-dependency upon the US, drove the oppositions underground and increased the probability that frustrated elements would resort to secret methods and acts of violence. Opposition to Al-Saud intensified from the time of the Iraqi invasion of Kuwait in 1990 as a result of the presence of hundreds of thousands of Western troops in the kingdom. The most violent disorderly behaviour of the early 1990s happened in Saudi Arabia and Bahrain – the two states least tolerant of political criticism; both were without any practical representative institutions.

However, by using a combination of several strategies, the GCC states have been successful in promoting social order and remaining stable. As Byman and Green remark,

> Ruling families have proven skilled at anticipating, and preventing political violence before it explodes. The regimes employ mixtures of carrots and sticks, using aggressive security services to monitor, and at times suppress, opposition, while co-opting potential opposition leaders with wealth, jobs, and high-status positions. In addition, regime leaders are cunning political chameleons, changing their outside appearance to match the issues of the day, while maintaining their hold on power.[21]

In this regard, this book will examine Saudi Arabia's role as the main GCC member and the likelihood of success of Riyadh's traditional strategies to control the social order in the future. For a better understanding of the socio-political issues in Saudi Arabia, it is vital that much attention is given to its geography and political ideology – as a tribal monarchy whose constitutional organisation is established on Salafi or Wahhabi Islamic law – and the political processes of its decision-making.

Internal threats to the stability of the Saudi regime

Oil wealth, besides its significant impact on the whole process of development and modernisation, economic and social features in Saudi Arabia, has given the kingdom great legitimacy over the years.

Oil revenue has enabled the regime to make the opposition noiseless, by controlling the economy to ensure its domestic socio-political stability via not just the rentier system but also by using bounty. Additionally, it has contributed to conciliate and repel potential foreign threats with the government's offers of generous amounts of aid.[22]

Oil wealth has also enabled the royal family to ensure the regime's survival via empowering the Bedouin or White Army, and old tribal elements from Najd loyal to the Saudi family, to be known as the Saudi Arabia National Guard (SANG). The SANG exists on the bounty of the rulers and has operated as independent units under direct command of King Abdullah since 1963. Its mission is to safeguard sensitive domains like oil installations and the royal family from internal rebellion, and it is a counterbalance within the royal family, who control the regular armed forces.

The regular Saudi Army, under the command of the Defence Minister, Prince Sultan, is small in number and comprises unskilled local military personnel that must rely on imported technology and foreign employees in order to operate complex and sophisticated weaponries. This situation results in a lack of any possible political antagonism incentives towards the regime. The Saudi ranks are swelled by foreign nationals, especially from Muslim countries – including Pakistanis, Jordanians, Syrians, Palestinians and Egyptians. Also, large numbers of American, British and French expatriate military technicians and trainers run the Saudi military modernisation programmes.

The qualitative superiority of Saudi arms sale policy, which influenced the kingdom towards progressive diversification of arms suppliers, has made the Saudis' personnel training and the issue of weaponries maintenance harder; the regime will remain even more dependent on Western suppliers in the future.

As Murden remarks, the aim of Riyadh's cautious military strategy, besides keeping Saudi armies inefficient in order to maintain the regime's security, also serves to postpone the reformation process in the country.[23] This is related, as Cordesman remarks, to "the commercial motives of foreign suppliers, and certainly the presence of so much foreign support".[24] Gause adds to this analysis the financial interests of those in the GCC states (including Saudi Arabia) who benefit from these large-scale arms deals[25] (see Figures 6.1 and 6.2).

In general, oil revenue has enabled Riyadh to spend extravagantly on its defence system. Regarding national defence and repelling external threats, after Iraq's invasion of Kuwait the military use of these kinds of arms purchases was doubted by the Saudi people, and the inability of the imported military technology to provide the kingdom with the security needs was proven. However, from an internal security point of view, it has improved the power and coercive capabilities of the regime to a degree sufficient to stay in power and, in general, to preserve social peace.

Social peace in Saudi Arabia, besides the use of a variety of government strategies to promote social order, is provided by the security forces, which are often staffed by foreigners who do not hesitate to suppress dissent.[26] This is particularly evident in the response to the seizure of the Grand Mosque in Mecca by Sunni radicals during the

Hajj in 1979, and the anti-American attacks in the kingdom during the 1980s and 1990s, which led to dozens of deaths and hundreds of arrests in both cases.

FIGURE 6.1
Cumulative Saudi Arabian arms imports relative to those of the other Persian Gulf states: 1986–1999
(value of deliveries in constant US$ millions)

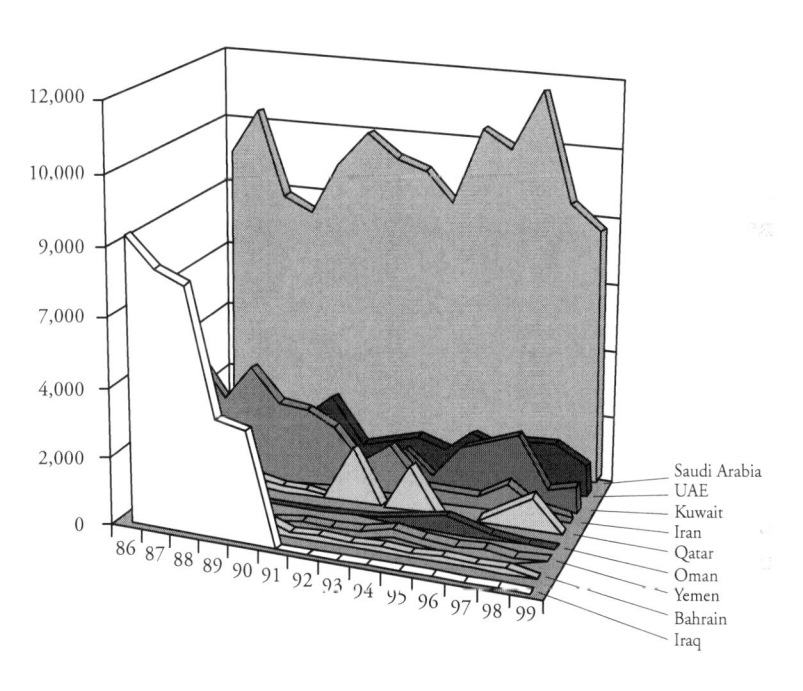

	86	87	88	89	90	91	92	93	94	95	96	97	98	99
Iraq	8,288	7,448	7,078	3,407	3,279	0	0	0	0	0	0	0	0	5
Bahrain	91	418	126	97	328	79	122	86	106	72	132	90	101	70
Yemen	564	1,045	1,523	1,554	35	41	6	22	275	145	81	110	30	30
Oman	178	157	38	73	12	57	11	140	307	445	376	160	30	30
Qatar	7	12	38	219	117	23	1,552	11	1,375	52	5	625	1,015	120
Iran	3,305	2,221	3,286	2,312	2,225	1,812	942	1,512	412	342	356	850	376	150
Kuwait	271	248	152	316	316	374	1,109	1,080	412	1,346	1,728	2,000	457	725
UAE	247	261	404	1,187	1,874	532	804	891	793	1,346	1,118	1,400	1,471	950
Saudi Arabia	8,978	10,320	7,710	7,423	8,900	9,968	9,312	8,962	8,143	10,350	9,862	11,600	8,424	7,700

Source: Adapted by Anthony Cordesman from State Department, *World military expenditures and arms transfers* (Washington D. C.: GPO), various editions.

FIGURE 6.2
Comparative military expenditures of the Persian Gulf powers as a percentage of GNP: 1989–1999

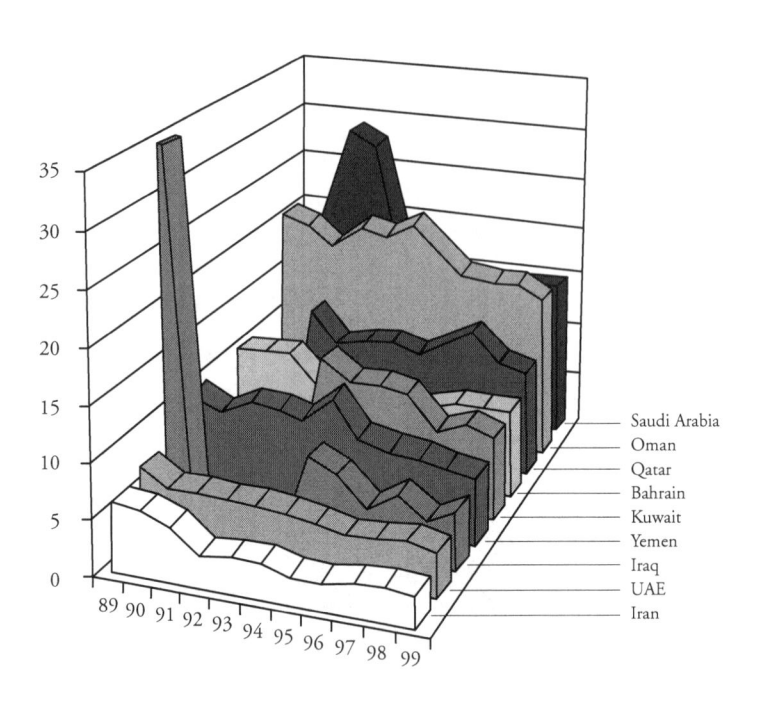

	89	90	91	92	93	94	95	96	97	98	99
Iran	6.4	6	5	3	3.4	3.3	2.6	2.5	3	3.1	2.9
UAE	7.3	5.8	5.8	5.6	5.5	5.3	4.8	4.3	4.4	4.7	4.1
Iraq	34.3	–	–	–	–	8.3	7.1	4.3	6	4.1	5.5
Yemen	9.9	8.6	9.8	9.8	9.2	11.4	8	7.2	7.1	6.7	6.1
Kuwait	6.1	(53.1)	(101.9)	(77.0)	12.8	11	11.1	10.7	7.6	8.6	7.7
Bahrain	10.5	10.5	10.8	8.2	7.9	7.5	7.7	7.5	8.2	8.1	8.1
Qatar	–	–	13.2	10.2	10.9	11.1	10.4	11.9	13.3	10.6	10
Oman	21.1	20.1	18.4	20.5	20	21.5	19.1	16.8	16.6	16.7	15.3
Saudi Arabia	15.9	20.6	28.5	27.2	16.4	14.1	13.2	14.9	14.9	14.9	14.9

Source: Adapted by Anthony Cordesman from State Department, *World military expenditures and arms transfers* (Washington D. C.: GPO), various editions.

Although calling in the US to protect the state against direct foreign threats seems reasonable according to Saudis who – like other GCC states – lack the military means to defend themselves, it has increased regimes' challenges and has enhanced a legitimacy crisis among the GCC citizens, including Saudi people. Such a crisis for Riyadh has acquired wider dimensions through the regime's resistance to any mobilised organisations of individuals or groups of citizens aimed at forming an alternative defence strategy, such as the Islamic activists' suggestion after the Kuwait crisis for the creation of a 500,000-man Saudi army to prevent dependence on outside forces for defence. The strategic umbrella provided by the US, and the numerous problems caused for the regime through its dependency on Saudi forces for national security (especially intensifying the present request for citizens' greater political participation, and also preventing Arab military coups during the 1950s and 60s), is firm evidence of Saudi Arabia's continued dependency on foreign forces in this regard.

Oil wealth has also promoted, according to Drysdale and Blake, "national integration by greatly strengthening the central government and by making possible ambitious development projects", especially by building a comprehensive air and road transportation network all around the kingdom. In return, this could promote the Saudi rulers' geopolitical superiority over the whole Arabian Peninsula. Moreover, as Drysdale and Blake remark, oil revenue has improved unity in the kingdom via the spread of public education as an element of promoting feelings of citizenship, and is also a way of strengthening national loyalty instead of tribal devotion.[27]

However, as the Saudi economy has remained heavily dependent on the oil sector – oil as the main source of foreign exchange still accounts for approximately 90–95 per cent of export earnings, 70–80 per cent of budget revenues and about 40 per cent of the country's gross domestic product (GDP) – the inherent vulnerability of such a reliance could be the greatest threat to the kingdom's integration and its long-term stability, which has been ensured by oil wealth (see Figure 6.3).

Such threats are rooted not only in a decrease of oil revenues (see Figure 6.4) but also in the lack of a native technological base and the skilled and unskilled labour force, specifically in oil sections, with its cultural consequences. In this respect, Drysdale and Blake's 1985 prophecy regarding the impact of the presence of numerous foreigners and their capacity to alter the character and cultural features of the country has proven to be accurate. They suggested that the major challenge facing Riyadh in the future might be how to survive in its present form when an increasing percentage of the population believes neither in Wahhabism nor in loyalty to the Saudi family.[28]

FIGURE 6.3
Saudi Arabia's oil production and consumption, 1980–2006

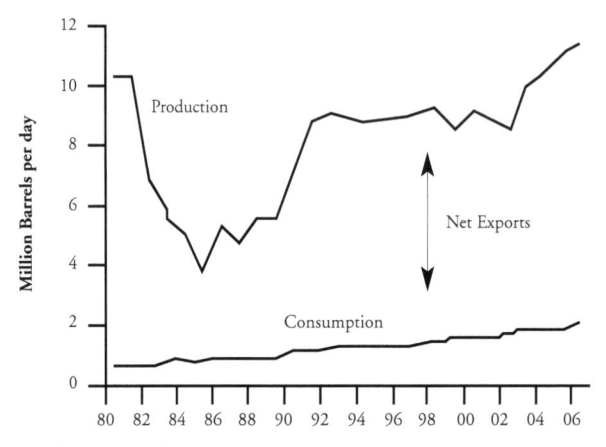

Source: http://www.eia.doe.gov/emeu/cabs/saudi.html

FIGURE 6.4
Share of OPEC net oil export revenues for selected countries, 1972–2006

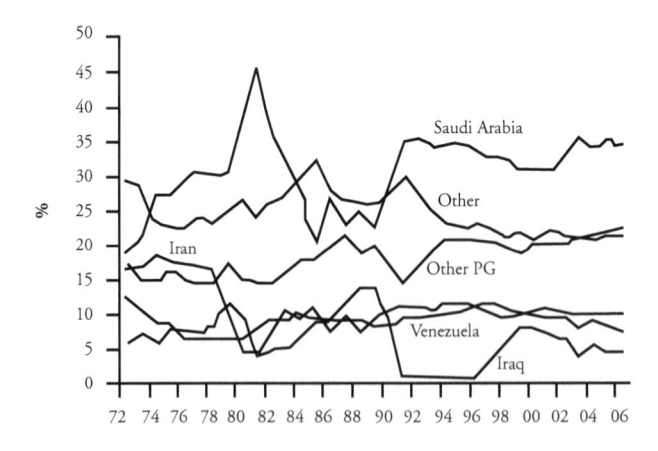

Source: http://www.eia.doe.gov/cabs/opecrev.html

However, due to various economic and social developments in the kingdom, the rulers are under pressure to address their inactivity in political development by accepting greater political participation for Saudi citizens. This has become a serious matter, not only because of the influence of Western culture in Saudi Arabia – specifically by a new generation of educated and unemployed citizens who had travelled and studied in the West – but also, besides high expectations, rapid population growth, high unemployment and falling oil revenues per capita, the profligate royal spending leading to economic stagnation has exacerbated resentment over corruption and wealth disparities. When newly educated technocrats and also religious scholars observe poorly educated family members indulging in rampant corruption and inefficiency in the government, this causes anger and resentment. Such social discontent will inevitably create instability. The major long-term socio-economic challenges confronting the regime, in spite of the recent increase, in its oil incomes will be as follows.

- Rapid population growth; estimated to average around 4.3 per cent annually for the period 1980–1997 with around 60 per cent of Saudis under 21 years of age.
- Emergence and gain in power of the middle class as a result of distribution of rent in society, with its own independent interests including demand for some reforms.
- High rates of Saudi nationals' unemployment; figures ranging from 10–25 per cent.
- High rate of expatriates in the kingdom as a demographic, cultural and political threat.
- Economic problems, almost two decades of heavy budget and trade deficits – the expenses of two wars of Iraq against Iran and Kuwait in 1980–1988 and 1990–1991 – total public debt of around US$175 billion and also a decline in real per capita oil export revenues since 1980 (from US$22,589 per person to US$4,564 in 2004).
- Wider gap between poor and rich, more corruption of the ruling family and the development of double standards.
- The strategic and economic relationship with the West, particularly the US, is a permanent controversy and may be the most disturbing problem for the Saudi monarchy. The relationship has become a liability for the internal legitimacy of Al-Saud, especially during

continued crises over Iraq until its occupation and the Saudi government's strict association with Washington in that regard. The economic relationship between the US and Saudi Arabia led to further internal security for Saudi Arabia. Riyadh, since the end of the twentieth century, has taken steps towards economic diversification to support its infrastructure against downturns in the oil markets as well as decreasing its reliance on oil revenues. However, Saudi Arabia, with a shortage of the managerial and technical potentiality and ability to operate different manufacturing industries, will remain a mere consumer of Western products. Its major economic activities are concerned with trade and investment and their prerequisites, so at a time of declining oil revenue the regime will be dependent on the West even more than before. As also mentioned in the August 2005 report of the Energy Information Administration (EIA), "Saudi Arabia is eager to maintain and even expand its market share in the United States for a variety of economic and strategic reasons."[29] Consequently, Washington's major technique to control the flow of oil from the PG via preserving promising political and economic ties with Riyadh has been built through increasing bilateral investment and trade. Therefore "the Saudi state, unlike the contemporary Iranian and Iraqi states (...) [is] wrapped up with the interests of Western states and business to a far greater extent".[30]

Under such a situation, alongside the regional socio-political changes, unrest may increase as government resources diminish in the future; this will probably contribute towards further socio-political instability. Any decline in socio-economic opportunities may motivate requests for political reforms and deliver greater political participation to citizens. Despite the considerable stability of Saudi Arabia, the regime has recognised the need for political and economic reforms, although limited in kind, to prevent any possible confrontation with its citizens, especially the large and restless younger generation who are unemployed and have high expectations.

Therefore, in order to deal with the new financial realities Saudi Arabia has moved cautiously and slowly towards extending the reform process and taking some unwanted economic choices, e.g. privatisation, subsidy cuts, tax increases and financial sector reforms. These reforms can have political consequences but not necessarily lead to a real change in its content. In this regard, big state-owned corporations that control the Saudi economy have not been under any transaction of state shares and wealth to private sections. Since a principal motive of Saudi privatisation has been its wish to join the World Trade Organisation (WTO), the approval of its membership in 2005 may postpone even its very slow attempts to perform privatisation in the country.

In fact, besides domestic and structural factors of Saudi society, globalisation, as Nonneman notes, is the main external factor of the apparent paradox of the GCC having taken a lead over most of the Arab world with regard to political liberalisation.[31] Therefore, privatisations, like all other features of economic globalisation, including WTO membership, free economy and liberal market operations (in other words, opening the kingdom's economy to free trade and foreign investments and capital flows) are such great advantages that Riyadh cannot ignore them. Hence, Saudi Arabia's membership of the WTO was approved on 11 November 2005 after a twelve-year negotiating process slowed by the country's participation in the Arab League's boycott of Israel. While the Saudi regime also looks at this accession as an element to help bolster energy security, liberal Saudi citizens hope it will accelerate economic reforms as a prerequisite and leverage to "open up" the political atmosphere. In addition, despite the economic benefits of accession to the WTO, the government may specifically face radicals' threats regarding the Saudi market opening towards Israel in the future.

With the new trend towards globalisation, the Al-Saud, who seem to be quite interested in finding solutions to Saudi Arabia's economic problems, are not yet ready to discuss other aspects of economic reform, which include greater transparency, anticorruption, good governance, and social and political reform, in accordance with the priorities of world economic organisations such as the International Monetary Fund (IMF), the WTO, the Organisation for Economic Cooperation and Development (OECD) and the World Bank. Therefore, Saudi policy was perceived as an attempt to select only those aspects of globalisation that Riyadh accepts in order to enjoy economic benefits without having to implement any real and major reforms.

Since any economic reform is accompanied by belt-tightening and a decline in the rentier system, the kingdom, in order to confront the political consequences, has been unenthusiastic about removing the financial cushion and increasing prices closer to market levels by decreasing subsidies. The political consequences of the Kuwait crisis in 1990 and fiscal crisis of Saudi Arabia, both of which accompanied the government decision to introduce indirect taxation and reduce some subsidies, paved the way for Saudis to ask about the absence of political participation and public consultation in the state's affairs. So, to make a gesture and give at least the appearance of more institutionalised consultative mechanisms for eliciting the populations' views on politics, since 1990 Riyadh has appointed new *majlis al-shura* (consultative councils), and in 1995 also made sweeping changes in the non-political parts of the cabinet by employing new faces to deal with economic problems.

In other words, Riyadh has chosen a limited reform as a strategic solution. It has realised that a slow opening up and reform process displaying a move away from authoritarian rule and transition towards democracy need not be harmful but could actually extend the rulers' legitimacy. However, as Nonneman remarks, those countries that have merely selectively appropriated democratic features without further democratisation will end up in a "grey zone" – Nonneman following here the argument of Daniel Bromberg that "liberalisation may not bring democratisation but rather a state of liberalised autocracy".[32]

Nevertheless, as Malik and Niblock note, the reforms undertaken by the Saudi regime so far suffer from two problems:

> First, they have mostly been implemented slowly and partially. There is the danger, already apparent in the country, that economic reform may become more difficult the longer it is left. Rising unemployment and deteriorating social conditions, fed by one of the highest rates of population growth in the world (...), will intensify political unrest and social disruption. Second, the reforms are still inadequate. The wider reforms that are needed are in many ways the most difficult, and will require a greater social and political transformation than has so far been envisaged. Greater transparency and accountability will be needed, and the educational and social facilities offered to Saudis must enable Saudi labour to be as productive as migrant/expatriate labour. While the problem of unemployment may gain temporary redress through the imposition of Saudi labour on unwilling employers, this will not create a productive economy for the long term. Saudi labour must be able to compete with expatriate/migrant manpower. The balance needs to be re-adjusted on both sides: making Saudi labour more productive and less expensive to employers; and improving the working conditions of migrant labour, thereby making it more expensive.[33]

Therefore, they emphasise the need for a "new social contract between the state and the population" to build a significant level of trust based on governmental transparency and a stronger commitment to socio-economic equity and greater popular accountability.[34]

Nonetheless, under new regional circumstances, especially in Iraq since the overthrow of Saddam's regime, the global trends towards democracy, and political reform plans not just in several GCC countries, e.g. Qatar, Bahrain, Oman and Kuwait, but also in revolutionary Islamic Iran, it is impossible for Al-Saud to rely much on its traditional strategies to keep social peace in an area of turbulence. As was explained earlier, parallel to modernisation and development process two major threats have confronted the kingdom: the traditionally discriminated-against and oppressed Shiites, who form about 10 per cent of the population (mostly concentrated in the oil-rich Eastern Province, formerly al-Hasa), and the growing anti-government religious militancy, specifically Sunni radical Muslims, in Saudi Arabia.

In general, the goal of Shiite opposition movements in Saudi Arabia has not been to overthrow the Al-Saud and the system of government, but the removal of all kinds of discrimination against them. Hence, since 1988 the Saudi Shiites have chosen democratic ways to achieve their socio-political demands. The Shiite community does not seem to pose the internal security threat that was a concern in the early 1980s, although, following new developments in Iraq after Saddam and greater sectarian tensions in the region, the Saudi regime is under more pressure to show greater tolerance. However, should Shiites succeed to power in Iraq, and Al-Saud delay in producing a proper reaction to the Shiites' demands for reforms, they might become a serious threat to the regime.

However, since the opposition in Saudi Arabia has always been fragmented and there is serious doubt about this changing in the foreseeable future, analysts mainly consider religious militancy the most dangerous threat to stability in the country. In order to understand the impact of Saudi Arabia's political development on the region's security, Riyadh's security concerns, especially those directed towards the other two major regional actors, and its foreign policy should be analysed.

External threats to the stability of the Saudi regime

Saudi Arabia's foreign policy has traditionally followed three fundamental objectives: security, Islamic solidarity and pan-Arabism. Its most fundamental goal is the preservation of the Al-Saud monarchy and maintaining and enhancing the security of its territory from external aggression.

The most important factors for the Saudi's very existence and prosperity are peace and stability in the PG region. Therefore, Saudi Arabia's most essential interest has been the preservation of the status quo with the management of relations with Iran and Iraq to prevent any superiority or expansion of these as its two major questions of security. In order to face external threats, achieve peace and security, and maintain the status quo, Riyadh found a regional military balance of power the most favourable solution. Nevertheless, being a relatively weak military power in comparison to Iran and Iraq, diplomatic and economic means tended to be the preferred options by which the Saudis chose to affect, in their limited capacity, the regional military balance of power. They traditionally prefer diplomatic methods and political influence, whether via adaptable diplomacy or generous aid.

Oil revenues have provided the means through which these goals have been pursued. However, vast economic wealth is not sufficient compensation for military weakness. To bolster its security and compensate for its military inadequacies, Saudi Arabia's foreign policy has traditionally preferred the West, specifically the US and its Arab neighbours. Hence, Riyadh's two major security resources are its influence, which originates from Saudi Arabia's prominent role within the region, and an informal alliance with Washington.

In this regard, Saudi Arabia's desire to be seen as a leader in the PG through its attempts to unify the other PG states in opposition to Riyadh's two major obstacles to security – Iran and Iraq – was realised by the occurrence of the Iran–Iraq war. Saudi Arabia established the GCC, a *de facto* military alliance, with five other PG states, each of which had either a formal or informal military alliance with the US. Also, Riyadh improved its already very close and cooperative connection with the US since the 1980s, specifically with regards to oil production and marketing. This improvement, which was primarily based on the Saudis dependence and need for more technically modern arms, continued on account of Riyadh's reliance on the US for vital technical assistance. The

US, which relies on Saudi Arabia for oil and the geopolitical aspects of oil, could thus alter the balance of power during 1980s and 1990s by interfering in the region on behalf of the GCC by deploying US forces against Iran and Iraq, respectively. Because of the interdependency between Riyadh and Washington, in contrast to Iran and Iraq, the Saudi Arabian acknowledgment of Western interests in this region resulted in the ascendancy of its regional influence. As Alaolmolki notes, "Saudi Arabia was in many respects the weakest but it was also the most influential of the Gulf Powers."[35]

Since the Saudi–Yemeni War in 1934, Riyadh, unlike Iraq and Iran, has not been confronted with any direct and serious foreign or even domestic conflict, such as foreign invasion, coup or revolution. Despite Saudi Arabia's three independent military and security entities (the Ministry of Defence and Aviation; the National Guard; and the Ministry of the Interior), which provide the kingdom's internal and external security, it has been proven that in case of crisis and war they are incapable of repelling potential attacks.

Riyadh required the help of the US to deter potential external threats posed by Iran and Iraq. With the occurrence of the Islamic revolution in Iran, Riyadh was deeply conscious that its very existence was threatened by the new theocratic and revolutionary regime in Tehran. Besides many different disagreements between Saudi Arabia and Iran, the conflict became particularly concentrated on Al-Saud control of the Holy Cities of Mecca and Medina, and the Hajj celebration. This issue, even in the early 1990s, and the need for a balance of power against Iraq's threat, put a significant limitation on Saudi policy options. To restrain Iran, the Saudis thought the best way was to increase deterrence via strengthening their military forces by acquiring large amounts of the most advanced military equipment from the US, and also providing military assistance to the other small and weak PG monarchies.

After Iraq's invasion of Kuwait, to deter further Iraqi aggression against Saudi Arabian territories with huge oil reserves, which would pose a serious threat to its very existence, the insufficient Saudi military force had no choice but to be supplemented with a large foreign military force. However, the Saudis were well aware that a large US military presence in Saudi Arabia would cause an anti-American backlash both within Saudi Arabia and in the rest of the world, in addition to the possibility that they could appear as a lackey of the US, so they asked other countries as well as the Arab League and the GCC to send military forces to Saudi Arabia too.[36]

Besides the Saudis' confidence of having friends to help them during war and crisis, wars and international sanctions against Iran and Iraq have weakened these two major regional rivals of Riyadh. Saudi Arabia and the rest of the GCC members seem more secure and stable than their powerful neighbours. Also, as previously mentioned, Yemen, which along with Iraq was considered to be a major external threat, now has less intention of threatening Riyadh since the Saudi resolution of border disputes with Sana'a and because it has been involved in its own domestic crisis.

Therefore, Saudi Arabia faces no urgent potential external threats; however, besides non-state threats from within Yemen and Iraq, and Riyadh's appreciation of the potential threat from a nuclear-armed Iran, a threat should not be ignored from one of the GCC members. Many of these have more worries about each other than about Iran or Iraq. Also, a potential threat from the Western powers, especially the US, which could develop from a critical domestic crisis to secure energy resources, should not be disregarded.

As was explained more fully in Chapter 4, the significant vulnerability of Saudi Arabia to energy terrorism, the limited ability of the US to control Saudi Arabia's internal security problems and the American view about the paradox of Washington's desire to become a long-term ally of an undemocratic and politically conservative regime, especially since 9/11, has led to some extreme outlooks concerning Saudi Arabia's future relations with the US, e.g. declaring war on Wahhabism, and invasion of the country and seizure of its oil fields.

Hence, the lack of domestic reforms, except its internal impacts, could result in a serious external threat from Riyadh's Western allies too. The GCC's statesmen and elites see Washington's pressure to carry out political and economic reform as the major external threat facing their country.[37]

Moreover, Saudi Arabia's foreign policy, with its domestic and regional impacts, has not helped the development of security in general. Domestically, it has generated anti-regime and anti-US sentiments with political discontent and radicalism and a high potential of terrorist actions. Regionally, especially by inviting US forces to enter the region and remain present for a long period, it has increased the security concerns of the other two major players in the PG. Since then, one of these, Iraq, has been invaded and occupied, and the other, Iran, is under permanent threat of military invasion by these foreign forces.

Conclusion

After the overthrow of Saddam's regime in 2003, the kingdom's most important security threat no longer seems to be foreign military invasion but rather the threat of Islamic extremism and terrorism. Saudi Arabia, which lacks strong civil-society institutions, suffers a direct internal threat from Islamic extremists, many relating to Al Qaeda and similar extremist groups. With continuing insecurity in Iraq and the presence of foreign troops, the extension of religious militancy will be unavoidable in Saudi Arabia as well as in the whole region – a situation that could become even worse because of Saudi support of Sunni insurgency in Iraq. Only major and real reforms in Saudi Arabia can safeguard the regime from these attacks and anti-government pressures. Major suggestions centre round steps that should be taken to defuse a potential crisis and to prevent violent sectarian confrontation. An inclusive national/inter-sectarian dialogue, encouraging tolerance and diversity, alongside political and religious reforms, and facilitated by the help and involvement of key members of the Sunni clergy, is necessary to fight both hatred and anti-Shiite sentiments.[38]

Therefore, to meet its major internal and external threats, Riyadh's only choices are taking real steps for domestic reforms and making significant attempts to prevent any further war and crisis in the region. Unfortunately, the current crisis in Iraq has made the whole situation, and especially the security concerns of the major PG players, more complicated. However, by cooperating with Iraq's new regime and its neighbours – especially Iran – Saudi Arabia could secure its long-term interests as well as the region's durable security. A long-term and comprehensive political strategy to broker CBM with Tehran is needed, the first step of which for Riyadh could be preventing the US and its allies from making the current crisis in the region worse with further military action against Iran. Also Riyadh needs to provide more harmony and coordination with Iran over its policies in Iraq, to assist Baghdad in overcoming its domestic unrest (as a critical element of regional instability) as soon as possible.

Despite the GCC states', including Saudi Arabia's, concerns regarding the possible decline in their role in further security arrangements in the region, consequent upon improving Iran–US relations it is obvious that their security can be provided only through CBM and by intensified and sustained diplomacy in a peaceful and non-confrontational atmosphere. The current US military presence in the PG only fans the flames of domestic and regional discontent; therefore, only by pursuing a comprehensive and long-term political strategy to broker CBM with neighbours could Riyadh encourage a moderate foreign policy in all PG states, including Iran. A process which could result in assuring the ultra-regional players' interests is acknowledged in this region – an important factor that would result in the foreign forces' withdrawal from the region.

In the next chapter, Iraq's political behaviour and its internal and external security concerns that have broadly affected the regional security will be studied.

NOTES

1 Daniel Byman and Jerrold Green, "The enigma of political stability in the Persian Gulf monarchies". In Barry Rubin (ed.), *Crises in the contemporary Persian Gulf* (London and Portland, OR: Frank Cass, 2002), 78.
2 Nozar Alaolmolki, *The Persian Gulf in the twenty-first century: stability and change* (Maryland, US and London, UK: University Press of America, 1996), 32.
3 Shahram Chubin, *Security in the Persian Gulf 1: Domestic political factors* (England: Gower, 1981), 2.
4 Byman and Green, op. cit., 90.
5 Chubin, op. cit., 1.
6 Mahmood Sariolghalam, "*Shenakht-e Khalij-e Fars dar ghaleb-e mabani-e nazari-e Khavar-e Mian-e shenasi*" [Cognition of the PG according to theoretical basis of acknowledging the Middle East], presented in *the International Conference on the Persian Gulf* (Tehran: Institute for Political and International Studies (IPIS), 1994).
7 Turki Al-Hamad, "Imperfect alliances: will the Gulf monarchies work together?" In Barry Rubin (ed.), op. cit., 30.
8 The US' reflagging operation was the war on tankers initiated by Iraq and resulting in Iran escalating its attacks on shipping serving Arab ports in the PG.
9 Gary Sick, "The coming crisis in the Persian Gulf". In Gary Sick and Lawrence Potter (eds), *The Persian Gulf at the millennium: Essays in politics, economy, security, and religion* (New York: St. Martin's Press, 1997), 12; also Gregory Gause, cited in Turki Al-Hamad, op. cit., 27.

10 Byman and Green, op. cit., 87.
11 English *Al-Jazeera* broadcasting (2007) http://english.aljazeera.net/NR/exeres/884C6F3B-846E-4E7B-A140-31D8828C2A0C.htm (accessed 8 September 2007).
12 Al-Hamad, op. cit., 30–31.
13 Byman and Green, op. cit., 79.
14 Details in Sick, op. cit., 21.
15 Al-Hamad, op. cit., 29; and Byman and Green, op. cit., 83, 85.
16 Gregory Gause, III, "The political economy of national security in the GCC states". In Sick and Potter (eds), op. cit., 66–67.
17 Shafeeq Ghabra, "Kuwait and the dynamics of socio-economic change". In Rubin (ed.), op. cit., 121–122.
18 Ibid., 84.
19 Ibid., 86, 91.
20 John Esposito, "Contemporary Islam: reformation or revolution?", *Arab World* (by permission of Oxford University Press, 2000), http://arabworld.nitle.org/texts.php?module_id=2&reading_id=211&print=1 (5 October 2005; can no longer be accessed).
21 Byman and Green, op. cit., 87.
22 For details see ibid., 89–94.
23 Simon Murden, *Emergent regional powers and international relations in the Gulf: 1988–1991* (Reading: Ithaca Press, 1995), 167–168.
24 Cited in ibid., 167.
25 Gregory Gause, III, "The political economy of national security in the GCC states". In Gary Sick and Lawrence Potter (eds), op. cit., 64, 65.
26 Byman and Green, op. cit., 88.
27 Alasdair Drysdale and Gerald Blake, *The Middle East and North Africa: A political geography* (New York: Oxford Press, 1985), 213–214.
28 Ibid.
29 See EIA, August 2005, http://www.eia.doe.gov/emeu/cabs/saudi.html (accessed 1 December 2005).
30 Murden, op. cit., 154.
31 Gerd Nonneman, "Political reform in the Gulf and Arabian Peninsula", lecture in Sir William Luce Memorial Fund (UK: Durham University, 21 June 2005).
32 Ibid.
33 Monica Malik and Tim Niblock, "Saudi Arabia's economy: the challenge of reform". In Paul Aarts and Gerd Nonneman (eds), *Saudi Arabia in the balance* (London: Hurst and Company, 2005), 103–104.
34 Ibid., 110.
35 Alaolmolki, op. cit., 136–137.
36 Ibid., 144–146.
37 See for instance, Al-Hamad, op. cit., 28.
38 Among many for details see, "The Shiite question in Saudi Arabia", *Middle East Report*, no. 45 (2005, September 19) http://www.crisisgroup.org/home/index.cfm?id=3678&l-1 (11 September 2007; can no longer be accessed).

7

Iraq

Introduction

In order to understand Iraq's domestic and foreign policy, particularly the nature of its response to realities in the PG that have significantly affected regional security, it is necessary to study factors that have shaped Iraq's evolution into the present Iraqi state.

The explanation of Iraq's political behaviour is grounded not only in political history but also in the energetic nature of Iraq's cultural, ethnic and religious affiliations, the people's self-image and beliefs. Iraq's political life has long been influenced by family relationships, tribalism, religion, climatic and geographical constraints, and natural resources such as water and oil, which still continue to have a significant influence over governmental decision-making. Iraq's conception of its security and national interests regarding relations with its immediate neighbours has not been an exception in this respect: specifically, its economic vulnerability is partly explained by its virtually landlocked position, which was determined in the twentieth century by European powers after WWI.

Drawing upon levels of analysis framework in international relations, social analysis and elite theory, the following discussion, which is based on the political sociology of the country, explains the influence of the above factors on the Iraqi government's conceptions of the state's strategic interests. It also studies the most sensitive internal priorities regarding Iraq's foreign relations that would ensure the state's continuity and stability, as well as the effect of Iraq's political system on the security of the region.

Political history

Since the *Uqair* Conference in 1922, which was held to settle border disputes between territories under British occupation, modern Iraq (which was a part of the Ottoman Empire until 1918) has been unhappy with its insufficient border outlet to the PG compared with Kuwait and Saudi Arabia. The new border arrangements, which were designed on purpose in order for Britain to control the ME and to limit Iraq's power in the region, remained a source of instability and anti-British sentiments in Iraq. Moreover, the state structure and imposed borders, which ignored the affiliations and ethnicity of the people who lived in the regions of Baghdad (Arab Sunni dominated), Mosul (Kurdish dominated) and Basra (Arab Shiite dominated), presented successive Iraqi governments with internal conflicts and difficulties in unifying effective political control and institutionalising the legitimacy of a central government.

In 1932, Iraq became formally independent. Following the 1958 military coup by Brigadier Abdul-Karim Qassim against the Hashemite monarchy, known as the 14th of July Revolution, a republic system was announced; however, the Iraqis have been ruled by different military successors since then, ending with Saddam Hussein.

The Iraqi revolutionary ideology, with its anti-monarchical sentiments, posed an intimidating message to the conservative monarchical systems of the PG, particularly Iran and Saudi Arabia. The secular system of the Arab Ba'th Socialist Party of Iraq was a republic based on the interim constitution of the 1968 coup led by Hassan al-Bakr. The government was under one-party rule, and following Saddam's alleged coup attempt of 1979, it was under his absolute personal authority. Saddam was president, prime minister, secretary general of the Ba'th Party Regional Command, chairman of the Revolutionary Command Council (RCC) and commander-in-chief of the armed forces. He was aided by cadres in his party, the military and political elite and by the tribal group Takritis. Islam was the state religion, (97 per cent of the population are Muslim – Shiite 70–75 per cent; Sunni 22–27 per cent), and the political economy of the state was based on socialism.

Sources of political behaviour
Besides the major influence of the ideological and political goals and concerns of the Ba'th party – as the single dominant political organisation from 1968–2003 – and the significant role of Saddam on all governmental decisions, Iraq's domestic circumstances also affected the country's political behaviour. Elements such as Iraq's geographic features and remarkable resources, pluralism, economical vulnerabilities, and geographic and

strategic location on the fringe of the Arab world bordering non-Arab regional powers, Iran and Turkey, all played an important part.

On the international scene, Iraq's perception of its internal dynamics and strategic vulnerabilities has featured a tendency to minimise them. This has always impacted on its foreign relations. On the domestic scene, the most important challenges for the government were the constant attempts at political legitimacy, via forging internal consolidation of a nation-state that had arisen out of Iraq's pluralism into a national identity, and establishing a stable central governing authority. In this respect, besides successive governments' attempts to establish economic and political coordination and integration of the three dominant Iraqi cities – Mosul, Baghdad and Basra – and to increase the links between rural and urban areas, it was concerned mostly with the vulnerability of their domestic affairs to external interference. In sum, opinions such as that of Moss Helms about the definite failure of any policy or treaty of Iraq with any foreign country without addressing these enduring Iraqi concerns are understandable; a requirement for preventing the risk of further disputes and cold or antagonistic relations of Iraq with the outside world.[1]

Political ideology: the Ba'th Party

To understand Iraq's policy in general and particularly in the PG, it is important to consider some basic ideological objectives of the Ba'th party, with the central idea of unifying the Arab states into one great and boundless state. In developing the biggest military force in the Arab world, and introducing a new brand of pan-Arabism, Iraq was looking forward optimistically to its role as a regional power and leader of the Arab world. The high expectation of the Iraqi regime, regardless of the reality of Iraq's potentialities and position, set the regime on a course of wars, boycotts, international isolation and finally the overthrowing of the regime in 2003.

The new pan-Arabism of Iraq was developed under Saddam, with its main message that "due to its heroic and rich history starting with ancient Sumer and Babylon and ending with Saddam, Iraq is the natural leader of the Arabs. As a result, everything that benefits Iraq will eventually benefit all the Arabs."[2] In this regard, as Murden remarks, Saddam's strategy for his regime's very survival was his exacting and effective ideological arguments, even more so than his sustaining a sense of crisis to justify his extreme practices of violence and dictatorship, as well as employing the security apparatus. As he explains, "Saddam (…) represented a parochial and pragmatic strain in Iraqi Ba'thism in which the imperatives of the Iraqi state would become paramount." Therefore, the Iran–Iraq war paved the way for the most practical dictatorship. "Within Iraq, the concentration on power required a direct approach to society's resources. Within the region, the regime sought to project its power (…) [without any regard for the Arabs who were] too passive and timid [from Saddam's point of view]."[3]

By applying various mechanisms (such as pre-Arab/Islamic historical myths and icons, the introduction of some Islamic principles into the Iraqi legal system in opposition to the secularism of Ba'thists, the selective return to tribal values and affinities, etc.), the Ba'th party dominated the political life of Iraq for 35 years and in attempting to face Iraq's challenges, similar to earlier governments, deviated from its ideological principles and adopted a pragmatic posture, even establishing relations with the US. Although the Ba'th were not successful in bringing stability to Iraq, establishing a system that had few institutional checks on executive power ensured an unprecedented continuity for more than three decades. The rise of Saddam to power was based on political cunning, but most of all, on an incomparable brutality. However, two major problems facing every Iraqi government were still unsolved during the time of Ba'th authority; domestically, how to achieve political legitimacy for the population, and regionally, how to secure good relations with neighbouring countries.

However, Murden's perception of Saddam's extraordinary influence on Iraqis' life was proven after his regime was overthrown in 2003. As Murden warned in 1995, regardless of people's hatred and fear, his sudden disappearance could cause "a gap in the identity of every Iraqi, and twenty years of state-building and ideology would almost immediately collapse". Consequently, Saddam was the major axis of the nation-state process and, as Murden affirms, "The new Iraqi nationalism was harnessed to the power of the Iraq state. The era of Saddam was presented as one of the re-emergence of Iraqi and, therefore, of Arab greatness."[4]

Internal threats to the stability of Iraq

Socio-political issues

Saddam was much more worried about an internal revolt as the major security threat to his regime than any external threat or invasion from regional or ultra-regional powers. This was accentuated in a report by the US Defence Department, which was produced after interviewing more than 110 Iraqi senior officials and military officers, freely and forcefully, along with an extensive review of captured documents from Iraq after its occupation in 2003:

> In Saddam's mind, the uprising of 1991 was the closest thing to almost ending his regime. It was much more important to him than the Iran-Iraq War, Desert Storm and all the sanction periods, because, according to his own calculations, he lost control of all but one province, Al Anbar.[5]

The distribution of political power in Iraq never reflected the diversity of its population, and Saddam's political manipulation of religious and ethnic identities using different symbols coloured his regime's political behaviour, to evoke emotional bonds and connections which provided an easier control of dissidents. However, such political tools were also used by opposition groups which put the regime under pressure, as Moss Helms notes: "Even Iraqi authority [was] acutely aware that pluralism [had] acted, at times violently, as a disruptive force in government affairs." As she also mentions, the significance of this issue was illustrated by Saddam's insistence that ethnic or religious connections should not replace one's first loyalty as an Iraqi national; Baghdad placed a significant emphasis on this order during the Iran–Iraq war. It is noteworthy that after Saddam's regime was overthrown, religious and ethnic political manipulation, as Moss Helms also had predicted, is still being used by different groups of the population to frame their opposition to the current political situation in Iraq and to achieve their associations' political goals. However, the regime was aware that its ability to minimise internal conflicts would have a great impact on Baghdad's capacity to achieve its ambitions for leadership in the PG. Therefore, besides the impact of ethnic and sectarian divisions within the country on the Iraqi national identity, one of the regime's main concern was that potentially dissident groups were geographically separated from other parts of Iraqi society; the Sunni Kurds in the northern oil field cities, the Shiite Islamists in the south and the mostly Sunni nationalists in the centre and the capital.[6]

Shiites and Kurds had constantly looked for political influence through political organisations, although the tribal policies of Saddam, with their domination by the Sunni Arab clans, as well as the systematic repression and clearance policies against them, did not leave any chance for Kurds or Shiites to legitimise the regime. Therefore, any political unrest in the Kurdish-dominated regions seeking independence and autonomy could threaten economic activity in the rest of the country, since the northern oil fields production was between 50 and 80 per cent of Iraqi petroleum during situations of both peace and war. In addition, the regime was confronted by Shiite moral ties with Iran and their underground movements with connections to Tehran. Basra in the south was the second major oil field of Iraq and the place where pipelines carried oil to the Mediterranean Sea through Turkey and Syria.[7] (See Figure 7.1.)[8]

FIGURE 7.1
Kurdish- and Shiite-dominated areas in Iraqi oil resources and facilities

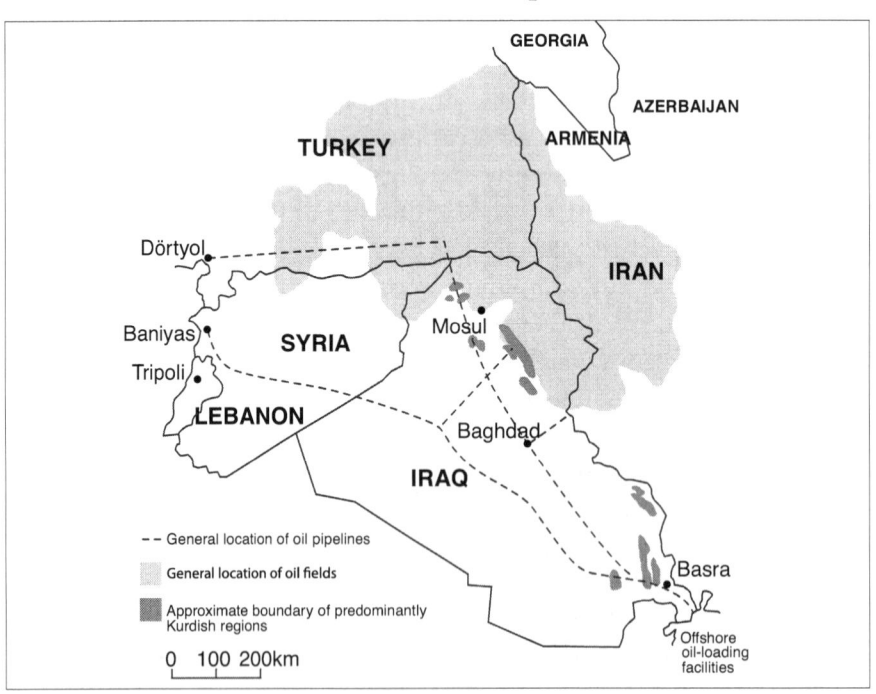

Furthermore, other countries, especially neighbouring states of Iran and Syria, which supported opposition groups in Iraq, were assisting and deepening internal divisions, similar to the way Iraq had worked in other countries.[9]

The post-1973 increase in oil revenues and the Algiers agreement with the Shah of Iran in 1975 that effectively ended Iranian military support for the Kurds in Iraq, enabled Saddam for a while not just to forge a national identity out of Iraq's diverse social structure, but also to control opposition movements. After the Iranian revolution in 1979, Iraq faced an Islamic Republic system which did not hide its wishes for its Islamic ideology to be distributed to other countries. Therefore, such a successful socio-political process did not last long and in September 1980 Saddam embroiled the country in a war against Iran. Opposition activities, which had accelerated even more since the Ba'th party's rule in 1968 and particularly after Saddam's presidency in 1979, entered a new phase with the onset of the Iran–Iraq war. These activities once again provided the opportunity for regional countries, particularly Iran and Syria, to try to control the opposition groups' agendas by developing close ties for their own purposes and also to attempt to check the power of Saddam's regime, a tactic similar to that which Iraq had employed in their countries.[10]

Moreover, in the course of time the problems posed by opposition groups were becoming much more complicated for the Ba'th regime. As Rabil observes, despite foreign support for Iraqi oppositions, the Ba'th government from 1968 to 1980 faced mainly local issues, and so was able to suppress the opposition and solidify its own rule. However, the Iran–Iraq war resulted in the "opposition's shift from a local to a regional phenomenon"; it placed the influential counterbalance of regional countries, especially Iran and Syria, against Saddam's power. The Kuwait crisis (1990–1991) and the March 1991 uprisings by Shiites and Kurds after the regime's defeat in Kuwait, transformed opposition to an "international phenomenon, letting the groups free themselves from the leverage of regional states. The Iraqi National Congress (INC) was born and Kurdish autonomy was secured in the north under US and UN sponsorship." Simultaneously, opposition groups started to solve their old problems of fragmentation caused by rivalries and ideological differences. The 11 September (9/11) attacks on the US not only accelerated this process but also made the opposition groups the focus of US efforts to effect regime change, which had become the Bush administration's high priority for Iraq.[11]

Another major concern of the Ba'th regime was its inability to control religious gatherings, such as Friday praying or Islamic holidays in mosques. At a time when all kinds of political or professional associations were forbidden or tightly controlled, these gathering became potential occasions for revolutionary and anti-governmental turmoil formented by dissident groups. This was particularly crucial since Iraq contains many holy Shiite sites including one of the holiest Shiite mosques, al-Kazimain, and two of the most revered Shiite cities, al-Najaf and Karbala.

Moreover, the tribal policies of Saddam, especially the domination of the Tikrit-centred Sunni Arab clans by the end of the Iran–Iraq war, exacerbated the dissatisfaction of Kurd and Shiite dissidents. While under a fully developed totalitarianism system, the entire society, particularly the Shiites and Kurds, was heavily controlled by military discipline, suspicion and pre-emptive violence, monitored by security apparatus and informers, and excessive and collective punishments were applied for any deviancy or disloyalty.

Indeed, the most critical problem facing Saddam, beside threats from within Ba'thist ranks, was relations with the military. Given the lack of freedom for any political movement in opposition to the government, the military, with a positive record of involvement in all successful coups during the twentieth century, was the most capable and organised group for making crucial political changes. Hence, the basic problem for the regime's security emerged after the Iran–Iraq war when the armed forces had not much to do. This could have been one of Saddam's reasons for getting involved in another war with Kuwait soon after the invasion of Iran. Fearful of revolt, Saddam was deeply distrustful of his own commanders and soldiers. Hence, Iraq's military capability was eroded by irrelevant guidance from the political leadership, the creation of "popular" militias, the prominent placement of Saddam's relatives and sycophants in key leadership positions, and an onerous security apparatus. He made crucial decisions himself, relied on his sons for internal security and military counsel, and imposed security measures that had the effect of hobbling his forces, according to the report by the US Defence Department of March 2006.

Therefore, by the end of the Iran–Iraq war, a huge guard (Republican Guards Corps) was created, which founded more than four divisions and was even placed between all army units and the capital city. The Guards and their special brigades represented the regime's ultimate tool of coercion and no level of violence was forbidden. However, during the collapse of Saddam's regime with no serious resistance, Baram's opinion was confirmed that only as long as the regime looked reasonably stable would this security apparatus remain loyal to Saddam.[12]

Between 1988 and 2002 Saddam was able to handle some serious family confrontations, along with two unconfirmed military coup attempts from 1991–1992. Nevertheless, his decision in 1991 to allow the Iraqi National Assembly to pass a law regulating a multi-party system to portray the regime as reintroducing democracy, also holding a national referendum on 15 October 1995 – the first since 1968 – showed his feeling of domestic vulnerability. His aim also was to demonstrate to the world that he would stay the only leader of the Ba'th party and of Iraq.

It is noteworthy that at the start of the new millennium, despite Iraq's economic sanctions and international isolation, the Ba'th regime was not facing serious internal resistance. The opposition abroad was divided and benefited from very limited help from both the US and Britain. The Shiite opposition at home was not strong enough to place the regime's stability in danger, and the Kurds were reluctant to enter into any other significant anti-regime activities. Accordingly, since Saddam was so convinced that the US was unwilling to accept casualties that he never believed the country would invade Iraq, he also believed that Russia and France would protect their own economic interests by blocking any United Nations Security Council authorisation of an invasion, and thus he gave all his attention to preventing a domestic revolt, specifically a palace *coup d'état*.

Wars and military development
Military development
Goals

Iraq was a highly militarised country with a desire to remain a major regional military power. This was the result of its incredible military spending in the course of the arms race with Iran since the 1960s. Before the Kuwait crisis, between 1972 and 1990, Iraq imported well over US$100 billion worth of conventional arms. During the Iran–Iraq war, Iraq spent between 40 and 75 per cent of its GDP on military expenditures at the cost of worsening the plight of Iraq's people. Iraq was concerned with both external and internal threats: its vulnerability to external forces lay in its borders, its access to the sea, its economy and provision of its water. Meanwhile the Kurdish and Shiite uprisings, Iran's contending for domination, Syria's being ruled by a rival faction of the Ba'th Party, Turkey's cooperation with Allied Forces and, most of all, Israel were all seen as a threat within the region. These internal and external threats, combined with Saddam's ambitions for regional hegemony and desire to become the leading Arab state, were the main contributory factors to instability in the PG.[13]

To achieve its goals of stability, Iraq first needed to provide better living conditions and build a strong army; this was to be achieved by increased oil revenues. In the 1950s the Ba'thist had raised the slogan of "Arab oil belongs to the Arabs" but it was not until 1972 that the first stage of nationalisation began, with the second stage concluding in 1975. Nationalisation changed not only the economic balance in Iraq but also its interest in the PG. The growing economy of Iraq increased the economic and strategic importance of the PG, so this waterway found an important place in Iraq's foreign policy. Iraq's land-locked position, with its only access to free waters a 19-kilometre coastline at the northern end of the PG guarded by Iran and Kuwait, meant that the country faced economic security risks from the increasing power of its neighbours, especially Iran. Two islands of Kuwaiti, Warbah and Bubiyan, that dominate the estuary on which Iraq's new port of Um Qasr is located, were a key strategic location in the PG and if reclaimed would ease Iraq's coastal limitation (see Figure 7.2).

In facing these threats Saddam, as Murden remarks, needed the capability for economic growth, which meant ideological aspirations had to be compromised. To achieve his goals, he would have to embark on an interdependent route through the export of Iraq's oil and move away from the local ideology and desire for independence from the West. This pragmatic outlook was one of the consequences of Iraq's increased capability for development over the period 1975–1980, which attended its status as an Emergent Regional Power. However, despite this more pragmatic attitude, the Iraqi regime (like most of the other ME countries) perceived military development as a short-cut to aspirations and status. Hence, Iraq's growth was oriented towards military applications and the expansion of military capabilities, allowing greater independence and military options to achieve foreign policy goals; this led to the application of aggressive strategies towards its neighbouring countries.[14]

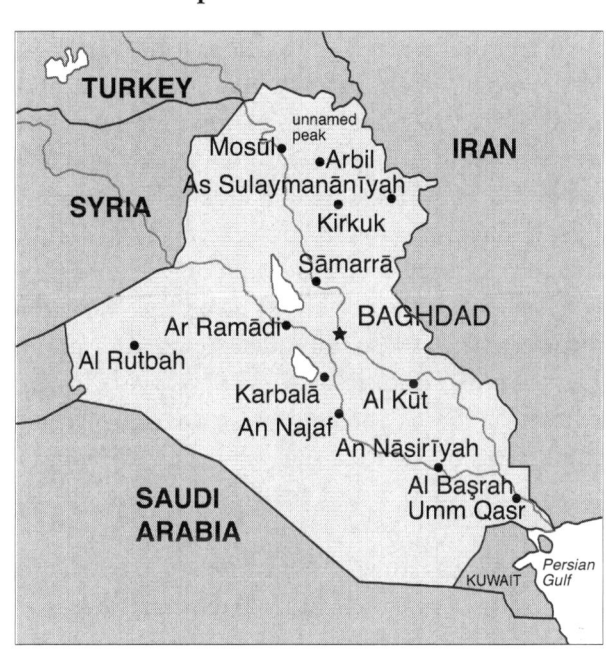

FIGURE 7.2
Iraq's land-locked location

Meanwhile, Saddam's ambition to challenge the balance of power in the PG, which was swinging towards Iran in the 1970s, was given an opportunity for fulfilment by the occurrence of revolution in Iran. On the one hand, the anti-status quo revolution of the Iranian Shiite population was perceived to be a real issue of security on the Arab side of the PG, and also a disturbing element in Iraq's internal balance, with domination of the secular Sunni clique from central Iraq over the majority Arab Shiite (70–75 per cent) and Kurdish (15–20 per cent) population. On the other hand, as Murden notes, the revolution coincided with some developments in Iraq that increased the choice of inter-state war. The post-1973 increase in oil revenues and the Algiers agreement with the Shah had resolved the issue of Kurdish rebels, fostered a period of growth for Iraq and also broadened Iraq's regional and international political horizons, specifically with the West. While the Revolution promised instability for Iran, and Tehran was isolated, Saddam was ready to challenge Iran to prove the dominant power and finally resolve the border dispute and Iraq's remaining economic insecurities.[15]

However, according to Alaolmolki, the Ba'th regime, through its massive militarisation programme, experienced the classic security dilemma. By developing Iraq's military capabilities, Saddam's attempt to increase his own regime's security itself led to a perception of insecurity on the part of the other regional actors. The fear grew in the region that Saddam planned to be the regional dominant power. Iraq's greater military ability and his own ambition for power convinced Saddam as well that Iraq would be the leading Arab state.[16] Saddam's pragmatic attitude was interrupted by his Ba'thist, pan-Arabist ideological justification for the expansion of his regime's security by focusing on war-making to secure the vital interests of Baghdad at the expense of other regional and international players – for instance, Iraq's invasion of Iran and Kuwait, and Saddam's serious consideration of invading Saudi Arabia, with Iraqi oil pipelines across its territory. Saddam's ideological attitude of extreme self-belief became apparent when he claimed that Iraqi military capabilities were a shield for the sovereignty and independence of the entire Arab nation. He believed that the Arab world owed Iraq a great debt; Iraq had saved it from the Persian threat and was now the safeguard against all Arab enemies. However, lack of respect from the other Arab states and the mixture of expectation and disappointment resulted in Saddam's frustration.[17]

Military technology
After the war with Iran, Iraq emerged as the most capable military power in the Arab world. In 1988, Iraq's armed forces claimed to number nearly 1 million, with 480,000 active reservists and 475,000 regular troops containing a core of 140,000 Republican Guard. To improve its weapons capability Iraq used two methods: importation and the build-up of domestic arms. Before the war the importation of sophisticated weapons was mainly from the USSR, and after the war the West also became a viable market through the involvement of the Iraqi diplomatic, intelligence and business sectors. About 80 per cent of Iraq's supply of weapons technology and expertise came from Germany. The main supplier was the high-technology company Messerschmitt-Bolkov Blohm (MBB), which is also a contractor to the Department of Defense of the US, as well as other countries.

Iraq integrated chemical weapons into its military doctrine and such weapons were used during the Iran–Iraq war. They were deployed extensively against Iranian forces and the Iraqi Kurdish population. Evidence suggests that the German government was not only informed of the dealings but also participated in them. It allowed German companies to export dual-use items to Iraq and sponsor counter-terrorist activities, namely Kurdish and Shiite insurgents. The French traded weapons for Iraqi oil and the United Nations (UN) found the equipment of eleven US companies, in various Iraqi military facilities, assisting in Iraq's development of chemical, biological and nuclear programmes. It was the extensive chemical and biological weapons programmes, discovered by the UN after the defection of Saddam's son-in-law, General Hussein Kamel Al-Majid, to Jordan, that were of fundamental importance to the entire ME. The Iraqi programme of nuclear development had been one of the most highly sophisticated programmes in the undeveloped world before the beginning of the Kuwait crisis. However, no report verified the existence or non-existence of further development after the UN inspection.[18] Baghdad's considerable efforts to secure significant military contracts, even after the war with Iran, increased the scale and potential of Iraq's military threat to the whole region.

The war's impact on military strength

While encouraging the illusion that Iraq was consolidating a form of pragmatic Ba'thism, Saddam took advantage of the Iran–Iraq war to build up his military and industrial empire. He continued to insist on the threat posed by an ideological Iranian Revolution and the PG states, believing such threats rallied to Iraq's aid. Iraq was seen as protection against political unrest both on a domestic level, against the Shiite population, and on an international level. Although Iraq's initiation of the war created arms supply problems, when the balance of fighting fell in Iran's favour, restrictions were eased. The Great Powers sought to prevent an Iranian expansion and re-initiated trading with Iraq. Soviet arms shipments that had been curtailed were restarted and military equipment from the Western states was exported to Iraq, both authorised and covertly. Saudi Arabia alone committed at least US$25 billion to Iraq and the relationship developed between Iraq and the US, until the latter became one of Iraq's top trading partners. Without access to such foreign resources from the PG states, the Soviet Union and the West, the Iraqi economy would have collapsed. The stabilising of the economy and access to foreign aid also enabled Iraq to build up its military capabilities.

It is believed that the support Iraq received from the PG states indirectly contributed to Iraq's invasion of Kuwait, because the conditions for the Kuwait crisis were initiated in the aftermath of the Iran–Iraq war. After the Iran–Iraq war, Kuwait and the UAE were becoming concerned that Iraq was a more serious and immediate threat than Iran, given its recently gained war experience. Iraq chose to fund its economic recovery without cutting back on its military expenditure. There was no threat of attack from Iran or any other neighbours and Iraq only engaged in civil conflict with Kurds and Shiites. Iraq poured huge amounts of resources into rebuilding and maintaining its military operational readiness. This choice increased the impact of its debt burden and created the economic crisis that helped lead Iraq to invade Kuwait. Iraq claimed that to prevent its financial recovery Kuwait violated its OPEC production quotas and demanded repayment of the "loans" provided in the war. However, in contrast, Saudi Arabia forgave the debt in recognition of Iraq acting as the bulwark for the PG against Iran for eight years. Saddam took a similar viewpoint. Iraqi Foreign Minister Tariq Aziz accused Kuwait of directly undermining Iraq, and called it an act of war.

Saddam took a somewhat understandably miscalculated step when he invaded Kuwait. He had not thoroughly contemplated the reaction of the West. However, even if he had, considering the context of Iraqi–US relations in the late 1980s and the Western aid provided during the Iran–Iraq war, Saddam may have simply overestimated the administration's commitment to this strategy of political appeasement and aid.[19] Moreover, after 1988, Saddam did not consider the increasing concern the US and Israel felt towards its military build-up since it had received the US green light. By letting him invade Kuwait the US was justified in destroying Iraq's powerful military and was able to resolve its concerns.[20]

After the war with Iran, Iraq may have emerged as the most capable military force in the Arab world, but Iraq's defeat in the "Desert Storm" operation in 1990–1991 reduced its military capabilities and its political capacity. The manpower of the military was severely downsized. Only about half of Iraq's pre-war equipment survived "Desert Storm"; its air force was no less than half of what it was before this operation. Yet still Iraq constituted one of the largest armed forces in the ME and posed a great threat to this region. The inability to prevent a significant decline in operational readiness because of the sanctions did not prevent the military showing signs of improving performance based on realistic standards and expectations. It would require time to rectify lost logistical capabilities and readiness, even after sanctions were lifted. However it was certain the military would be built back up as quickly as possible once Iraq regained access to its oil wealth.[21]

Economic vulnerability
The survival of the regime depended on its economic development. Despite Iraq's great economic potential after the end of the war with Iran, there were several serious issues, various political and economic uncertainties confronting Iraq, that continued to obstruct Saddam's path. The geographical difficulties, including the limited access to water, the 1975 Algiers Accord and Kuwait's refusal to lease its islands, all added to the worsening economic situation after the war with Iran. The mounting debt continued to undermine Iraq's credibility and perceived security in the eyes of potential investors. Unlike Iran, Iraq had a considerable foreign exchange debt and, all the while, it had to try to keep up with the economic power of Iran. Various methods were applied to solve Iraq's economic difficulties and to return to the peaceful economic growth it had enjoyed before the war. Privatisation, for instance, was sought as a means of gap filling the lack of efficiency and provision strengthened rather than weakened the regime's grip on the country. By 1989 control of foreign companies in Iraq was eased but restrictions on the activities of foreign and private sector liaison did remain. This included restrictions of working in the south, as secure access to the sea remained an unresolved question and so a potential security issue. Also, to compensate for the low oil returns and the damage oil refineries suffered during the war, the regime had to turn to exportation of non-oil produce, which involved the south. In addition, the political effect of increased food prices pushed the regime to depend more on imports to meet the substantial needs of its people. Internal expectations were much higher after the war, increasing social and political unrest, which added to the existing economic problems when it became clear that the country's revenue could not live up to such expectations. All these social-economic pressures on the regime and the demands for resources from armed forces, from debt, civil reconstruction and corruption, were heavy. Iraq's

only leverage was the high price of oil. So in the beginning of 1990, when overproduction by the PG states sent OPEC oil prices heading from US$18 to US$14 per barrel, Iraq lost its last viable option to regain economic stability and security, making a bad situation worse. According to the regime, for every US$1 per barrel decrease in oil price, Iraq lost US$1 billion of oil income per year. Oil prices dropped and Iraq's capacity to export was another real shortfall. The regime knew the way to success lay in its oil reserve and so began oil pipeline construction projects – Baghdad's most ambitious scheme. However the increase in oil prices would be frustratingly slow and ultimately insufficient[22] (see Figure 6.4).

For power and stability, and in order to solve its economic problems, the regime opted to invade another country, once again making itself secure by making another country insecure. Iraq's invasion of Kuwait caused a boycott of Iraqi oil, which prevented Iraq using its recently constructed facilities for the duration of the conflict. Many other problems faced Iraq after the Kuwait crisis, including the increase in civil strife, international sanctions like the no-fly zones, the catastrophic breakdown of the healthcare system, with acute shortages of medicines and medical supplies, and a serious increase in the child mortality rate. These all threatened the continued stability of the country. It was estimated by *The New York Times*, April 1991, that it would cost at least US$30 billion to rebuild the physical infrastructure, five years to repair the electrical grid and maybe even years to activate the water purification plants. The sovereignty of the regime was weakening and the important issue now was survival.

The impact of Iraq's internal problems on Persian Gulf security
The Ba'th social foundations were greatly undermined by both "Desert Storm" and the sanctions imposed afterwards. These events had a huge impact on the political, military and economic aspects of Iraq and challenged the security of the PG. The Kuwait crisis caused great human loss, and along with civilian migration to other countries, including neighbouring ones, reduced Iraq's skilled population.

Iraq looked towards its oil reserves to solve its problems and so was determined to loosen the sanctions. However, from a regional perspective, either removing or maintaining the sanctions would cause concerns among neighbouring states. To not remove the sanctions would hurt the people of Iraq and potentially force Baghdad to seek a more radical method of release. It could even lead to the gradual collapse of the government and the disintegration of state institutions. Such disintegration of Iraqi institutions would lead to cross-border activities in the whole region that would be destabilising. Iraq's weakness was also a concern for the GCC and its Western partners as it further shifted the balance of power in Iran's favour. However, to remove the sanctions would allow Iraq to use its oil revenues to rebuild its military power and continue on its previous destructive path, simply creating an alternative threat to the PG. Therefore, from the 1990s until the invasion of Iraq in 2003, the major challenge was how to balance the constraint on Baghdad's rearmament with its need for economic resuscitation.

External threats

As mentioned earlier, the key elements of Iraq's political interaction with the outside world is shaped by the country's geographical location, its pluralistic society, its acknowledged position as the eastern flank of the Arab world, its own perception of its immediate strategic interests and concern for the wider Arab world, and also the dynamics of oil politics in the region. Theses elements, combined with Saddam's keen interest in power and leadership, established the foundations for Iraq's foreign policy during the Ba'thists' rule.

Furthermore, Iraq's foreign policy had been extremely dependent on the character of its leadership and the domestic political situation it faced. In this regard, the high degree of volatility of foreign policy had not allowed Iraq to play a stable, continuous and constructive role in the region's security, but rather in various periods of time it played a disruptive role. On the one hand, the lack of domestic opportunities and even Iraq's lack of interest to become involved in the PG region until the time the Ba'th party came to power under the leadership of Saddam, did not leave any room for Iraq in the regional equation. On the other hand, although the regional situation was ready in 1970s for Iraq's activities and also in the 1980s when Iraq emerged as a regional power, the ambitious political and ideological policies of the Ba'th party could not provide for Iraq a central, basic or continuous role in the region. Political upheavals and the instability of Iraq's foreign policy, from Socialist Arab Revolutionary to Pragmatism and the change of international orientation, meant the country was confronted with instability in its foreign relations with both its neighbours and the Great Powers. Also the radical, aggressive and ambitious policies of the Ba'thist regime, without recognising the real potential of the country, pushed Iraq in several different periods to war and desolation. The policies used to ensure the regime's security not only seemed difficult to comprehend and unpredictable to the outside world but misled the regional and international countries and caused a lack of global confidence in Iraq's notions and goals. In order to understand the unsteadiness of Baghdad's behaviour, Iraq's foreign policy during the period of this study will now be analysed.

The goals of Iraq's foreign policy
The foreign policy goals of Iraq can be summarised in the following stages.

1) Iraq was to be the model state and leader of the Arab world. The Ba'th party was determined to maintain its authority and establish the prerequisites for the regime's stability.
2) Arab unity was to be achieved by the implementation of Ba'thist ideological visions, once stability was reached, and the termination of all foreign control over the Arab world.
3) Non-alignment and the idea of reliance on Europe as an alternative to entanglement with the superpowers, which was achieved by strengthening its relations with Europe, particularly the West, through military, economic, cultural and technical means and expanding financial and oil trade with those it considered friends, e.g. France, Brazil, India, Spain and Africa.
4) Assigning a greater role to the Ba'thist ideology as a catalyst among Arab nations and undeveloped countries, combined with Iraq's financial and agricultural capabilities, meant that Iraq could become a leader of the non-aligned movement. For example Iraq donated millions of dollars to different countries including Syria, Jordan and also the PLO (Palestine Liberation Organization).
5) Maintaining the economic security of the country, which relied heavily upon Iraq's general situation and also its accessibility to the PG. Thus, Iraq was vulnerable to the increasing power of neighbouring PG states, particularly Iran.

6) Iraq's analysis of its security in the PG was based on its self-reliance, which stemmed from its being able to strengthen and modernise its military capabilities through its oil revenues, and to exclude the role of any superpower in the region. In this regard, it rejected all foreign bases in the PG and any regional security pacts, e.g. the proposal from Oman in 1975, and foreign control of the strategic Strait of Hormuz. Iraq depended heavily on the Hormuz Strait for its imports and exports and thus required freedom of navigation. Saddam asked for cooperation from Arab states in the PG, on the basis of Arab national interest, on commercial and economic projects and bilateral agreement among the countries of the region, including Iran.

7) After the 1990s the real security goals of Baghdad were not entirely clear but survival was the first priority of the regime, and avoiding the fragmentation of the state. To secure its objectives, Saddam needed to exploit Iraqi oil revenues, to give the impression of possessing a powerful military strength to deter internal and external threats, and to mend his damaged image as an Arab leader. The possession of weapons of mass destruction (WMDs) was recognised as an element to enhance the regime's security and image. Therefore, Saddam sought to end UN-imposed sanctions to fulfil his goals. For the achievement of his goals after 1990, the new policy agenda focused on taking a greater stand against Israel, where he believed disarmament should start. Even under sanctions and in spite of its efforts to build up its military capabilities, Iraq, according to Hollis, was looking for another war and for a political position because there was no insurance of the permanency of the Ba'th regime.[23]

Barriers to Iraq's foreign policy

Until 1970 Iraq had no interest in and was not capable of influencing the political situation of the PG. One possible reason for this was the West's negative attitude towards Iraq. According to Edmund Ghareeb, "Iraq was portrayed as a xenophobic land plagued by violent political upheavals and instability" with a determined anti-Israel policy. There was also an assumed close relationship with the Soviet Union, which would have coloured such attitudes further. According to Ghareeb, these views overlooked Iraq's real and significant geopolitical position as a PG state with legitimate interests of its own in the area. However, Ghareeb goes on to explain the real barrier to Iraq's ability to become involved in PG affairs, which was mainly a lack of long-standing economic and political interests in this region, a lack of funds for initiating major development projects and providing naval forces to play a role in the PG, and particularly its reliance on Britain with its wide domination and influence over the PG as Iraq's protector. After the 1958 Revolution, Iraq's economic weakness and its ethnic, religious and sectarian problems caused a lack of social cohesion, which impacted on the development of the entire country. Hence, the oil industry and Iraq's claim of sovereignty over Kuwait (for its substantial oil income) had a significant impact on Iraq's interest in the PG affairs. Nevertheless, active Iraqi involvement in PG affairs only emerged after the Ba'th Party rose to power in 1968. Although the problem of sectarianism continued, the regime's main preoccupation was with the task of warding off plots against the party, consolidating its authority, and the conflict with the Kurdish rebels, all of which continued to limit Iraq's foreign policy alternatives. However, at this period of time some factors led to an increased emphasis in Iraqi foreign policy on PG affairs. Theses factors were: Britain's decision to withdraw from East of Suez by 1971 and Iraq's concern about the future power structure in the PG, the decline of Nasserism in the region following his 1967 defeat which left a new opportunity for the Ba'thists' influence, the growing importance of oil, especially after the 1973 energy crisis, and antagonistic relations with Syria which limited Baghdad's influence in the Fertile Crescent area.[24]

Still in the 1970s, Iraq's most serious obstacle was the regional powers of Iran and Saudi Arabia – which will be studied in the following chapter – both of which were supported politically and militarily in this role by the US. Despite the removal of Iran from such a regional position because of the occurrence of the revolution, Saddam was not able to continue taking advantage of this opportunity, which might have allowed Baghdad to become a regional power and improve its political relations with the West and also its Arab neighbours in the PG. The war with Iran in this period caused vast economic damage, social and political unrest and left the country with high foreign debts, which threatened the credibility of the regime.

A series of events occurred in the period 1988–1990, which resulted in Iraq returning to its original ideological position and a gathering hostility to the West. The first alarming events could be seen in the Eastern European countries – from the overthrowing of the Ceausescu regime in Romania (as a pariah state in which change was said to be desirable) in 1989, to the decline of Soviet power in early 1990. The demise of the communists left the US as the only remaining superpower and decreased Iraq's political manoeuvrability to apply its own foreign policy.

Feeling the shift in US attitude, Iraq created propaganda to discredit the US. In an attempt to gain the support of the Arab world, the Ba'th regime focused on the Anglo-American policy of supporting Israel and the control of Arab developments; this was understandable to the majority of Arabs. Baghdad's debates embraced the sensitive issues of sovereignty and technology transfer, and the West's denial of military technology to the Arabs. In the eyes of the Iraqi regime the ultimate suspicion was that the West was preparing the ground for an Israeli attack on the military infrastructure of Iraq. However, the response of the Arab world to the Ba'th regime was not what Saddam had hoped for and Western powers appeared to have a common concern about Iraq's core military interests as they noticed a build-up in Iraq's armament, including its interest in the development of WMDs. Despite some events that deepened the cycle of mutual Iraqi–Western recrimination, political blocks to Iraqi growth required pragmatism.

Even after Saddam's subsequent rejection of international pleas for clemency for Farzad Bazoft, a reporter from the British newspaper *The Observer*, who was sentenced to death for espionage and duly executed on 15 March 1990, he attempted to keep a pragmatic stance and ruled out any severe policy action against the West, particularly Britain and the US. Since Iraq was an important market, from the West's point of view the diplomatic rupture was likely to be controllable too. However after the Anglo-American intelligence "sting" at Heathrow airport, in March 1990, which exposed illegal Iraqi procurement of switches which could be used in nuclear weapons, and later the seizure of components for Iraq's so-called Supergun at Teesport by UK Customs, huge amounts of negative worldwide publicity for Iraq were generated that seemed to demonise the Iraqi regime. This situation was alarming for Iraq, whose major supply networks were blown open. Then, while talk of sanctions persisted in the US Congress, ministers from the West were scrutinising the exportation of dual-use technology. Despite growing pressure on

Iraq, a major policy crackdown on Baghdad by the West, on the basis of political criteria, did not occur. Iraq was not prevented from importing specialised equipment, and the exportation of military-related equipment was not stopped until the invasion of Kuwait in 1990. It was these events, which embedded frustration and anger in Iraq, combined with Iraq's failure to make significant economic progress after the end of the Iran–Iraq war, that in the early 1990s effected a reorientation of the regime, to take a more ideological approach.[25] However, as mentioned earlier, in the aftermath of the 1991 Kuwait crisis the main difficulties facing Iraq were political and international isolation, and economic sanctions. This situation left both its neighbours in the PG and the Western Community with the question of how best to deal with Iraq: containment or change.

Iran

Iran was always a serious impediment to Iraq's ambitions in its regional foreign policy, especially in the PG. Suspicion and hostility characterised Iran–Iraq relations throughout the period 1968–1975. Even after the Iran–Iraq war, the two countries never reached a full peace settlement. However, the West and the GCC were always concerned about the potential for a strategic rapprochement between Iran and Iraq. The reasons for such continuous conflict were not just ideological but contained historical, territorial and political factors too. Chubin and Zabih emphasise that "domestic politics and inter-Arab politics have been an important constraint, hindering and at times precluding the possibility of Iraqi compromise with Iran". As they explain, "The salient issues between [the] two states [were]: the Shatt al-Arab, the Kurdish question, and the shaping of Gulf politics." They go on to argue that the key tendencies of Iran–Iraq relations were to allow differences in one area to spill over into other areas in their relationship, and for Iran to take a strict approach with Iraq.[26]

At different times each country would wait for an opportunity when the balance of power in political and military terms was in their favour to solve their border issues by ignoring previous agreements. The interest in contrasts between Iran–Iraq, particularly the Arvand Roud (Shatt al-Arab), was augmented after the withdrawal of the British. The questions now were who would achieve hegemony in the PG, the political evolution or revolution of the Sheikhdoms and the roles of each state in PG politics spreading rivalry into all areas of Iran–Iraq relations. Iran sought regional security and unimpeded passage of maritime traffic. To achieve this, Iran looked for cooperation with and between the PG states to prevent a takeover bid from a non-regional power and as a barrier against disruptive local or domestic forces. On the other hand, Iraq encouraged and sponsored revolutionary movements, including the Bahrain Liberation Front, the Popular Front for the Liberation of the Occupied Gulf and dissident Kurds in Iran – a new instrument of pressure. Iraq also took advantage of the Iranian claim to Bahrain and Iran's opposition to the Union of Arab Emirates to promote itself as the Arab protector and also by appealing to all the Arab states in the name of the Gulf's "Arabism" to isolate Iran in PG politics. However, both Iran and Iraq's rival attempts to attract the other PG states and ignore each other's security concerns and role in the regional security arrangement were rejected. For instance, Kuwait and Saudi Arabia rejected both Iran's proposal for establishing a formal collective defence system and Iraq's July 1970 Al-Bakr proposal, because neither state seemed to consider the smaller countries' desires not to become entwined in the Iran–Iraq dispute.[27]

The 1975 Agreement between the two sides was, however, of such importance in the PG that both Iran and Iraq promised to work for better relations among the littoral states. This Iranian–Iraqi rapprochement, combined with the resolving of the Saudi Arabia–Iraqi border disputes, diminished tensions in the PG and established a better environment for communication and cooperation between PG states, while Iraq undertook a friendlier, if still slightly cautious, policy towards Iran. However security in the PG remained a matter of disagreement among the coastal states.

Saddam declared in 1976 that "Iranian–Iraqi rapprochement permitted discussions for establishing a collective Gulf security agreement".[28] However, the spirit of the accord never materialised and after the overthrow of the Shah, the revolutionary regime did not disclaim Iranian hegemony. Nonetheless, Iraq emerged as the major power in the PG and concluded that the best opportunity for Iraqi hegemony in this region, and the solution to the problem of the Arvand Roud, was to start the war in 1980.

Despite the very similar positions of the two states regarding the security model in the PG (e.g. their self-reliant nature and exclusion of the role of any superpower in the region), the great ideological differences, as well as the orientation of the two regimes in international politics, were always part of the quarrelsome Iran–Iraq relations. Until 1979, the nationalist and socialist regime of Iraq faced a conservative monarchy that sought to retain the throne and preserve a key role in the region, particularly in the PG. After 1979, Iraq faced an Islamic Republic system, which did not hide its wishes for its Islamic ideology to be distributed to other countries. The Arab states of the PG, including Iraq, were concerned about the impact of the revolution, particularly in Shiite-populated countries, and also about the possibility of a similar fate for their regimes.

Expecting hostilities from each other, Iran and Iraq searched for and exploited opportunities to act against the other. Conflict was usually fuelled by the support of opposition groups on both sides, which could act as a suitable and effectual leverage for further hostile actions or even for improving mutual relations of the two countries. The Kurdish and Shiite populations were always the victims of the tactical manoeuvres of these two countries, through both support and pressure. Therefore, the opposition groups all had significant variable roles in the relations between Iran and Iraq, and consequently had both an impact on and were affected by bilateral and regional circumstances. The use of such groups and the inconsistencies of the two countries made it hard to achieve any lasting rapprochement.

Saudi Arabia (the GCC)
Except for a short period in the PG's history, Iraq was never successful in gaining the confidence of other Arab states. Even in the most important period of such relations, during 1975–1990, the Arab states did not trust Iraq or have any long-standing strategic relationship with it. They saw Iraq as a means to fulfilling their need and the only option in facing the threat of Iran. This is a major reason why Iran has always had a major role in determining the kind of relationship between Iraq and the GCC. Even as an Arab country, Iraq continued to feel isolated because the other states would not rely on it. They treated Saddam's "revolutionary" regime, his claim to Kuwait, Iraq's international orientation towards the USSR, its military policy and attempts for regional hegemony with caution and scepticism, so no stable relations could be established.[29] Chronologically reviewing Iraq's foreign policy and the GCC's reactions to it supports this contention.

From 1968–1975 the Ba'th regime could not expand its political or ideological relations with other PG states and mobilise them against Iran's role as *gendarme* of the region. Such failure, which, according to Chubin and Zabih, was due mainly to Baghdad's own inept diplomacy and only partly due to Iranian statecraft, encouraged Iraq to seek an ideological confrontation, not just against Tehran but against all the conservative Arab regimes too. Iraq's relations with its Arab neighbours were significantly influenced by the return of the Ba'th to power. The Ba'thists advocated a radical ideology committed to replacing the prevailing configuration of power and to effecting radical social and economic change, which did not appeal to Iraq's more conservative neighbours.[30]

In May 1969, Saudi Arabia rejected the Iraqi offer of a military agreement. Later, when Iraq failed to gain Saudi support for its response to Iran's abrogation of the 1969 Arvand Roud, it began to look beyond the PG for support. An isolated Iraq offered and accepted an agreement with the Soviet Union. Consequently, Saudi Arabia, with US support, started a plan for the modernisation of its armed forces. These events widened the gap in relations between Iraq and the other Arab states, including Saudi Arabia. Only in 1974–1975 could Iraqi–Saudi relations improve because of concern for Iran's role in Oman and the policy of rapprochement and *détente* with Iran and other PG countries. In 1979–1980, as a result of revolution in Iran, the opposition of the Camp David pact and the appearance of the desire to keep the big powers out of the PG, Iraqi–Saudi relations moved closer.

Both Riyadh and Baghdad were interested in releasing each other from reliance on the superpowers. Fortunately, the Iranian revolution forced Riyadh to distance itself from the US and oppose the peace treaty of Camp David. With Egypt and Iran tied up, Iraq was given the opportunity to fill the gap as the leading power in the region. However, Iraq did not want to be seen leaving the rapprochement or interfering with the internal affairs of other countries, as this would damage Iraq's recently improved relations with Saudi Arabia and isolate it again. Nevertheless, under the pretext that the Iranian revolution was a threat to the whole region Iraq started a war as the Arab Protector and so was able to maintain good relations, achieve regional hegemony and sort out the issue of Arvand Roud in one go.

In 1990, Iraq once again faced an economic problem and sought a violent solution. Iraq faced demands for the repayment of Iran–Iraq war loans without the ability to pay, so it changed its rhetoric, starting an anti-Western campaign, focusing on security and the Arab community. However, Iraqi diplomacy was a screen for many grievances towards other Arab countries. Saddam believed overproduction of oil was benefiting the West and costing Iraq revenues and development potential. After the Baghdad conference of 28 May 1990, the Iraqi regime took a more threatening course, which was a diverging point for Arabs. Saddam sought an ideological rationale for dominating the region, which included war with Israel and the liberation of the Palestinian people. However, the conference also exposed the reality that, at least among the Arab states, Iraq was not trusted. Over-estimating Arab public support and acting without the assistance of regional governments, Saddam began another risky war.

After 1990, Iraq faced yet more barriers to its foreign policy from the global condemnation of its invasion of Kuwait and from the application of wider international sanctions. Despite some differences between the GCC members on how to deal with Iraq, which appeared as early as 1993, they were united in opposing Iraq and in their common mistrust of the Ba'thist regime. Kuwait and Saudi Arabia in particular rejected the UAE's initiative for Arab reconciliation with Iraq and called for the UN Security Council to ensure complete destruction of all Iraq's WMDs. The UK and the US also stressed the need to overthrow Saddam by continuing sanctions and isolating Iraq, but it was not yet time for them to remove him from power.

Contributory elements to Iraq's foreign policy
Previous chapter in this book have shown that, in achieving its foreign policy goals, Iraq had benefited from various elements, such as ideology, diplomacy, military and propaganda methods, as well as aiding un-developed countries, establishing economic partnerships and internal developments. In addition to Iraq's methods of pursuing its foreign policy objectives, the contributory elements to Baghdad's foreign policy can be classified in the following ways.

1) Different kinds of international political systems, as well as the US security strategies, in the ME/PG provided constraints upon or opportunities for Iraq to play a role in the region and achieve its foreign policy goals. In the 1970s, US security policy was based on

the twin-pillar system emphasising the emerging regional powers. Iraq was not part of this system; however, the removal of the Great Powers from the region provided it with the opportunity to consider the future power structure of the PG. In the 1980s, the international political concerns regarding the impact of the Iranian Revolution on the ME and the Western fear of disruption to the oil supply provided an opportunity for Saddam to pursue its own goals by invading Iran. However, in the 1990s the bipolar system and the Cold War ended and the US attempted to consolidate its interests globally. The new international political system focused on cooperation rather than confrontation. Hence, this presented an obstacle to Iraq's ambitions, particularly its military build-up, which had been noticed by the West.

2) Iraq's oil revenues furthered good relations with the rest of the PG states and the West. The latter enabled Iraq to diversify its purchases of arms, goods and technology, lessening its dependence on the USSR in this regard.

3) Economic development and reducing Kurdish issues through the attempt of the 1970 Manifesto and finally through the 1975 Algeria Accord with Iran gave Iraq a freer hand in consolidating its role in the PG.

4) The Iran Revolution and Camp David peace agreement improved Iraq's position and enabled it to fill the power gap left by the decline of Iran, Egypt and Saudi Arabia. Also, no longer isolated, Iraq would be able to establish its own influence in the PG.

5) The Ba'th regime never faced serious internal resistance. The geographical features of Iraq and the differing ideologies and aims of opposition groups combined with Saddam's tribal policy and totalitarian political system — consisting of strong information and security apparatus – meant that the regime could control the opposition's activities. Opposition groups were used by Iraq's neighbouring states, including Syria and Iran, to undermine Saddam's power for their own purposes; however, the opposition was weak, divided and benefited from only limited help from the US and Britain. According to Hollis, even two years after "Desert Storm" Saddam Hussein was still very much in power. In Iraq, those who would destroy Saddam were afraid of both him and the consequences of his demise. They believed that the coalition

members, both Arab and Western, who built up Saddam and armed him in the first place should be responsible for his removal. In reply, those on the outside claimed that until the Iraqi army moved against the regime they could not effect this.[31]

6) The lack of US commitment to overthrow Saddam stemmed mainly from the desire that the fall of the regime was to occur under US control. Although the region's stability was dependent on the development of Iraq, whose territorial integrity and social cohesion after 1991 were weakening, the US ignored these dilemmas to make changes in its own favour. Also, according to Adel Abdul Mahdi, an Iraqi thinker and director of Centre of Islamic Studies and Documents in Paris, it was Iraqi society and not its ruler that was the concern of the US. Washington did not want to disturb the regional balance and cause social upheaval against US interests. So, after the liberation of Kuwait, President George H. W. Bush did not seek military action against Iraq; instead, he only continued the policy of containment. This gave the US the use of Iraq as the Eastern Flank against some countries, including Iran, but left the country unable to decide its own fate, as Abdul Mahdi observes.[32] In addition, the 1991 attack provided the impetus for unity in adversity for Iraq and the multinational coalition did not want to take the steps, or deal with the consequences, of fighting for a replacement of the Iraqi regime.[33] Also, the coalition powers were divided over how to treat Iraq after Kuwait was released, with France in the lead. This lack of cohesion also influenced the regional players and opposition groups, the latter being disorganised and insufficiently equipped to struggle against the regime. They even involved themselves in military and political disputes with each other. This weakness, particularly in Iraq, provided Israel, whose interests were similar to the US, with the best regional security situation it had ever known. All this prevented the US from entering Iraq and so allowed Saddam to continue his regime.[34]

7) After 1991 a weak Iraqi regime suffering UN sanctions and coalition control was preferred by its neighbours to a federation of Kurds or the disintegration of the country. Iraq's neighbours were also tired of waiting for a change of government in Baghdad. The regional countries, specifically Iran, Syria and Turkey, supported the territorial integrity and unity of Iraq and feared that the no-fly-zones were

eroding the cohesion of the country. Also, there was no consensus concerning a powerful opposition group that would replace the Ba'th regime. In addition, the West preferred Saddam to remain so that the UN could continue to justify its search for WMDs in the name of regional security. Meanwhile, Western countries continued to keep communication with opposition groups open.

8) Attempts to establish a link between economic cooperation and political interests through ties with non-aligned countries, Russia and the EU. For instance, in an effort to remove the sanctions on it, Iraq sought to take advantage of the division between the UN's real power brokers using a two-tiered strategy: Steadfastness and Diplomatic Activity. In the latter part of this strategy Iraq's aim was to influence France, Russia and China into lifting the sanctions. In the mid-1990s, these three permanent members of the Security Council resisted any military action against Iraq and favoured the removal of sanctions, even when it meant abandoning the UN inspection system.

9) Some countries were doubtful whether the continuation of the sanctions would help to overthrow Saddam and were concerned they might worsen the situation by increasing the human cost and the sympathy Iraq received from the outside world. Iraq was able to exploit these sympathies and divisions.

10) The American hard-line policy against Iran paved the way for some Iranian attempts for closer relations with Iraq – although major differences such as the Mujahedin's military activity or the problem of how to deal with prisoners of war (POW) meant that such relations were never fully established. Nonetheless, Iran was another country calling for the lifting of sanctions.

Conclusion

Security, the most important issue in the PG region, was significantly influenced by the Ba'thist regime of Iraq in its interaction with other littoral states. In studying Iraqi political behaviour, the importance of its geopolitical elements has been acknowledged; in particular their impact on Iraq's definition of security, national interests and strategic concerns. In addition, Saddam's aggressive foreign policy, his high expectations,

Iraq's lack of regional credibility and isolation, the consequence of war and failure of state development, as well as the interests of external powers in contrast with Iraq's behaviour combined can be seen as the divergent elements that prevented a collective security arrangement, which meant the PG continually encountered crisis and instability.

Iraq's periodically changing political ideology, from radical to pragmatic, was seen as a short-term tactical advantage increasing Iraq's political manoeuvrability and meant relationships with both regional and international powers were constantly changing, leaving Iraq with an unstable policy.

Despite the very similar positions of Iraq and Iran as the two major regional powers, regarding the security model in the PG, the great ideological differences as well as the orientation of the two regimes in international politics were always parts of the quarrelsome Iran–Iraq relations. In addition, other regional and ultra-regional players viewed closer ties between Tehran and Baghdad as a threat to their interests in this region and towards the weaker PG states of the GCC; consequently, these states encouraged competition between Iraq and Iran.

Also, except for a short period, Iraq was never accepted by the other Arab states in the PG region as a reliable member. The GCC never trusted Iraq or had any long-standing strategic relationship with it and they treated the Ba'th regime with caution and scepticism. They mainly saw Iraq as a means to fulfilling their need and the only option in facing the threat of Iran.

Iraq was serving the interests of external powers, whose main claim was regional stability and security. However, as soon as Iraq attempted to pursue its own security and economic interests, which conflicted with the major powers', they embarked on a war against Baghdad, despite it formerly having been an ally.

The desire of both regional and non-regional actors to exclude Iraq from any collective regional security arrangements, and Saddam's overconfident and unrealistic opinion of Iraq's military potential, which encouraged him to underestimate his enemies, highlighted the impossibility of shaping stable regional security arrangements.

After the fall of the Ba'th regime, further attempts to establish regional security will be even harder because the geopolitical variables have been increasingly highlighted, particularly the role of ethnic and religious groups. With the establishment of internal stability, the other geopolitical concerns of Baghdad, specifically its land-locked location, will need to be considered very seriously.

The Ba'thist regime never managed to solve the two major dilemmas of political legitimacy and good relations with its neighbours. Any future party able to solve these problems would have to establish a stable and realistic policy that does not threaten or confuse littoral states. It will only be through collective regional cooperation and respect for Iraq's geopolitical concerns that Iraq can be prevented from further violent policies and the region protected from another crisis from an Iraqi regime with any political ideology.

At the second regional security summit of the International Institute for Strategic Studies (IISS) in Bahrain, December 2005, it was emphasised that, although an orderly exchange of views in public and private is taking place, the region is a long way from establishing a solid foundation that could build confidence, settle disputes and deter conflict. However, those who might take part in any future regional security arrangements may be able to encourage a better framework for conflict resolution and diplomatic cooperation. In this summit it was also stated that development must be made to improve security allowances, particularly as the "balance of power, good governance, wise internal security arrangements, political and economic reform, improving rights for minorities, intense diplomatic exchanges, well-managed links with external powers, are all vital sinews in the regional security body politic, and even so, in both these areas, crises with military dimensions can emerge".[35]

One significant result of studying Iraqi political behaviour is the recognition of the important impact of the international system and the necessity of achieving a fair political system in international relations for assuring security and stability in any region in the world, including the PG. The outcome of Iraq's two invasions of its neighbours shows how similar wars, fought in two different periods, could have such widely contrasting outcomes. The first made Iraq the greatest military state in the region, whereas the second resulted in economic, military and political ruin. These opposing results also had an effect on the regional security for the whole of the PG. The international communities' behaviour exposed a double-standard attitude; claiming that they were acting to benefit the security of the region, when within a decade, by 1997, they had left Iraq as a greater threat to the region than in any previous time.

Iraq was a country whose own policies did not change dramatically and yet they were faced with a complete turnabout of attitudes from the international countries: from offering aid to open hostility. There appears no basis for such a shift in attitude, just the unfortunate fact that one single and unique standard does not apply to every country because there is not a fair international system.

To complete the discussion about insecurity components in the PG, in particular to sketch the future shape of collective security arrangements in the region, Iran's political behaviour and its internal and external security concerns and threats will be studied in the next chapter.

NOTES

1. Christine Moss Helms, *Iraq: Eastern flank of the Arab world* (Washington D. C.: The Brookings Institution Press, 1984), 202.
2. Amatzia Baram, "Saddam's state, Iraq's politics and foreign policy". In Barry Rubin (ed.), *Crises in the contemporary Persian Gulf* (London and Portland: Frank Cass Publisher, 2002), 201.
3. Simon Murden, *Emergent regional powers and international relations in the Gulf: 1988–1991* (Reading: Ithaca Press, 1995), 106, 108.
4. Murden, op. cit., 107.
5. *The New York Times*, http://www.sundaytimes.co.za/zones/sundaytimesNEW/basket7st/basket7st1142226590.aspx (accessed 25 June 2006).
6. Moss Helms, op. cit., 24.
7. Ibid., 25.
8. Figure is cited in ibid., 26.
9. Ibid., 27.
10. Ibid.; also Robert Rabil (2002) "Iraqi opposition: from conflict to unity", *Middle East Review of International Affairs (MERIA) Journal*, vol. 6, no. 2. Cited from *Asia at Times*, http://atimes.com/atimes/Middle_East/EA18Ak04.html (accessed 20 July 2006).
11. Rabil, op. cit.
12. Baram, op. cit., 205.
13. See, Anthony Cordesman and Ahmed Hashim, *Iraq, sanctions and beyond* (Colorado and Oxford: Westview Press, 1997), 218; also Nozar Alaolmolki, *The Persian Gulf in the twenty-first century, stability and change* (Maryland, US and London, UK: University Press of America, 1996), 98–99.
14. Murden, op. cit., 8–10.
15. Ibid., 24–25; also Rosemary Hollis, *Gulf security: No consensus* (London: Royal United Services Institute for Defence Studies, 1993), 18.
16. Alaolmolki, op. cit., 99.
17. Murden, op. cit., 124–126.

18 See, Alaolmolki, op. cit., 99, 102; also Murden, op. cit., 114.
19 Alaolmolki, op. cit., 106.
20 Ezzatollah Ezzati, *Tahlili bar Geopolitic-e Iran va Eragh* [An Analysis on Geopolitics of Iran and Iraq] (Tehran: Foreign Ministry Press Centre, Institute for Political and International Studies (IPIS), 1381 Solar Calendar [2002]), 196–197, 201.
21 Murden, op. cit., 108; also Phebe Marr, "Iraq faces the twenty-first century: potential challenges for Gulf states". In David Long and Christian Koch (eds), *Gulf security in the twenty-first century* (Abu Dhabi, UAE: The Emirates Center for Strategic Studies and Research, 1997), 35–36.
22 Murden, op. cit., 116–123.
23 Hollis, op. cit., 18, 24.
24 For details see, e.g. Edmund Ghareeb, "Iraq: emergent Gulf power". In Husein Amirsadeghi (ed.), *The security of the Persian Gulf* (London: Croom Helm London, 1981), 197–204.
25 Details in Murden, op. cit., 129–137.
26 Shahram Chubin and Sepehr Zabih, *The foreign relations of Iran: A developing state in a zone of great-power conflict* (Berkeley, Los Angeles, London: University of California Press, 1974), 192, 171.
27 Details in ibid., 184–192.
28 Ghareeb, op. cit., 213.
29 Chubin and Zabih, op. cit., 184–185, 189; also Ghareeb, op. cit., 205.
30 Details in Chubin and Zabih, op. cit., 192; also Ghareeb, op. cit., 205–206.
31 Hollis, op. cit., 27.
32 Adel Abdul Mahdi (winter 1997) "*Miz-e gerd: Aragh, sahn-e bazi-e ghodratha*" [Roundtable: Iraq, theatre of the Great Power's game], *Faslnameh Motaleaat-e Khavar-e* Mianh [Middle East Studies Quarterly] vol. 4, no. 4, 18–30.
33 Hollis, op. cit., 18–19.
34 Abdul Mahdi, op. cit., 18–30.
35 *The Gulf Dialogue*, the bulletin of the Second Regional Security Summit of the International Institute for Strategic Studies (IISS) in Bahrain, December 2005 (Britain: Chandlers, East Sussex), 114–115.

8

Iran's security threats and challenges

Political system

Introduction

The purpose of this chapter is to highlight the convergence of Iran's policy towards PG security from 1962 to 1997. Although Iran's political regime pre-revolution and post-revolution differed, there remained fixed factors that concerned Iran as a country. These included the geopolitics of Iran, the countries' geostrategic situation and the significance of stability and security of the PG as a subsystem of international system for the country's process of development. Its foreign policy towards the PG shows Iran's continuing aim and need to establish stability and security within the region and cooperate with its neighbours – particularly emphasising the necessity that PG security should be provided by the regional countries, implying a desire to see the removal of all foreign presence in the region.

In regard to Iranian pronouncements on the issue of PG security, which expose Iran's deep-rooted sense of its own strategic importance, there were two key concerns for Iran: the first was its economic dependence on the Hormuz Strait as its only means of exporting oil. Iranians sought to ensure free passage of oil while preventing others gaining control of the PG. The second is that Iran sees itself as playing a central role in PG security.

The main reason for choosing 1962 as the starting year of this study is the significant effect the successes and failures in Iran's foreign policy towards the PG have had on the stability and security of the region. A further, and important, reason is that at that time the ME was acquiring a new role in international relations, especially due to the great decrease of intensity of the bipolar system manifested in the Cold War, and that Iran was becoming a major power in the ME. According to the international system there was more possibility for smaller countries to manoeuvre. The evolution of Iran's role for the US and the USSR, combined with its intentions and the opportunity to play a greater role on a regional and intention lever, meant that it placed greater attention on the PG, in line with its own interests in security.[1] Covering this period up until 1997, this book will study Iran's failures and successes in its policy towards the PG in three different phases: 1962–1979 under the Muhammad Reza Shah's rule and within the Cold War as a successful period; and the periods of 1979–1989 and 1989–1997 in post-revolution Iran within the bipolar and unipolar system of international system. While the first phase post-revolution was a failure in the second phase Iran could regain much of its regional and international legitimacy, which included the adoption of a pragmatic and active policy in the PG, to manage affairs in this region.

Drawing upon the level of analysis framework in international relations, the task of this chapter is threefold: first, to study the power structure and decision-making process with relation to security in pre- and post-revolutionary Iran. Second, to examine the internal threats during the study period of 1962–1997 including socio-political issues and also economic and military development. Third, to understand Iran's trends and options in its foreign relations concerning security of the PG with key countries including the Great Powers and its PG neighbours by applying the observations of previous chapters regarding Iran's political history and its external threats.

Interaction of domestic and foreign policy

Iranians are known as proud nationalists, pursuing independence, equality and a more important role and prestige in international level. There is a possibility that Iran intends to return to its pre-revolution stage of regional hegemony in the PG, it perceiving itself as a strong Middle Eastern state that has the privilege of supervising affairs in the PG. Therefore, "religion, nationalism, ethnicity, economics, and geopolitics all are important in explaining Iran's goals and tactics in its relationship with the outside world, as are the agendas of key security institutions and the ambitions of their leaders (...) [Hence], politics and even basic structure of government are in flux."[2] In this regard, there have been rigid links between domestic, foreign and security policies in all aspects of Iran's political history. As Ramazani in 1975 observed, "there is little doubt that the twin goals of autonomy abroad and authority at home are the most salient features of interaction between foreign policy and domestic politics in Iran (...) [In other words] every major foreign policy objective and decision of Iran has its domestic counterpart."[3] Also, as Chubin and Zabih remarked in 1974,

> Because the security of the Shah's regime and the state as a whole were equated, foreign policy was expected to strengthen the internal and external requirements for stability and survival of the regime. This meant a concerted search for external sources of military support from those powers which accepted this equation of regime security and were able and willing to support it.[4]

Iran's post-revolutionary major policies also included "a complex calculus of Iran's overall vulnerability, its need to ensure the regime stays in power, and its commitment to revolutionary ideals. Iran's leaders weigh all these factors when making their decisions."[5] Hence, notions, perceptions, attitudes and the individual characteristics of all policy-makers are influential in Iran's foreign policy as much as in other developing countries, which, unlike developed countries with different foreign policy-making institutions, are dependent on direct decisions of the states' leaders. Though some Iranian policies seem difficult to comprehend and unpredictable to the outside world, this book gives consideration to the different systemic sources of input into Tehran's foreign policy decision-making. It studies internal elements as well as the global and regional variables and their interaction, and treats them as contributors to Iranian foreign policy.

The theoretical basis is established by acknowledging the policies of a small power, and also the link between national and international systems. In other words, a state's foreign policy, within a system of international politics, can be analysed by comparative foreign policy, and its public policy formation and political structure can be analysed with particular attention to the link between domestic and foreign policy decision-making. In this regard, James Rosenau's theory is concerned with two factors: the political link between national and international structures, and the penetration of domestic policies of political systems that are affected by external affairs.[6] Also, if we focus on the policies of a small power and the evolution of Iran's foreign policy there is a question about how to survive during the Cold War when situated next to a superpower renowned for its aggressive behaviour and expansionist attitude, in an area with entrenched power struggles.[7] Under such circumstances, Iran's long-term security depends largely on the persistence of those external and internal political factors that can contribute to successful Iranian diplomacy.

Power structure
Imperial Iran
For a clearer understanding of Iran's policy, the impact of the type of decision-making system and leadership factor on the policy process is essential. The major theme of this part of the study deals with domestic sources of Iran's foreign policy, which explains the impact of domestic elements' priority over international variables on foreign policy, as well as domestic uses of foreign policy.

The decision-making system of the pre-revolution era was a hierarchical structure: the Shah was at its head, with his decisions and orders being imposed from above. As Chubin and Zabih note,

> It is recognized that the Shah is the sole and ultimate source of decisions affecting foreign policy, in all its manifestations (…) the penetration of Iran's political system and the interrelationship between domestic politics and foreign alignment have diminished in the course of the decade, although the influence of the West, and particularly the United States, remains pervasive in Iran's politics.[8]

As Ramazani mentions, after the fall of the Mosadegh government, the Shah's personal control became supreme and unchallenged. He was the central player in foreign policies even more than domestic, as evidenced by his influence in establishing and implementing all major decisions from oil agreements and the Baghdad Pact to the Irano–Soviet negotiations and the Bahrain dispute, climaxed by his frequent foreign goodwill visits to countries in both political blocs as well as the superpowers. These visits were also made by the royal family and even the prime minister to direct and support the Shah's decisions when the Shah himself preferred not to become directly involved; this was also the role of Parliament.[9] The consequences of this type of decision-making system for Iran's foreign policy during the Shah's rule, as Chubin and Zabih observe, were the following.

1) Iran's foreign policy in broad terms was remarkably stable; where foreign policy was personal it reflected the leader's wish to demonstrate his stability and consistency. In this regard, foreign policy was formulated by pragmatism rather than ideological attentions.
2) This type of state is both less and more adaptable. In the first instance the prestige of the leader would be at stake, and in the second the Shah's acknowledged, almost total, control would provide an immeasurably strong negotiating hand and decisiveness that comes from the lack of serious economic, political or social constraints – e.g. between 1970–1971 the dropping of the Bahrain claim and the pursuing of the claim to PG islands.
3) Foreign policy controlled by one person manifests a person's temperament. The world is seen from their viewpoint and observes other governments as equally personal – e.g. an insult to the state is a personal slight and a government's views are represented by its newspapers. Iran evidenced this hypothesis in its insistence that Nasser, the President of Egypt, "apologise", especially regarding its confronting the Iranian government in PG politics, before diplomatic relations could be resumed. The emphasis on personality is a dangerous feature in a state's foreign policy that can cause misunderstanding and confusion.
4) The temptation arises, when personal control of foreign policy aligns with the domination of internal affairs, to enhance the leadership's prestige internationally to legitimise and strengthen the regime. Such domestic uses of foreign policy can be seen in the celebration of 2,500 years of monarchy, emphasising military sophistication, sensitivity to the naming of the Gulf, regular discussions on Iranian responsibility in the PG, and encouragement of sloganeering to mobilise the populace on regional issues. However, it cannot be a substitute for policy. Iran's hurriedly prepared and aborted 1965 continental shelf agreement with Saudi Arabia, its short-run issues in international politics, and its reluctance to establish long-range policies are characteristic of the diplomacy of a small state.
5) This type of system retards the professionalism of foreign policy. Although this theory has not really been tested, the absence of continuous policy direction, the unavailability of diplomats who can authoritatively state Iran's position, the absence of expertise

evident in Iran's regional relations particularly with the Arab world, its personalised and improvised decisions, and hesitation reflected in its failure to prepare for Britain's withdrawal with no active initiative suggested until the leadership returns to the issue demonstrates this danger and the potential of a bottleneck arising at times of great foreign affairs activity.

6) The merger of pure diplomacy and pure coercion, with a greater reliance on the latter, tends to occur wherever the same individual dominates both foreign and military affairs. In dealing with the superpowers Iran relied on diplomacy while in local relations it preferred to emphasise its might – e.g. the Arvand Roud dispute. Its reaction to Jamal Nasser's campaign in Yemen was to increase arms purchases. When Britain withdrew it emphasised military preparation rather than seeking complementary diplomatic options. However, it has not been proven that Iran's reliance on military solutions or its underestimation of diplomacy in its foreign policy arose from its decision-making structure – although it can be seen that military inputs into foreign policy were considered more significant than diplomatic ones.

7) The only learning process that could take place was a personal one, requiring a change in the decision-makers' own attitudes, as there was no formalised foreign policy process. This brought with it inherent long-term disadvantages including an increase in the strain on the Iranian leadership, particularly considering the increasing diversification of Iran's foreign relations, the many technical features of diplomacy at that time and Iran's desire for a wider regional role.[10]

Islamic Republic of Iran

Iran's post-revolutionary complex political system combines elements of a modern Islamic theocracy with democracy. Its decision-making system is a compromise of a kind. Its vital decisions are usually made by consensus rather than decree.

Despite constitutional law detailing the different institutions of government, their makeup and their duties, individuals still substantially influence the final decisions, attempting to use institutions as mere instruments to implement them. Despite the existence of different councils and institutions, there is no formal or routine policy process;

instead, a complex system of compromises between institutions and individuals has been accepted. Hooshang Amirahmadi praises the decentralising process of Iran's power structure, suggesting it is a step towards greater pluralism, and goes on to explain that the structure of "the Iranian government is not pyramid-like [but] (...) it is a structure of power comprised of many inter-connected and autonomous rings". The central ring is made up of a group of elite individuals, mostly clergymen of great influence; that rarely hold official government positions because who they are is more important than the positions they occupy. The second ring contains those elite with senior posts, composed of clergymen and civilians, and then beyond that are the forces that manage the various elements of the system described as the "roots of power", including revolutionary foundations and religious security forces.[11] Under such circumstances, it is not unusual to see many senior posts exclusively given to close relatives of those in power who, as Amirahmadi also remarks, in turn appoint their own relatives and friends to sensitive positions.[12] As Nourbakhsh comments, this complex network of patronage, both personal and patrimonial, established and controlled everything, including the government.[13]

The foreign policy decision-making process in Iran is extremely complex, involving interfacing between many official and unofficial forces. Policy outcomes are difficult to predict owing to the varied and varying composition of institutions, the personal influence of their members and the manoeuvrability of pressure groups associated with them. Although there is general agreement that observers can identify most of the significant players, the actual process of decision-making remains vague,[14] and uncertainty surrounds the rules by which state and non-state players decide objectives and more importantly reach final decisions.[15] The chaotic impression this system gives to external observers hides what is described by Daniel Byman (et al.) as a "highly stylised and ritualised mode of interaction". According to the authors, this interaction is based on the impromptu trading of support, information and unspoken approval, preserving solidarity and consensus. However, the consequence of such a system is that decisions are subject to a back-and-forth process, with individuals withholding support and the differing objectives and enthusiasm of institutions resulting in inconsistent policy, policy slippage and policy setbacks, all leading to mixed signals in Iran's foreign policy.[16] According to Byman (et al.), the institutions and organisations in Iran have important political and military roles, with many duties, beliefs and aims overlapping considerably – most institutions, however, are weak while the personal networks of leaders are strong and thus power shifts according to the fortunes of the individual leaders rather than the scope of institutions. Decision-making is characterised by both seemingly chaotic complexity and consensus; no one institution or individual has complete control, so a majority of institutional and non-institutional actors, family ties, personal relationships, overlapping institutional authority and the mixture of religion and politics must be gained to reach one's end.[17]

Nourbakhsh attempts to describe the process of decision-making as follows: an opportunity or threat is discovered; the message passes through all the different institutional sources to the president, the Supreme National Security Council (SNSC), the *Majlis* (Parliament), the Guardian Council (GC), the Expediency Council (EC) and the Supreme Leader (see Figure 8.1). Even though the ultimate decision may be the leader's choice, through official and unofficial means, all the institutions and individuals are able to influence it to a certain extent. Also, the leader may choose to delegate or simply be influenced by the victor of a factional debate; in this regard it is not always the leader who is the final decision-maker.[18] Despite the explanation of Kamal Kharrazi, the head of the new Strategic Council for Foreign Relations (*Shora-yi Rahbordi-yi Ravabet-i Khareji*) – which was created by a 25 June decree from the Supreme Leader – that such a lack of coherence in foreign relations strategy was the reason for the foundation of this council, this council does not seem to be able to offer a more coherent and organised foreign policy decision-making process. This is because, on the one hand, there are some uncertainties regarding the new council's purpose given that there are various political bodies oriented toward foreign policy decision-making. On the other hand, despite Kharrazi's emphasis on the consultancy dimension of the council's purpose and the impossibility of its interference in other foreign policy organisations, according to his explanation of the obligation laid on executive organs to obey the approved strategy presented to Ayatollah Khamenei, such a situation would provide a more tangible influence for the Supreme Leader in the foreign policy decision-making process.

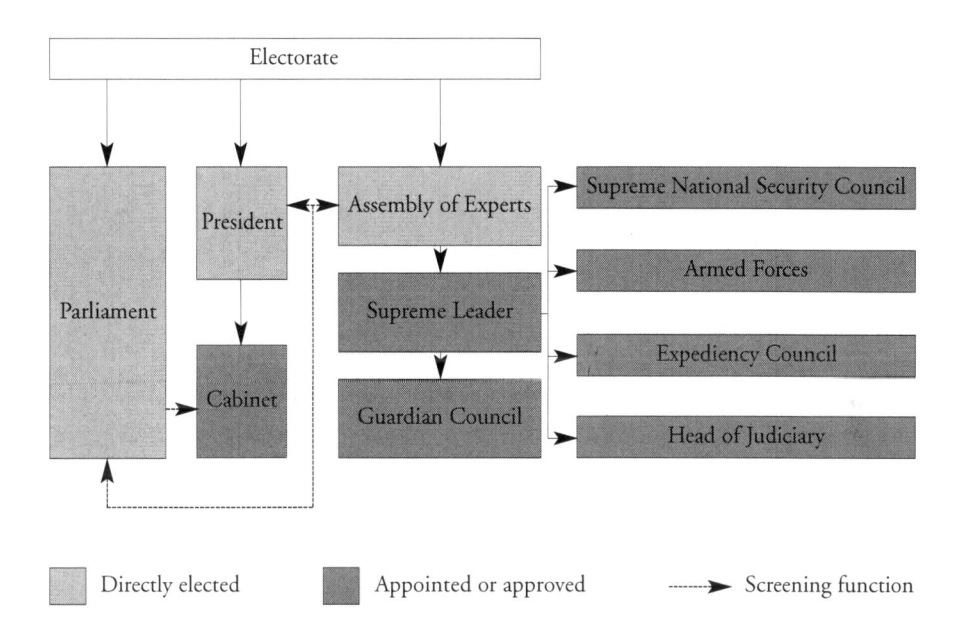

FIGURE 8.1
Islamic Republic of Iran's power chart

[Figure: Power chart showing Electorate at top, connecting to Parliament, President, and Assembly of Experts (directly elected). President connects to Cabinet. Assembly of Experts connects to Supreme Leader, which connects to Guardian Council. Supreme Leader also connects to Supreme National Security Council, Armed Forces, Expediency Council, and Head of Judiciary (appointed or approved). Dashed arrows indicate screening function between Guardian Council and Parliament/Cabinet.]

Legend: Directly elected | Appointed or approved | ------> Screening function

According to Byman (et al.), when it comes to formal decisions about Iran's security policy, the Supreme Leader simply oversees while the President handles the daily decision-making; however, informally the leader exerts considerable control over day-to-day implementations. Also, concerning Iran's security policy several institutions are of particular significance, including the intelligence services, the Islamic Revolutionary Guard Corps (IRGC) and the Artesh (regular armed forces). The first two organisations are concerned with the defence of the revolution against domestic enemies, while the Artesh concentrates its efforts on potential attacks from the outside or other traditional threats. Hence, the sharing of responsibilities and overlap of duties and beliefs often creates duplication and rivalry.[19]

Iran's strategies and its foreign policy's orientation and goals have not only been a revolutionary reaction against the Shah's regime, but have also been influenced by the revolutionary leaders. Houman Sadri categorises Iran's revolutionary leaders into two groups: idealists and realists. As he explains, the revolutionary idealists believe that in time the revolution will spread everywhere. Their desire is to focus resources in support of movements abroad; they hold onto an anti-status quo belief and apply their revolutionary values in foreign relations – all of which seems to pose a threat to the national security of other states, especially Iran's PG neighbours, and consequently contributes to the isolation of Iran. This is evidenced by the support of Arab states in the PG for Iraq's invasion of Iran a year after the revolution. Although, Sadri continues, revolutionary realists had the same aim as idealists – to export the revolution – their methodology differed. The realists dealt with problems of national rather than international concern, prioritising the building of a model revolutionary state in their own country. However, they understood real politics, the limits of their country's revolutionary powers and the country's need for external assistance in modernisation, and so concerned themselves with the reaction the revolution met with on the international stage. They were also pragmatic enough to realise the importance of good diplomatic relations and that internationally isolating the country would not pay off. As Sadri mentions, an example of a revolutionary realist is Ali Akbar Hashemi Rafsanjani, who worked against the isolationist tendencies within the new leadership. Despite such differences, a common belief on both sides was that the new regime needed a fresh approach to foreign relations.[20]

After 1989, the evolution of Iran's foreign relations was implemented by Hashemi Rafsanjani. He began confidence building, established a *détente* policy and strengthened Iran's regional position. Also, by managing PG relations and by adopting a pragmatic and active regional policy, he began rebuilding much of Iran's international credibility. Despite the tendency of revolutionary states to forge a close-knit relationship between domestic and foreign policies, when its state security was at risk ideological Iran managed to temper its ideology with pragmatism. However, the primacy of foreign policy in Iran's scheme continued, even during the Hashemi Rafsanjani period, when he preferred to deal with national rather than international concerns, maintaining the same problems as the Shah during his period. It was not until 1997 that this policy was altered. During the presidency of Mohammad Khatami urgent domestic issues brought with them the realisation that foreign policy could no longer replace domestic performance; internal crisis could not be met by foreign-policy activism. However, by ending isolation and increasing access to external resources, Iran could alleviate some of the pressures on the regime through foreign policy.

As Byman (et al.) mentions, Iran's security policy is a combination of Islamic and nationalist objectives. However, in recent years the necessity of preserving regional stability and improving Iran's economy has dictated the influence of geopolitics, economics and even ethnicity in shaping Iran's security policy. Also, from 1997 the presidency of Khatami added to the elements of the regime's security policy a clearer superiority and urgency of domestic issues. These additional influences led to the development of better relations with regional neighbours at the expense of revolutionary principles and to the following of more cautious policies than Iran's Islamic and nationalist ethos might otherwise have dictated.[21] However, since the presidency of Ahmadinejad, the IRI has once again returned to its previous radical priorities.

In sum, Iran's foreign policy is infused with a desire for autonomy as well as for influence on its regional and even the international stage. Therefore, the concept of "national interests" as a guide for foreign policy has been mostly missing from Iran's policies, whether under the Shah's regime or that of the IRI. Iran's relationship to the international environment is described by Chubin as follows: "[L]ike those of other small states Iran's security and ability to manoeuvre largely depends on an international environment which it can little affect."[22] Both national interests and the international environment have, from the period of the Shah, continued to present a real challenge to Iran's foreign policy.

Imperial Iran's security challenges

Introduction

> The modern Iranian State is the product of many very complex and long-term social relations, deep-rooted political interactions and socio-economic processes.
>
> A. Ehteshami (2000)[23]

Domestic, foreign and security policies are not divided issues. It must be recognised that the major threat to Iranian society comes from within, which is evidenced by the revolution. However, Iranian political regimes' endeavour has been characterised mainly by two factors: ignoring or being unaware of national interests, and laying blame on other internal or external events. An examination of domestic threats, particularly during the study period of 1962–1997, will involve consideration of the major socio-political issues, and economic and military development, both pre- and post-revolution.

Mohammad Reza Pahlavi's regime

Two interpretations are put forward of the internal threats to the security of the Mohammad Reza Pahlavi's regime (1941–1979), which was ended by the Islamic revolution, as Abrahamian explains:

> One interpretation – accepted by supporters of the Pahlavi regime – claims that the revolution occurred because the shah modernized [1963–1977] too much and too quickly for his traditional-minded and backward-looking people. The other – favoured by opponents of the regime – argues that the revolution occurred because the shah did not modernize fast enough and thoroughly enough to overcome his initial handicap of being a CIA-installed monarch in an age of nationalism, neutralism, and republicanism.[24]

However, according to Abrahamian both interpretations are only half right. The revolution began because the Shah modernised the socio-economic level, increasing both the middle and industrial working classes, but did not modernise the political level. This imbalance created strained links and blocked communications between the political system and the general population. The few bridges that had connected the traditional social forces, particularly the bazaars and religious authorities, collapsed. By 1977, the widening gulf between the two levels meant that an economic crisis was able to pull down the whole regime. The revolution took place not because of over- or under-development but because of uneven development.[25] Subsequently, under the Shah's rule, Iranian society was plagued by the following four major crises.

1) The crisis of justice, which was rooted in social relations, the living conditions of the people, the unjust distribution of wealth, social discriminations and the gap between the poor and rich. This gap

was created by the modernisation plan and social development, which was made possible by increasing oil revenues. It is also true, as Abrahamian remarks, that substantial amounts of money were wasted on royal extravagances, bureaucratic consumption, outright corruption, nuclear installation and ultra-sophisticated weapons. However, greater amounts were channelled into the economy and into the government-subsidised Industrial and Mining Development Bank of Iran.[26]

2) The participation crisis emerged because of the Shah's personal fear of the people demanding the right to play a more active role in determining their own fate, which went completely against the ethos of his totalitarian and autocratic regime. Consequently, although he modernised the structure of socio-economics, he made little effort to develop the political system, thus preventing the formation of pressure groups and other social forces.

3) A moral and spiritual crisis shook the legitimacy of the regime to its foundations in terms of public opinion and conscience. The prevailing notion that "modernisation brings secularity", or "modernisation is a fundamental break with spirituality", together with the Shah's efforts to foster a Western-oriented culture, his glorification of pre-Islamic Persia (such as his celebration of the 2,500th anniversary of the founding of the Persian Empire, which was held at the site of Persepolis in 1971, or the imposition of a new calendar dating from the pre-Islamic monarch Cyrus the Great instead of from the prophet of Islam's *higra*), the presence of thousands of Westerners in Iran, the increasing number of cinemas showing "decadent" Western films, as well as discos, bars and casinos for gambling (all against *Sharia* law), represented an ascending perfidious culture. These developments were against the beliefs of most Iranians and were construed by *Ulema* as destructive of Shiism. They were perceived by many as an effort on the Shah's part to destroy Islam and seemed inextricably bound to a decline in Islamic practices.[27]

4) The prevailing security atmosphere that controlled opposition groups and the media was mainly led by a new secret police named *Sazman e Ettela'at va Amniyat-e Keshvar* (National Security and Information Organisation, SAVAK). This organisation was set up by the Shah who, after the Mosadegh[28] experience, wanted an effective

internal security service. However, he also maintained additional intelligence services, partly to check on each other.

The regime's modernisation was unlike what was successfully experienced in other societies. The Shah's main motivation was his dream of developing Iran into a "Great Civilization" and making it one of the most powerful nations of the world: not only secure, but self-sufficient via oil money. However, by late 1974 the oil boom brought a completely different result than the "Great Civilization" promised by the Shah. The moderate decline of oil revenues in 1974–1975, which was followed by a sharp decline in the final year of the Shah's regime, brought an alarming increase in inflation and a widening gap between the rich and poor. By mid-1977, an economic recession, with high government deficits and high inflation, urban overcrowding, government policies that damaged the bazaar classes, and lack of political freedom contributed to the widespread perception that the "Great Civilization" was just a hollow dream without firm buttresses.

The modernisation of Iran had three shortcomings. First, it was forced upon the people from above, without allowing them to participate (due to the lack of political development), creating expansive dualism between traditional beliefs and modern secular ideas. This dualism was seen in the economy, in the culture, in the forms of thinking and particularly with regard to religious beliefs. The lack of an overarching ideology meant that the Shah failed to attract the population to the process of modernisation. The second shortcoming was the uneven development of the economic and political systems, as explained earlier. The third shortcoming was the lack of a single unique ideology to reconcile the people's beliefs and the Shah's modernisation. This absence was partly because the modernisation package was designed by America, enabling the introduction of American capitalism into Iranian society, which encouraged secular ideas.[29]

Political policy
Far-reaching political, social and economic reforms, known as the Shah's White Revolution (1963), were encouraged by the US, which was happy to support the Shah's placing of great emphasis on reinforcing Iran's internal security. Consideration of the Shah's agricultural and oil policies demonstrates how the regime politically alienated the population and

increased its dependency on the West for survival, which ultimately destabilised the regime. The consequences of the Shah's economic strategy, especially in these two major areas of development, may, as Keddie notes, be seen as:

> contributing to a capitalist type of agricultural and industrial growth, with a natural emphasis on state capitalism, given the autocratic nature of the regime and its monopoly control of the ever-growing oil income. (…) The years 1962–77 may be seen as a unit in this building up of a predominant state capitalism, undermining of semifeudal forms of landownership seen as a bar both to development and to central government control of the countryside, and encouragement and subsidy to private capitalists.[30]

In the decade after the 1953 coup d'état, the Shah worked to consolidate his power and became increasingly interested in modernising the Iranian economy and society in a Western manner, and developing its military strength. In this regard he carried to the extreme displays of ultra-sophisticated and expensive weaponry, which, combined with his economic policy that had turned Iran into a huge consumer of Western goods, made Iran substantially dependent on the West – specifically the US. So, to achieve his goals, the Shah needed financial aid, which he received from America. He was able to solve his oil dispute with Britain and form a contract with a British consortium, which resulted in an increase in oil revenues. All theses events assisted the Shah in gaining control of most of Iran's economy and the state itself. The additional revenues also increased Iran's military strength, which was necessary for the regime's survival.

Economic development
There were contrasting views concerning the Shah's socio-economic policies. Some, especially those outside Iran, thought they were a great success citing in support of this the increase in Iran's GNP, the impressive industrial, agricultural and infrastructural projects, and the number of social welfare activities. However, opponents of the regime saw the policies as artificial and fraudulent, arguing that the development had only benefited the regime and its Western supporters. Opponents also claimed there were no structural changes, and that the social and economic projects undertaken by the Shah's regime served only to reinforce

a capitalist system of agriculture and industrial growth, with the emphasis on state capitalism, as evidenced by the autocratic character of the regime and the monopoly it held on oil income. Increased oil revenues simply increased the disparity between the rich and poor because the Shah's over-ambitious fantasy led to associations with multinational corporations, which left the day-to-day needs of most Iranians unfulfilled. The government did not even try to use taxation to its advantage, yet this could more justly have distributed income and signalled that the people had a role in the government they paid for.[31]

Although the Shah's first major programme of modernisation ended because of economic difficulties, his later plan resulted in major transformations in Iran's society and economy, such as economic expansion, unequal distribution of wealth, profound changes in the class structure and a decline in the agriculture sector. These transformations were the result of a focus on an industrialisation programme that depended heavily on Western technology and managerial skills.

As Milani explains, when the Shah introduced land reforms in 1963 as part of his White Revolution, the coalition (made up of landlords, rich merchants, some top clergy, armed forces and the US) that overthrew Mosadegh in 1953 began to disintegrate. The subsequent establishment of the Triangle of Fortune or Triple Alliance, which was made up of the combined forces of the Iranian state, the industrial bourgeoisie and foreign capitalists, particularly the US, was necessary to ensure the survival of the Pahlavi regime and its modernisation plan for Iran. The drive behind each group was a desire for the speedy development of Iran's economy and an "open-door" policy, especially towards the West.[32]

However, a major pernicious consequence of such economic expansion, which was not seriously considered, was the shifting of Iran's focus from agriculture to industry, resulting in an increased labour force with all its disadvantages such as rapid urban migration as well as excessive inflation. This massive movement of mainly young people from a very religious and political culture in the country actually assisted the ultimate downfall of the regime because, in the end, the strength of the revolution came from the urban areas where the political culture of the masses was Islamic so they could easily lend their support to Grand Ayatollah Khomeini.

Such a significant change from land ownership for agricultural production to investment in commercial and industrial projects also resulted in the allocation of a considerable amount of the state's resources for the development of industries, as well as encouraging involvement in the private sector. Official records show that in 1980, out of 5,288 industrial units, more than 89 per cent were owned by the private sector while only 409 (around 7 per cent) were state controlled. Unsurprisingly, the Pahlavi family benefited the most from the economic boom; indeed, by the early 1970s they had established a huge financial empire and were controlling almost everything. They invested considerable funds – borrowed from state banks, often on very favourable terms – in various commercial and industrial businesses. Their other source of wealth was oil income. According to *The Washington Post*, in the last few years of the Shah's regime significant amounts (possibly about US$2 billion), with no trace in the state treasury, were transferred directly from the state's oil income into the royal family's secret foreign bank accounts. As long as the royal family remained in control the strength of the private sector increased, due to extravagant financial incentives and the fact that Iran was introduced to foreign capital, the foreign banking industry and various economic agreements between Iran and the West, specifically the US.[33] The consequence of all this, as Milani notes, was that:

> As the role of the state and indigenous industrialists increased, so did that of foreign capital. (…) The foreign role in the banking industry also increased. (…) Concomitant with increased foreign involvement was the deepening of Iran's dependence on the West. The imports of capital and intermediate goods rose from $89 million in 1963 to $886 million in 1977. The dependent industrialists of Iran had become the junior partners of elites in the metropolis countries. They identified with and emulated the West to such an extent that they became alienated from their own culture. This created a ubiquitous cultural gap between his small portion of the population and the bulk of Iranians.[34]

The Shah's power was based on the three pillars of the armed forces, the court patronage network and the vast state bureaucracy, which enabled the state's control to expand into the day-to-day lives of its citizens. In the towns the state hired 50 per cent of full-time employees giving it control of a vast percentage of the population's salaries and benefits. Although this network did not yet include the *bazaaries* (market merchants), it did penetrate the countryside. It managed to supplant the local *khans* (landowners), demolishing the barrier that had once prevented absolute government authority over the rural population. Now the government could reorganise the whole countryside. As the final step, in 1975, the Shah established the additional and fateful fourth pillar of a one-party state. Giving way in the late 1950s to growing pressure for more democracy, the Shah created two parties: the Melliyun (Nationalist) party and the Mardom (People) party. However, both parties were introduced simply for the sake of appearances and, with little difference between them, they remained under the control of their creator. It was not until more than fifteen years later that the Shah dissolved these existing two parties and created the Resurgence party (*Hizb-i Rastakhiz*) – headed by Amirabbas Hoveyda, the prime minister – whose main aim, as Abrahamian expresses it, was to turn the old-fashioned dictatorship into a modern totalitarian state.[35]

Military development
Another part of the Shah's attempt to consolidate his power was his effort to increase his regime's military strength. His ambition was for Iran to become a leading military power, which would also provide the means to subdue domestic political opposition. To achieve his goal the Shah obtained US aid. The military relationship between the US and Iran began in the late 1940s. However, the real increase in Iran's dependency on the US occurred after the 1953 restoration of the Shah to power. This dependency was not only military but also financial, and lasted up until 1967 when Iran's oil revenues increased. The consequent increase in wealth, as well as the US' political agenda and the Shah's eagerness to buy sophisticated weapons, prompted the US to ignore Iran's attempts to prevent domestic or regional instability through the build-up of arms. Instead it established a new interdependent partnership.

After Britain's withdrawal from the region, the US was reluctant to involve itself directly. Consequently it needed a powerful and friendly state to protect US interests in the PG. Hence US strategic interests led to the creation of a regional security system and a strong Iran that remained independent of the USSR, which was increasing its military potential. Therefore, in May 1972, as a result of the Nixon–Kissinger decision to expand America's commitment to Iran's military build-up, Washington allowed the Shah to buy conventional (non-nuclear) arms. This indicates that the US–Iran relationship was seen as beneficial to both countries and did not require a direct US military role or significant

American expense. However, it did mean that the US had changed from being what Chubin described as a "restraining patron to [being an] acquiescent partner". This bound the US' interests to the fate of the Shah's regime – even the Carter administration continued US agreements with Iran.[36] From 1973, when the price of oil began to rise, the West found it convenient to recycle Iran's petrodollars and thus allowed the Shah to purchase large amounts of up-to-date and sophisticated military equipment, which led to Iran's role as the policeman of the PG.

The main strain on the relationship was the Shah's desire for more and newer military equipment, which led the US to forcibly encourage greater economic reforms to ensure stability and prevent upheaval or revolution. However, this was unbalanced by the Shah's insistence on spending more of Iran's growing oil revenues on weaponry rather than on Iran's economy.

Dimensions of Iran–US military ties
Advantages
Iran's military build-up, Chubin remarks, "held the potential for a regional equilibrium less susceptible to disturbance by outside powers". This, as he explains, was because Iran's arms were supplied by the US and thus the US' ability to react quickly in this area was improved because of the compatibility between the US' military equipment and that of Iran. In addition, the relationship meant that the US could use Iranian territory to gather intelligence and monitor Soviet missile testing.[37]

Although the Shah's ambition was for Iran to gain influence and become a leading military power, not just in the PG but throughout the ME and the Indian sub-continent, the deployments of its ground forces had the character of being almost solely concerned with defence and internal security. In this regard, as Canby remarks, a full three-fifths of Iran's army was deployed near the borders with Iraq, and half of the remainder was located in the capital. The air force comprised only one brigade able to provide domestic reinforcement or be of use in the rest of the PG region. This meant that the Shah would only really have been effective in intervening in areas near his own borders. This concentration of forces near the borders, particularly the Iraqi frontier, with nearly all the Iranian army's armour oriented towards Iraq, reflected both the obvious need to face the Iraqi threat and the American belief that such forces would be able to contain and delay any Soviet threat until the arrival of US reinforcements. Forces were not placed any closer to the Soviet border because they would only be lost early on, and may have appeared confrontational during times of peace.[38]

So a relative political stability was brought to the PG for about ten years as a result of the intensification of the US–Iran military relationship. The closeness of this relationship was promoted by Iran's desire to assume the responsibility neither the UK nor the US wanted, combined with increasingly significant political developments of the region, especially in the context of the Cold War. Moreover, as no other states besides Iran could ensure the region's security, a close military relationship was essential.

Disadvantages
The close military ties between the US and Iran had disadvantages for both the Shah's regime and Washington, as outlined below.

- It led to an unwelcome number of foreign technical advisers, instructors and their families, who contributed to inflation and often caused justified indignation among Iranians. By 1976 there were some 25,000 military-related personnel (and their dependants) in Iran, and it was estimated that by 1980 there would be 50,000 to 60,000. One rise led to another and in industry the lack of training in Iran meant that the Iranian population lost out again as more foreigners were brought in to deal with the bigger, more technical and complex projects. This further contributed to over-crowding, shortages, inflation and an anti-American feeling.
- The aid and technical assistance given by the US, together with Israel, to the SAVAK, which was the most dreaded internal security agency, increased popular resentment toward the countries that helped the SAVAK.
- The Shah's insistence on spending more of Iran's growing oil revenues on weaponry rather than on Iran's economy had serious socio-economic consequences.
- During Iran's revolutionary period, the close military ties between the two countries became a disadvantage for the Shah; although it had contributed to his regime's stability in a peaceful era. Moreover, during this period of crisis a demonstrative use of US force as a deterrent against external intervention in Iran could have

backfired, as it could have been construed as an indication of opposition to the revolution.[39]
- Regarding the possibility that purchasing arms from the US was among the causes of the revolution, Chubin remarks that it is uncertain whether the purchase of arms actually contributed to the economic problems that led to the revolution. However, if the Shah had been refused the weapons it would have weakened the Iran–US relationship. This in turn would have created a weaker, unstable Iran, which was eventually the case after 1976. It became clear that a weaker Iran was a greater destabilising regional force as well as a threat to US interests.

Opposition groups
The Shah, with his dictatorial character and zero tolerance – which had alienated all social groups and classes with the possible exception of the upper layer of the bourgeoisie – perceived opposition groups as a threat to his regime. Their demands that the regime observe the constitution, free political prisoners, and respect freedom and human rights, were ignored and they were severely oppressed by the regime, especially in the post-1953 coup d'état.

SAVAK had the main responsibility for identifying and destroying all who opposed the Shah's dictatorship in any way. It had headquarters in London, Geneva and Washington and developed ties with intelligence agencies from America, Britain and Israel. SAVAK was particularly suspicious of groups of intellectuals, students and religious clerics both at home and abroad. Due to its efforts the Shah's regime was stable and able to control discontent for a time. However, it could not last long; via a strong revolutionary movement started in 1978 the regime was overthrown within months and the Shah had to face the consequences of his oppressive policy.

The first problem for the regime was that of legitimacy, which for Iran was linked to the form and nature of governance of a Muslim society. The regime had alienated the masses. Discontent increased when the promised decentralisation of the political and economic systems failed to be realised. However, instead of destroying the roots of dissension the regime's oppressive policies actually resulted in the radicalisation of opposition groups. The response to the regime's oppression varied greatly from passive to violent. Many remained silent, not in support of the regime but because economic benefits of developments outweighed the negative impacts of rapid changes. Some analysts indicate other reasons, including pessimism and a sense of hopelessness over traditional leaders' ability to confront the regime, combined with the massive losses of the 1963 uprising, which highlighted the Shah's greater power, as well as the lack of opportunity for mobilising people and forming political gatherings. All this paved the way for militia activities and the establishment of small secret groups, ranging from Nationalist to Marxist to Islamist, to carry on the struggle against the regime, thus politicising a generation of Iranians both at home and abroad to shake the foundations of the Pahlavi rule.

In order to understand the Islamic-led revolution in Iran the tactics and aims of opposition groups need to be studied. Generally speaking, several groups were opposed to the regime, including both secular and religious entities. With the exception of the Mujahedin-e Khalq, which adopted the strategy of armed struggle, those that held or supported Islamic ideology sought to replace the Pahlavi regime with an Islamic system through political and cultural actions. In contrast, those from secular backgrounds simply rebelled, with the aim of opposing the political participation crisis. They believed that an armed struggle was the path to political freedom. Opposition groups with secular backgrounds included the National Front, the Tudeh and the Fadaiyan-e Khalq. These groups were not interested in replacing the regime with an Islamic system. However, the regime had alienated them by centralising power and ceasing to act in accordance with institutionalised rules; as a result, parties were replaced by movements as an alternative form of political organisation.[40] Lack of influence and communication with the majority of people, whose political culture was Islamic, and also the adoption of strategies of leftist leaders in Latin-America which focused on armed action and ignored the potential or exploration of non-violent political channels, resulted in the failure of these leftist guerrilla movements. This strategy brought them into direct conflict with the regime, which damaged their networks and organisations.

Therefore, a growing number of oppositionists voiced their views in Islamic terms and many opposition groups had ties with the Islamic opposition. This was because Islamic ideology was linked to the political culture of the masses in such a way that the Shah could not easily contain them. The clergy had a significant influence on the masses and had been a political voice – for example, in 1964 Grand Ayatollah Khomeini's opposition to capitulation or the granting of diplomatic immunity by the Shah to American military personnel.

In addition, the failure of the Fadaiyan-e Islam, the main Islamic armed opposition, led Islamic groups to recognise the need for cultural and political tactics rather than military ones when mobilising people against the Shah's regime. Although there were some other secret groups led by Ayatollah Beheshti and Ayatollah Taleghani, opposition activity took place mainly within religious settings, such as mosques (there were 100,000 mosques and 200,000 clerics), which gave more of a chance to mobilise the masses without the interference of the security forces. There were many reasons to form a new coalition – which included almost all different social classes and political forces, whether related to the Islamists or focused on a non-religious leadership outside the control of the regime. Among the most important were: the prevailing ideology, Islam, continuing political-cultural activity in mobilising the masses, and a charismatic, unique and popular leader in the form of Grand Ayatollah Khomeini "emerging before the Shah was overthrown".[41] In addition, as Abrahamian notes, the new leader's promise to bring social justice, in contrast to the regime's inability to satisfy people's increasing expectations, and also his "timely statements to woo the secular opposition and to assure all that the autocracy would not be superseded by a theocracy", were important elements of forming the new coalition against the Shah's regime.[42]

Although it was obvious that the regime would end sooner or later, the human-rights policy enunciated by President Carter, in hopes of making US foreign policy more benevolent post-Vietnam, helped to bring about the downfall sooner. Under domestic and international pressure the Shah began to make gestures in favour of public opinion, although these were later and less than people had expected. He eased pressure on political prisoners, cancelled the censorship of the writings of Dr Ali Shariati, an influential modernist Islamist leader, and, in 1977, after the economic crisis seriously worsened, replaced the prime minister. His new choice, Jamshid Amuzegar, was meant to be the solution to Iran's growing economic problems, given his background in economics and oil. However, the economic crisis continued and discontent increased. In 1978 opposition escalated, with widespread street protests. The revolution was spontaneous but not led by armed opposition, as in the 1970s, or by a political organisation backed by the Soviet Union. The revolutionaries were led instead by Grand Ayatollah Khomeini, an exiled religious leader who had lived for fourteen years in Iraq and later in France and who was able to gather a unique coalition of opposition against the Pahlavi monarchy.

The Shah's regime had been economically and politically stable both internally and externally, particularly in its regional and international position. However, because this security was achieved through a system of oppression and fear, the regime was ultimately undermined from within. The Shah's regime was not considered a threat to the regional security of the PG because it had the same political orientation towards the West, which it lost after the revolution ignited anti-status-quo rhetoric and policies. Revolutionary Iran's problem was seen as a security matter for its neighbours. Although the post-revolution system, especially through the first decade, had more political legitimacy, it was faced with many different problems that resulted in the political and economic instability of Iran.

The Islamic Republic's security challenges

Introduction

A revolution, by its very nature as a significant change in a relatively short period of time, causes instability within a political system which appears as insecurity. In this regard the focus of the new regime in Iran, despite its efforts to manage the revolutionary fever, was on the struggle for survival against both external and internal opposition. Similar insecurity was felt by neighbouring countries, along with ultra-regional players, because of the new regime's anti-status-quo and revolutionary policies.

The main internal threats causing instability after the revolution were political and economic unsteadiness. These encouraged both internal and external threats because the regime was considered at its weakest position and, as such, the opposition saw a way to achieve its goals, e.g. the Mujahedin-e-Khalq armed struggle and Iraq invasion. However, the Islamic Republic of Iran (IRI), despite suffering many losses, has more or less been able to overcome such problems.

Despite the general stability of the regime since the revolution, the IRI has been strategically and structurally quite vulnerable. Such vulnerabilities will be investigated in this section through studying Iran's most significant internal challenges during the first two decades of the revolution: 1979–1988 and 1989–1997, both of which will be considered from a political, economic and military point of view.

The first decade of the Islamic revolution: 1979–1988
Political issues
In the first decade of the revolution the IRI followed the "neither East nor West" policy. It was an independent power and had significant regional influence, particularly politically, affecting both east and west of Iran, including the Arab world. The revolution was widely popular in Iran and there was no real domestic threat, nor has there been any serious opposition since. However, this does not mean that none existed; many of those who initally supported the political system ultimately came to oppose it but it was not enough to amount to an effective offensive.

According to many observers it is incredible that the IRI has survived so many attempts, both Iranian and foreign, to destroy it. This survival has been credited to a mixture of social elements, economic control, and fear. A social base has supported the regime and its Islamic programme, motivated partly by a feeling of insecurity arising from the belief that the US is committed to the elimination of the Islamic Republic. A strong ideological commitment has thus powered the continuation of the revolution. Resistance to any foreign-inspired change or interference remains a strong undercurrent of nationalistic feeling among Iranians.[43]

The economic system was central to the foundation of the regime, as it enabled direct control of employment. This control mechanism was strengthened by an increasing dependency on government subsidies, made possible by recruiting new supporters of the revolution into the government administration for civilian and military purposes, and also by using the oil revenues to influence Iran's economy. Finally, it is supposed that the regime's survival was also owed to fear because of the ideological confrontation against dissent. The combination of all three elements prevented the expression of open political opposition, and narrowed the options of resistance to either internal exile or armed action.[44]

The most serious internal threat to the regime in this period was the Mujahedin-e-Khalq group. This organisation started an armed uprising in June 1981, which later attracted several small leftist parties. Although immediately after the revolution it was widely popular among Shiite youth, it eventually lost its popularity and its members were deemed traitors by the Iranian people as a result of their support for Iraq in its war against Iran. Masoud Rajavi, the leader of the Mujahedin, failed in his attempt to achieve the sharing of political power through street demonstrations, so he joined forces with Bani Sadr, who was then president, and declared war on the Islamic regime, initiating a three-step strategy: destabilisation of the Islamic leadership; pressuring the government through street demonstrations; and finally creating a mass uprising. The Mujahedin spread terror throughout the population, from officials to ordinary people. Six of the seven well-respected elderly religious deputies whom Grand Ayatollah Khomeini had put in charge of different regions of the country were killed or seriously wounded. The Mujahedin claimed in the summer of 1982 that it had killed over a thousand members of the state security forces. Rajavi also claimed that the organisation had assassinated more than two thousand top political and religious leaders in 1981, the year before they went underground. However, these tactics proved to be counter-productive, and by 1982 numerous members had been killed or imprisoned, which enabled the regime to easily tear down the group. They continued with underground activities but left the country and began cooperating with Saddam in 1986, and in 1988 accompanied Iraqi forces on their offensives into Iran. In July 1988, after the IRI had announced its acceptance of UN Resolution 598 (which called upon Iran and Iraq to cease hostilities and observe a ceasefire as a first step towards a negotiated settlement), several hundred of the Mujahedin stayed behind to occupy the town of Islamabad in Bakhtaran (Kermanshah) province; however, Iranian forces of the Islamic Revolutionary Guard Corps (IRGC), in an operation named *Mersad*, destroyed a significant number of them. Hooglund alludes to the fact that the local population assisted the IRGC in defeating the Mujahedin and concludes from this that, "Most Iranians, whether they are fanatical supporters of the Islamic Republic, indifferent to politics or even opposed to the regime, including monarchists and leftists, consider the actions of the Mojahedin [Mujahedin] as unforgivable treason."[45]

The regime faced other opposition, including Kurdish resistance, which supported the Mujahedin forces in the western mountains until the attacks of 1982. Some plots attempted to overthrow the regime – for example, former Foreign Minister Sadegh Ghotb-zadeh was accused of and executed for plotting a coup and working for the US. Other opposition came from left-wing groups. After the rise of Hojjatieh, an extreme secret organisation that opposed communism and Bahaism, left-wing forces that had supported the regime appeared to lose their influence. Tudeh members were removed from the civilian and security forces, even though left-wing support continued for the regime's anti-imperialist and anti-capitalist policies. However, with the exception of Bazargan, the former prime minister, no prominent personality spoke out against the regime. After the regime consolidated itself it was faced with other emerging issues, including the absence of political parties because of resistance to the idea of giving representation to the people. Even the Islamic Republic Party (IRP), established by Ayatollah Beheshti and other official members, never served as a cohesive party and was disbanded by its prominent members at the consent of Grand Ayatollah Khomeini in 1987.[46] Another problem that emerged was the result of the continuation of previous political institutions, including the parliament, ministries and armed forces. Even the titles of the main newspapers remained the same, although with different orientations. Furthermore, only certain issues of specific interest to Islamist ideology were addressed, such as the status of women, who were ordered to wear religious clothing in public, and the harmonisation of the judicial system with Islam by removing all secular laws. Little attention was spared for other pressing matters, specifically civil rights. According to Halliday, this was mainly an attempt to win back support from the middle classes. These policies were criticised by Bazargan, who attacked the corruption, inefficiency, demagogy and violations of human rights in Iran. However, despite such problems, the regime, according to Halliday, was successful because it attracted new workers to the old administration, and used the system of Friday prayer leaders, the IRGC and the *Basij* (a paramilitary volunteer force) mobilisation forces. This network was, to all intents and purposes, fulfilling the role of a ruling party; it was through mosques and associated institutions that forms of popular mobilisation and ideological strategy were being carried out.[47] Although the regime was no longer facing any internal threat to its power, the Kurdish and Mujahedin-e-Khalq opposition being weaker than before, other problems were arising.

Economic problems

The Islamic regime had little to show for its monopoly of power; there were major unemployment figures, the urban population was increasing, the rate of literacy decreasing and the non-oil sectors of the economy stagnating. Also, corruption within the regime was growing. All these factors compounded the difficulties of Iran's foreign policy and significantly affected the survival of the regime.

Furthermore, people's frustration about the continuation of war – with no sign of victory, no successful international peace delegations, mounting casualties on both sides, and growing anti-war sentiment, particularly among the young – and the 1988 attack by the USS *Vincennes* on an Iranian civilian passenger plane in the PG (which killed all 290 people on board), persuaded Iranian authorities to consider the domestic effects of the war and look for a political solution. By 1988 most of the country's leaders believed that continuation of the war posed a serious threat to the stability, even survival, of the IRI. Thus on 18 July 1988, Iran notified the UN's Secretary General, Perez de Cuellar, that it accepted the Security Council's document of Resolution 598 for ceasefire without reservations. Tehran was thus able, at last, to respond to the demands of its people, ease the international situation and escape from its isolation so that it could begin economic and social reforms.

The eight-year war, which had begun immediately after the revolution, had resulted in the deceleration of some major economic plans. The economic situation and people's expectations of the revolutionary leaders to do what they had promised pushed Iran to turn its energies to the enormous task of rebuilding the agricultural, commercial, cultural, industrial and social infrastructure destroyed during eight years of war. Iran's economy was a key issue in this reconstruction. The government wanted to release the economy from the hold of foreigners, especially the West; however, it realised that while Iran's economy relied on its oil reserves this goal would continue to be just a dream. Also, the Iranian goal of building an Islamic model by increasing standards of living, helping the poor and improving the agricultural system presented a major challenge to the regime and still remains unfulfilled.

Over the first decade, the IRI was confronted with several major economic difficulties. However, since everything depended on the balance of internal forces the post-revolution reforms were by no means smooth or organised. This weakness and the continuing internal debate meant that

Iran was so occupied with its own problems that it could not possibly have been perceived as a regional threat.

The second decade of the Islamic revolution: 1989–1997

As the regime entered its second decade it did not face any serious threats, just the challenge of reconstructing the war-damaged industrial and social infrastructures and keeping the promises made before the revolution, particularly those concerning greater economic and social justice. However, there was enormous disagreement within the country over Iran's domestic and foreign policy. The two major events of the second decade were the end of the eight-year war with Iraq and the death of Grand Ayatollah Khomeini, the founder and dominant personality within the IRI, in 1989. Both events disturbed the balance of the existing social, political and economic order.

Economic problems

Economic problems ranged from high inflation to unemployment, mass migration to the cities, growing corruption within the administration, underproduction, too inefficient utilisation of industrial capacity and lack of basic foods (especially wheat and rice). Also, the fall in oil prices and decrease in oil exports from the pre-revolutionary level resulted in low foreign exchange earnings. These problems were made worse by a dramatic population increase. However, the greatest challenge was the ad hoc management of the wartime economy and the regime's inability to decide on a method for the development of economic and social policy, and whether the policy should be centralised and state-run or left to the decision of the private sector, or both. The key issue was the level of integration of Iran into the international economy. Long-term survival of the regime hinged upon its success in rationalising the economy and improving living standards. After the death of Grand Ayatollah Khomeini a new team led by Hashemi Rafsanjani and Ayatollah Khamenei was quickly put in place and enacted several constitutional reforms aimed at strengthening the executive to the determinant of a multitude of competing centres of power. The team also eventually formulated an economic agenda in the form of a five-year (1989–1993) development plan. These reforms marked a new phase in the revolution, called the Second Republic, which, according to Kaveh Ehsani, abandoned the dream of an Islamic development model.[48]

The discussion about rebuilding Iran and the roles of both the government and the private sector was really a continuation of the ideological struggle between interventionists and the laissez-faire proponents from the IRI's early days. However, the current debate had more to do with political decisions in the future concerning the economic role of the government. Another key factor in the debate, from as early as September 1988, was the inclusion of foreign involvement offered from both Eastern and Western Europe and also Asia.

The debate was closely bound to the discussion about national reconciliation, some believing that an offer should be made to Iranian opponents of the regime in order to encourage them to contribute their talents towards rebuilding Iran. The most important issue was the financing of reconstruction and whether this should be undertaken by the government, the private sector, or both. As the private sector did not have sufficient resources the government relied heavily upon oil revenues. But as other OPEC members were over-producing, this lowered oil prices, which meant that Iran's oil revenues – from which came 90 per cent of the state budget – averaged less than US$10 billion for the year. The solution was for Iran to align its foreign policy with its economic needs. This meant it had to gain influence over the limiting of output in OPEC, which would increase oil prices. To achieve this it was necessary to re-establish relations with the GCC, and particularly Saudi Arabia.

A long-term industrialisation strategy was needed to reduce this dependency, as was the persistent need to court the private sector for its resources, to enable reconstruction and reduce the size of the public and services sectors, as well as to expand the productive sectors, especially industry. To achieve a real structural transformation it was necessary to embark on comprehensive political and legal reforms that would allow Iran to replace oil as the income-generating basis of the national economy. Hence, as well as importing technology and hardware, it was important to build the social consensus necessary to mobilise available resources. This would have required the establishment of greater pluralism, national reconciliation, and some form of participatory democracy. However, as Ehsani observes, in the early 1990s Iran had no luck applying a long-term strategy; the resulting economic crisis is confirmation of this view. The economic crisis was the result of applying a selective version of a "mixed" economy on the basis of the Five-Year Plan and the policies recommended by the International Monetary Fund. This version rhetorically stressed the leading role of the private sector but did not include any real economic reform, especially regarding the tax system and privatisation process.

Iran's torpid economic performance has continued up to the present. Even despite re-emphasising the importance of privatisation in the Fourth Five-Year Economic Development Plan (2005–2010), it has only been since 2007, and by the Supreme Leader's request, that government officials have begun to speed up the implementation of the policies outlined in the amendment of Article 44, though there have been some efforts to apply privatisation more widely. The Second Republic did not hesitate to seek international loans and direct foreign investments; however, such efforts in the early 1990s were counteracted by the negative image of Iran held abroad exacerbated by its countenancing the death sentence on Salman Rushdie and its continued support of certain movements – e.g. Hizballah in Lebanon.

Other economic features of the Second Republic were as follows.

1) The significant effect of favourable international circumstances on Iran's economic performances – e.g. access to capital and technology for growth and development during 1988–1991 as an effective element in achieving many targets of the Plan – and, in contrast, Iran's failure to gain access to such facilities in the years 1991 to around 1997.
2) The lack of social reforms and poor management after 1991, which resulted in massive foreign debt, inflation and economic stagnation. After 1992 this resulted in urban riots, anti-government demonstrations and vocal criticism of the development policies. Also, while the trade deficit and foreign debt shot up, oil revenues remained lower than forecast. This exposed Iran's seriously neglected internal structural problems and poor grasp of the global economic situation, as well as the extent of Iran's international isolation.

The whole situation, which had divided Iranian society, far from providing national reconciliation, led to the acceleration of the delegitimisation of the regime, whose major slogan promised to eliminate the gap between poor and rich. The government's mishandling of the economy – which as Ehsani notes was the result of "a development strategy that emphasised growth over employment and export-oriented, government-owned industry over a privately-owned, grass roots national industrial base" – neutralised Iran's industrialisation efforts. Alongside US pressure on its allies not to reschedule Iran's debt or issue new credit, foreign investors were deterred by both the unstable economy and the insecurity of an unreformed political system.

Therefore, since 1993 Iran has experienced even more economic chaos due to poor political and economic leadership, a lack of government interest in applying real political and structural reforms, and the failure to formulate a long-term development strategy. The alternative Islamic model of development was not realised; in its place was created a model that, although generating popular and local initiatives, lacked the basic foundations of political and legal reforms.[49]

Socio-political issues
As mentioned earlier, the debate over reconstruction was closely bound to discussions concerning national reconciliation. Two major events in the Second Republic provided the regime with an opportunity to overcome its strategic problems. A major socio-political result of the end of the war and the new political atmosphere after the death of Grand Ayatollah Khomeini, according to many observers, was a new era of civil society discourse. This not only resulted in increasing awareness among the various social forces but also contributed to competition among political elites and the formation of new political groupings. Additionally, it caused the diffusion of social and political powers into multiple centres with the opportunity to share power through various efforts, bargains and pacts.

However, despite the advantages of the new political environment, the regime could not achieve its domestic or foreign policy goals. Domestically, this was due to the inability of the government to address sensible if controversial internal debates, especially regarding demands from secular Iranians for more cultural freedom, which were in contrast to the demands of the lower classes, or received criticism from religious sides asking for greater political tolerance.

Solutions like the "China model" were discussed and implemented during Rafsanjani's presidency, 1989–1997. The model aimed to liberalise the economy and improve people's livelihood, while maintaining sole control of political power. This was to be achieved by preoccupying the people with either the threat of foreign enemies or the promise of economic welfare. However, the model failed, just as it had done on similar occasions in 1925–1941 under Reza Shah and in 1941–1979 under Muhammad Reza Shah, and it is unlikely to work in Iran any time in the future. According to Abbas Milani, these failures were because, on the one hand, China has a strong industrial basis for its export sector and an impressive ability to attract foreign investment; in comparison, Iran has failed to export much more than oil and has a poor record in attracting foreign investments. On the other hand, economic needs are not the only ones in people's lives, especially in an era in which democracy has become an essential part of every nation's basic rights and demands. Milani points to historical evidence that economic riches not only lead to greater political demands but also provide the new affluent classes with the political, social and economic means to see their demands are met. This applies in Iran's vibrant civil society, which is far from dead.[50]

Hence, at the end of the second decade of the revolution, despite Iran's tactical stability, it was confronting serious strategic challenges, including: Rafsanjani's failure to develop a civil society based on social justice; incorporating a sizeable middle class with political knowledge; forming a free market economy system. Such failures prevented Iran from establishing a democratic society able to attract the essential investments needed to solve Iran's economic difficulties and endemic unemployment problems. It also resulted in the absence of the rule of law in government policy, which led to a system of regular corruption, economic incompetence, ideological impoverishment, interference in the private lives of citizens, socio-political intolerance, oppressive policy against dissidents,[51] millions of unemployed youth and the growth of the women's movement. All these issues, especially the last two, resulted in the second Khordad event at which the populace rejected existing policy and emphasised the need for real social, economic and specifically political reforms. This event ended with extraordinary support for Khatami's reforms in 1997. It was only after 1997 that civil discussions expanded from a small hesitant circle of intellectuals and assumed their current importance at the level of national politics in Iran.

Regarding Iran's foreign policy in the second decade of the revolution, there was a general wish to face domestic issues and economic problems by improving relations with the outside world and to change Iran's international relations. However, the multiplicity of power centres, the lack of a single centre for designing foreign policy, and the great dependency of external relations on politics within Iran dominated by rivalries and significant disagreements between left and right wings (later, reformist and conservatives forces) over domestic and foreign policies, all meant that vigorous debates among the factions prevented a clear foreign policy being formulated. As a result, Iran was not able to establish constructive and cooperative relations with the West, especially regarding its negative international image.

In sum, all internal and external challenges during the first two decades of the IRI decreased the regime's legitimacy, added imperativeness and motivated the democratic movement. But what helped to strengthen the tactical stability of the IRI was the continuance of Western, especially US, antagonistic policy, including long-term embargoes. This helped the regime to justify its failure to implement the revolutions' promises; by opposing the US it could still count on the support of some part of the population. As foreign threats increased, strong Iranian nationalism was added to the equation, strangling reforms and the democratic movement. Embargoes placed on Iran imposed heavy costs on the population. Meanwhile, according to Abbas Milani, domestic right-wing allies, particularly the *bonyads* and the IRGC, gained much benefit. They attained power, privilege and illicit gains through "import licenses" for embargoed goods. Without such embargoes, Iran could have integrated into the global economy, resulting in more legal and economic transparencies and the emergence of a more vibrant middle class, which would have strengthened the private sector and civil society.[52]

Domestic military: the role of military forces on Iran's society
Socio-politically
Historically, the Iranian military has always played a significant role in Iran's society. However, it is impossible to separate its security role from its role in domestic politics. As well as being used to secure national sovereignty, it has also been used to control the masses and strengthen the government – although the IRI has tried to limit its influence on

society and has purposely excluded it from everyday politics, like previous regimes.[53]

This study will first describe the military's role in the IRI's politics and then explore the question of whether the armed forces might be a threat to the regime or to the people. It also will consider their role in Iran's policy with respect to its difficulties in the PG. Particular consideration will be given to the increase of political strife and the surrounding ideological issues.

After the revolution one of the most important steps taken to institutionalise the regime was the establishment of the Islamic Revolution Guards Corps (IRGC), which gained a permanent position in the security of the regime. The IRGC offset the distrusted regular military at the beginning of the revolution and became a popular force during the diplomatic hostage crisis, which threatened a possible US invasion. Also, a huge number of volunteers (of the *Basij*) were trained by the IRGC and were established to fight Iraq as an auxiliary to frontline operations. In addition, these were used to confront the revolution's domestic threats and uphold Islamic norms in society.

The division of Iran's armed forces affected the unity of command, resulting in rivalry, and decreased the military's effectiveness. There were distinct differences in the methodology of the two branches regarding their preparation for war. The regular military focused on hardware, technology and the human component, while the IRGC concentrated on the human element, particularly ideological commitment and morale beliefs. However, the regime could develop a more balanced understanding of these various elements of the military.

The second decade of the revolution saw some success in the structural reform of the security system. This included integrating the visions and values of the regular army and those of the IRGC, allowing there to be more of a balance of power between the two forces. Examples of this include the establishment of the Ministry of Defence and Armed Forces Logistics (MODAFL), under which both the IRGC and the regular army were to operate, and choosing commanders from each side for the other organisation.

In the first decade of the revolution, all military forces were engaged with Iraq's invasion. Subsequently, they have been making preparations for the eventuality of a foreign attack, procuring and developing new armaments. In particular, they have also re-engaged with civilian plans.

[191]

The Artesh has done the latter both in strategic and practical terms. Strategically, it has emphasised its ability to defend Iran against its external enemies. It has also carefully given the impression that it has stayed above the factional politics of the regime not because it is unable to engage in national politics, but for the good of the nation. Practically, it has assisted civilian projects with the manpower and expert technical knowledge required, playing a central role in the reconstruction of those areas of the country damaged by the war and generally opening up access to its assets. The IRGC, as well as being massively involved in civil society plans, perceives itself as the vanguard of the revolutionary regime and feels that it has a right to intervene in internal politics. However, it has its own interpretation regarding what socio-political reforms are necessary. It has also reacted to political issues according to the makeup of the political leadership and the scale of the violence. For instance, despite massive popular support many among the IRGC and the *Basij* interpreted President Khatami's reforms "as challenges to the interests of those who have been loyal supporters of the Islamic Republic and defenders of the *Faqih*". Such interpretations, and even criticism of the president's reforms, are often encouraged by conservative political forces, which encourage radical groups like *Ansar-e Hezballah* and the *Basij* to become politically involved.[54] Both these factors have raised serious concerns to Iranian society as well as the defence system.

1) President Khatami's reform process became contentious within the defence establishment and its constituent parts in the *Entezamat* (the law and security enforcement agencies). Inaction towards it on the part of the political establishment could threaten the complex defence structure that had been so carefully created. In this regard, for example, the IRGC responded differently to the 1994 Qazvin riots and the July 1999 Tehran student riots. In the Qazvin riots, some IRGC officers refused to carry out orders that they thought were unnecessarily against the people, believing that the IRGC should not always defend the existing political regime when it is attacked by domestic pressure or criticism. However, during the 1999 student riots IRGC commanders publicly criticised President Khatami and his reforms, believing that his reforms were the cause of the riots and were endangering the regime.[55]

2)   From the social perspective, the IRGC's self-interpretations about the socio-political issues have been criticised by the Artesh, the intelligentsia and the reformists, who have maintained that the defence establishment should not have a view on political matters. These groups also voiced concern over the military's determining the fate of the country, fearing that the gap between Iranian society and its political leaders is likely to get wider as the IRGC becomes more involved in socio-political matters and Iran's youth grow in numbers and in culturally diversity. This factor may contribute to the country's tendency to secularise. As a result the regime's reliance on coercion as a mean of control may well increase. Iran's intelligentsia, however, prefers to avoid direct confrontation and will take any conciliatory means possible towards opposition.[56] Since the advent of Ahmadinejad's presidency and a concomitant increase in the IRGC's involvement in affairs of state, the problem has become all the more salient.

There are no signs that the armed forces are lacking in loyalty towards the regime, despite some differences of opinion and disputes between them. Traditionally, the armed forces have always had close ideological affinities to the conservative elements of the regime, and have far from presented a threat to them. Historically, the Artesh has always been dependent on a political master, and the political establishment has deliberately deprived it of having one. It would thus only interfere in internal politics in a situation of social chaos or where the government was facing near-collapse, as Byman (et al.) mentions. The IRGC leadership is closely allied to the regime, and is unlikely to become politically active against it. Furthermore, both the Artesh and the IRGC consider the stability of the regime to be the red line, though if the IRGC perceives a danger to Islamic or revolutionary values it may feel compelled to intervene. Although there is no serious dispute between them, the IRGC's leaders have different points of view regarding Iran's socio-political issues. According to Byman (et al.), "some believe that this can be done only through reform and openness, while others believe that such reforms pose a mortal threat to the character and nature of the Islamic Republic".[57]

As Byman (et al.) also remarks, there are concerns about the IRGC's inaction or slow response to social crises, which may be due to the large numbers in the IRGC's rank and file who are less ideological, more sympathetic to calls for reform, and are likely to prefer political discourse to the use of force. In addition, there has been a large presence of IRGC (and other pillars of the revolution) members' children at anti-establishment demonstrations – for instance, at the July 1999 student demonstrations in Tehran. This is of special concern because it is unclear how the IRGC would respond to the elite's splitting, particularly if those who currently support the Supreme Leader were divided. According to Byman (et al.), however, what is most unclear is how the IRGC would react to an extensive reform movement that was popularly supported by Iranians claiming to be upholding an Islamic system. It is hard to predict how the IRGC would react in the event of further riots like those in Qazvin in 1994 and Tehran in 1999. Whether or not it would support the official response would largely depend on the makeup of the political leadership and the scale of the violence. According to Byman (et al.), in an effort to respond to concerns regarding the IRGC's inaction or slow response to civil strife, the political leadership has formed special units (the Ashura, Zahra, Sayid-ul Shohoda battalions) specifically designed to handle problems of popular unrest.

Although there is consensus in Iran, the possibility of military intervention in Iranian politics has not been ruled out by analysts if certain red lines are crossed. These red lines include threats to the rule of the *Vali-e Faqih*, open disrespect of Grand Ayatollah Khomeini and his legacy, overly dramatic social reforms, and relations with the US and Israel. In the context of a process of socio-political and economic reform, these red lines are beginning to fade, however. In addition, as Byman (et al.) argues, despite the intervention that would ensue were these red lines to be crossed, Iran's military apparatus is likely to be a force for the stability of the country. Further, it is much harder to arrive at consensus on economic and social policies than on security policy, since there are more interests and revolutionary sensitive issues involved in the former.[58] However, arriving at a consensus on Iran's security policy is getting more difficult. This is due to the military and security organisations' (especially the IRGC, *Basij* and the police) greatly increased involvement in various political and economic projects in the country as well as the impact of their emphasis on cultural and religious issues.

However, provided that Iranian politics remain stable and avoid widespread strife, "the IRGC leadership would prefer to devote its attention to improving its military standards and competing more effectively with the Artesh".[59] Yet, the recent experience of "unified governance" after 2005 under the control of the conservatives has shown that the IRGC is not content with developing its military capabilities, but will also seek to secure for itself a wider and more influential role in Iranian society.

The IRGC already has a very influential economic network as a result of the privatisation of the economy in the 1990s. Its strong military-economic role was given a political dimension by the majority secured at the seventh parliamentary election for its members and the conservatives, and by Ahmadinejad's victory in the 2005 presidential election.

According to Byman (et al.), the probability of military intervention on the part of the major military forces (i.e. the IRGC and Artesh) is likely to increase if Iran's elite becomes increasingly divisive and political factionalism turns into widespread violence. If this view is correct, then such a scenario would in turn culminate in the armed forces' (especially IRGS, *Basij* and the police) increased interference in Iranian society. But such a reaction (including more direct interference, less tolerance, and the closure of the political space) would pave the way for more opposition, an increased tendency towards secularisation and even more direct public confrontation with the regime as well as with the military forces. The IRGC should recognise that aggressively opposing any reform of conservative policies would result in further aggravating its existing internal ruptures, galvanise its external opposition and lead to further marginalisation of its position.[60]

Economically

One of the major regional and domestic impacts of the Iran–Iraq war was the growth and empowerment of Iran's military forces' manpower. What was to be done with this during peacetime proved to be a major dilemma. Iraq used its surplus troops to wage another war against Kuwait. By contrast, Iran used the privatisation of its economy in the 1990s as a way to occupy a significant number its soldiers during peacetime, in order to prevent them from becoming embroiled in any anti-government activities such as coups.[61]

The soldiers were given various opportunities, including buying shares or working at local (as well as international) industrial, commercial and housing companies. This was achieved on a large scale – for example, by 2007 *Khatam-ol-Anbia* headquarters (known in English as Ghorb Khatam) had already completed more than 1,200 projects and had been contracted to work on 250 others.[62] This process gave the IRGC a strong economic network, which, especially since Ahmadinejad's presidency, it continues to enjoy. The conservative forces have thus been able to take advantage of the IRGC's economic influence in the struggle for absolute power. However, according to a former general manager of one of Iran's largest steel factories, this solution has created another problem – namely, involving troops in economic affairs risks abandoning in them the idea that the state is worth sacrificing oneself for.[63] While this has indeed been a problem, it is also true that military men tend to prefer military solutions and to that extent a sense of selflessness has remained.

Although the new situation benefited the IRGC's high ranks, many of its lower ranks, especially in the *Basij*, were left marginalised in the post-war reconstruction period. Ahmadinejad addressed this issue, which, together with his militant view of politics, re-enfranchised those feeling marginalised and ensured the IRGC's support during the presidential election. Today, this translates into a continued relationship between the IRGC and the presidency of mutual reinforcement and support. This relationship has meant that the IRGC has gained control of huge assets in the country and heightened its economic role, which began during Rafsanjani's administration. It has profited more than anyone from Ahmadinejad's election in 2005. For example, the government has awarded the IRGC (and its associate companies) in excess of US$3.4 billion to pursue engineering projects in the oil and gas industry, and in one case alone was given US$1.3 billion to pursue a civilian services project.[64]

The IRGC has been criticised by reformists for its lack of accountability and for its monopoly on contracts that no outside party can bid for and for which the IRGC does not necessarily have any expertise. Although this enormous economic role can partly be accounted for by the official distrust of foreign and private sector companies, these factors have, in recent years, fed speculation that the government's vast generosity in handing out contracts to the IRGC is fuelled by its increasing dependence on the IRGC and the need to pay back its dues incurred by the IRGC's support during Ahmadinejad's election. The international embargoes imposed upon Iran have also helped ensure the IRGC's economic domination, including in the energy sector. They have put obstacles in the way of international financing, which has given state-run companies the upper hand in their battle with private companies. According to Abbas Milani, they have also made it possible for IRGC's domestic allies, such as the right wing and the *bonyads*, to profit from the illegal trade of goods that, because of the embargo, have become hard-to-find commodities. Ending embargoes, as he suggests, would thus have a number of positive effects: it would reduce the power of radical right-wing groups, and it would challenge the IRGC's economic monopoly by encouraging international companies to do business in Iran, thus taking away the IRGC's concessions. As Milani concludes, this would thereby assist the development of an emerging middle class closely allied to the presently restrained democratic movement. If the international community would like to give Iran's process of democratisation a chance, it should end its sanctions upon it.[65]

Military development
Policies
Having been engaged in a revolution and a war, and having faced embargoes, Iran's military has been somewhat depleted. Its main focus since 1988 has not therefore been on expansion due to an increased willingness to use force but, rather, on the rebuilding and replacement of its forces in an effort to remedy its deficiencies, particularly with regard to technological advancement. Its arms programmes are designed to deter attacks from those parties whom it consider it is under potential military threat from, such as the US, Israel and, until 2003, Iraq.[66]

The official line following the revolution was that Iran no longer serves American interests in the PG and would discontinue all military agreements with the US. However, despite this and its handling of the war with Iraq, Iran has continually displayed a pragmatic side to itself with regard to its defence strategy, visible in both military procurements and domestic defence production. Soon after the end of the war, the government made it clear that the country's rearmament strategy was one of its main priorities, and increased the governmental budget for military expenditure. As explained earlier, since the Second Republic, Iran has been attempting to replace, rationalise and modernise its military structures as well as accelerate the development of its defence industries, partly engendered by a review of its rearmament strategy. A pragmatist-led move towards "moderation" in foreign policy properly began in the mid-1980s when President Rafsanjani himself made diplomatic visits to China and North Korea. The President's support enabled the pragmatists to begin to take fuller control of the country's military affairs, and between 1988 and 1992 they had managed to ensure that about a quarter to one-third of overall government expenditure was on defence and defence-related matters.[67] All this raises the general consideration of how and when Iran intends to use its growing military strength: is it becoming a source of regional concern, or does its military strategy merely reflect local realities and the regional arms race?

Rearmament
Under the Shah, most of Iran's weapons were imported from the West and Iran's military industry was limited to the assembly of such foreign weapons. After the Islamic revolution, Iran faced growing isolation and a weapons embargo imposed upon it by the West. This meant that Iran was subsequently dependent on a domestic arms industry lacking in technological expertise and thus had to also rely on military imports from various Eastern countries as well as its existing Western weaponry.

Iran has the lowest military budget in the PG and, due to continuing sanctions and economic problems, cannot compete in the region's arm race. Moreover, not only are its military imports overly disparate and of questionable quality, but it is also not guaranteed the long-term aftersales service required for aircraft and so forth, since exporters such as Russia, China and North Korea are susceptible to US pressure. Furthermore, it has had to abandon the idea that domestic arms production will provide a significant solution to these problems and has decreased its expenditure since the end of the Iran–Iraq war to less than one half of what it was spending previously. Although, according to certain sources, it continued to spend US$4 billion a year on its military,[68] in 1989, according to Michael Eisenstadt, the *majlis* allocated US$10 billion over a five-year-period for arms imports in support of its conventional arms build-up, for instance. It has sought to increase its role in the market for military technology (for which domestic arms production can serve as a medium) and powerful arms transfer; it is also using missiles and fast attack boats in order to become less dependent on problematic aircraft imports.[69]

Although Iran's rearmament since the end of the war in 1988 has been comprehensive, it has been limited due to the Western embargo and Iran's resultant inability to acquire exactly what it might have done had the embargo not been in place. As Terrence Taylor of the International Institute for Strategic Studies (IISS) puts it, "There is certainly an attempt to increase the capabilities of the Iranian military, although the full extent of it is not clear."[70]

The Iranian military is one of the largest in the region. It totals about 545,000 personnel, 420,000 of whom serve with the regular armed forces and 125,000 with the IRGC. It also includes a paramilitary volunteer force called the *Basij*, which is made up of 90,000 full-time uniformed members, up to 300,000 reservists, and a further 11 million men and women who could be mobilised. Despite its size, the Iranian military also spends less as a percentage of GNP than any other PG nation, except the UAE. Nevertheless, it has been described, for example by General John Abizaid, the US commander in the region, as the most powerful force in the ME.

Aside from the different problems regarding Iran's military already outlined, there is a general concern regarding Iran's attempt to develop its unconventional weapons. Despite the fact that Iran has publicly condemned the use of chemical weapons, from whose use it greatly suffered during the 1980–1988 Iran–Iraq war, and in that in 1997 it ratified the Chemical Weapons Convention, many worry about its intentions regarding unconventional weapons. As Chubin remarks, "Iran's policies are a product of various factors including its recent experience, its world view, its capabilities, the global and regional opportunities and its other values. Its intensions are thus variable although its inclination is fairly steady." He then concludes that Iran's strategic inclinations towards developing unconventional weapons are predictable.[71] Like Chubin, most Western analysts assume Iran's strategic weapons programme to be its top priority. Some, such as Eisenstadt, believe that in trying to develop its strategic weapons programme, Iran is displaying its wish to become the dominant power in the PG, as well as expressing how vulnerable it is feeling.[72] Others, Barry Rubin for instance, believe that Iran is pursuing the development of missiles and perhaps nuclear weapons as a cheaper substitute to fully addressing the needs of its run-down conventional military.[73]

Together with these assumptions, the lack of transparency in Iran's military statistics has further compounded suspicions, despite Tehran's denial of developing unconventional weapons. Iran's military capabilities are largely kept secret. Only in recent years have official announcements highlighted the development of weapons such as a large arsenal of missiles as well as its own tanks, armoured personnel carriers, submarines and a fighter plane (it is known that the IRGC is responsible for the development of Iran's military industry and for making procurements such as those listed earlier). However, despite allegations made by US officials, in its February 2006 report on Iran's nuclear programme, the International Atomic Energy Agency (IAEA) found no evidence to support the claim that Iran is developing nuclear weapons.

As Jerrold Green remarks, some Middle Eastern strategic analysts, such as Ahmed Hashim, have highlighted the fact that regional actors Israel and Pakistan have nuclear weapons, that some of Iran's northern neighbour states may be littered with stray former Soviet weapons, that the Arab states in the PG are protected by the US, and that the US as a consequence is militarily active all along the PG's coastline. According to such analysts, not only do these factors make Iran's nuclear ambitions likely, they also make them understandable. However, although Iran may well have the intention to develop WMDs, it has limited possibilities available to achieve this, rendering "reports of secret nuclear sites being built unsubstantiated". A major difficulty facing Iran's putative unconventional weapons programme has been acquiring the requisite technological expertise. While Russia and China have not altogether toed the US line, most countries, partly down to US pressure, have been unwilling to provide Iran with the assistance it needs in order to properly develop its nuclear and chemical weapons capabilities, as Green mentions. Iran is also likely to be mindful of Iraq's ill-destined putative nuclear programme which caused an Israeli air attack on its Osirak nuclear reactor and, following years of UN inspections, culminated in its eventual invasion by the US and its allies. This has meant that while most Middle Eastern strategic analysts agree that Iran could potentially become a nuclear power, they are uncertain as to how and when such a capability could surface.[74] This is specifically true following the release of a report of the US National Intelligence Estimate (NIE), in December 2007, which acknowledged that Iran has no weapons programme.

Defence role in the Persian Gulf
In general, particularly because Iran's economy is centred on the PG's

natural resources, the continuing presence of foreign forces in the region has resulted in Tehran feeling very threatened. This has led it to the conclusion that it should adopt a policy of strengthening its military capabilities dovetailed with a foreign policy that will deal with external threats (especially from the US) to change the regime, prevent another experience such as the unexpected eight-year war from occurring again, and will, as Brigadier General Rahim Safavi puts it, "better defend Islamic ideals and safeguard territorial integrity".[75]

As Chubin remarks, Iran's military weakness, which was in part due to US sanctions, as well as poor relations between the US and Iran, paved the way for an Iraqi invasion. Iraq perceived these as ideal conditions for it to attempt to change the balance of power in the PG and dominate the region. Iran's military weakness thus proved to be a destabilising force in the PG threatening instability for all interested parties. It is no surprise then that Iran felt the need to strengthen its military power after the revolution.[76]

The US strategy also appears premised on a faulty analysis of Iranian politics. The US argument has been that putting pressure on the regime will expedite a change in Iranian policy as well as restoring the respect in the US necessary for a more balanced dialogue to take place. US strategy has thus been to increase its military presence in the PG, place embargoes on Iran and hint at intentions towards regime change, all in an effort to prove to Iran that it means business. However, such a strategy is more likely to retard than accelerate an Iranian policy change; all it has achieved is to make Iran feel under threat and that it must engage in escalating its own military agenda as well as adopt a more radical and sceptical policy towards the US. The same goes for the policy of exaggerating Iran's military threat to its neighbours in the PG, which has had the added disadvantage of increasing the destabilisation of the region by encouraging an arms race in the GCC. GCC countries have felt compelled to purchase expensive, and sometimes unnecessary, weapons, and the recent emphasis on Iran's nuclear ambitions (albeit denied by Tehran) has led many states to consider undertaking their own nuclear projects (though they have announced plans for achieving nuclear energy, they have not announced any intention to develop nuclear weapons). Such a potential arms race in the ME is highly unlikely to lead to regional security and only benefits Western arms companies.

As has been discussed, although Iran's military growth has been fairly extensive, it is built upon foreign and sometimes incompatible weapons system imports and still has a long way to go. It is also questionable whether Iran's unhealthy economy is capable of enabling it to compete with its wealthy neighbours in the region. For instance, in 1996 Saudi Arabia's defence budget was US$13.9 billion; Israel's was US$7 billion, while Iran's was only US$3.4 billion. This has led many analysts to believe that Iran's displays of military strength are merely cases of diplomatic posturing born out of a sense of its own weakness in the face of overwhelming US military strength.[77]

A confrontational US policy also has some internal impacts. Under heavy pressure from the US, Iranian nationalist and radical anti-foreigner sentiments, as well as government support for these, are likely to increase. As a result, the government will come under decreasing criticism and be able present domestic failures as the effect of such external threats, thereby assuring that the domestic process of democracy continues to be in trammels. In the words of a prominent reformist, Behzad Nabavi: "Those who threaten and pressure from the outside forget that we still think in traditional ways about national sovereignty. If we have to choose between individual freedom and national sovereignty, we will choose the latter. We hope we don't have to choose."[78]

Iran's perception, as articulated by Ayatollah Khamenei, that the US will not be satisfied until it goes back to the same patron–client relationship it enjoyed during the Shah's regime, is shaping some of its foreign policy. In particular, it has allowed the armed forces and intelligence services to influence many of its decisions, especially in regard to its security challenges.[79]

Much of Iran's use of the armed forces in pursuing its foreign policy goal in the PG is really just "diplomatic posturing" on the part of Tehran. As Rathmell observes, the intensification of Iran's military exercises and procurement (constituting part of the aim of becoming the dominant power in the region, as mentioned in the 20-year development plan) are attempts to assert Iran's right to the PG. Or, as Chubin argues, they are there for the dual purpose of reminding the Arab states that Iran is a major power, and reminding the Americans that an attack on Iran would be against their interests.[80]

By developing relations with its neighbours in the PG, Iran has sought to encourage them to enter into collective security arrangements that exclude outside powers. It has also assured them that "as long as the territorial integrity of Iran is not threatened, the military and defence power of Iran will not be a threat to any country" (Mohsen Rezaei, then Commander in Chief of IRGC) while at the same time warning them of its slogan "security for all or for none".[81]

As Eisenstadt observes, Iran's military build-up is motivated by a number of factors: first, by its perception that it faces threats from regional and non-regional potential enemies. Second, by its religious and nationalistic desire to become a regional power. The IRI believes that it ought to play a major role in world affairs and that, as the defender of the interests of all Muslims and the guardian of Iran's national interests, it should be treated as a beacon for revolutionary Islam throughout the world. Finally, by its leadership's belief that Iran is geographically optimally situated to become the dominant power in the PG. After all, it has the largest coastline of any PG state and has vital interests in the region.[82]

Iran has pursued a dual policy of economic and political engagement with its non-Arab neighbours and a sceptical, unstable attitude towards the GCC. This, together with an inability to estimate Iran's true military capabilities due to a lack of transparency, has fuelled concerns and uncertainties on the part of the GCC and the West.[83] Added to these concerns is Iran's desire to dominate the PG, in order to have a more powerful position regarding outstanding border and territorial disputes with its Arab PG neighbours, and its willingness to considerably influence oil production levels and prices, Iran having the ability to close the Strait of Hormuz, through which about 20 per cent of the world's oil flows.[84] However, analysts do not believe that the Iranian army is in a position where it could successfully carry out any meaningful invasion. It could pose only a limited threat to GCC targets through its missiles and the laying of mines by submarines.

In the event of a US attack, Iran has announced its reservation to attack US interests around the world as a means of defending itself. Ayatollah Khamenei, for instance, on different occasions throughout 2007, stated that a US invasion of Iran would cause it to target US interests worldwide. Iran has portrayed the current situation as a win-win case for itself, as Ayatollah Khamenei has stated: "If the US doesn't attack us we will become stronger. And if it does attack us, we will become more united and find a lot of friends throughout the world"; the US "is the main loser because it boycotts Iran".[85] From the US' perspective, increases in Iran's military activity as well as the potential use of terrorism as a means of hitting its targets around the world constitute a great threat. Meanwhile, Iran sees its current foreign policy as vital to the prevention of any threat to its sovereignty, even if it is in reality only political posturing. The result is an escalating security chain that threatens to worsen regional stability and assures neither regional nor global security.

In sum, disturbance in the military balance of power in the PG has been followed by an unstable situation, which has consequently proved to be a threat to all internal and external players. Such instability has also attracted foreign forces to the region in order to protect their interests. This has caused complaints from some regional states and led to a rise in anti-Western sentiments among people in the whole region. It has isolated weaker players and compelled them to implement more radical policies, which in turn has encouraged all sides to build up their military capabilities and has engendered a new arms race. Although such a situation has set the scene perfectly for arms suppliers, it has created a more unstable climate by causing regional players to have increasingly antagonistic and sceptical attitudes towards one another. Under such circumstances, a violent reaction from internal or external players is inevitable. These parties may use invasion or terrorist attacks as a way of implementing their foreign policy objectives, both of which would affect the regional, as well as the international, community.

The prevailing view on US foreign policy is solely coloured by security and military concerns. Thus, only those who place more emphasis on their security and military capabilities can follow their foreign policy goals in such a situation. So the US could only enter into dialogue with those who have power in these two fields, as Akbar Ganji argues.[86]

Facing such an attitude, the empowerment of military forces, especially the IRGC, in the decision-making system of Iran looks like an inevitable solution to the country's survival. Even though Iran has not announced an intention to seek nuclear weapons, the current situation, together with the US' continued threats of regime change, makes it reasonable for it to do so in an effort to defend itself in a region where some of its neighbours have, or may subsequently develop, nuclear capabilities and the support of the US.

The IRI is also partly responsible for the current tense political situation. It has failed to establish a stable relationship with its neighbours or the West (especially the US), or to acknowledge Western interests in this geopolitical region. It has also failed to reconcile its differences with the West and assure it of its vital interests in the PG. This has meant that Iran's goal of establishing collective regional security arrangements excluding foreign powers has not been achieved, and has therefore contributed to the wider presence of foreign forces.

Nevertheless, the question is: what is the reason for the US' strategy in this region, especially its antagonistic policy towards Iran – particularly considering the negative impact US embargoes have had towards the security and stability of the region as a sub-system of the ME, significant to the international community? This is a question that featured prominently in the old discussion between the EU and US regarding Iran, with the EU taking the opinion that threatening, or indeed using, force against Iran would only make the situation deteriorate, since crises work like chains: one instance generates several more.

Perhaps there are two lines of response to this question. The first is that US decision-makers are ignorant of regional sensitivities and issues. If this is true, which is unlikely, the US should discontinue its insistence on pursuing the dream of global leadership. The second is that they are aware of the negative consequences an antagonistic policy may harbour, but that they are motivated by some hidden political or economic agenda. For instance, perhaps the secret US agenda is to turn Iran into the domestic ME enemy in an effort to solve the problem of Israel's regional recognition. This would not only deflect attention away from Israel, but, in maintaining a regional enemy, would create a scenario suitable for the continuation of a divide-and-rule strategy to implement US foreign policy objectives, including its desired effects on oil prices and increasing arms sales.

If something like this is the case, which looks more likely than the first response, then all the US allegations concerning ME states' military ambitions drastically begin to lose credibility – particularly since its antagonistic policy and foreign policy's prevailing view on security and military concerns has created a haven for undemocratic governments as well as strengthening the military's role in the whole socio-political life of ME nations. The US should thus stop pretending that it is trying to instigate democracy in the ME.

In sum, despite all the foreign threats and antagonistic policies against the IRI since the revolution, the major challenges to its survival have been internal issues. In particular, the IRI should be extremely worried about political and economic instability as well as the social pressures in people's lives. Tension in foreign relations (especially with its neighbours in the PG and also the West, particularly the US), as well as international isolation and sanctions, which have resulted in Iran's failure to integrate in the global economy (e.g. not becoming a member of WTO), could constitute a threat to bring the regime down. If uneven economic and political development in Iranian society forced the Shah's regime to be overthrown, the threat to the new regime cannot be ignored or underestimated.

Therefore, the regime's survival depends upon opening up the political system to more democratic participation and economic reforms in order to address its strategic weakness. As Abbas Milani remarks, the IRI is relatively stable despite serious problems such as: having millions of unemployed youths; peoples' exclusive dependence on patronage and subsidies of the regime whose transparency and ability in economic policies have been criticised and are under question even by statesmen; its failure to curb growing poverty, despite the wide wealth sources in Iran; and the existence of women's and democratic movements that are a response to unanswered demands. Despite existing tensions and disagreements between political groups, such as the regime's divine legitimacy in contrast to popular sovereignty, a popular uprising, or less violent government change, seems very unlikely at the moment; a view shared by Abbas Milani and other observers.[87]

However, the regime's failure to establish a government based on the rule of law, or to deliver on the revolution's reform promises, as well as temporary and unsuccessful policies like the "China model", will not help it displace the political demands made upon it. As Abbas Milani also observes, the new regime's supposed stability is comparable to that which the Shah enjoyed in the mid-1970s when none of the major Western powers (nor the Shah and his powerful secret service, SAVAK) had any suspicion at all that there was a revolution to follow. Therefore, because of the revolution in particular, democracy is a necessity, not a luxury, for Iran more than for any other state in the ME. Democracy, and its promise to attract the investments Iran needs to put an end to high unemployment, is the only solution to its huge economic problems. External pressures and antagonistic policies, such as the threat of invasion and the imposition of sanctions, risk further postponing the advent of such democracy and the integration of Iran in the global economy.[88] Furthermore, the IRI's authorities should not, as Mohsen Milani mentions, assume they have more time than the previous Iranian leaders had to implement their promises.[89]

Domestic issues are the pivotal problems facing Iranian society. Hence, as long as satisfying its people, the provision of wealth (as a major element in the success of a society,[90] as well as a significant element of power and influence), and preparations towards democracy (giving the government soft and hard power as well as political legitimacy) are not the top priority of the IRI, Iran cannot become a stable regional power. This will especially be the case if Iran fails to reduce tension in its relations with its neighbours in the PG and with the West – particularly the US. Military strength with the support of the masses alone (assuming that Iran's foreign policy is supported by the people of other countries) cannot help in this regard without the administrational lever of the governments with whom it has tensions.

Democracy is indispensable to Iranian society with its long history of independent thought. However, implementing democracy takes time and requires patience and sustained effort. It faces three major challenges in Iran: first, in overcoming people's impatience, especially on the part of the youth; second, in overcoming anti-Western sentiments that the conservative and more religious factions of society wish to instil; and finally, in the reconciliation it must attain with *Sharia* law. Facing up to the last two challenges means facing up to the perennial social tension between the demands of the traditionalists and modernists – an issue that the reformist government of President Khatami also had to address.

The US' use of military force to attain its foreign policy objectives in the ME has helped to ensure the empowerment of deep-rooted security and intelligence organisations in the whole socio-political life of Iran, as well as in other countries in the region. This has in turn slowed down and encumbered Iran's domestic process of democratisation, the potential impact of which should not be underestimated as has been evidenced since the presidency of Khatami.

Thus, like any other country, a shift in Iran's political climate in particular can only be achieved if it is initiated within the framework of domestic debate. Attempts to impose it from outside will only stifle the process of change; however, the international community could support democratisation by encouraging an atmosphere that is germane to such a process (for instance, by ending the current embargoes and thereby helping Iran solve its economic problems and actively participate in the global system). This means that the internal challenges facing Iran could translate into security concerns. These issues, together with the IRI's relative political immaturity, show that Iranian society needs time to educate itself about its rights, needs, and the methods (such as establishing powerful parties) it can use to achieve its goals.[91]

As Bernard Hourcade observes, "Today we are facing a new political landscape with the emergence of a new generation of leaders and political actors [who have] (…) a new political history, originating from the Islamic Revolution and not from the imperial regime."[92] This new generation of leaders should be given a chance to develop the kinds of reform that are needed, especially since these will only work if they are sensitive to local cultural and religious norms, such as being consistent with *Sharia* law.

Conclusion

Iran's domestic history during most of the latter part of the nineteenth century consisted of efforts to defend itself against British and Russian attempts to dominate the country as part of the "Great Game". Russia, Britain and later the US helped to end Iran's democratic revolutions by a series of occupations, by supporting undemocratic, totalitarian regimes, intervening when such regimes were under internal threat, and by overthrowing nationalist and democratic governments in Iran. Based on their geopolitical world-picture, not only did they have a political vested interest in doing so, but also they gained economically from it. Although all of these factors contributed to a growing antipathy towards the West, Iran continued to serve Western interests under pro-Western regimes like the Shah's. However, after the Islamic revolution in 1979, when Tehran discontinued such a pro-Western policy, the West re-engaged its old policy of interference in Iran's internal affairs and has since made numerous attempts to depose the existing regime through war, isolation, sanctions and threats of direct invasion. Therefore, Iran's foreign policy, and its ability to achieve its objectives as well as its political orientations, has mainly depended on its security environment, which is influenced by the international system. In a cooperative international environment and through the use of a *détente* policy, imperial Iran was able to build

CBM with the PG states and assure the extra-regional powers that their interests in the PG were being maintained. This meant that the presence of foreign forces in the region was prevented. However, the emergence of the IRI was not welcomed by the superpowers, who found that the IRI was disturbing their influence and the balance of power in the ME. The new republic, with its commitment to political Islam and revolutionary rhetoric, was perceived to be a threat to the Arab PG states (the CBM with whom were thereby in decline) and was unable to ensure the maintenance of the extra-regional powers' interests in the region. These factors, as well as policies ranging from a revolutionary stance to pragmatism evidenced in the three decades of the IRI's existence, provided a good pretext for extra-regional direct interference in PG states' affairs and regional military presence.

As Mohsen Milani observes, this was especially the case for the US, for whom the demise of the USSR had threatened the conceptualisation of the world as consisting of two rival camps of good and evil. The demise of the USSR had also created a geopolitical crisis for the US and some of its allies in the ME, since some of the latter had lost their strategic value, which could only be regained if they became influential in dealing with a new threat. Thus, the threat posed by Iran was greatly exaggerated in order to replace that posed in the eyes of Arabs by Israel. After the end of the Cold War the Iranian and Islamic ideological threat was played up to replace that posed by Soviet Communism, much to the benefit of US–PG states' arms sales, which were now given a reason to continue.[93]

There is a sense in which both Iran and the US were in a dilemma: both sides needed each other but realised that positively engaging with one another came at a price. As Abbas Milani remarks, the IRI needed US approval in order to secure the flow of capital necessary for Iran's economic problems to subside, as well as a guarantee that the US would not seek to overthrow the regime; however, much of the regime's legitimacy rested on its opposition to the US. Similarly, the US needed to engage with Iran, qua influential PG power, in order to secure regional stability and thereby US interests; however, Washington feared that engaging with Iran would strengthen a regime it opposed. The US has been unable to develop an effective and permanent strategy towards Iran; its policies have been reactionary and have thus only lasted until the next crisis.[94] The IRI did make some attempts to improve US–Iranian relations. For instance, it supported the liberation of Kuwait after the

Iraq invasion, and it has had a positive role in Afghanistan. Also, in order to face its greatest challenges (reconstruction and economic problems), and although the rise of the IRI was considered to have "subdued those voices in favour of pursuing an accommodation with the US",[95] a pragmatic Iran was prepared to forge such relations. However, in doing so, it faced two problems: first, it was not willing to give up its policy regarding independence; and second, conservative forces, in a climate of relative internal instability, wanted to be seen as the ones who rebuilt relations with the US; they did not want a rival camp, especially the leftists/reformists, to have this accolade.

The US, however, did not display any intention of reciprocating such conciliatory gestures and mending its frustrated relationship with Iran. This meant that the bilateral relationship between them remained stagnant. It also meant that the Arab PG states were being persuaded to take up a similarly isolationist stance towards Iran. The corollary of all this has been that the IRI has had to operate in a difficult international environment, which has pushed it towards more independent policies and has delayed its better and closer integration with the West.

Three decades of such a policy has caused many crises in the ME and a growing fear on the part of Arab PG rulers regarding their political stability. It has also caused an increase in anti-Western (especially anti-US) sentiments, which has highlighted that, first, the ME/Arab PG states are tired of the economic and socio-political impacts of regional crises and that even though the instability of the situation has been exaggerated by the US, they prefer a peaceful atmosphere. Second, the importance of Iran's role in the security and stability of the region has been stressed; by ignoring and diminishing its role, the security of both regional and extra-regional states is threatened, as well as effects on the oil supply and market. Due to Iran's geopolitical situation, all its political regimes, despite their differing political orientations, including those both before and after the revolution, have converged on what Iran's general security policy should be. This is that Iran should develop its natural role in the PG's security.

The regional importance of Iran makes it vital for there to be relations between it and those extra-regional powers with interests in the region. Attempts to circumvent this necessity, such as the US' strategy of placing the GCC instead of Iran as the region's most influential player, have not been successful. The IRI perceives Iran's value in this respect, as well as the US need to cooperate with it in order to solve its crisis in Iraq, for instance. The IRI has, in this recognition, shown a diminishing tendency to accept US pressure – for instance, regarding its nuclear programme. The lesson to be learned from the experience of the most geopolitical region in the world, the PG, is that in order to attain regional security it is imperative that the major regional and external players have suitable relations. No other alternative strategy would be able to fulfil regional and ultra-regional interests, and meet security concerns.

However, what Iran needs is coalition-building with the West to feature in its foreign policy. As Sariolghalam observes, "Iran's unique political ideology and foreign policy objectives prevents it from entering into meaningful coalition with other countries in its neighbourhood as well as in the entire Muslim World." Thus, the main way it can acquire technology, wealth, science and power in the contemporary world is via the West. This is why, as Sariolghalam continues, the IRI needs to reach a consensus on the issue of relations with the West. Only by doing so can Iran grow and develop economically, improve its global image, and secure its national interests[96] – a matter that can pave the way for stable CBM with the PG states too.

The antagonistic relationship of Iran and the West has provided the GCC with the opportunity to take advantage of Tehran's political isolation to sort the issue out in a way that has benefited its members. For example, even Iran's territorial disputes became a lever for the GCC on different political occasions. Before the revolution, the PG Arab states placed little emphasis on the islands dispute because of their Western orientation and fear of the Shah, who was supported by the US. After the revolution, however, the advent of the IRI's revolutionary rhetoric made Arab states more frightened of Iran and so they increased their claims regarding the islands on different occasions as leverage against Iran.

The lack of relations between Iran and the US, as the major regional and ultra-regional powers in the PG, has been a major obstacle to the establishment of a stable regional security system. This has resulted in more international pressure being put on Iran. This international pressure has helped the IRI to justify its domestic failure and to keep the country unified. Due to its geostrategic position, its Islamic political ideology, its energy resources and its nuclear programme, Iran is currently at the forefront of international concerns. However, as Hourcade observes, being the focus of such attentions has made Iran work towards independence; its perception of the balance of power has made Iran become more confident that it will not be attacked by external players. This has also united the country against the West, making it harder for it to integrate with the rest of the world, the opposite of what the international community would have liked. Iran is now protected from the imposition of heavy sanctions due to its building strong and efficient ties with several different countries, organisations, and economic and oil lobbies.[97] In the interest and security of all, the need to have CBM between Iran and the West (especially the US) should therefore now be understood.

By applying the outcome of the previous chapters dealing with the different security concerns and different perceptions of regional and ultra-regional players of what constitutes a threat to regional security, in the next and final chapter this book will study the future shape of security arrangements in the PG, addressing the need for a stable and peaceful structure of relationships to provide security.

Notes

1. Shahram Chubin and Sepehr Zabih, *The foreign relations of Iran: A developing state in a zone of great-power conflict* (Berkeley, Los Angeles, and London: University of California Press, 1974).
2. Daniel Byman, Shahram Chubin, Anoushiravan Ehteshami and Jerrold Green, *Iran's security policy in the post-revolutionary era* (USA: National Defense Research Institute (RAND), 2001), xi, 1.
3. Rouhollah Ramazani, *Iran's foreign policy 1941–1973; A study of foreign policy in modernizing nations* (USA: The University Press of Virginia, 1975), 442, 444.
4. Chubin and Zabih, op. cit., 4.
5. Daniel Byman (et al.), op. cit., 2.
6. James Rosenau, "Introduction: political science in a shrinking world". In James Rosenau (ed.) *Linkage politics: Essays on the convergence of national and international systems* (New York: The Free Press, 1969), 1–17; also James Rosenau, "Toward the study of national-international linkages". In ibid., 44–63.
7. Details in Chubin and Zabih, op. cit.
8. Ibid., 18.
9. Ramazani, op. cit., 452–453.
10. Chubin and Zabih, op. cit., 300–304.
11. Hooshang Amirahmadi, "Iran's power structure", *Internet Concepts*, http://www.iranian.com/Mar96/Opinion/AmirIran.html (accessed 24 August 2006).
12. Ibid.
13. Amir Ali Nourbakhsh (July–August 2004), "Who calls the shots in Iran's foreign policy offensive?", *Iran Focus* [a political-economic monthly publication], http://216.109.125.130/search/cache?p=iran+domestic+sources+of+foreign+policy&fr=FP-tab-web-t500&toggle=1&ei=UTF-8&u=www.iranexpert.com/2004/foreignpolicy1august.htm&w=iran+domestic+sources+foreign+policy&d=fOZZByQ8NRGN&icp=1&.intl=us (28 August 2006; can no longer be accessed).
14. Ibid.
15. Byman (et al.), op. cit., xiii.
16. Ibid., xiii–xii.
17. Ibid.
18. Nourbakhsh, op. cit.
19. Byman (et al.), op. cit., xii.
20. Houman Sadri, "Trends in the foreign policy of revolutionary Iran", *Journal of Third World Studies,* vol. 15, no. 1, April 1998.
21. Byman (et al.), op. cit., xi.
22. Chubin and Zabih, op. cit., 296.
23. Cited in the foreword section of Ali Ansari, *Iran, Islam and democracy: The politics of managing change* (London: Royal Institute of International Affairs, 2000), vii.
24. Ervand Abrahamian, *Iran between two revolutions* (Princeton, New Jersey: Princeton University Press, 1982), 426–427.
25. Ibid.
26. Ibid., 427.

27 Nikki Keddie, *Roots of revolution* (New Haven and London: Yale University Press, 1981), 240–224; also Mohsen Milani, *The making of Iran's Islamic revolution: From monarchy to Islamic republic* (Boulder, San Francisco, and Oxford: Westview Press, 1994), 64.
28 Mossadegh, who was the prime minister of Iran from 1951 to 1953, aimed to establish democracy and end the foreign presence in Iranian politics, especially by nationalising the Anglo–Iranian Oil Company's (AIOC) operations in Iran. His leadership resulted in the Shah's exile from the country. He was removed from power in a coup d'état on 19 August 1953, organised and carried out by the US Central Intelligence Agency (CIA) at the request of the British Secret Intelligence Service, MI6.
29 Details in, e.g., M. Milani, op. cit., 70; and Asaf Hussain, *Islamic Iran: Revolution and counter* (London: Frances Printer Publishers, 1985), 44–45.
30 Keddie, op. cit., 160.
31 Ibid., 160, 170.
32 Statistical details in M. Milani, op. cit., 60.
33 Details in ibid., 61.
34 Ibid.
35 Abrahamian, op. cit., 435–441.
36 Chubin, *Security in the Persian Gulf 4: The role of outside powers* (UK: Gower, 1982), 10, 13–14.
37 Ibid., 11.
38 Steven Canby, "The Iranian military: political symbolism versus military usefulness". In Husein Amirsadeghi (ed.), *The security of the Persian Gulf* (London: Croom Helm, 1981), 101–102.
39 Chubin, *Security in the Persian Gulf 4*, op. cit., 14–15.
40 Adam Przeworski, "Institutionalisation of voting patterns and mobilisation", *American Political Science Review*, vol. 69, March 1975, p. 67, cited in Hussain, op. cit., 119.
41 M. Milani, op. cit., 246.
42 Abrahamian, op. cit., 533, 535.
43 Among many, see Fred Halliday, "Year IV of the Islamic Republic", *MERIP Reports*, no. 113, *Iran since the Revolution* (March–April 1983), 7.
44 Ibid., 7–8.
45 Eric Hooglund, "The Islamic Republic at war and peace", *Middle East Report*, no. 156, *Iran's Revolution Turns Ten* (January–February 1989), 12.
46 According to some sources the debate over power distribution and economic policy in Iran, which began in 1986, sufficiently stalled the IRP party for members to disband for political expediency.
47 Fred Halliday, "The revolution's first decade", *Middle East Report*, no. 156, op. cit., 20; also Halliday, "Year IV of the Islamic Republic", op. cit., 4, 7.
48 Kaveh Ehsani, "Tilt but don't spill: Iran's development and reconstruction dilemma", *Middle East Report*, no. 191, November–December 1994, 16–17.
49 Details in ibid., 11–20.
50 Abbas Milani, "US foreign policy and the future of democracy in Iran", *The Washington Quarterly*, vol. 28, no. 3, summer 2005, 47.
51 Such as the series of assassinations known as "serial killing", which eliminated dissident political and intellectual figures.

52 For details see Abbas Milani, op. cit., 49–50.
53 Byman (et al.), op. cit., 53–54.
54 Ibid., 46.
55 Ibid.
56 Ibid., 47–48.
57 Such a difference was indicated in a poll in 1997. "Reportedly, 73 percent of the IRGC and 70 percent of the Basij voted for Khatami." Ibid.
58 Details in ibid., 48–52.
59 Ibid.
60 Ibid., 52.
61 For details see International Crisis Group (ICG), "Iran: Ahmadi-Nejad's Tumultuous Presidency" (Tehran/Brussels), no. 21, 6 February 2007, ICG interviews in Iran, Tehran, 2006.
62 According to Brigadier-General Abdolreza Abed, deputy commander of IRGC and head of Ghorb, cited in ICG, op. cit., 13.
63 ICG interview, Tehran, 9 July 2006, op. cit.
64 ICG interview, former senior diplomat, Tehran, 6 August 2006, op. cit., 12–13.
65 More details in Abbas Milani, op. cit., 49–50.
66 Shahram Chubin, "Iran's military intentions and capabilities". In Patrick Clawson (ed.), *Iran's strategic intentions and capabilities* (Washington, D. C.: Institute for National Strategic Studies – National Defense University, 1994), 73–75; also Michael Eisenstadt, "DÉJÀ VU all over again? An assessment of Iran's military buildup". In ibid., 118.
67 Ibid., Ehteshami, *After Khomeini: The Iranian second republic* (London: Routledge, 1995), 168–169, cited from *Kayhan Havai*, 29 January 1992.
68 Cordesman (30 October 2000), http://www.iranwatch.org/privateviews/CSIS/csis-iranarmstransf-103000.pdf.
69 More details in Eisenstadt, op. cit., 99; and Darius Bazargan, "Iran: politics, the military and Gulf security", *MERIA Journal*, vol. 1, no. 3, September 1997.
70 Bazargan, op. cit.
71 Chubin, "Iran's military intentions and capabilities", op. cit., 66.
72 Eisenstadt, op. cit., 101.
73 Barry Rubin, "The Persian Gulf after the Cold War: old pattern; new era", *MERIA Journal*, vol. 3, no. 2, June 1999, http://www.biu.ac.il/SOC/besa/meria/journal/1999/issue2/jv3n2a6.html (accessed 23 September 2004).
74 More details in Jerrold Green, "Iran and Gulf security". In David Long and Christian Koch (eds), *Gulf security in the twenty-first century* (Abu Dhabi, UAE: The Emirates Center for Strategic Studies and Research, 1997), 22–24.
75 Bazargan, op. cit., cited from the Iranian news agency IRNA quoting the Revolutionary Guards' Deputy Commander, Rahim Safavi.
76 Chubin, *Security in the Persian Gulf 4*, op. cit., 30, 35.
77 Bazargan, op. cit.
78 ICG, op. cit., 25.
79 Byman (et al.), op. cit., 53.
80 See Bazargan, op. cit., for citations.
81 Ibid.
82 Eisenstadt, op. cit., 95–96.
83 Green, "Iran and Gulf security", op. cit., 21.

84 See Eisenstadt, op. cit., 95.
85 ICG, op. cit., 25.
86 Akbar Ganji, speaking in the Council on Foreign Relations of the US, in 2007.
87 Abbas Milani, op. cit., 45–46, 49.
88 Ibid., 45.
89 Mohsen Milani, op. cit., 65.
90 For example, Adam Smith argues in his *The Wealth of Nations* that the notion of justice is inextricably allied to that of wealth, so that a government cannot provide justice to its people without eliminating their poverty and evenly distributing its revenues. He also argues that a political economy should make it possible for both the people and the sovereign to enrich themselves, and he criticises those groups who use their political influence to manipulate the government in order to gain economic advantage for themselves. This analysis seems relevant to the situation vis-à-vis Iran's economic problems, and suggests a reason why Iran's economic policy is not working.
91 See Bernard Hourcade, "Iran's internal security challenges". In Walter Posch (ed.) *Iranian Challenges*, Chaillot Paper (Institute for Security Studies – EU) no. 89, May 2006, pp. 41–41, http://www.iss-eu.org/chaillot/chai89.pdf (13 June 2006; can no longer be accessed); also Abbas Milani, op. cit., 50.
92 Hourcade, op. cit., 42, 57–58.
93 Mohsen Milani, op. cit., 243.
94 Abbas Milani, op. cit., 41, 55.
95 Analysts like Calabrese, op. cit., 7.
96 Mahmood Sariolghalam, "Theoretical renewal in Iranian foreign policy (Part II)", *Discourse; an Iranian Quarterly*, vol. 3, no. 4, (spring 2002), II, 58. Ibid.
97 Hourcade, op. cit.

9

Final conclusion: shape of security arrangements in the Persian Gulf

Introduction

The intention in this chapter is to provide a conceptual and analytical foundation for a discussion about the future shape of security arrangements in the PG in order to address the need for a stable and peaceful structure of relationships that provides security for all littoral states, as well as protecting the interests of the external powers. To this end, three fundamental schools of thought in international security will be briefly examined in order to explain the major strategic choices available to both the PG and the external powers' decision-makers. The schools of thought that will be explored are: the realist school; the hegemonic or counterproliferation school; and the neo-liberalism or cooperative school.

Through a historical and theoretical study of the security systems in the PG during the 1960s–1990s, this chapter will identify the different models' elements of success and failure and suggest a more durable and pervasive system. Some key factors, such as inclusiveness (for all regional players), legitimacy and authority, will be investigated in order to cast light on the issues involved in creating a regional security regime.

The goal of the suggested system is that of any security system, namely to "be able to reduce, prevent, or meet potential threats"[1] or, as Kraig expresses it, "to create a stable and peaceful structure of relationships that allows every state to meet its minimum security needs and develop its economy and political institutions without at the same time increasing the level of threat toward its neighbors".[2]

This chapter will also include a study of the failure of the existing security situation as well as a look at scholars' diverging solutions to it. Doing so will make it possible to assess what a more ideal endpoint could be. Once the latter is achieved, it will be possible to suggest better future security arrangements – for instance, one whose agenda is to manage relations between states, or whose grand strategy is the management and regulation of power.

The perception of what constitutes a threat to regional security varies among Arabs, Iranians and the ultra-regional powers, and all accordingly have different solutions to what they perceive is the problem. The West sees the potential use of force by regional players armed with WMDs, domestic instability, social and economic decline and terrorism as cause for grave concern. The regional PG states, on the other hand, are worried that their national sovereignty is under threat, via domestic problems and the danger of political instability contributing to socio-political turmoil, or via external pressure. All the PG states are in different ways victims of non-regional states' interventionist policies. Some have experienced invasions, others sanctions, and others again have endured the presence of foreign forces, all of which have resulted in regional crises. Nevertheless, regardless of the relevant parties' differences of opinion, all these issues, along with three decades of crises in the PG, illustrate how urgent it is that the problem regarding regional security be resolved.

Thus, to be able to analyse the determinant factors of a security system this study has drawn upon the level of analysis framework in international relations. As Steven Spiegel (UCLA political science professor and author) notes,[3] a state's foreign policy, within a system of international politics, can be analysed on three levels. Doing so makes it possible to identify the forces that affect policy at each level. The implications of such identification can then be used to suggest ways in which innovative methods for attaining more stable regional relations can be developed. The first, or "systemic" level, concerns the interaction between different states. At this level the nation-state in the central unit of analysis, which is driven by national interests, is defined in terms of power. This means that the sovereign nation-state is the main factor to consider when an outline for security and stability is being drafted. It also means that national security is essentially "a relationship between the state and its external environment", according to Maoz,[4] and thus that states' behaviour will partly depend on the international security system's structure.[5] At the second and third levels, the "domestic" and "individual (leaders)" levels respectively, the domestic dimensions of stability are recognised. Indeed, based on the outcomes of previous chapters, the greatest dangers in the PG, according to many analysts are more the potential internal socio-economic and political changes than any regional or non-regional aggression.

All three levels of the PG states' foreign policies and the forces that affected them, especially the debate that occurred at the domestic and individual levels, have been studied in the previous chapters. However, using analysis framework, it will be argued that the best solution to the regional security problems in the ME, including its sub-region the PG, is through dialogue – that is, to promote unofficial, informal contacts and negotiations in creating a functional regional security arrangement, a matter that puts emphasis on soft, as opposed to hard, power. Some analysts, such as Kraig, believe that such a strategy presents a good model for defence and economic policy. According to him, the proposal recommends "a situation in which the financial and human capital of nations is used primarily for social, political, economic and spiritual development, rather than for military and security/police forces". The proposed framework also addresses the question of legitimacy and authority, and sees them as inextricably linked to that of sustainability. It acknowledges the need to persuade regional states that the security framework is not purposely disadvantageous to them and that if it is to last it must be supported by most, if not all, of the players involved. This is only possible if all parties concerned consider the security framework's aims to be the attainment of mutually beneficial results.[6]

Security theories

When faced with perceived threats from other states, the reactionary choices nation-states make (as units of international politics) determine the structure and various institutions of the security system, which will, in turn, define the options available to such states. To understand nation-states' choices concerning the use of their power, whether political or military, to attain national security in response to threats from other states in various international systems (see Table 9.1), three fundamental competing schools of thought regarding the practice of international security will be examined. The following text will attempt to define these schools of thought as well as evaluate some of their strengths and weaknesses.

Security Arrangements in the Persian Gulf

TABLE 9.1
Security models

	Unit level: national security strategies				
	Unilateral action		**Multilateral action**		
Military means	Security through strength		Alignment		Collective security "Humanitarian intervention"
	Offensive strength	Defensive strength	Against power	Against threats	
Non-military means	Diplomacy Neutrality Accommodation		Containment Trade		Arbitration
	Systems level: structure and institutions				
	Anarchy		**International society**		**World order**
Military means	Balance of power		Alliances Confidence-building Arms control Security regimes		Collective security Peacekeeping
	Parity	Mutual defensive superiority			
Non-military means	Common security		Cooperative security Institutionalization		International law "Democratic Peace" Integration

Source: Bjørn Møller

The realpolitik/realist school

The main assumption of (neo)realists is that states naturally prefer conflict rather than cooperation in their relationships. In such an atmosphere of anarchy, their behaviour is motivated by a desire for power and security, influenced by the key political players in the system with regard to their relative strength. As Møller notes, a system of international relations entirely based on either "national self-help" (unilateral action) or "collective self-help", where states create alliances against one another, will unavoidably result in anarchy. Realists believe the main principle of order in such an anarchical environment is the balance of power, limited by how polarised the system is. This is especially dependent upon the number of factions within it and how closely integrated these camps or blocs are. Although realists will regard unipolarity to be at best a transitory stage, they will regard the distinction between bipolarity and multipolarity as central in a debate as to how best to achieve a balance of power. Whether the system becomes bipolar or multipolar will depend mainly on whether the states attempt to achieve balance against absolute strength or against strength combined with hostile goals. Also, the level of conflict produced by the system will largely depend on which security approach is chosen.[7]

Realpolitik as a guideline for foreign policy is related to realism and can be considered one of the foundations of realism. It is the pragmatic notion that politics or diplomacy is based principally on practical considerations rather than ideological thoughts. It was, for example, introduced by the US Secretary of State, Henry Kissinger, to the Nixon White House to help develop a new relationship with communist China.

Due to the emphasis in realpolitik on securing national interests via the most practical means, pursing its directives can sometimes mean violating ideological principles. For instance, the US under the Nixon, Carter and Reagan administrations supported authoritarian regimes in the ME/PG, such as those of the Shah in Iran and Saddam in Iraq, despite their violations of human rights, in order to secure the US' national interest in the stability of this region.

While supporters of realpolitik would consider actions such as these defensible given the restrictions of practical reality, which preclude a fixed set of rules, political ideologues would label them amoral. According to the latter group, realpolitik is the selfish pursuit of national interest in a well-calculated play of power to which ethical norms are inappropriate. Political ideologues, who prefer principled action above all other considerations, usually reject any compromises and accept failing to achieve their short-term political gains in favour of adhering to principles.

As mentioned earlier, realpolitik can be regarded as one of the foundations of realism because both implicate power politics and concentrate on the balance of power between nation-states. They act in one direction with two different tasks. Realism acts like a theoretical paradigm, providing a description and prediction of international relations, while realpolitik is a normative outline for policy-making. As Kraig notes, realpolitik prescribes diplomacy on the basis of military threats but it never ignores other sovereign states' core national interests or security concerns. It also recognises commonalities as well as areas of competition for all nation-states and rejects any definition of allies and enemies on a permanent basis. Such kinds of realpolitik diplomacy were developed during 1648–1789, the years of nation-state development in Europe, prior to the French Revolution. During this period, most competition was centred round expansion and the reinforcement of the state, with little connection to people. National expansion was not ideologically motivated but mainly pragmatic. However, traditional realpolitik started to dissipate as radically diverse ideologies and value systems among nation-states began to emerge in Western Europe, with a wide range of mutual misperceptions about security. This worsened when those states that wanted to secure some relative advantage over their rivals were able to guarantee security via traditional methods of weakening or eliminating the rivals, while, as Kraig notes, "[T]he conflicting value systems made cooperative efforts look too costly and even immoral." In addition, in the nineteenth century, the activities of the growing number of sub-national or trans-national actors (many of whom were part of ethnic nationalist movements and terrorist groups), subverted the strong sovereign control that is essential for a security system based on principles of balance of power to be rational. When this occurred during WWI it resulted in greater interstate competition between the Great Powers and eventually undermined the use of power balancing as a conflict-management mechanism.[8]

While, in general, a balance of power signifies parity or stability between competing forces, as a term in international law it also expresses intention to prevent any one nation from becoming strong enough to compel others to obey its political agenda. According to the traditional balance-of-power logic, conflict management operates best under particular circumstances. Nation-states, says Kraig, should define national security and stability in kind (according to their common values and interests) and should rely on their rivals to respect the system and the independence of all other states more than their interest in spreading their doctrine or ideologies. The central role of sovereign states is not undermined because of the existence of trans-national or intra-national movements. Eventually, by applying stable domestic and foreign policies, states will be able to prevent radical changes in ideology from shaping foreign policy. This is a major element that allows mutual trust to build up and to pave the way for stable confidence-building measures.[9]

With these considerations in mind, as well as the different political ideologies and foreign policy objectives of the PG states, the major factor of balance of power cannot be ignored in any PG security system.

The hegemonic or counterproliferation school

Another strategy for regional security is provided by the hegemonic or counterproliferation school, which justifies the operational use of military and economic instruments to achieve the interests of one state, or one set of states over the others, through compliance and deterrence. This is a strategy the US is pursuing, based on a network of friends and allies who share the US' foreign policy goals. In this regard, confronting new challenges of the post-Cold War era, the US seeks to further strengthen and adapt its Cold War security relationships with its allies to establish new security relationships.

Different tools for implementing this kind of strategy have been introduced, such as export control (especially the denial of technology to the developing world), methods of deterrence including advanced technology and powerful military equipment (e.g. nuclear arsenal), and proactive techniques of defence based on pre-emptive strikes and reactive measures. The main aim of Washington's national security planning has been to improve the implementation of this strategy by applying such methods. As Kraig remarks, there is some similarity between a hegemonic strategy and the mercantilism of the eighteenth and nineteenth centuries, which held the belief that traditional alliances would guarantee collective security for them and their friends and allies. According to this vision of international politics, a selective globalisation of the free market was necessary while developing countries were being denied dual-use commercial advances with military applications with the intention of gaining political or military power. Therefore, security was only seen in terms of cooperation of allies in their joint military and economic relations against their enemies, who were perceived as stubborn and impossible to integrate within the hegemonic security framework. To summarise, in the hegemonic or counterproliferation theory, diplomatic relations is defined largely in terms of bilateral and selectively multilateral relationships between friends and allies. For the US, for instance, such relationships in the ME have been formed with Israel and the GCC. Similar to the balance-of-power principle, this theory depends on both the explicit and implicit use of threats. However, unlike traditional realpolitik, as Kraig notes, "[T]he goal of these threats is not to establish a roughly equal balance among all sovereign actors but rather to consolidate economic and military supremacy among friends and allies." Under this framework there is no attempt to build conceptual bridges between a nations ideology and those of its enemies; rather it is an explicit attempt to make its interests and those of its allies predominant.[10]

The cooperative school
The last and most relevant school of thought to be considered in terms of this study is neo-liberalism or cooperative theory. According to this school of thought cooperation is possible and will occur when states calculate that it is in their best interest. There is no argument between neo-realists and neo-liberalists that the state is a rational, unitary actor driven by its interests; however, their disagreement is centred round the nature of states and their interests. The neo-liberals believe cooperation is feasible among states because they are motivated by their interest in wealth and are concerned with absolute and not relative gains. While liberals emphasise the significant role institutions can play in negotiations, realists see them as an extension of a state's interest. Hence, according to Spiegel, neo-realism seems to have the best conceptual resources to explain modern ME history. However, while in neo-realism much of the focus for achieving security is on predicting conflict rather than cooperation, neo-liberalism suggests the theoretical possibility of the prospect of cooperation through institutions as a way that the creation and acceptance of cooperative norms will influence states' interests. The various approaches discussed here emphasise the importance of providing solutions to security concerns, and at the

same time, an attempt is needed to create an environment encouraging cooperation.[11]

The main hypothesis of the cooperative school of thought is that it is not only a nation-state's friends and allies who should participate in security arrangements. This school's fundamental tenet is that "all nation-states will find greater relative security through mutual obligations to limit their military capabilities rather than through unilateral or allied attempts to gain dominance". The thesis works via certain assumptions such as, all nation-states (friends and foes alike), despite the existence of considerable mutual mistrust, will accept the terms of such proposed mutual obligations, and also, that such obligations will be mutually advantageous and verifiable. Therefore, according to this school of thought, security can be obtained only through the outlawing of policies that aim to achieve inter-state dominance.[12]

The most important strategic problem facing the theory, according to the Brookings study group, is reassurance and not deterrence as in the Cold War. In order to achieve the reassurance sovereign states need to address their national security, cooperation must first be instigated and then maintained. The key to such reassurance is a reliable normative and institutional structure. Achieving cooperation depends variously on economic incentives and inducements, political legitimacy, threats against bad behaviour such as the imposition of sanctions, and an inclusiveness that rewards nation-states for their involvement and continued compliance.[13] To summarise, according to the cooperative framework, due to the globalisation of social and economic trends, security is increasingly clarified as a collective good. Therefore, nation-states cannot be divided into the categories of "friends" and "enemies" but, rather, should all be treated as mutual partners struggling to achieve mutual security, even when different states are ideologically radically different.

The differences between and similarities of these theories have been summarised by Kraig as follows: proponents of traditional realpolitik consider international security to be a balance of interests based on a rough balance of power, whereas the more recent US strategic model is based on an imbalance of power and interests (hegemony) and on the use of both offensive and defensive threats. According to neo-liberals, however, the cooperative model can be considered a balance of interests based upon mutual reassurance. Nonetheless, despite the similarity of realpolitik and the cooperative theory, in that both strategies advocate the importance of brokering a balance of interests, they differ in their preferred model of guaranteeing this balance. Realpolitik relies to a great extent on implicit military and economic threats (and temporary alliances to build up power), while cooperative theory relies on promises and reassurances as firm and impenetrable factors. Both of these schools are quite different to the evolving US hegemony strategy, which is increasingly focused on establishing a unitary and dominant value system based on a network of friends and allies supportive of US foreign policy objectives. The hegemonic approach brooks no competitors with different goals and values, while the realpolitik and cooperative security models believe that each nation-state's national interests should be guaranteed at some minimal level. In addition, the cooperative school of thought shares some of its theoretical assumptions with realism, e.g. requiring a set of geopolitical circumstances. Both assume that the primary actor is the sovereign state and that such states will be domestically stable, immune from the sort of domestic turmoil evident in Iran's 1979 revolution, and therefore that the mutual agreements ordering relations will remain stable.

Thus, in order to achieve durable security, it is necessary to design a security model that will be able to give such basic assurances to all its members. The security model should construe the gains it aims to achieve as mutual gains for all participants, not as gains for one particular player or set of players, and thereby be able to assure that remaining in the system will be in all the relevant parties' interests. The model should also be immune to any internal turmoil or changes (in this particular case) to the littoral states. With these constraints in mind, as well as the results of our earlier study of security theories and that which follows, concerning these models' history in the PG, an attempt will be made to suggest and develop an appropriate model for security in the region.

The Persian Gulf's security systems

The aim of this book is to attempt to create a comprehensive strategy for peace and stability in the PG. In order to do this the relative strengths and weaknesses of the three theories, as well as the various historical challenges in applying the frameworks to the PG security environment, need to be assessed.

In the period between the collapse of the Ottoman Empire and Britain's departure from the ME, the security system in the PG was founded on realpolitik's balance-of-power principle. The security system at this time worked due to a number of factors. First, the complex policies pursued by Britain included the application of the policy, which stated that "to dominate a region it is necessary to weaken regional powers". As explained earlier (Chapter 5), for this reason Iran's efforts to establish power in the PG were totally unacceptable to and annulled by Britain. Britain severely vetoed every action, measure, or proposal by Iran to establish a navy for security in the PG. Second, Britain combined consolidating its military superiority in the region by placing troops in well-chosen bases, supported by offshore naval forces and the secondment of officers in key areas, with the installation of proxy regimes, which thus created and supported friendly governments in this region. Third, the Sheikhs were at this time ready to welcome the help and support of Britain in making the political changes that led towards the establishment of their new countries, despite London's action in keeping competition among them within limits.[14]

Following Britain's departure, the PG region, particularly because of its huge oil reserves, became a platform on which the feuding Cold War powers could compete. Competing for control over this geopolitical region, the US assumed the role of regional security guarantor from the British, and could thereby take over the role of security manager of the region. Nevertheless, numerous attempts to find an effective regional security arrangement after the British departure were ended ineffectually. At first the US followed its containment policy against the USSR by supporting the Baghdad Pact (1955–1958); however, the 1958 military coup in Iraq converted such formal alignment to bilateral ties and agreements between the US and every state in the region. From the late 1960s through to the late 1970s, seeking to maintain regional stability, the US persisted in a realpolitik strategy of attempting to support a rough balance of military power between the most dominant powers in the region, Iran and Iraq. Iran, as the military pillar of Nixon's doctrine, was supported by the US against socialist, anti-Western Iraq. Nixon's "Twin Pillars", or the strategy of local hegemony with US dependence on local powers, did not work; however, this was mainly due to the US' underestimation of the domestic side of security. The lack of the US' regional allies' political legitimacy due to their carelessness about domestic developments and political reforms was in large part responsible for security failure in this region. Hence, as Kraig notes, the strategy of local hegemony, which eventually led to Iran's revolution in 1979 and later to the terrorist attacks by Saudi citizens on the US on 11 September 2001, also failed. Consequently, the factor of legitimacy is essential for establishing any new PG security order, as is the awareness that a strategy based on structures of power, particularly when one relies on local military powers that are prone to fail or change, is bound to be unsuccessful.

Following the Iranian revolution of 1979, which effectively removed one of the "pillars" of Nixon's "Twin Pillar" doctrine, and also the USSR's invasion of Afghanistan, US policy for PG security became based on what was to become known as the "Carter doctrine". According to this strategy, Washington would resist any outside forces' attempts to gain control over the PG and its oil flow.

During the 1980s, the US' aim was to achieve a pure balance of power in order to keep the peace, by limiting both Iran and Iraq from growing too powerful. This included the support of Baghdad in its war with Tehran in order to prevent the emergence of revolutionary Iran as the local hegemony, also providing immediate security to the newly established GCC. Simultaneously, because of the military weakness of the GCC states and their ideological opposition to socialist, anti-Western Iraq (and hence the lack of a strong pro-West pillar to fill the place of the Shah), the US was persuaded to be drawn more directly into the region. Therefore, the Rapid Deployment Force (RDF) was established and Washington invested in regional military bases. Regarding the RDF, in 1983, a new US Central Command (US CENTCOM) was established by the Reagan administration to project power and command, particularly regarding the US, which was ill-prepared to project power in the PG. RDF, as its central base, was extended from the East Mediterranean to Pakistan and from the shared Turkish and Iraq borders (NATO frontiers) in the north to the African Horn region in the south with Diego Garcia Island in the Indian Ocean. Besides the US' major nuclear facilities in Western Europe under NATO command, nuclear weapons were also deployed in the ME and PG region (Southwest Asia) under US central command. As Nassar comments concerning this issue, "[T]hese weapons had been deployed with the full consent and approval of European countries, whereas these weapons can be deployed at any time in South West Asia (…) without any agreement concluded with the countries concerned."[15] Regarding regional military bases, while US military help in the event of absolute emergencies was highly esteemed, the GCC states were not interested in institutionalising a US military role, preferring whenever possible to take advantage of diplomatic manoeuvring, including providing financial aid to thwart any potential threats. Being aware of their military weakness and comparatively small population, the GCC (with the exception of Oman) was pleased that the RDF was located "over the horizon", believing that a direct US military presence in the region could provoke the anger of Iran, Iraq and several other Arab states as well as arguably the USSR. Therefore, none of the GCC members took part in any official agreement with the US over defence until two events that resulted in volatility in the region in the period between the early 1980s and 1990s, viz. the war on tankers and the Iraqi seizure of Kuwait. The US, which had little physical or institutional involvement in regional defence schemes, responded to the former with a reflagging operation and embarked on direct military activity by escorting GCC tankers carrying a US flag. The operation, which was an escalation in terms of intervention and was sanctioned by the UN Security Council and the participation of other Western states, convinced both the US and Kuwait (which had initiated the idea) to take steps to characterise the operation as merely an international policing activity rather than US defence of GCC stases. Therefore, the reflagging operation, with wide international dimensions and very limited GCC states' assistance, was not a new kind of US–GCC alliance but rather a limited US military operation.

Disadvantages of the US' strategy in the 1980s
There were several disadvantages to the US' use of the balance-of-power strategy in the PG. First, ignoring Iran's security concerns and national interests as the major regional player resulted not only in the failure of the US–PG security system but also compelled Iran to take a more radical approach to a foreign policy that placed more emphasis on military empowerment. Second, the strategy authorised Iraq to proliferate offensive military power and entailed ignoring Iraqi human rights transgressions, including the replacement of WMDs.

Until 1990 the US had stuck to a strategy of maintaining a low-cost security system in the PG. Until then it had relied merely on a naval presence and on its regional allies, mainly the GCC and, to some extent, Iraq. However, Iraq's invasion of Kuwait in August 1990 indicated the failure of this policy. In contrast to previous situations, in a direct reaction to Iraq's invasion and the growing threat to Saudi Arabia, the US assumed its new role as main military defender in the region. This security approach was not welcomed by the GCC and included extensive forward basing and regular military engagements of US forces that sometimes turned into significant deployments. However, it was the GCC's best choice, since none of its allies in the Arab world could offer help.

As mentioned earlier, the additional factor resulting in Washington changing its strategy and causing the US' reflagging operation was the war on tankers initiated by Iraq and resulting in Iran's escalating its attacks on shipping serving Arab ports in the PG. Furthermore, according to some sources, the invasion of Kuwait was the consequence of the US green light to Iraq to do so. Arguably then, both of the "reasons" for an increased US military role had been part of a US premeditated and engineered scheme. In any case, regardless of whether these speculations seem logical and consistent, by the end of the "Desert Storm" operation in 1991, the US was practically the major military force in the region.

Shortly after "Desert Storm", the 1991 "Damascus Declaration" (a US-encouraged treaty that entrusted GCC land defences to Syrian and Egyptian infantry and armoured divisions) was signed to show that the US did not seek to be the dominant force in all PG defences. However, the GCC states were not eager to accept the declaration, since they did not trust Egypt and Syria, politically or militarily. This meant that Washington was able to sign several different military agreements with GCC states and seemed enthusiastic about accepting its new role of offering security and selling arms. These military treaties were different: there was no US–GCC pact, and Washington had to deal with each state separately and with varying success. For instance, while Saudi Arabia decided not to endorse an official agreement with the US (because of certain technical problems with Washington as well as a fear of the consequences of angering Iran and Syria), Kuwait did (following it up with pacts with Britain and France) and so did Bahrain.

Despite stationing several thousand infantry and armoured forces in the PG, US forces mainly relied on air power. However, although this strategy had been successful in the "Desert Storm" operation, the use of such air power demonstrated major deficiencies faced by US military power in the region. The importance of physical occupation was realised, whether for a conclusive victory in battles or to bring about the political change Washington saw as necessary to prevent future threats in the region. This shortcoming, however, was overcome later by the US invasion of Iraq in 2003. However, shortly after the "Desert Storm" operation, the new strategy of "Dual Containment" marked the US' distance from reliance on regional allies via the balance-of-power doctrine and movement towards its more muscular regional attendance. Washington's strategy of "Dual Containment", to some extent a response to the deficiencies that were made evident during the Kuwait crisis, sought during the Clinton administration to replace Saddam Hussein, establish a new government in Iraq and force Iran to change its foreign policy through military and economic sanctions. It also included new military agreements with the GCC states, with whom the US now entered into increased arm sales to equip pro-US local military, who, despite their inability to operate the less sophisticated arms they had bought previously, planned to use these new arms as supplemental weaponries to US forces. Since 1991 in particular, due to the removal of Soviet threats to Europe and East Asia, the PG region has become the centre stage in terms of US strategic thinking and force planning. Therefore, the new strategy of both Iran and Iraq containment also indicated that a large portion of total US military operating, force-structure and investment costs were devoted to military issues in the PG. Consequently, these developments signified a growing interdependent US–GCC relationship which, before 1990, had largely been a potential alliance, but since then has been implemented as a very real and strategically crucial one for both sides.[16]

After "Desert Storm", besides military protection, the GCC's other expectation concerning its military pacts with Washington was that the US would make some efforts to resolve the Arab Israeli conflict, in order that the PLO and Syria would not be angered by this newly implemented alliance or seek retribution against the GCC states. In response to this, Presidents George H. W. Bush and Bill Clinton had initiated a multilateral security approach known as the "Madrid process", which included producing a practical Israeli–Palestinian peace process among its goals.

However, in the second half of the 1990s, with the fading of the Arab–Israeli peace process and with the US bombing raids in response to

Saddam's not completely cooperative attitude towards the UN inspection regime, the new US security approach failed to achieve its major objectives. In particular, the cooperative mode of the GCC with the US evolved into a more critical position. This was especially due to Egyptian and Syrian anger with Washington, which inspired the GCC states to seek additional security cooperation (in the event of a new crisis with Iraq) with these two countries and Iran. The other reason was that the US bombing raids, which were very unpopular throughout the whole Arab world, caused great sympathy in both Iraq and other Arab states, where public opinion felt strongly for the Iraqi people's suffering caused by UN sanctions. Moreover, there was growing criticism and voiced concerns from many regional intellectuals, journalists and others who felt that, in addition to the cost of the US presence for the GCC states, the crisis in Iraq was only helping to establish US dominance in the PG. These factors convinced the GCC states to seek Washington's military intervention only in times of need, believing that by seeking supplemental security cooperation with the assistance of Egypt, Syria and Iran, led by President Khatami, tensions in the region would dissipate.[17]

Disadvantages of the US' security strategy in the 1990s

During the 1990s, the occurrence of some intra-regional developments undermined the US security system in the PG. In the case of the GCC, Qatar emerged as an independent player. This shook up the kaleidoscope of relationships within the GCC six-member grouping. More importantly, Iran gradually moved towards receiving a more moderate security approach, although still with Tehran's stipulation that Iran be recognised as the natural regional hegemony. Iran's regional policy of *détente* was accompanied by various domestic democratic developments, including democratic elections. Consequently, the dual containment policy begin to look futile as, on the one hand, Iran's moderation brought hopes that at least cooperative measures such as CBM could be established between the GCC and Iran, and, on the other, Washington failed to contain Iraq, the immediate threat to the region.

In the post-Cold War world, the security arrangement under the desired US unipolar system did not work for a number of reasons. While Europe was mostly hospitable to American forces after WWII and during the Cold War, the PG was not.[18] Neither was the PG as hospitable to American forces as it was to Britain before its departure in 1971. It was also a mistake to exclude key players, viz. Iran and Iraq, from security arrangements in the most geopolitically significant region in the world. In order to attain peace in such circumstances one needs good relations between the strongest global and regional players, in particular Iran. Moreover, the US military presence was costly, dysfunctional and shifted from being reliant on regional allies to a more immediate presence. The dual containment policy, which was designed to strangle Iran via economic sanctions, was largely unfeasible, as some GCC members as well as European and Asian countries continued and even extended their economic ties with Iran in the absence of American companies. In addition, many security problems of the GCC were internal and mostly connected to potential foreign threats or to a local reaction to their governments' cooperation with the US. Since "Desert Storm" these states have been harassed by local opposition and terrorism, in particular from religious extremists. Furthermore, GCC states that suffered from inter-state disputes and differences (especially regarding non-demarcated borderlines and security cooperation with Iran) also had serious concerns about the backlash of dissatisfaction from Arab states such as Egypt and Syria regarding their alliance with the US, or feared that they would be left unsupported in times of need. Washington was unable and also was not asked by GCC governments to deal with their domestic issues, while Egypt, Syria and Iran's contribution to ease domestic and inter-group problems and to cooperate for the sake of regional security, in particular as a way to counter Iraq, was welcomed. Hence, there was a great divergence in the threat perceptions of the GCC and the US, as among GCC states themselves. These were some important diversities and variations that were not considered in the simplistic dual containment strategy.

Furthermore, as Kraig explains, the Madrid process had various structural problems and so was unable to tackle any of these concerns. It too was founded on a selectively multilateral approach of collective security, relying on friends and allies to provide security for the whole region; thus it suffered from the systematic exclusion of key regional players, viz. Iran and Syria. Furthermore, it was part of a US foreign policy that was overly focused on military strategy and tactics rather than on a consistent political scheme for the PG as an ME sub-region.

The Madrid process' only political objective was to broker peace between the Israelis and Palestinians as the answer to all problems in the ME, including the PG. However, such an assumption left the political and security questions in the PG unanswered and no political structure for a contained Iraq and Iran was drawn, except continuing to rely on military tools as well as economic strangulation as the strong option to bring down regimes in Tehran and Baghdad. It was a quite different approach to regional security to that adopted in Europe during and after the Cold War, in which security was brokered by a combination of military means in the form of NATO, and extremely strong and inclusive political and economic frameworks to create a system based upon common norms, institutions and the rule of law.

Similarly, despite the successful experience of applying the Marshall Plan for Europe after WWII, the defeat of Iraq in 1991 only resulted in bilateral defence pacts. This process weakened any potential regional security interdependency and, in contrast, increased the security dependence of the GCC on the US. Moreover, domestic issues in the GCC, the rulers' major security problem, were being given no consideration. From the military point of view too, US security strategy in the ME had structural problems. Of the three major goals of the US Pentagon for security in this region, namely: improving the capabilities of the RDF through bilateral defence-cooperation agreements, strengthening the local defence capabilities of GCC states, and promoting intra-GCC cooperation, only the first easy goal was accomplished. These failures in US strategy have had several repercussions. Besides the inherent regional geopolitical dynamics, they too have been responsible for the maintenance of traditional notions of realpolitik to form the political agenda among the littoral states. Consecutively, these states have stuck to the security calculus of a rough balance of power and thus continue to rely on external powers (e.g. the US, China and Russia), sometimes by proxy such as via the importation of weapons technology and in other cases via actual US military deployments, to defend their sovereignty, regimes' permanence and domestic identity.[19] In addition, it is very likely, if not definite, that the surge in active US military deployments since the early 1990s has radicalised many against the US and thus indirectly contributed to the attacks of 9/11.

Present security problems of the key players in the Persian Gulf
The United States
The US hegemonic approach to security is increasingly focused on ensuring a stable and pro-Western system via the establishment of a commanding value system that includes promoting regional political change. So the start of the twenty-first century has seen the US attempting to broker security in the PG by putting in place an extensive, growing military presence. On the one hand, this presence was motivated by the US understanding that, over time, intervention had failed to be a strong enough deterrent. On the other hand, it was motivated by its national interests and foreign policy goals. Economically speaking, the US arms market profits from this stance. Furthermore, the US needs a well-integrated world economy, and the latter depends on stable oil supplies and suppliers, secured in past by impeding the development of WMDs by those regimes that may threaten PG oil flow. Politically speaking, this stance helps bring about its hegemony in the international system and assures its own domestic security.

Despite the failure of its security policy, the US is still trying to convince the GCC to continue its reliance on the US security umbrella and to purchase US arms. However, as in the inter-World War period in Europe, the absence of an inclusive security arrangement has only made the possibility of insecurity and warfare look more likely. This means that the Arabs have been made dependent on a security arrangement they consider increasingly unreliable.

Washington faces a strategic dilemma: it wants to secure its national interests and its need for a well-integrated world economy. But in doing so it has not chosen the best options, pursuing instead a costly and dangerous military strategy, and supporting the weakest and politically least stable of the three regional powers in the PG. Further, political discontent and radicalism within the GCC pose a direct threat to US national security. Both are fuelled by US support for Israel and regional dictatorial regimes as well as by the socio-economic woes that grip the region. The current US military presence in the PG only fans the flames of such discontent and, since September 2001, it has become obvious that, as well as being very expensive, the US strategy in the PG has caused dangers to its homeland security to become very real and immediate.

It also puts in danger whatever remaining regional allies the US has left, especially Saudi Arabia. Hence, although as Rathmell (et al.)

argue, "the United States does not have the option of withdrawing from the Gulf as the British did 30 years ago", Washington does have some alternative options available, and which it should take. For instance, it could pursue a comprehensive political strategy to broker CBM with Iran (with whom it is the only nation in the PG not to have relations). Iran is a key regional player with direct interests and security concerns in both its very long western and eastern borders with Iraq and Afghanistan, and so building CBM with it could help engender a situation where the US could more easily withdraw from the region. Such a political process between two adversary countries is likely to take time; however, not pursuing this option would have far greater long-term negative consequences for the US. This is especially true for a number of reasons, as outlined below.

First, Iran's influence is rising due to the US' removal of its local enemies, namely Saddam Hussein and the Taliban, an influence that was always largely due to its advantageous geopolitical position. It is thus unlikely that Iran will easily surrender when it feels under threat. Second, although the Arab PG states feel under threat from Iran, the latter is unlikely to present a real threat, particularly if it is included in a comprehensive regional security apparatus. Third, the Arab PG states are unenthusiastic about putting their security solely in the hands of the US, and their leaders have recently supported the idea of a collective security arrangement for the region that includes Iran (as voiced, for instance, by Saudi Foreign Minister Saud al-Faisal at the 2004 Gulf Dialogue in Bahrain) and are growing increasingly frustrated with US reluctance to have any dealing whatsoever with the Iranians. Furthermore, the recent US invasion of Iraq has led to much regional anti-US sentiment that has put Arab leaders under a great deal of domestic pressure to discontinue their US security alliance. In addition, there is considerable fear of a US–Iran battle, which would overflow into the Arab countries.

Finally, Iraq's internal crisis has had a considerable impact on the GCC, which now faces the serious possibility of a shift in the political balance of power between Sunnis and Shiites by losing the Eastern flank of the Arab world through Iraq's conversion to a Shiite state and thus becoming Iran's ally. Due to its geopolitical features, Iraq will always be both politically ambitious and a major player in the Arab world as well as the PG, regardless of who rules it. This fact, together with the deep insecurities felt by Iraq about its geopolitical restriction in the PG and the fact that actual and potential enemies sit astride its oil export routes, all encourage the GCC to deal with Iran in a more peaceful manner in the interests of maintaining a balance of power.

Therefore, Washington has no real choice as to whether to postpone or deny its need to enter into positive dialogue with Tehran. The US also needs to invest in a less expensive and more sustainable PG security system that promotes, rather than resists, political change. It is uncertain how political change is best achieved; however, it is clear that the worst way to decrease tension and radicalism is the US strategy of putting pressure on the region's rulers to develop domestically.

Iran
Iran wishes to be recognised as a regional power (a position it feels has been ignored) and to play its role accordingly. It has the capability of posing a sea-denial threat in the PG and could develop nuclear weapons. Nevertheless, despite the US confrontational policy, the West's concern regarding Tehran's threat to regional stability by, for instance, spreading its revolution, and the GCC's fear of Iranian ambitions, is unfounded; some analysts, such as Rathmell (et al.), feel it is unlikely to present a threat at all, depending on its role in the security system. This is because the PG is the major lifeline of Iran's economy and so requires its stability. Also, the future of US security policy in the PG looks uncertain, both to Iran and the Arabs in the southern peninsula who, along with the Arab World in general, question the US' role and intentions in the region.

The GCC
The GCC's concerns are: its weakness in terms of defending itself, the impacts of a direct US presence and Iran's ambitions (i.e. will it pursue a policy of expansionism, or develop nuclear weapons?), and the impact of Iraq's internal crisis on its political as well as socio-economic situation, especially with regards terrorism. The GCC also fears the introduction of a rival democratic system and the shift in the political balance of power between Sunnis and Shiites. Finally, it questions the competence of foreign powers in their dealings in the region, including the US, with which it originally wanted to keep an "over the horizon" relationship and which is still its *de facto* partner in PG security arrangements.

Strategic conditions of the Persian Gulf

The PG has some strategic properties that affect how successful a security system will be, and which have not been effectively dealt with in the attempt to construct a new and viable multilateral PG framework for security. These properties are as follows.

First, the PG comprises three poles – Saudi Arabia (including the GCC), Iran and Iraq – which all need to be taken into account when designing a lasting security system. None of these countries, including Saudi Arabia, is happy with the existing balance of power, which is kept in check by the threat of American intervention. The relationship between the three poles is asymmetric, with Iran's geography and population giving it a naturally dominant position and strategic depth. Though Iraq was able to compete with Iran in the 1970s and 80s, this was only via an unsustainable and oppressive militarisation of its people and economy as well as through help from the GCC and the Great Powers during its eight-year war with Iran. The GCC is powerful from a financial point of view (largely acquired from oil revenues), but it has been unable to turn this strength into the strategic leverage necessary to balance Iran or Iraq. The asymmetrical dynamic that exists in the PG has meant that it has been along the lines of realpolitik. However, this has been done in a situation where it is impossible to find balance and a general acceptance of the status quo, and this has meant that the region has remained insecure and dangerous to its people and the rest of the world.[20]

Second, the new global security thinking of cooperation, which indicates the decline of traditional realist perceptions of international relations and an end to a zero-sum notion of national security, is difficult to implement in the PG. This security thinking was initiated by the USSR's President Gorbachev in terms of arms control in the late 1980s and coincided with certain Western definitions of security, evidenced in cooperative security theories with an emphasis on economic and political legitimacy. The cooperative security system succeeded in Europe, East Asia and Latin America during the 1990s mainly because these systems were supported by political transformation, meaningful reform and, thus, stability, a necessary political element missing in the PG, where – despite some debates regarding a regional cooperative security system in the mid-1990s – it was not taken seriously. Therefore, the balance of power in the PG has remained unstable. None of the three major PG players, including the GCC (as a cooperative organisation), has displayed a functional interest in cooperating with the other two. So, while the US was able to depend more on an organic regional progress in lieu of mere military force in its security approach in Europe, East Asia and Latin America, the contextual aspects of the PG have made this impossible.[21]

Despite these issues, as well as those regarding potential American unwillingness to countenance it, there are some good reasons in favour of establishing a regional multilateral security arrangement. These reasons include, as Kraig observes, the comprehensive failure of different unilateral or selective bilateral or multilateral security frameworks in the PG via foreign power intervention, as well as the systematic exclusion, economic and military, of major state and non-state actors from the prevailing security mandate. Furthermore, it is conceptually impossible to have a system that is considered to legitimately be in all the involved parties' interests when the prevailing strategy is to create a coalition whose existence is defined in terms of being opposed to one or more of those involved parties.

Kraig has similar views to those of Sariolghalam, who has serious misgivings about the possibility of Iran entering into coalition (cooperative)-building with the GCC, because of different cultural, ideological and political differences. As Kraig mentions, it seems that the preferred form of achieving stability and security is not via a multilateral coalition in the PG, but via a two-party coalition across regions' bilateral agreements with an outside power (based on the hegemonic principles or on traditional realpolitik).[22] Hence, regional multilateralism only plays a secondary role in PG security. For instance, the GCC, qua multilateral organisation, does not have the necessary expansion potential via its membership or the organisation's authorisation to be able to be the basis for a new PG security arrangement.

First, its too exclusionist character does not allow for easy expansion (to include Iraq, Iran and Turkey, for instance), unlike analogous European organisations. The GCC is limited to Arab monarchies with mostly similar domestic structures and foreign policies which share similar interactions with the US. Other similarities among the GCC members are that they all see Islamic fundamentalism a threat, widely agree about intra-GCC trade expansion, and share similar political alignments with other PG and non-PG countries. However, despite their similarities, GCC states have often been engaged in arms-buying as a means to deter and balance one another or as a way to obtain leverage within the organisation. Unlike NATO in Europe during the Cold War, which was able to harmonise and conduct its different countries' military capabilities towards a collective and overarching political objective, such integration in the case of the GCC states looks to have limited potential. While GCC states may have established viable deterrents against each other and Iran, they have not done so with regard to other potential foes and remain a net consumer, as opposed to net producer, of security. Under such conditions, it is hard to accept that the GCC can have a serious role in a regional collective cooperation model for the PG.

Second, reconciling the GCC's relatively new nation-states to a greater authorisation of this organisation is debatable. Consensus on such a strong multilateral security organisation requires conceding some of their sovereignty over diplomatic, economic and military affairs. It also requires much liberalisation and transparency and GCC states are less than enthusiastic about joining a wide cooperative effort that would give every member the power to oversee and influence the domestic issues of other members, and thereby lose control over information, finance and defence choices. Generally speaking, it is the GCC states' fragile political base, along with an emerging sense of each state's national identity, that have thus far alleviated attempts to cooperate more productively in different fields of foreign policy. Thereby, economic and military levers have thus remained largely under these states' sovereign control rather than been applied through a joint plan for action. Moreover, the reliance of each member of the GCC (instead of the whole organisation) on outside powers has been to the benefit of cooperating partners, especially the smaller ones, at the regional level when dealing with large nation-states. Accordingly, due to the relative deficiency of technology and industry and in some cases population among many ME countries, it would be impossible to deal with crises without considerable contributions from external powers.

Other studies, such as that by the Bertelsmann Group, also highlight the importance of foreign actors' contribution to ensuring security in the PG, due to the enormous amount of mutual suspicion in the region. However, the Bertelsmann Group, while emphasising the positive contribution of foreign actors, stresses the necessity of reducing the foreign military presence in the region and emphasises that the main responsibility for establishing a new approach to PG security should lie with regional states. The problem, as this study explains, is that:

> Regional actors do not share a common threat perception, let alone a joint approach to regional security. They have tended to view interaction as a zero-sum game, and their relations have almost exclusively been conducted on a bilateral basis. A shared approach to regional security has never emerged and multilateral designs have never been seriously considered.[23]

US hegemonic power in the region, Kraig notes, significantly contributes to such a network of merely bilateral relationships. It signifies that in any future PG security plan, US actions should be taken into account, a matter that could easily become a prohibitive factor and de-motivate the spending of large amounts of political or financial capital in constructing a security model when Washington gets what it wants through bilateral means regardless. In addition, there is not any certainty about the US trend for multilateral local cooperation in the economic fields; evidently it is in its interests to sustain oil prices as low as possible. Cooperation in the PG would result in its attaining more economic power, particularly if an independent regional energy organisation was established. Such regional cooperation has been successfully experienced in Europe, where the US goals have been to promote a strong side-by-side EU and NATO for concurrent growth of economic and military power. Yet, there is no resemblance between US goals in Europe and its goals in the PG. However, without greater economic cooperation between littoral states, a basis for stronger security interactions in the PG does not seem to be approaching. In order for there to be regional security, the US has to prepare for higher oil prices, which will seriously examine Washington's security strategy in the PG.[24]

Furthermore, from a political point of view, the US does not support any kind of coalition or regional cooperation of the GCC with Iran. As James Bill notes:

> The US seeks to prevent the rise of independent-minded regional hegemons [such as Iran] (...) [and] seeks to control the behaviour of regional hegemons in regions rich in geostrategic significance and natural resources. (...) [Hence], as part of its policy of containment and control, the US enlists the support of regional allies. In the Middle East, this role is played by the GCC countries and Israel.[25]

Nevertheless, Kraig provides some reasons why the multilateral policy options should at least be tested alongside traditional bilateral ties: stating, for example, that the reliance on bilateral coalition with external powers has had numerous negative consequences that contribute to domestic instability by showing the government's inability to defend the country, thus giving the impression that the state is dependent on "neo-imperial powers". The role of external powers arguably prevents any possibility of the regional states creating their own defence frameworks. It contributes to the current policy inertia that favours bilateral, and not multilateral, agreements for defence. Such outside contributions may also remove the need for greater regional cooperation in general, and may bring with them the particular ideological value systems and associated foreign policy goals of the outside players. The latter includes the effects of systemic competition between external powers, such as the US, China and Russia. Aid to ME/PG countries with antipathy towards the US, especially Iran, is widely seen, for instance, as uncooperative practice by China and Russia against the US. It may also embrace the domestic, political and economic objectives of the non-regional powers, i.e. the fact that the US, Europe, Russia and China need to keep their arms industries at high levels to satisfy domestic lobbies and facilitate employment.

Most important, external powers' interference – particularly the US' preferred strategy of bilateralism – may in the end overwhelm the stabilising aspects of the balance of power in the region; in such a context, actions such as the purchase of weaponry and the forging of alliances would have completely different meanings for competitors; what one side might see as a deterrent action the other side might perceive as an offensive action. The latter can evidently be perceived in the differing perceptions of Arabs and Iran related to whether Israeli nuclear weapons are there only as a deterrent. After all, there is a fundamental security dilemma in the region – that is, the lack of systematic interregional relationships, specifically in respect to political and military affairs. Consequently, there is no specific interaction between the large and small regional states, nor between the three PG poles (Iran, Iraq and Saudi Arabia), nor a systematic way for Iraq and Iran to interact with the GCC states. Moreover, no serious process or forum exists for this interaction to take place.

To sum up the results: different policies of selective multilateralism, bilateralism and unilateralism have been ineffective and even disastrous in bringing about security in the PG. The reason for such a failure is simply that the most prominent states inextricably support exclusionary types of coalition. The outcome of all of the mentioned policies, besides a general political isolation, is the systematic exclusion, economically or militarily, of a major state and of non-state actors in the security order. If the major idea of a coalition is being opposed to someone else, then it is in principle impossible for that coalition to be seen as legitimate to all, and therefore it would be unable to assimilate all the regional actors' major interests.[26]

Alternatives

Various changes in the global political landscape, most especially those that have occurred since the end of the Cold War, have provided a fresh opportunity to develop a new approach to international security. This new approach places particular emphasis on patterns of cooperation. One viable path towards a more sustainable security situation in any region would be to stress the growing importance of economic developments and the role of regional and international organisations in increasing security. Examples of this would be the European Union (EU) and Asia-Pacific Economic Cooperation (APEC), which increase security by fostering interdependency with other regions through increased cooperation; or the UN, which affects regional security affairs by means of its different peacekeeping missions. Not only have the changes in the global political landscape enabled the development of a new general approach to international security, they also offer an opportunity to develop a sustainable form of security in the PG, which is the most geopolitical region of the world. This can be achieved by a close analysis and evaluation of various successful cooperation models that are to be found in other regions of the globe.

Given the new global landscape, the best proposal for a new security framework for the PG would be one that relied on fostering cooperative relationships among national military establishments, rather than confrontational relationships. The justification for this is that according to many theorists, such as Nolan, traditional security methods that are based on massive military confrontation are no longer particularly effective or even acceptable to global public opinion.[27]

Furthermore, as Ehteshami, Russell and Kraig observe, in any appropriate alternative strategy for security in the PG that aims to ensure sustainability it is crucial to maintain a clear distinction between short-term requirements and long-term goals or expectations.[28] *Apropos* this distinction, see the argument of the previous chapter on Iran. There it was argued that in addition to the need to construct comprehensive multilateral coalitions, it is important to recognise the significance of the relationship between major regional and non-regional powers to achieve a durable and long-term security situation in any region.

In addition to these conditions, the situation since 2003 and the downfall of Saddam's regime (which was the greatest obstacle to developing lasting security in the PG), has also created a greater and unprecedented opportunity for regional cooperation. Moreover, in doing so, this has inadvertently provided the conditions for the creation of new security arrangements in the region.

One possible approach to the issue of security in the PG is to study security models applied in other regions of the world and consider whether they may be profitably applied to the PG. Among the various alternatives, the Asian model in the form of trade, financial and political arrangements among countries of East Asia has been proposed as that most suitable for developing a better partnership between Iran, the GCC and the EU. The types of arrangements of the new Asian regional architecture include bilateral free trade agreements (FTAs), regional trade pacts, currency and monetary arrangements, and political and security arrangements. The East Asian regional architecture is supported by two distinct pillars. The economic pillar is strong and growing more intense through plans to develop a web of bilateral and regional bilateral free trade agreements – like an East Asian Economic Community (with 13 nations), an East Asian FTA (with 16 nations), and an Asia Pacific FTA (with 21 nations) – where the political and security pillar has remained relatively underdeveloped. Regarding security, the most progress has been made through the Association of South East Asian Nations acting as convener and has taken the form of the ASEAN Security Community (10 Southeast Asian nations) and ASEAN Regional Forum (25 nations, including the United States). As the Bertelsmann Group, and others such as Jones, remark, as a starting point this model is likely to be the most appropriate one for the PG, because it offers a set of arrangements that in the fullness of time could be extended to the rest of the ME too. This model is supported by a set of overlapping bilateral and multilateral dialogue structures that have, in turn, been built around several general principles of regional conduct.

Here, the EU will be looked at as an interesting framework for PG security, as it is itself a successful model using the supporting method of dialogue structures. In any case, an alternative approach would be to encourage the involvement of Asian-Pacific countries, such as China, India and Japan, whose growing dependence on energy supplies from the PG has increased their desire to have a greater geopolitical role in maintaining security in the PG independent from the US. This may be a key to promoting regional stability.[29]

In general, what the discussion thus far has shown is that the important interlocking elements needed to establish a workable, legitimate and authoritative security model in the PG can be categorised as follows: an inclusive and multilateral approach; a balance of power, preferably through arms control negotiations among all three regional key players; and domestic developments and reforms in the littoral states, such as those suggested by different authors including Rathmell (et al.). This study proposes that these would add to an appropriate international political environment with a proper international security system's structure.

The key issue for achieving a durable collective security approach will remain Iran–US relations. However, it is possible to create a counter-balance to the US hegemony through dialogue within the region, as well as dialogue with the non-regional powers with interests in this region. By building partnerships with major international powers, such as China and the EU, so that they take a greater role in the PG security matters, the US hegemony could be reduced.

Lessons from the establishment of the European Union

The issue in this section is whether the lessons learned during the transformation of Europe from an area of conflict into a security community could be validly applied in the PG region. If the lessons are applicable to the PG region, then studying the EU's security framework will be instructive and useful. Bjørn Møller's study of security models and their applicability to the PG is one of the best and most comprehensive studies of the European transformation. Consequently, the discussion here will mainly follow his.

Bjørn Møller
During the Cold War, realists argued that the West's political strategy of containment, with its purpose of maintaining the status quo and preventing the USSR from expanding towards Western Europe, would result in stability. This was subsequently shown to be mistaken. As a defence strategy, containment soon became militarised and even nuclearised. It was perceived as a matter of impeding or deterring a military attack by military tools. The result was the necessity of a military alliance similar to NATO, which resulted in a rough and disproportionate balance of power between the Eastern and Western pacts of NATO and Warsaw. Another consequence was a permanent arms race. However, there was little support in the West for alternative security models, such as "defensive", "non-provocative" or "confidence-building defence" models, which place more burden on the balance of "mutual defensive superiority" rather than military strength to deter an attack from the other parties. Anyhow, Europe's military security problem was only solved when in the late 1980s President Gorbachev's initiative for arms control was suggested.[30]

In discussing the concept of "mutual defensive superiority" as an integrated issue with the political strategy of common security, Møller argues that it was perceived as a way of obtaining the most advantage from the military stand-off. This is because of the implication that there would be no absolute winner from conflicts but mutual losses, particularly in respect of the use of nuclear weaponry. Hence, despite constraints on security concerns that arose from national interest and also in spite of divergent conceptions of common security, collaboration – even between opponents – was the more reasonable course. Trade was the major factor of the European security approach that engendered peaceful interaction, a real interdependency, and led to integration. The evidence for this lies in the fact that the EU, which evolved from the "European Coal and Steel Community", is the most successful of all European security models.[31]

This model of developing security through interdependency, which offers a completely non-military path to security and peace, may nonetheless, as Møller remarks, be combined with such military safeguards through collective security arrangements. Hence, even after the Cold War and in spite of the dissolution of the Warsaw Pact and the Soviet Union in 1989 and 1991 respectively, NATO is still active and even seeks out new activities in other parts of the world. Among the new activities its role was limited to being a peacekeeping force within its traditional geographical bounds and to providing so-called "training" for former Eastern bloc member states on the civil–military relations befitting a democracy. However, it has recently extended its ventures beyond such geographical limits with the new role of military interventionism. As Møller notes, though, despite some humanitarian interventions, "suggestions to the effect that for NATO this was the logical behavior of an alliance that had simply abandoned its geopolitical self-definition in favour of seeing itself as a 'community of values' ring rather hollow".[32]

However, the task of the Organisation for Security and Co-operation in Europe (OSCE), one of the most important European organisations after the EU, which during the Cold War had a major role in maintaining regional peace, has since had a low profile. This is an organisation with a long history during the Cold War of supporting and encouraging the signing of agreements on CBM, as well as confidence and security-building measures. Even some attempts, such as those pursued by Moscow, to raise the OSCE's role by developing this organisation into a major institution in Europe tasked with maintaining collective security, have effectively been made redundant by NATO. Møller observes that, despite this barrier, the OSCE can still play an important role in fostering peace and security in the region via democratisation.[33]

Hence, Møller, in a review of the old theory of "democratic peace" (which has its origins in Immanuel Kant's "Perpetual Peace" of 1795) by authors such as Bruce Russett, Nils Petter Gleditsch and Havard Hagre, concludes that this theory has experienced a significant renaissance since 1990. Møller finds the "monadic" version of this theory implausible on account of its claim that democratic countries are inherently peaceful: the pre-emptive military actions of the US and Israel are cases in point. The "dyadic" version, despite involving the less radical claim that democracies do not go to war against each other, also comes under criticism. It is unable to give a clear definition of war or an adequate answer to the question of how high to determine the standards for democracy (e.g. NATO's war against Serbia).

Møller also rejects the third version of "democratic peace", the "strong systemic" version, as unrealistic insofar as "it envisages a democratic structure for the world". Møller himself suggests a "weak systemic" version according to which, as he explains, "the system would be more democratic the more its constituent parts are so. The number of state dyads, between which war would be possible, would simply decline with the spread of democracy". He concludes that if the "democratic peace" theory is correct, then it would be rational for states, including democracies, to democratise their neighbours, not just peacefully but using force if needed. The EU, being an organisation that offers various economic and security advantages, is a unique community that every European state would like to be part of. Therefore, the EU has the power and influence to require them to meet demanding standards of reforms before they are permitted to join the organisation.[34]

To explore whether European security models are applicable to the PG region, Møller examines the fact that the PG states interact on security issues more than they do with other countries (except the US). For this, Møller employs Barry Buzan's concept of a regional security complex (RSC), which places emphasis on the undividable relationship between the common primary security concerns of a group of states and their individual national security concerns. As a means of understanding regional dynamics from both inside states and beyond states to international organisations, Møller places his emphasis on the interaction among states. The assumption of stable regional dynamics is that states have "socio-political cohesion based on a well-defined 'idea' of the state, as well as the appropriate physical basis and institutional expression". This is a stable base for preventing states from being driven by domestic political agendas to cause regional instability.[35]

However, the PG states are categorised as "weak states" because of their domestic and regional problems, such as religious or ethnic minority issues, lack of democracy, unresolved border disputes with each other, and what Møller calls "procedural legitimacy". They also suffer from a low amount of "maturity", where mutual recognition of sovereignty is still an unsolved issue among neighbours and there is the risk of conflicts and war developing between neighbours as well as with ultra-regional states. In sum, such domestic political instability with its impact on inter-state relations would result in regional instability as a whole. Despite the lack of common threat perception among the PG states, and notwithstanding such fragile interstate relations and the absence of experience in coordinating a collective security approach, Møller notes that, "[T]he region does exhibit certain patterns of restraint, based on a shared commitment to important values and a certain commitment among states to the survival of all as well as an embryonic institutional framework."[36]

However, especially in reference to the present situation, Møller concludes that there is definitely not a unipolar system; neither is there any possibility of fostering a new form of bipolarity or a stable security approach to the balance of power in the PG. In this regard he notes that the new definitions, like Huntington's, which divide the globe between the West and the rest of the world, might even work as a unifying agent for the region. Regarding the region's lack of a major divisive issue over which there could develop bipolarity among neighbouring states and further encourage clashes between them, Møller notes that despite the great divergence between Shiite and Sunni groups, the division is not strong enough to serve as the basis for entrenched polarisation and conflict between and within the PG states. Given the existence of the three major poles of Iran, Iraq and Saudi Arabia (GCC), Møller believes that a tripolar structure is likely. However, the problem is that the balance of power between these three is delicate and very asymmetrical (see Table 9.2); also, temporary alignments of the classical kind of two against the third pillar have proved fragile. The other problem is that, in comparison with Europe, institutionalisation in this region is far more promising; there are no inclusive regional arrangements or institutions dealing with the various issues facing the PG. Most regional problems are discussed bilaterally. The GCC is the only form of institutionalised security cooperation but, as Møller points out, "rather than seeking to involve Iran and Iraq, the GCC has (so far) merely sought to deter them, mainly by serving as a vehicle for ensuring US support". Another problem is that despite the significance of indirect means to achieve security, such as establishing a network of economic and other ties for promoting peace and stability via interdependency, as did the EU, PG states have not been able to take advantage of such methods.[37]

TABLE 9.2
The balance of power between the three regional powers

Rank order	Population	Wealth	Military power	Friends
Iraq	2	3	2/3	3/1
Iran	1	2	1	2/3
Saudi Arabia	3	1	3/2	1/2

Source: Bjørn Møller
Note: Legend: Normal: prior to 2003, italics: after 2003

Consequently, as Møller also recognises, the security situation up to 2003 was the best opportunity to provide a stable security approach in the PG. Iraq was weak, Iran's military threat was much weaker than it is today, with Tehran's more pragmatic foreign policy looking for normalisation with the GCC, especially under the presidency of Khatami and his dynamic *détente* foreign policy. The weak GCC, which was taking advantage of the US security umbrella, instead of making war against Iraq had the opportunity to stabilise the situation via diplomatic means as well as arms control negotiations (see Table 9.3). However, by electing to pursue a dual containment strategy against Iran and Iraq Washington missed this great opportunity.[38]

TABLE 9.3
Possible stabilisation measures (–2003)

	Iraq	Iran	GCC
Dual containment	Roll back (military, economically)	Contain (economically, militarily)	Support (militarily)
Alternative			
Phase 1	Contain (militarily)	Normalise (integrate)	Support (militarily, defensively)
Phase 2	Normalise (integrate)	Support (security guarantee)	Support (security guarantees)
Phase 3	Support (security guarantee)	Support (security guarantees)	Support (security guarantees)
Phase 4	(Security community, collective security, general security guarantees)		

Source: Bjørn Møller

Other studies of security models

Other analysts, like Richard Russell, also believe that for stable security architecture in the volatile region of the PG (even in the post-Saddam era) there is no alternative to balance-of-power politics, nor can Iran be excluded from any regional security arrangements. As Joseph McMillan, Richard Sokolsky and Andrew Winner argue, "[T]he region needs regularized multilateral connections on security and related issues that encompass all the key players in the region, namely, Iraq, Iran and Saudi Arabia."[39]

Such multilateral connections will promote transparency and build trust that will enable the development of a new security network with more formal security institutions, similar to those used in Europe during the Cold War. As Pollack, Takeyh, Cook and Ehteshami, for instance, have detailed in various ways, the PG needs a gradual approach, which would begin with the establishment of a regional-security forum for debates, the exchange of information and even the formulation of agreements. This could be a move towards confidence-building measures, such as exchanges of views, information and even observers, or also building links for multilateralism with the final intention of developing arms control pacts. Eventually, these would lead to a full security system similar to institutions such as the OSCE.[40]

Hence, Russell praises the flexibility of a balance-of-power strategy for the PG and argues that this would be a very good thing for the US. He emphasises that if this strategy is employed alongside over-the-horizon military capabilities, it would be beneficial to the mutual interests of both the US and the regional-security partners.[41]

Analysts and scholars, as well as policy-makers, have drawn similar conclusions concerning the two dominant contending frameworks for PG security: US hegemony and principled multilateralism. These conclusions are viewed as even more valid in the post-Saddam era.

Rathmell (et al.), for instance, argue that in the post-Saddam era none of the US alternative models of security, either to unilaterally attempt to enforce a democratic system or to act merely as an external balancer in the traditional balance-of-power approach, will work. They emphasise the disadvantages of the US hegemony strategy and the heavy dependence on a forward US military presence to provide the region's security. Instead, Rathmell (et al.) suggest that, because of a wide range of national, regional and international issues related to developments in the PG, the US and Europe need to work together to construct a more sustainable PG security system based on a combination of balance of military power between Iran, Iraq and the GCC, and broad political and economic reforms to tackle the political and socio-economic problems causing reasons for discontent and extremism in the region. Besides Europe's strategic interest in the PG, such as its greater dependency than the US on PG energy supplies, close ties with the region by a network of economic and political linkages and deep concerns regarding US permanent hegemony in the ME/PG, the EU's perception that it needs military power to back up its soft power and prove its ability to be a more effective partner to the US in this region is understandable.[42]

However, what makes the European Union's role in the PG security especially valuable is its less confrontational policy towards the region than that of the US. Also, it has the power and influence to foster practical reforms. Its policy of "critical dialogue" with Tehran in the 1990s, despite US discontent, and its demanding standards of reform before expanding its economic ties with the GCC, are some examples of when it has used its considerable economic and institutional ties to make a real contribution to moderation and stability in the region. Moreover, as was mentioned in previous chapters, since 2004 the EU decision to create a rapid reaction force (RRF) independently of NATO, in spite of its small and limited size, could be a starting point for the EU to take a more significant geopolitical role in the strategic region of the PG. Hence, there is a long list of reasons for not only the US, but also the littoral states, to involve Europe/the EU more in any future PG security system.

Kraig is another writer who has questioned the continuing strategy of US hegemony. He suggests that an alternative, quite different, security approach would be a "principled multilateral" approach, distinguished by its inclusiveness and basic recognition of the inherent rights of all PG states – especially those regarding legitimate measures for self-defence and regime survival. It also includes a rules-based system in which international law is applicable to all actors in the PG, including the US. The major hypothesis of principled multilateralism is that, "[S]ecurity is sought with other states, rather than against them, and that domestic developments in the Gulf will follow a more beneficial course if all states are gradually intertwined in a web of military and economic agreements that create strong interdependence."[43]

An alternative: A PG Pyramid Security Model

In designing a model that addresses the need for collective security architecture for the PG region, this study has come up with a model of developing security through the feelings of attachment and interdependency that should occur when the littoral states have a single geopolitical vision. The following factors, with some new mechanisms, are its major principles.

- Geopolitics, which, being the most fixed and firm feature of the region, will provide the basis for discussion. Geopolitics is the major convergent element among the PG states: it shows that every state, as a part of this geopolitical region, has a unique and non-ignorable place in the security system. Regardless of their size, all states have a similar, though unequal, weight. Geopolitics also shows how important it is for regional states to take advantage of the geopolitical significance of the PG as a power/knowledge which would enable them to play a major role in balance-of-power politics in the international system and be able to take advantage of various opportunities resulting from geopolitical developments, to their best interests as well as to the region's security and stability. Urging littoral states to have global and not merely regional geopolitical perspectives would result in a single geopolitical vision as a power/knowledge for all the regional states in the PG. Only by addressing this fragile region as a whole, not as divided states and groups of individuals ranged against the other states or groups, would it be possible to prevent further geopolitical problems in this region and change the traditional disruptive role of geopolitical significance of the PG in the region's security to enable it to become a convergent element. Under such circumstances, geopolitics would work as an element for encouraging cooperation among all beneficiary parties instead of being an expansion lever of the external powers.
- The need to include all littoral states. The attitude of all PG states should be that of mutual partners attempting to achieve global and regional security, regardless of a diversity of dissimilar state ideologies.
- The balance of military power between the region's three major players: Iran, Iraq and Saudi Arabia (GCC). This balance should not be of the classical kind of two against the third, but should preferably be maintained through arms control negotiations.
- The need to assure the interests of all regional and non-regional players.
- Acknowledging the necessity of a proper and positive relationship between the strongest regional actor and the non-regional player

(with great influence and interest in that region), as a general and certain principle to attain regional security in any region, including in the PG. Based on the single successful occurrence of the twin-pillar security model in the PG, as well as the need to construct comprehensive multilateral coalitions, the key factor in achieving a durable collective security approach in the PG will remain Iran–US relations.

- The need for there to be no foreign military presence (in the long term) or dominance (in the short term) in the region, as this affects the regional balance of power and is a source of instability. It is also a cause of radicalism and a major obstacle to reform.
- Introducing a fourth element to previous categories of the important, interlocking elements needed to establish a workable, legitimate and authoritative security model in the PG. An appropriate international political environment with a proper international security system's structure is added to the other three elements of: an inclusive and multilateral approach; a balance of power, preferably through arms control negotiations among all three regional key players; and domestic developments and reforms in the littoral states.
- The last and most important element of integration is people's communication/interconnections. Developing and capitalising on these will increase a nation-state's soft power and also strengthen the regional security situation.

The importance of this model stems not just from the role that states have in its architecture and their effect on its functionality, but also that some consideration is given to the role of people (even sub-national groups), their interactions, as well as their satisfaction. The reasons for this emphasis are as follows.

1) As the fundamental part of any nation-state, people have a significant role in the success of any cooperation model. Therefore, in the process of reform in the PG, states' national governments will be obliged to consider their role more seriously, which in the current century should be a compulsory requirement.
2) Interpersonal communication is important to prevent an escalation of confrontational feelings between Arabs and Persians, or the further development of political theories that specify the clashes

between civilisations as a reason for the differences in cultural and religious identities (according to Huntington's theory). At present (the twenty-first century) this is a major challenge that confronts all littoral states.

3) President Khatami's theory of dialogue among civilisations in international relations should be acknowledged within the PG to be significant. The theory has been recognised internationally to correctly emphasise the importance of dialogue, despite cultural diversities. However, its particular applicability to the PG is owing to the experience of peaceful coexistence of the people in this region long before foreigners' dominance over the PG, which began in the fifteenth century, and the policy by foreigners to "divide and rule" to increase ethnic confrontational feeling among people in this region. Hence, emphasising this theory at present is specifically important because of current regional ethnic disputes, which have greatly increased since the US invasion of Iraq in 2003.

In other words, the emphasis of this model on the role of people is supported by the modern world's wider and more complex set of interactions, in addition to the growing capacity and importance of and emphasis on reforms that encourage nations and groups to have more influence on world affairs. Even expansionist geopoliticians such as Huntington acknowledge the growing influence of people (individuals and groups) where he downplays the continuing major power of the nation-states and assumes "cultures" of people as the dominant source of conflicts in the future global politics. It is in such a world that Huntington's post-Cold War strategic debate, with its aim of maintaining the US as the premier global power, is based, stressing the importance of "renewing its Western civilization from within and actively containing, dividing and playing off other civilizations against each other".[44] PG states should be aware of such a divide-and-rule policy and overcome their domestic and regional problems. This argument is supported by the efforts made to spread the concept of the new war against terrorism, and ideas like Huntington's perception of the potentially rough conflict between Western and Islamic civilizations as a defining feature of an evolving world order.

Moreover, the new political climate after Saddam, which has caused a growing sectarian divide in the region, would urge the PG states (especially the GCC, which has discriminated against and oppressed Shiites, who form a large segment of several of their populations, and the growing anti-government religious militancy, specifically Sunni radical Muslims) to overcome their domestic and regional problems. It is important to include Yemen in the Pyramid Security Model, since it is a major state in the vicinity, and a source of radicalism.

As was studied in previous chapters on internal threats, the GCC states are aware of the need for domestic reform to make their regimes more stable and their economies more vibrant; however their domestic socio-economic and political problems confront them with rigorous restrictions in their attempts to carry out real reforms. Despite this fact, the GCC states are advised to implement real reforms sooner rather than later.

Moreover, as Turki Al-Hamad states, due to issues, especially the consequence of very high corruption and uncountable government spending levels, "The unconditional social agreement of loyalty in return for free social services between the rulers and the ruled in the GCC states has been shaken."[45] Also, due to potential reductions in oil revenues (which have worked as a legitimate factor for all regional states), unrest may increase as government resources diminish in the future; this will probably contribute towards further socio-political instability. Any decline in socio-economic opportunities – e.g. imposing a tax system – may motivate requests for political reforms and deliver greater political participation to citizens. However, the reform process needs time and a specific education of the people (especially in this region with a combination of traditional values and modern culture and other current socio-political issues which have increased radicalism) to prevent social unrest or any possible confrontation with citizens – especially the large and restless younger generation who are unemployed and have high expectations.

Domestic issues are pivotal problems facing Iranian society, too. Uneven economic and political development in Iranian society caused the Shah's regime to be overthrown, so the threat to the new regime cannot be ignored or underestimated. Because of the revolution in particular, democracy is a necessity, not a luxury, for Iran more than for any other state in the ME. Democracy, and its promise to attract the investments Iran needs to put an end to high numbers of unemployment, are the only solutions to its huge economic problems. Hence, as long as satisfying its people, the provision of wealth (as a major element to the success of a society, as well as a significant element of power and influence) and preparations towards democracy (giving the government soft and hard power as well as political legitimacy) are not the priority of the IRI, Iran cannot become a stable regional power. This is particularly the case if Iran fails to reduce the tension in its relations with its neighbours in the PG and the West, particularly the US. Therefore, the regime's survival depends upon opening up the political system to more democratic participation and economic reforms in order to address its most strategic weakness.

In sum, wider economic reforms and creating a regional economic interdependency would be a solution to the difficulties that all the PG states are facing. In the pyramid model, NGOs, private sectors and people's communications/interrelations are employed to help shape dialogue as the basic step towards any CBM and interdependency.

The orientation of future global politics is important as to whether they serve the interest of a premier global power or serve the benefit of a world that appreciates diversity and contains different nations and civilizations. This study has thus come up with a fourth element in addition to the previous categories of the interlocking elements needed to establish a functional security model in the PG, "an appropriate international political environment with a proper international security system's structure". Therefore, it has stressed the necessity of considering more seriously President Khatami's theory of dialogue among civilizations in international relations. This theory, which was mainly provided in response to Huntington's, emphasises the importance of dialogue, despite cultural diversities, in a time where all nations and the globe itself need maximum cooperation and harmony; some major examples of present-day threats being global warming, environmental degradation and resource depletion.

Geometrical functionality of a pyramid model

I have designed this model as a pyramid (see Figure 9.1) with three sides comprising:

1) the policies of the littoral Arab states
2) the policies of ultra-regional powers, and
3) Iran's policies.

FIGURE 9.1
The Pyramid Security Model

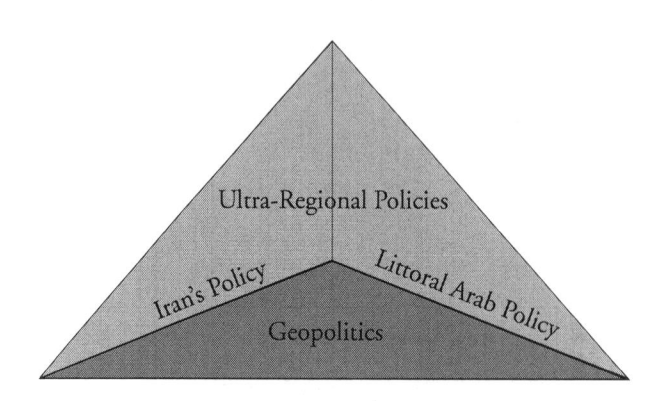

Ultra-Regional Policies
Iran's Policy
Littoral Arab Policy
Geopolitics

As the most powerful regional player, with its geopolitical features, Iran has strategic depth and a naturally dominant position in the PG.

One side of the pyramid is dedicated to Iran because, as mentioned earlier, to establish any long-term multilateral security approach a coalition of the strongest regional and global powers is needed to guarantee peace and stability.

In addition to the three sides, the base of the pyramid, which interacts with all three sides, is the geopolitics of the PG. The reasons for taking geopolitics as the base are as follows.

1) The geopolitics of the PG should be treated as the determining factor of all regional and ultra-regional interactions and relations, as geopolitics has an impact on every single nation-state's interests and national security, and hence must always be the base of pyramid. It is the major axis of the security model.
2) In any instance of an attempt by any of the three regional and non-regional elements to change the base of the pyramid in its favour, the model will be destabilised and regional instability will be the result. In other words, in a balance of power based on geopolitics (including military power, arms races, or cultural/nationalist issues),

if any party tries to ruin the balance (i.e. if there is too much movement of the vertex, which means the picture of vertex will not be seen on the base "geopolitics" any more), history will repeat itself. If one of the countries involved gains too much weight, the other two would feel threatened and try to compensate.

3) Each one of the three sides of the pyramid interacts with geopolitics as the regional axis, but also each member of any pair of sides has some interaction with each other. In other words, there is bilateral as well as multilateral interaction between the sides. Also, at the vertex of this pyramid, triple interactions come together as the basis of the models' balancer. So long as the vertex of the pyramid is projected onto the geopolitics base, the stability of the region is guaranteed.

Some factors influencing the functionality of the model
I believe this model can work on the basis of the mixed approaches of a cooperative-security (liberalism) framework and realpolitik (realism). What is needed is a balance of interests between the three sides of the pyramid. Without interaction and cooperation between these three sides, such that there is interdependency between them, this balance will not be achieved. Also, according to the cooperative model, the factor of equality and prosperity for all will mitigate any humiliations and weakness, and consequently reduce radical behaviour. This will also give all states and nations opportunities to improve their own opportunities for peace, security and prosperity, to lower hostility and increase cooperation and a healthy interdependency. This can be achieved by decreasing investment in military capabilities and investing more in social wealth and prosperity.

In this model the primary actor is the sovereign state, which will enter into verifiable agreements with other states; however, a wide role is allocated to the people. Since the interactions of the nation-states, people and governments are important to strengthen the cooperation model there should be a greater emphasis on promoting the convergence elements and eliminating the divergence elements. The stability of the pyramid arises from the interaction of nation-states through the axis of convergence elements existing between them. So, to prevent instability and preserve the authority of this model in the PG we should bear the following points in mind.

1) We must pay attention to all major strategic elements of the PG (in the long term), including the concerns of all states, which affect any regional security system. In insisting on this as a requirement of any new and viable multilateral PG framework, it would increase the possibility of all the littoral nation-states defining their national security in terms of their common values and interests, such as Islam, rather than their differences, such as the Shiite and Sunni division, or energy as the major economic source of all PG states.

2) This model, with its emphasis on a balance of power by means of negotiations for arms control, along with its CBM, also aims to establish and encourage a broad understanding of security that includes its economic and social dimensions. This would also include making issues such as political reform, economic diversification and educational reform the key pillars of any sustainable framework. This argument is supported by the prevailing global atmosphere, which, since the end of the Cold War, has placed particular emphasis on patterns of cooperation, as well as on real domestic reforms – a pre-eminent global security issue in the post-9/11 world. Added to this is the fact that, due to growing political discontent and radicalism within the GCC along with the spread and evolution of terrorism from radical religious militants in the whole region, which has intensified since 2003, the issue of applying domestic reforms is construed not simply in terms of political prestige but as a necessity. Moreover, recent regional developments support the argument that littoral states, both Iran and Arabian, have shown increasingly serious interest in supporting the idea of an inclusive collective security arrangement for the region.[46] Each state, by increasing its stability via improving its social-economic standards and values, can upgrade its weight in this security framework, so social-economic dimensions will gradually become the most important geopolitical features of each state, irrespective of the size of the country. In such circumstances (i.e. a broader understanding of security), communication will become increasingly important for a more stable region.

3) Construing geopolitics as the basis of this model could work as a deterrent system, due to its mentioned role as a convergent element among the PG states and as a shape of power/knowledge resulting

from a single geopolitical vision. As mentioned earlier, only by addressing this fragile region as a whole would it be possible to prevent further geopolitical problems in this region. However, the littoral states would be able to take advantage of a single geopolitical vision in the international system if they make efforts to solve their domestic problems as well as their long-standing regional disputes – e.g. territorial and boundary disputes. This could be done through the improvement of the political conditions via extending confidence-building measures and regional cooperation, especially by having greater economic interaction, and in particular by establishing various organisations to promote cooperation and the rule of law. Such a process, one that puts emphasis on soft, as opposed to exclusively hard, power, would pave the way for the creation of a functional regional security arrangement. It may also effectively deter aggression or hostile actions that would otherwise undermine the pyramid. One of the organisations for promoting the rule of law should be an organisation tasked with preventing aggression or antagonistic actions that would undermine the new system.

By emphasising the geopolitical elements, especially socio-political and economic power rather than military power, it is possible to maximise domestic stability and political legitimacy while at the same time minimising the strength of the fear of bigger states by smaller states. The pyramid model connects the issues of legitimacy and authority closely with the issue of sustainability. This is primarily because the model construes the gains it aims to achieve as mutual gains for all participants, not as gains for one particular actor, or set of actors. It can thereby more plausibly make the assurance that remaining in the system will be in the interests of all the relevant parties. This would in turn lessen the possibility of any states withdrawing from the model because of any sudden ideological or political changes.

Some details and suggestions
1) The role of people and the private sector: among the various possible socio-economic interactions, trade is a particularly significant element for creating interdependency, which would in turn be peace-promoting.

2) Europe and the key Asian Pacific region's states would also need to play a greater security role. However, the best security role can be obtained through increasing the interdependency of these regions with the PG states. Continuing efforts to strengthen the cooperation axis and interdependence between the EU–AP and the PG may result in the following corollaries for the region: encouraging domestic developments in the PG; encouraging greater CBM among PG states as well as regulating regional and non-regional powers' relations and in some cases, such as US–Iran, establishing new relations; and cooperating with all relevant parties to control insurgencies and terrorist attacks in the region. This could assist the PG states to stabilise this model of cooperation until their CBM have been sufficiently developed and they have been assured of the functionality of this model. After this the over-the-horizon presence can even be reduced to nil.

3) Given the considerable effect Iran can have on the security of the PG, its domestic stability as well as its permanent and stable foreign policy is very significant for the security and steadiness of this region. *Détente* foreign policy with an emphasis on the convergent elements with its neighbours is needed to assure regional and non-regional parties of Tehran's peaceful goals. These can pave the way for guaranteeing long-term security, which could result in foreign forces withdrawing from the region.

4) Arab states will need to understand that the idea of multilateral security structures and the improvement of relations between Iran and the US are in their interests. Furthermore, they need not be concerned about a devaluation of their political weight and of being excluded from future decision-making in this region. To assuage the Arab states, especially the smaller or weaker countries, of their fear of Iran they would need to be assured that the establishment of regionally based security structures will not result in a reduced US military umbrella with a reciprocal Iranian move. Moreover, they would need to know that even if Iran had such ambitions it should, within the Pyramid model's regulation, first develop bases like CBM to assure its neighbours of its peaceful goals.

5) Since integration in the PG has not been welcomed by the West, and any multilateralism in this region might face some resistance, it is especially important to emphasise that stability in this geopolitical

and geostrategic region has been proven to be essential to global peace and prosperity. So despite any possible resistance, forming such integration would be in the interests of everyone, rather than just flattering to the concerns of the Great Powers with huge interests in this region.

6) A further factor in favour of regional integration is that any regional cooperation and integrity within Islamic countries would be to the advantage of the Islamic world. Given that no unity can happen at once, it must occur region by region. This is an idea that is no doubt not particularly welcomed by the Great Powers, especially as they are spreading ideas like Huntington's or the concept of the new war against terrorism, which places great emphasis on reactions rather than its true causes. This can be addressed by considering and confronting real causes and problems, which is an approach that has been effective in other places, such as the recent IRA peace process in Northern Ireland. If there is any true desire for peace in the ME there are many examples to follow: a plan like the Marshall Plan could easily work here.

Some practical solutions
The pyramid model can avoid the typical problems that arise for models based on a competition for power between states with conflicting national interests and agendas, like Russell's,[47] as it does not base a balance of power on such confrontational foundations. The other tools for achieving this balance, like political-military contacts, confidence-building measures and arms control, can be provided via the following.

- Forums, used as initiatives for CBM in different fields. These forums could be the beginning of the establishment of different regional institutions in various fields (i.e. arms control, counter-terrorism, economic/trade, security, cultural/educational, etc.).
- Continuing current bilateral agreements and starting new multilateral agreements until there is real reassurance. New ties and agreements between Iran and the US, and with the GCC, should be explored, especially over geopolitical issues such as oil and gas, transportation networks, goods transition, etc.

- To increase the geopolitical position of the PG and decrease the security threat to the status quo, Yemen should be included as a member of this region.

Final outlines

Various developments in the modern world have generated greater interconnectedness and interdependency between nation-states. Traditional security approaches based on military confrontation rather than co-operative relations have become increasingly untenable and are unlikely to succeed at all, especially in a significant geopolitical region like the PG, where issues of security have wide local, regional and global effects.

It was observed that only a security model that contained interlocking elements of inclusiveness, power balance and domestic reform within an appropriate and just international political environment that has a proper international security system structure – whereas the region lacks all – would be able to manage relations between PG states and create a power regulation that would ensure the rule of "law" rather than the rule of "the powers".

As it was shown, in order to attain regional security, besides the importance of considering the security concerns and national interests of both regional and non-regional players, it is imperative that the major regional and external players have suitable relations. No other alternative strategy would be able to fulfil regional and ultra-regional interests and meet security concerns. In this regard, one of this study's major topics of analysis has been the behaviour of Iran and the US. Therefore, the pyramid model – a cooperative model for a security system – whereby one of its major mechanisms is such a relationship, has been developed.

It was noted that the general consensus among different authors and analysts is that dialogue between states and organisations is the best tool for building confidence, settling disputes and deterring conflict in the PG. It was emphasised that engaging in dialogue is the only way to promote transparency, build trust and create a new security network with more formal security institutions.

The result of such processes would be similar to the consistent political strategy (Marshall Plan) employed alongside a military strategy (NATO) in Europe during and after the Cold War. The PG states are wealthy enough not to require international financial aid to supplement regional collective cooperation; they would mainly need the political and technological support of ultra-regional powers for a multilateral security approach.

However, despite all the disadvantages of a selective security approach in the PG, Washington still prefers and employs bilateral defence arrangements and military tools rather than a political framework by offering to sell more arms to its regional allies against Iran. This is evidenced by the US Secretary of State Condoleezza Rice and the Defence Secretary Robert Gates' recent (August 2007) trip to the region with the aim of launching Washington's new ME strategy of containment against Iran, arming its allies, obtaining support for an Iraq Shiite-led government and arranging a new conference for peace between the Israelis and Palestinians. The arming of US Arab allies – e.g. the GCC states through deals worth US$30 billion – was announced as a response to the growing threat of Iran. The aim was to reassure them of long-term US support, especially after Washington and Tehran appeared to be entrenched in their stances on Iran's nuclear programme. In this regard, Gates remarked during his trip that, having been in the PG for some 60 years, the US has "every intention of being here for a lot longer".

Moreover, Iran's failure to recognise the geopolitical significance of this region from non-regional players' points of view and also its unstable and unwise foreign policy, especially towards its PG neighbours, has paved the way for the US to continue its hegemonic regional security strategy. Its policy, especially regarding its nuclear programme, has served as an opportunity for the US to make a wider front in the ME against Iran. It has also paved the way for closer ties between old enemies, the Arabs and the Israelis, as they both see Iran as a common threat.

However, US direct military involvement in the PG has not just been an expensive exercise for Washington, but has resulted in competing reactions from other parties with interests in this region, viz., China, the EU and Russia. It has also stimulated popular discontent in the host countries, particularly against Arab regimes. This situation has resulted in increasing militarism, either in the form of terrorist attacks or the extension of the military presence and power of different regional and non-regional parties, directly or indirectly. However, since the US' interests have been guaranteed in both peace and crisis situations in this region, some major questions are raised, and answered, especially with respect to the two most important traditional objectives of Washington's policy in the ME: the preservation of the oil flow at an affordable price; and the security of Israel. This causes some questions to arise. What are the US' real foreign policy goals in the ME/PG? Is there any willingness to build peace and security in this region or does Washington need at least one permanent enemy in the region to achieve its hidden hegemonic intentions, including arms sales? Or, does the US support any kind of collective regional arrangements in the PG, whether security or economic cooperation arrangements, which would create the assurance of a commitment to a common interest? This kind of idea seems very unwelcome to Washington – as well as other non-regional powers – because its long-term interests would be in contrast to the existence of a single powerful regional energy organisation in the PG. Also, greater economic interaction and cooperation would result in a basis for stronger security interactions among littoral states of the PG, interactions that, with the exception of Iran, would be greater than those they currently have with the US. Therefore, there would be no reason for a US military presence or a flourishing US arms market in the region; a very dangerous and alarming fact to US foreign policy concerns.

Under such circumstances the continuity of the West's expansionist geopolitical debates and the US' drive for control over the states and strategic resources and wealth of the world, with a determining influence on foreign policy and global strategy, becomes dependent on a description of the world map similar to that of the Cold War period, one of ideological identity and difference; such as foes or allies, "with us or against us", etc. Therefore, the recent model of emerging world order suggested by Samuel Huntington – namely, the "clash of civilizations" – as a dominant factor in future global politics for the continuance of dividing the world into good and evil has been highly welcomed. In his opinion the most fundamental of such clashes is the conflict between the West and the rest of the world,[48] where in his new post-Cold War geopolitical world-picture, the principal American strategic interest is to perpetuate the primacy of the US as the global power.[49] The continuity of this geopolitical debate and how US statesmen have conceptualised the role of their state in world affairs, which intensified since 11 September 2001 (9/11), can be seen in US terminology. Instead of "the evil empire" used by Ronald Reagan to describe the USSR, George W. Bush's phrase for the official enemies of the US in 2002 – particularly, Iraq, Iran and North Korea – is the "axis of evil".[50] His use of terms like "Islamic fascists" serves to link the actions of violent Muslims to their religion and thereby strengthen arguments about the clash of civilisations between Islam and the West.[51] Such definitions of a divided world are being propagandised where cooperation, most especially since the end of the Cold War, is the prevailing global atmosphere and is increasingly being practised within and by the West, although there is not any meaningful process or global support for collective cooperation and unity within the rest of world, viz. non-Western, developing and underdeveloped countries and more specifically the ME/PG.

Nation-states such as the Islamic Republic of Iran have a special place in these geopolitical debates addressing the new confrontation of Islam and the West. Besides its significant geopolitical situation, Iran's Islamic political ideology, its antipathy towards the US, and its growing influence in the ME with its intention of creating collective regional security arrangements, which would increase its regional role and simultaneously exclude foreign powers' presence, are all key factors. States such as Iran, whose foreign policies have considerable impact against US hegemonic unilateralism, specifically in the ME/PG, are currently meant to be disrupted and isolated; politically, militarily and economically. However, as was argued earlier, without a proper relationship between Iran and the US as the two major regional and non-regional powers, establishing peace and security would be impossible. Therefore, it has been argued that as long as the foreign policy goals of the US as the hegemonic power in the present international system are based on preventing a natural development of regional powers' roles, especially Iran's, none of the security arrangements can work. The consequences of the US' political strategy of containment in the PG could be similar to the defence strategy during the Cold War which soon became militarised and even nuclearised.

Such external threats and interferences are one of the reasons why the PG states have regional geopolitical perspectives rather than global views, a major prohibitive factor in establishing a collective regional security approach. Other reasons for the littoral states espousing a regional geopolitical perspective have been highlighted by studying the domestic and regional threats they are faced with.

In addition to the importance of the positive and cooperative role of Iran in the interconnected ME/PG issues, the major role of the littoral states in the establishment of durable security in the PG cannot be ignored; it remains a particularly glaring omission from the GCC's considerations. According to one high-ranking diplomat of Bahrain, for instance, the major reason for their reliance on a US security umbrella is the GCC's fear of Iran. However, in response to the author's question about the existence of plans for a short- or long-term agenda to develop CBM with Iran to overcome such fear, his response was completely negative. The point is that if the GCC has been able to continue to exist and overcome its members' differences and disputes to work as a group, an inclusive, multilateral cooperation model that is to the advantage of all involved should be able to work.

In addition, the role of other ultra-regional players, especially those emerging powers like the EU and some key states in the AP (viz. China, India, Japan), in building a durable security framework is significant. Their strategic interest in the PG, such as their growing dependency on PG energy supplies which exceed the US', their close ties with the region by a network of economic and political linkages and their deep concerns over US permanent hegemony in the ME/PG, have resulted in their recognition of a need for military power to back up their soft power. This military power is needed if they are to adopt a greater geopolitical role independently of Washington and if they are to counterbalance the balance of power controlled by the US in the PG.

To prevent wider militarism in this narrow and volatile geostrategic waterway, and promote a real and substantial process of development in the PG states, it is necessary to encourage all parties to work together to construct a more durable security system which would be in the interests of all, particularly via increasing global economic integration. By this process, the fourth interlocking element of the PG security system, which was described as an appropriate international political environment, would also be achieved.

This study holds that the Pyramid Security Model could be a solution to the very volatile situation in the PG, because in order to address major security issues this model is based on geopolitical realities as well as the political and economic concerns of all regional and ultra-regional parties.

The final conclusion of this study is that the entire situation, with its suspicions and mistrust among all regional and ultra-regional states combined with the neglect of other parties' interests and security concerns, has resulted in a daily escalation of crises in this most geostrategic region of the world. The people of the region in particular are the greatest losers in such an unstable and critical situation. The littoral states' regimes do not benefit from such circumstances either. All these factors, combined with the global loss of energy security and increases in the price of energy, and the more recent issue of the spread and evolution of terrorism by radical religious militants, should press all the different parties, both regional and non-regional, to support and assist the establishment of comprehensive security cooperation in this narrow but vital waterway for global peace, security and prosperity. As long as security rather than diplomacy is the priority in the foreign policy of external as well as internal players of the PG, and as long as the general aim is maximum security and political regimes' survival, meaning that security tools focused on military capabilities are a major necessity, stability and prosperity will not occur in this region.

Notes

1 Andrew Rathmell, Theodore Karasik, and David Gompert, "A new Persian Gulf security system", *RAND issue paper* (2003).
2 Michael Kraig (Fall 2004), "Assessing alternative security frameworks for the Persian Gulf", *Middle East Policy*, Washington, vol. 11, issue 3, cited in the site of *Gulf 2000* of Columbia University, NY, USA.
3 Steven Spiegel, "Regional security and the levels of analysis problem", *Journal of Strategic Studies*, vol. 26, issue 3, September 2003, 75–98.
4 Zeev Maoz, "Domestic politics of regional security: theoretical perspectives and Middle East patterns", *Journal of Strategic Studies* (Frank Cass and Company Ltd) Building Regional Security in the ME, 20–21, http://www.jstor.org.ezphost.dur.ac.uk/.
5 Kenneth Waltz, *Theory of international politics* (New York: McGraw-Hill, 1979), 73; cited by Steven Spiegel, op. cit.
6 Kraig, op. cit.
7 Bjørn Møller, "Security models and their applicability to the Gulf: the potential of European lessons applied". In Christian Koch and Felix Neugart (eds), *A window of opportunity: Europe, Gulf security and the aftermath of the Iraq war* (Dubai, UAE: Gulf Research Center, 2005), 56–57.
8 Kraig, op. cit.
9 Ibid.
10 Ibid.
11 Spiegel, op. cit., 76–77.
12 Kraig, op. cit.

13 Janne Nolan (ed.), *Global engagement: Cooperation and security in the 21st century* (Washington, D. C.: Brookings Institution Press, 1994), http://www.brook.edu/press/books/GLOBalen.htm (can no longer be accessed), cited in Kraig, op. cit.
14 J. E. Peterson, *Defending Arabia* (London: Croom Helm, 1986), cited by Andrew Rathmell (et al.), op. cit.
15 Bahig Nassar (n.d.), "US global strategy to maintain world order: the new role of NATO and the US Central Command", *International Network of Engineers and Scientists against Proliferation*, http://www.inesap.org/bulletin15/bul15art17.htm (6 November 2007; can no longer be accessed).
16 Joseph Kostiner (November 1998), "The United States and the Gulf states: alliance in need", *MERIA Journal*, vol. 2, no. 4, http://meria.idc.ac.il/journal/1998/issue4/jv2n4a6.html (accessed 10 May 2007); also Rathmell (et al.), op. cit.
17 Kraig, op. cit.; also Kostiner, op. cit.
18 Richard Russell (winter 2005), "The Persian Gulf's collective-security mirage", *Middle East Policy Council*, vol. XII, no. 4, 82–83.
19 Kraig, op. cit.
20 Rathmell (et al.), op. cit.
21 Ibid.
22 See also Mahmood Sariolghalam (spring 2002), "Theoretical renewal in Iranian foreign policy (Part II)", *Discourse; an Iranian Quarterly*, vol. 3, no. 4, pp. II, 58.
23 Bertelsmann Group for Policy Research Center for Applied Policy Research, "Europe and the Middle East: new ways and solutions for old problems and challenges?" (Munich: Felix Neugart, September 2006), 24.
24 Kraig, op. cit.
25 James Bill, "The politics of hegemony: the United States and Iran", *Middle East Policy*, vol. VIII, no. 3 (September 2001), 92.
26 Kraig, op. cit.
27 Nolan, op. cit.
28 See also Anoushiravan Ehteshami, "Iran, the GCC and Europe: alternative strategies". In Christian Koch and Felix Neugart (eds), op. cit., 45.
29 Peter Jones, *Towards a regional security regime in the Middle East: Issues and options* (Stockholm: SIPRI, 1998), cited in Ehteshami, op. cit., 48–49; also Bertelsmann Group, op. cit.
30 Møller, op. cit., 58–61.
31 Ibid., 61–63.
32 Ibid., 64–66.
33 Ibid., 66–67.
34 Ibid., 67–68.
35 Ibid., 69–70.
36 Ibid., 71–73.
37 Ibid., 73–76.
38 Ibid., 76–77.
39 Joseph McMillan, Richard Sokolsky, and Andrew Winner, "Toward a new regional security architecture", *The Washington Quarterly*, vol. 26, no. 3 (summer 2003), 167, cited in Russell, op. cit.
40 Russell, op. cit., 78–79; also Ehteshami, op. cit., 48–50.
41 Russell, op. cit., 85.
42 Rathmell (et al.), op. cit., 1, 2, 7, 10.

43 Kraig, op. cit.
44 Gearóid Ó Tuathail, "Samuel Huntington and the 'civilizing' of global space". In Gearóid Ó Tuathail, Simon Dalby, and Paul Routledge (eds), *The Geopolitics Reader* (US and Canada: Routledge, 1998), 174.
45 Turki Al-Hamad, "Imperfect alliances: will the Gulf monarchies work together?" In Barry Rubin (ed.), *Crises in the contemporary Persian Gulf* (London and Portland, Oregon: Frank Cass, 2002), 30–31.
46 For instance, statement of Saudi Foreign Minister Saud al-Faisal at the 2004 Gulf Dialogue in Bahrain, or President Ahmadinejad's proposals for collective economic and security cooperation addressed to the GCC summit in Doha in December 2007.
47 Russell, op. cit., 81.
48 Samuel Huntington, "The clash of civilizations?", *Foreign Affairs* (summer 1993), 2–49.
49 Ó Tuathail, "Samuel Huntington and the 'civilizing' of global space", op. cit., 171, 173.
50 Gearóid Ó Tuathail, "General introduction; thinking critically about geopolitics", in Gearóid Ó Tuathail, Simon Dalby, and Paul Routledge (eds), op. cit., 6. (2nd edition (2006), 3.)
51 Richard Allen Greene, "Bush's language angers US Muslims" *BBC News* (12 August 2006), Washington, http://news.bbc.co.uk/2/hi/americas/4785065.stm.

Selected bibliography

Aarts, Paul and Nonneman, Gerd (eds), *Saudi Arabia in the balance* (London: Hurst and Company, 2005).
Abrahamian, Ervand, *Iran between two revolutions* (Princeton, New Jersey: Princeton University Press, 1982).
Amirahmadi, Hooshang (ed.), *Small islands, big politics: The Tonbs and Abu Musa in the Persian Gulf* (New York: St. Martin's Press, 1996).
Bill, James, "The politics of hegemony: the United States and Iran", *Middle East Policy*, vol. VIII, no. 3 (September 2001).
Buzan, B., *States and fear: An agenda for international security in the post-Cold War era* (New York: Harvester Wheatsheaf, 1991).
Byman, Daniel, Chubin, Shahram, Ehteshami, Anoushiravan, and Green, Jerrold, *Iran's security policy in the post-revolutionary era* (USA: National Defense Research Institute (RAND), 2001).
Carter, H. and Ehteshami, Anoushiravan (eds), *The Middle East's relations with Asia and Russia* (London, USA and Canada: Routledge Curzon, 2004).
Chubin, Shahram, "Iran", in Yezid Sayigh and Avi Shalim (eds), *The Cold War and the Middle East*, (Clarendon: Oxford, 1997).
Chubin, Shahram and Sepehr Zabih, *The foreign relations of Iran: A developing state in a zone of great-power conflict* (Berkeley, Los Angeles, and London: University of California Press, 1974).
Clawson, Patrick (ed.), *Iran's strategic intentions and capabilities* (Washington, D. C.: Institute for National Strategic Studies – National Defense University, 1994).
Cordesman, Anthony, *Iran's military forces in transition: Conventional threats and weapons of mass destruction* (Westport, Connecticut, and London: Praeger, 1999).
Couloumbis, Theodore and Wolfe, James, *Introduction to international relations: Power and justice* (New Jersey: Prentice-Hall, 1990).
Doran, Charles and Buck, Stephen (eds), *The Gulf, energy, and global security* (Colorado and London: Lynne Rienner Publishers, 1991).

Drysdale, Alasdair and Blake, Gerald, *The Middle East and North Africa: A political geography* (New York and Oxford: Oxford University Press, 1985).

Ehteshami, Anoushiravan, *After Khomeini: The Iranian second republic* (London: Routledge, 1995).

Ezzati, Ezzatollah, *Tahlili bar Geopolitic-e Iran va Eragh* [An Analysis of the Geopolitics of Iran and Iraq] (1381 Solar Calendar [2002]) (Tehran Foreign Ministry Press Centre: Institute for Political and International Studies (IPIS)).

Hollis, Rosemary, *Gulf security: No consensus* (London: Royal United Services Institute for Defence Studies, 1993).

Holsti, Kalevi, *Peace and war: Armed conflicts and international order, 1648–1989* (Cambridge, UK: Cambridge University Press, 1991).

Huntington, Samuel, "The clash of civilizations?", *Foreign Affairs*, Summer 1993.

Kazemi, Ali Asghar, *Aba'd-e hoghoghi-e hakemiat-e Iran dar Khalij-e Fars* [Legal dimensions of Iran's authority in the Persian Gulf] (1368 Solar Calendar [1989]) (Tehran: Institute for Political and International Studies (IPIS)).

Keddie, Nikki, *Roots of Revolution* (New Haven and London: Yale University Press, 1981).

Kemp, Geoffrey and Harkavy, Robert, *Strategic geography and the changing Middle East* (Washington, D. C.: Brookings Institution Press, 1997).

Klare, Michael, "The Bush/Cheney energy strategy: implications for US foreign and military policy", Information Clearing House (2003), http://www.informationclearinghouse.info/article4458.htm (accessed 2 October 2004).

Koch, Christian and Neugart, Felix (eds), *A window of opportunity? Europe, Gulf security and the aftermath of the Iraq war* (Dubai, UAE: Gulf Research Center, 2005).

Kraig, Michael Ryan, "Forging a new security order for the Persian Gulf", *Middle East Policy*, vol. XIII, no. 1, spring 2006.

Long, David and Koch, Christian (eds), *Gulf security in the twenty-first century* (Abu Dhabi, UAE: The Emirates Center for Strategic Studies and Research, 1997).

Milani, Mohsen M., *The making of Iran's Islamic revolution: From monarchy to Islamic republic* (Boulder, San Francisco, and Oxford: Westview Press, 1994).

Møller, Bjørn, "Security models and their applicability to the Gulf: the potential of European lessons applied", in Christian Koch and Felix Neugart (eds), *A window of opportunity? Europe, Gulf security and the aftermath of the Iraq war* (Dubai, UAE: Gulf Research Center, 2005).

Moss Helms, Christine, *Iraq: Eastern flank of the Arab World* (Washington D. C.: Brookings Institution Press, 1984).

Murden, Simon, *Emergent regional powers and international relations in the Gulf: 1988–1991* (Reading: Ithaca Press, 1995).

Niblock, Tim (ed.), *Iraq: The contemporary state* (London: Croom Helm, 1982).

Peterson, J. E., *Defending Arabia* (London: Croom Helm, 1986).

Ó Tuathail, Gearóid, Dalby, Simon, and Routledge, Paul, *The geopolitics reader* (US and Canada: Routledge, editions of 1998 and 2006).

Ramazani, Rouhollah, *Revolutionary Iran: Challenge and response in the Middle East* (US and London: The Johns Hopkins University Press and The Johns Hopkins Press Ltd, 1986).

Rathmell, Andrew, Karasik, Theodore, and Gompert, David, "A new Persian Gulf security system", in *RAND issue paper* (2003).

Rubin, Barry (ed.), *Crises in the contemporary Persian Gulf* (London and Portland, Oregon: Frank Cass, 2002).

Saghafi-Ameri, Nasser, *Estrategy va Tahavvolat-e Geopolitic pas az Doran-e Jang-e Sard* [Strategy and geopolitical changes in the aftermath of the Cold War era] (1373 Solar Calendar [1994]) (Tehran: Foreign Ministry Printing and Publication).

Sariolghalam, Mahmood, *Theoretical renewal in Iranian foreign policy (Part II). Discourse; an Iranian Quarterly* (Spring 2002) vol. 3, no. 4.

Schofield, Richard (ed.), *Territorial foundations of the Gulf States* (London: UCL Press, 1994).

Sick, Gary and Potter, Lawrence (eds), *The Persian Gulf at the millennium: Essays in politics, economy, security, and religion* (New York: St. Martin's Press, 1997).

Spiegel, Steven, "Regional security and the levels of analysis problem", *Journal of Strategic Studies*, vol. 26, issue 3, September 2003, 75–98.

Wright, Steven, *The United States and Persian Gulf security: The foundations of the war on terror* (Reading: Ithaca Press, 2007).

Index

Page numbers in *italics* refer to figures, tables and maps.

9/11 attacks on the United States, xxiii, 129–30, 228, 234, 266
14th of July Revolution (1958), Iraq, 124

Abdullah, King of Saudi Arabia, 105
Abizaid, General John, US commander, 199
Abrahamian. Ervand, 168
Abu Dhabi–Saudi Arabia, border dispute, 67
Abu Musa, border dispute, 67, 71, 72, 84, 85, 86
  solving, 89–90
Achaemenid (Hakhâmaneshiyân) Dynasty (550–330 BCE), Iran, *81*
Afghanistan
  East Corridor, 39
  Iran, relationship with, 210
  Soviet invasion, 15, 228
Afsharid Dynasty (AD 1736–1802), Iran, *83*
Ahmadinejad, Mahmoud, President of Iran, 167, 193, 195, 196
Algeria, as a gas source, 20
Algeria Accord, Iraq–Iran (1975), 76, 78, 129, 133, 145
America *see* United States
Amirahmadi, Hooshang, 89–90, 163
Amuzegar, Jamshid, Iranian Prime Minister, 179
anarchy, 220–1
Ancel, Jacques, 73/75, 77
Ansar-e Hezballah, Iran, 192
Arab Ba'th Socialist Party *see* Ba'th Party
Arab–Israeli conflict, 231, 234
Arab League
  boycott of Israel, 113
  Saudi Arabia, military presence in, 118
Arabia, maps
  northern, delimited state territory (1913 to present day), *75*
  southern, contemporary framework, *76*
  southern and south eastern, territorial limits and claims (1903–1955), *74*
Arabian Peninsula, Iran as a threat, 55
Arak refinery, Iran, 41
arms
  and Iran, 197
  and Iraq, 131, 134
  to Saudi Arabia, imports (1986–1999), *107*

arms buying, GCC states, 239–40
arms negotiations, and the Pyramid Security Model, 260
arms race
  in Europe, 246
  in the GCC, 201
  Persian Gulf, 88
arms sales
  GCC states, 231
  Saudi Arabia, 106
  United States, 235, 265, 266
Artesh (regular armed forces), Iran, 165, 192, 193, 195
Arvand Roud (Shatt al-Arab) waterway, border dispute, 67, 72, 76, 77, 85, 144, 145
ASEAN Regional Forum, 244
ASEAN Security Community, 244
Ashkâniân (Parthian) Dynasty (247 BCE–CE 224), Iran, *82*
Asia-Pacific Economic Cooperation (APEC), role in increasing security, 243
Asia Pacific FTA, 244
Asian Great Powers, interdependency with Iran, 37–42
Asian-Pacific region, 22
  energy policy and security, 29–32
  geopolitical aspects, 32–7
  Iran and Asian Great Powers' interdependency, 37–42
  oil and gas demands, 17, 22
  Persian Gulf energy security, 29–44
  Persian Gulf policies, 15
  and the Pyramid Security Model, 262
  see also China; India; Japan; South Korea; Taiwan
Association of South East Asian Nations, 244
axis of evil, xxiii, 266
Ayatollah Beheshti, 179, 183
Ayatollah Khamenei, 164, 185, 202, 203–4
Ayatollah Khomeini, 172, 179, 180, 182, 183, 185, 188, 194
Ayatollah Taleghani, 179
Azadegan oil field, Iran, 40
Aziz, Tariq, Iraqi Foreign Minister, 136

Baghdad, Iraq, 124, 125

[277]

Baghdad Pact (1955–1958), 227
Bahrain
　opposition violence, 104
　Qatar, border dispute, 66, 69, 70, 72, 77
　Saudi Arabia, shared oil reserves, 70
　United States, relationship with, 230
Bahrain Liberation Front, 145
al-Bakr, Hassan, Iraqi coup leader, 124
Al-Bakr proposal (1970), 145
balance of power, 221
　definition, xiv
　disadvantages, 229–32
　in the Persian Gulf, *249*
Bandar Abbas, Iran, 90
Basij, Iran, 183, 191, 192, 194, 195, 196, 199
Basra, Iraq, 124, 125
Ba'th Party
　in Iraq, 124, 125–6, 132, 134, 142, 147, 149, 152–3
　and Iraq's foreign policy, 139–40, 140–1
Bazargan, Mehdi, Iranian Prime Minister, 183
Bazoft, Farzad, 143
Bedouin, in Saudi Arabia, 105
Bertelsmann Group, 240–1, 244
Bill, James, 241
biological weapons, xxix, 135
Blake, Gerald, xxiv, 4, 5, 7, 9, 67, 73, 109–10
boundaries, as a cause of instability, 73/75
Britain
　Iran, border disputes with, 79–84
　Iraq, border disputes, 123–4
　Persian Gulf
　　border disputes with, 65–6
　　policies, 142, 227
Brookings study group, 225
Brzezinski, Zbigniew, xiii
Bu Saafah offshore oil field, Saudi Arabia/Bahrain, 70
Bubiyan islands, border dispute, 76, 77, 132
budgets
　Iran, 186, 198, 202
　Israel, 202
　Saudi Arabia, 109, 111, 202
　United States, xxiii
Bundy, Rodman, 72–3
Bush, George H. W., US President, 150, 231
Bush, George W., US President, xxiii, 47–8, 266–7
Buzan, Barry, 248
Byman, Daniel, 96, 97, 102–3, 105

Calder, Kent, 30
Camp David peace agreement, 149
Carter doctrine, 228
Carter, Jimmy, US President, 47, 179, 221
Caspian Basin *see* Caspian Sea region

Caspian Sea region
　gas reserves, 11, 22
　obstacles as an energy supplier, 58–9
　oil and gas reserves, *24*
　potential as an energy supplier, 41, 58–9
CBM *see* confidence-building measures
Central Command (US CENTCOM), United States, 228
chemical weapons, xxix, 135, 199, 200
Chemical Weapons Convention, 199
Cheney, Dick, former US Secretary of Defence, 47
China
　Agreement of the Century with Iran, 38
　as a competitor, 242
　gas consumption, 31
　geopolitics, 33–4
　Iran, relationship with, 35, 198
　navy, 34
　as an oil importer, 32, 33
　oil production and consumption (1980–2003), 30, *30*
　Persian Gulf, relationship with, 33–4
　and Persian Gulf security, 245
　Russia, relationship with, 35
　United States, relationship with, 35–6, 221
China model, Iran, 188–9, 206
Chubin, Shahram, 97, 144, 159, 160, 160–2, 175, 199, 201
clash of civilizations, xxv
Clinton, Bill, US President, 231
coal, in the European Union, 17
Cohen, Mackinder and Spykman, geopolitical worldviews, *xxvi*
Cohen, Saul Bernard, xxiv–xxv, 6–7
Cold War, xxii–xxiii, xxviii, 227, 246, 247, 264
communication, importance of interpersonal, 254, 254–5
confidence-building measures, 91
　with Iran, 209, 232, 236
　and the Pyramid Security Model, 260, 262, 263
　with Saudi Arabia, 119, 120
Congress Hearings, United States, 109th (27 July 2005), 49, 50
cooperative school security theory, 224–6, 238–9
　and the Pyramid Security Model, 259
counterproliferation school security theory, 223–4
crime, as a social problem, 102
crude oil *see* oil
Curzon, Lord, 77

Damascus Declaration (1991), 79, 87, 230
Defence Policy Board, United States, 53
defence system, Saudi Arabia, 106
definitions, xiii–xiv
Desert Storm operation (1990–91), 51, 79, 87, 136, 138, 230

INDEX

Divided Zone oil field, Saudi Arabia/Kuwait, 70
Drysdale, Alasdair, xxiv, 4, 5, 7, 9, 67, 109–10
Dual Containment policy, 25, 26, 231, 232, 233

East Asia, security models, 244
East Asian Economic Community, 244
East Asian FTA, 244
East Corridor, 39
economic reforms, Saudi Arabia, 113–15
EEC (European Economic Community), 17
Egypt
   Damascus Declaration (1991), 79, 87
   United States, relationship with, 232, 233
Ehteshami, Anoushiravan, 33, 37–8
EIA (Energy Information Administration), 17, 30, 112
Eisenstadt, Michael, 203
Emergent Regional Power, Iraq as, 132
energy consumption
   primary, by type (2002), *19*
   world (2001), *18*
Energy Information Administration *see* EIA
energy security
   EU and Persian Gulf, 15–28
      energy supply policy, 17–20
      energy supply security strategy, 20–1
      EU challenges, 15–17
      security, 22–6
      terrorism as a threat, 49, 52–3
      threats in the Persian Gulf, 45–62
energy security definition, 45–6
   Iran's role, 54–9
   regional perspective, 50–2
   ultra-regional perspective, 46–53
   and War on Terror, 52–3
   The West's alternative solutions, 49–50
   The West's challenges, 48–9
   United States and, 46–7
energy supply indicators, EU and accession countries, *18*
energy types, primary consumption (2002), *19*
Ertan, Fikret, 40
Esposito, John, 104
EU (European Union)
   energy supply indicators, *18*
   foreign policy, 22
   as a framework for Persian Gulf security, 245
   and Iran, 25–6, 205
   and Iraq, 25
   lessons from the establishment of, 245–52
      Bjørn Møller, 246–50
      other studies of security models, 250–2
   and Persian Gulf
      energy security, 15–28, 22–6
      energy security challenges, 15–17
      energy security conclusion, 26–7

energy supply policy, 17–20
energy supply security strategy, 20–1
rapid reaction force (RRF), 252
role in increasing security, 243
and the United States, 241
Eurasia, xxiv, 4, 5, 6, 7
Europe
   arms race, 246
   and the Pyramid Security Model, 262
   realpolitik in, 222
European Coal and Steel Community, 17, 246
European Economic Community (EEC), 17
European Union *see* EU
Expediency Council (EC), Iran, 164
exports, Iran, *57*
Ezzati, Ezzatollah, xxi–xxii, xxiv, xxxi, 87

Fadaiyan-e Khalq, Iran, 178, 179
al-Faisal, Saud, Saudi Foreign Minister, 236
flow map, of world crude oil re Strait of Hormuz (2010), *xxviii*
foreign policy
   approach to security systems, xxxii–xxxiv
   EU, 22
   Iraq, 139–41
   levels of analysis, 218–19
   Saudi Arabia, 116–19, 120
foreigners
   in Iran, 176
   in Saudi Arabia, 106, 109–10
France, arms dealings with Iraq, 135
free trade agreements (FTAs), 244
Frontières de Convenance, 72

Gargash, Anwar, 78, 79
gas
   Caspian Sea region, *24*
   Persian Gulf, 8–13
      as a percentage of world (2006), *xxvi*
      political geography and geopolitics, 9–11
      strategic position, 11–13
Gates, Robert, US Defence Secretary, 265
GCC (Gulf Cooperation Council), 95–121, 248
   arms race, 201, 239–40
   border disputes, 77
   domestic and structural factors, 101–5
      economic structure, 102–5
      political legitimacy problems, 101–2
      social structure, 102
   formation, 8, 116, 228
   Iran
      attitude towards, 203
      as a threat, 55
   Iraq, as a threat, 55, 146–8
   leadership tradition, 96–8

as a pole of the Persian Gulf, 238–43, 249–50, 249, 250
present Persian Gulf security problems, 237
reform dilemmas, 98–9
Saudi Arabia, military presence in, 118
Saudi regime
  external threats to stability, 116–19
  internal threats to stability, 105–15
  security relationships with the United States, 51–2
threats and external factors, 99–101
trade with the EU, 24
United States, relationship with, 47, 224, 229, 232–3, 234
geopolitical worldviews, Mackinder, Spykman and Cohen, *xxvi*
geopolitics
  in the Asian-Pacific region, 32–7
  and China, 33–4
  definitions, xiv, xxi–xxii
  and India, 34–5
  non-regional states' geopolitical intention, xxii–xxx
  in the Persian Gulf, 4–8, 9–11
  and the Pyramid Security Model, 253, 258–9, 260–1, 264
  regional states' geopolitical intention, xxx–xxxii
geostrategy, definition, xiii
Germany, arms dealings with Iraq, 135
Ghareeb, Edmund, 141–2
Ghorb Khatam (*Khatam-ol-Anbia*), Iran, 196
Ghotb-zadeh, Iranian Foreign Minister, 183
globalisation, 113, 223, 225
GME (Greater Middle East) plan, 27
Gorbachev, Mikhail, President of the Soviet Union, 238, 246
Grand Mosque, Mecca, seizure by Sunni radicals (1979), 106–7
grand strategy, definition, xiv
Great Powers, xx, 6, 9, 11, 135, 222, 238
  Asian, 37–42
Greater Middle East plan, 27
Green, Jerrold, 96, 97, 102–3, 105, 200
Guardian Council (GC), Iran, 164
Gulf Cooperation Council *see* GCC

Hakhâmaneshiyân (Achaemenid) Dynasty (550–330 BCE), Iran, *81*
Al-Hamad, Turki, 99, 102, 256
Harkavy, Robert, 11–12, 17, 32, 33–4, 39, 59
Hashemi Rafsanjani, Ali Akbar, 166
Hashim, Ahmed, 200
Hawar islands, border dispute, 66, 69
heartland concept, xxiv, 5
hegemonic school security theory, 223–4, 225–6
hegemony, definition, xiii–xiv

Helms, Moss, 127
Hizballah movement, Lebanon, 187
Hojjatieh, Iran, 183
Hollis, Rosemary, 25
Hormuz, Strait of *see* Strait of Hormuz
Hough, Harold, 90
Hourcade, Bernard, 208
Hoveyda, Amirabbas, Iranian Prime Minister, 174
human rights, 177, 179, 183, 221, 229
Huntingdon, Samuel, theory, xxv, xxviii–xxix, xxx, 249, 255, 257
Hussein, Saddam
  and the balance of power in the Persian Gulf, 133–4
  and the Ba'th Party, 124
  and economic growth, 132–3
  internal threats, 127
  military strength, 135–7
  Mujahedin-e Khalq, Iran, cooperation with, 182
  need to overthrow, 148, 149–50, 231
  and politics, 125–6
  reasons for aggression, 77
  relationship with the military, 130–1
  and UN inspections, 232

IISS *see* International Institute for Strategic Studies
IMF (International Monetary Fund), 49, 187
imports
  to Iran, *57*
  from the Persian Gulf, oil, *23*
  to Saudi Arabia, arms (1986–1999), *107*
  of United States crude oil, by source, *16*
India
  Agreement of the Century with Iran, 38
  gas consumption, 31
  gas pipeline from Iran, 38–9
  geopolitics, 33, 35
  Government of, pre-Independence, 77
  International North–South Transport Corridor, 39
  Iran, relationship with, 35, 39
  navy, 35
  oil consumption, 30
  oil production and consumption (1990–2006), *34*
  and Persian Gulf security, 245
  Russia, relationship with, 35, 39
  United States, relationship with, 35
International Atomic Energy Agency (IAEA), 200
International Court of Justice (ICJ), the Hague, 66, 70
International Institute for Strategic Studies (IISS), 153, 199
International Monetary Fund *see* IMF
International North–South Transport Corridor, 39

INDEX

IRA peace process, Northern Ireland, 263
Iran
   Achaemenid (Hakhâmaneshiyân) Dynasty (550–330 BCE), *81*
   Afghanistan, relationship with, 210
   Afsharid Dynasty (AD 1736–1802), *83*
   arms programmes, 197
   and the axis of evil, 266
   Britain's interest in border disputes, 79–84
   and chemical weapons, 199
   China, relationship with, 35, 198
   China model, 188–9, 206
   confidence-building measures, 209
   and the cooperative school security theory, 239
   Damascus Declaration (1991), exclusion from, 79
   defence budget, 202
   defence role in the Persian Gulf, 200–8
   East Corridor, 39
   EU, relationship with, 205
   exports, *57*
   foreign policy, 190
   foreigners in, 176
   GCC (Gulf Cooperation Council), attitude towards, 203
   and geopolitics, xxv
   India, relationship with, 35, 39
   interdependency with Asian Great Powers, 37–42
   International North–South Transport Corridor, 39
   Iraq
      border disputes, 67, 72, 76, 77
      invasion by (1980), 85
      as a threat to stability, 144–6
   Islamic Revolution, 104, 133–4
   Israel, relationship with, 194
   Japan, relationship with, 40–1
   Kurds in, 145, 146, 182–3
   Kuwait, support for liberation, 209–10
   Medes (Mâdhâ) Dynasty (728–550 BCE), *81*
   military development, 197–208
      defence role in the Persian Gulf, 200–8
      policies, 197–8
      rearmament, 198–200
   modernisation, 170, 172, 197–8
   North Korea, relationship with, 198
   and nuclear technology, 200, 204
   as an obstacle to Saudi security, 116
   and OPEC, xxv
   Parthian (Ashkânîân) Dynasty (247 BCE–CE 224)–, *82*
   Persian Gulf, sovereignty, 80
   and Persian Gulf energy security threats, 54–9
   Persian Gulf peace and security alternatives, 88–91
   as a pole of the Persian Gulf, 238, 249–50, *249*, *250*
   potential as an energy supplier, 24
   power chart, *165*
   and present Persian Gulf security problems, 237
   and the Pyramid Security Model, 262
   Qatar
      alignment with, 69
      border dispute, 69
      joint exploration, 70
   role of military forces on society, 190–7
      economy, 195–7
      socio-political issues, 190–5
   Russia, relationship with, 39
   Safavid Empire (AD 1501–1722), *83*
   sanctions against, 48, 201
   Sasanid (Sâsânîân) Dynasty (CE 224–640), *82*
   Saudi Arabia, relationship with, 186
   security challenges, Imperial Iran, 167–80
      Mohammad Reza Pahlavi's regime, 168–80
   security challenges, Islamic Republic, 180–208
   security strategy 1990s, 232
   security threats and challenges, 157–216
      interaction of domestic and foreign policy, 158–60
      political system, 157–67
      power structure, Imperial Iran, 160–2
      power structure, Islamic Republic of Iran, 162–7
   Shah's dependence on the West, 171
   share of imports, *57*
   Sharia law in, 207, 208
   Sharjah, border dispute, 86
   Shiites in, 133, 146
   support for opposition groups in Iraq, 129
   as a threat to Arabian Peninsula states, 55
   today, *84*
   trade with the EU, 25–6
   Twin Pillars system, 85
   and unconventional weapons, 199, 200
   United Arab Emirates
      border dispute, 67, 84, 85
      border dispute, solving, 89–90
   United States
      arms imports, 175, 177
      interest in border disputes, 85–8
      relationship with, 49, 56, 58, 101, 194, 197, 203–5, 209–10
      sanctions against, 57
   and weapons of mass destruction, 200
   The West, relationship with, 203–4, 211–12
   White Revolution (1963), 170, 172
   see also Reza Pahlavi, Mohammad, Shah of Iran
Iran–Iraq War, 8, 99, 100, 129, 135, 136, 142, 184, 185, 199, 228
Iran–Pakistan–India gas pipeline, 38–9

Iran–US military ties, Imperial Iran, 174–5, 175–7
Iraq, 123–55
  1958 coup, 227
  arms dealings, 131, 134, 135
  and the axis of evil, 266
  Ba'th Party, 124, 125–6, 132, 134, 142, 147, 149, 152–3
  biological weapons in, 135
  border arrangements, 123–4
  border disputes, 67, 72, 76, 77
  chemical weapons in, 135
  Damascus Declaration (1991), exclusion from, 79
  as an Emergent Regional Power, 132
  external threats to stability, 139–51
    foreign policy barriers, 141–4
    foreign policy contributory elements, 148–51
    foreign policy goals, 140–1
    Iran, 144–6
    Saudi Arabia/GCC, 146–8
  foreign policy, 139–41
  foreign support for opposition groups, 129
  geographical location, 124–5
  internal threats to stability, 127–39
    economic vulnerability, 137–8
    effect on Persian Gulf security, 138–9
    military development, 131–4
    military technology, 134–5
    socio-political issues, 127–31
    war's impact on military strength, 135–7
  invasion of Kuwait, 55, 68, 136, 229, 230
  Iran
    border disputes, 67, 72, 76, 77
    invasion of (1980), 85
  Islam as state religion, 124
  Israel, as a threat to, 132
  Kurdish- and Shiite-dominated areas, oil resources and facilities, *128*
  Kurds in, 124, 128, 129, 130, 132, 133, 135, 146
  Kuwait, border dispute, 66, 72, 76–7, 77
  location as land-locked, *133*
  nationalism in, 126
  and nuclear technology, 143–4, 200
  as an obstacle to Saudi security, 116
  oil fields, 128
  Persian Gulf
    foreign policy and, 140–1
    as a pole of, 238, 249–50, *249, 250*
    relationship with, 76–7
  political history, 123–6
    political ideology: the Ba'th Party, 125–6
    sources of political behaviour, 124–5
  Republican Guards Corps, 130–1, 134
  sanctions against, 48, 138, 141, 151, 232
  Saudi Arabia
    relationship with, 135, 136
    as a threat to, 230
  security threats, 100
  Shiites in, 124, 128, 130, 132, 133, 146, 236
  Sunnis in, 124, 128, 130, 133, 236
  Syria
    relationship with, 142
    as a threat to, 132
  trade with the EU, 25
  Turkey, as a threat to, 132
  UN weapons inspection, 135
  United States
    discredited, 143
    military force against, 47, 48
    policy towards, 150
    relationship with, 135
  United States Defence Department report, 127, 130
  weapons of mass destruction, 141, 143, 148, 151, 229
  The West, attitude towards, 143
  Western attitude towards, 141–2
  see also OPEC
Iraqi National Congress (INC), 129
Ishida, Susumu, 36–7
Islam
  as a security threat, xxix
  Shah of Iran's attitude towards, 169
  as state religion of Iraq, 124
Islamabad, Iran, 182
Islamic fundamentalism, 119, 239
Islamic Republic Party (IRP), Iran, 183
Islamic Revolution, Iran, 104, 133–4, 168, 178–80
  1979–1988, 181–5
    economic problems, 184–5
    political issues, 181–3
  1989–1997, 185–90
    economic problems, 185–8
    socio-political issues, 188–90
Islamic Revolutionary Guard Corps (IRGC), Iran, 165, 182, 183, 190, 191, 192–5, 196–7, 199–200
Israel
  attack on Osirak nuclear reactor, Iraq, 200
  boycotted by the Arab League, 113
  defence budget, 202
  Iran
    attitude towards, 85
    relationship with, 194
  Iran–Arab disputes, role in, 87
  National Security and Information Organisation (SAVAK), Iran, aid to, 176, 177
  and nuclear technology, 200
  as a threat to Iraq, 132

INDEX

United States, relationship with, 224
Israeli–Arab conflict, 231, 234

Japan
  Caspian Sea region, equity stakes in, 41
  geopolitics, xxviii, 36–7
  Iran, relationship with, 40–1
  oil consumption, 30
  as an oil importer, 36
  Persian Gulf, relationship with, 36
  and Persian Gulf security, 245
  Russian Far East, equity stakes in, 41
  United States, relationship with, 36
Jiang Zemin, President of China, 33
Jufeir oil field, Iran, 38

Kant, Immanuel, 247
Kazemi, Ali Asghar, 72
Keddie, Nikki, 171
Kemp, Geoffrey, 11–12, 17, 32, 33–4, 39, 47, 59
Khafus border post incident (1992), 69, 71, 77
Kharrazi, Kamal, Iranian Foreign Minister, 39, 164
Khatam-ol-Anbia (Ghorb Khatam), Iran, 196
Khatami, Mohammad, President of Iran, 166–7, 189, 192, 207, 232
  theory of dialogue, xxx, 255, 257
Khordad event, Iran, 189
Khuzestan, Iran, 85
Kissinger, Henry, US Secretary of State, 221
Klare, Michael, 47–8, 52
Kraig, Michael, 217, 219, 222, 224, 225, 241–2
Kurds
  in Iran, 145, 146, 182–3
  in Iraq, 124, 128, 129, 130, 132, 133, 135, 146
    oil resources and facilities, *128*
Kuwait
  Iran, support for liberation, 209–10
  Iraq, border dispute, 66, 72, 76–7, 77
  Iraqi invasion, 55, 136, 229, 230
  Saudi Arabia
    border dispute, 66, 72
    shared oil reserves, 70
  United States, relationship with, 230
  United States military intervention, 47
  see also OPEC

Larson, Alan, US government spokesman, 46
Law of the Sea (UN Convention), 72
liberalism, and the Pyramid Security Model, 259

Mackinder, Halford, xxiv, 4–5
Mackinder, Spykman and Cohen, geopolitical worldviews, *xxvi*
Mâdhâ (Medes) Dynasty (728–550 BCE), Iran, *81*

Madrid process, 231, 233–4
Mahan, Alfred, xxiv, 4
Mahdi, Adel Abdul, 150
Majlis (Parliament), Iran, 164, 198
Malik, Monica, 114–15
Manning, Robert, 30, 31
Mardom (People) party, Iran, 174
marginal crescent concept, 4, 5–6
maritime delimited areas, 71–3
Marshall Plan, 234, 263, 264
McLachlan, Keith, 69
Mecca, Grand Mosque, seizure by Sunni radicals (1979), 106–7
Medes (Mâdhâ) Dynasty (728–550 BCE), Iran, *81*
Melliyun (Nationalist) party, Iran, 174
Memorandum of Understanding (MOU), Abu Musa (1971), 67, 78, 86
MENA region, 7, 67
mercantilism, 223
Mersad operation, Iran, 182
Messerschmitt-Bolkov Blohm (MBB), 134
Middle East
  and international relations, 157
  major oil fields, *10*
  oil and gas, timespan, 60
  United States, relationship with, 40, 205
  United States Pentagon, security goals, 234
  see also Persian Gulf
Middle East and North Africa (MENA) region, 7, 67
Middle East and Persian Gulf, map, *viii*
Milani, Abbas, 189, 197, 206, 209
Milani, Mohsen, 173
military expenditure and GNP, Persian Gulf powers (1989–1999), *108*
Ministry of Defence and Armed Forces Logistics (MODAFL), Iran, 191
Møller, Bjørn, 221, 246–50
Morgenthau, Hans, 4–5
Mosadegh government, Iran, 160
Mosul, Iraq, 124, 125
Moynihan, Joseph, 47, 55–6
Mubarak oil and gas field, Sharjah, 90
Mujahedin-e Khalq, Iran, 178, 181–2, 183
Murawiec, Laurent, 53
Murden, Simon, 125–6
Muslims, radical, 103, 104

Nabavi, Behzad, 202
Nassar, Bahig, 228–9
Nasser, Jamal, President of Egypt, 100
National Front, Iran, 178
National Intelligence Estimate (NIE), United States, 200
National Iranian Oil Company, 38

National Security and Information Organisation (SAVAK), Iran, 169, 176, 177
nationalism, 77, 100, 104, 126, 190, 208
NATO (North Atlantic Treaty Organisation)
    and the Cold War, 234, 240
    and Europe, 24, 246, 247, 264
    and the United States, 241
navies
    Chinese, 34
    Indian, 35
    Iranian, xx
    Persian Gulf (proposed), xviii, xix, 227
neo-liberalism, 224–6
neo-realism, 224
New York Times, The, 138
Niblock, Tim, 114–15
Nixon, Richard, US President, 221, 227, 228
North Africa
    as a gas source, 15, 23
    instability concerns, 23–4
    oil and gas, timespan, 60
North Atlantic Treaty Organisation *see* NATO
North Dome gas field, Qatar, border dispute, 69
North Korea
    and the axis of evil, 266
    Iran, relationship with, 198
Northern Ireland, IRA peace process, 263
Norway, as a gas source, 20
Nourbakhsh, Amir Ali, 163, 164
Nowrooz offshore oil field, Iran, 40–1
nuclear technology
    and Iran, 200, 204
    and Iraq, 143–4, 200
    and Israel, 200
    and Pakistan, 200
    possible attacks on, 101
    and the United States, 60, 228–9

oil
    Caspian Sea region, reserves, *24*
    OPEC, export revenues (1972–2006), *110*
    Persian Gulf, 8–13
        exports by route (2002), *xxvii*
        imports, *23*
        as a percentage of world (2006), *xxvi*
        political geography and geopolitics, 9–11
        strategic position, 11–13
    production and consumption
        China (1980–2003), *30*
        India (1990–2006), *34*
        Saudi Arabia (1980–2006), *110*
    resources and facilities, Iraq, *128*
    Saudi Arabia, dependence on, 109
    Strait of Hormuz flow map (2010), *xxviii*
    United States
        importance for transportation, 49–50
        imports, by source, *16*
        world reserves (1980–2006), *xxvii*
oil corridor, *10*
oil fields
    in Iraq, 128
    Middle East, *10*
Oman
    Saudi Arabia, border dispute, 90
    United Arab Emirates, border dispute, 67
    Yemen, border agreement, 77
OPEC (Organisation of the Petroleum Exporting Countries), 12
    European Union, supplies to, 19
    export revenues (1972–2006), *110*
    global market, 49
    Iran and, xxv
    oil prices, 55, 138, 186
    production quotas, 136
Organisation for Security and Co-operation in Europe (OSCE), 247
Organisation of the Petroleum Exporting Countries *see* OPEC
Osirak nuclear reactor, Iraq, Israeli air attack, 200
Ó Tuathail, Gearóid, xxi, xxiii, xxix, xxxii
Ottoman Empire
    Iran, competition, 72
    Iraq in, 123
    Persian Gulf, role in, 77

Pakistan
    gas pipeline from Iran to India, 38–9
    and nuclear technology, 200
Palestine
    United States policy, reaction of Saudi Arabia, 50
Palestine Liberation Organisation (PLO), 140, 231
Palestinian–Israeli peace process, 231, 265
Parthian (Ashkâniân) Dynasty (247 BCE–CE 224)–, Iran, *82*
Perez de Cuellar, Javier, UN Secretary General, 184
Persian Gulf
    arms race, 88
    balance of power, 133–4
    border disputes, 65–7, 91
    Britain, border disputes, 65–6
    definition, xiii
    energy security threats, 45–62
        energy security definition, 45–6
        Iran's role, 54–9
        regional perspective, 50–2
        ultra-regional perspective, 46–53
        and War on Terror, 52–3
        The West's alternative solutions, 49–50
        The West's challenges, 48–9
    and EU energy security, 15–28

[284]

gas, 8–9
   as a percentage of world (2006), *xxvi*
   political geography and geopolitics, 9–11
geographical location, 3–13
geopolitical perspectives, 4–8
military expenditure, and GNP (1989–1999), *108*
oil, 8–9
   as a percentage of world (2006), *xxvi*
   political geography and geopolitics, 9–11
   strategic position, 11–13
oil and border disputes, 67–71
oil exports, by route (2002), *xxvii*
oil imports, 23
political, geographical and legal disputes over borders, 71–8
Portuguese in, 80
security arrangements, future, 217–71
   alternatives, 243–52
   Bjørn Møller, 246–50
   cooperative school theory, 224–6
   EU establishment lesson, 245–52
   final outlines, 264–9
   GCC security problems, 237
   hegemonic or counterproliferation school theory, 223–4
   Iran security problems, 237
   present security problems, 235–7
   Pyramid Security Model, 252–64
   Pyramid Security Model details and suggestions, 261–3
   Pyramid Security Model functionality, 257–61
   Pyramid Security Model practical solutions, 263–4
   realpolitik/realist school theory, 220–3
   security models, other studies, 250–2
   security systems, 226–43
   security theories, 219–26
   strategic conditions, 238–43
   US 1980s strategy disadvantages, 229–32
   US 1990s strategy disadvantages, 232–4
   US security problems, 235–7
strategic conditions, 238–43
ultra-regional powers' interest in border disputes, 78–9
see also Iran; Iraq
Persian Gulf and Middle East, map, *viii*
PG *see* Persian Gulf
Pierce, Ray, 53
Pike, David, 68–9
pivot regions, 4–5
PLO (Palestine Liberation Organisation), 140, 231
police, in Iran, 169, 194, 195
Popular Front for the Liberation of the Occupied Gulf, 145

Portuguese, in Persian Gulf, 80
power
   balance of
      definition, xiv
      disadvantages, 229–32
      in the Persian Gulf, *249*
Prescott, J., 67
Pyramid Security Model, xxxvi–xxxix, *xxxvii*, 252–64, *258*, 268
   details and suggestions, 261–3
   factors influencing the functionality, 259–61
   geometric functionality, 257–9, *258*
   practical solutions, 263–4

Al Qaeda, 52–3, 119
Qaruh island, border dispute, 66
Qassim, Brigadier Abdul-Karim, Iraqi coup leader, 124
Qatar
   Bahrain, border dispute, 66, 69, 70, 72, 77
   deposition of rulers, 97
   geographical location, 90
   independence in GCC, 232
   Iran
      alignment with, 69
      border dispute, 69
      joint exploration, 70
   Saudi Arabia, border dispute, 66, 69, 69–70, 77
Qazvin riots (1994), Iran, 192

Rafsanjani, Hashemi, Iranian President, 185, 188, 189, 196, 198
Rajavi, Masoud, 182
Ramazani, Rouhollah, 58, 158–9
Rapid Deployment Force (RDF), United States, 228
rapid reaction force (RRF), European Union, 21, 252
RCC (Revolutionary Command Council) Iraq, 124
Reagan, Ronald, US President, xxiii, 221, 228, 266
realpolitik/realist school security theory, 220–3, 225–6, 238, 259
reflagging operation, United States, 229, 230
regional security complexes (RSCs), 248
religion
   in Iraq, 124
   and militancy, 103, 104
rentier system, 102, 103
Republican Guards Corps, Iraq, 130–1, 134
Resurgence party, Iran, 174
Revolutionary Command Council (RCC), Iraq, 124
Reza Pahlavi, Mohammad, Shah of Iran
   economic development, 171–4

Iran–US military ties, 175–7
military development, 174–5
opposition groups, 177–80
personal control, 160
political policy, 170–1
regime, 168–80
Rezaei, Mohsen, Commander in Chief of IRGC, 203
Rice, Condoleezza, US Secretary of State, 265
Riedel, Bruce, 58
rimland concept, xxiv, 5–6
Rogers, Paul, 40
Rumailah oil field, Iraq, 68, 69
Rushdie, Salman, 187
Russell, Richard, 251
Russia
   Asian-Pacific region, relationship with, 35
   as a competitor, 242
   as a gas source, 15, 20, 23
   geopolitical importance, 20, 23
   India as energy partner, 39
   International North–South Transport Corridor, 39
   Iran, relationship with, 39
Russian Far East, Japanese equity stakes in, 41

Sadr, Bani, President of Iran, 182
Sadri, Houman, 165–6
Safavi, Brigadier General Rahim, 201
Safavid Empire (AD 1501–1722), Iran, *83*
Salameh, Mamdouh, 42
Salari, Alireza, 89, 90
sanctions
   against Iran, 48, 57, 201
   against Iraq, 48, 138, 141, 151, 232
Sariolghalam, Mahmood, 97–8, 211, 239
Sâsâniân (Sasanid) Dynasty (CE 224–640), Iran, *82*
Saudi Arabia
   anti-American attacks, 107
   Arab League, military presence in, 118
   arms imports (1986–1999), *107*
   arms sales, 106
   Army, 106
   Bahrain, shared oil reserves, 70
   Bedouin in, 105
   confidence-building measures, 119, 120
   defence budget, 202
   defence system, 106
   Eastern Province, oil reserves, 47
   economic reforms, 113–15
   external threats to stability, 116–19
   foreign policy, 116–19, 120
   GCC (Gulf Cooperation Council), military presence in, 118
   and globalisation, 113
   internal threats to stability, 105–15
   Iran, relationship with, 186
   Iraq
      relationship with, 135, 136
      as a threat to stability, 146–8, 230
   Islamic fundamentalism in, 119
   Kuwait
      border dispute, 66, 72
      shared oil reserves, 70
   monarchy, Twin Pillars system, 85
   oil, dependence on, 109
   oil production and consumption (1980–2006), *110*
   Oman, border dispute, 90
   opposition violence, 104
   as a pole of the Persian Gulf, 238, 249–50, *249, 250*
   policy on Palestine, reaction to, 50
   political participation, 111
   Al Qaeda in, 119
   Qatar, border dispute, 66, 69, 69–70, 77
   religious militancy as a threat to stability, 104
   Shiites in, 115, 119
   socio-economic challenges, 111–12
   Sunnis in, 115, 119
   terrorism as a threat to energy security, 52–3
   unemployment, 111
   United Arab Emirates (Abu Dhabi), border dispute, 67
   United States
      military presence in, 117
      protection, 109
      relationship with, 50, 52, 54, 112, 116–17, 230, 235
   White Army in, 105
   World Trade Organisation membership, 113
   Yemen, border dispute, 68–9
   see also OPEC
Saudi Arabia National Guard (SANG), 105–6
Saudi Aramco, 52
Saudi Army, 106
Saudi–Yemeni War (1934), 117
Schofield, Richard, 70–1, 87–8
seas, importance of controlling, 4
Second Republic, Iran, 185–6, 187, 188
Second World War, xxii, 6
security approach to security systems, xxxiv–xxxix
security models, *220*, 244, 250–2
   see also Pyramid Security Model
security system, definition, xiii
security theories, 219–26
   cooperative school theory, 224–6
   hegemonic or counterproliferation school theory, 223–4
   realpolitik/realist school theory, 220–3

Senate Armed Services Committee, United States, 47
September 11 attacks on the United States, xxiii, 129–30, 228, 234, 266
Shah of Iran *see* Reza Pahlavi, Mohammad
Sharia law, in Iran, 207
Shariati, Dr Ali, 179
Sharjah
  Iran, border dispute, 86, 90
Shatt al-Arab (Arvand Roud) waterway, border dispute, 67, 72, 76, 77, 85, 144, 145
shatter belt concept, 6–7
Shiites
  discrimination against, 103–4, 256
  in Iran, 133, 146
  in Iraq, 124, 128, 130, 132, 133, 146, 236
    oil resources and facilities, *128*
  in Saudi Arabia, 115, 119
  as a threat to GCC regimes, 103
Sinopec, 38
socio-economic challenges, in Saudi Arabia, 111–12
Sokolsky, Richard, 52
Soroush offshore oil field, Iran, 40–1
South Korea
  gas consumption, 31
  oil consumption, 30
South Pars gas field, Iran, 41
  border dispute, 69
Soviet Union
  Afghanistan, invasion of, 15, 228
  during the Cold War, 246
  Iraq, arms dealings with, 135
  United States, relationship with, xxii, 5, 209, 227
Spiegel, Steven, UCLA professor, 218
Spykman, Mackinder and Cohen, geopolitical worldviews, *xxvi*
Spykman, Nicholas John, xxiv, 5–6
stabilisation measures (-2003), *250*
Strait of Hormuz, xxv, 89, 90
  crude oil, flow map (2010), *xxviii*
  importance to Iran, 157, 203
  importance to Iraq, 141
  Persian Gulf oil supplies through, 50
Strategic Council for Foreign Relations, Iran, 164
Strategic Petroleum Reserve, United States, 50
Sultan, Prince, Saudi Defence Minister, 106
Sunnis
  in Iraq, 124, 128, 130, 133, 236
  in Saudi Arabia, 119
  seizure of the Grand Mosque, Mecca (1979), 106–7
  as a threat to GCC regimes, 103, 104, 115, 256
Supreme National Security Council (SNSC), Iran, 164

Syria
  Arab–Israeli conflict and, 231
  Damascus Declaration (1991), 79, 87
  Iraq, relationship with, 129, 132, 142
  United States, relationship with, 232, 233

Taiwan, gas consumption, 31
Takritis, in Iraq, 124
Tanker War (1987), 99, 229
Taylor, Terence, 199
Tehran student riots (1999), Iran, 192, 194
terrorism
  as a social problem, 102
  as a threat to energy security, 49, 52–3, 260
transportation, importance of oil in the United States, 49–50
Triangle of Fortune (Triple Alliance), Iran, 172
Tudeh, Iran, 178, 183
Tunb islands, border dispute, 67, 71, 72, 84, 85, 86
  solving, 89–90
Turkey
  Iran, attitude towards, 40
  as a threat to Iraq, 132
Twin Pillars system, 54, 85, 149, 227, 228, 254

UAE *see* United Arab Emirates
Umm al-Maradim island, border dispute, 66
UN (United Nations)
  and border disputes, 66, 72
  Iraq weapons inspections, 135, 200
  Resolution 598 (1988), 182, 184
  role in increasing security, 243
  Security Council
    Chinese veto, 38
    destruction of Iraq's WMDs, 148
    Kuwait invasion, 229, 230
unemployment
  in Saudi Arabia, 111
  as a social problem, 102
UNIDO (United Nations Industrial Development Organisation), 42
Union of Soviet Socialist Republics (USSR) *see* Soviet Union
United Arab Emirates
  Iran, border dispute, 67, 84, 85, 86
    solving, 89–90
  Oman, border dispute, 67
  territorial divisions, 73
United Arab Emirates (UAE), Abu Dhabi, 67
United Nations *see* UN
United Nations Industrial Development Organisation (UNIDO), 42
United States
  9/11 attacks, 129–30
  1980s strategy, 228–9

[287]

disadvantages, 229–32
1990s strategy, disadvantages, 232–4
Abu Musa border dispute, 86
anti-American attacks in Saudi Arabia, 107
arms sales, 175, 177, 235, 265, 266
Bahrain, relationship with, 230
Caspian Sea region, viewpoint, 58–9
China, relationship with, 35–6, 221
Congress Hearings, 109th (27 July 2005), 49, 50
Defence Policy Board, 53
Egypt, relationship with, 232, 233
energy consumption, 17
energy security, 46–7
GCC (Gulf Cooperation Council), relationship with, 224, 229, 232–3, 234
India, relationship with, 35
Iran
  aid to Shah, 171
  arms to, 175, 177
  border disputes, 85–8
  relationship with, 37, 49, 56, 58, 101, 194, 197, 203–5, 209–10
  sanctions against, 201
Iraq
  discredited by, 143
  military force against, 47, 48
  policy towards, 150
  relationship with, 135
Israel, relationship with, 224
Japan, relationship with, 36
Kuwait
  military intervention in, 47
  relationship with, 230
Middle East, relationship with, 40, 205
national interest, 221
NATO (North Atlantic Treaty Organisation) and, 241
nuclear weapons deployment, 228–9
oil imports, by source, *16*
Pentagon goals for Middle East security, 234
Persian Gulf
  policy towards, 15, 16, 54
  present security problems, 235–7
  security system, dependence on, 88
reflagging operation, during Kuwait invasion, 229, 230
Saudi Arabia
  military presence in, 117
  protection, 109
  relationship with, 50, 52, 53, 54, 112, 116–17, 230, 235
security policy, 148–9
security relationships with the GCC, 51–2
South Asia, policy towards, 35–6
Soviet Union, relationship with, xxii, 209, 227

strategic interests, xxviii–xxix
Strategic Petroleum Reserve, 50
Syria, relationship with, 232, 233
transportation, importance of oil, 49–50
use of the hegemonic or counterproliferation school security theory, 223–4
United States Defence Department, report on Iraq, 127, 130
Uqair Conference (1922), 123–4
US/USA *see* United States
USS *Vincennes* attack, 184
USSR *see* Soviet Union
Uzbekistan, East Corridor, 39

Vali-e Faqih, Iran, 192, 194
Velayati, Ali Akbar, Iranian Foreign Minister, 86
Venezuela *see* OPEC

Walker, Julian, 66
War on Terror, 52–3
Warbah island, 132
  border dispute, 76, 77
Warsaw Pact, 246
Washington Post–Kuwait, The, 51–2
Washington Post, The, 38, 53, 173
weapons of mass destruction (WMDs)
  and Iran, 200
  in Iraq, 141, 143, 148, 151, 229
weapons, unconventional, and Iran, 199, 200
welfare system, 102, 103
West, The
  Iran, relationship with, 203–4, 211–12
  Iraq, attitude towards, 141–2
  Iraq attitude towards, 143
  and Persian Gulf energy security threats, 48–50
White Army, in Saudi Arabia, 105
White Revolution (1963), Iran, 170, 172
Wilkinson, John, 66
WMDs *see* weapons of mass destruction
World Trade Organisation (WTO), Saudi Arabian membership, 113
WWII, xxii, 6

Yadavaran oil field, Iran, 38
Yemen
  civil war, 100
  Oman, border agreement, 77
  and the Pyramid Security Model, 256, 264
  Saudi Arabia, border dispute, 68–9

Zabih, Sepehr, 144, 159, 160, 160–2
Zeihan, Peter, 52–3
Zhang Guihong, 35–6

Entire	Dentate	Serrate	Crenate	Lobed

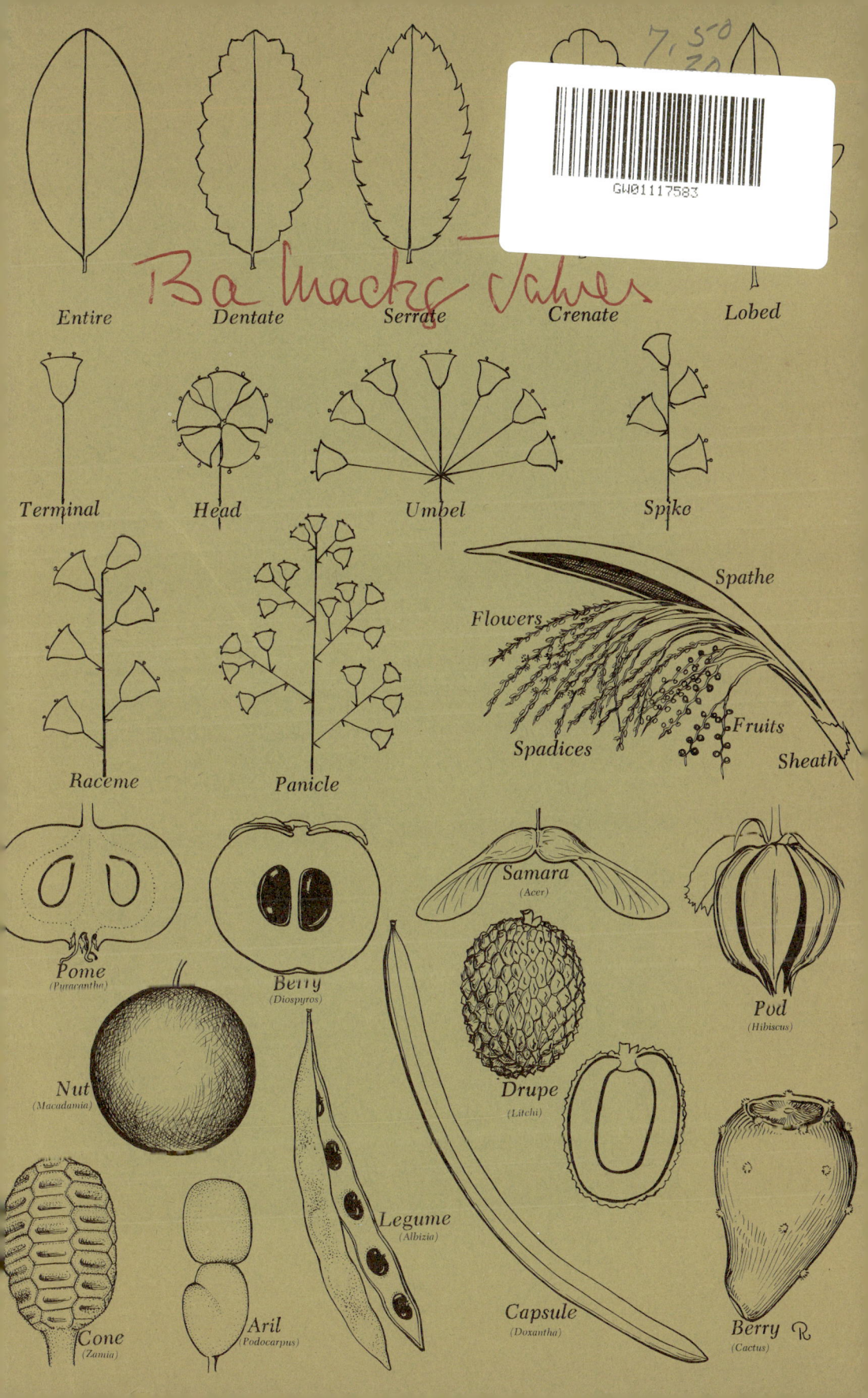

Ba Macks Jahies

Terminal	Head	Umbel		Spike

Raceme   Panicle

Spathe
Flowers
Spadices   Fruits
Sheath

Pome *(Pyracantha)*

Berry *(Diospyros)*

Samara *(Acer)*

Pod *(Hibiscus)*

Nut *(Macadamia)*

Drupe *(Litchi)*

Cone *(Zamia)*

Aril *(Podocarpus)*

Legume *(Albizia)*

Capsule *(Doxantha)*

Berry *(Cactus)*

Florida Landscape Plants
Native and Exotic

JOHN V. WATKINS

Florida Landscape Plants
Native and Exotic

Drawings by
MARION RUFF SHEEHAN
and other delineators

UNIVERSITY OF FLORIDA PRESS
GAINESVILLE

A University of Florida Press Book

COPYRIGHT © 1969 BY THE BOARD OF COMMISSIONERS
OF STATE INSTITUTIONS OF FLORIDA
Second Impression, 1970
Third Impression, 1971
ISBN 0-8130-0283-4
LIBRARY OF CONGRESS CATALOG CARD NO. 74-92045
PRINTED IN FLORIDA

Preface

THIS ALL-FLORIDA garden book is a combination of *Your Guide to Florida Landscape Plants*, published in 1961, and its companion volume on tropical exotics that came out two years later. I have retained the distinctive, tabular format that proved to be popular with homeowners, students, and nurserymen. Illustrator Marion Ruff Sheehan has contributed many original drawings, and I have renovated the pest control guide.

Although there are more than 350 entries in this book, a few favorite landscape plants may be absent because it would be impossible to describe and illustrate all of Florida's horticultural material in a single volume of popular size.

Manual of Cultivated Plants (L. H. Bailey, Macmillan, New York, rev. ed. 1949) is the authority for plant names, their pronunciation, and their derivation. Plant heights in the present volume represent average sizes of aged specimens growing in Florida, and may vary from dimensions printed in Bailey's *Manual*. Systematic arrangement used here for your convenience, and for orderly presentation, follows phylogeny in that great work.

Gardeners should consult *Your Florida Garden*, 5th edition, for detailed information on the design of home grounds, the culture of garden flowers, bulbs, and lawns.

Exotica III, the world's best pictorial record of ornamental plants of hot countries, is ever useful to Florida gardeners.

JOHN V. WATKINS

Gainesville, Florida

Contents

FLORIDA ZONE MAP - viii

INTRODUCTION BY JOHN POPENOE - 1

FLORIDA LANDSCAPE PLANTS - 2

MODEL PLANTING PLAN - 353

PEST CONTROL GUIDE - 355

GLOSSARY OF HORTICULTURAL TERMS - 356

INDEX - 361

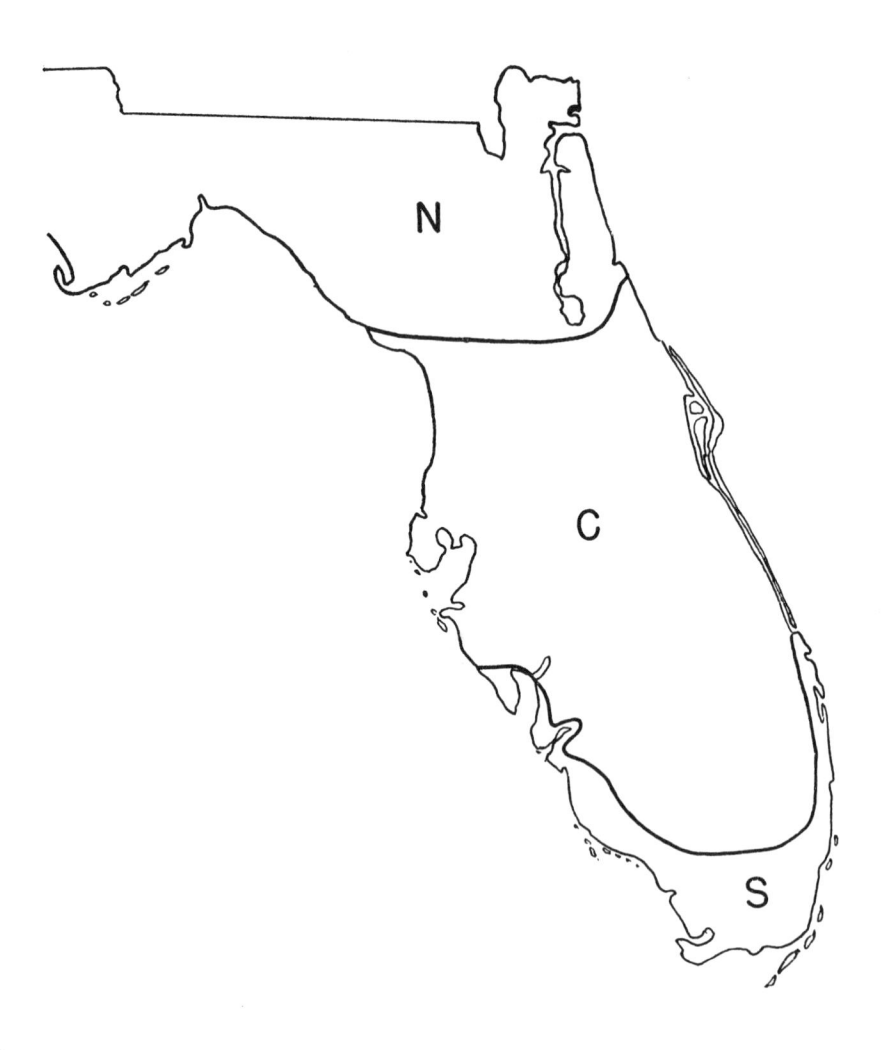

Zone map for Florida gardeners.

N = Northern Florida
C = Central Florida
S = Southern Florida

Introduction

To produce this handbook of easy reference, Professor John Watkins combined, and brought up to date, material from two of his garden manuals that have gone out of print. Progress in scientific research necessitates periodic revision of garden books.

Professor Watkins has selected over 350 of Florida's best landscape plants and he writes about them with the assurance of one who spent a professional lifetime teaching courses in landscape horticulture. The excellent illustrations on each page make for quick, easy identification, and the text tells about their cultural needs and their approved uses in home ground plantings.

Residents who have gardened in colder climates are often confused because of drastically different conditions. They will find in *Florida Landscape Plants: Native and Exotic*, authoritative information that will help them in the selection of plants for their gardens and in their care.

Miami, Florida   John Popenoe, *Director*
                                                      The Fairchild Tropical Garden

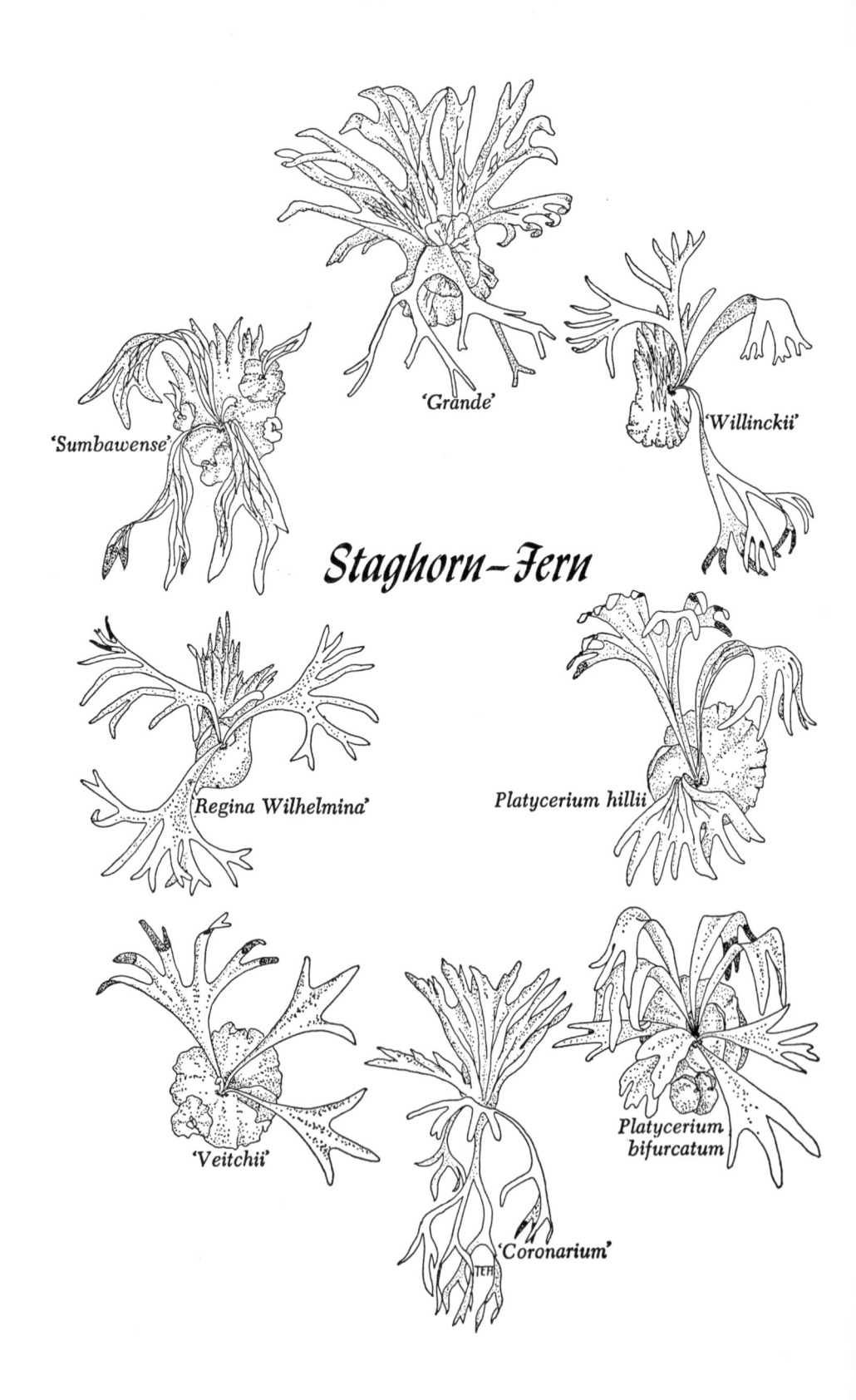

Staghorn-Fern

'Grande'

'Sumbawense'

'Willinckii'

'Regina Wilhelmina'

Platycerium hillii

'Veitchii'

'Coronarium'

Platycerium bifurcatum

3
Staghorn-Fern

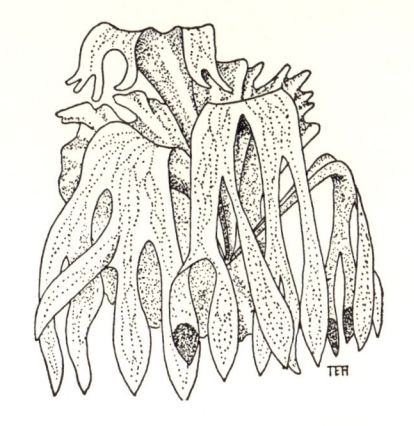

Platycerium (platty-SEAR-ee-um): Greek for broad horn.
SPP.: several species grow in Florida.

FAMILY: Polypodiaceae.   RELATIVES: Holly-fern and leather-leaf fern.
TYPE OF PLANT: Epiphytic perennial.   HEIGHT: 3'. ZONE: S
HOW TO IDENTIFY: These spectacular tree-dwelling ferns have leaves of 2 types—the flat, rounded, brown sterile fronds, that contrast with the outward-thrusting antler-forked, green fertile fronds.
HABIT OF GROWTH: Brown sterile fronds grow tight on the substratum and send out attractive, lobed, green fertile fronds.
FOLIAGE: Of two sorts—parchment-like, round, flat, barren fronds lie flat to the substratum, while freestanding, forked, green, reproductive leaves thrust outward.
FLOWERS: Absent.
FRUITS: Sori, in dense pads, are produced near the tips of fertile fronds.
SEASON OF MAXIMUM COLOR: Little seasonal variation.
LANDSCAPE USES: To cast the spell of the tropics and to add interest to a patio wall, nothing surpasses staghorn-fern. In frostless areas, specimens thrive on palm trunks or on branches of woody trees. These great epiphytes are quite fashionable.
HABITAT: Eastern tropics.
LIGHT REQUIREMENT: Reduced light is optimum, staghorns will not endure the Florida sun.
SOIL REQUIREMENT: Osmundine, sphagnum moss, tree fern, or combinations of these.
SALT TOLERANCE: Not tolerant.
AVAILABILITY: Nurseries on the peninsula have staghorn-ferns in containers upon occasion.
CULTURE: Fasten to a slab of pecky cypress, redwood, or tree fern with a blanket of one or more of the media mentioned above; keep constantly moist and shaded; supply liquid fertilizer once a month during warm weather.
PROPAGATION: Division; or sowing spores on moist, sterile peat.
PESTS: Mites and chewing insects.

4
House Holly-Fern

Cyrtomium (sir-TOE-me-um): Greek word for bow.
falcatum (fal-KAY-tum): sickle-shaped, alluding to the form of the pinnae.

FAMILY: Polypodiaceae. RELATIVES: Leather-leaf fern and staghorn-fern.

TYPE OF PLANT: Herbaceous perennial. HEIGHT: 24″. ZONE: N,C,S

HOW TO IDENTIFY: Upright, very shaggy stems bear dark, heavy pinnae that resemble holly leaves.

HABIT OF GROWTH: Compact, forming tight, knee-high evergreen clumps.

FOLIAGE: Dark, heavy, remotely resembling holly foliage.

FLOWERS: Absent.

FRUITS: Large sori scattered over the undersides of fertile fronds.

SEASON OF MAXIMUM COLOR: No seasonal variation.

LANDSCAPE USES: As a ground cover for very shady locations, and for planters under eaves, house holly-fern has long been a favorite in Florida. As a porch plant, it has served generations of Floridians.

HABITAT: Warm parts of eastern Asia.

LIGHT REQUIREMENT: Shady locations are necessary.

SOIL REQUIREMENT: Tolerant of varying soils throughout Florida.

SALT TOLERANCE: Tolerant of salt air back from the strand.

AVAILABILITY: House holly-ferns are available in retail nurseries.

CULTURE: Plant in a shaded location; protect from frost; water moderately during periods of drought.

PROPAGATION: Division of matted clumps.

PESTS: Mites, caterpillars, grasshoppers, and a leaf-spotting disease.

5
Leather-Leaf Fern

Polystichum (pol-is-tee-cum): Greek for many rows, alluding to sori.
adiantiforme (aye-dee-ant-ee-FORM-ee): resembling adiantum.

FAMILY: Polypodiaceae.   RELATIVES: Boston-fern and holly-fern.

TYPE OF PLANT: Herbaceous perennial.   HEIGHT: 3'.   ZONE: N,C,S

HOW TO IDENTIFY: Triangular fronds, which may grow as much as a yard high, are made up of stiff, leathery, coarse-toothed, heavy-textured pinnules.

HABIT OF GROWTH: Compact, clump-forming.

FOLIAGE: Bold, heavy, leathery, sometimes 3' high, of excellent keeping quality when cut.

FLOWERS: Absent.

FRUITS: Spores are borne in prominent sori midway between the edges and the midribs of the pinnules.

SEASON OF MAXIMUM COLOR: No seasonal variation.

LANDSCAPE USES: For many years leather-leaf fern has been popular as a pot plant for porches, and it is often planted, too, in earth of shaded garden spots and patios. Grown commercially for florists, cut leather-leaf fern is sometimes used instead of the old stand-by *Asparagus plumosus*.

HABITAT: World tropics.

LIGHT REQUIREMENT: Broken shade of hammocks, or constant shade of porches.

SOIL REQUIREMENT: Tolerant of varying soils.

SALT TOLERANCE: Grows back from the strand with some protection.

AVAILABILITY: Frequently seen in containers on retail sales lots.

CULTURE: Plant divisions slightly deeper than the plant grew originally; water periodically when there is little rain; fertilize with balanced fertilizer in water solution during warm months.

PROPAGATION: Division or sowing spores on sterilized, moist peat.

PESTS: Mealy-bugs, leaf-hoppers, and leaf-miners.

6
Tree Fern

Alsophila (al-SOPH-ill-a): Greek for grove-loving.
Cibotium (si-BOAT-ee-um): Greek for little seed-vessel.
Cyathea (si-ATH-ee-a): Greek for cup referring to the fruiting bodies.
Dicksonia (dick-SON-ee-a): for J. Dickson, English botanist.
SPP.: species from each of these genera grow in Florida.

FAMILY: Cyatheaceae. RELATIVES: The tree ferns.
TYPE OF PLANT: Tree fern. HEIGHT: 20'. ZONE: C,S
HOW TO IDENTIFY: Striking tree fern with distinct trunk.
HABIT OF GROWTH: Single, brown trunks bear beautiful heads of lacy fern foliage.
FOLIAGE: Evergreen, huge, feather-leaved, of fine texture and yellow-green color.
FLOWERS: None.
FRUITS: Fruiting bodies on the backs of some mature leaf segments.
SEASON OF MAXIMUM COLOR: No variation.
LANDSCAPE USES: For creating true tropical effects nothing can surpass tree ferns.
HABITAT: Tropics of both hemispheres.
LIGHT REQUIREMENT: Partial shade or dense shade of live oaks is suitable.
SOIL REQUIREMENT: Almost any reasonably fertile, well-drained soil is suitable.
SALT TOLERANCE: Not tolerant.
AVAILABILITY: Certain specialty nurseries have tree ferns in containers.
CULTURE: Plant with care in well-made site; water faithfully; keep atmosphere moist by frequent misting; fertilize every month during growing weather.
PROPAGATION: By sowing spores.
PESTS: Mites and mealy-bugs.
NOTE: Under any name, a tree fern is a topflight landscape plant where winter temperatures do not cause its death.

7
Queen Sago

Cycas (sy-kus): Greek name for a palm tree.
circinalis (sir-sin-al-is): coiled.

FAMILY: Cycadaceae.   RELATIVES: The cycads, including Florida's coontie.

TYPE OF PLANT: Cycad.   HEIGHT: 20'.   ZONE: S

HOW TO IDENTIFY: Palm-like with dark green feather-leaves; the foot-long pinnae, with flat margins, droop gracefully.

HABIT OF GROWTH: Stout, unbranching trunk with beautiful drooping foliage atop.

FOLIAGE: Evergreen, pinnate, of fine texture and darkest green color.

FLOWERS: Felty inflorescence in the center of the leaf mass.

FRUITS: Orange-colored, smooth, the size and form of bantam eggs.

SEASON OF MAXIMUM COLOR: When seeds ripen on mature plants.

LANDSCAPE USES: Because of its tropical aspect, and very graceful habit, queen sago is highly regarded as a freestanding specimen for large properties in areas that are nearly frostless.

HABITAT: Tropical Africa; in Florida, warmest spots only.

LIGHT REQUIREMENT: Shade is quite suitable, but not necessary.

SOIL REQUIREMENT: Tolerant of varying soil types.

SALT TOLERANCE: Not tolerant.

AVAILABILITY: Queen sago is popular and rather widely available in containers.

CULTURE: When well established in a frost-protected location, queen sago grows well with usual care.

PROPAGATION: Seedage or division of offsets.

PESTS: Scales and leaf-spotting disease.

NOTE: *Cycas revoluta*, the hardy relative that is seen in northern Florida, is not recommended because of its susceptibility to leaf-spotting disease. A fungicide, such as Bordeaux mixture, destroys the appearance of sago plants, and offers no sure protection against leaf-spotting.

8
Coontie

Zamia (ZAY-me-a): Latin for pine nut.
floridana (flor-ee-DAY-na): Floridian.

FAMILY: Cycadaceae.   RELATIVES: Queen sago.

TYPE OF PLANT: Dwarf herbaceous perennial.   HEIGHT: 3′.   ZONE: N,C,S

HOW TO IDENTIFY: Feather-like, evergreen leaves emerge from a very large storage root; and there are very often reddish-brown reproductive cones at the ground line.

HABIT OF GROWTH: Dwarf herbaceous perennial of fern-like appearance.

FOLIAGE: Evergreen, fern-like, fine in texture, in tones of green.

FLOWERS: None.

FRUITS: Large, reddish-brown reproductive cones at ground level; staminate and pistillate cones on separate plants.

SEASON OF MAXIMUM COLOR: No seasonal variation.

LANDSCAPE USES: No native plant is better for foundation plantings for low, rambling houses of contemporary design. Set 1½′ o.c. As a transition plant for larger species and in planters and urns, coontie excels, as it does as an atmosphere-creator when planted by pine trunks in woodland developments. Tropical species from Central America with very broad pinnae are worthy landscape plants for frostless locations.

HABITAT: Sandy soils throughout the state.

LIGHT REQUIREMENT: Full sun or dense shade, latter preferred.

SOIL REQUIREMENT: Tolerant of various types of well-drained soil.

SALT TOLERANCE: Tolerant of salt drift.

AVAILABILITY: Coonties are often sold in retail sales lots.

CULTURE: Coontie is most difficult to transplant because of the far-reaching tap root. Plant in well-drained locations; water with moderation; protect against red scale.

PROPAGATION: Seedage. This is difficult and high mortality is the rule.

PESTS: Florida red scale, a major pest must be controlled by regular spraying, lest it cause the death of plants.

9
Fern Podocarpus

Podocarpus (po-do-CAR-pus): Greek for foot and fruit.
gracilior (gra-SILL-ee-or): more graceful.

FAMILY: Podocarpaceae.   **RELATIVES:** The genus stands alone.

TYPE OF PLANT: Tree, usually maintained as a shrub in Florida.
                                               HEIGHT: 20'. **ZONE:** S

HOW TO IDENTIFY: Evergreen, narrow foliage is held by gracefully drooping branches.

HABIT OF GROWTH: Tree with drooping leader and pendulous branches.

FOLIAGE: Evergreen, very fine in texture, medium green in color, excepting new growth which is silvery.

FLOWERS: Inconspicuous catkins or scale-enclosed ovules.

FRUITS: Drupe-like, each standing above its edible red aril.

SEASON OF MAXIMUM COLOR: New growth in springtime is silvery.

LANDSCAPE USES: Fern podocarpus is an outstanding accent plant and atmosphere-creator for tropical plantings on the warmer part of the peninsula. As an espalier on a north wall, as a specimen near a terrace, or as a screening plant, it is most highly recommended.

HABITAT: South Africa; in Florida, sparingly planted in warm locations.

LIGHT REQUIREMENT: Tolerant of shade, but grows equally well in full sun.

SOIL REQUIREMENT: Tolerant of varying soils.

SALT TOLERANCE: Grows back from the strand with some protection.

AVAILABILITY: Infrequently seen in containers on retail sales lots.

CULTURE: Plant carefully in fertile, well-drained soil; water moderately; keep lawn grasses from encroaching; fertilize twice annually.

PROPAGATION: Cuttage and marcottage.

PESTS: Usually none of major importance.

NOTE: Possibly most fern podocarpus in Florida belongs in *P. gracilior*.

10
Nagi

Podocarpus (po-do-car-pus): Greek for foot and fruit.
nagi (nag-eye): native Japanese name.

Family: Podocarpaceae.   Relatives: The genus stands alone.

Type of Plant: Tree; used as a shrub in Florida. Height: 40'. Zone: N,C,S

How to Identify: Strong central leader, hatrack type branching, evergreen leaves, the broadest in the genus (1" x 3").

Habit of Growth: Strongly upright central leader with symmetrical branching in geometric pattern.

Foliage: Evergreen, medium in texture, dark green in color.

Flowers: Inconspicuous male catkins or ovules in scales on separate plants.

Fruits: Drupe-like, ½" in diameter, purple, with bloom.

Season of Maximum Color: No seasonal variation.

Landscape Uses: As a strong accent, no plant excels podocarpus nagi. Thus, it is rather widely used throughout the state. For cut foliage this plant excels, as the cut branches stand up very well in flower arrangements. Pistillate plants that bear heavy crops of fruit are likely to exhibit yellow-tipped foliage.

Habitat: Japan; in Florida, popular in foundation plantings.

Light Requirement: Tolerant of shade, grows equally well in full sun.

Soil Requirement: Tolerant of varying soils.

Salt Tolerance: Endures salt drift back from the strand.

Availability: Many nurseries offer plants in containers and B & B.

Culture: Plant carefully in fertile, made-up sites; water moderately; keep lawn grasses from encroaching; fertilize twice annually while young.

Propagation: Seedage and cuttage.

Pests: Usually none of major importance.

11
Yew
Podocarpus

Podocarpus (po-do-CAR-pus): Greek for foot and fruit.
macrophylla (mac-roe-PHIL-a): large leaf.

FAMILY: Podocarpaceae.   RELATIVES: The genus stands alone.

TYPE OF PLANT: Tree; usually a shrub in Florida. HEIGHT: 50'. ZONE: N,C,S

HOW TO IDENTIFY: Evergreen, flat linear leaves about 2"-3" long, with prominent midrib, lighter green beneath. Green seeds standing above purple arils on pistillate plants.

HABIT OF GROWTH: Compact, dense, heavily foliated well to the ground.

FOLIAGE: Evergreen, very fine in texture, dark green in color.

FLOWERS: Inconspicuous, male catkins or ovules in scales on separate plants.

FRUITS: Drupe-like, green, ovoid, ½" in diameter, each standing above its purple, edible aril.

SEASON OF MAXIMUM COLOR: No seasonal variation.

LANDSCAPE USES: Podocarpus is one of Florida's leading landscape plants. As an accent in foundation plantings, for interest in skyline above an enclosing shrubbery barrier, as a clipped hedge, it serves with distinction.

There are several excellent named varieties that have been chosen for one or another outstanding characteristic.

HABITAT: Japan; in Florida, planted everywhere as a garden shrub.

LIGHT REQUIREMENT: Tolerant of shade, grows equally well in full sun.

SOIL REQUIREMENT: Tolerant of varying soils.

SALT TOLERANCE: Endures salt drift back from the strand.

AVAILABILITY: All nurseries sell podocarpus plants in containers or B & B.

CULTURE: Plant carefully in fertile, made-up sites; water moderately; keep lawn grasses from encroaching; fertilize twice annually while young.

PROPAGATION: Seedage and cuttage.

PESTS: Usually none of major importance.

12 Japanese Plum-Yew

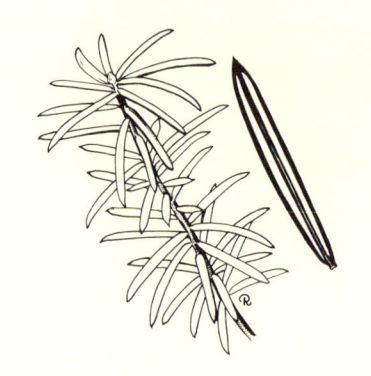

Cephalotaxus (sef-al-oh-TACKS-us): Greek for head and taxus.
harringtonia (hair-ing-TONE-ee-a): no doubt honors a Mr. Harrington.
'Drupacea' (drew-PAY-see-a): drupe-like.

FAMILY: Cephalotaxaceae. RELATIVES: This genus is alone in its family.

TYPE OF PLANT: Dwarf shrub. HEIGHT: 6'. ZONE: N

HOW TO IDENTIFY: Stiffly upright habit of growth; evergreen leaves in 2 rows, with 2 glaucous bands beneath; with staminate heads on stalks ¼" long.

HABIT OF GROWTH: Stiffly upright.

FOLIAGE: Evergreen, 2" long, abruptly pointed, very fine in texture.

FLOWERS: Inconspicuous catkins.

FRUITS: Usually none in Florida.

SEASON OF MAXIMUM COLOR: No variation.

LANDSCAPE USES: In seeking for dwarf, fine-scale shrubs, we must not overlook this slow-growing, shade-tolerant plum-yew. As an edging, plant it 14" o.c.; as a facer shrub in front of larger, leggy kinds, plant 18" o.c.

Popular with an older generation, Japanese plum-yew went out of favor, but with contemporary architecture demanding minimum plant material and with the wide use of planter bins under broad eaves, this diminutive shrub should enjoy a revival of popularity.

HABITAT: Japan; in Florida, landscape plantings in northern counties.

LIGHT REQUIREMENT: Shade-tolerant, a very good north-side plant.

SOIL REQUIREMENT: Fertility and moisture-holding capacity above average are needed for good appearance.

SALT TOLERANCE: Not tolerant of front-line conditions.

AVAILABILITY: Some nurseries in northern Florida display specimens.

CULTURE: On good soil, with northern exposure, plant carefully; water with moderation; fertilize once each spring.

PROPAGATION: Cuttage.

PESTS: Nematodes.

13
Bunya-Bunya

Araucaria (ah-rah-CARE-ee-a): from Arauco, a province in southern Chile.
bidwillii (BID-will-ee-eye): for J. Bidwill, a nineteenth-century botanist.

FAMILY: Araucariaceae. RELATIVES: Araucaria trees of both hemispheres.

TYPE OF PLANT: Tree. HEIGHT: 70'. ZONE: N,C,S

HOW TO IDENTIFY: Juvenile leaves lanceolate, 2" long; adult leaves spirally imbricated, ovate, ½" long, woody; cones 9" long x 8" in diameter.

HABIT OF GROWTH: Upright, symmetrical from single central leader.

FOLIAGE: Evergreen, fine in texture, dark green in color.

FLOWERS: Inconspicuous in tight catkins.

FRUITS: Very conspicuous cones 9" long x 8" in diameter.

SEASON OF MAXIMUM COLOR: No seasonal change.

LANDSCAPE USES: Bunya-bunya is recommended as a strong, single accent for large developments. Small trees are popular urn subjects for patios, terraces, and Florida rooms. In this plant, northern Floridians can have hardy monkey-puzzle-like specimens.

HABITAT: Australia; in Florida, infrequently planted as a lawn tree.

LIGHT REQUIREMENT: Full sun for best compact, symmetrical growth.

SOIL REQUIREMENT: Sandy soil of varying acidity is acceptable.

SALT TOLERANCE: Probably tolerant of salt drift back from the strand.

AVAILABILITY: Upon rare occasion, small trees may be found in containers.

CULTURE: Plant carefully in prepared site; water well, and repeat when there is no rain; fertilize twice or thrice annually while young.

PROPAGATION: Seedage or cuttage.

PESTS: None of major concern.

NOTE: *Araucaria* is represented by 12 species in both hemispheres. This is the most hardy and the one most often seen, therefore, in sections where frosts occur annually. Bunya-bunya is usually quite dependable under home-garden conditions in Florida.

14
Norfolk-Island-Pine

Araucaria (ah-rah-CARE-ee-a): from Arauco, a province in southern Chile.
excelsa (ex-SELL-sa): tall.

FAMILY: Araucariaceae. RELATIVES: Damar-pine and bunya-bunya.

TYPE OF PLANT: Large tree. HEIGHT: 50'. ZONE: C,S

HOW TO IDENTIFY: Strong, straight, central leader with horizontal branches in symmetrical whorls; tiny, sharp-pointed, evergreen leaves.

HABIT OF GROWTH: Geometrically symmetrical with branches in even whorls.

FOLIAGE: Evergreen, very fine in texture, dark green in color.

FLOWERS: Inconspicuous.

FRUITS: Cones 3"-6" in diameter almost globular with spiny scales.

SEASON OF MAXIMUM COLOR: Little seasonal change.

LANDSCAPE USES: As a strong, single accent to enhance a feeling of the tropics, this striking tree is popular, and well-grown lawn specimens are highly prized. Small trees are admired as urn subjects for patios, terraces, and Florida rooms.

While there are a dozen species in this genus, Norfolk-Island-pine is by all odds the most popular in Florida. In some resort cities, specimens of this subtropical plant are well known for the mood that they create.

HABITAT: Norfolk Island; in Florida, warmer coastal positions.

LIGHT REQUIREMENT: Full sun for best, compact, symmetrical growth.

SOIL REQUIREMENT: Sandy soil of varying acidity is acceptable.

SALT TOLERANCE: Quite tolerant of salt air back of the first dune.

AVAILABILITY: Retail sales lots offer beautiful little trees in containers.

CULTURE: A well-made planting hole containing an acid, fertile mixture is recommended to give a young tree a good start. Careful watering, a mulch, and annual fertilization should be supplied.

PROPAGATION: Cuttage of terminal shoots for symmetrical trees.

PESTS: Scales and mushroom root-rot.

15
Callitris

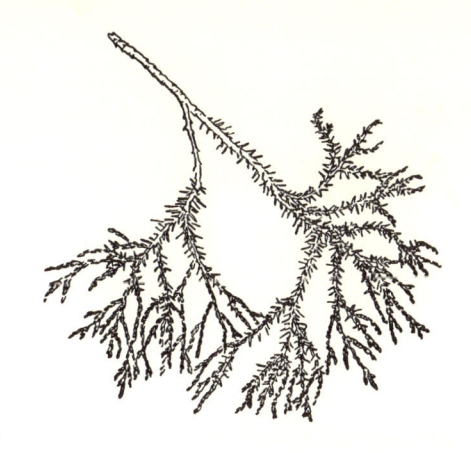

Callitris (cal-IT-ris): Greek for beautiful.
robusta (roe-BUS-ta): robust.

FAMILY: Pinaceae.   RELATIVES: Pine and cedar.
TYPE OF PLANT: Tree.   HEIGHT: 45'. ZONE: N,C,S

HOW TO IDENTIFY: Scale-like, evergreen leaves; jointed, angled branchlets; subglobose cones 1" through. The graceful habit is characteristic.

HABIT OF GROWTH: Very compact, dense, symmetrical evergreen.

FOLIAGE: Evergreen, minute, of finest texture and dark green color.

FLOWERS: Staminate flowers in small catkins, pistillate cones of 6 unequal scales.

FRUITS: Subglobose cones about an inch across.

SEASON OF MAXIMUM COLOR: No variation.

LANDSCAPE USES: As an unusually dense, graceful freestanding specimen, callitris is notable. It is almost universal in its appeal while young because of its neat, compact growth.

There are 3 or 4 species in Florida, all likely to be mislabeled in nurseries. Very popular in the nineteen-twenties, callitris has lost ground as a specimen plant partly because of its susceptibility to mushroom root-rot and partly because the same effect can be had more easily, more quickly, and more cheaply with Australian-pines.

HABITAT: Australia; in Florida, sparingly planted on the peninsula.

LIGHT REQUIREMENT: Full sun for symmetrical, compact growth.

SOIL REQUIREMENT: Tolerant of sandy soils.

SALT TOLERANCE: Tolerant of light salt drift at some distance from the sea.

AVAILABILITY: Nurseries in central Florida may stock this and other species.

CULTURE: Plant with reasonable care in enriched sites; water faithfully during the first year; thereafter little or no care is needed.

PROPAGATION: Seedage.

PESTS: Mushroom root-rot, which can be very serious.

16
China-Fir

Cunninghamia (cunning-HAM-ee-a): for J. Cunningham, its discoverer.
lanceolata (lance-ee-oh-LAY-ta): lance-shaped.

FAMILY: Taxodiaceae.   RELATIVES: Cypress, redwood, and sequoia.

TYPE OF PLANT: Tree.   HEIGHT: 60'. ZONE: N

HOW TO IDENTIFY: Narrow, evergreen leaves 2½" long, with 2 white bands running lengthwise beneath; and the bases running down the twigs. Tree *always* suckering around the base.

HABIT OF GROWTH: Narrowly upright always with suckers around the base.

FOLIAGE: Evergreen with 2 white bands below. The leaf bases run down the twigs.

FLOWERS: Inconspicuous.

FRUITS: Roundish cones with leathery, toothed, pointed scales.

SEASON OF MAXIMUM COLOR: No seasonal change.

LANDSCAPE USES: In northern Florida where freezes occur, China-fir can be used as a freestanding specimen to approach the effect that the more tender monkey-puzzle-trees give in warmer sections. Cold-tolerant and disease-resistant, China-fir is planted rather widely in northern Florida and it is deeply appreciated for its many good qualities in states just north of the Florida line. Where China-fir can serve, if it is in the spirit of the scene, it is most highly recommended as a maintenance-free evergreen.

HABITAT: China; in Florida, northernmost counties only.

LIGHT REQUIREMENT: Full sun or north-side location in the shade.

SOIL REQUIREMENT: Tolerant of many soils found in northern Florida.

SALT TOLERANCE: Not tolerant.

AVAILABILITY: Some few nurseries may display small China-fir trees in gallon containers, but these are not widely offered in Florida.

CULTURE: After establishment in superior soil, no care is needed.

PROPAGATION: Cuttage or seedage.

PESTS: None of major importance.

17
Portuguese Cypress

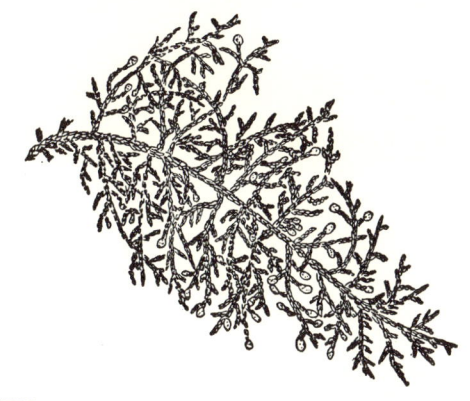

Cupressus (coo-press-us): a classical name.
lusitanica (loo-si-tan-ee-ca): Portuguese, but native in Central America.

FAMILY: Cupressaceae.   RELATIVES: Arbor-vitae, false-cypress, and juniper.

TYPE OF PLANT: Tree.   HEIGHT: 50'.   ZONE: N

HOW TO IDENTIFY: Reddish bark, pendulous branches, usually blue-green foliage.

HABIT OF GROWTH: Dense, compact, beautifully symmetrical.

FOLIAGE: Evergreen, needle-like, of fine texture, blue-green color.

FLOWERS: Inconspicuous.

FRUITS: Cones ½" in diameter composed of 6-8 scales, with glaucous bloom.

SEASON OF MAXIMUM COLOR: No seasonal change.

LANDSCAPE USES: Clonal propagations from special trees that have good habit, pendulous branches, and glaucous foliage are very popular as freestanding specimens in northern Florida. These are rare and hard to come by. Seedlings, grown from imported seeds, are easy to bring along, but they are quite variable in form, habit, and color, and most of them lack the strong appeal of the selected blue clones. These latter will be hard to find and expensive to buy.

HABITAT: Mountains of Central America; in Florida, northern section.

LIGHT REQUIREMENT: Full sun.

SOIL REQUIREMENT: Fertile, well-drained soil in the northern counties.

SALT TOLERANCE: Not tolerant of dune conditions.

AVAILABILITY: Portuguese cypress is rare in nurseries.

CULTURE: Plant in well-prepared site; water moderately until well established; thereafter, no attention, other than light fertilization, will be needed.

PROPAGATION: Cuttage is used for best blue clones, but cuttings root slowly. Seedlings grow easily, but they are quite variable and very subject to damping-off disease.

PESTS: None of major consequence.

18
Italian Cypress

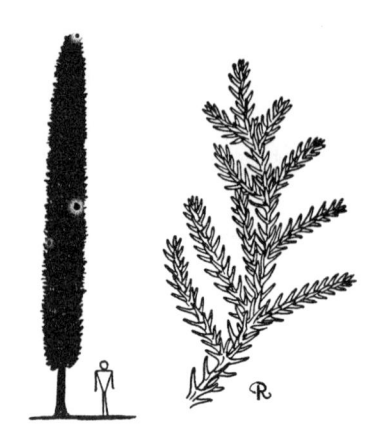

Cupressus (coo-press-us): a classical name.
sempervirens (sem-per-vie-rens): evergreen.

FAMILY: Cupressaceae.   RELATIVES: Arbor-vitae, false-cypress, and juniper.

TYPE OF PLANT: Tree.   HEIGHT: 50'. ZONE: N

HOW TO IDENTIFY: Strict, upright habit of growth, much taller than broad; needle-like foliage that does not turn plum-colored during cold weather.

HABIT OF GROWTH: Narrow, upright, much taller than broad.

FOLIAGE: Evergreen, needle-like of fine texture, dark green color.

FLOWERS: Inconspicuous.

FRUITS: Cones 1" in diameter with 8-14 scales, usually not seen in Florida.

SEASON OF MAXIMUM COLOR: No seasonal change.

LANDSCAPE USES: As a strong accent, Italian cypress, in the variety 'Stricta,' which is the one most often seen, is unequaled. This columnar tree is unsuitable for home landscaping; rather, its use will be restricted to college campuses and arboretums where plantings on a large scale could be complemented by strong accents 50' in height.

HABITAT: Southern Europe; in Florida, northern tier of counties.

LIGHT REQUIREMENT: Full sun.

SOIL REQUIREMENT: Fertile soil.

SALT TOLERANCE: Not tolerant.

AVAILABILITY: Italian cypress is rarely seen in Florida nurseries.

CULTURE: Plant in well-prepared site; water periodically until well established; thereafter, no attention will be needed.

PROPAGATION: Cuttage or marcottage.

PESTS: None of major concern.

19 White-Cedar

Chamaecyparis (cam-ee-sip-ar-is): Greek for dwarf cypress.
thyoides (thigh-oy-dez): like thuja.

FAMILY: Cupressaceae.   **RELATIVES:** China-fir, cypress, and arbor-vitae.

TYPE OF PLANT: Tree.   **HEIGHT:** 80'. **ZONE:** N

HOW TO IDENTIFY: Attractive ascending growth; tiny, evergreen leaves closely overlapping or spreading at apex on leading shoots, with conspicuous glands on the back.

HABIT OF GROWTH: Attractive, symmetrical, dense crown.

FOLIAGE: Evergreen, of fine texture, medium green color.

FLOWERS: Inconspicuous.

FRUITS: Cones about ¼" across that have a glaucous bloom while immature, turn brown at maturity.

SEASON OF MAXIMUM COLOR: No variation.

LANDSCAPE USES: As a strong, permanent accent, this native tree may serve well. For woodland or public plantings, white-cedar is highly recommended.

This is another example of a native tree that is not nearly so widely planted as it should be. Completely adapted to our state, of course, notably resistant to insects and diseases, beautifully symmetrical in growth, white-cedar should appear in more plantings. Seeds germinate satisfactorily and growth is moderately rapid. There is seedling variation in form, but this is not objectionable.

HABITAT: Moist soils in certain locations in northern Florida.

LIGHT REQUIREMENT: Native in wooded areas, but grows well in sun.

SOIL REQUIREMENT: Native stands grow on fertile, moist soils.

SALT TOLERANCE: Not tolerant.

AVAILABILITY: Although this is one of our very best needle evergreens, it is not often found in nurseries.

CULTURE: Plant small seedlings in moist, organic soil, and no additional care will be required.

PROPAGATION: Seedage.

PESTS: None of major consequence.

20
Oriental Arbor-Vitae

Thuja (THOO-ya): classical name.
orientalis (oh-ree-en-TAL-is): oriental.

FAMILY: Cupressaceae.   RELATIVES: True cypress, false-cypress, and juniper.

TYPE OF PLANT: Tree or shrub.   HEIGHT: 40'.   ZONE: N,C,S

HOW TO IDENTIFY: Narrow-leaved, coniferous evergreen that produces its branchlets in vertical plane; shape of the plant often runs to the globular or columnar.

HABIT OF GROWTH: Columnar or globular, with dense foliage.

FOLIAGE: Evergreen, very fine in texture, in various tones of green and/or yellow according to the variety. Fall color often purple toward tips of foliage.

FLOWERS: Inconspicuous.

FRUITS: Cones ½"-1" long, usually 6 woody scales.

SEASON OF MAXIMUM COLOR: Winter, when foliage is purple.

LANDSCAPE USES: Florida landscape developments are best completed without this strongly geometrical shrub; nonetheless, oriental arbor-vitae is very popular with homeowners and is much planted.

HABITAT: Orient; in Florida, much planted.

LIGHT REQUIREMENT: Full sun for best compact habit.

SOIL REQUIREMENT: Tolerant of varying soils.

SALT TOLERANCE: Not tolerant.

AVAILABILITY: Widely offered in containers and B & B.

CULTURE: Plant with reasonable care; water faithfully until well established; fertilize very lightly because of rapid growth. Juniper blight, a very serious disease, is controlled by very frequent applications of fungicides.

PROPAGATION: Cuttage.

PESTS: Juniper blight and mites are bad in Florida.

21 Southern Red-Cedar

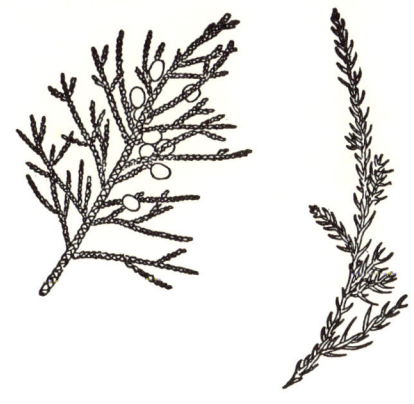

Juniperus (june-IP-er-us): old classical name.
silicicola (sill-ee-SICK-oh-la): having silicles (capsules broader than long).

FAMILY: Cupressaceae.   RELATIVES: True cypress and false-cypress.
TYPE OF PLANT: Tree.   HEIGHT: 25'. ZONE: N,C,S
HOW TO IDENTIFY: Coniferous evergreen tree with reddish-brown, very thin bark; green flexible twigs that contain two kinds of leaves, the juvenile form being sharp-pointed and spreading; the adult form, scale-like, closely appressed and 4-ranked.
HABIT OF GROWTH: Very symmetrical while young, becoming picturesque, flat-topped, often windswept, with age.
FOLIAGE: Evergreen, minute, finest texture and dark green color in the usual forms.
FLOWERS: Inconspicuous strobili (sexes on different trees) in very early spring.
FRUITS: Succulent, dark blue, drupe-like cones less than ¼" long, in winter.
SEASON OF MAXIMUM COLOR: Not much variation, excepting for the brown cones.
LANDSCAPE USES: As a freestanding specimen, southern red-cedar has long been popular. For beach cottages and woodland plantings, it excels. Windbreaks made by planting these trees in double, staggered rows have been used for centuries.
HABITAT: Limestone areas of Florida as far south as Sarasota County.
LIGHT REQUIREMENT: Full sun or partial shade of hammocks.
SOIL REQUIREMENT: Calcareous soils are acceptable, as are beach-front locations.
SALT TOLERANCE: Very tolerant of salt, recommended for dune planting.
AVAILABILITY: Some commercial nurseries sell 1-year seedlings in containers and B & B, and some state agencies distribute seedlings for reforestation.
CULTURE: Set in moderately fertile soil if possible; water until well established, and during dry times thereafter; fertilize once or twice annually.
PROPAGATION: Seedage.
PESTS: Juniper blight is a very serious disease that browns the interiors of infected plants. Mites attack junipers, too.
NOTE: Red-cedar, *Juniperus virginiana,* grown farther north, is easily confused.

22
Japanese Juniper

Juniperus (june-IP-er-us): old classical name.
chinensis (chi-NEN-sis): Chinese.
'Columnaris' (col-um-NARE-is): columnar.

FAMILY: Cupressaceae.   RELATIVES: True cypress and false-cypress.

TYPE OF PLANT: Tree.   HEIGHT: 30'. ZONE: N,C

HOW TO IDENTIFY: Tree-like, owing to strong, single, central leader with 2 kinds of leaves (needle-like and scale-like) on every branch.

HABIT OF GROWTH: Columnar, with a strong, erect trunk.

FOLIAGE: Evergreen, of 2 types, needle-form and scale-form, on every branch. Texture is fine and color is dark green, even during the winter.

FLOWERS: Inconspicuous.

FRUITS: Usually not formed in Florida.

SEASON OF MAXIMUM COLOR: No seasonal changes.

LANDSCAPE USES: For accent, both freestanding, and in shrubbery groups, Japanese juniper is the best exotic, columnar, needle-leaved evergreen for Florida. It rightly enjoys considerable popularity.

HABITAT: China; in Florida, cultured in northern counties.

LIGHT REQUIREMENT: Full sun for compact growth.

SOIL REQUIREMENT: Fertile, well-drained soils are recommended for good growth.

SALT TOLERANCE: Not tolerant.

AVAILABILITY: Northern Florida nurseries display plants B & B or in containers.

CULTURE: On well-drained, reasonably fertile soil, no special measures are needed except to control juniper blight and mites upon occasion.

PROPAGATION: Cuttage.

PESTS: Juniper blight and mites.

23
Shore Juniper

Juniperus (june-IP-er-us): old classical name.
conferta (con-FERT-a): crowded.

FAMILY: Cupressaceae.   **RELATIVES:** True cypress and false-cypress.

TYPE OF PLANT: Dwarf shrub.   **HEIGHT:** 2'. **ZONE:** N

HOW TO IDENTIFY: Evergreen leaves all needle-like in whorls of 3, each with 2 longitudinal lines on the upper surface. Most branch-tips upward-pointing.

HABIT OF GROWTH: Low, mat-forming.

FOLIAGE: Evergreen, needle-form with 2 white lines, very fine in texture and light gray-green in color.

FLOWERS: Inconspicuous.

FRUITS: None, usually, in Florida.

SEASON OF MAXIMUM COLOR: No seasonal variation.

LANDSCAPE USES: Shore juniper excels as a low transition plant or ground cover for positions in full sun. In sunny planters it looks particularly fine. This, the best of the ground-clinging conifers for our state, enjoys considerable popularity in northern counties.

HABITAT: Japan; in Florida, northern counties.

LIGHT REQUIREMENT: Full sun for compact growth.

SOIL REQUIREMENT: Sandy soils are acceptable.

SALT TOLERANCE: Tolerant of moderate salt spray.

AVAILABILITY: Shore juniper, in containers or B & B, is widely stocked.

CULTURE: On reasonably fertile sandy soil in upper Florida, no special care is needed. The usual watering and fertilization will suffice.

PROPAGATION: Cuttage.

PESTS: Mites and juniper blight.

24
Pfitzer Juniper

Juniperus (june-IP-er-us): old classical name.
chinensis (chi-NEN-sis): Chinese.
'Pfitzeriana' (fits-er-ee-ANE-a): of Herr Pfitzer.

FAMILY: Cupressaceae.   RELATIVES: True cypress and false-cypress.

TYPE OF PLANT: Dwarf shrub.   HEIGHT: 5'.   ZONE: N,C

HOW TO IDENTIFY: Low shrub of horizontal-spreading growth, with branch tips always outward-pointing, or slightly nodding, never upright.

HABIT OF GROWTH: Horizontal-spreading.

FOLIAGE: Evergreen, very fine in texture, light gray-green in color.

FLOWERS: None in Florida.

FRUITS: None in Florida.

SEASON OF MAXIMUM COLOR: No seasonal changes.

LANDSCAPE USES: As a transition plant and planter subject, this dwarf, needle-leaved evergreen is very useful in western Florida. Southward, down the peninsula, Pfitzer juniper becomes increasingly less good as a garden shrub. Unfortunately, there is confusion in naming in nurseries.

HABITAT: China; in Florida, the northern counties.

LIGHT REQUIREMENT: Full sun only.

SOIL REQUIREMENT: Looks best on fertile, well-drained land.

SALT TOLERANCE: Tolerant of salt air well back of the dunes.

AVAILABILITY: Nurseries in northern Florida feature Pfitzer junipers B&B during the winter season. There is often incorrect labeling.

CULTURE: In northern Florida, fertile, well-drained earth that has adequate moisture is a requirement for success.

PROPAGATION: Cuttage, using tips in December-January.

PESTS: Mites and juniper blight.

25
Common Screw-Pine

Pandanus (pan-DAY-nus): Latinized Malayan name.
utilis (YOU-till-us): useful.

FAMILY: Pandanaceae.
TYPE OF PLANT: Tree.
RELATIVES: This genus stands alone.
HEIGHT: 25′. ZONE: S

HOW TO IDENTIFY: Stout, branching tree with many brace roots; outward-pointing leaves 3′ long by 3″ broad, with many sharp, ascending, red spines on margins and midrib. During parts of the year there are conspicuous rough fruits hanging on stout cords.

HABIT OF GROWTH: Coarse tree with scaffold-like branches that support groups of spirally arranged, ribbon-like leaves at their tips.

FOLIAGE: Evergreen, ribbon-like, yard-long, spine-edged, reddish-toned.

FLOWERS: Ball-like, 8″ in diameter, hanging from cord-like peduncles.

FRUITS: Round, rough, compound fruits, with prism-like sections, on pistillate trees.

SEASON OF MAXIMUM COLOR: No seasonal variation.

LANDSCAPE USES: To create the atmosphere of the tropics, use pandanus as a freestanding specimen. For terrace, patio, or Florida room, potted individuals are in favor.

HABITAT: South Sea islands; in Florida, widely planted in warmest parts.

LIGHT REQUIREMENT: Full sun for fruiting specimens, small plants endure shade.

SOIL REQUIREMENT: Grows well in soils of many different types.

SALT TOLERANCE: Tolerant of salt air back of the front-line dunes.

AVAILABILITY: Many nurseries, chain stores, and garden centers market screw-pines.

CULTURE: Set in a site that has been improved by the addition of organic matter; water periodically until established; thereafter keep lawn grasses away from the root zone; fertilize twice each year.

PROPAGATION: Division or seedage.

PESTS: Scales.

NOTE: Veitch pandanus (*P. veitchii*), much used as a pot plant, has spiny leaves with white bands at the margins.

Sander pandanus (*P. sanderi*) with denser, more tufted foliage, has golden yellow bands from midrib to margin. Botanical status is uncertain and labeling may not always be correct.

26
Licuala Palm

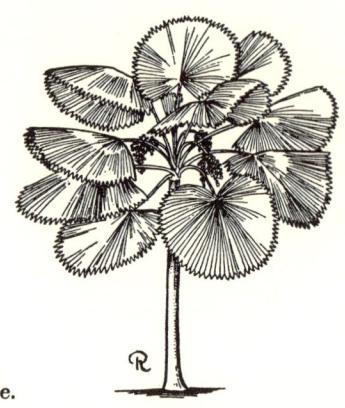

Licuala (lick-you-ALE-a): aboriginal Moluccan name.
grandis (GRAN-dis): large.

FAMILY: Palmaceae.

RELATIVES: The palm trees.

TYPE OF PLANT: Dwarf palm tree.

HEIGHT: 8'. ZONE: S

HOW TO IDENTIFY: Dainty, shade-demanding, dwarf, single-trunked palm with orbicular, yard-broad, undivided, much-pleated leaves.

HABIT OF GROWTH: Single-stemmed, with the dainty, pleated leaves held by slender, spiny petioles.

FOLIAGE: Evergreen, palmate, bold in design, dark green in color.

FLOWERS: Inconspicuous, mostly perfect.

FRUITS: Showy clusters of scarlet, pea-like pointed drupes.

SEASON OF MAXIMUM COLOR: When fruits mature.

LANDSCAPE USES: As a diminutive subject for an urn in a patio or Florida room, licuala palm is ideal. While this species is perhaps the best known, it is not the only one in *Licuala*.
These scale-model palms require shade and warmth.

HABITAT: New Britain Island; in Florida, greenhouses, nurseries, and patios.

LIGHT REQUIREMENT: Dense shade is a requirement for success.

SOIL REQUIREMENT: Moderately fertile, well-drained medium.

SALT TOLERANCE: Not tolerant.

AVAILABILITY: Specialty nurseries may have small licuala palms in gallon containers.

CULTURE: Plant in good soil in a shaded spot; water faithfully; fertilize twice annually; keep grass back. Protection must be supplied on cold nights.

PROPAGATION: Seedage.

PESTS: Nematodes, scales, and mites.

27
Paurotis Palm

Paurotis (paw-ROE-tis): Greek for small ear, application unclear.
wrightii (RIGHT-ee-eye): for C. Wright, American botanist.

FAMILY: Palmaceae.
TYPE OF PLANT: Palm tree.
RELATIVES: The palm trees.
HEIGHT: 30'. ZONE: C,S
HOW TO IDENTIFY: Clump-growing, small-scale fan palm with armed petioles. Slender trunks grow with tufts of fan leaves atop, always with many suckers around their bases.
HABIT OF GROWTH: Clump-forming by many slender trunks.
FOLIAGE: Evergreen, palmate, tropical in appearance, of medium green color.
FLOWERS: Inconspicuous, on long, branching spadices among the leaves, but protruding beyond the leaf mass in untidy array.
FRUITS: Shining, black, globular drupes ⅜" in diameter.
SEASON OF MAXIMUM COLOR: When flowers open in early summer.
LANDSCAPE USES: In highest favor for landscaping houses of contemporary design, for palm groups, and for parts of enclosing borders, is this native of the Florida Everglades. Beloved of landscape architects and palm fanciers, most available native clumps have been transplanted to landscape compositions. Paurotis palms, also known as Cape Sable palms, are attractive while small and trunkless, yet they are particularly picturesque and handsome in maturity, when several leaning trunks reach roof-tree height. Old fruiting stalks should be pruned out regularly for neat appearance, as should old leaves that turn brown.
HABITAT: Moist locations in the Florida Everglades and Caribbean islands.
LIGHT REQUIREMENT: Full sun or partial shade.
SOIL REQUIREMENT: Tolerant of many soils, native in wet places but grows well on elevated, sandy soil; tolerates alkalinity.
SALT TOLERANCE: Tolerant of salt air; slightly brackish water.
AVAILABILITY: Some nurseries will offer small seedlings in containers.
CULTURE: Set slightly deeper than the palm grew formerly, into fertile, acid soil; water periodically until the palm is well established. Keep lawn grasses back from the roots.
PROPAGATION: Seedage and/or division.
PESTS: None of major concern.

28 Gru-Gru Palm

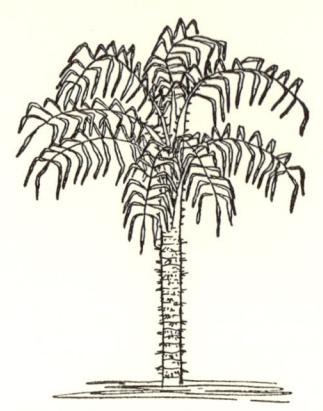

Acrocomia (ack-roe-COM-ee-a): from a tuft of leaves at the top. SPP.: several species are grown in Florida.

FAMILY: Palmaceae.

RELATIVES: The palm trees.

TYPE OF PLANT: Palm tree.

HEIGHT: 50'. ZONE: C,S

HOW TO IDENTIFY: Vicious thorns arm the trunk and leaf-stalks.

HABIT OF GROWTH: Straight-trunked palm that develops a bulge in middle age.

FOLIAGE: Evergreen, pinnate, fine in texture, light green in color.

FLOWERS: Inconspicuous, in branched, drooping spadices, among the leaves.

FRUITS: Large, round, oil-bearing, sometimes edible.

SEASON OF MAXIMUM COLOR: Possibly when fruits mature.

LANDSCAPE USES: For palm groups, because of the curiosity of the heavily armed trunks, gru-grus must be included.
 Palms of this genus have real atmosphere-creating character, much appreciated by tourists to lands of the Caribbean.

HABITAT: Tropical America; in Florida, warm locations.

LIGHT REQUIREMENT: Full sun.

SOIL REQUIREMENT: Tolerant of sandy soils of many types.

SALT TOLERANCE: Tolerant of salt drift, back of front-line dunes.

AVAILABILITY: Gru-gru palms in containers will be found in specialty nurseries.

CULTURE: Plant in enriched site during warm months; water faithfully; keep lawn grasses back; fertilize during each rainy season.

PROPAGATION: Seedage.

PESTS: Scales and palm weevils in old age.

29 Lady Palm

Rhapis (RAY-pis): Greek for needle.
excelsa (ecks-SELL-sa): tall.

FAMILY: Palmaceae.

RELATIVES: The palm trees.

TYPE OF PLANT: Dwarf palm.

HEIGHT: 10'. ZONE: N,C,S

HOW TO IDENTIFY: Growing in matted clumps, lady palm makes a dense mass of foliage. The blades of the leaves are 5- to 10-parted nearly to the base, 1⅛" wide at the middle; the apexes are short-toothed.

HABIT OF GROWTH: Clump-forming by underground, running stems.

FOLIAGE: Evergreen, digitate, attractively divided, of medium green color.

FLOWERS: Inconspicuous, unisexual, in branched spadices among the leaves.

FRUITS: Small, 1- to 3-seeded berries.

SEASON OF MAXIMUM COLOR: No color variation.

LANDSCAPE USES: For foundation plantings on north sides of buildings, lady palms are in great favor. As urn subjects for terrace, patio, or Florida room, they are unexcelled. Lady palms are among the most-wanted dwarf palms in Florida, and, as a consequence, they are rare and expensive. One rare clone has variegated foliage.

HABITAT: Eastern Asia; in Florida, shady locations in all areas.

LIGHT REQUIREMENT: Shade is requisite for success with lady palms.

SOIL REQUIREMENT: The best looking plants grow on moist, fertile soil.

SALT TOLERANCE: Not tolerant.

AVAILABILITY: Nurseries offer small seedlings or little divisions in containers, but large specimens are rare and expensive.

CULTURE: Plant only in shady locations, in well-prepared, fast-draining soil that is high in organic matter. Water faithfully but moderately.

PROPAGATION: Division, seedage when seeds are to be had.

PESTS: Scales and caterpillars.

NOTE: Dwarf lady palm (*Rhapis humilis*) has more slender stems and narrower (¾") leaf segments. There is confusion in naming in the genus *Rhapis*.

30
Windmill Palm

Trachycarpus (tray-key-CAR-pus): Greek for rough fruit.
fortunei (FOR-tune-eye): for R. Fortune, Scottish botanist.

FAMILY: Palmaceae.
RELATIVES: The palm trees.
TYPE OF PLANT: Palm tree.
HEIGHT: 20'. ZONE: N,C

HOW TO IDENTIFY: Slender palm with single trunk clothed in brown fiber and yard-broad palmate leaves attached to rough-edged petioles.

HABIT OF GROWTH: Upright, from a single, erect trunk with neat crown.

FOLIAGE: Evergreen, palmate, coarse in texture, gray-green in color.

FLOWERS: Small, yellow, in small, branching spadices among the leaves.

FRUITS: 3-parted, angled fruits, the size of peas, if present.

SEASON OF MAXIMUM COLOR: No seasonal variation.

LANDSCAPE USES: This diminutive, slow-growing palm is of greatest usefulness with structures of contemporary design. In foundation plantings or in shrubbery borders it may serve as an excellent accent.

Popular in Mediterranean gardens and in tropical arboretums, too, windmill palm is enjoying public favor in Florida. *Trachycarpus* will not be injured by cold, and will remain in scale for many, many years. It has, in truth, many admirable qualities.

HABITAT: Eastern Asia; in Florida, infrequently seen in gardens of the upper peninsula and the panhandle.

LIGHT REQUIREMENT: Tolerant of shade, yet grows in full sun, too.

SOIL REQUIREMENT: Fertility above average is recommended.

SALT TOLERANCE: Tolerant of salt air back of the front-line dunes.

AVAILABILITY: Windmill palm is found in specialty nurseries.

CULTURE: Make sites carefully with an acid, organic mixture; plant a little below original growing depth; water faithfully; keep lawn grasses back from the root zone. Fertilize twice or thrice annually.

PROPAGATION: Seedage.

PESTS: Scales.

31
European Fan Palm

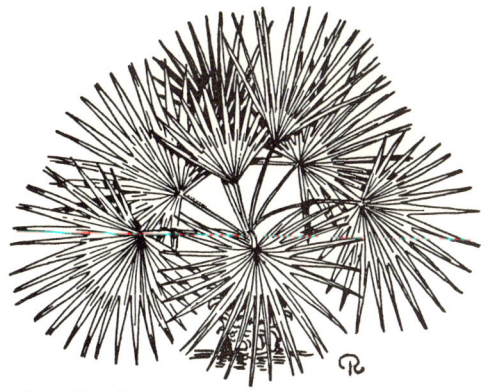

Chamaerops (cam-EE-rops): Greek for dwarf bush.
humilis (HUME-ill-is): dwarf.

FAMILY: Palmaceae.

RELATIVES: The palm trees.

TYPE OF PLANT: Palm tree.

HEIGHT: 15'. ZONE: N,C,S

HOW TO IDENTIFY: Clump-growing; palmate foliage is held by armed petioles. The leaf segments do not droop.

HABIT OF GROWTH: Clump-forming by suckers around the base.

FOLIAGE: Evergreen, palmate, of attractive form, and gray-green color.

FLOWERS: Inconspicuous, in dense spadices among the leaves.

FRUITS: Small, globular berries, reddish or yellowish in color.

SEASON OF MAXIMUM COLOR: No variation in color.

LANDSCAPE USES: As a tiny lawn specimen; many seedlings never grow over 5' in height. As a part of a palm group, set these dwarfs 5' o.c. As an urn subject for terrace, patio, or Florida room, European fan palm excels.

HABITAT: Southern Europe; in Florida, all sections.

LIGHT REQUIREMENT: Sun or shade.

SOIL REQUIREMENT: Tolerant of many kinds of soil.

SALT TOLERANCE: Tolerant of light salt drift, back from the dunes.

AVAILABILITY: Only rarely is this little palm found in nurseries, yet it warrants much wider use.

CULTURE: Set in well-prepared planting sites; water faithfully; keep lawn grasses back from the root zone. Fertilize lightly once or twice during the rainy season.

PROPAGATION: Seedage or division.

PESTS: Scales.

NOTE: There are some named clones, there is extreme seedling variation, and many individuals may never reach the maximum height of 30', but remain for many years true dwarfs.

32
Washington Palm

Washingtonia (wash-ing-TONE-ee-a): for G. Washington.
robusta (roe-BUS-ta): robust, referring to the height of the tree.

FAMILY: Palmaceae.	RELATIVES: The palm trees.
TYPE OF PLANT: Palm tree.	HEIGHT: 60'. ZONE: N,C,S

HOW TO IDENTIFY: Leaves palmate, with many gray threads, petioles heavily armed; growth rapid.

HABIT OF GROWTH: Straight trunk and close, compact head with shag.

FOLIAGE: Evergreen, palmate, bold in aspect, medium green in color.

FLOWERS: Bisexual, inconspicuous, in long, panicled spadices among the leaves, but longer than the foliage mass.

FRUITS: Black, shining drupes that are ellipsoid in shape.

SEASON OF MAXIMUM COLOR: No variation.

LANDSCAPE USES: As an avenue tree, plant 25'-35' apart. Washington palm serves admirably as a central feature in a palm group in large public landscape plantings, but it is too tall for small home ground plantings.

HABITAT: Mexico, in Sonora and Baja California; in Florida, ubiquitous.

LIGHT REQUIREMENT: Full sun for best growth, yet it endures some shade while young.

SOIL REQUIREMENT: Tolerant of light, open sands of low fertility.

SALT TOLERANCE: Tolerant of salt drift back of the front dunes.

AVAILABILITY: Small Washington palms are offered by nearly all nurseries.

CULTURE: After proper planting, no special attention is needed.

PROPAGATION: Seedage.

PESTS: Scales while young, palm weevil in old age.

NOTE: California Washington palm (*Washingtonia filifera*), indigenous to California and so widely used as an avenue tree there, is not often seen in Florida. The Californian has a thicker, heavier trunk and is less tall than its Mexican relative. The shag of hanging dead leaves adds to the picturesque quality, but it presents a fire hazard and a breeding place for rats, so it is unlawful to leave the shag in some California communities.

33
Chinese Fan Palm

Livistona (liv-is-TONE-a): for Livistone, Scotland.
chinensis (chi-NEN-sis): Chinese.

FAMILY: Palmaceae.

RELATIVES: The palm trees.

TYPE OF PLANT: Palm tree.

HEIGHT: 25'. ZONE: C,S

HOW TO IDENTIFY: The ringed trunk is usually straight; the palmate leaves have long, bifid segments that hang downward with age. The bases of the green petioles of young plants are edged with downward-pointing, single spines.

HABIT OF GROWTH: Gracefully fountain-like, causing this species to be called Chinese fountain palm in some localities.

FOLIAGE: Evergreen, palmate, with bifid segments that bend sharply downward.

FLOWERS: Inconspicuous, bisexual, in thin spadices amidst the foliage.

FRUITS: Black, olive-like, ellipsoid-oblong, 1" in length.

SEASON OF MAXIMUM COLOR: No seasonal variation.

LANDSCAPE USES: As a freestanding specimen the little Chinese fountain palm is noted for its outstanding beauty, and as an urn subject a young seedling is much admired as well. Although Chinese fan palm has long been known to horticulture, it has not been much planted by homeowners within its climatic range. It is hoped that this may be remedied as gardeners learn of this fine little palm.

HABITAT: China; in Florida, sparingly planted over the peninsula.

LIGHT REQUIREMENT: Shade while young, sun is tolerated in maturity.

SOIL REQUIREMENT: Soil of moderate fertility is recommended.

SALT TOLERANCE: Not tolerant.

AVAILABILITY: Nurseries offer small Chinese fan palms in containers.

CULTURE: Plant in reasonably fertile soil; shade while young; mulch with organic litter; water during dry spells; fertilize thrice annually.

PROPAGATION: Seedage.

PESTS: Scales.

34 Cabbage Palm

Sabal (SAY-bal): unexplained.
palmetto (pal-MET-oh): little palm.

FAMILY: Palmaceae.
RELATIVES: The palm trees.
TYPE OF PLANT: Palm tree.
HEIGHT: 90'. ZONE: N,C,S

HOW TO IDENTIFY: Smooth-edged petioles continue through the palmate blades of the leaves. The trees are quite variable in aspect and foliage color.

HABIT OF GROWTH: Variable as to trunk diameter, curvature, and presence of boots, yet with a small, dense crown of deeply-cut palmate leaves. Rarely specimens with branched trunks and 2, 3, or 4 crowns of foliage are seen in Florida.

FOLIAGE: Evergreen, with petiole continuing through the blade, variable in color.

FLOWERS: Inconspicuous, hermaphroditic, in branched inflorescences.

FRUITS: Black, globular berries with short, tapering bases.

SEASON OF MAXIMUM COLOR: No variation.

LANDSCAPE USES: As peerless avenue tree, 20'-40' o.c. As a framing tree for buildings, as a member of a palm group, as a freestanding specimen, and as a patio or terrace tree, the native cabbage palm cannot be excelled.

    This is Florida's state tree, and here it is appreciated for its many sterling qualities.

HABITAT: Much of Florida is inhabited by this picturesque palm.

LIGHT REQUIREMENT: Sun or shade.

SOIL REQUIREMENT: Extremely tolerant of varying soil conditions.

SALT TOLERANCE: Very tolerant of salt; recommended for seaside plantings.

AVAILABILITY: Landscape-size trees are dug from the wild upon order.

CULTURE: Plant deeply in well-prepared sites during summer months; water copiously for a time, after new growth is well under way, no more attention will be needed.

PROPAGATION: Seedage.

PESTS: Palm leaf skeletonizer, palmetto weevil.

NOTE: *Sabal peregrina*, 25' high, planted in Key West, has very fruitful spadices that are shorter than the leaves.

35
Fiji Fan Palm

Pritchardia (prit-CHAR-dee-a): for W. Pritchard, an Englishman.
pacifica (pa-SIFF-ee-ca): of the Pacific Ocean.

FAMILY: Palmaceae.
TYPE OF PLANT: Palm tree.
RELATIVES: The palm trees.
HEIGHT: 30'. ZONE: S

HOW TO IDENTIFY: Straight, slender bole; 5-foot leaves, deeply neatly pleated, held by 3-foot, spineless petioles; globe-like fruit clusters hung on 3-foot cords.

HABIT OF GROWTH: Neat, distinctive fan-leaved crown atop a slender, straight trunk.

FOLIAGE: Evergreen, palmate, neatly pleated to form a beautiful design, in dark green.

FLOWERS: Inconspicuous bisexual, in globes at the ends of cords.

FRUITS: Globular ½" black berries with tapered bases borne in large balls on yard-long cords.

SEASON OF MAXIMUM COLOR: No color variation.

LANDSCAPE USES: As a framing tree or as a freestanding specimen in a protected garden in extreme southern Florida, Fiji fan palm is without superior. It is easily injured by wind and frost.

HABITAT: Fiji Islands; in Florida, protected locations only.

LIGHT REQUIREMENT: Partial shade is desirable.

SOIL REQUIREMENT: Fertile, well-drained organic soil is recommended.

SALT TOLERANCE: Very intolerant of salt air.

AVAILABILITY: Fiji fan palm will be found in containers in some specialty nurseries in the warmest parts of the lower peninsula.

CULTURE: Plant this delicate palm carefully in a well-prepared site in a most protected location; water faithfully; mulch and fertilize three times a year.

PROPAGATION: Seedage.

PESTS: Scales, mites.

NOTE: Thurston fan palm (*Pritchardia thurstonii*) thrusts its fruits well beyond the leaves on 6-foot cords. This one grows to about 15' in height and has beautifully pleated leaves. There are numerous other species in *Pritchardia*, but these are rare in Florida gardens.

36
Canary Island Date Palm

Phoenix (FEE-nicks): ancient Greek name for the date palm.
canariensis (can-ar-ee-EN-sis): of the Canary Islands.

FAMILY: Palmaceae.

TYPE OF PLANT: Palm tree.

RELATIVES: The palm trees.

HEIGHT: 60'. ZONE: N,C,S

HOW TO IDENTIFY: Stocky, single trunk marked with diamond pattern from the sloughed boots, pinnate leaves with murderous thorns on the petioles and small, orange, decorative dates borne by pistillate individuals.

HABIT OF GROWTH: Straight, single trunk with heavy head of pinnate leaves.

FOLIAGE: Evergreen, feather-leaved with stiffish pinnae, murderous thorns at the bases of the leaf stalks. The foliage is of fine texture and yellow-green color.

FLOWERS: Unisexual, inconspicuous, in short spadices amidst the leaves.

FRUITS: Ovoid, about 1" in length, of a bright orange-yellow color.

SEASON OF MAXIMUM COLOR: Early summer when fruits are fully colored.

LANDSCAPE USES: As an avenue tree, spaced 50' apart, when there is sufficiently broad planting strip, Canary Island date palm is unsurpassed. For single specimens on lawns of public buildings it is majestic. Its huge bulk makes this palm unsuitable for residential plantings.

HABITAT: Canary Islands; in Florida it is planted in every community.

LIGHT REQUIREMENT: Full sun for best development.

SOIL REQUIREMENT: Any well-drained soil will suffice.

SALT TOLERANCE: Tolerant of salt somewhat back from the front-line dunes.

AVAILABILITY: Most nurseries offer Canary Island date palms in containers.

CULTURE: Plant in reasonably fertile sites; water moderately; mulch the root zone; keep lawn grasses back; protect the leaves from leaf-spotting diseases while young, and from palm leaf skeletonizer when mature.

PROPAGATION: Seedage.

PESTS: Leaf-spot, palm leaf skeletonizer, palm weevil in old age.

NOTE: Hybridization within the genus *Phoenix* has been recognized in Florida for many years. Many garden palms may be crossbred.

37
Senegal Date Palm

Phoenix (FEE-nicks): ancient Greek name for the date palm.
reclinata (reck-lin-AH-ta): leaning.

FAMILY: Palmaceae.

TYPE OF PLANT: Palm tree.

RELATIVES: The palm trees.

HEIGHT: 35'. ZONE: N,C,S

HOW TO IDENTIFY: A clump-forming palm with many leaning, bowed trunks and feather-leaves whose pinnae are stiffish and sharp-tipped. The petioles are heavily armed with very sharp spines.

HABIT OF GROWTH: Clump-forming by gracefully curving stems.

FOLIAGE: Evergreen, pinnate, with thorns at the bases of the leaf-stalks. The texture is fine, the color medium green.

FLOWERS: Unisexual, inconspicuous, in short spadices amidst the foliage.

FRUITS: Ovoid little dates about 1" in length of bright orange color.

SEASON OF MAXIMUM COLOR: In early summer when fruits turn orange.

LANDSCAPE USES: As a freestanding specimen to create atmosphere or mood, Senegal date, or cluster date as it is frequently called, is highly regarded and much used in landscape compositions.

HABITAT: Africa; in Florida, all areas.

LIGHT REQUIREMENT: Full sun or partial shade.

SOIL REQUIREMENT: Any well-drained soil seems to be adequate.

SALT TOLERANCE: Tolerant of salt air back from the strand.

AVAILABILITY: Senegal date palms are fairly abundant in small sizes in containers. Landscape-size B&B specimens are rare and expensive.

CULTURE: Plant in fertile soil; water moderately; fertilize once or twice a year; keep lawn grasses from encroaching upon the root zone for a few years.

PROPAGATION: Seedage and/or division of suckers from the base of old trees.

PESTS: Palm leaf skeletonizer and leaf-spot.

NOTE: Cliff date (*Phoenix rupicola*) grows with a single bowed trunk which supports leaves with soft, drooping pinnae emerging from a single plane. Hybridization within the genus *Phoenix* has been widespread in Florida for many years, and many garden specimens are crossbred palms.

38
Pygmy Date Palm

Phoenix (FEE-nicks): ancient Greek name for the date palm.
roebelenii (roe-bell-EEN-ee-eye): for Mr. Robeleni.

FAMILY: Palmaceae.

RELATIVES: The palm trees.

TYPE OF PLANT: Dwarf palm tree.

HEIGHT: 8'. ZONE: C,S

HOW TO IDENTIFY: A dwarf palm of fine proportions with delicate pinnate leaves and murderous thorns at the bases of the leaf-stalks.

HABIT OF GROWTH: A graceful, fine-scale crown above a single, straight trunk.

FOLIAGE: Evergreen, pinnate, with spines on the petiole, of fine texture.

FLOWERS: Unisexual, inconspicuous, in short spadices among the leaves.

FRUITS: Cylindrical little jet-black dates about 1" long.

SEASON OF MAXIMUM COLOR: No variation unless fruits mature.

LANDSCAPE USES: Unquestionably one of Florida's leading dwarf palms, pygmy date is used as a freestanding specimen, planter subject, or urn plant for patio, terrace, or Florida room.

Thousands are propagated here and sold for landscape use and for shipping to northern markets.

HABITAT: Burma; in Florida, protected spots on the peninsula.

LIGHT REQUIREMENT: Partial shade or full sun.

SOIL REQUIREMENT: Well-drained, fertile soil with moderate moisture.

SALT TOLERANCE: Not tolerant.

AVAILABILITY: Most retail nurseries on the peninsula, many chain stores everywhere, offer this excellent little palm for sale.

CULTURE: Plant in fertile soil; water moderately; fertilize three times each year; protect from frost.

PROPAGATION: Seedage.

PESTS: A leaf-spotting disease, scales, and caterpillars.

39
Fishtail Palm

Caryota (carry-oh-ta): Greek name first applied to the cultivated date.
mitis (my-tis): mild.

FAMILY: Palmaceae.

RELATIVES: The palm trees.

TYPE OF PLANT: Palm tree.

HEIGHT: 25'. ZONE: S

HOW TO IDENTIFY: Clump-growing palm whose leaf-blades are divided into many segments, each of which resembles the tail of a fancy gold fish.

HABIT OF GROWTH: Clump-growing by many suckers around the base.

FOLIAGE: Evergreen, of fishtail form and medium texture.

FLOWERS: Inconspicuous, in scurfy, much-branched spadices amidst the foliage.

FRUITS: Globose drupes ½" in diameter and bluish-black in color.

SEASON OF MAXIMUM COLOR: No seasonal variation.

LANDSCAPE USES: As a part of shrubbery borders and foundation plantings for large buildings, fishtail palms are popular, but, perhaps their best use is for urns for household decoration.

HABITAT: Tropical Asia; in Florida, warmest locations only.

LIGHT REQUIREMENT: Resistant to deep shade.

SOIL REQUIREMENT: Tolerant of varying soils, but fertile soil is best.

SALT TOLERANCE: Not tolerant.

AVAILABILITY: Fishtails are in high demand, and they are widely offered in containers by nurseries in warmest sections of the state.

CULTURE: Plant in carefully made sites; water faithfully; keep lawn grasses from encroaching upon the root zone.

PROPAGATION: Seedage or division.

PESTS: Red spider mites and scales.

NOTE: Wine palm (*C. urens*), seen in southern Florida, may grow to a height of 80' or more to become too large to use with small homes. This species does *not* sucker at the base.

40 Madagascar Palm

Chrysalidocarpus (kris-al-id-oh-CAR-pus): Greek for golden fruit.
lutescens (loo-TESS-enz): becoming yellow.

FAMILY: Palmaceae.

RELATIVES: The palm trees.

TYPE OF PLANT: Palm tree.

HEIGHT: 30'. ZONE: S

HOW TO IDENTIFY: Clump-growing palm with ringed, bamboo-like stems and yellow leaf-ribs.

HABIT OF GROWTH: Clump-forming by means of gracefully bending stems.

FOLIAGE: Evergreen, pinnate, of fine texture and yellow-green color.

FLOWERS: Inconspicuous in short clusters below the crownshaft, yet hidden in foliage.

FRUITS: Oblong, ¾" in diameter, nearly black when mature.

SEASON OF MAXIMUM COLOR: No seasonal variation.

LANDSCAPE USES: This beautiful soft palm is one of Florida's favorites for use in foundation plantings, as a featured patio plant, or as an urn subject for terrace or Florida room. Madagascar palm is very subject to injury by cold.

    Gardeners know this attractive plant under various names, and so nursery labels may designate it as areca palm, bamboo palm, yellow palm, or cane palm. Under any appellation this is one of the most useful palms of the tropics the world around.

HABITAT: Madagascar; in Florida, widely planted in nearly frostless sections.

LIGHT REQUIREMENT: Tolerant of rather dense shade in patios or Florida rooms.

SOIL REQUIREMENT: Grows best in fairly rich soil, slightly acid in reaction.

SALT TOLERANCE: Quite intolerant of salt.

AVAILABILITY: Most nurseries in southern Florida offer Madagascar palms in varying sizes in containers.

CULTURE: Plant in fertile, acid soil; water moderately during dry periods; protect against scale insects and frost.

PROPAGATION: Seedage or division.

PESTS: Scales followed by sooty-mold.

41
Royal Palm

Roystonea (roy-STONE-ee-a): for R. Stone, an American engineer.
SPP.: two species grow in Florida.

FAMILY: Palmaceae.
TYPE OF PLANT: Palm tree.
RELATIVES: The palm trees.
HEIGHT: 75'. ZONE: S

HOW TO IDENTIFY: Majestic palm trees with cement-gray trunks that are thickened at about the middle or above; bright green crownshafts and beautiful heads of soft, pinnate leaves.

HABIT OF GROWTH: Majestic, clean, upright.

FOLIAGE: Shedding at maturity, unarmed, of medium texture and bright green color.

FLOWERS: Inconspicuous, unisexual, in huge spadices below the crownshaft.

FRUITS: Black or bluish drupes about ½" long.

SEASON OF MAXIMUM COLOR: Perhaps when fruits mature.

LANDSCAPE USES: Southern Florida's most popular palm tree is widely used for avenue plantings, (30'-50' o.c.), for framing large buildings and for palm groups. The species most used in landscaping is Cuban royal palm (*Roystonea regia*). Less frequently planted by nurseries is our own native Floridian royal palm (*R. elata*). This one, so effectively employed at the famed Hialeah racecourse, has the thickening toward the upper part of the bole, with a shoulder at the top; the pinnae lack longitudinal nerves, and the black fruits are nearly round.

HABITAT: Tropical America; in Florida, nearly frostless locations.

LIGHT REQUIREMENT: Full sun or broken, shifting shade.

SOIL REQUIREMENT: Rich soil is best.

SALT TOLERANCE: Tolerant of salt drift.

AVAILABILITY: Small trees in containers and B&B are offered by most nurseries in southern Florida.

CULTURE: Start off well by setting in fertile holes and supplying adequate moisture; during dry times water as needed; fertilize young trees twice each year.

PROPAGATION: Seedage.

PESTS: Scales while young.

NOTE: *Roystonea* species vary from island to island in the West Indies, but the palm was never found on the Florida keys.

42 Manila Palm

Veitchia (VEECH-ee-a): for the English horticultural family.
merrillii (MER-ril-ee-eye): for E. Merrill, American horticulturist.

FAMILY: Palmaceae.

RELATIVES: The palm trees.

TYPE OF PLANT: Palm tree.

HEIGHT: 25'. ZONE: S

HOW TO IDENTIFY: Resembles small royal palm, with broad, flat pinnae. Prominent clusters of bright red fruits are borne below the crownshaft in winter and spring. The stocky trunk is ringed.

HABIT OF GROWTH: Straight-trunked palm tree of stocky appearance.

FOLIAGE: Evergreen, pinnate, with flat, broad pinnae, of fine texture and light green color. The rachis bends gently to give a graceful effect.

FLOWERS: Inconspicuous, unisexual, in branched spadices below crownshaft.

FRUITS: Drupe-like, bright red, 1" in diameter, very showy; gracefully placed on bone-white spadix in winter and spring.

SEASON OF MAXIMUM COLOR: Late winter and early spring when fruits mature.

LANDSCAPE USES: Avenue tree, plant 25'-35' apart, framing tree, member of a palm group.

Manila palm is usually called adonidia palm in the Miami area. Under any name this lime-enduring, sturdy little tree, that resembles a scale-model royal, is worthy of the high esteem with which it is regarded in frostless areas. Important dividend is the highly decorative red fruits that are produced during the height of the tourist season.

HABITAT: Philippine Islands; in Florida, warmest locations.

LIGHT REQUIREMENT: Full sun when mature, partial shade while young.

SOIL REQUIREMENT: Tolerant of the limestone soils of southern Florida.

SALT TOLERANCE: Tolerant of salt air back from the beach.

AVAILABILITY: Manila palm is very popular in extreme southern Florida where it is widely available in nurseries in all sizes.

CULTURE: Set slightly deeper than former level in well-made sites; water faithfully; keep lawn grasses away from root zone; fertilize thrice annually.

PROPAGATION: Seedage.

PESTS: Scales.

43
Alexandra Palm

Archontophoenix (ar-kon-toe-FEE-nicks): Greek for majestic palm.
alexandrae (alex-AN-dree): for Alexandra, Queen Dowager of Great Britain.

FAMILY: Palmaceae.
RELATIVES: The palm trees.
TYPE OF PLANT: Palm tree.
HEIGHT: 45'. ZONE: S
HOW TO IDENTIFY: A slender palm that grows from a single thin, ringed trunk with a swollen base that holds pinnate leaves with heavy side ribs and red fruits ½" across. The fruits are held by green spadix-branches which are quite long.
HABIT OF GROWTH: Neat, upright, symmetrical from single, ringed trunk.
FOLIAGE: Evergreen, pinnate, medium fine in texture, medium green in color. The rachis curves gracefully to give a very pleasant aspect.
FLOWERS: Inconspicuous, in many-branched spadices below the crownshaft. The spadix-branches are green, the tiny flowers white.
FRUITS: Red, ½" in diameter on green, many-branched clusters below the crownshaft.
SEASON OF MAXIMUM COLOR: When fruits mature.
LANDSCAPE USES: As a single specimen, as a framing tree, and as an avenue tree, Alexandra palm is well liked. It will serve as a container subject, too, for years. This species is very tender to cold.
HABITAT: Queensland; in Florida, planted in most nearly frost-free locations.
LIGHT REQUIREMENT: Full sun or broken, shifting shade.
SOIL REQUIREMENT: Reasonably fertile, well-drained soil seems to be best.
SALT TOLERANCE: Not recommended for direct exposure to the surf.
AVAILABILITY: Nurseries in the warmest part have Alexandra palms.
CULTURE: Plant carefully in well-prepared, frost-protected sites; water faithfully in dry times; protect the foliage against scale insects, the roots against grass.
PROPAGATION: Seedage.
PESTS: Scales and caterpillars.
NOTE: The identity of this palm, and closely related *Archontophoenix cunninghamiana*, is not always clearly defined in nurseries and parks in Florida. The last-named species is much the hardier of the two and has lilac flowers and broader pinnae.

44 Seaforthia Palm

Ptychosperma (tie-koe-SPERM-a): folded seed.
elegans (ELL-ee-gans): elegant.

FAMILY: Palmaceae.
TYPE OF PLANT: Small palm tree.
RELATIVES: The palm trees.
HEIGHT: 25'. ZONE: S

HOW TO IDENTIFY: Small size, ringed single trunk 3"-4" in diameter, thickened near the base; open head of small, pinnate leaves above a green crownshaft; red fruits hanging below the crownshaft.

HABIT OF GROWTH: Small-scale, erect little palm from a single, slender trunk.

FOLIAGE: Evergreen, pinnate, medium fine in texture, bright green in color.

FLOWERS: Inconspicuous, below the crownshaft in bushy spadices.

FRUITS: Bright red, oblong, ¾" long.

SEASON OF MAXIMUM COLOR: Warm months when fruits color.

LANDSCAPE USES: For small home grounds, this small-scale palm can serve as a framing tree or as a patio subject. As a tubbed specimen it has been grown for generations, north and south, as "Seaforthia elegans." It has a long history of popularity in American horticulture, despite confusion in nomenclature.

HABITAT: Tropical islands of the Old World; in Florida, warmest areas.

LIGHT REQUIREMENT: Tolerant of shade.

SOIL REQUIREMENT: Tolerant of many different soils.

SALT TOLERANCE: Not tolerant of front-line dune conditions.

AVAILABILITY: Small seaforthia palms in containers are offered by nurseries in southern counties.

CULTURE: Set slightly deeper than formerly in made-up planting site; water faithfully until well established; apply mulch; keep grasses from the root zone.

PROPAGATION: Seedage.

PESTS: Scales and mites.

NOTE: MacArthur palm (*Ptychosperma macarthurii*), with its clustered slender stems and red fruits, is very popular in the Miami area for planters and urns. There are other species and there are some hybrids, all of which are rare in Florida gardens.

45 Coconut Palm

Cocos (COKE-os): Portuguese for monkey.
nucifera (noo-SIF-er-a): nut-bearing.

FAMILY: Palmaceae.

RELATIVES: The palm trees.

TYPE OF PLANT: Palm tree.

HEIGHT: 60′. ZONE: S

HOW TO IDENTIFY: Palm with leaning, slender, bulbous trunk, heavy crown of graceful pinnate foliage, and nuts, much of the year around.

HABIT OF GROWTH: Graceful, bending trunks hold heavy, graceful crowns.

FOLIAGE: Evergreen, pinnate, of medium texture and medium green color.

FLOWERS: Unisexual, in panicles among the leaves.

FRUITS: The well-known coconuts.

SEASON OF MAXIMUM COLOR: Little seasonal variation.

LANDSCAPE USES: The ubiquitous coconut is greatly beloved and deeply appreciated by those persons who dwell in hot countries. As an avenue tree, coconut palm can stand at intervals of 25′-35′. As a background tree, as a framing tree, and as a freestanding specimen, it is without peer for frost-free locations.

There are strains that have been selected for different characters. One of the most popular now is the so-called dwarf yellow, or dwarf golden, with its bright, little fruits. Another is the dwarf green, whose fruits are vivid green at maturity.

HABITAT: Tropical strands around the world; in Florida, southern counties.

LIGHT REQUIREMENT: Intense light of tropical seashores.

SOIL REQUIREMENT: Tolerant of many diverse soils.

SALT TOLERANCE: Unexcelled for salt tolerance.

AVAILABILITY: Small coconut palms are available in containers in nurseries in southern Florida.

CULTURE: After establishment, no care is required save for semiannual fertilization.

PROPAGATION: Seedage; set coconuts into the earth about one-half their depth.

PESTS: Nematodes, virus diseases, and fungi.

46
Pindo Palm

Butia (bew-tee-a): corruption of a native name.
capitata (cap-ee-tay-ta): in compact head.

FAMILY: Palmaceae.

TYPE OF PLANT: Palm tree.

RELATIVES: The palm trees.

HEIGHT: 20'. ZONE: N,C,S

HOW TO IDENTIFY: Blue-green, pinnate leaves have strongly recurving leafstems that emerge from heavy, stocky trunks. Decorative orange dates may mature in summertime.

HABIT OF GROWTH: Stout trunks hold recurving, graceful leaves.

FOLIAGE: Evergreen, pinnate, fine in texture, blue-green in color.

FLOWERS: Small, in dense spadices about 3' long, amidst the foliage.

FRUITS: Decorative, orange, date-like, in showy clusters.

SEASON OF MAXIMUM COLOR: Summer when dates color.

LANDSCAPE USES: As a freestanding specimen on large properties, or as a member of a palm group, this hardiest of pinnate palms is highly recommended. Much space is required for the short, broad top to develop. There is great variation among pindo palms in Florida landscape plantings; botanical status is unclear. In years past this palm was known as *Cocos australis*.

HABITAT: Brazil; in Florida, every community in the state.

LIGHT REQUIREMENT: Full sun for best fruiting and compact habit of growth.

SOIL REQUIREMENT: Tolerant of varying soils throughout Florida.

SALT TOLERANCE: Tolerant of salt air back from the strand.

AVAILABILITY: Pindo palms are available in retail nurseries.

CULTURE: After careful planting in fertilized earth, periodic watering and the removal of encroaching lawn grasses will assure good growth.

PROPAGATION: Seedage.

PESTS: Palm leaf skeletonizer.

NOTE: A striking palm is a natural cross between pindo palm and queen palm. This bigeneric hybrid is a beautiful, hardy plant that has many of the good qualities of each parent.

47
Household Palms

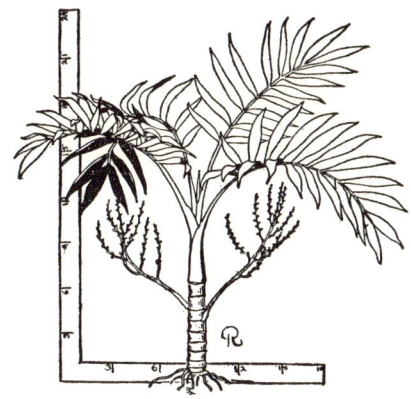

Chamaedorea (cam-ee-DORE-ee-a): Greek for dwarf and gift.
SPP.: several species are grown in Florida.

FAMILY: Palmaceae.
RELATIVES: The palm trees.
TYPE OF PLANT: Dwarf palm trees.
HEIGHT: 10'. ZONE: S
HOW TO IDENTIFY: Dwarf, pinnate palms, with single or multiple trunks and branched spadices among the leaves. The Chamaedoropsis complex, to which these little palms belong, is incompletely understood, and current study should cast light upon true botanical status within the group.
HABIT OF GROWTH: Upright, with tiny, symmetrical crowns.
FOLIAGE: Evergreen, pinnate, of fine texture and pale green color.
FLOWERS: Inconspicuous, unisexual flowers, borne on separate plants.
FRUITS: Globular little drupes.
SEASON OF MAXIMUM COLOR: None.
LANDSCAPE USES: As urn subjects for shady locations, for planter bins, and for accents in north-side foundation plantings, these tiny palms are in high favor in frostless locations.

Chamaedorea elegans (illustrated) is usually single-trunked, and widely planted.

Chamaedorea erumpens is a clump-grower that requires full shade and freedom from frost. The horticultural variety 'Fairchild' is characterized by foliage in which terminal pinnae are united into two broad blades. Both are much admired in frostless gardens.

Chamaedorea seifrizii is a scrambling palm that may endure more light than the others in this group.

Other species in *Chamaedorea* are offered by nurserymen in southern Florida.
HABITAT: Central America; in Florida, shady locations in nearly frostless locations.
LIGHT REQUIREMENT: Shade is necessary for health and a deep green color.
SOIL REQUIREMENT: Fibrous leaf mold with fertility above average is best.
SALT TOLERANCE: Not tolerant.
AVAILABILITY: Chain stores, filling stations, and garden centers offer household palms in containers. Specialty nurseries stock rarer species and varieties.
CULTURE: Shade is a requirement; limey soil is tolerated if it is open and fibrous; protection from frost is necessary for success with these diminutive tropical palms.
PROPAGATION: Seedage.
PESTS: Mites and scales.

48
Sentry Palms

Howeia (how-ee-a): for Lord Howe Islands in the southern Pacific Ocean. SPP.: two species are grown in Florida.

FAMILY: Palmaceae.
TYPE OF PLANT: Palm trees.
RELATIVES: The palm trees.
HEIGHT: 35'. ZONE: S
HOW TO IDENTIFY: Erect, smooth, single trunk; pinnate leaves 8' long with rachises gently curving downward.
HABIT OF GROWTH: Appealing, neat, and clean.
FOLIAGE: Evergreen, pinnate, of fine texture and dark green color.
FLOWERS: Inconspicuous, unisexual, in spadices amidst the foliage.
FRUITS: Yellow-green, ovoid drupes the size of pecans.
SEASON OF MAXIMUM COLOR: No difference in color.
LANDSCAPE USES: As urn subjects, sentry palms (or kentia palms) have been prime favorites for generations. In southern Florida they serve as small framing trees and as lawn specimens with distinction.

Howeia belmoreana "makes like a bell," and is notably the more graceful of the two. This one has short petioles.

Howeia forsteriana, Forster's sentry palm, has leaves with long petioles and fewer pinnae and these stand away from the rachis horizontally for half their length, then become pendent. The fruits of Forster's are long-attenuate to the apex, not beaked. Forster's sentry palm is the more rapid grower.

Sentry palms are very sensitive to cold.

HABITAT: Lord Howe Islands; in Florida, frost-free locations.
LIGHT REQUIREMENT: Tolerant of shade in patios, terraces, and Florida rooms.
SOIL REQUIREMENT: Fertile, well-drained, organic soils for best growth.
SALT TOLERANCE: Not tolerant.
AVAILABILITY: Specialty nurseries have small sentry palms (they call them kentias) in containers.
CULTURE: Plant carefully in acid compost; water faithfully; protect from cold, from lawn grasses, and from scale insects.
PROPAGATION: Seedage.
PESTS: Scales of many types.

49
Queen Palm

Arecastrum (ary-CAST-rum): *Areca*-like.
romanzoffianum (roman-zof-ee-AY-num): for N. Romanzoff of Russia.

FAMILY: Palmaceae.
RELATIVES: The palm trees.
TYPE OF PLANT: Palm tree.
HEIGHT: 40'. ZONE: C,S

HOW TO IDENTIFY: Single, usually straight, ringed trunk with untidy boots just below foliage; pinnate, unarmed leaves; decorative orange fruits during cool months.

HABIT OF GROWTH: Straight, single trunk, and graceful crown of soft leaves.

FOLIAGE: Evergreen, pinnate, fine in texture, dark green in color.

FLOWERS: Inconspicuous, on very large interfoliar spadices.

FRUITS: Decorative, orange, drupe-like, 1-seeded dates.

SEASON OF MAXIMUM COLOR: Cool months when dates mature.

LANDSCAPE USES: Central Florida's most popular palm is used for avenue plantings (25'-35' o.c.), as a framing tree, as a background tree, and as a member of palm groups.

There is considerable seedling variation in populations of queen palms.

HABITAT: Brazil; in Florida, widely planted in central Florida.

LIGHT REQUIREMENT: Full sun for best habit and fruiting.

SOIL REQUIREMENT: Tolerant of various types of sandy soil.

SALT TOLERANCE: Not very tolerant.

AVAILABILITY: Queen palms in containers and B & B are for sale in almost all nurseries in central Florida. They are often labeled *Cocos plumosa*.

CULTURE: If planted in holes made up with fertile compost, watered during dry times, and fertilized at the beginning of the rainy season, queen palms should grow well.

PROPAGATION: Seedage, volunteers often appear under fruiting trees.

PESTS: Mineral deficiency on calcareous soils and scales.

NOTE: A notable palm is a natural cross between queen palm and pindo palm. This bigeneric hybrid is a beautiful, hardy plant that has many of the good qualities of each parent.

50
Spindle Palm

Mascarena (mass-car-EE-na): for the Mascarene Islands, home of the palm.
verschaffeltii (ver-sha-FELT-ee-eye): for A. Verschaffelt, Belgian horticulturist.

FAMILY: Palmaceae.   RELATIVES: The palm trees.
TYPE OF PLANT: Palm tree.   HEIGHT: 25'. ZONE: S

HOW TO IDENTIFY: The straight, smooth, gray trunk is swollen prominently just below the green crownshaft. The leaves are short-petioled, and a prominent yellow band extends the full length of the midrib. Fruit clusters are sent out just below the crownshaft.

HABIT OF GROWTH: Dwarfish palm with straight, heavy, bulging trunk, holding a very close, compact head of short pinnate leaves.

FOLIAGE: Evergreen, pinnate, with very short petiole; unarmed.

FLOWERS: Inconspicuous, yellowish, very numerous in spadices below the crownshaft.

FRUITS: Plum-like, less than 1 inch long, produced abundantly.

SEASON OF MAXIMUM COLOR: Little seasonal variation.

LANDSCAPE USES: For the curiosity of the markedly bulging trunk and the yellow-banded midribs, spindle palm may be set as a free-standing specimen.

HABITAT: Mauritius; in Florida, warmest locations.

LIGHT REQUIREMENT: Full sun or broken shade.

SOIL REQUIREMENT: Many soils appear to be suitable.

SALT TOLERANCE: Tolerant of salt drift back from the strand.

AVAILABILITY: Specialty nurseries in southern Florida may carry a few *Mascarena* palm seedlings in containers.

CULTURE: Plant with care in a place that has been enriched with peat; water carefully; place a mulch over the root zone, and keep lawn grasses clear of the mulched area.

PROPAGATION: Seedage.

PESTS: Mites, scales, and nematodes.

NOTE: Bottle palm (*Mascarena lagenicaulis*), also from Mauritius, has the bulge nearer the base of the trunk to lend a bottle-shape to the stout little cement-gray stem.

51
Galingale

Cyperus (si-PEAR-us): ancient Greek name for these plants.
SPP.: several species are grown in Florida.

FAMILY: Cyperaceae.   RELATIVES: Bulrushes and sedges.
TYPE OF PLANT: Herbaceous perennial.   HEIGHT: Variable.   ZONE: N,C,S
HOW TO IDENTIFY: Triangular stems bear tufts of leaves atop. Strong clumps of many stems are formed under good conditions.
HABIT OF GROWTH: Upright, symmetrical form.
FOLIAGE: Leaves round or flat, clustered at the tips of the triangular stems somewhat like the ribs of umbrellas.
FLOWERS: Inconspicuous, in spikelets covered by subtending bracts.
FRUITS: Tiny achenes of sedges.
SEASON OF MAXIMUM COLOR: Little seasonal variation.
LANDSCAPE USES: In conjunction with water gardens, lily pools, or basins in Florida rooms, the galingales are very useful in helping to create the feeling of tropical living. Actually, these plants grow in garden soil as well.
HABITAT: World-wide tropics.
LIGHT REQUIREMENT: Tolerant of shade, grows equally well in full sun.
SOIL REQUIREMENT: Tolerant of varying soils, grows well in water.
SALT TOLERANCE: Endures salt drift back from the strand.
AVAILABILITY: Many nurseries offer plants in containers.
CULTURE: Plant in a boggy place and forget.
PROPAGATION: Division of matted clumps. Small plants arise from leaf axils if foliage heads are placed in moist sand. These are potted separately.
PESTS: Mites.
NOTE: Umbrella-plant (*Cyperus alternifolius*), with many long, flat spreading leaves, the most common species, is pictured above. There is a clone with mottled foliage. Papyrus (*C. papyrus*), with many long, wire-like clustered leaves is preferred for water gardens. Papyrus grows two or three times the height of umbrella-plant. For tiny water-garden arrangements, there is *C. haspan* 'Viviparus', the smaller, right-hand sketch. Dwarf, broad-leaved *Cyperus diffusus* makes an attractive pot plant for pool or Florida room.

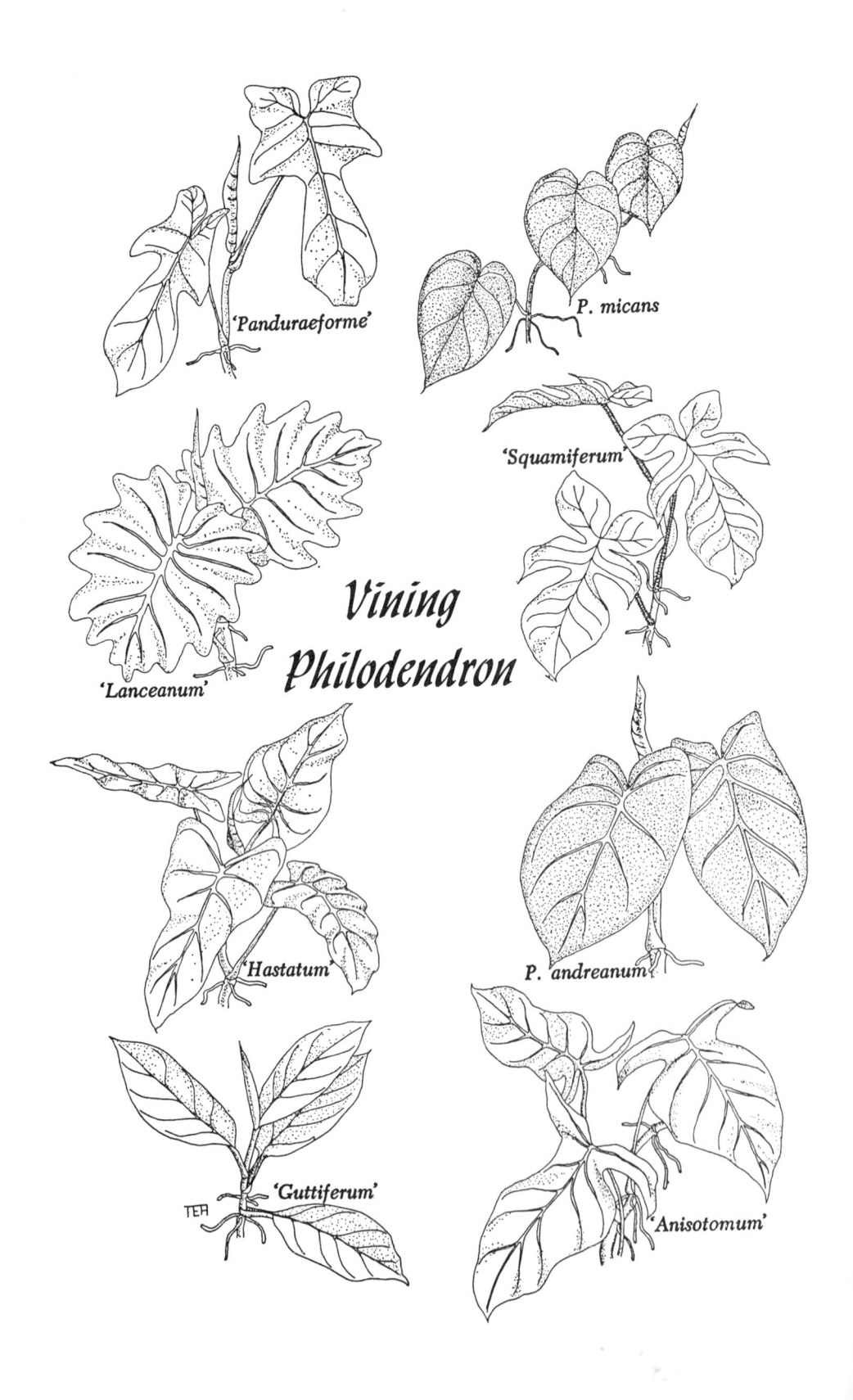

Vining Philodendron

'Panduraeforme'

P. micans

'Squamiferum'

'Lanceanum'

'Hastatum'

P. andreanum

'Guttiferum'

'Anisotomum'

53
Vining Philodendron

Philodendron (fil-oh-DEN-dron): Greek for tree-loving.
SPP.: many species and countless varieties grow in Florida.

FAMILY: Araceae.
RELATIVES: Caladium and ivy-arum.
TYPE OF PLANT: Vine.
HEIGHT: Variable. ZONE: S

HOW TO IDENTIFY: Vigorous tropical lianas, with leaves in infinite variety of shapes, sizes, and colors. Strong, brown, twine-like roots hold tenaciously to supporting trees or walls.

HABIT OF GROWTH: Vining herbaceous perennial.

FOLIAGE: Variable, always evergreen, usually of bold form, variable in color, frequently dark green, sometimes variegated.

FLOWERS: Spadices within thick, persistent, boat-like spathes.

FRUITS: Fleshy, densely packed, ripened ovaries.

SEASON OF MAXIMUM COLOR: No seasonal variation.

LANDSCAPE USES: Landscape planners and homeowners use philodendrons in every conceivable landscape application. For planters in Florida rooms or for urns on terraces philodendrons are highly approved. The vining types are ever popular for training on trees and patio walls.

HABITAT: Tropical America; in Florida, widely cultured indoors and out.

LIGHT REQUIREMENT: Variable, some thrive in sunlight, others in shade.

SOIL REQUIREMENT: A fertile, well-drained, organic soil, slightly acid in reaction, is always best.

SALT TOLERANCE: Not tolerant of dune conditions.

AVAILABILITY: All nurseries and garden centers offer philodendrons.

CULTURE: After establishment in nearly frostless locations, philodendrons require reasonable attention in the matter of watering and fertilization. They are not temperamental plants, and they respond well to moderately good care and mulching.

PROPAGATION: Vining types by cuttage; self-headers by seedage.

PESTS: Scales.

NOTE: The genus *Philodendron* contains 200 species; with these countless hybrids have been produced.

P. selloum

Seedling

Self-Heading

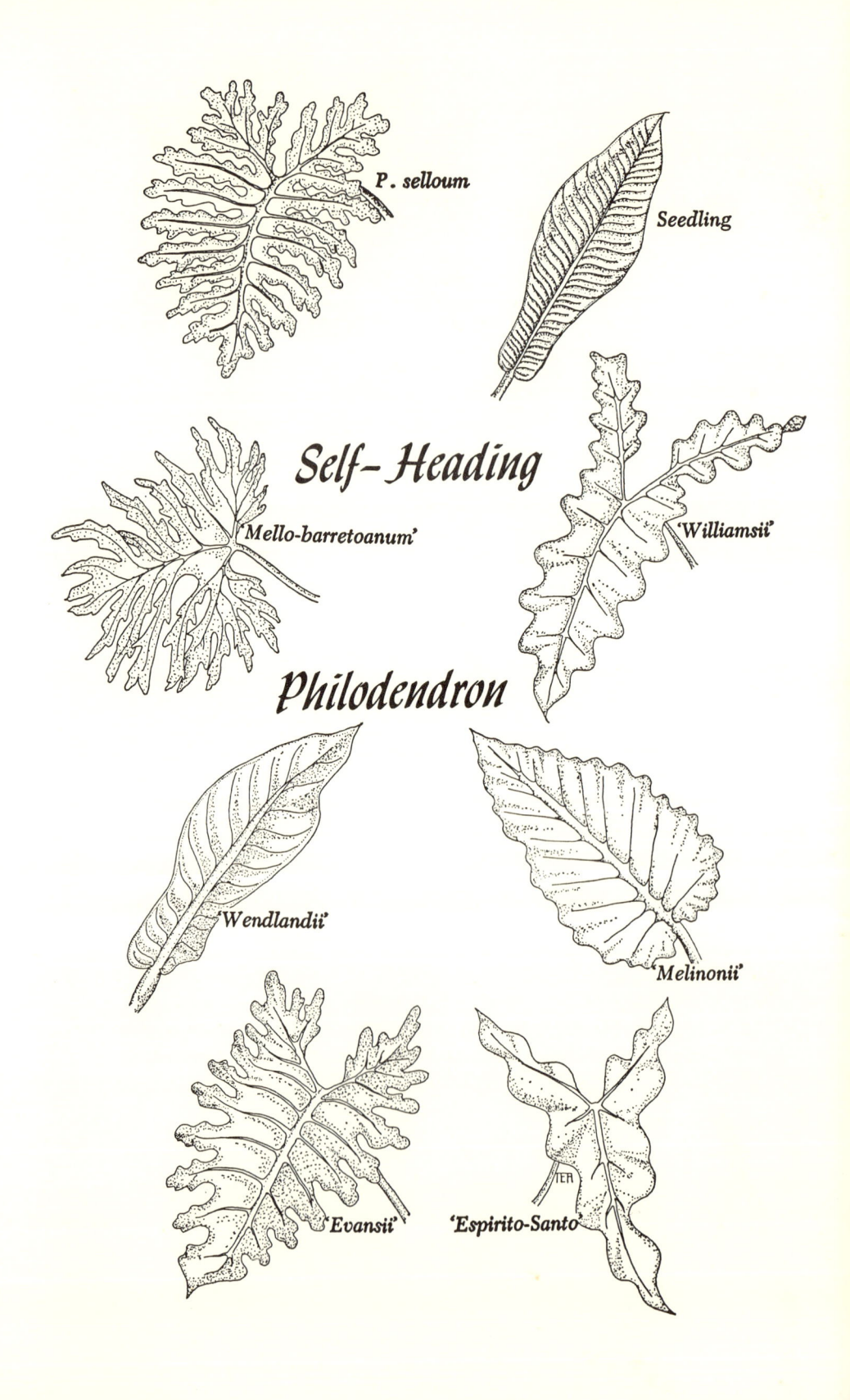

'Mello-barretoanum'

'Williamsii'

Philodendron

'Wendlandii'

'Melinonii'

'Evansii'

'Espirito-Santo'

55
Self-Heading Philodendron

Philodendron (fil-oh-DEN-dron): Greek for tree-loving.
SPP.: many species and countless varieties grow in Florida.

FAMILY: Araceae.   RELATIVES: Caladium and ivy-arum.

TYPE OF PLANT: Herbaceous perennial.   HEIGHT: Variable. ZONE: S

HOW TO IDENTIFY: Arborescent herbaceous perennials with leaves in an infinite variety of shapes, sizes, and colors.

HABIT OF GROWTH: Very compact.

FOLIAGE: Highly variable in size, shape, and color; usually bold and showy.

FLOWERS: Spadices within thick, persistent, boat-like spathes.

FRUITS: Fleshy, densely packed ripened ovaries.

SEASON OF MAXIMUM COLOR: Summer when new growth appears.

LANDSCAPE USES: Landscape planners and homeowners use philodendrons in every conceivable landscape application. They excel as subjects for planters in Florida rooms and for urns on terraces.

HABITAT: Tropical America.

LIGHT REQUIREMENT: Variable: some thrive in sunlight, others in shade.

SOIL REQUIREMENT: Fertility and moisture-holding capacity above average are needed for good appearance.

SALT TOLERANCE: Not tolerant of front-line conditions.

AVAILABILITY: Most nurseries display specimens.

CULTURE: After establishment in nearly frostless locations, philodendrons require reasonable attention in the matter of watering and fertilization.

PROPAGATION: Self-heading philodendrons are propagated by seedage.

PESTS: Mites and scales.

NOTE: The genus *Philodendron* contains 200 species; with these, countless hybrids have been produced. On the opposite page are leaf drawings of self-headers. Naming is not always consistent. Above is the popular *Philodendron cannaefolium*.

56
Dieffenbachia

Dieffenbachia (deef-en-BOCK-ee-a): for J. Dieffenbach, German physician.
SPP.: several species, and many varieties are grown in Florida.

FAMILY: Araceae.   RELATIVES: Philodendron, monstera, and caladium.
TYPE OF PLANT: Herbaceous perennial.   HEIGHT: 8'.   ZONE: C,S
HOW TO IDENTIFY: Ringed, hose-like stems, with many prominent root initials and bold, variegated leaves with long petioles which clasp or ensheath the stems.
HABIT OF GROWTH: Stems bent or almost upright, usually unbranched, with the huge, alternate, evergreen leaves growing out in all directions.
FOLIAGE: Evergreen, large, bold, usually variegated in striking patterns.
FLOWERS: Spadices within thick, persistent, boat-like spathes.
FRUITS: Fleshy, densely packed, ripened ovaries.
SEASON OF MAXIMUM COLOR: No seasonal variation.
LANDSCAPE USES: Dieffenbachias are in great demand as accent plants in outdoor plantings and as urn subjects for Florida rooms, patios, and terraces.
HABITAT: Tropical America; in Florida, widely cultured indoors, and out.
LIGHT REQUIREMENT: Very tolerant of shade, yet grows in sun.
SOIL REQUIREMENT: Tolerant of many soil types and reactions, but grows best with moderate moisture and freedom from nematodes.
SALT TOLERANCE: Not tolerant of dune conditions.
AVAILABILITY: All nurseries and garden center stores offer dieffenbachias.
CULTURE: Plant in moderately fertile soil of acid reaction; water with moderation; fertilize lightly once each month during growing weather; control mealy-bugs.
PROPAGATION: Cuttage of stem pieces, and marcottage.
PESTS: Mealy-bugs, mites, scales, nematodes, and root-rot.
NOTE: The genus *Dieffenbachia* contains a score of species that have been used to make many varieties. Naming may not be consistent. Above is *Dieffenbachia amoena*, popular, fast-growing, king-size dumb-cane.

57
Monstera

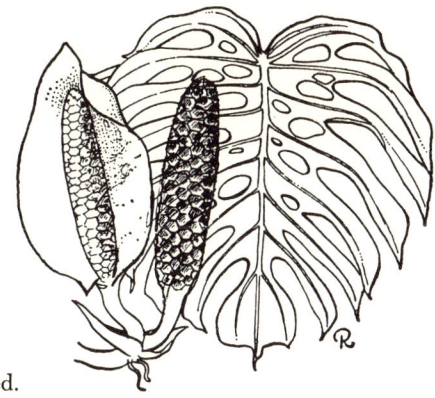

Monstera (mon-STER-a): name unexplained.
deliciosa (de-lis-ee-OH-sa): delicious.

FAMILY: Araceae.   RELATIVES: Dieffenbachia and philodendron.

TYPE OF PLANT: Vine.   HEIGHT: Variable. ZONE: S

HOW TO IDENTIFY: Yard-long, thick, evergreen leaves that are pinnately cut with elliptic spaces, from a rampant, fast-growing tropical vine, also known as ceriman in some localities.

HABIT OF GROWTH: Rampant vine that climbs by strong aerial rootlets.

FOLIAGE: Evergreen, huge, of tropical appearance and dark green color.

FLOWERS: Thick, densely flowered spadix about a foot long.

FRUITS: Thick, densely packed fruits cohering into a cone-like body.

SEASON OF MAXIMUM COLOR: No variation.

LANDSCAPE USES: For creating a tropical atmosphere, outdoors or in the house, nothing can surpass ceriman, and it is widely employed, in consequence, in every conceivable landscape and interior decorating use in Florida.

HABITAT: Tropical American mainland; in Florida, widely cultured.

LIGHT REQUIREMENT: Shade of forests is natural habitat.

SOIL REQUIREMENT: Rich forest soils are best.

SALT TOLERANCE: Not tolerant.

AVAILABILITY: Monsteras are for sale in almost every nursery and garden center.

CULTURE: In a nearly frostless location, plant pieces of stem; water faithfully during dry times; fertilize thrice annually; protect from scale insects and from frost.

PROPAGATION: Cuttage of pieces of the stem.

PESTS: Scales, mites, mealy-bugs.

NOTE: Swiss-cheese plant, *Monstera friedrichstahlii*, has smaller, elliptical leaves with most holes enclosed, not forming deep sinuses.

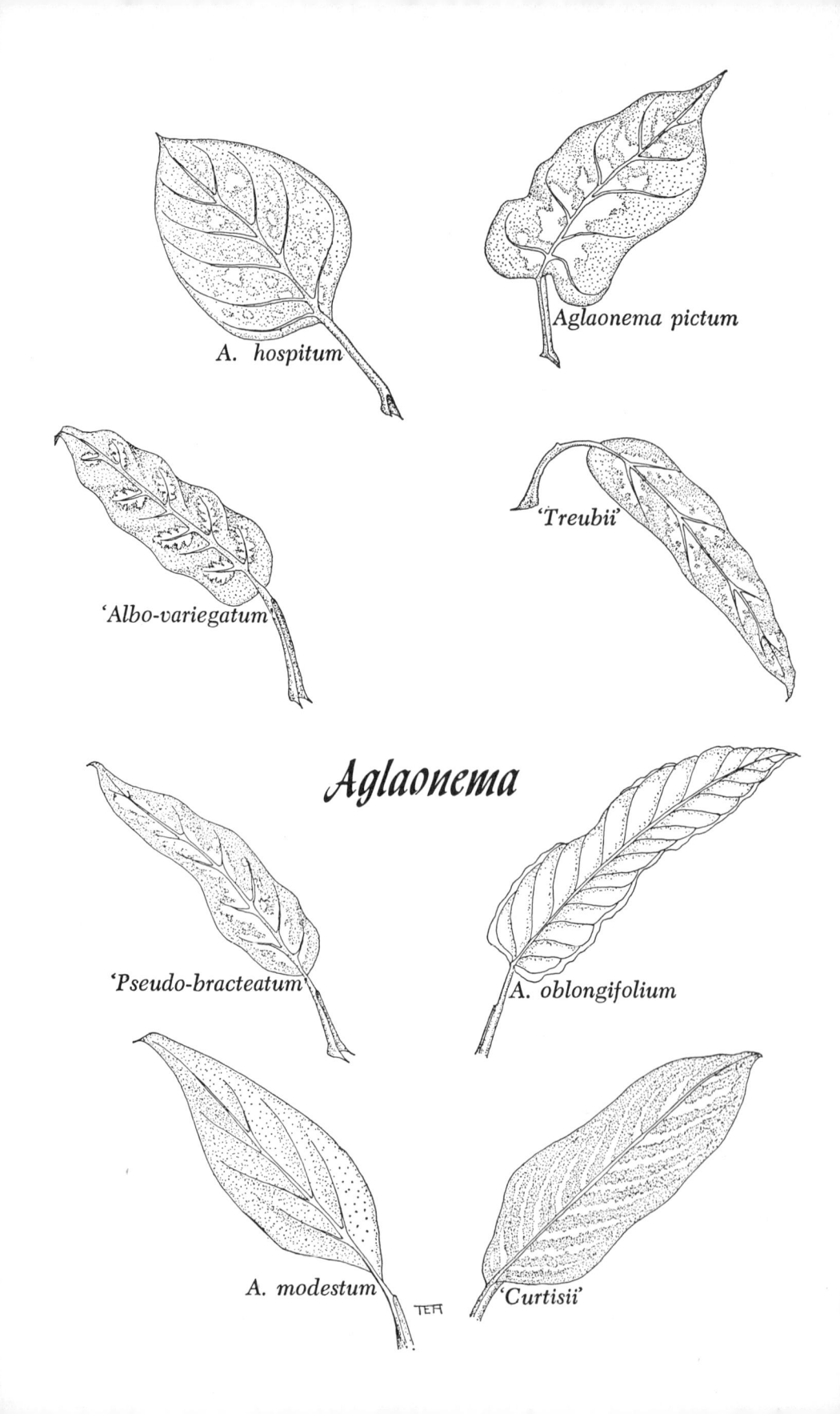

Aglaonema

A. hospitum

Aglaonema pictum

'Albo-variegatum'

'Treubii'

'Pseudo-bracteatum'

A. oblongifolium

A. modestum

'Curtisii'

59
Aglaonema

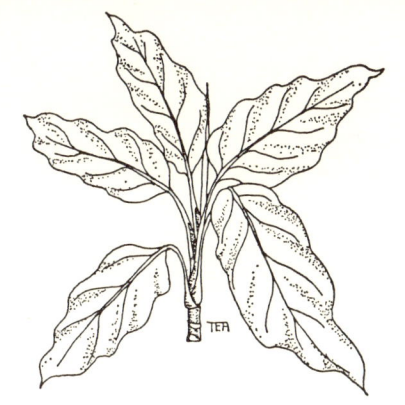

Aglaonema (ag-low-NEE-ma): Greek for bright thread, referring to the stamens. SPP.: several species grow in Florida.

FAMILY: Araceae. RELATIVES: Monstera and philodendron.
TYPE OF PLANT: Herbaceous perennial. HEIGHT: Variable. ZONE: S
HOW TO IDENTIFY: Round, thumb-sized stems bear attractive leaves by ensheathing petioles that are equal to, or shorter than, the blades. Tiny spadices are protected by little green or yellow spathes which soon wither to reveal attractive red or yellow fruits.
HABIT OF GROWTH: Neat, upright-spreading, with leaves attractively arranged at stem-ends.
FOLIAGE: Bold and attractive, held horizontally by ensheathing petioles shorter than blades. Patterns of white markings vary with the species or variety.
FLOWERS: Little spadices with tiny spathes resemble diminutive callas.
FRUITS: Conspicuous, bright red or yellow, in little clusters, held on slender stalks.
SEASON OF MAXIMUM COLOR: Late summer when fruits ripen.
LANDSCAPE USES: For locations with reduced light, aglaonemas are outstanding. Use them in planter bins, urns, pots, or, in frostless areas, in north-side arrangements in the foundation scheme.
HABITAT: Malaysia.
LIGHT REQUIREMENT: Tolerant of reduced light that would be unsuitable for many tropical exotics.
SOIL REQUIREMENT: Fertile, nematode-free compost is highly suitable, yet aglaonemas will survive in peat and perlite, in sand, or in water if fertilizer salts (in small amounts) are added regularly.
SALT TOLERANCE: Not tolerant of dune conditions.
AVAILABILITY: Nurseries and garden centers offer aglaonemas.
CULTURE: These plants should not be subjected to low temperatures, nor should they be planted in media that might contain nematodes. Regular applications of dilute fertilizers should be made during growing weather.
PROPAGATION: Cuttage and marcottage.
PESTS: Nematodes, pythium root-rot under some conditions, and mites.
NOTE: Chinese evergreen (*Aglaonema modestum*), illustrated above, is the most popular of the several species grown in Florida. Other well-known aglaonemas are portrayed on the facing page.

60
Schismatoglottis

Schismatoglottis (skis-mat-o-GLOT-is): Greek for falling tongue, referring to the shedding spathe.
picta (PICK-ta): painted.

FAMILY: Araceae. RELATIVES: Aglaonema and dumb-cane.
TYPE OF PLANT: Herbaceous perennial. HEIGHT: Variable. ZONE: S
HOW TO IDENTIFY: Very closely allied to dumb-cane, schismatoglottis is most difficult to differentiate. The leaves are held in much the same fashion, variegation is similar to that in some dumb-canes, and growth habits are much alike.
HABIT OF GROWTH: Stems usually upright, unbranched, with large, alternate, evergreen leaves growing out in all directions.
FOLIAGE: Bold and attractively marked with white, some cultivars show translucent spots. The sheathing petiole is longer than the blade.
FLOWERS: Unisexual flowers in spadices, typical for the family; the stamens are free, the ovaries L-celled, the spathe falls free.
FRUITS: Oblong, green or yellowish.
SEASON OF MAXIMUM COLOR: Possibly when the little fruits develop color.
LANDSCAPE USES: Schismatoglottis enjoys the same popularity for indoor uses as do its close relatives dieffenbachia, aglaonema, and monstera. This aroid serves well in planters that receive reduced light.
HABITAT: Malaya.
LIGHT REQUIREMENT: Reduced light found in Florida rooms and patios is satisfactory.
SOIL REQUIREMENT: A fertile, well-drained, organic soil, slightly acid in reaction, is always best, yet mixtures of peat and perlite are frequently used for schismatoglottis.
SALT TOLERANCE: Not tolerant of dune conditions.
AVAILABILITY: Chain stores, garden centers, and nurseries offer potted plants of this species under a variety of names.
CULTURE: Regular attention to watering, fertilization, and pest control will keep plants growing satisfactorily.
PROPAGATION: Cuttage and marcottage.
PESTS: Mites, nematodes, and scales.

61
Ivy-Arum

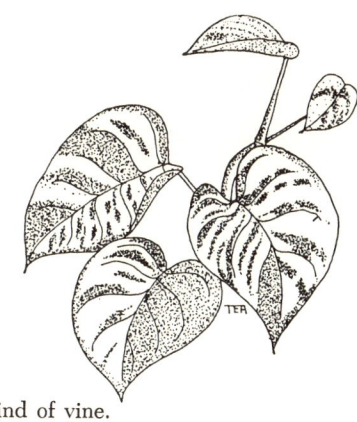

Scindapsis (sin-DAP-sis): Greek name for some kind of vine. SPP.: 2 species and a number of varieties grow in Florida.

FAMILY: Araceae.
RELATIVES: Calla and spathiphyllum.
TYPE OF PLANT: Vine.
HEIGHT: Variable. ZONE: S

HOW TO IDENTIFY: Huge, variegated, ovoid leaves with 1 or more deep clefts are produced by wrist-thick, vigorous, climbing vines.

HABIT OF GROWTH: Rampant tropical vine that climbs into tallest trees.

FOLIAGE: Gigantic, bizarre, mottled leaves, often with clefts, are characteristic of vines growing vigorously on vertical supports in the open. Indoors and on earth-bound individuals, leaves may be heart-shaped, about 6″ long.

FLOWERS: Densely packed spadices within white, deciduous spathes, when present.

FRUITS: Typical, cone-like aroid fruits, if present.

SEASON OF MAXIMUM COLOR: Springtime when colors of new growth are fresh.

LANDSCAPE USES: To highlight palm trunks, ivy-arums are in great favor in most nearly frost-free sections. As ground cover, earth-bound vines are excellent for shady spots. For indoor decoration, these plants are popular as pot items, planter-bin subjects, and for growing in bowls of water.

HABITAT: Tropical islands of the Pacific.

LIGHT REQUIREMENT: Tolerant of shade, but color is better in full light.

SOIL REQUIREMENT: Tolerant of many soil types.

SALT TOLERANCE: Endures mild salt air back from the strand.

AVAILABILITY: Chain stores, garden centers, and retail nurseries offer ivy-arums in pots.

CULTURE: Plant slightly deeper than formerly, water faithfully during dry times; fertilize during warm months.

PROPAGATION: Cuttage of stem joints.

PESTS: Scales, mites, and mealy-bugs.

A. crystallinum

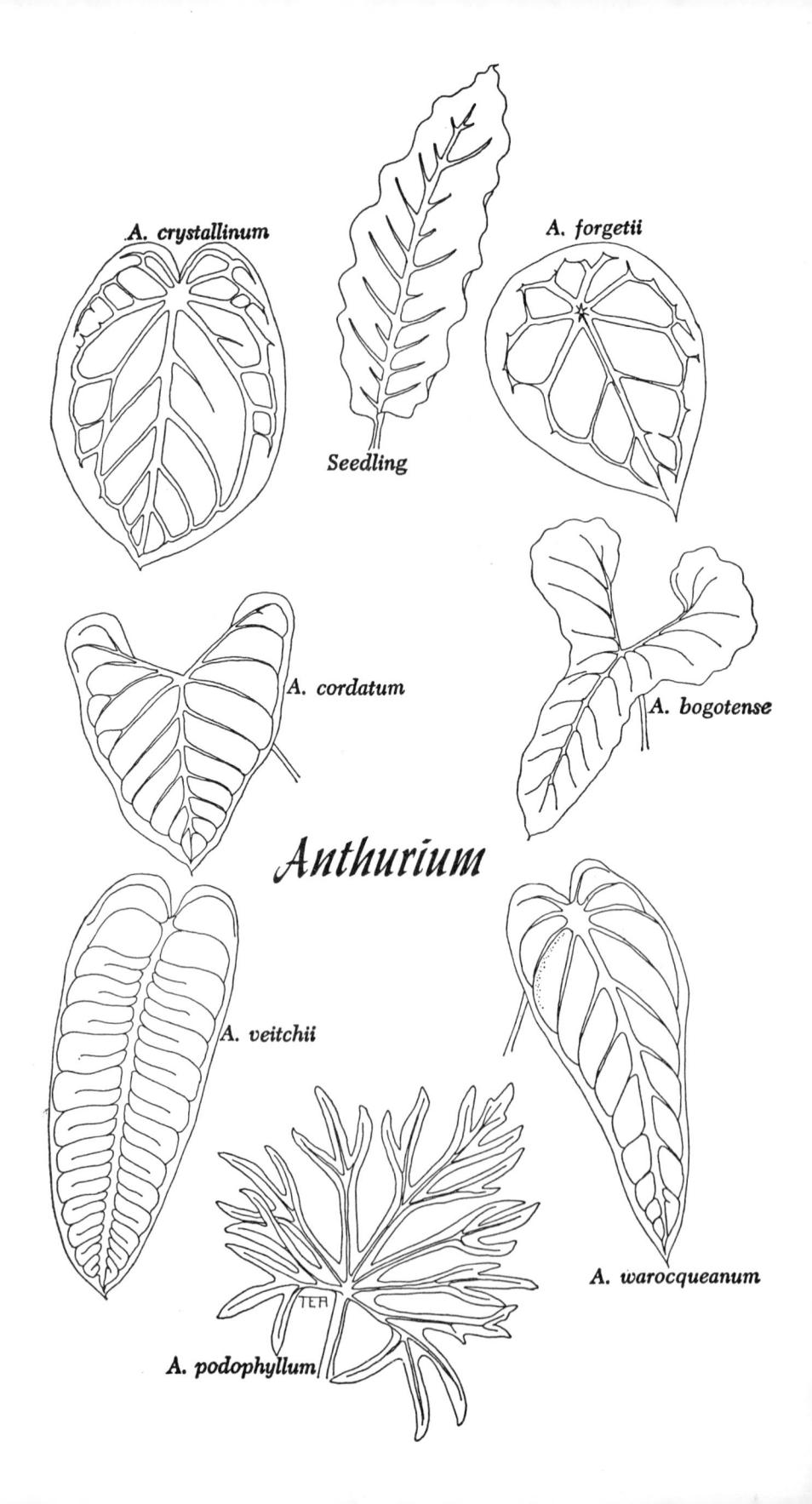

Seedling

A. forgetii

A. cordatum

A. bogotense

Anthurium

A. veitchii

A. warocqueanum

A. podophyllum

63
Anthurium

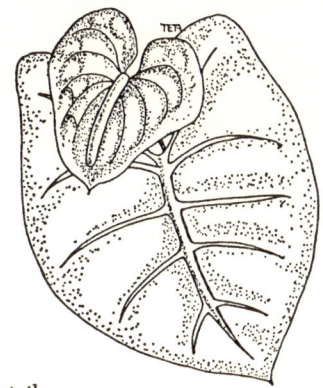

Anthurium (an-THOO-ree-um): Greek for flower and tail.
SPP.: several species and many hybrids are found in Florida.

FAMILY: Araceae.   RELATIVES: Alocasia and colocasia.
TYPE OF PLANT: Herbaceous perennial.   HEIGHT: Variable. ZONE: S
HOW TO IDENTIFY: Many anthuriums are grown for their very showy, highly decorative spathes, the most colorful in the aroid family. These are called "flamingo-flowers." Others are cultured for their decorative leaves (the rat-tail anthuriums).
HABIT OF GROWTH: Compact herbaceous perennial.
FOLIAGE: Extremely variable, usually decorative, bold and persistent.
FLOWERS: Extremely variable; flamingo-flowers are most beautiful; rat-tail types are considerably less attractive.
FRUITS: Fleshy berries.
SEASON OF MAXIMUM COLOR: Warm months when blossoms appear.
LANDSCAPE USES: As specimens in frostless, shady spots outdoors, or in pots, anthuriums are greatly admired. Flamingo-flowers, noted for their beautiful clear colors and amazing keeping-quality, are popular corsage subjects.
HABITAT: American tropics.
LIGHT REQUIREMENT: Reduced light is optimum.
SOIL REQUIREMENT: Organic potting compost, sawdust, peat, osmundine, and tree fern fragments, or combinations of these, are used as growing media for anthuriums.
SALT TOLERANCE: Not tolerant.
AVAILABILITY: Small plants in containers are for sale in some nurseries and garden centers on the peninsula.
CULTURE: Plant slightly deeper than the plant grew formerly; water carefully daily; fertilize once each month during the summer.
PROPAGATION: Cuttage and seedage.
PESTS: Mites, nematodes, scales, mealy-bugs, and grasshoppers.
NOTE: Possibly a dozen of the 500 species in *Anthurium* have been used to make hybrids. Both wild types and hybrids of complex lineage are popular in Florida, and some of each are illustrated on the facing page. Above right is a sketch of a flamingo-flower, a hybrid of *Anthurium andreanum*.

64
Spathiphyllum

Spathiphyllum (spath-i-FIL-um): Greek for leaf-spathe.
SPP.: 2 species and several hybrids grow in Florida gardens.

FAMILY: Araceae.   RELATIVES: Elephant-ear and ivy-arum.

TYPE OF PLANT: Herbaceous perennial.   HEIGHT: 2'. ZONE: C,S

HOW TO IDENTIFY: Thin, lanceolate, sharp-acuminate, plantain-like leaves are held gracefully by long petioles; flowers with persistent white (or greenish-white) spathes are produced freely during warm months. Usually spathiphyllums in Florida grow as clusters of leaves, without an above-ground stem.

HABIT OF GROWTH: Clump-growing herbaceous perennial.

FOLIAGE: Foot-long, lanceolate, sharp-acuminate, dark-green leaves are held by petioles of about their same length.

FLOWERS: Bisexual, fertile flowers are packed on little spadices which are backed by attractive white or greenish spathes.

FRUITS: Fleshy, berry-like.

SEASON OF MAXIMUM COLOR: Spring and summer when blossoms are out.

LANDSCAPE USES: As ground cover for shady spots, as pot plants, or as components of planter arrangements, spathiphyllums are good for those who would like to have easy-to-grow white anthuriums.

HABITAT: American tropics.

LIGHT REQUIREMENT: Tolerant of considerable shade.

SOIL REQUIREMENT: Reasonably fertile soil that is free of nematodes is best.

SALT TOLERANCE: Not tolerant.

AVAILABILITY: Many nurseries, garden centers, and chain stores offer plants in containers.

CULTURE: Turn a specimen out of its container; plant at the same level at which it grew formerly; water during periods of drought; and fertilize each month during the summer.

PROPAGATION: Division of matted clumps.

PESTS: Mites, scales, and mealy-bugs.

Fancy-Leaved Caladium

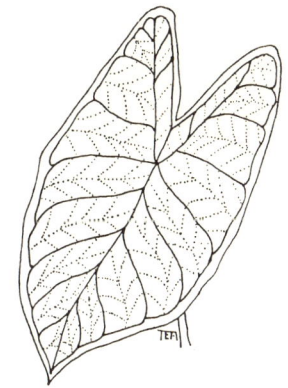

Caladium (cal-AYE-dee-um): name of East Indian origin.
SPP.: at least 2 species have been used to make the many hybrids.

FAMILY: Araceae.
RELATIVES: Monstera and aglaonema.
TYPE OF PLANT: Tuberous perennial.
HEIGHT: 2'. ZONE: N,C,S
HOW TO IDENTIFY: The strikingly beautiful fancy-leaved caladiums are so well known that description should be unnecessary. There is remarkable variety in form and color of leaf.
HABIT OF GROWTH: Bright leaves on tall stems arise from tubers to form clumps.
FOLIAGE: Deciduous, variously heart-shaped or of lance-form, in a multitude of color combinations.
FLOWERS: Boat-shaped, persistent spathes enclose somewhat shorter spadices.
FRUITS: Fleshy berries may mature after pollination.
SEASON OF MAXIMUM COLOR: Warm months.
LANDSCAPE USES: For bright spots of summertime color in front of green shrubbery, or in planters, fancy-leaved caladiums have long been great favorites. Best landscape effects are attained when many plants of a single clone are bedded together, but some homeowners prefer to mass mixed foliage for a great riot of color.
HABITAT: Tropical America.
LIGHT REQUIREMENT: Full sun or high, shifting shade.
SOIL REQUIREMENT: Rich, organic earth is best.
SALT TOLERANCE: Not tolerant.
AVAILABILITY: Garden centers offer, at appropriate seasons, both dormant tubers and potted plants in full leaf.
CULTURE: Plant tubers when days lengthen in springtime; water during dry times; and fertilize once each month. As days shorten (October-November), the leaves may be cut away. In northern Florida, where freezes are the rule, tubers should be dug at this time and stored in dry peat until the following spring.
PROPAGATION: Division of offsets from old tubers.
PESTS: Soil-borne fungus diseases, mites, and grasshoppers.

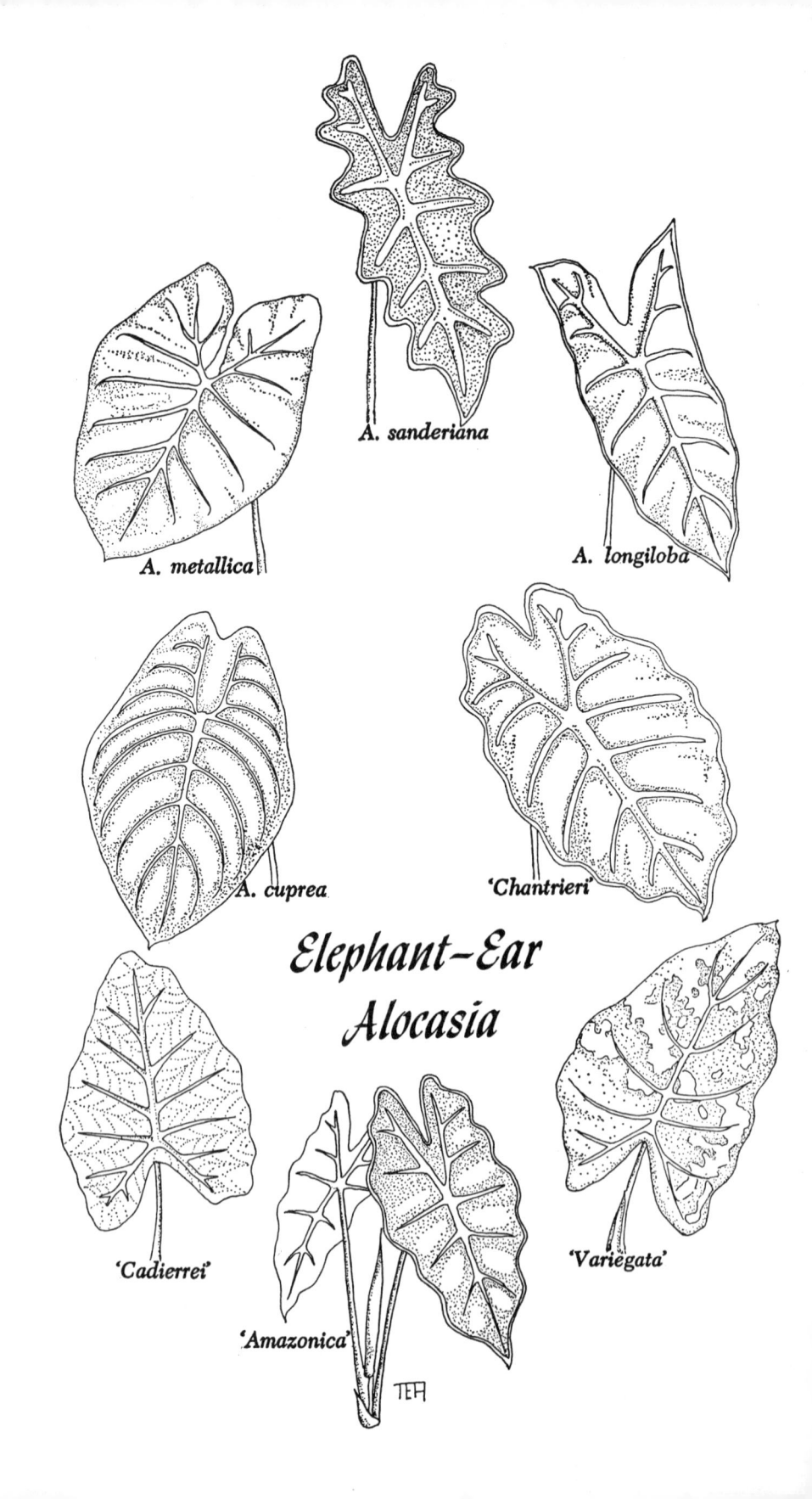

Elephant-Ear Alocasia

67
Elephant-Ear

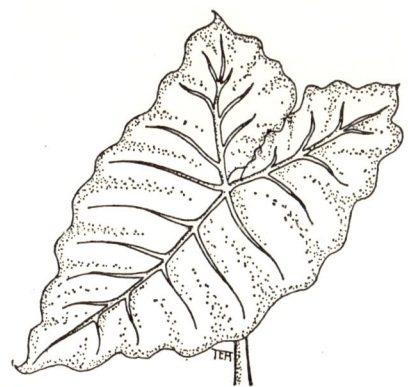

Alocasia (al-o-CAZ-ee-a): name made from *Colocasia*.
Colocasia (col-o-CAZ-ee-a): old Greek name.
Xanthosoma (zan-tho-SO-ma): Greek for yellow body, referring to the stigma.
SPP.: many species and innumerable varieties belong in this great complex.

FAMILY: Araceae. **RELATIVES:** Aglaonema and dieffenbachia.
TYPE OF PLANT: Tuberous or rhizomatous perennial. **HEIGHT:** Variable.
ZONE: N,C,S
HOW TO IDENTIFY: Bold, shield-like leaves (peltate or sagitate) are held by fleshy petioles. Leaf colors, sizes, shapes, and ornamentation beggar description.
HABIT OF GROWTH: Huge, coarse, sprawling, many-stemmed.
FOLIAGE: Bold, decorative, variable in size, color, form, and ornamentation.
FLOWERS: Spadices are protected by boat-like spathes.
FRUITS: Fleshy berries, if present.
SEASON OF MAXIMUM COLOR: Warm months when fresh leaves appear.
LANDSCAPE USES: To enhance the feeling of the tropics, elephant-ears may be grouped at the far end, or a low corner, of the out-of-door living area. The outsize foliage does not combine well with that of most woody shrubs. As pot plants, the diminutive, fancy-leaved types (see opposite page) are very popular. For planters, medium-sized clones can be selected.
HABITAT: The tropics the world around.
LIGHT REQUIREMENT: Full sun or broken, shifting shade, depending upon the kind.
SOIL REQUIREMENT: Rich, organic, moisture-retentive earth is best.
SALT TOLERANCE: Not tolerant.
AVAILABILITY: Garden centers sell canned plants.
CULTURE: Once they are established, the large elephant-ears growing in the earth receive little attention. The miniature, pot-plant types, on the other hand, require reasonable care in the matter of watering and fertilization.
PROPAGATION: Division of underground storage organs.
PESTS: Soil borne fungus diseases.
NOTE: Uncounted numbers of aroids in this huge complex are grown in Florida for garden ornament; yet, in tropical lands, the world around, these are important sources of dietary starch. On the facing page are depicted some of Florida's favorites in the genus *Alocasia*. Naming may not always be in perfect agreement in different garden centers.

'Auritum'

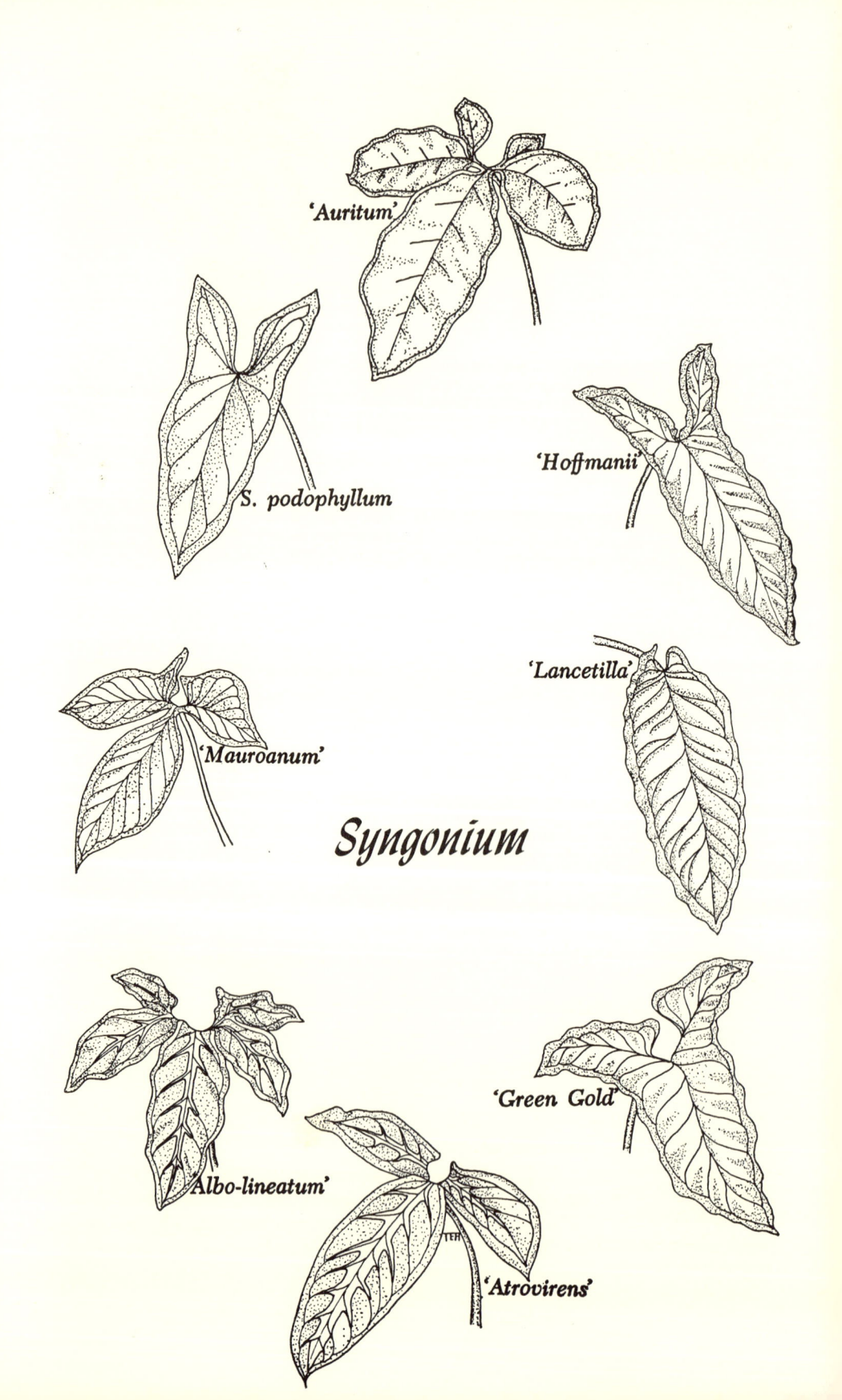

S. podophyllum

'Hoffmanii'

'Mauroanum'

'Lancetilla'

Syngonium

'Albo-lineatum'

'Atrovirens'

'Green Gold'

69
Syngonium

Syngonium (sin-go-nee-um): Greek, referring to cohesion of the ovaries.
spp.: several species and many cultigens are in Florida.

Family: Araceae.   Relatives: Elephant-ear and caladium.
Type of Plant: Herbaceous perennial.   Height: Variable. Zone: S
How to Identify: These creeping plants bear small, delicate, more or less lance-shaped leaves while young, then huge, peltate, deeply lobed foliage on long petioles at maturity. The rooting stems yield milky sap when wounded. Juvenile leaves remotely resemble those of fancy-leaved caladiums.
Habit of Growth: Fast-growing tropical vine.
Foliage: More or less lance-shaped or 3-pointed; marbled with white while young; giant, lobed, nearly green leaves are borne by old vines.
Flowers: Yellowish or greenish spathes surround shorter spadices.
Fruits: Black seeds may mature after pollination.
Season of Maximum Color: Spring, when new growth emerges.
Landscape Uses: For Florida room urns, juvenile syngoniums are very popular, as they grow well and are most attractive, delicate, little aroids. Yard syngoniums assume mammoth sizes as they adorn palm trunks to enhance the tropical effect.
Habitat: Tropical America.
Light Requirement: Reduced light of dwellings is acceptable, as is the high, shifting shade from palms.
Soil Requirement: Moderately fertile, fibrous, slightly acid compost is good.
Salt Tolerance: Not tolerant.
Availability: Chain stores and retail nurseries carry potted syngoniums.
Culture: Be cautious in watering and fertilization in order that compact, nonclimbing, juvenile form with bright variegation may be maintained.
Propagation: Cuttage.
Pests: Nematodes, mites, and soil-borne diseases.
Note: Named varieties in Florida are many, some of the choicest being illustrated on the opposite page. Juveniles are delicate, little, variegated-leaved pot plants; old vines on palm trunks become jungle giants with wrist-thick stems that hold huge, fingered, outsize leaves. Above right is shown *Syngonium wendlandii*.

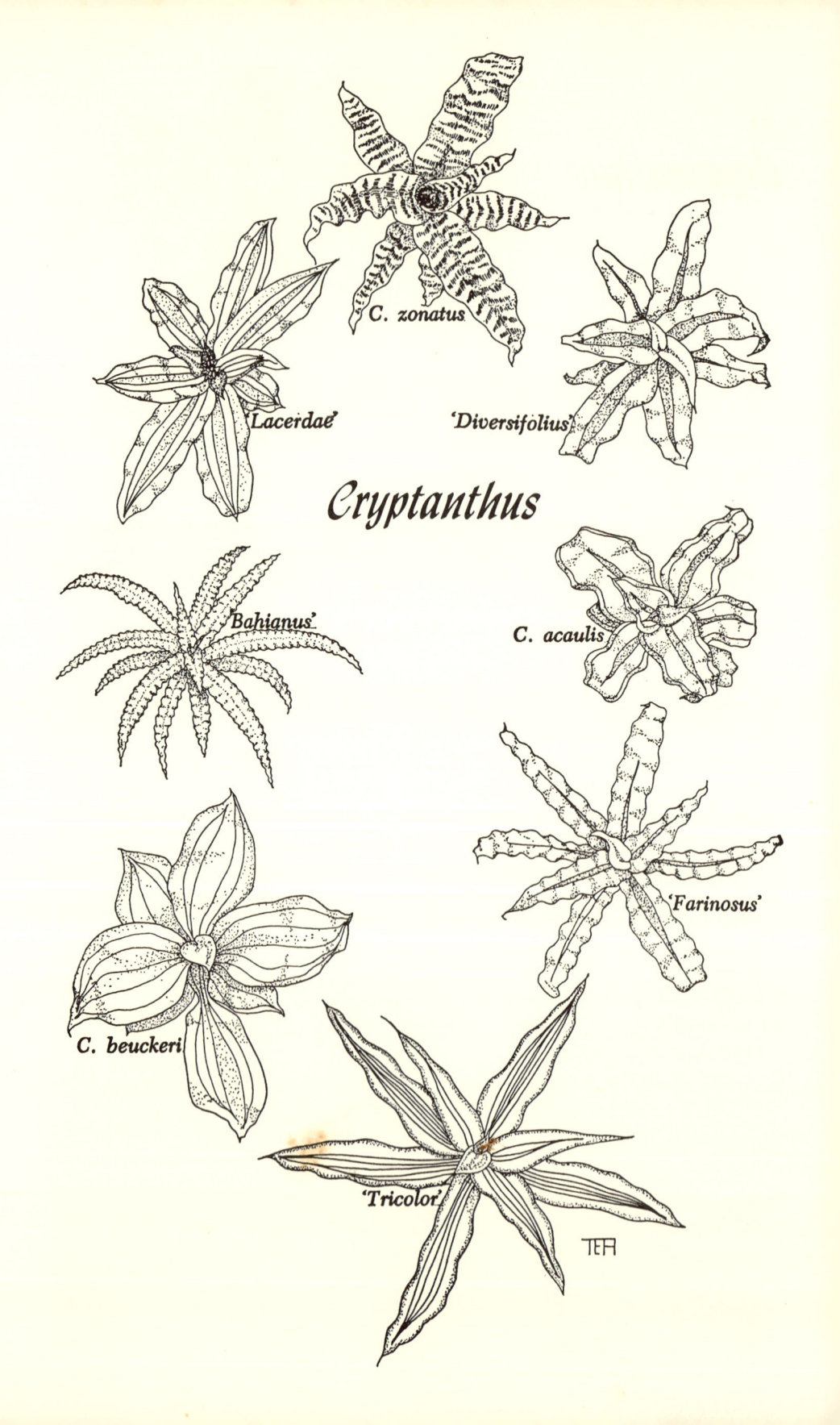

Cryptanthus

- C. zonatus
- 'Lacerdae'
- 'Diversifolius'
- 'Bahianus'
- C. acaulis
- C. beuckeri
- 'Farinosus'
- 'Tricolor'

71
Cryptanthus

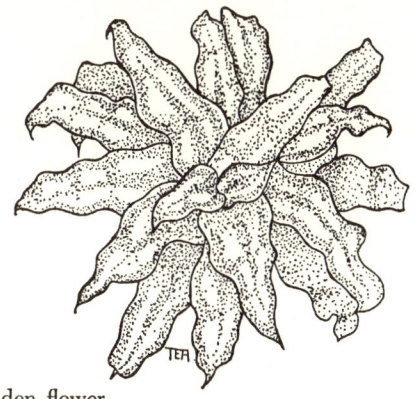

Cryptanthus (crip-TAN-thus): Greek for hidden flower.
SPP.: several species and a number of hybrids grow in Florida.

FAMILY: Bromeliaceae. RELATIVES: Aechmea and billbergia.
TYPE OF PLANT: Epiphytic perennial. HEIGHT: 2″-10″. ZONE: S
HOW TO IDENTIFY: These are the pygmies of the Bromeliaceae. Tiny, flat rosettes of smooth or scurfy, spine-edged leaves are typical. Flowers are hidden in the hearts of the rosettes, and mature specimens usually produce offsets in abundance.
HABIT OF GROWTH: Tight, little rosettes of stiff leaves.
FOLIAGE: Diminutive rosettes are formed by little, undulate, prickly leaves. These may be all green, all red, or variously striped, banded, or spotted.
FLOWERS: Inconspicuous white flowers hide in the hearts of the rosettes.
FRUITS: Tiny, dry berries.
SEASON OF MAXIMUM COLOR: Springtime when new growth emerges.
LANDSCAPE USES: For little indoor planters and dish gardens, these miniature bromels are much admired. Outdoors as ground cover or for decorating limbs of rough-barked trees, they are used, too.
HABITAT: Tropical America.
LIGHT REQUIREMENT: Shifting sun-and-shade or reduced light of dwellings.
SOIL REQUIREMENT: Osmundine, or a mixture of peat, leaf-mold, and sand.
SALT TOLERANCE: Not tolerant of dune conditions.
AVAILABILITY: Small plants in pots are offered by nurseries, garden centers, and chain stores.
CULTURE: Fasten to limbs of rough-barked trees with aluminum wire, or pot in your chosen medium. Keep water in leaf bases, and the medium moist, and set potted plants out in the rain during warm weather. Apply dilute liquid fertilizer to the growing medium once each summer month.
PROPAGATION: Division of offsets (these will be unrooted).
PESTS: Scales; mosquitoes might breed in water-holding leaf bases of outdoor plants.

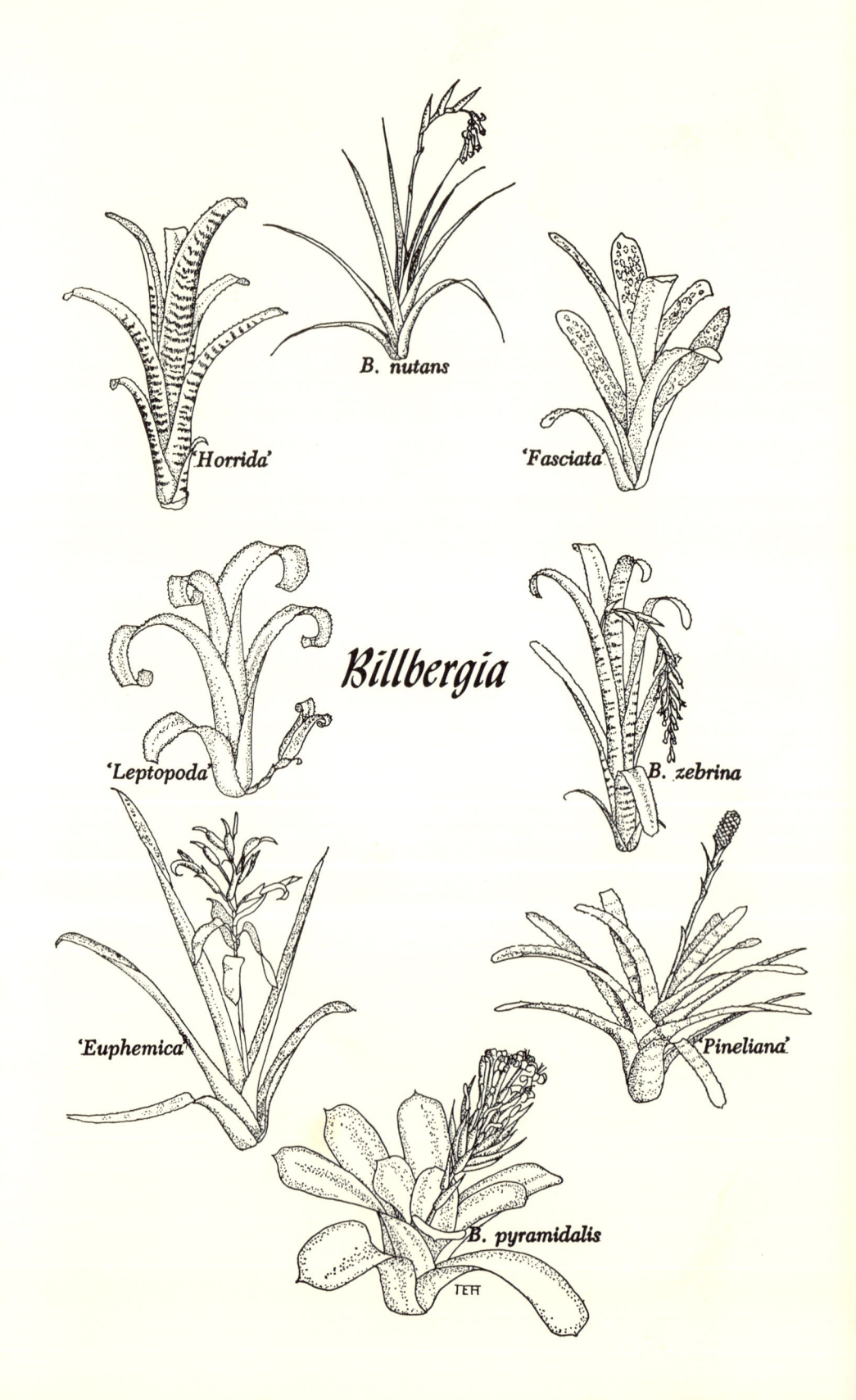

Billbergia

'Horrida'
B. nutans
'Fasciata'
'Leptopoda'
B. zebrina
'Euphemica'
'Pineliana'
B. pyramidalis

Billbergia

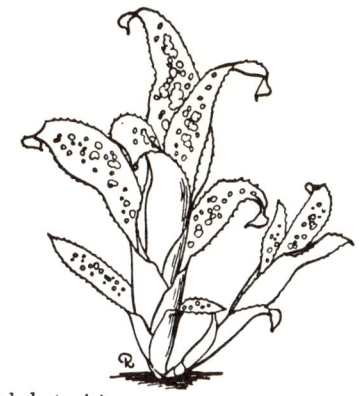

Billbergia (bill-BURR-jee-a): for J. Billberg, Swedish botanist.
SPP.: several species and numerous hybrids grow in Florida.

FAMILY: Bromeliaceae.   RELATIVES: Aechmea and Spanish-moss.
TYPE OF PLANT: Herbaceous perennial.   HEIGHT: 3'. ZONE: S
HOW TO IDENTIFY: Plants composed of stout rosettes of scurfy or smooth, usually spine-edged, leaves, that may be spotted or blotched. Some are epiphytic, others terrestrial.
HABIT OF GROWTH: Clump-growing by offsets of stiff leaves.
FOLIAGE: Stiff rosettes of mostly spine-edged leaves in varying color patterns.
FLOWERS: Usually spectacular spikes contain bright, showy bracts beneath the true flowers.
FRUITS: Many-seeded berries.
SEASON OF MAXIMUM COLOR: Late summer and early fall when spikes appear.
LANDSCAPE USES: For adding interest to trees, for planters, urns, and for earth-culture in warm locations, billbergias, like so many bromeliads, are very popular. These are leading plants for hobby collections.
HABITAT: Tropical America.
LIGHT REQUIREMENT: Ordinarily billbergias thrive in fairly bright light. Intensity of coloration may be lost inside some homes.
SOIL REQUIREMENT: Osmundine; a mixture of peat, leaf-mold, and sand; or rotted leaves worked into the earth beneath oak trees.
SALT TOLERANCE: Not tolerant of dune conditions.
AVAILABILITY: Most nurseries and garden centers carry billbergias in pots.
CULTURE: Fasten to limbs of rough-barked trees with copper or aluminum wire, or pot in chosen medium. Keep cups at leaf bases full of water and apply dilute liquid fertilizer to the growing medium once each summer month.
PROPAGATION: Division of offsets and seedage.
PESTS: Scales; mosquitoes may breed in water held in cups of outdoor billbergias.
NOTE: This genus, among the most popular of the bromels, has been used extensively in plant breeding. Shown opposite are some of Florida's favorites; above right is 'Fantasia'.

74
Aechmea

Aechmea (eke-ME-a): Greek, referring to the pointed sepals.
SPP.: several species and numerous hybrids grow in Florida.

FAMILY: Bromeliaceae. RELATIVES: Pineapple and billbergia.
TYPE OF PLANT: Herbaceous perennial. HEIGHT: 3'. ZONE: S
HOW TO IDENTIFY: Stiff rosettes of scurfy or smooth, usually spine-edged, variously colored leaves make up the plants that hold aloft spikes of usually bright-colored bracts in winter and springtime. Some are epiphytic, others terrestrial.
HABIT OF GROWTH: Clump-growing by offsets of stiff leaves.
FOLIAGE: Stiff rosettes of leaves of varying widths and colors.
FLOWERS: Usually spectacular spikes of varying bright bract coloration.
FRUITS: Many-seeded berries.
SEASON OF MAXIMUM COLOR: March-April when blossoms are out.
LANDSCAPE USES: For adding interest to trees, for planters, urns, and for earth-culture in warm locations, aechmeas, like so many bromeliads, are very popular. These are indicated for general landscapes and are much admired by hobbyists.
HABITAT: Tropical America.
LIGHT REQUIREMENT: Shifting light-and-shade is acceptable; some highly colored varieties may become paler in the reduced light of homes.
SOIL REQUIREMENT: Osmundine; a mixture of peat, leaf-mold, and sand; or rotted leaves worked into the earth beneath oak trees.
SALT TOLERANCE: Not tolerant of dune conditions.
AVAILABILITY: Most nurseries in Florida offer aechmeas in containers of various sizes.
CULTURE: Fasten to branches of rough-barked trees with copper or aluminum wire; pot in your chosen medium in containers or plant in the rotted leaf-mold beneath live oak trees. Keep the cups full of water and apply dilute liquid fertilizer to the growing medium once each summer month.
PROPAGATION: Division of offsets or seedage.
PESTS: Scales; mosquitoes may breed in the water standing in the cups of outdoor aechmeas.
NOTE: Hybridization has been extensive within this very large genus (140 species) and with other genera, with the result that many hybrid forms are seen in Florida landscape arrangements. It must be realized that definitive study in the Bromeliaceae is badly needed, as the botany is now incompletely understood.

75
Pinguin

Bromelia (bro-MELL-ee-a): for M. Bromel, a Swedish botanist.
pinguin (PIN-gwin): native vernacular name.

FAMILY: Bromeliaceae. RELATIVES: Pineapple and Spanish-moss.

TYPE OF PLANT: Herbaceous perennial. HEIGHT: 3'. ZONE: C,S

HOW TO IDENTIFY: Rosettes of stiff, spine-edged foliage; underground ratoons spread the cultures over large areas.

HABIT OF GROWTH: Rosettes of stiff leaves.

FOLIAGE: Evergreen, spine-edged, ribbon-like, gray-green in color.

FLOWERS: Central spikes with bright red bracts hold inconspicuous little flowers.

FRUITS: Small, globular, fuzzy fruits along the upper parts of the spikes.

SEASON OF MAXIMUM COLOR: Springtime when the bracts turn red.

LANDSCAPE USES: To help create a tropical atmosphere, clumps of pinguin are useful. The plants, in vegetative condition, are not in the least dramatic, but in springtime, when reproductive spikes appear, they are most spectacular because of the glowing red bracts. Visitors are invariably pleased with the effect.

In tropical lands, hedges of pinguin are used to check livestock.

HABITAT: Tropical America; in Florida, frost-free locations.

LIGHT REQUIREMENT: Full sun or broken shade.

SOIL REQUIREMENT: Tolerant of a wide range of soils.

SALT TOLERANCE: Tolerant of salt.

AVAILABILITY: Pinguin is usually not a nursery item; homeowners may exchange plants.

CULTURE: Pinguin requires no care whatsoever.

PROPAGATION: Division of matted clumps.

PESTS: None of major concern.

76
Wandering-Jew

Tradescantia (trad-es-CANT-ee-a): for J. Tradescant, English gardener; and *Zebrina* (zee-BRINE-a): referring to the striped leaves.
SPP.: several species of both genera grow in Florida.

FAMILY: Commelinaceae.   RELATIVES: Oyster-plant and spiderwort.

TYPE OF PLANT: Herbaceous perennial.   HEIGHT: 10". ZONE: N,C,S

HOW TO IDENTIFY: Wandering-Jew is grown by homeowners so widely that description here seems unnecessary.

HABIT OF GROWTH: Sprawling, mat-forming, by horizontal, rooting stems.

FOLIAGE: Succulent, soft, furnished with long, sparse hairs; leaf-bases ensheath their stems.

FLOWERS: Tiny, nestling within protective leaf-like bracts. Tones may vary with the variety.

FRUITS: Tiny, inconspicuous.

SEASON OF MAXIMUM COLOR: Little variation, even when blossoms are out.

LANDSCAPE USES: As ground cover for shady, frostless locations, wandering-Jew has long been a favorite with Floridians. To cover the soil in planters and to soften their top lines, these perennials serve. Very often single pots of fancy-leaved types are featured porch plants.

HABITAT: Tropical America.

LIGHT REQUIREMENT: Reduced light is optimum.

SOIL REQUIREMENT: Tolerant of widely varying well-drained soils.

SALT TOLERANCE: Not tolerant.

AVAILABILITY: Offered in containers by most nurseries in central and southern Florida. Frequently received from neighbors.

CULTURE: Simply stick pieces of stems where plants are wanted; water carefully until established, thereafter moderately during times when rains are infrequent; fertilize lightly at the onset of warm weather.

PROPAGATION: Cuttage.

PESTS: Mites, but these plants are notably pest-free.

77
Setcreasea

Setcreasea (set-CREASE-ee-a): derivation unclear.
SPP.: several types are cultured in Florida.

FAMILY: Commelinaceae. RELATIVES: Spiderwort and wandering-Jew.
TYPE OF PLANT: Herbaceous perennial. HEIGHT: 14". ZONE: N,C,S
HOW TO IDENTIFY: Fleshy, hairy leaves grow oppositely from erect or trailing stems. Three-petaled, ephemeral blossoms nestle in leaf-like bracts in terminal positions. Ubiquitous 'Purple Queen' has rich, purple foliage, other types have green leaves or ones striped with white.
HABIT OF GROWTH: Sprawling, mat-forming.
FOLIAGE: Succulent, fleshy, with many, long, fine hairs; leaf-bases ensheath their stems.
FLOWERS: 3 flaring pink petals, highlighted by golden anthers, characterize the flowers that nestle within their large, protective, leaf-like bracts during warm months.
FRUITS: Tiny, inconspicuous.
SEASON OF MAXIMUM COLOR: Spring when new leaves emerge.
LANDSCAPE USES: As ground cover for frostless locations, setcreaseas are in high favor. For sunny, exposed rock-'n'-gravel gardens, in shady planters, beneath pines and palms, these creeping perennials serve with distinction. Most popular is 'Purple Queen' (large drawing in center). Cultivated here are all-green 'Pallida' (right-hand sketch) and striped 'Striata' (left-hand sketch). Botanical status in *Setcreasea* is unclear.
HABITAT: Tropical America; in Florida, nearly frostless locations.
LIGHT REQUIREMENT: Full sun or broken, shifting shade.
SOIL REQUIREMENT: Rich soil is best, but setcreasea grows in poor sand as well.
SALT TOLERANCE: Tolerant of salt drift.
AVAILABILITY: Plants in containers are offered by most nurseries in Florida.
CULTURE: Simply stick pieces of stem where plants are wanted; water carefully until established, thereafter moderately when rains are infrequent; fertilize lightly once each summer month.
PROPAGATION: Cuttage.
PESTS: Mites, but these plants are notably pest-free.

78
Oyster-Plant

Rhoeo (RE-o): name obscure.
discolor (DIS-col-or): of two colors.

FAMILY: Commelinaceae.   RELATIVES: Spiderwort and wandering-Jew.
TYPE OF PLANT: Herbaceous perennial.   HEIGHT: 2'.   ZONE: C,S

HOW TO IDENTIFY: Broad, tender, succulent leaves that are green above and purple beneath, grow in little clumps; conspicuous boat-shaped bracts enclose little, white flowers.

HABIT OF GROWTH: Dense lanceolate leaves make this a formal, neat, little herbaceous perennial.

FOLIAGE: Evergreen, long-lanceolate, green above, purple beneath.

FLOWERS: Inconspicuous, white blossoms are held within boat-shaped bracts.

FRUITS: Little capsules mature within the bracts.

SEASON OF MAXIMUM COLOR: No seasonal variation.

LANDSCAPE USES: Oyster-plant enjoys great popularity as a groundcover, as an edging, and for planting bins. Usual planting interval is 1' o.c.
 There is a variety 'Vittata' or 'Striata,' that has longitudinal lines of yellow down the centers of leaves.
 Tender to cold, oyster-plant must be taken indoors for the winter in northern counties.

HABITAT: American tropics; in Florida, ubiquitous where winters are not severe.

LIGHT REQUIREMENT: Full sun or deep shade is acceptable.

SOIL REQUIREMENT: Almost any growing medium will support oyster-plant.

SALT TOLERANCE: Tolerant of salt air back of the first dune.

AVAILABILITY: Available in almost every plant-merchandising establishment.

CULTURE: Oyster-plant has few cultural requirements, and these are very easily supplied.

PROPAGATION: Seedage, cuttage, and division.

PESTS: Caterpillars and mites.

79
Spironema

Spironema (spy-roe-NEE-ma): Greek for spiral thread for winding filaments.
fragrans (FRAY-grans): fragrant.

FAMILY: Commelinaceae. RELATIVES: Dichorisandra and setcreasea.

TYPE OF PLANT: Herbaceous perennial. HEIGHT: 4'. ZONE: C,S

HOW TO IDENTIFY: Broad, foot-long leaves encircle their stems in rosette form; stolons are readily sent out, many twine-like roots grow from these, and maturing individuals send up yard-long spikes of tiny, very fragrant flowers.

HABIT OF GROWTH: Mat-forming by stoloniferous growth.

FOLIAGE: Lush, bold, succulent, 4" x 12", green with purple shadings, held in rosette form to make a symmetrical plant.

FLOWERS: Yard-long spikes bear little, white, fragrant blossoms in summer.

FRUITS: Small pods.

SEASON OF MAXIMUM COLOR: No variation.

LANDSCAPE USES: Spironema usually serves as a pot plant or hanging-basket subject, yet it can be used in planters, and as a ground cover under large-leaved trees where coarse texture is not objectionable. The summertime flower spikes make for an untidy effect. In years past, botanists used *Spironema* to study transport of fluids.

HABITAT: Mexico.

LIGHT REQUIREMENT: Full sun or partial shade of porches.

SOIL REQUIREMENT: Tolerant of a wide range of soil types.

SALT TOLERANCE: Not tolerant.

AVAILABILITY: Occasionally spironemas appear in nurseries.

CULTURE: Minimum care keeps spironema in growing condition. Like so many members of the Commelinaceae, this plant demands little from its owner.

PROPAGATION: Cuttage and division.

PESTS: Mites, but this plant is notably pest-free.

A. humilis

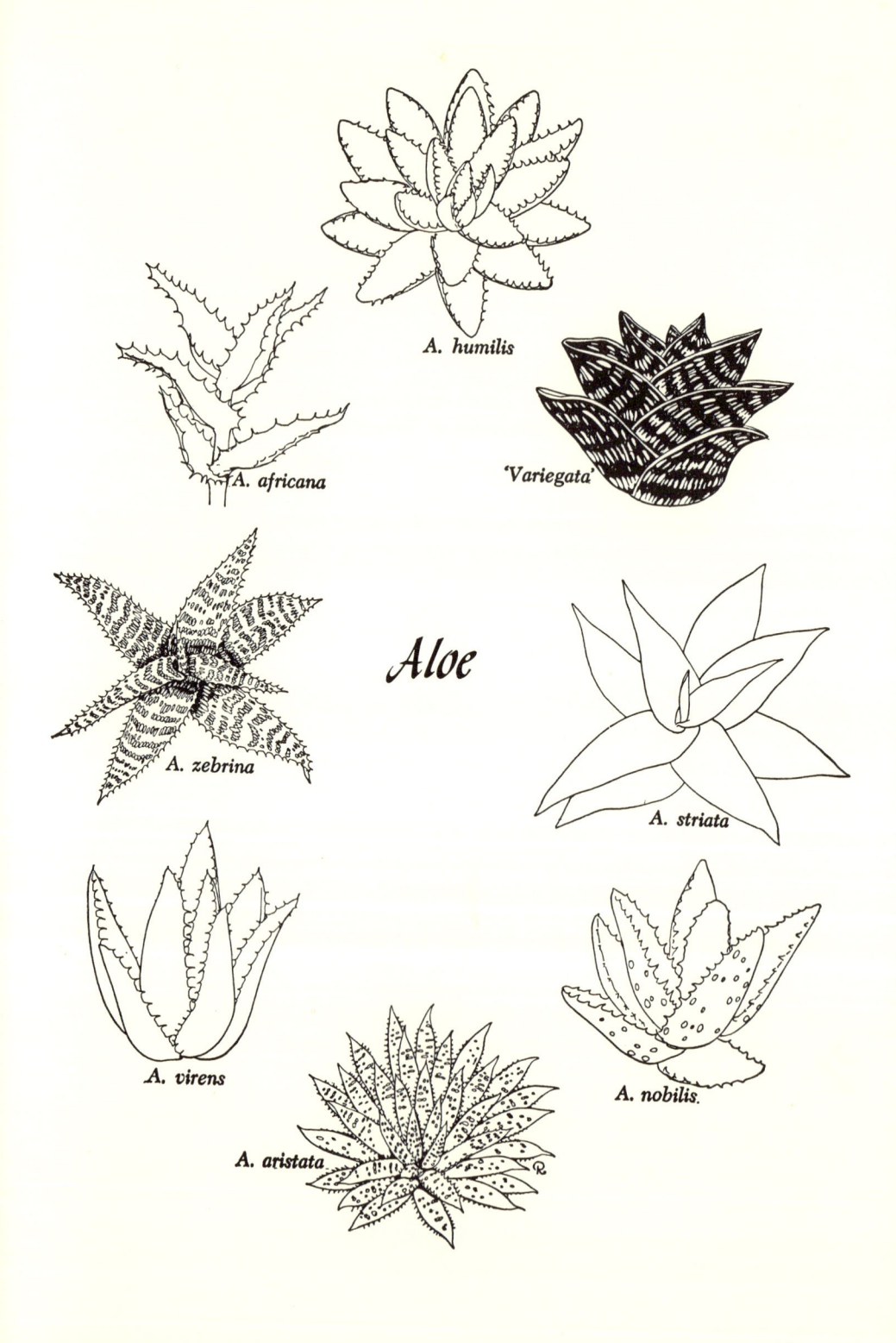

A. africana

'Variegata'

Aloe

A. zebrina

A. striata

A. virens

A. aristata

A. nobilis

81
Aloe

Aloe (AL-oh): ancient Arabic name.
SPP.: several species are grown in Florida.

FAMILY: Liliaceae. RELATIVES: Lily, daylily, and asparagus.
TYPE OF PLANT: Succulent perennial. HEIGHT: Variable. ZONE: C,S
HOW TO IDENTIFY: Stiff rosettes of thick, succulent, spike-edged, or smooth leaves, usually mottled; erect scapes with red, orange, or yellow tubular flowers.
HABIT OF GROWTH: Compact because of many closely held succulent leaves.
FOLIAGE: Succulent, usually mottled with purple or white.
FLOWERS: Showy spikes of tubular blossoms in tones of red, orange, or yellow produced during warm months.
FRUITS: 3-angled capsules.
SEASON OF MAXIMUM COLOR: Spring, when blossoms unfurl.
LANDSCAPE USES: To help create the feeling of the tropics, aloes are in vogue. For rock-'n'-sand gardens, urns, and sunny planter-bins, they are in demand. For seaside arrangements, aloes excel.
HABITAT: Old World tropics and warm temperate regions.
LIGHT REQUIREMENT: Full sun or shady situations.
SOIL REQUIREMENT: Most soils seem to be entirely adequate. Basic reaction and dry conditions are tolerated.
SALT TOLERANCE: Most tolerant of salt, grows on front-line dunes.
AVAILABILITY: Canned plants are stocked by most nurseries in southern Florida.
CULTURE: After establishment, water moderately during periods of extreme drought. Fertilize once at the beginning of the rainy season.
PROPAGATION: Division of offsets from around old plants; seedage.
PESTS: Caterpillars may chew holes in young, tender leaves.
NOTE: Most widely grown is Barbados aloe (*Aloe barbadensis*) illustrated above. Leaves are spiny-toothed, 1" yellow flowers are produced on 4' scapes in summer.

Coral aloe (*Aloe striata*) (right opposite) may form a 2' trunk that bears leaves 4" x 20", striate, with entire white margins and spikes of coral-red flowers.

Tree aloe (*Aloe arborescens*) develops a trunk that bears spreading leaves 2" x 24" with prickly, wavy margins, and red flowers that are 1½" long. This is widely grown in the type and is the parent of some hybrids.

Other aloes grown in Florida appear on the opposite page.

82
Pony-Tail

Beaucarnea (bo-CAR-nee-a): derivation obscure.
recurvata (ree-curv-ATE-a): recurved, referring to the downward-bending foliage.

FAMILY: Liliaceae.   RELATIVES: Lily, gloriosa, and aloe.

TYPE OF PLANT: Tree.   HEIGHT: 15'. ZONE: C,S

HOW TO IDENTIFY: The greatly swollen trunk base and the recurving, narrow leaves are certain identification.

HABIT OF GROWTH: Upright, with long, flowing, ribbon-like leaves.

FOLIAGE: Evergreen, fine in texture, light green in color.

FLOWERS: Inconspicuous.

FRUITS: Usually none are produced in Florida.

SEASON OF MAXIMUM COLOR: None.

LANDSCAPE USES: As an urn subject for terrace, patio, or Florida room, pony-tail excels. As a freestanding specimen out-of-doors it is sometimes seen in frostless locations.

Pony-tail is one of Florida's most dramatic plants because of its much-expanded trunk at the soil line. This is a tried-and-true conversation piece.

HABITAT: Mexican highlands; in Florida, sandy soils in warm locations.

LIGHT REQUIREMENT: Full sun.

SOIL REQUIREMENT: Sandy, well-drained neutral soils.

SALT TOLERANCE: Tolerant of salt drift well back from the sea.

AVAILABILITY: Many nurseries sell small pony-tails in containers.

CULTURE: Plant in a well-drained site that is not subjected to low temperatures; fertilize once at the beginning of warm weather; keep lawn grasses back from the trunk.

PROPAGATION: Seedage.

PESTS: Chewing insects, root-rot diseases may cause death on wet soils.

Lily-Turf

Liriope (leer-EYE-o-pee): for the nymph Liriope.
muscari (mus-CARE-ee): referring to musky odor.

FAMILY: Liliaceae. RELATIVES: Lily and dwarf lily-turf.
TYPE OF PLANT: Herbaceous perennial. HEIGHT: 1'. ZONE: N,C,S
HOW TO IDENTIFY: This dwarf, rhizomatous herb forms close, green mats. The dark-green, grass-like foliage is interspersed with spikes of pretty blue flowers in springtime, and conspicuous, shiny, black fruits during the winter.
HABIT OF GROWTH: Grass-like, mat-forming.
FOLIAGE: Evergreen, long-linear, grass-like, growing in tufts.
FLOWERS: Lax spikes of pretty blue flowers, ¼" across, in spring and summer.
FRUITS: Globose capsules, ⅓" in diameter, persist during fall and winter.
SEASON OF MAXIMUM COLOR: Spring and summer when blossoms are out, fall and winter when fruits mature.
LANDSCAPE USES: As a ground cover for densely shaded spots, lily-turf is widely accepted. Plant 6" or 12" o.c. As an edging for shady walks, it excels.
HABITAT: Eastern Asia; in Florida ubiquitous in shady gardens.
LIGHT REQUIREMENT: Shady situations are recommended.
SOIL REQUIREMENT: Tolerant of many soil types; however, growth is more attractive in fertile earth.
SALT TOLERANCE: Tolerant of salt air back from the strand.
AVAILABILITY: Most nurseries stock lily-turf.
CULTURE: Plant divisions of old matted clumps in well-prepared soil, water moderately until well established, then during periods of severe drought only. Fertilize once each springtime.
PROPAGATION: Division and seedage.
PESTS: Scales and a very serious tip-burn.
NOTE: Confusion exists in this genus, and labeling may be inaccurate. Giant, broad-leaved types and others with striped leaves are popular in western Florida.

84 Dwarf Lily-Turf

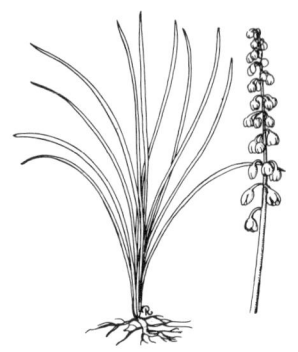

Ophiopogon (o-fee-o-POE-gon): Greek for snake's beard.
japonicus (jap-ON-i-cus): Japanese.

FAMILY: Liliaceae.   RELATIVES: Aloe and cast-iron plant.

TYPE OF PLANT: Herbaceous perennial.   HEIGHT: 10″. ZONE: N,C,S

HOW TO IDENTIFY: This is the finest-textured of the liliaceous, non-grass ground covers. The leaves are ⅛″ broad, the flowers are usually hidden below the foliage, and the fruits, if present, are inconspicuous.

HABIT OF GROWTH: Grass-like, mat-forming by stolons.

FOLIAGE: Evergreen, long-linear, very fine in texture, very dark green when growing in the shade.

FLOWERS: Inconspicuous, bluish, 3/16″ long, few on short scapes that are lower than the leaves.

FRUITS: Small, fleshy capsules when present.

SEASON OF MAXIMUM COLOR: Little change throughout the year.

LANDSCAPE USES: For covering the earth under trees, for shaded planters, and to edge woodland walks, dwarf lily-turf excels. Set divisions 6″ o.c.

HABITAT: Eastern Asia; in Florida, ubiquitous in shady gardens.

LIGHT REQUIREMENT: Full shade is quite acceptable.

SOIL REQUIREMENT: Adapted to many soils.

SALT TOLERANCE: Tolerant of salt air back from the strand.

AVAILABILITY: Most nurseries stock dwarf lily-turf.

CULTURE: Plant divisions of old matted clumps in well-prepared soil, water moderately until well-established, then during periods of severe drought only. Fertilize once each springtime.

PROPAGATION: Division.

PESTS: Scales.

NOTE: Dwarf lily-turf is offered for sale under many strange vernacular names. Giant types and others with striped foliage are much used in western Florida to edge garden walks.

85
Cast-Iron Plant

Aspidistra (as-pi-DIS-tra): Greek for small, round shield, describing the stigma.
elatior (ee-LAY-tee-or): taller.

FAMILY: Liliaceae.   RELATIVES: Daylily and Easter lily.

TYPE OF PLANT: Herbaceous perennial.   HEIGHT: 3'. ZONE: N,C,S

HOW TO IDENTIFY: Clusters of tall, broad, evergreen leaves are sent up from strong, persistent rhizomes. These tough leaves, either all green or striped with white, endure low light intensities and low atmospheric humidity which would be unsuitable to many foliage plants.

HABIT OF GROWTH: Clump-forming.

FOLIAGE: Yard-long by 6" broad, atop erect petioles, produced in dense clusters from tough rootstocks.

FLOWERS: Inconspicuous, borne close to the earth.

FRUITS: Inconspicuous, little 1-seeded berries.

SEASON OF MAXIMUM COLOR: No seasonal variation.

LANDSCAPE USES: Since earliest times, this has been a dependable porch plant, always noted for its ability to endure adverse growing conditions. Now contemporary designers approve its use.

HABITAT: China; in Florida, frequently seen in shady gardens.

LIGHT REQUIREMENT: Reduced light is optimum; full sunlight cannot be tolerated.

SOIL REQUIREMENT: Moderately fertile, fibrous soil is best, yet cast-iron plant shows tolerance for widely varying growing media.

SALT TOLERANCE: Tolerant of moderate salt air back of first-line dunes.

AVAILABILITY: Nurseries offer aspidistras in containers.

CULTURE: Plant slightly deeper than former growing depth in shady locations; water during periods of drought; fertilize once each summer month.

PROPAGATION: Division of old matted clumps.

PESTS: Leaf-spotting disease.

Agave filifera

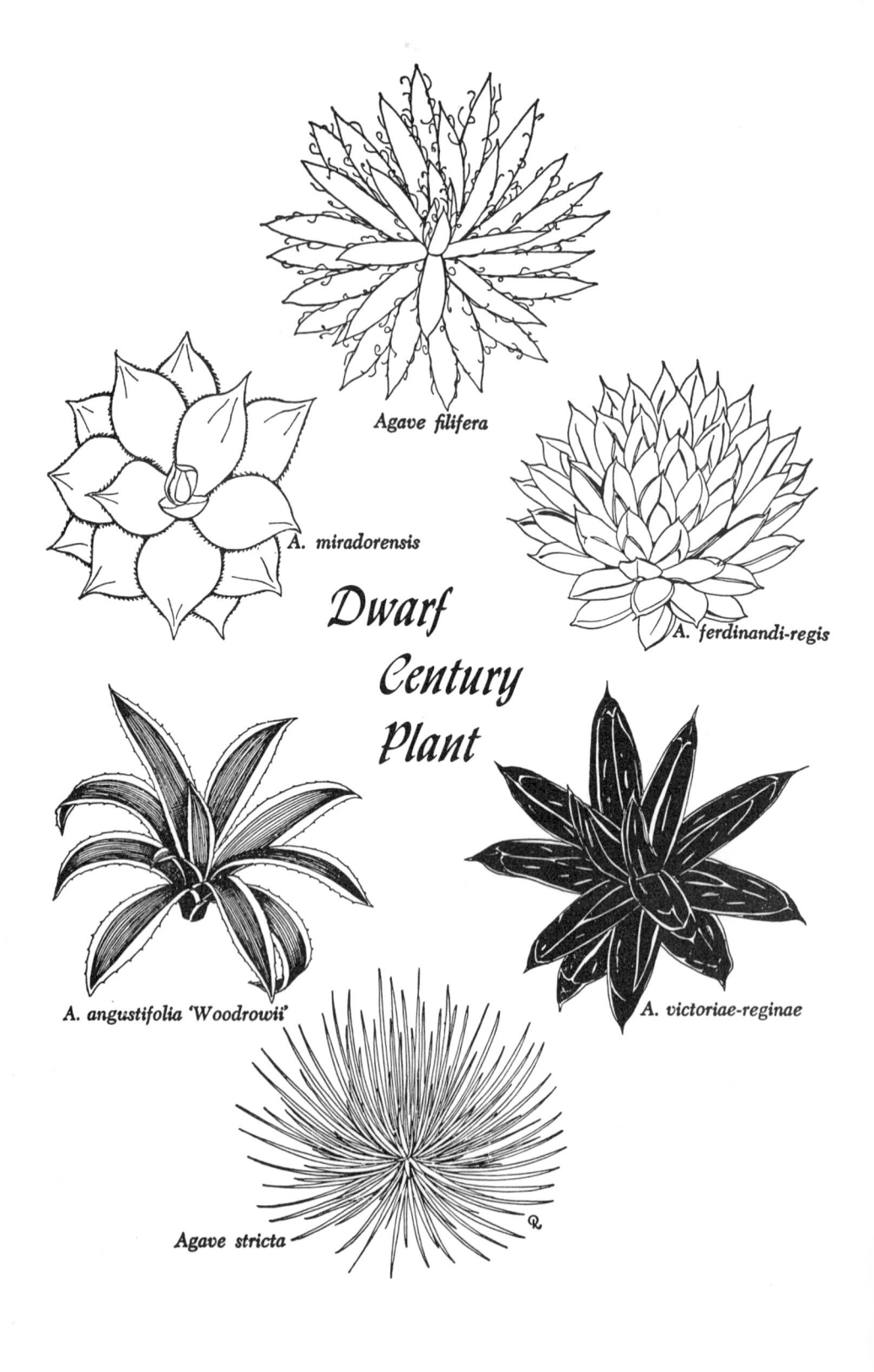

A. miradorensis

Dwarf Century Plant

A. ferdinandi-regis

A. angustifolia 'Woodrowii'

A. victoriae-reginae

Agave stricta

87
Century Plant

Agave (a-GAY-vee): Greek for admirable.
americana (a-mer-ee-CANE-a): American.

FAMILY: Agavaceae.   RELATIVES: Spanish bayonet, dracena, and ti.
TYPE OF PLANT: Succulent herbaceous perennial.
　　　　　　　　　　　HEIGHT OF LEAF MASS: 6'. ZONE: N,C,S
HOW TO IDENTIFY: Great, stiff, heavy, persistent leaves in rosettes.
HABIT OF GROWTH: Tight rosettes.
FOLIAGE: Very coarse in texture, gray-green or banded with yellow.
FLOWERS: Yellowish-green on horizontal branches, high in the air.
FRUITS: Capsules the size of large eggs that split to release black seeds or germinating seedlings.
SEASON OF MAXIMUM COLOR: No seasonal variation.
LANDSCAPE USES: As a strong accent, where a bold tropical effect is wanted, century plant excels. As a tubbed specimen, it may serve, if terminal spines are carefully clipped away.
　　Here in Florida, landscape architects and homeowners employ agaves often in landscape compositions to enhance the feeling of the tropics. In spite of their wide use, many, many more could be planted. In rock-'n'-sand gardens, agaves make harmonious compositions with tropical succulents.
HABITAT: Dry, sandy regions; in Florida, very widely planted.
LIGHT REQUIREMENT: Full sun for best growth, but endures heavy shade.
SOIL REQUIREMENT: Any well-drained soil is suitable.
SALT TOLERANCE: No plant is better adapted to seaside conditions.
AVAILABILITY: Nurseries, garden centers, and chain stores offer century plants of many kinds.
CULTURE: The sharp spines that terminate the leaves must be removed so that they do not injure children and pets.
PROPAGATION: Division of clumps, or aerial plants from the inflorescence.
PESTS: Scales, but these are not of great consequence.
NOTE: There are more than 300 species, and many varieties of *Agave*.

'Compacta Goldeana'

Sansevieria trifasciata

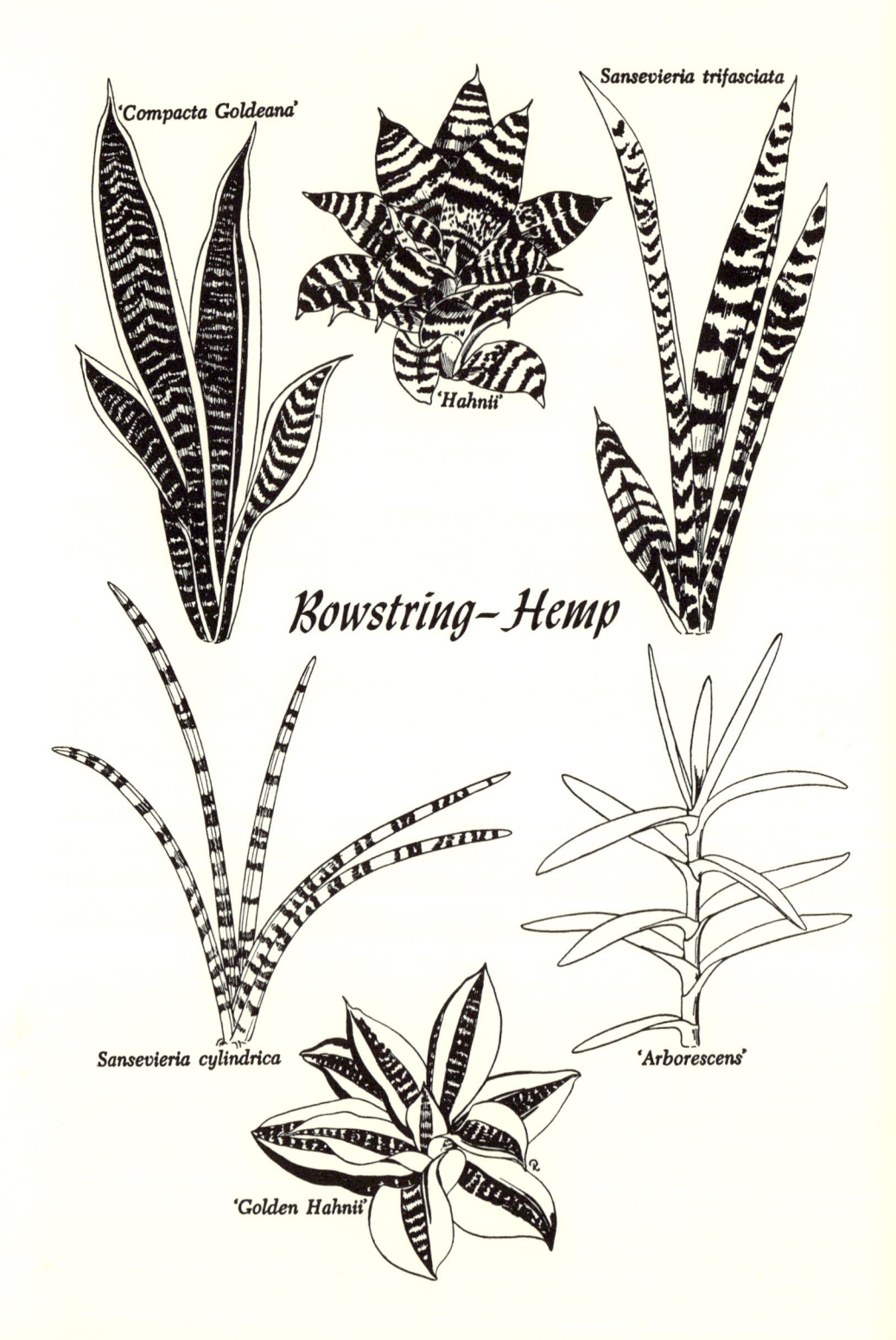

'Hahnii'

Bowstring-Hemp

Sansevieria cylindrica

'Arborescens'

'Golden Hahnii'

89
Bowstring–Hemp

Sansevieria (san-see-VERE-ee-a): for an Italian prince.
SPP.: many kinds grow in Florida.

FAMILY: Agavaceae.

TYPE OF PLANT: Herbaceous perennial.

RELATIVES: Dracena and ti.

HEIGHT: Variable. ZONE: S

HOW TO IDENTIFY: Stiff, mottled, blotched or striped leaves, succulent, and fiber-bearing, characterize this great group of tropical exotics. Scapes support white, tubular, very fragrant flowers.

HABIT OF GROWTH: Very compact, rosette-like.

FOLIAGE: Stiff, succulent, mottled, blotched or lined, of many shapes and sizes.

FLOWERS: White, tubular, fragrant, held by scapes that are usually taller than the leaf mass.

FRUITS: Green pods may follow pollination.

SEASON OF MAXIMUM COLOR: Little variation over the seasons.

LANDSCAPE USES: Sansevierias are planted in every conceivable landscape application in Florida. As accent plants in foundation arrangements, in planters, for Florida room urns, as porch plants, even for tiny dish gardens, these African tropicals are in high favor.

HABITAT: Tropical Africa.

LIGHT REQUIREMENT: Full sun or reduced light of dwellings is acceptable.

SOIL REQUIREMENT: Tolerance of widely varying soils is notable.

SALT TOLERANCE: Tolerant of salt air and saline soils.

AVAILABILITY: Usually found in chain stores and nurseries.

CULTURE: Simply plant, water, and forget.

PROPAGATION: Division or leaf cuttage.

PESTS: Caterpillars may chew tender foliage.

NOTE: Many clones are widely grown in our state. Pictured opposite are popular kinds with their Florida names. As the botany is imperfectly understood, naming is subject to question. New kinds arise in horticultural establishments, and acceptance by the public has been quite marked. Above is the popular birds-nest sansevieria.

90
New Zealand Flax

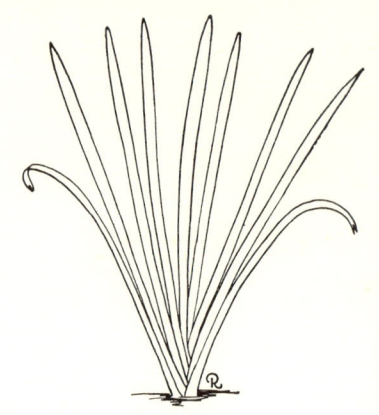

Phormium (FOR-me-um): Greek for basket, referring to uses of the fiber.
tenax (TEE-nax): strong.

FAMILY: Agavaceae. **RELATIVES:** Century plant and bowstring-hemp.
TYPE OF PLANT: Herbaceous perennial. **HEIGHT:** 6'. **ZONE:** C,S
HOW TO IDENTIFY: Tall, sword-shaped, equitant, keeled leaves rise to man-height from fleshy rhizomes. Tubular red or yellow flowers may be produced on 15' scapes under good conditions.
HABIT OF GROWTH: Stiffly upright by long, lance-form leaves.
FOLIAGE: Man-high, 5" broad, sword-shaped, equitant, highlighted with orange-red lines at the keeled midrib and at the margins. Old leaves will split at their apexes.
FLOWERS: Tubular, red or yellow, borne in 15' scapes under favorable conditions.
FRUITS: Capsules 2"-4" long if present.
SEASON OF MAXIMUM COLOR: Warm months when flowers appear.
LANDSCAPE USES: For the strong tropical character of the tall, dusky leaves, New Zealand flax is in high favor with garden designers. An established clump may be used near a doorway, gate, or passage, particularly with structures of contemporary design. A clump is effective near a water feature as well.
HABITAT: New Zealand.
LIGHT REQUIREMENT: Full sun or broken, shifting shade.
SOIL REQUIREMENT: Moist, rich soil high in organic matter is recommended.
SALT TOLERANCE: Not tolerant of dune conditions but thrives near tidal lagoons.
AVAILABILITY: Nurseries offer New Zealand flax in cans.
CULTURE: Once established in good, moist soil, this tough fiber-bearing relative of the century plant requires little care.
PROPAGATION: Division or seedage.
PESTS: Usually none of major importance.
NOTE: Ordinarily the type (depicted above) is displayed in Florida landscape plantings, but the clone 'Variegatum' has striped leaves, and a selection with leaves that display a rich, reddish cast is attractive.

91 Adam's Needle

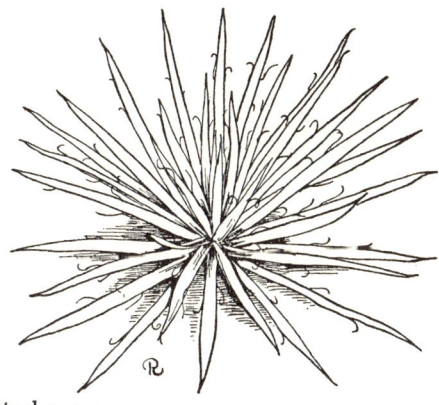

Yucca (YUCK-a): modification of an aboriginal name.
smalliana (small-ee-AY-na): for J. Small, American botanist.

FAMILY: Agavaceae.   **RELATIVES:** Dracena, century plant, and tuberose.

TYPE OF PLANT: Dwarf succulent shrub in landscaping.

HEIGHT: 2½'.   **ZONE:** N,C

HOW TO IDENTIFY: Rosettes of gray-green, lance-shaped, sharp-tipped, thread-edged leaves have led to the use of bear-grass as one local name.

HABIT OF GROWTH: A strong basal rosette, with no erect trunk.

FOLIAGE: Evergreen, ribbon-like with gray threads, gray-green in color.

FLOWERS: White, nodding, on tall, erect panicles which arise from the center of the foliage rosette. The white petals are edible.

FRUITS: Conspicuous, fleshy capsules, which turn black and dry at maturity.

SEASON OF MAXIMUM COLOR: Early summer when flower spikes are sent up.

LANDSCAPE USES: As a transition plant for a group of Spanish bayonets and/or century plants, bear-grass serves admirably. Set these 2' apart. To edge driveways or walkways in woodland plantings, use the same interval. For urns and planters this native plant can be used, too.

HABITAT: Sandy ridges and hammocks in Florida.

LIGHT REQUIREMENT: Full sun or broken shade below tall pines or oaks.

SOIL REQUIREMENT: Any well-drained soil seems to suffice.

SALT TOLERANCE: Very tolerant of salt.

AVAILABILITY: Occasionally nurseries will offer bear-grass plants in containers.

CULTURE: Bear-grass transplants with difficulty, often plants will die after they have been in garden locations for many months. Plant in well-drained sites, water with moderation.

PROPAGATION: Seedage and division of matted, native clumps.

PESTS: Possibly soil-borne diseases cause death in gardens.

92
Spanish Bayonet

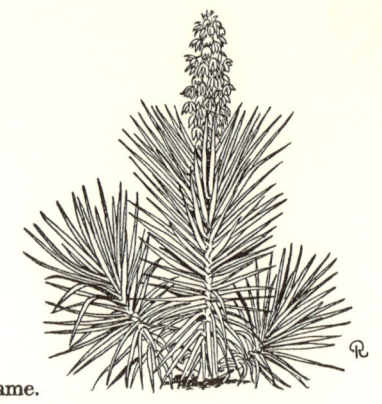

Yucca (YUCK-a): modification of an aboriginal name.
aloifolia (al-low-i-FOL-ee-a): aloe-leaved.

FAMILY: Agavaceae.   RELATIVES: Century plant, dracena, and tuberose.
TYPE OF PLANT: Herbaceous perennial.   HEIGHT: 25'.   ZONE: N,C,S
HOW TO IDENTIFY: Evergreen dagger-like leaves 2½' long x 2½" wide, tipped with sharp spines grow outward from many inclining thick trunks. Spikes of white nodding blossoms appear in springtime.
HABIT OF GROWTH: Clump-forming, by means of many inclining trunks.
FOLIAGE: Evergreen, dagger-like, coarse in texture, in tones of green.
FLOWERS: White, hanging, cup-like, 3" in diameter are held by erect, terminal panicles in springtime. The petals are edible.
FRUITS: Fleshy capsules about 5" long which dry and turn black at maturity.
SEASON OF MAXIMUM COLOR: Spring, when spikes of white flowers come out.
LANDSCAPE USES: For seaside planting, nothing equals Spanish bayonet. For barriers, enclosures, foundation plantings, set plants or unrooted cuttings 1½'-3' apart. Inland, this native plant serves equally well to enhance the tropical atmosphere.
   The vicious thorns must be removed with sharp pruning shears from the leaf-tips as new foliage unfurls. *Yucca elephantipes* does not have harmful spines.
HABITAT: Well-drained sands in Florida, notably, the coastal dunes.
LIGHT REQUIREMENT: Sun or shade.
SOIL REQUIREMENT: Any well-drained soil.
SALT TOLERANCE: Very tolerant of salt, therefore, highly recommended for dune plantings.
AVAILABILITY: Occasionally Spanish bayonets are offered in containers by nurserymen, but more often they are simply cut from native cultures as they are needed.
CULTURE: Plant rooted plants or unrooted cuttings in well-drained sites. These need not be fertile or rich in organic matter. Water sparingly at all times.
PROPAGATION: Cuttage, using pieces of any size at any season.
PESTS: Yucca moth larvae may destroy buds of low plants.
NOTE: There are clones with foliage variously striped with gold or gold and pink.

93
Spineless Yucca

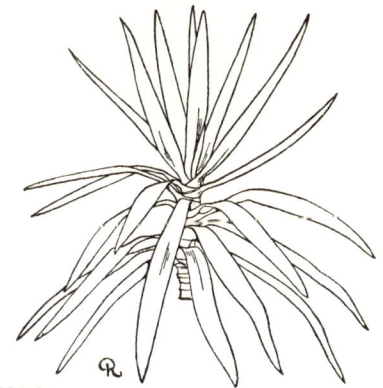

Yucca (YUCK-a): modification of an aboriginal name.
elephantipes (el-e-FAN-ti-pez): elephant foot.

FAMILY: Agavaceae.   RELATIVES: Spanish bayonet and ti.
TYPE OF PLANT: Succulent shrub.   HEIGHT: 25'. ZONE: C,S

HOW TO IDENTIFY: Spanish bayonet-like, but with pliable leaves terminated by harmless tips.

HABIT OF GROWTH: Clump-forming by means of inclining trunks.

FOLIAGE: Evergreen, dagger-like, coarse in texture, colored in tones of green.

FLOWERS: White, cup-like, hanging from erect panicles. The petals are edible.

FRUITS: Purple-black capsules in summertime.

SEASON OF MAXIMUM COLOR: Springtime, when the spikes of white flowers elongate.

LANDSCAPE USES: To enhance the tropical effect wherever Spanish bayonets have been used, this related species may be preferred because of the harmless leaf-tips. As accents in foundation arrangements and for large planters, spineless yucca is highly regarded. In succulent groups by antique brick walls and in rock-'n'-gravel gardens it is almost an essential component.

HABITAT: Central America; in Florida, now widely planted.

LIGHT REQUIREMENT: Sun or shade.

SOIL REQUIREMENT: Any well-drained soil appears to be suitable.

SALT TOLERANCE: Tolerant of salt.

AVAILABILITY: Many nurseries stock this desirable plant.

CULTURE: Plant in well-drained site; water and fertilize with moderation.

PROPAGATION: Cuttage, using pieces of any size.

PESTS: Yucca moth may kill low plants.

NOTE: Spineless yuccas with striped foliage are to be found in some nurseries.

Dracaena goldieana

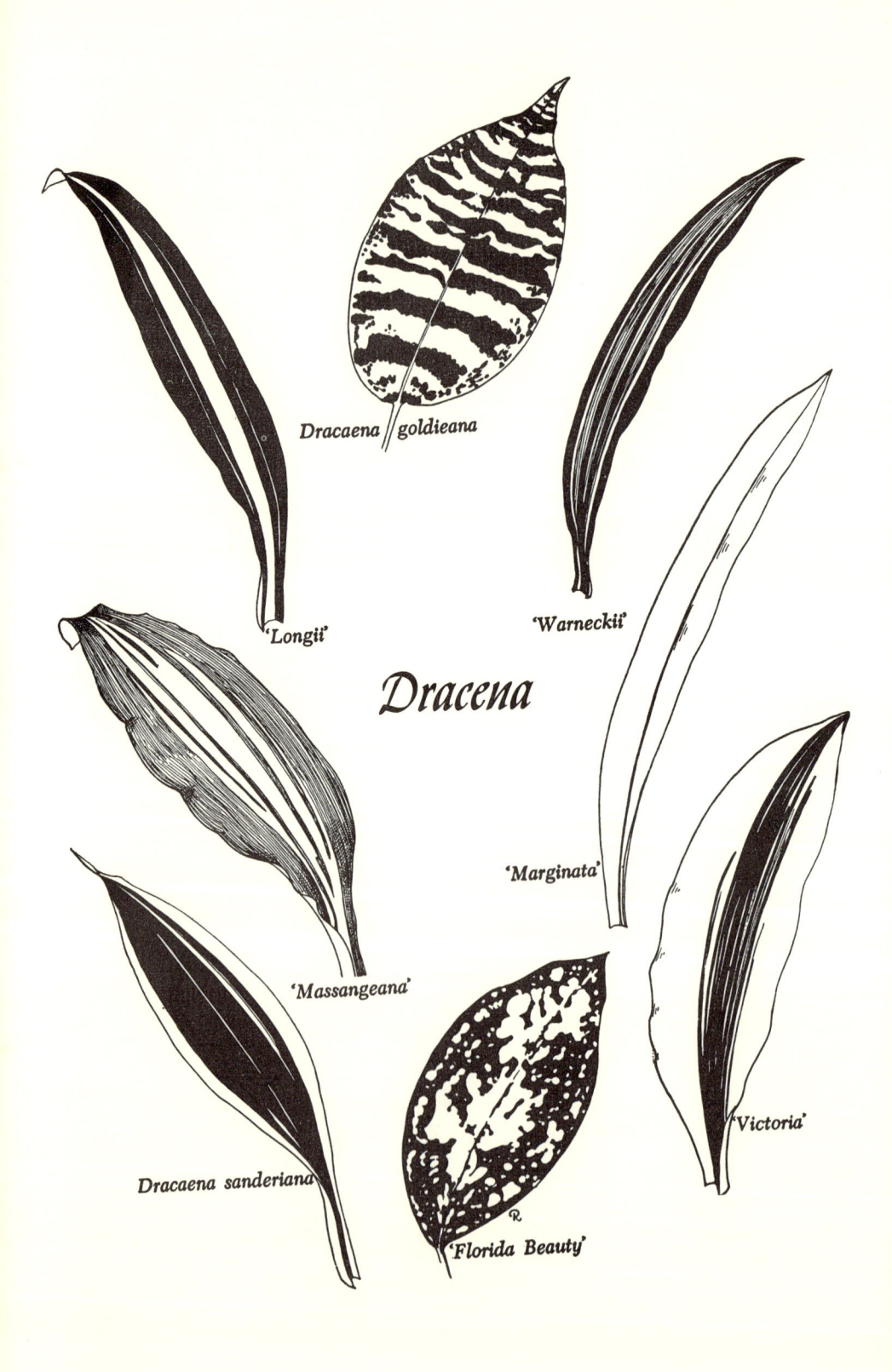

'Longii'

'Warneckii'

Dracena

'Marginata'

'Massangeana'

Dracaena sanderiana

'Florida Beauty'

'Victoria'

95
Dracena

Dracaena (dray-SEEN-a): Greek for female dragon.
SPP.: several species are grown in Florida.

FAMILY: Agavaceae.　　　　　　　　RELATIVES: Century plant and ti.
TYPE OF PLANT: Shrub.　　　　　　　　　　　　HEIGHT: 15'. ZONE: S
HOW TO IDENTIFY: Woody-stemmed shrubs with prominent corn-like leaves more or less clustered near the tips. The leaves, which have no petioles, are variable in size and color, depending upon the species and variety. Flowers, which are held in branched, upright panicles, have an unpleasant odor.
HABIT OF GROWTH: Strongly ascending, single-trunked in some species, branched in others.
FOLIAGE: Evergreen, without petioles, of bold, tropical aspect, of variable color.
FLOWERS: Inconspicuous, in upright panicles, dark red outside, white inside, with unpleasant odor.
FRUITS: Globose berries with 1 to 3 seeds when present.
SEASON OF MAXIMUM COLOR: No seasonal variation.
LANDSCAPE USES: For the attractive tropical aspect, landscape dracenas are popular in garden compositions in southern Florida. Tender to cold, these tropical exotics must be kept in Florida rooms or in greenhouses in more northerly locations.
HABITAT: Tropical Africa; in Florida, landscape plantings in the southern part; Florida rooms of all sections.
LIGHT REQUIREMENT: Tolerant of considerable shade.
SOIL REQUIREMENT: Fertile, moisture-retentive soils are requisite for good-looking foliage.
SALT TOLERANCE: Not tolerant.
AVAILABILITY: Dracenas are widely offered in containers in southern Florida.
CULTURE: Plant in reasonably fertile soil that has been made free of nematodes; water moderately and fertilize about three times each year.
PROPAGATION: Cuttage and marcottage.
PESTS: Anthracnose leaf-spot is sometimes serious.
NOTE: Landscape dracenas in Florida are many, botanical status is unclear, and labeling may be inconsistent. Portrayed across are Florida favorites under names that may be at variance with those in use in your community. On this page is delicate, little 'Marginata'.

96
Ti

Cordyline (core-dee-LINE-ee): Greek for club, referring to the thickened roots.
terminalis (ter-min-ALE-is): at the end of the stem.

FAMILY: Agavaceae.   RELATIVES: Dracena and Spanish bayonet.
TYPE OF PLANT: Shrub.   HEIGHT: 8'. ZONE: S

HOW TO IDENTIFY: Showy, persistent leaves of many colors and sizes are always held by distinct, clasping petioles. Flowers are produced on foot-long panicles among the leaves.

HABIT OF GROWTH: Stiffly upright, some forms are branched, others are not.

FOLIAGE: Evergreen, with channeled, clasping petioles, of variable color.

FLOWERS: Inconspicuous, in various tones, held on branched panicles.

FRUITS: Globose berries, rather freely produced by some varieties in Florida.

SEASON OF MAXIMUM COLOR: The year around, if not injured by cold.

LANDSCAPE USES: To enhance the tropical effect, colorful ti is popular in extreme southern Florida. It is set in foundation arrangements, and in bins and urns. A group of 3 ti of a single color forms an effective focal point in front of green shrubbery. The clones are many, some of which have English names, some French, some Japanese, and some Hawaiian. Consistency in naming may not be the rule. Ti is very tender to cold.

HABITAT: Eastern Asia; in Florida, landscape plantings in southern part.

LIGHT REQUIREMENT: Tolerant of considerable shade.

SOIL REQUIREMENT: Reasonably fertile soil that is free of nematodes is best.

SALT TOLERANCE: Not tolerant.

AVAILABILITY: Many nurseries, garden centers, and chain stores offer plants in containers and small pieces of stem in plastic bags for home propagation.

CULTURE: Plant in reasonably fertile soil that has been made free of nematodes; water moderately; fertilize about three times each year; protect the foliage against leaf-spot.

PROPAGATION: Cuttage and marcottage.

PESTS: Anthracnose leaf-spot, nematodes, and mites.

97
Banana

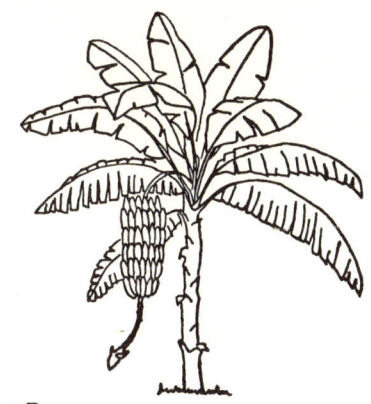

Musa (MEW-sa): for A. Musa, physician to the first Roman emperor.
paradisiaca (para-dis-EYE-a-ca): of gardens.

FAMILY: Musaceae.   RELATIVES: Bird-of-paradise flower and travelers-tree.

TYPE OF PLANT: Tall herbaceous perennial.   HEIGHT: 20′.   ZONE: N,C,S

HOW TO IDENTIFY: Tall, stoloniferous herbaceous perennial with evergreen leaves some 7′ long x 1½′ wide, with a bunch of bananas emerging from the axies of mature specimens.

HABIT OF GROWTH: Tree-like, from underground rootstocks.

FOLIAGE: Evergreen, of coarse texture and deep green color when well fertilized.

FLOWERS: Terminal hanging inflorescences borne under protective purplish bracts.

FRUITS: Long, berry-like bodies with thick, shining rinds, hang in clusters.

SEASON OF MAXIMUM COLOR: Summer when purple bracts are present.

LANDSCAPE USES: For lending an air of the tropics, nothing surpasses banana. Plant bananas in bold clumps behind walls or hardy shrubs so that they will not be missed when frost cuts them to the earth.

HABITAT: Tropics around the globe; in Florida, ubiquitous.

LIGHT REQUIREMENT: Full sun or broken shade.

SOIL REQUIREMENT: Fertile, moist soil makes for best growth.

SALT TOLERANCE: Not tolerant.

AVAILABILITY: Most sales lots offer bananas in containers during the summer months.

CULTURE: Plant, water, and forget.

PROPAGATION: Division of matted clumps.

PESTS: *Cercospora* leaf-spot, Panama disease, scales, and nematodes.

NOTE: There are many, many kinds of bananas. Some persons are attracted by clones with leaves marbled with white, or foliage that is predominately red with purple blotches.

98 Travelers-Tree

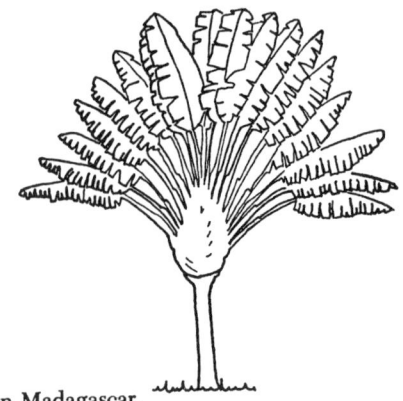

Ravenala (rav-en-ALE-a): name of the plant in Madagascar.
madagascariensis (mad-a-gas-car-ee-EN-sis): of Madagascar.

FAMILY: Musaceae. **RELATIVES:** Banana and bird-of-paradise flower.

TYPE OF PLANT: Tree. **HEIGHT:** 25'. **ZONE:** S

HOW TO IDENTIFY: Huge leaves are held in two ranks to give a fan-like effect atop a stout, palm-like trunk.

HABIT OF GROWTH: Two-ranked foliage forms a huge, symmetrical fan.

FOLIAGE: Evergreen, bold in aspect, medium green in color.

FLOWERS: Small white flowers are held in erect series of canoe-like bracts.

FRUITS: Three-celled woody capsules with many indigo seeds.

SEASON OF MAXIMUM COLOR: No seasonal change.

LANDSCAPE USES: To help create a tropical atmosphere, travelers-tree is one of Florida's most popular plants; surely none is more striking. Travelers-tree is used as a freestanding specimen, often as a focal point in the outdoor living area. There is no truth in the oft-heard idea that the foliage fan must face a certain point of the compass.

HABITAT: Madagascar; in Florida, planted as a lawn specimen in warm locations.

LIGHT REQUIREMENT: Full sun for best growth, but small plants in pots may be shaded for a time.

SOIL REQUIREMENT: Fertile soil, high in organic matter is best.

SALT TOLERANCE: Not tolerant of dune conditions.

AVAILABILITY: Most nurseries on the lower peninsula offer plants.

CULTURE: In locations protected from frost, plant in fertile earth; water carefully; fertilize several times during growing weather.

PROPAGATION: Seedage or division.

PESTS: *Cercospora* leaf-spot is a very serious disease.

99
Heliconia

Heliconia (hell-i-CONE-ee-a): For Mt. Helicon.
SPP.: several species and variants are cultured in Florida.

FAMILY: Musaceae. RELATIVES: Banana and travelers-tree.
TYPE OF PLANT: Herbaceous perennial. HEIGHT: Variable. ZONE: S
HOW TO IDENTIFY: Plants resemble slender or dwarf bananas and produce inflorescences with highly decorative bracts. The plants, their foliage, and their bracts are variable with the species or the variety.
HABIT OF GROWTH: Upright, banana-like.
FOLIAGE: Banana-like and highly decorative.
FLOWERS: Inconspicuous, held within various kinds of highly colored, very beautiful bracts, for which these plants are cultivated.
FRUITS: Blue capsules which break into berry-like parts.
SEASON OF MAXIMUM COLOR: Spring and summer when bracts develop color.
LANDSCAPE USES: For the beautiful, colorful bracts, heliconias are in high favor in frostless locations. While these inflorescences are usually cut for indoor decoration, if left in place they become sure-fire conversation starters.
HABITAT: Tropical America; in Florida not very widely cultured.
LIGHT REQUIREMENT: Full sun or partial shade.
SOIL REQUIREMENT: Fertile, moist soil makes for best growth and flowering.
SALT TOLERANCE: Quite tolerant of salt air back of the first dune.
AVAILABILITY: Retail sales lots offer heliconias in containers.
CULTURE: Plant, water, and continuously protect the foliage against *Cercospora* and *Helminthosporum* leaf-spots. Fertilize once during each summer month.
PROPAGATION: Division of matted clumps.
PESTS: *Cercospora* and *Helminthosporum* leaf-spots, scales, and nematodes.
NOTE: Shown above are some Florida favorites. Common names are many—wild plantain, balisier, flowering banana, and lobster-claw are some of those most frequently heard.

100
Bird-of-Paradise Flower

Strelitzia (strel-IT-zee-a): for the wife of King George III.
reginae (ree-JINE-ee): of the queen.

FAMILY: Musaceae. **RELATIVES:** Banana and travelers-tree.
TYPE OF PLANT: Herbaceous perennial. **HEIGHT:** 4'. **ZONE:** C,S

HOW TO IDENTIFY: Two-ranked evergreen foliage with channeled, erect, succulent petioles which support the waxy blades that are 6" x 18"; spectacular bird-like blossoms atop long scapes as tall as, or taller than, the foliage mound.

HABIT OF GROWTH: Clump-forming, trunkless, herbaceous perennial.

FOLIAGE: Evergreen, waxy, bold in form and dark green in color.

FLOWERS: Spectacular orange-and-blue floral parts emerge from horizontal, boat-shaped bracts atop vertical, leafless scapes.

FRUITS: Three-angled capsules that split to release seeds that are edible.

SEASON OF MAXIMUM COLOR: Whenever flowers are produced.

LANDSCAPE USES: For the curiosity of the flying birds, strelitzia is much admired. In planters or in front of evergreen shrubbery, clumps may stand with 3' between individuals. Improved strains produce birds which fly well above the foliage. Bird-of-paradise flower does not always bloom as freely as it does in California.

HABITAT: South Africa; in Florida, sparingly cultured in gardens.

LIGHT REQUIREMENT: In Florida, high shade is recommended during part of the day.

SOIL REQUIREMENT: Rich, moisture-retentive, acid soil is recommended.

SALT TOLERANCE: Not tolerant.

AVAILABILITY: Nurseries on the peninsula offer plants in containers.

CULTURE: Plant in well-prepared sites; water faithfully; protect from cold and scale insects.

PROPAGATION: Seedage or division.

PESTS: Scales.

NOTE: *Strelitzia nicolai*, to 20' in height, with palm-like trunk and leaves, resembles an untidy travelers-tree. In this, the larger, more hardy strelitzia, the spathe is reddish, the sepals white, the tongue blue.

101
Pine Cone-Lily

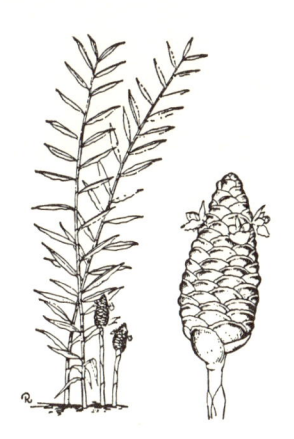

Zingiber (ZIN-gy-burr): classical name.
zerumbet (zur-RUM-bet): aboriginal name.

FAMILY: Zingiberaceae.
RELATIVES: Ginger and shell-flower.
TYPE OF PLANT: Herbaceous perennial.
HEIGHT: 4'. **ZONE**: N,C,S
HOW TO IDENTIFY: Leafy stems of ginger-like foliage are sent up in springtime, to be followed in the autumn by short bracted inflorescences which resemble pine cones. These flower heads, which become bright red at maturity, are much admired for indoor decoration.
HABIT OF GROWTH: Leaning, heavily foliated stems form strong clumps.
FOLIAGE: Alternate, long, narrow leaves like ginger foliage are held almost horizontally by the 4' stems. Plants die down during short days of autumn.
FLOWERS: Bracted heads form red, pine cone-like bodies on short stems after the rainy season.
FRUITS: Capsules.
SEASON OF MAXIMUM COLOR: Fall and winter when bracted heads develop red coloration.
LANDSCAPE USES: Because they are so popular for indoor arrangements, Floridians cultivate pine cone-lilies as separate plantings in the out-of-door living area or the service area. During the cold months there is nothing above ground.
HABITAT: South Sea Islands.
LIGHT REQUIREMENT: Full sun or shifting, broken shade.
SOIL REQUIREMENT: Fertile, moist soil makes for best growth and flowering.
SALT TOLERANCE: Tolerant of salt air back from the beach.
AVAILABILITY: Retail nurseries throughout the state sell pine cone-lilies.
CULTURE: Plant rootstocks in springtime just below the surface of the earth; water moderately; fertilize lightly once during each summer month.
PROPAGATION: Division of matted clumps.
PESTS: Mites.
NOTE: Variegated ginger (*Zingiber zerumbet* 'Darceyi') is admired for its glistening white-and-green foliage. It can be grown in herbaceous borders and as a pot plant.

102
Torch-Ginger

Phaeomeria (fee-o-ME-ree-a): Greek for dark and part.
speciosa (spee-see-OH-sa): showy.

FAMILY: Zingiberaceae. RELATIVES: Ginger-lily and shell-flower.

TYPE OF PLANT: Herbaceous perennial. HEIGHT: 12'. ZONE: N,C,S

HOW TO IDENTIFY: One of the most vigorous plants in its family, torch-ginger will form huge clumps of tall, heavily foliated stems under good conditions. Spectacular reddish flower heads stand terminally on separate yard-tall, leafless scapes.

HABIT OF GROWTH: Dense, close clumps are formed by leafy stems.

FOLIAGE: Evergreen, lush, and attractive.

FLOWERS: Spectacular reddish or pinkish heads of waxy bracts terminate separate, one-flowered, leafless scapes.

FRUITS: Berries massed together somewhat resembling small pineapples.

SEASON OF MAXIMUM COLOR: Autumn, when flowers expand.

LANDSCAPE USES: For the lush, tropical effect of the vigorous foliage and the very handsome, waxy inflorescences, torch-ginger enjoys popularity in warm sections of the state. Bold clumps standing by bodies of water are striking.

HABITAT: South Sea Islands.

LIGHT REQUIREMENT: Partial shade is recommended.

SOIL REQUIREMENT: Rich, acid, moist soil is needed for best growth.

SALT TOLERANCE: Tolerant of mild salt air back from the strand.

AVAILABILITY: Most retail nurseries in warm areas sell torch-ginger plants in containers.

CULTURE: Plant divisions of old matted clumps in springtime; water until established; after that, little care is needed. Fertilize once at the beginning of the rainy season.

PROPAGATION: Division of old clumps; seedage.

PESTS: Mites, nematodes on light sandy soils.

NOTE: Formerly in *Amomum*, torch-ginger is now in the genus *Phaeomeria*.

103
Shell-Flower

Alpinia (al-PIN-ee-a): for P. Alpinus, early Italian botanist.
SPP.: several species and clones are seen in Florida.

FAMILY: Zingiberaceae.   RELATIVES: Ginger and pine cone-lily.
TYPE OF PLANT: Herbaceous perennial. HEIGHT: Variable. ZONE: N,C,S
HOW TO IDENTIFY: Bold clumps of heavily foliated stems come up from vigorous rootstocks. The persistent leaves may measure a foot in length by half this width. In *Alpinia*, flowers are borne at stem-ends, not on separate peduncles near the earth.
HABIT OF GROWTH: Dense, graceful, compact clumps are formed by leafy stems.
FOLIAGE: Persistent, bright, deep green. Some cultivars are variegated.
FLOWERS: Shell-like, fragrant, in drooping clusters at stem-ends.
FRUITS: Capsules.
SEASON OF MAXIMUM COLOR: Summer and autumn, as flowers open.
LANDSCAPE USES: For the lush effect of the huge clumps and the interest of the attractive warm-weather blossoms, shell-flowers have long been Florida favorites. In warm locations, stems will persist; in cold sections, they will be cut to earth each winter, but new shoots will appear with the spring.
HABITAT: South Sea islands.
LIGHT REQUIREMENT: Full sun or high, shifting shade.
SOIL REQUIREMENT: Fertile, moist soil makes for best growth.
SALT TOLERANCE: Somewhat salt tolerant, but not for dune plantings.
AVAILABILITY: Nurseries in warmer parts of the state stock shell-flowers in containers.
CULTURE: Plant rootstocks in springtime just below the surface of the earth; water periodically until established; and fertilize once at the beginning of the summer rainy season.
PROPAGATION: Division of matted clumps.
PESTS: Mites, yet these pests are usually not of major concern.
NOTE: Most popular shell-flower is *Alpinia speciosa*, above right. Its clone 'Vittata' has foliage attractively splotched with white. At the lower left is depicted *A. mutica* which produces small erect spikes of attractive open flowers that are followed by persistent, felty, red fruits. The top sketch illustrates red-ginger, *Alpinia purpurata,* which is distinguished by vivid, terminal clusters of red bracts which subtend tiny white flowers.

Ginger-Lily

Hedychium (he-DICK-ee-um): Greek for sweet snow, referring to the flowers. SPP.: several species and hybrids grow in Florida.

FAMILY: Zingiberaceae. RELATIVES: Ginger and shell-flower.
TYPE OF PLANT: Herbaceous perennial. HEIGHT: 6'. ZONE: N,C,S
HOW TO IDENTIFY: This genus produces heavy clumps of leafy stems from strong rhizomes, and terminal inflorescences. In *Hedychium* the fragrant, long-tubed flowers have large, flaring lips. White in the most popular species, yellow or pinkish blooms are borne by lesser-known kinds.
HABIT OF GROWTH: Heavily foliated stout stems form huge clumps.
FOLIAGE: Evergreen, alternate, 24" x 6", held attractively by man-high stems. Ginger-lily foliage is killed in northern Florida, but may persist in warmer sections.
FLOWERS: Fragrant, long-tubed flowers with lobed lips extend from terminal, bracted heads.
FRUITS: Capsules which split to reveal red seeds.
SEASON OF MAXIMUM COLOR: Warm months when blossoms are out.
LANDSCAPE USES: In common with other gingerworts, hedychiums have long been popular with Floridians for the beauty of the lush foliage and for the interesting inflorescences. Clumps can form parts of herbaceous borders, or they may stand near bodies of water. Travelers to Hawaii have seen leis made of these attractive, scented blossoms.
HABITAT: Eastern Asia.
LIGHT REQUIREMENT: Full sun or broken, shifting shade.
SOIL REQUIREMENT: Fertile, moist soil makes for best growth and flowering.
SALT TOLERANCE: Tolerant of salt air back of the first-line dunes.
AVAILABILITY: Nurseries sell ginger-lilies in cans.
CULTURE: In springtime, plant rootstocks just below the surface of the earth; water moderately; and fertilize once at the beginning of each rainy season.
PROPAGATION: Division of matted clumps.
PESTS: Mites, possibly nematodes in light, open, sandy soils.
NOTE: Most widely grown ginger-lily is white-flowered *Hedychium coronarium*, illustrated above. *H. flavum* has yellow blooms, and *H. gardnerianum* has light yellow blossoms. There are hybrids among these species.

105
Spiral-Flag

Costus (cost-us): old classical name.
spp.: perhaps a half dozen species may be found in Florida gardens.

FAMILY: Zingiberaceae.   RELATIVES: Shell-flower and torch-ginger.
TYPE OF PLANT: Herbaceous perennial. HEIGHT: Variable. ZONE: N,C,S
HOW TO IDENTIFY: Large, lush leaves are spirally arranged around stems that arise from underground rootstocks. Terminating these may appear bracted, cone-like inflorescences, from which emerge colorful flowers in season.
HABIT OF GROWTH: Sprawling to form huge mounds by spiral-leaved stems.
FOLIAGE: Evergreen, abundant, spirally arranged; the tone of green varies with the species.
FLOWERS: Conspicuous, colorful, in terminal positions, arising from cone-like, bracted heads.
FRUITS: Seeds may form between bracts.
SEASON OF MAXIMUM COLOR: Warm months when blossoms appear.
LANDSCAPE USES: For the interest of the spirally arranged foliage and the cone-like flower heads, spiral-flags are rather widely planted in Florida. Clumps may stand in moist locations near watercourses, or they may be featured against masonry walls if the soil there is rich and retentive of moisture.
HABITAT: Tropics of both hemispheres.
LIGHT REQUIREMENT: Full sun or high, shifting shade.
SOIL REQUIREMENT: Fertile, moist soil makes for best growth; therefore spiral-flags are often planted near water.
SALT TOLERANCE: Tolerant of conditions back of the front-line dunes.
AVAILABILITY: Spiral-flags are staple items in retail nurseries.
CULTURE: Plant rootstocks or offsets in springtime; water moderately until established; fertilize once at the beginning of the rainy season; and keep grasses back from the root zone.
PROPAGATION: Division of matted clumps, separation of offsets that form below flower heads, and cuttage of stems.
PESTS: Mites, possibly nematodes in light, open, sandy soils.
NOTE: Of the hundred or more species recorded, no more than a half dozen are likely to be seen in Florida. *Costus speciosus* (left-hand sketch) has foot-long green leaves that are downy beneath. The 10-foot stems are topped by bracted cones from which appear white, papery flowers. *Costus igneus* (right-hand sketch), orange-spiral-flag, grows a foot in height, and bears 6″ leaves that are purple beneath.

Calathea

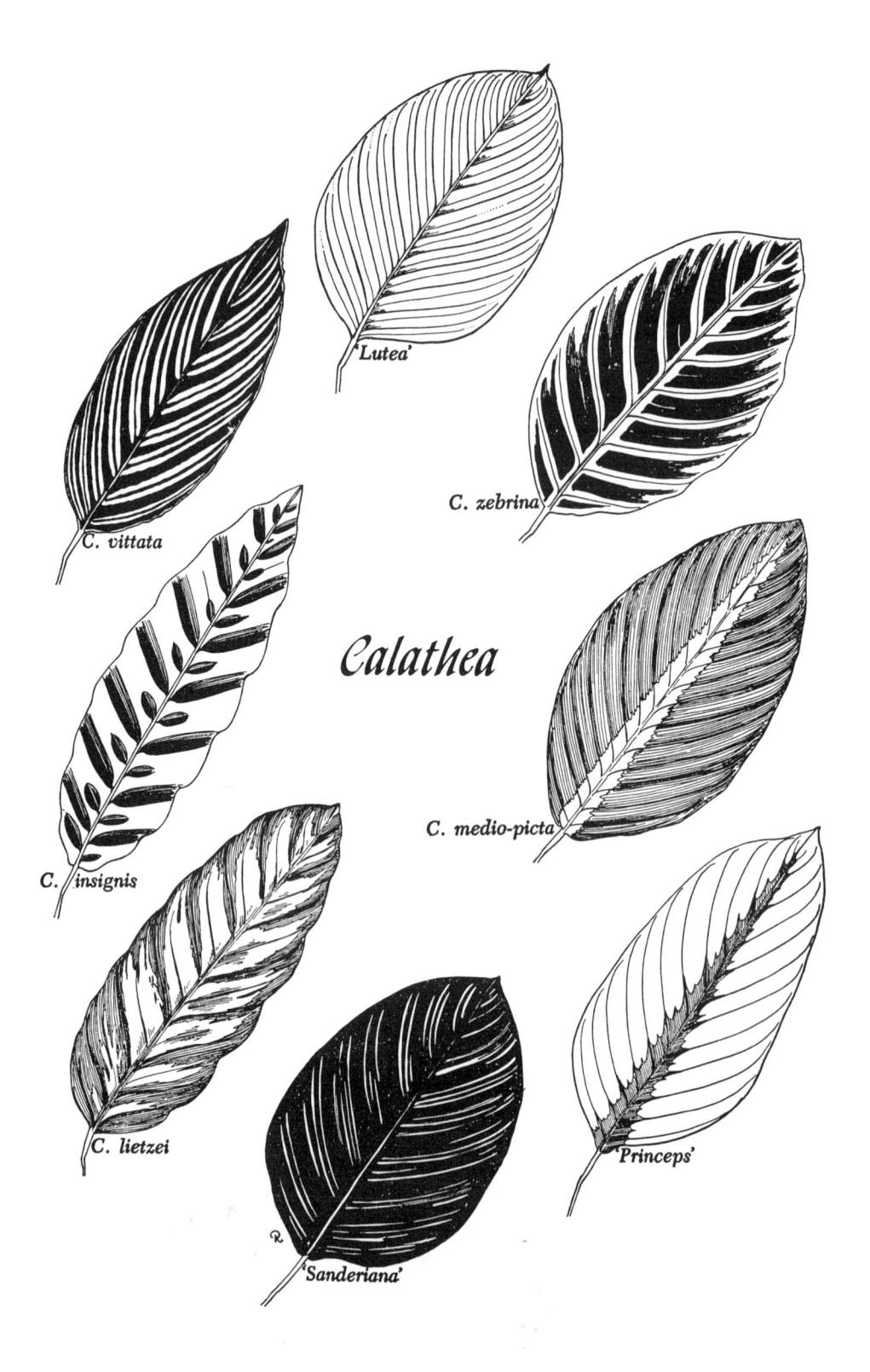

- C. vittata
- 'Lutea'
- C. zebrina
- C. insignis
- C. medio-picta
- C. lietzei
- 'Sanderiana'
- 'Princeps'

107
Calathea

Calathea (cal-a-THE-a): Greek for basket, referring to the setting of the flowers. SPP.: many kinds are cultured in our state.

FAMILY: Marantaceae.

RELATIVES: Arrowroot and thalia.

TYPE OF PLANT: Herbaceous perennial.   HEIGHT: Variable. ZONE: S

HOW TO IDENTIFY: Sheathing leaves noted for their appealing markings grow during warm, moist months to delight gardeners. To distinguish varieties and species, and to be certain that a plant in question is a calathea and not a maranta, is a most difficult assignment.

HABIT OF GROWTH: Mottled leaves are held gracefully by wiry stems.

FOLIAGE: Very appealing, because of the beautiful patterns of lines, blotches, and spots.

FLOWERS: Little spikes, not particularly showy.

FRUITS: Little berries or capsules.

SEASON OF MAXIMUM COLOR: Spring when new foliage comes out.

LANDSCAPE USES: As pot plants, these are very popular because of their attractively marked foliage. Protection from cold is essential.

HABITAT: Tropical America.

LIGHT REQUIREMENT: Reduced light is optimum, bright sunlight is not recommended.

SOIL REQUIREMENT: Rich, moisture-retentive, but fast-draining soil is needed for good growth and bright coloration.

SALT TOLERANCE: Not tolerant of ocean-front conditions.

AVAILABILITY: Nurseries sell calatheas in pots.

CULTURE: Plant at the same level as the plant grew formerly, in a pot that has an abundance of coarse material in the bottom to assure good drainage and aeration. Supply high humidity and high temperature continuously, and light fertilization once in each summer month.

PROPAGATION: Division.

PESTS: Mites.

NOTE: Above is *C. vandenheckei* 'Wendlinger'; illustrated on the opposite page are some of Florida's most popular calatheas. Clear-cut distinction between these many kinds is hard to define. All of these are called marantas in Florida.

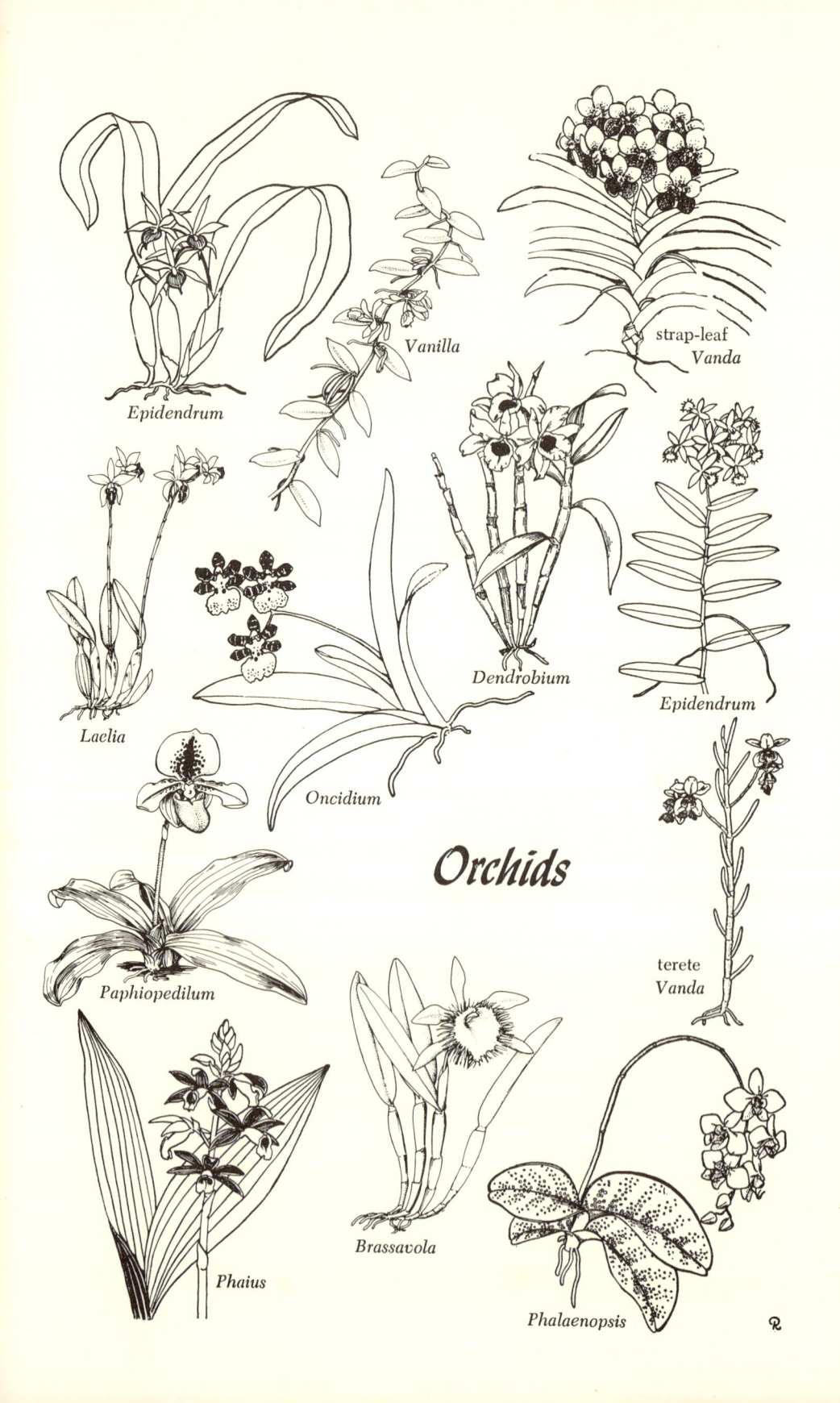

Epidendrum

Vanilla

strap-leaf *Vanda*

Laelia

Oncidium

Dendrobium

Epidendrum

Paphiopedilum

Orchids

terete *Vanda*

Phaius

Brassavola

Phalaenopsis

109 Epiphytic Orchid

1. *Cattleya* (CAT-lee-a): for W. Cattley, English horticulturist.
2. *Dendrobium* (den-DRO-bee-um): Greek for tree and life.
3. *Epidendrum* (ep-ee-DEN-drum): Greek for on trees.
4. *Oncidium* (on-SID-ee-um): Greek for tubercle, for lobed labellum.
5. *Phalaenopsis* (fal-ee-NOP-sis): Greek for moth-like.
    SPP.: many kinds are seen in Florida.

FAMILY: Orchidaceae.   RELATIVES: The orchids.
TYPE OF PLANT: Epiphytic perennial.   HEIGHT: Variable. ZONE: S
HOW TO IDENTIFY: Tree-dwelling perennials that produce white, velamen-coated roots that lodge in bark crevasses. Plants often have pseudobulbs, usually with green leaves.
FOLIAGE: Usually green, persistent, but there are many exceptions.
FLOWERS: Extremely variable, some minute, others large and spectacular, the most wanted blossoms in the plant kingdom.
FRUITS: Angled pods that may contain millions of dust-like seeds.
SEASON OF MAXIMUM COLOR: Usually springtime, but some epiphytic orchids may be found in flower every month in the year.
LANDSCAPE USES: To add interest to lawn trees, epiphytic orchids are wired to branches of trees in nearly frost-free locations. In colder sections, pot culture in greenhouses is standard.
HABITAT: Tropics of both hemispheres.
LIGHT REQUIREMENT: Light, shifting shade is acceptable; dense shade is unsuitable.
SOIL REQUIREMENT: Osmundine, shredded tree fern, or chipped bark from lumber trees can be used to pot epiphytic orchids.
SALT TOLERANCE: Not tolerant.
AVAILABILITY: Orchid nurseries, garden centers, and chain stores sell epiphytic orchids.
CULTURE: Secure landscape epiphytes to branches of rough-barked yard trees with copper wire; pot greenhouse epiphytes after flowering, in one of the media listed above. Soak weekly, syringe lightly each day, tie new growths to wire stake.
PROPAGATION: Division and seedage.
PESTS: Scales, mites, and fungus diseases.

110 Terrestrial Orchid

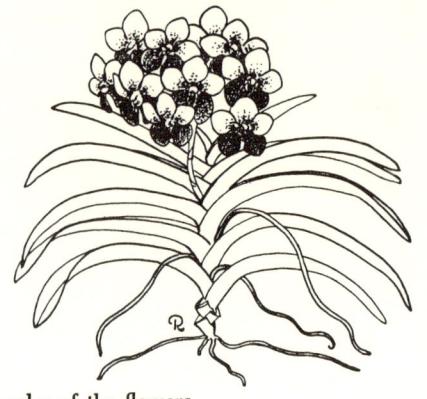

Phaius (FAY-us): Greek for swarthy, for the color of the flowers.
Vanda (VAN-da): Sanskrit name.
and numerous other genera.
SPP.: many kinds are seen in Florida.

FAMILY: Orchidaceae.

RELATIVES: The orchids.

TYPE OF PLANT: Terrestrial perennial.

HEIGHT: Variable. ZONE: S

HOW TO IDENTIFY: Positive identification depends upon flowers, as the plants are so variable.

HABIT OF GROWTH: Extremely variable.

FOLIAGE: Extremely variable, evergreen or deciduous.

FLOWERS: True orchids in many sizes and colors.

FRUITS: Angled capsules that may contain myriads of tiny seeds.

SEASON OF MAXIMUM COLOR: Usually springtime, yet terrestrial orchids may flower at other seasons.

LANDSCAPE USES: For the curiosity of orchids as garden flowers, earth-dwellers can form color highlights in frost-free gardens. In cooler sections of Florida these plants are grown in containers in greenhouses.

HABITAT: Tropics of both hemispheres.

LIGHT REQUIREMENT: Variable; some demand full sun, others thrive in partial shade, none grow well in deep shade.

SOIL REQUIREMENT: Open, friable, gritty, reasonably fertile, fast-draining soils are needed.

SALT TOLERANCE: Not tolerant.

AVAILABILITY: Terrestrial types are for sale in all orchid nurseries.

CULTURE: Plant carefully, slightly deeper than formerly, water during periods of drought, apply dilute, liquid fertilizer once during each summer month. Furnish wooden trellises for vining types to cling to.

PROPAGATION: Cuttage by pieces of stem, or division of clump-growers.

PESTS: Scales.

111
Australian-Pine

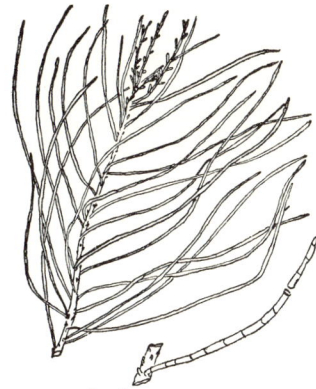

Casuarina (cas-you-are-EYE-na): with branches like cassawary feathers.
equisetifolia (eck-we-seat-ee-FOL-ee-a): with leaves like the horsetail.

FAMILY: Casuarinaceae. RELATIVES: The genus is alone in its family.
TYPE OF PLANT: Tree. HEIGHT: 60′. ZONE: S
HOW TO IDENTIFY: Horsetail-like branch tips, green, leafless; cones very short-stalked, globular, ½″ in diameter. This species self-seeds but does *not* sucker at the roots.
HABIT OF GROWTH: Spire-like, with open crown; seedlings make huge cultures.
FOLIAGE: Absent; branch texture very fine, of dark green color.
FLOWERS: Inconspicuous.
FRUITS: Brown cones, very short-stalked, globular, ½″ in diameter.
SEASON OF MAXIMUM COLOR: No variation.
LANDSCAPE USES: For clipped hedges and topiary near the sea nothing surpasses this species. For windbreaks and roadside trees, Australian-pines are much used. They serve notably to help hold sand and build keys in southern Florida.
HABITAT: Australia; in Florida, warmest locations, often at seaside.
LIGHT REQUIREMENT: Full sun or shady situations.
SOIL REQUIREMENT: Most soils seem to be entirely adequate.
SALT TOLERANCE: Most tolerant of salt, grows on front-line dunes.
AVAILABILITY: Canned trees are stocked by most nurseries in southern Florida.
CULTURE: Plant in a prepared site; water until established; thereafter prune rigorously to keep within size desired.
PROPAGATION: Seedage. *C. lepidophloia* may be grafted upon *C. equisetifolia*, thus making sucker-free plants.
PESTS: Mushroom root-rot.
NOTE: *C. cunninghamiana*, the hardiest species, has upright, spire-like habit, dense green foliage, and brown cones 1″ in diameter.
   C. lepidophloia forms countless suckers to encompass large plots of ground. This one does not produce fruits in Florida, and it is *not* tolerant of salt.

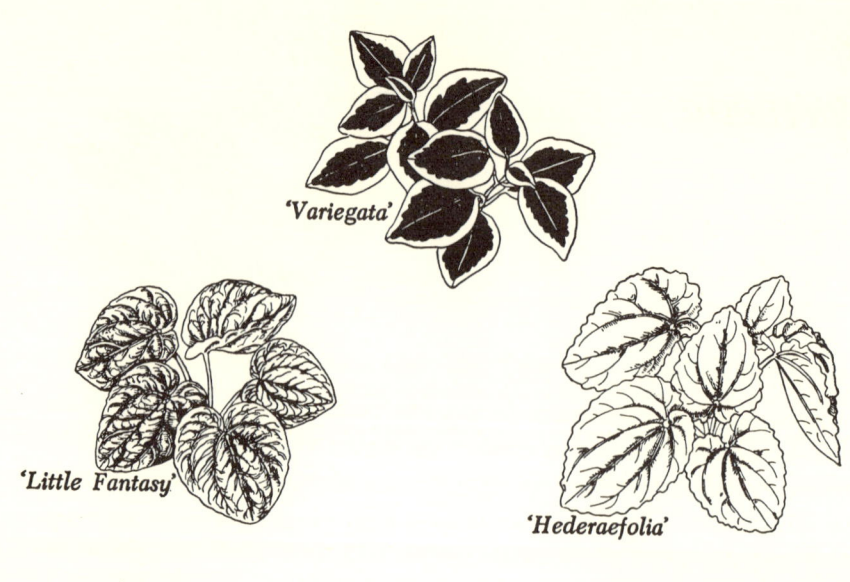

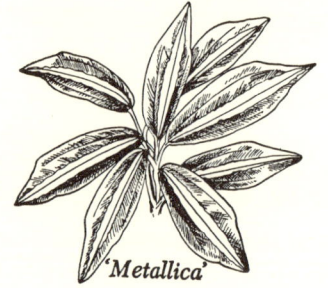

Peperomia

'Variegata'

'Little Fantasy'

'Hederaefolia'

'Metallica'

'Bicolor'

P. nivalis

'Tricolor'

'Argyreia'

113
Peperomia

Peperomia (pep-er-oh-me-a): pepper-like.
spp.: many kinds are seen in Florida.

FAMILY: Piperaceae.
RELATIVE: Pepper of commerce.
TYPE OF PLANT: Herbaceous perennial.
HEIGHT: Variable. ZONE: S

HOW TO IDENTIFY: Small, succulent, clump-growing perennials send up decorative leaves of many shapes, sizes, and colors and little spikes of inconspicuous flowers.

HABIT OF GROWTH: Diminutive clump-grower.

FOLIAGE: Evergreen, succulent, diverse in size, shape, and color.

FLOWERS: Little spikes of inconspicuous flowers.

FRUITS: Little, thin-coated berries.

SEASON OF MAXIMUM COLOR: Possibly when new growth first emerges.

LANDSCAPE USES: Long favorite pot plants, latterly popular as ground cover for shady, frostless spots and for planters, peperomias are to be found in many households. They are frequently planted in pockets in rockery-water-features in home landscapes.

HABITAT: Tropical America.

LIGHT REQUIREMENT: Shaded locations are right for peperomias.

SOIL REQUIREMENT: Rich, fibrous, quick-draining soil is best.

SALT TOLERANCE: Not tolerant.

AVAILABILITY: Peps in containers are offered in chain stores and retail sales lots.

CULTURE: After potting in soil described above, keep humidity very high by frequently syringing with very light mist.

PROPAGATION: Cuttage and division.

PESTS: Mites, leaf-spots, and rots.

NOTE: To visit Florida nurseries and garden centers and to study the 7 pages devoted to the genus in *Exotica* is to realize that the cultivars are many, the naming not necessarily consistent. Shown above and across are some of Florida's favorite peps.

114 Southern Wax-Myrtle

Myrica (mir-EE-ca): Greek for the tamarisk.
cerifera (sir-IF-era): wax-bearing.

FAMILY: Myricacae.   RELATIVES: Northern bayberry and sweet gale.

TYPE OF PLANT: Large shrub or small tree.   HEIGHT: 25'.   ZONE: N,C,S

HOW TO IDENTIFY: Aromatic leaves are coarsely serrate toward their tips, rusty-glandular on both sides; waxy-gray-green fruits are borne by some individuals.

HABIT OF GROWTH: Clump-forming by stolons; picturesque shapes are often seen.

FOLIAGE: Semievergreen, alternate, medium in texture, variable in color.

FLOWERS: Inconspicuous, unisexual; there are pistillate and staminate plants.

FRUITS: Grayish-green, waxy drupes are borne by pistillate plants.

SEASON OF MAXIMUM COLOR: Possible when fruits color in autumn.

LANDSCAPE USES: For enclosure (5' o.c.) no native shrub is more appreciated. Wax-myrtle becomes too open below for clipped hedges, too large for foundation plantings. As a small specimen tree, wax-myrtle can be a good selection.

HABITAT: Ubiquitous in every county in Florida.

LIGHT REQUIREMENT: Full sun or partial shade.

SOIL REQUIREMENT: Wet swamplands or dry locations on high ground.

SALT TOLERANCE: Tolerant of salt air and saline soils.

AVAILABILITY: Usually not a nursery item, native clumps are dug as needed after permission has been granted by the property owner.

CULTURE: Cut branches back to 10" stubs and dig clumps with generous mats of roots. Water and forget.

PROPAGATION: Transplant wild clumps with permission of the property owner.

PESTS: Caterpillars tie terminal leaves, cankers may form on old branches.

115
Laurel Oak

Quercus (KWARE-cuss): ancient Latin name.
laurifolia (law-rye-FOL-ee-a): laurel-leaved.

FAMILY: Fagaceae.   RELATIVES: The beeches and the chestnuts.

TYPE OF PLANT: Tree.   HEIGHT: 100'.   ZONE: N,C,S

HOW TO IDENTIFY: A fast-growing tree that bears alternate, thin smooth leaves that are shining on both sides; round acorns that mature the second year and are enclosed for ¼ or less of their height in thin, saucer-like cups.

HABIT OF GROWTH: Upright tree that is taller than broad, with round head.

FOLIAGE: Deciduous or partially evergreen, alternate, medium fine in texture.

FLOWERS: Inconspicuous, in catkins near the branch-tips.

FRUITS: Round acorns, maturing the second year, are enclosed ¼-way in flattish cups.

SEASON OF MAXIMUM COLOR: No variation.

LANDSCAPE USES: Laurel oak grows rapidly, reaches senility and begins to break up near the half-century mark. For occasional planting on home grounds where fast growth is required and short life is no disadvantage, this native might be indicated. However, ultimate size is great and cost of removal may be considerable. Laurel oak is not recommended for municipal planting because of its comparatively short life.

HABITAT: Moist soil north of the Everglades.

LIGHT REQUIREMENT: Sun or shade; mature specimens require much space in full sun.

SOIL REQUIREMENT: Widely tolerant of the many varying soils found in Florida.

SALT TOLERANCE: Not tolerant.

AVAILABILITY: Most nurseries would dig young laurel oak trees on order.

CULTURE: No special care is needed after properly planted young trees become established.

PROPAGATION: Seedage.

PESTS: Mushroom root-rot.

116
Live Oak

Quercus (KWARE-cuss): ancient Latin name.
virginiana (vir-gin-ee-AY-na): Virginian.

FAMILY: Fagaceae.   RELATIVES: The beeches and the chestnuts.
TYPE OF PLANT: Tree.   HEIGHT: 60'. ZONE: N,C,S
HOW TO IDENTIFY: Noble tree with wide-spreading horizontal branches covered with deeply corrugated, light gray bark; evergreen alternate leaves that are thick, shining green above, downy beneath with revolute edges. The acorns, which mature the first season, are nearly black, elliptical, enclosed for ⅓ their length in top-shaped cups.
HABIT OF GROWTH: Wide-spreading, horizontal branches from short, buttressed trunks which often assume picturesque shapes, allow branch-tips to bend down to the earth.
FOLIAGE: Evergreen, medium fine in texture, dark green above, lighter beneath.
FLOWERS: Inconspicuous, in catkins near the branch-tips.
FRUITS: Elliptical black acorns, enclosed ⅓ their length in deep cups.
SEASON OF MAXIMUM COLOR: No variation.
LANDSCAPE USES: Live oak is Florida's shade tree par excellence. As an avenue tree it has the highest rating; set individuals 90' apart. The life of live oak trees is measured in centuries; stability in high winds is widely recognized; the picturesque forms are greatly admired.
HABITAT: Hammocks and lake margins in every county in Florida.
LIGHT REQUIREMENT: Shade or sun; for maximum development, allow great space in full sun.
SOIL REQUIREMENT: Moist soil of good fertility.
SALT TOLERANCE: Very tolerant of salt and alkaline soil.
AVAILABILITY: Good, small live oak trees are not readily available. Small native seedlings might be dug on order.
CULTURE: Plant carefully in well-prepared planting sites; wrap trunks; water faithfully; fertilize twice a year; remove moss periodically.
PROPAGATION: Seedage.
PESTS: Mushroom root-rot.
NOTE: Twin live oak, *Q. virginiana,* 'Geminata' grows on sandy soil, is more upright in habit, has thick revolute leaves and acorns growing as twins.

117
Aluminum-Plant

Pilea (pie-lee-a): Latin for felt cap, for the fruit cover.
cadierei (cad-year-eye): for M. Cadiere.

FAMILY: Urticaceae.   RELATIVES: Artillery-plant and panamigo.

TYPE OF PLANT: Herbaceous perennial.   HEIGHT: 8". ZONE: C,S

HOW TO IDENTIFY: The quilted and puckered leaves marked with silver bands are sure identification.

HABIT OF GROWTH: Mat-forming to cover the earth in shady locations.

FOLIAGE: Evergreen, puckered, lined with silver-colored bands.

FLOWERS: Inconspicuous, in little spikes.

FRUITS: Tiny pods.

SEASON OF MAXIMUM COLOR: Early spring when new growth appears.

LANDSCAPE USES: In shaded rock-'n'-sand gardens and indoor planters and pots, aluminum-plant is extremely popular.

HABITAT: Tropical regions.

LIGHT REQUIREMENT: Tolerant of considerable shade; sunlight is unsuitable.

SOIL REQUIREMENT: Rich fibrous, fast-draining soil is best.

SALT TOLERANCE: Tolerant of salt drift back from the strand.

AVAILABILITY: Almost all nurseries have small plants for sale.

CULTURE: Plant sections of stems in pots, planters, or pockets of the soil mentioned above and maintain high humidity by frequent syringing with light mist.

PROPAGATION: Cuttage and division.

PESTS: Mites.

Dwarf Elm

Ulmus (ULM-us): ancient Latin name for the elm.
pumila (PEW-mill-a): dwarf.

FAMILY: Ulmaceae.

RELATIVES: The elm trees.

TYPE OF PLANT: Tree.

HEIGHT: 25'. ZONE: N,C

HOW TO IDENTIFY: Very rapid, upright growth; deciduous or semievergreen foliage with unequal bases, almost simply serrate, pubescent in axils of veins beneath.

HABIT OF GROWTH: Strongly upright, rapid growth.

FOLIAGE: Deciduous or semievergreen, of fine texture and medium green color.

FLOWERS: Inconspicuous catkins in early spring, if present.

FRUITS: Small winged fruit, called samara, if present.

SEASON OF MAXIMUM COLOR: Possibly autumn, when leaves turn yellow.

LANDSCAPE USES: For a very fast-growing tree, this little elm is popular. It is not recommended for permanent street use, however, because of rapid growth and possible short life.

HABITAT: Siberia; in Florida, rather widely planted in the northern section.

LIGHT REQUIREMENT: Full sun.

SOIL REQUIREMENT: Any soil seems to be adequate.

SALT TOLERANCE: Not recommended for dune planting.

AVAILABILITY: Nurseries in central and northern Florida offer this elm.

CULTURE: Plant with reasonable care; water until established; fertilize once each winter while young.

PROPAGATION: Seedage by means of imported seeds; cuttage, as well.

PESTS: Mites.

NOTE: There may be confusion with Chinese elm (*Ulmus parvifolia*), which is inclined to have a more weeping habit and smaller leaves. This one may be sold as evergreen elm or weeping evergreen elm in south-central Florida nurseries.

119
Creeping Fig

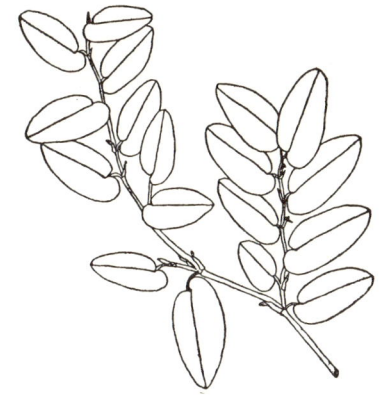

Ficus (FYE-cuss): ancient Latin name for the fig.
pumila (PEW-mill-a): dwarf.

FAMILY: Moraceae. RELATIVES: The fig trees, mulberry, and hops.

TYPE OF PLANT: Vine. HEIGHT: Variable. ZONE: N,C,S

HOW TO IDENTIFY: Vigorous vine that clings by tenacious, aerial rootlets, yields milky sap when wounded, and produces large, green figs on stiff, horizontal fruiting branches at maturity.

HABIT OF GROWTH: Vining, with excessively rapid growth on most vertical surfaces.

FOLIAGE: Evergreen, fine texture on vertical shoots, coarse foliage on horizontal branches; the color is usually dark green or medium green.

FLOWERS: Absent.

FRUITS: Green figs the size and shape of hens' eggs, on mature, horizontal branches.

SEASON OF MAXIMUM COLOR: Spring, when new growth is reddish.

LANDSCAPE USES: To soften masonry walls, plant 5'-10' o.c. Do not plant this vine unless time can be devoted to pruning to regulate size, and do not plant near wooden structures.

HABITAT: Eastern Asia; in Florida, ubiquitous in landscape plantings.

LIGHT REQUIREMENT: Not critical, most light intensities are acceptable.

SOIL REQUIREMENT: Not critical, most soils are acceptable.

SALT TOLERANCE: Not critical, endures conditions back of the dunes.

AVAILABILITY: Fig vines in containers are occasionally offered in sales lots.

CULTURE: Creeping fig grows so vigorously, that containing the root system in a deep, bottomless container in the earth is recommended. Periodic clipping is essential to keep the vine within bounds.

PROPAGATION: Simple layerage or cuttage.

PESTS: None of major concern.

NOTE: Variety 'Minima' has very small leaves held by slender twigs. *Ficus radicans* has oblong-lanceolate leaves 2" long. Its variegated form is popular for hanging baskets and planter bins.

F. rubiginosa 'Variegata'

F. religiosa

F. altissima

F. elastica 'Doescheri'

F. elastica 'Decora'

Ficus

F. vogelii

F. lyrata

121
Large-Leaf Ficus

Ficus (FYE-cuss): ancient Latin name for the fig.
SPP.: several species and a number of cultivars grow in Florida.

FAMILY: Moraceae.   RELATIVES: Mulberry and cecropia.
TYPE OF PLANT: Tree.   HEIGHT: 50'-120'. ZONE: S
HOW TO IDENTIFY: Milky sap exudes when bark is broken, most species send down aerial roots which become multiple trunks to form huge, spreading trees.
HABIT OF GROWTH: Widely sprawling with aerial roots, multiple trunks.
FOLIAGE: Evergreen, as much as a foot long, bold in aspect.
FLOWERS: Absent.
FRUITS: Figs of various sizes, shapes, and colors.
SEASON OF MAXIMUM COLOR: When figs ripen.
LANDSCAPE USES: Because of their huge sizes, they are useful in public plantings. In homes they are grown in urns.
HABITAT: World tropics; in Florida, warmest locations.
LIGHT REQUIREMENT: Full sun or broken shade.
SOIL REQUIREMENT: Tolerant of many soil conditions.
SALT TOLERANCE: Not tolerant of dune conditions.
AVAILABILITY: Most nurseries in southern Florida sell tropical fig trees.
CULTURE: Plant with a little organic matter around the root ball, water, and forget. For container culture, select a soil mixture that is not excessively fertile, always water with moderation in an attempt to control growth.
PROPAGATION: Cuttage or marcottage.
PESTS: Scales.
NOTE: Depicted across are leaves of *Ficus* planted in hot countries.
Ficus lyrata, fiddle-leaf fig (lower right), has evergreen leaves 15" long shaped like violins.
F. vogelii (lower left) holds pubescent foliage almost horizontally.
F. elastica 'Doescheri' has leaves marbled with yellow.
F. religiosa, bo tree (upper left), has long-pointed, heart-shaped leaves that hang downward from long flexible petioles.
F. rubiginosa 'Variegata' (top) has downy leaves 4" long, with short, obtuse apices.
F. altissima, lofty fig (upper right), has glossy foliage with white veins. The two lowest veins form a distinct V.
F. elastica 'Decora' (right center) produces broad reddish leaves that are quite brilliant while young.

122 Benjamin Fig

Ficus (FYE-cuss): ancient Latin name for the fig.
benjamina (ben-jah-MINE-a): refers, incorrectly, to this as a benzoin source.

FAMILY: Moraceae.   **RELATIVES:** The fig trees, mulberry, and hops.
TYPE OF PLANT: Tree.   **HEIGHT:** 50'. **ZONE:** S
HOW TO IDENTIFY: Weeping habit, no aerial roots in the usual Florida forms; evergreen leaves resistant to thrips, tiny figs becoming deep red.
HABIT OF GROWTH: Weeping branches drape gracefully from a very symmetrical, dense head; aerial roots are lacking in the usual forms seen in Florida.
FOLIAGE: Evergreen, alternate, thrips-resistant, of fine texture.
FLOWERS: Lacking.
FRUITS: Red figs ⅓" in diameter, in sessile, axillary pairs.
SEASON OF MAXIMUM COLOR: Summer when figs color.
LANDSCAPE USES: As a street tree (set 35'-50' o.c.) benjamin fig is very popular in southern Florida. The beautiful weeping habit, resistance to foliar thrips, and freedom from aerial roots, make for its excellence as an avenue tree. There are several selections in this excellent species, the outstanding one being 'Exotica.'
HABITAT: India; in Florida, very widely planted in frost-free areas.
LIGHT REQUIREMENT: Full sun or broken shade.
SOIL REQUIREMENT: Any soil seems to be suitable.
SALT TOLERANCE: Not tolerant of dune conditions, but grows back of the strand.
AVAILABILITY: Nurseries in southern Florida sell small trees in containers and B & B.
CULTURE: Water during periods of drought; keep lawn grasses back; fertilize annually while young. In maturity, pruning should be all the care that is required.
PROPAGATION: Cuttage and marcottage of very large branches.
PESTS: Scales.
NOTE: Cuban-laurel (*Ficus retusa*, 'Nitida') is very widely grown in southern Florida as a clipped hedge or sheared specimen shrub. This upright-growing, robust tree has upright habit, aerial roots emerging from trunk and branches, and foliage that is almost always malformed by the feeding of thrips.

123
Cecropia

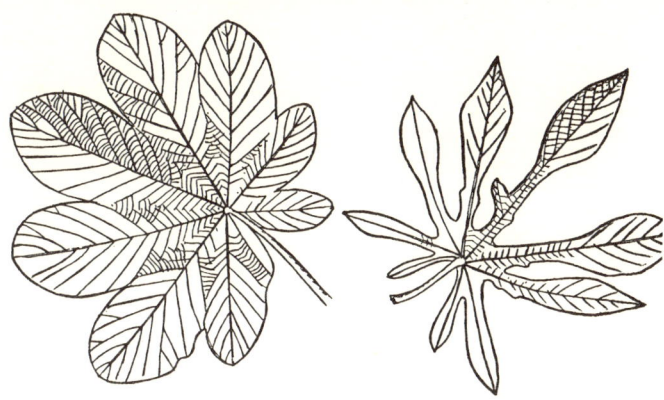

Cecropia (see-CROW-pea-a): Greek, refers to use of wood in wind instruments. *palmata* (pal-MAY-ta): divided in a hand-like fashion.

FAMILY: Moraceae.   RELATIVES: Mulberry and ficus trees.

TYPE OF PLANT: Tree.   HEIGHT: 50′. ZONE: S

HOW TO IDENTIFY: Slender trunk with smooth bark, open branching; huge palmate leaves (right-hand sketch) with white under surfaces clustered at the ends of branches, cut to middle or below.

HABIT OF GROWTH: Tall, ungainly, open.

FOLIAGE: Evergreen, palmate, of most interesting form, dark green above, white beneath.

FLOWERS: Inconspicuous catkins.

FRUITS: Pencil-like pods to 6″ long.

SEASON OF MAXIMUM COLOR: No variation.

LANDSCAPE USES: The curled-inward dried cecropia foliage is useful in dry arrangements. The tree may stand free as a horticultural curiosity on large grounds in nearly frostless locations.

HABITAT: Tropical America; in Florida, most nearly frost-free areas.

LIGHT REQUIREMENT: Broken shade of wooded areas.

SOIL REQUIREMENT: Fertile soil above average in quality.

SALT TOLERANCE: Not tolerant of seaside conditions.

AVAILABILITY: Specialty nurseries in warmest parts may stock small cecropia trees.

CULTURE: Plant with great care in warmest location; water faithfully; keep lawn grasses from encroaching; fertilize annually.

PROPAGATION: Seedage and/or cuttage.

PESTS: Ants inhabit hollow branches, but apparently do no damage.

NOTE: *Cecropia peltata* (left-hand sketch) has foot-broad leaves divided only ⅓ of the distance to the center, with petiole attached near the center, and with fruits about 3″ long. Cecropia trees are killed by frost.

124
Silk-Oak

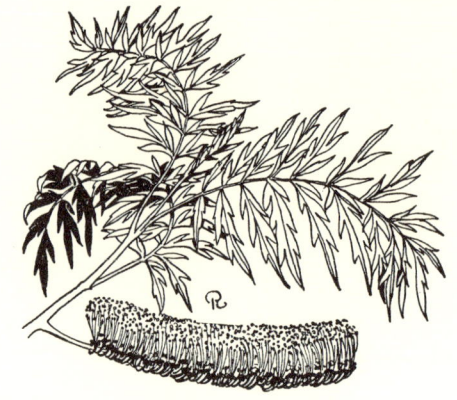

Grevillea (gray-VILL-ee-a): for C. Greville, a patron of botany in England.
robusta (roe-BUS-ta): strong.

FAMILY: Proteaceae.　　RELATIVES: Queensland nut and silver-tree.

TYPE OF PLANT: Tree.　　　　　　　　HEIGHT: 75'. ZONE: C,S

HOW TO IDENTIFY: Evergreen dissected leaves, gray-green in color; young branches covered with gray hairs; showy orange blossoms in springtime.

HABIT OF GROWTH: Robustly upright with compact head, and thick trunk.

FOLIAGE: Evergreen, fern-like, of fine texture and gray-green color.

FLOWERS: Showy, orange, in short (4") racemes on old wood.

FRUITS: Broad, assymetrical follicles, about ¾" long.

SEASON OF MAXIMUM COLOR: Springtime.

LANDSCAPE USES: Silk-oak is such a huge tree that there are few places in modern residential arrangements that it will serve. For large municipal developments, within its climatic range, silk-oak may be indicated where rapid growth and great size are acceptable. The trees may stand 50'-60' o.c.

HABITAT: Australia; in Florida, sandy soils of the warmer counties.

LIGHT REQUIREMENT: Full sun for best flowering.

SOIL REQUIREMENT: Open sands of central and southern Florida.

SALT TOLERANCE: Not tolerant.

AVAILABILITY: Most nurseries sell small silk-oak trees in containers.

CULTURE: Within its climatic range, silk-oak grows rapidly without special care.

PROPAGATION: Seedage.

PESTS: Caterpillars and mushroom root-rot.

NOTE: Clones with special characteristics have been selected, but these are not widely grown in Florida.

125
Banks Grevillea

Grevillea (gray-VILL-ee-a): for C. Greville, English patron of botany.
banksii (BANKS-ee-eye): for J. Banks, English patron of horticulture.

FAMILY: Proteaceae.   **RELATIVES:** Queensland nut and Australian silk-oak.

TYPE OF PLANT: Tree or large shrub.   **HEIGHT:** 20'.   **ZONE:** S

HOW TO IDENTIFY: Small tree with evergreen, pinnate leaves that have revolute margins and are silky beneath; terminal red blossoms in 4" spikes.

HABIT OF GROWTH: Shrubby little tree.

FOLIAGE: Evergreen, fern-like, of fine texture and gray-green color.

FLOWERS: Red, in dense, erect, terminal spikes in springtime.

FRUITS: Shaggy little capsules less than 1" long.

SEASON OF MAXIMUM COLOR: Spring, when red flowers are out.

LANDSCAPE USES: As a source of red in a shrubbery border, or as a little yard tree, Banks grevillea serves. It may grow as an urn subject as well. Banks grevillea is much preferred to its huge relative, the silk-oak, because it does not grow so large. This plant may not be completely successful everywhere in Florida, but gardeners in moderately warm locations should try Banks grevillea.

HABITAT: Queensland; in Florida, sparingly cultured in warmest parts.

LIGHT REQUIREMENT: Partial shade of high tree tops.

SOIL REQUIREMENT: Fertile, well-drained soil that is free of nematodes.

SALT TOLERANCE: Not tolerant.

AVAILABILITY: Specialty nurseries may have small trees in containers.

CULTURE: Plant carefully in soil that has been made free of nematodes; water carefully; fertilize three times each year; mulch the root zone; keep lawn grasses hoed back.

PROPAGATION: Seedage or cuttage.

PESTS: Borers, scales, mites, and nematodes.

126
Coral-Vine

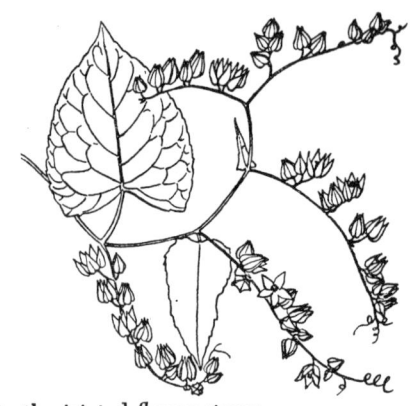

Antigonon (an-TIG-o-non): Greek, referring to the jointed flower stems.
leptopus (LEP-to-pus): slender-stalked.

FAMILY: Polygonaceae.   **RELATIVES:** Sea-grape and pigeon-plum.

TYPE OF PLANT: Herbaceous vine.   **HEIGHT:** Variable.   **ZONE:** N,C,S

HOW TO IDENTIFY: This is a tendril-climbing, tender, herbaceous vine with heart-shaped leaves. Showy pink or white flowers are produced during late summer and autumn. Frost cuts coral-vine to the earth.

HABIT OF GROWTH: Climbing by tendrils.

FOLIAGE: Evergreen, heart-shaped, coarse in texture, and light green in color.

FLOWERS: Slender racemes of bright pink, or white, flowers in late summer and autumn.

FRUITS: Three-angled, pointed pods.

SEASON OF MAXIMUM COLOR: Late summer and fall.

LANDSCAPE USES: To veil a fence, pergola, or arbor, coral-vine has long been the choice of many southern homeowners. Where frosts occur, it cannot produce a permanent effect, yet the seasonal flowers are most attractive.

HABITAT: Tropical America; in Florida, ubiquitous.

LIGHT REQUIREMENT: Full sun for best flowering.

SOIL REQUIREMENT: Most soils are suitable.

SALT TOLERANCE: Not tolerant.

AVAILABILITY: Coral-vine is a popular home-gardening plant that is usually given away by people who have old vines; seldom does it appear in nurseries.

CULTURE: Plant with reasonable care; water for a month or so if there is no rain. During the winter, cut the canes back to the ground.

PROPAGATION: Seedage. Volunteer seedlings abound under old vines.

PESTS: Caterpillars chew holes in the leaves.

127
Ribbon-Bush

Homalocladium (hoe-mal-oh-CLAY-dee-um): Greek for leaf-like branches.
platycladum (platty-CLAY-dum): wide-branched.

FAMILY: Polygonaceae.   RELATIVES: Coral-vine and sea-grape.

TYPE OF PLANT: Shrub.   HEIGHT: 4'. ZONE: C,S

HOW TO IDENTIFY: One of the distinctive plants of tropical horticulture, this woody shrub bears branches that are flat, jointed, ribbon-like. Leaves may be absent entirely, or restricted to young, sterile shoots.

HABIT OF GROWTH: Scraggly, loose assemblage of many slender, drooping branches.

FOLIAGE: Absent, or if temporarily present on young shoots, lanceolate, lobed at bases, about 2" long.

FLOWERS: In small clusters at joints in the flattened branches.

FRUITS: Purplish, berry-like, ridged, if present.

SEASON OF MAXIMUM COLOR: Best color is summer green.

LANDSCAPE USES: For the unique, ribbon-form branches, this plant is sometimes included in homeground arrangements. It may appear as a member of a shrubbery border, or as a conversation-piece in an urn on a terrace.

HABITAT: Solomon Islands.

LIGHT REQUIREMENT: High, shifting shade is excellent.

SOIL REQUIREMENT: Moderately fertile, moist, well-drained soil is acceptable.

SALT TOLERANCE: Not tolerant of dune conditions.

AVAILABILITY: Ribbon-bush is occasionally seen in Florida nurseries.

CULTURE: Ordinary care as a pot-plant or as a shrub in frost-free gardens should make for success with ribbon-bush.

PROPAGATION: Cuttage.

PESTS: Scales and nematodes.

128
Sea-Grape

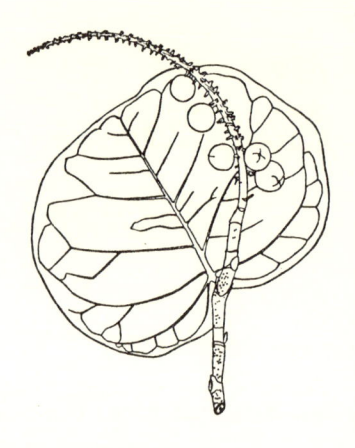

Coccoloba (coco-LOBE-a): Greek for lobed berry.
uvifera (oo-VIFF-er-a): grape-bearing.

FAMILY: Polygonaceae.   RELATIVES: Coral-vine and pigeon-plum.
TYPE OF PLANT: Tree or shrub, depending upon training.
HEIGHT: 25'. ZONE: S

HOW TO IDENTIFY: Evergreen leaves, almost circular in outline, 8" in diameter, red-veined; purple grapes hang in long bunches during warm months.
HABIT OF GROWTH: Low-spreading to form dense shrub clumps, or small trees.
FOLIAGE: Evergreen, almost circular, coarse in texture. Mature leaves have red veins and turn completely red before they fall; young foliage is a beautiful bronze.
FLOWERS: Inconspicuous ivory blossoms in foot-long racemes.
FRUITS: Purple grapes ¾" in diameter, which are excellent for jelly.
SEASON OF MAXIMUM COLOR: Warm months when grapes ripen.
LANDSCAPE USES: No tropical plant is more dramatic than sea-grape, none better for seashore landscape. Use as a terrace tree or as a part of an enclosing border (set 7'-10' o.c.). Because of its coarse texture and large size, sea-grape is not best for foundation plantings for small homes, but it is in high favor for use with large buildings in tropical settings. There is a clone with strikingly variegated leaves.
HABITAT: Sea beaches in tropical America, including southern Florida.
LIGHT REQUIREMENT: Intense light of ocean front is optimum.
SOIL REQUIREMENT: Beach sand.
SALT TOLERANCE: Most tolerant of salt; widely used on the ocean front.
AVAILABILITY: Nurseries in southern Florida feature sea-grapes.
CULTURE: Plant in moderately rich sites; water faithfully until well established; thereafter, prune to control shape.
PROPAGATION: Seedage.
PESTS: Pith borer.
NOTE: Pigeon-plum (*C. laurifolia*), also native in southern Florida, becomes a tree 40' in height. The evergreen leaves are oval, 4" long; the purple fruits are smaller than those of sea-grape. This is a most beautiful and desirable landscape tree for seaside locations.

129
Big-Leaf Sea-Grape

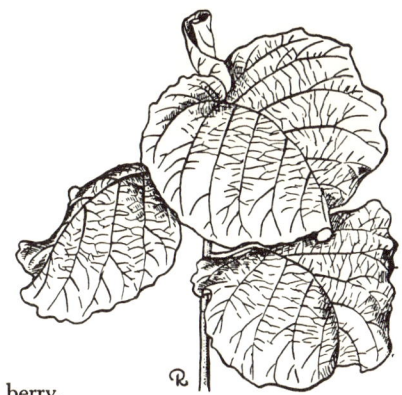

Coccoloba (co-co-LOBE-a): Greek for lobed berry.
grandifolia (grand-i-FOL-ee-a): large-leaved.

FAMILY: Polygonaceae.   RELATIVES: Coral-vine and native sea-grape.

TYPE OF PLANT: Tree.   HEIGHT: Variable. ZONE: S

HOW TO IDENTIFY: The largest (yard-broad) disc-form leaves of any woody plant in Florida horticulture make it easy to identify this tropical exotic.

HABIT OF GROWTH: Stout, upward-thrusting trunks, sometimes with little branching, hold the huge, circular leaves.

FOLIAGE: Yard-broad, disc-shaped, puckered, with prominent veins, rolled-down edges, and rusty pubescence below.

FLOWERS: Small, greenish, in erect, terminal spikes when present on mature trees.

FRUITS: Berry-like, if present.

SEASON OF MAXIMUM COLOR: Little seasonal variation.

LANDSCAPE USES: For the striking king-size leaves, this tropical relative of buckwheat is cultivated as a freestanding specimen. Certain to evoke comment, it can be grown as a tubbed individual, or as a point of emphasis in a border of tropical shrubbery.

HABITAT: Tropical America.

LIGHT REQUIREMENT: High, light, shifting shade is quite suitable.

SOIL REQUIREMENT: Gritty, open, moderately fertile, well-drained soil is best.

SALT TOLERANCE: Locations just back of front-line dunes are acceptable.

AVAILABILITY: Landscape nurseries in extreme southern Florida might stock big-leaf sea-grapes.

CULTURE: Do not overwater or overfeed, lest big-leaf sea-grape grow too rapidly.

PROPAGATION: Marcottage or cuttage of large-leaved, juvenile individuals.

PESTS: Mealy-bugs, mites, scales, and pith-borers.

130
Blood-Leaf

Iresine (eye-ree-SIGN-ee): Greek, alluding to woolly flowers and seeds.
lindenii (lin-DEN-ee-eye): for J. Linden, Belgian horticulturist.

FAMILY: Amaranthaceae. RELATIVES: Amaranth and cocks-comb.

TYPE OF PLANT: Herbaceous perennial. HEIGHT: 3'. ZONE: C,S

HOW TO IDENTIFY: Blood-red opposite leaves about 2½" long are produced in great profusion, to give a very compact habit. Little, round, chaffy heads of flowers, greenish to straw-colored, are produced during much of the year.

HABIT OF GROWTH: Slender, upright, yet forming dense mounds of red.

FOLIAGE: Opposite, blood-red, 2½" long, acuminate.

FLOWERS: Prominent, chaffy, or woolly little bracted heads on long peduncles.

FRUITS: Little woolly 1-seeded fruits.

SEASON OF MAXIMUM COLOR: Summer.

LANDSCAPE USES: For a mound of glowing red in full sun, blood-leaf is popular. As a pot plant in very light shade, it serves as well.

HABITAT: Tropical America.

LIGHT REQUIREMENT: Full sun for best color and compact habit.

SOIL REQUIREMENT: Sandy soil of open character is suitable.

SALT TOLERANCE: Tolerant of salt drift back from the shore.

AVAILABILITY: Nurseries in southern Florida offer blood-leaf in containers.

CULTURE: In a sunny spot, plant as a garden perennial after danger of frost has passed. Pinch out terminal buds for best compact habit. Blood-leaf thrives in light, sandy soil despite presence of nematodes.

PROPAGATION: Cuttage.

PESTS: Mites.

NOTE: The botany of this section of the amaranth family is in need of definitive study.

131
Bougainvillea

Bougainvillea (boo-gain-vil-ee-a): for M. de Bougainville, the French navigator. spp.: two species are widely grown in Florida.

Family: Nyctaginaceae.   **Relatives:** Four-o'clock and sand-verbena.
Type of Plant: Vine.   **Height:** Variable. **Zone:** C,S
How to Identify: Long, thorny canes with alternate, heart-shaped leaves and flowers enclosed by conspicuous, highly colored bracts during the cool months.
Habit of Growth: Sprawling by far-reaching canes. Support is usually provided.
Foliage: Evergreen, of medium texture and medium green color.
Flowers: Small, tubular, enclosed by large, showy, highly colored bracts.
Fruits: Inconspicuous, little ribbed pods.
Season of Maximum Color: Winter and spring when this becomes Florida's favorite vine.
Landscape Uses: Bougainvillea sprawling over a masonry wall is a sight long to be remembered. Plant every 10'. Trained beside and across doorways, the vine is very popular, and it is sometimes used to veil wire fences.

   Most clear-colored, wanted varieties come from *B. spectabilis,* great bougainvillea. Hardier, cosmopolitan, purple bougainvillea is in *B. glabra.* This one is sometimes trained as a tree.
   In northern Florida, bougainvilleas freeze to the ground almost every winter.

Habitat: Brazil; in Florida, widely planted in central and southern areas.
Light Requirement: Full sun for best flowering.
Soil Requirement: Tolerant of various soils, but may develop chlorosis on calcareous earth.
Salt Tolerance: Endures salt air back from the front-line dunes.
Availability: Nurseries on the peninsula have bougainvilleas in containers.
Culture: Plant in carefully made sites of fertile, acid medium in full sun; attend to watering carefully; spray for leaf-chewers and keep lawn grasses off the roots. Fertilize lightly about three times each year.
Propagation: Cuttage.
Pests: Caterpillars and mineral deficiencies on lime-bearing soils.

132
Hottentot-Fig

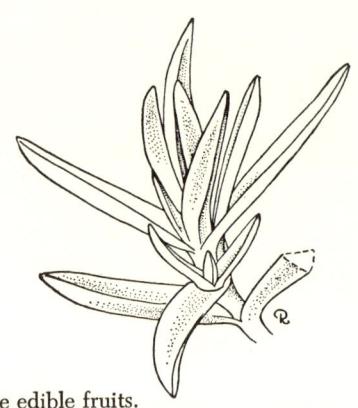

Carpobrotus (car-poe-BRO-tus): in reference to the edible fruits.
edulis (ed-YOU-lis): edible.

FAMILY: Aizoaceae.

RELATIVES: Ice-plant and stoneface.

TYPE OF PLANT: Perennial.

HEIGHT: 6″. ZONE: C,S

HOW TO IDENTIFY: Stems, which become woody, creep for great distances along the earth and bear 4″ triangular leaves in clusters. Usually in Florida this plant is seen in seaside gardens.

HABIT OF GROWTH: Wide-spreading branches form a mat as they run across the earth.

FOLIAGE: Evergreen, succulent, triangular; keels finely serrate growing in little bunches along the prostrate stems.

FLOWERS: Yellow to rose-purple, 3″ across, bright, and glistening.

FRUITS: Large and edible, if present.

SEASON OF MAXIMUM COLOR: Summer when flowers are out.

LANDSCAPE USES: For covering sandy expanses, especially at the seashore, Hottentot-fig is extremely popular in Florida, as it is in California. An outstanding demonstration of this use in the Sunshine State is at Marineland. For sunny planter-bins, this African succulent is also very useful.

HABITAT: South Africa.

LIGHT REQUIREMENT: Full sun of tropical and subtropical strands.

SOIL REQUIREMENT: Sandy, fast draining soil of low or moderate fertility is optimum.

SALT TOLERANCE: Very tolerant of salt, recommended for ocean-front planting.

AVAILABILITY: Garden centers and nurseries may supply plants.

CULTURE: Plant sections of stem in open, sandy soil; water moderately until established; then forget.

PROPAGATION: Cuttage and division.

PESTS: A fungous disease attacks Hottentot-figs under some conditions.

NOTE: Taxonomy of the Aizoaceae, which includes many succulent, ground-cover-type plants for sandy locations, is imperfectly understood, and confusion may be the rule.

133
Wintergreen Barberry

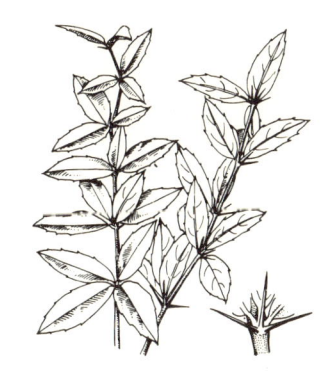

Berberis (bur-bur-is): ancient Arabic name.
julianae (jewel-ee-ann-ee): for Mrs. Julia Schneider.

FAMILY: Berberidaceae. RELATIVES: Nandina and holly-grape.
TYPE OF PLANT: Shrub. HEIGHT: 6′. ZONE: N

HOW TO IDENTIFY: A shrub which bears 3″, spiny-toothed leaves and 3-parted spines. Bright yellow inner bark is revealed when outer bark is broken.

HABIT OF GROWTH: Dense, by many stems, under good conditions.

FOLIAGE: Evergreen, alternate, of medium texture, dark green color.

FLOWERS: Yellow, ¼″ across, in groups of about 15.

FRUITS: Black berries, about ⅓″ across contain 1 seed each.

SEASON OF MAXIMUM COLOR: When blossoms are out and fruits color.

LANDSCAPE USES: For foundation plantings in extreme northern Florida, set plants 18″ o.c. North-side locations are satisfactory. Under high pine shade, wintergreen barberry can be used for low hedges. Set the plants 18″ o.c.

HABITAT: China; in Florida, superior soils of the panhandle.

LIGHT REQUIREMENT: Full sun on superior soils, or part-shade from high pines.

SOIL REQUIREMENT: Clay-loam soils support the best plants.

SALT TOLERANCE: Tolerant of light salt drift back from the Gulf shore.

AVAILABILITY: Nurseries in northwestern Florida offer plants in containers.

CULTURE: Plant in heavy soil; water with moderation; fertilize twice annually while young. On the upper peninsula, plant only in heavy soil either on north-side locations or close to pine trunks. Always mulch barberry plants for best growth.

PROPAGATION: Cuttage.

PESTS: Nematodes and mites.

NOTE: Japanese barberry (*Berberis thunbergii*), especially the red-leaved clone, 'Atropurpurea,' behaves well on heavy soil in western Florida, and can be employed where a fine-scale, slow-growing plant is needed in foundation arrangements. Red-leaved barberry looks nice growing by white masonry.

Nandina

Nandina (nan-DEAN-a): Japanese name.
domestica (dough-MES-tee-ca): domesticated.

FAMILY: Berberidaceae.   **RELATIVES:** Barberry and mahonia.
TYPE OF PLANT: Shrub.   **HEIGHT:** 8′. **ZONE:** N

HOW TO IDENTIFY: Many, nonbranching, ringed stems with lacy, compound leaves atop; panicles of white blossoms in springtime followed by bright red berries in winter.

HABIT OF GROWTH: Stiffly upright, unbranching, to give stilt-like effect.

FOLIAGE: Deciduous, alternate, 2- to 3-compound, lacy, to give very fine texture. The summer color is medium green and the fall color is red.

FLOWERS: Small, white, in long terminal panicles.

FRUITS: Berries, ¼″ in diameter, bright red by cool weather.

SEASON OF MAXIMUM COLOR: Autumn after fruits color.

LANDSCAPE USES: Singly, or in groups of three against pine trunks, nandina looks best. As a facer shrub against larger shrubs, allow 3′ between plants. Groups of 3 nandinas at the backs of planters may serve to give interest against masonry walls. Here, the plants can be set 18″ o.c. This Japanese shrub does so much better in western Florida than it does on the sandy soil of the peninsula, that it is highly recommended for the former area, not endorsed for the latter.

HABITAT: Eastern Asia; in Florida, superior soil of upper counties.

LIGHT REQUIREMENT: Tolerant of shady locations, endures full sun on heavy soils.

SOIL REQUIREMENT: Superior soils of the panhandle are best for nandina.

SALT TOLERANCE: Not tolerant.

AVAILABILITY: Small plants in gallon cans and larger plants B&B are offered by nurseries in northern Florida.

CULTURE: On good soil, culture is easy, no special procedures are needed.

PROPAGATION: Seedage and division.

PESTS: Mites, scales, and mushroom root-rot.

135 Cocculus

Cocculus (COCK-you-lus): Greek for small berry.
laurifolius (laur-ee-FOL-ee-us): laurel-leaved.

FAMILY: Menispermaceae. **RELATIVE:** Moonseed.

TYPE OF PLANT: Shrub or small tree. **HEIGHT:** 25′. **ZONE:** N,C,S

HOW TO IDENTIFY: Declinate, round, green branches that hold alternate, evergreen leaves with 3 prominent veins. Little racemes of tiny blossoms appear in April-May.

HABIT OF GROWTH: Weeping, or clambering if supports are available.

FOLIAGE: Evergreen, alternate, coarse in texture, dark green in color.

FLOWERS: Inconspicuous, in axillary racemes, in April-May.

FRUITS: Subglobose drupes $1/8''$ in diameter, when present.

SEASON OF MAXIMUM COLOR: Little seasonal variation.

LANDSCAPE USES: As a part of a shrubbery border or as a foundation plant for a very large building, set 5′ apart. Cocculus is an excellent shrub that deserves wider use when its large size and coarse texture will not be disadvantageous. Plants will freeze to the ground some winters in unprotected north-Florida locations.

HABITAT: Himalayan region; in Florida, warmer parts of the peninsula.

LIGHT REQUIREMENT: Full sun or partial shade.

SOIL REQUIREMENT: Soils of many types are acceptable.

SALT TOLERANCE: Not tolerant of salt wind.

AVAILABILITY: Container-grown plants are in many nurseries in warmer parts.

CULTURE: After cocculus is growing well in moderately fertile soil, little care will be required other than regular pruning.

PROPAGATION: Standard or leaf-bud cuttings under mist in springtime.

PESTS: Scales.

Starry Magnolia

Magnolia (mag-NO-lee-a): for P. Magnol, an early French botanist.
stellata (stel-ATE-a): starry.

FAMILY: Magnoliaceae.

RELATIVES: The magnolias and banana-shrub.

TYPE OF PLANT: Large shrub or small tree.   HEIGHT: 25'.   ZONE: N

HOW TO IDENTIFY: Robust shrub or small, many-stemmed tree, with showy white blossoms in wintertime that have petals and sepals alike. The foliage is deciduous, and all leaves, buds, and new twigs are densely pubescent.

HABIT OF GROWTH: Open, upright-branching large shrub or small tree.

FOLIAGE: Deciduous, alternate, of coarse texture and medium green color.

FLOWERS: Showy, white, 3" across, sepals and petals alike, 12 or more in number, 2" in length, outward-flaring. There are clones with all-pink flowers.

FRUITS: Cone-like burs that are usually few-seeded in Florida.

SEASON OF MAXIMUM COLOR: January-February when blossoms are out.

LANDSCAPE USES: Known for its outstanding beauty in late winter, starry magnolia is the best of the Oriental species for Florida. Though the white form is the one most often sold here, there are other clones that should be used in landscaping. One with pink flowers is especially nice. Starry magnolia may be a freestanding specimen or a member of a shrubbery border.

HABITAT: Japan; in Florida, better soils of northern counties.

LIGHT REQUIREMENT: Full sun or shifting shade from tall pine trees.

SOIL REQUIREMENT: Fertile, acid, well-drained soils.

SALT TOLERANCE: Not tolerant.

AVAILABILITY: Starry magnolia is not widely offered by retail nurseries.

CULTURE: Plant in fertile, well-drained spot; water periodically until well established; mulch the root zone; fertilize once each year while young.

PROPAGATION: Cuttage.

PESTS: Scales and nematodes.

137
Saucer Magnolia

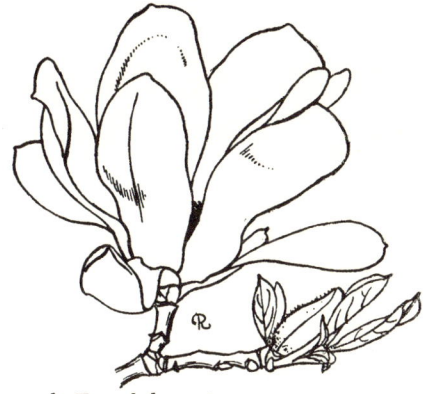

Magnolia (mag-NO-lee-a): for P. Magnol, an early French botanist.
liliflora (lily-FLOR-a): with flowers like a lily.
'Soulangeana' (soo-lon-gee-ANE-a): for the originator, Soulange-Bodin.

FAMILY: Magnoliaceae.   RELATIVES: The magnolias and banana-shrub.
TYPE OF PLANT: Shrub in Florida.   HEIGHT: 15'. ZONE: N
HOW TO IDENTIFY: Shrubby growth, deciduous, alternate leaves that emerge from furry buds; showy tulip-like blossoms in late winter from fur-coated buds; the sepals, usually purplish or pinkish outside, are ½ as long as the petals.
HABIT OF GROWTH: Shrubby, upright-branching.
FOLIAGE: Deciduous, alternate, very coarse in texture, medium green in color.
FLOWERS: Showy, upward-pointing, bell-like, purplish or pinkish outside, white inside, with little fragrance.
FRUITS: Cone-like, 4-inch burs that are usually few-seeded in Florida.
SEASON OF MAXIMUM COLOR: January, when flowers unfurl.
LANDSCAPE USES: As a freestanding specimen, saucer magnolia is a long-time favorite. It may be set into a shrubbery border to lend seasonal color interest, as well.

This group of plants does best in the northwestern section of the state, and is not generally recommended for the peninsula. The tendency is for the blossoms to appear a few at a time during the warm winter weather rather than to make a great burst of color as they do farther north where lower winter temperatures keep the plants dormant until spring.
HABITAT: Gardens of the temperate zone; in Florida, upper tier of counties.
LIGHT REQUIREMENT: Full sun or high, shifting pine shade.
SOIL REQUIREMENT: Superior, well-drained soils of upper counties.
SALT TOLERANCE: Not tolerant.
AVAILABILITY: Saucer magnolias are not widely offered in Florida.
CULTURE: In northwestern Florida, plant with care in fertile, well-drained spot; water until established, then during periods of drought; fertilize once each winter while young.
PROPAGATION: Cuttage or graftage.
PESTS: Scales, nematodes, and mushroom root-rot.

138 Magnolia

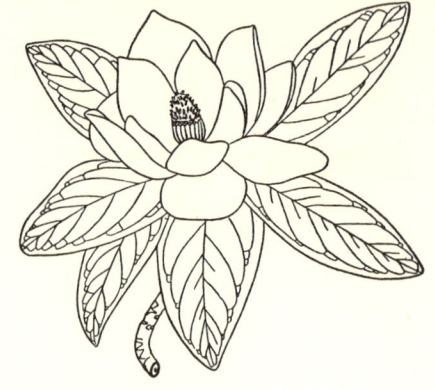

Magnolia (mag-no-lee-a): for P. Magnol, an early French botanist.
grandiflora (gran-da-flor-a): large-flowered.

FAMILY: Magnoliaceae.

RELATIVES: The magnolias and banana-shrub.

TYPE OF PLANT: Tree.

HEIGHT: 75'. ZONE: N,C

HOW TO IDENTIFY: Huge, stiff, evergreen leaves that are shining, dark green above and brown-tomentose or light green below; huge, waxy, white, fragrant blossoms in springtime.

HABIT OF GROWTH: Upright, often with straight central leader and compact head.

FOLIAGE: Evergreen, alternate, bold in outline, dark, shining green in color.

FLOWERS: Huge, white, waxy fragrant blossoms in springtime.

FRUITS: Cone-like 4-inch burs that split to reveal showy scarlet seeds.

SEASON OF MAXIMUM COLOR: Spring, when blossoms unfurl.

LANDSCAPE USES: As a street tree (50'-60' o.c.), magnolia is superb; as a freestanding specimen, framing tree, or shade tree in home-ground developments it is a long-time favorite. Grouped informally on broad highway rights-of-way, this native tree is one of great distinction. Some seedlings have leaves that are attractively coated with brown tomentum on their lower surfaces.

HABITAT: Hammocks of central and northern Florida.

LIGHT REQUIREMENT: Full sun for best habit and flowering.

SOIL REQUIREMENT: Fertile hammock soil for best growth and flowering.

SALT TOLERANCE: Quite tolerant of salt drift and dune sand.

AVAILABILITY: Nurseries sell magnolia seedlings in containers or B & B.

CULTURE: In fertile, moist soil, magnolia grows well without special attention save for the usual fertilization and watering while young.

PROPAGATION: Seedage, yet fine selections are increased by cuttage or graftage.

PESTS: Magnolia scale, algal leaf-spot.

139
Banana-Shrub

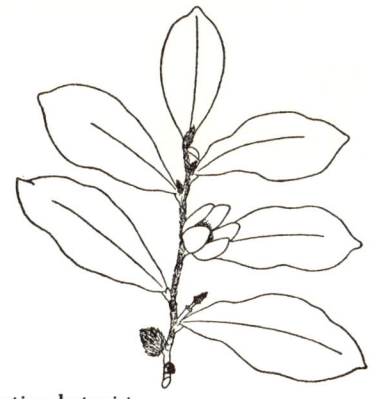

Michelia (me-SHELL-ee-a): for P. Michel, a Florentine botanist.
fuscata (fuss-KAY-ta): dark brown.

FAMILY: Magnoliaceae. RELATIVES: The magnolias and the tulip-tree.
TYPE OF PLANT: Shrub.   HEIGHT: 20'. ZONE: N
HOW TO IDENTIFY: A large, much-branched shrub that bears evergreen, alternate, dark green leaves; buds with fuzzy coverings and yellow flowers with the odor of banana.
HABIT OF GROWTH: Much-branched, low-headed, compact shrub.
FOLIAGE: Evergreen, alternate, of medium fine texture and dark green color.
FLOWERS: Yellow, magnolia-like, 1½" across, with the odor of banana.
FRUITS: Small, rough burs.
SEASON OF MAXIMUM COLOR: Springtime when little, yellow blossoms open.
LANDSCAPE USES: As a freestanding specimen banana-shrub has been a favorite in northern Florida for generations. It can be used as an accent in the foundation planting for a multistoried building and as a member of an enclosing barrier. In this last use, the planting interval may be 5' o.c.
HABITAT: China; in Florida, fairly common in gardens of upper counties.
LIGHT REQUIREMENT: Broken, shifting shade from tall pine trees is ideal.
SOIL REQUIREMENT: Fertile, well-drained soils, rich in organic matter are best.
SALT TOLERANCE: Not tolerant.
AVAILABILITY: Small shrubs in containers are offered in many retail sales lots.
CULTURE: Plant in fertile, well-drained soil; water periodically until established; fertilize once each winter; protect from scale insects.
PROPAGATION: Cuttage.
PESTS: Magnolia scale is a very serious pest and must be controlled by periodic spraying; mushroom root-rot.

140
Anise-Tree

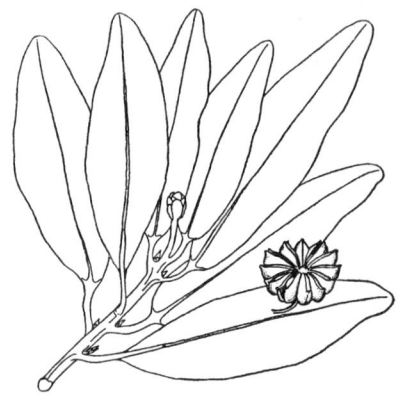

Illicium (ill-ISS-ee-um): Latin for allurement, for the pleasant odor.
anisatum (an-ee-SAY-tum): for the anise-scent of crushed leaves.

FAMILY: Illiciaceae.
RELATIVES: Florida anise-tree.
TYPE OF PLANT: Shrub or tree.
HEIGHT: 20'. ZONE: N,C

HOW TO IDENTIFY: Strong scent of anise is released when leaves are crushed.

HABIT OF GROWTH: Very compact, dense close to the earth.

FOLIAGE: Evergreen, alternate, bold in pattern, light green in color.

FLOWERS: Very small, nodding, greenish-yellow, not fragrant.

FRUITS: Fluted pods split at pie sections to release dark brown seeds.

SEASON OF MAXIMUM COLOR: No variation.

LANDSCAPE USES: For enclosure, no shrub surpasses anise. Plant 5' o.c. For foundation plantings for massive public buildings, the plants may stand at the same interval.
  Anise-tree is one of Florida's best large exotic shrubs.

HABITAT: Japan and Korea; in Florida, gardens in upper counties.

LIGHT REQUIREMENT: Very tolerant of shade; grows well in full sun, too.

SOIL REQUIREMENT: Very tolerant of a wide range of soils.

SALT TOLERANCE: Not tolerant of seaside locations.

AVAILABILITY: Rather widely available in nurseries in upper Florida.

CULTURE: Rich soil, moderate moisture, and a mulch over the roots should make for success. Annual pruning is needed if the plant is to be maintained as a shrub.

PROPAGATION: Cuttage, simple layerage, and seedage.

PESTS: Mites, scales upon occasion.

NOTE: Florida anise-tree (*Illicium floridanum*) grows to a height of 20' and bears aromatic leaves; red-purple flowers with 20-30 petals, making each about 1½" across, and much more showy than those on the exotic species. Fruits, the fluted pods, are quite similar.

141
Camphor-Tree

Cinnamomum (sin-a-MO-mum): ancient Greek name.
camphora (cam-FOR-a): of camphor.

FAMILY: Lauraceae.   RELATIVES: Avocado, redbay, and sassafras.
TYPE OF PLANT: Tree.   HEIGHT: 50'. ZONE: N,C,S

HOW TO IDENTIFY: Crushed leaves have the odor of camphor; twigs, petioles, and leaves are all the same color.

HABIT OF GROWTH: Closely branched to make a dense, round symmetrical head.

FOLIAGE: Evergreen, alternate, aromatic, of medium texture and dark green color.

FLOWERS: Inconspicuous, produced in springtime in axillary panicles.

FRUITS: Shining black berries ⅜" in diameter, produced in abundance to become a nuisance on walks, terraces, and driveways.

SEASON OF MAXIMUM COLOR: Springtime when new growth emerges.

LANDSCAPE USES: Shade tree for large properties and for avenue plantings, planting distance 50'. Sheared hedges are made from camphor. Set seedlings 2' o.c. and clip very frequently for best appearance. Mature trees have such dense heads that it is difficult to grow grass beneath them.

HABITAT: Eastern Asia; in Florida, ubiquitous.

LIGHT REQUIREMENT: Full sun or light, high shade.

SOIL REQUIREMENT: Tolerant of many soils, may be chlorotic on calcareous earth.

SALT TOLERANCE: Not tolerant.

AVAILABILITY: This is not a lucrative nursery item, as small camphor seedlings grow abundantly under old trees, and many are given away by homeowners.

CULTURE: Camphor-trees transplant with great difficulty in larger sizes, and so plants from gallon containers only are recommended. These will grow very rapidly with but little care.

PROPAGATION: Seedage.

PESTS: Scales, mites, and chlorosis on calcareous soils.

Jade-Plant

'Tricolor'

Crassula arborescens

'Portulacea'

C. tetragona

C. lycopodioides

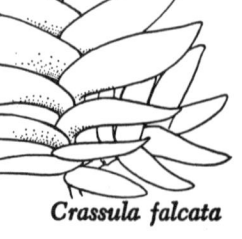

'Albiflora'

Crassula falcata

'Pagoda'

143
Jade-Plant

Crassula (CRASS-soo-la): Latin for thick.
argentea (are-GENT-ee-a): silvery.

FAMILY: Crassulaceae.   RELATIVES: Kalanchoë and sedum.
TYPE OF PLANT: Shrub.   HEIGHT: 4'. ZONE: S
HOW TO IDENTIFY: A thick, succulent, brown trunk bears thick, succulent branches in comely aspect, which hold very thick, oval leaves clustered near their tips. Growth is very slow; the demand for water, small. This indeed, resembles a diminutive tree with leaves of jade.
HABIT OF GROWTH: Diminutive, tree-like.
FOLIAGE: Thick, heavy, succulent, oval, not petioled, usually with red edges.
FLOWERS: Jade-plant may grow for many years without blooming. When flowers do appear, they are small, white, or rosy-red in close panicles.
FRUITS: Little pods, when present.
SEASON OF MAXIMUM COLOR: Springtime when foliage matures with full color.
LANDSCAPE USES: For the attractive branching and the tolerance of shade and dry atmosphere, jade-plant has been a household favorite since the beginning of gardening. Alone in a decorative container, or with other little plants in a bin, this South African succulent is sure to please.
HABITAT: South Africa.
LIGHT REQUIREMENT: Tolerant of very dense shade, yet compact habit and attractive red leaf-margins can be had only in bright light.
SOIL REQUIREMENT: Open, free-draining, sandy soil, rather low in nutrients, is recommended.
SALT TOLERANCE: Tolerant of conditions back of the first dunes.
AVAILABILITY: Small plants can be had at most nurseries and chain stores.
CULTURE: Plant in a container, with plenty of drainage, that is filled with a medium as described above; water very lightly, allowing the soil to become quite dry between applications. Keep in a shaded location.
PROPAGATION: Cuttage.
PESTS: Rots, if overwatered.
NOTE: Above is a picture of the species. Clones, some with striped leaves, and also related species which bear succulent leaves of various forms, are often seen. Some are portrayed on the opposite page.

Kalanchoe marmorata

K. verticillata

K. beharensis

K. synsepala

Kalanchoe

K. blossfeldiana

K. pinnata

K. daigremontiana

K. tomentosa

145
Kalanchoe

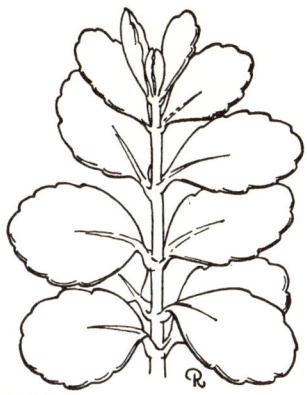

Kalanchoë (cal-ANN-ko-ee): adapted from the Chinese name.
SPP.: several species are grown in Florida.

FAMILY: Crassulaceae. RELATIVES: Jade-plant and houseleek.
TYPE OF PLANT: Herbaceous perennial. HEIGHT: Variable. ZONE: S
HOW TO IDENTIFY: Thick, succulent leaves, often with crenatures where small plants arise in profusion. Leaf shape, size, and mottling vary with the species or variety.
HABIT OF GROWTH: Loose habit by several stems that may shed lower leaves.
FOLIAGE: Coarse, bold, often netted with purple or red, usually with crenatures from which plantlets arise for vegetative increase.
FLOWERS: Showy, numerous, in terminal clusters during the warm months. The bell-like corollas hang downward below their calyces.
FRUIT: Little follicles, usually inconspicuous.
SEASON OF MAXIMUM COLOR: Summer and fall when flowers appear.
LANDSCAPE USES: As a ground cover for frostless locations, *Kalanchoë fedtschenkoi*, illustrated above (erroneously called "gray sedum"), is in high favor. All species are wanted for rock-'n'-sand gardens and for planters. Large, fuzzy-leaved species and hybrids are good for urns.
HABITAT: Old World tropics.
LIGHT REQUIREMENT: Full sunlight or partial shade of greenhouses, patios, or Florida rooms.
SOIL REQUIREMENT: Light, gritty, open, well-drained soil of moderate fertility is recommended. Basic reaction, high salt content, and dry conditions are tolerated.
SALT TOLERANCE: Tolerant of salt air and saline sands.
AVAILABILITY: Nurseries and chain stores everywhere sell kalanchoes in containers.
CULTURE: Freedom from frost and invading weeds are necessities for success. One light fertilization at the beginning of the rainy season should supply adequate nutrients for the year.
PROPAGATION: Simply lay a leaf where small plants are wanted, or break plantlets from leaf margins. *K. fedtschenkoi* and *K. blossfeldiana* are grown from conventional tip cuttings commercially.
PESTS: Caterpillars occasionally attack leaves, and leaf-spotting fungi appear on some varieties under humid conditions.

146
Oak-Leaf Hydrangea

Hydrangea (hy-DRAIN-jee-a): Greek for water vessel, from the shape of the capsules. *quercifolia* (kware-see-FOL-ee-a): oak-leaved.

FAMILY: Saxifragaceae. RELATIVES: Currant, saxifrage, and philadelphus.

TYPE OF PLANT: Shrub. HEIGHT: 6'. ZONE: N

HOW TO IDENTIFY: Deciduous, opposite, deeply cleft, oak-like leaves 8" long on pubescent twigs, with fuzzy axillary buds; showy white spikes appear in late spring.

HABIT OF GROWTH: Spreading, with up-pointing twigs.

FOLIAGE: Deciduous, opposite, striking in form, light green. Fall color: rusty.

FLOWERS: Showy, elongated panicles 1' long, calyces white, turning purplish.

FRUITS: Capsules with 2-5 cells, splitting down from the top.

SEASON OF MAXIMUM COLOR: Early summer.

LANDSCAPE USES: For wooded areas, oak-leaf hydrangea can be used effectively against the trunks of large trees. This native shrub is admired by advanced gardeners for its value in landscaping naturalistic areas, but it is seldom seen in home plantings. Here it grows too tall, the foliage is too coarse in texture and, like that of most hydrangeas, it falls to the earth in autumn. This free-flowering outsized shrub is completely maintenance-free when grown on hammock soil in northern counties.

HABITAT: Hammocks of northern Florida.

LIGHT REQUIREMENT: Partial shade of hammocks, north side of tree trunks.

SOIL REQUIREMENT: Fertile, slightly acid well-drained hammock soil.

SALT TOLERANCE: Not tolerant.

AVAILABILITY: Oak-leaf hydrangea is seldom seen in Florida nurseries.

CULTURE: In hammock soil, when it is planted on the north side of a tree trunk, no attention will be needed after this shrub becomes established.

PROPAGATION: Cuttage and seedage.

PESTS: None of major concern.

147
Hydrangea

Hydrangea (hy-DRAIN-jee-a): Greek for water vessel, from the shape of the capsules.
macrophylla (mak-roe-PHIL-a): large-leaved.

FAMILY: Saxifragaceae.   RELATIVES: Currant, saxifrage, and philadelphus.

TYPE OF PLANT: Shrub.   HEIGHT: 4'.   ZONE: N,C

HOW TO IDENTIFY: Huge, opposite, deciduous leaves; prominent axillary buds; showy blossom-heads in summer.

HABIT OF GROWTH: Compact, much-branched with up-pointing twigs.

FOLIAGE: Deciduous, opposite, coarse in texture, medium green. Fall color: spotted yellow.

FLOWERS: Prominent calyces are the showy parts of the inflorescences. These are usually blue on acid soil, pink on basic, and a dirty white on earth of neutral reaction. Buds and young leaves are poisonous.

FRUITS: Capsules, seldom formed in Florida.

SEASON OF MAXIMUM COLOR: Early summer.

LANDSCAPE USES: Along north walls or under oak trees, hydrangeas look best in generous drifts, with about 2' between individuals. The clones in this species, most popular in Florida, number a score or more.
   Summertime blossoms, deciduous foliage, and very coarse texture limit the usefulness of hydrangeas near houses of contemporary design, but the blue, pink, or white heads that appear so dependably endear hydrangeas to all garden-lovers. Pruning must be done immediately after flowering, otherwise new flower buds will be sacrificed.

HABITAT: Japan; in Florida, north sides of buildings or under trees on the upper peninsula and on the panhandle.

LIGHT REQUIREMENT: As indicated above, shade is recommended in Florida.

SOIL REQUIREMENT: Fertile, well-drained soil is best.

SALT TOLERANCE: Not tolerant.

AVAILABILITY: Many retail sales lots offer hydrangeas in containers.

CULTURE: A shaded site, moderate moisture, fairly high fertility, and good drainage should be supplied for hydrangeas. Pruning directly as flowering ends is suggested to keep plants compact.

PROPAGATION: Cuttage.

PESTS: Nematodes, mites, and scales.

Pittosporum

Pittosporum (pit-TOSS-poe-rum): Greek for pitch and seeds.
tobira (toe-BYE-ra): native Japanese name.

FAMILY: Pittosporaceae.   RELATIVES: Hymenosporum and sollya.
TYPE OF PLANT: Shrub.   HEIGHT: 15'. ZONE: N,C,S
HOW TO IDENTIFY: Thick, clustered stems bear whorled, revolute, leathery leaves that have a disagreeable odor when crushed. Little, white, fragrant flowers are followed by angled, green capsules containing red-coated seeds.
HABIT OF GROWTH: Compact, much-branched shrub.
FOLIAGE: Evergreen, whorled, medium in texture, dark green in color.
FLOWERS: Fragrant, white, 5-petaled, ½" long, in terminal umbels.
FRUITS: Angled, globose capsules, ½" in diameter. In western Florida, these fruits may contain viable, red-coated seeds; on the peninsula, the capsules may be sterile.
SEASON OF MAXIMUM COLOR: Spring when blossoms are out.
LANDSCAPE USES: For hedges (plant 18" o.c.) pittosporum cannot be excelled; for foundation arrangements, allow 3' between individuals, and in informal shrubbery borders, set the plants 5' apart. For seaside plantings and for partially shaded situations, pittosporum is highly recommended.
   For pleasantly variegated foliage that gives an olive-green effect, choose the popular variegated clone.
HABITAT: Eastern Asia; in Florida, much used as a garden shrub.
LIGHT REQUIREMENT: Tolerant of shade, recommended for north-side locations.
SOIL REQUIREMENT: A fertile, slightly acid medium is best.
SALT TOLERANCE: Very tolerant and highly recommended for seaside plantings.
AVAILABILITY: Both green and variegated plants are offered by Florida nurserymen.
CULTURE: Plant in enriched, acid site; furnish with mulch; combat cottony cushion scale and *Cercospora* leaf-spot continually.
PROPAGATION: Cuttage and seedage.
PESTS: Cottony cushion scale and *Cercospora* leaf-spot.
NOTE: *Pittosporum undulatum*, rather subject to attack by pests, grows in Florida, but it is not as dependable here as it is in California.

149
Loropetalum

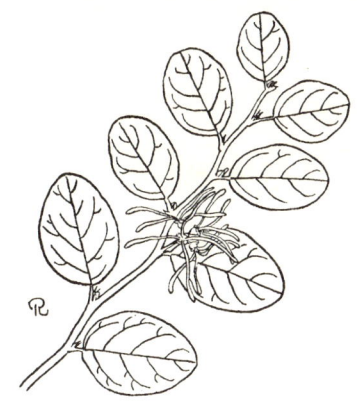

Loropetalum (lor-oh-PET-a-lum): Greek for strap and petal.
chinense (chy-NEN-see): Chinese.

FAMILY: Hamamelidaceae.   RELATIVES: Witch-hazel and sweet-gum.

TYPE OF PLANT: Shrub.   HEIGHT: 12'.   ZONE: N,C

HOW TO IDENTIFY: Compact shrub with outward-pointing branches; alternate, simple, rough, evergreen, ovate leaves to 2" long; white or yellowish flowers in clusters in early spring.

HABIT OF GROWTH: Compact, leaves closely packed on outward-pointing branches.

FOLIAGE: Evergreen, rough chlorotic of medium fine texture.

FLOWERS: Whitish flowers with feathery, strap-shaped petals about 1" long.

FRUITS: Woody capsules that split to release two seeds.

SEASON OF MAXIMUM COLOR: Little variation, even when white blossoms are out.

LANDSCAPE USES: Foundation plants for small houses, plant 3' o.c.
Loropetalum is not very widely planted in Florida, but in some locations it performs well. Landscape architects and homeowners have found merit in the medium-fine texture of the rough foliage and the horizontal growth of the branches with the result that loropetalum is seen in home plantings.

HABITAT: China; in Florida, sparingly cultured.

LIGHT REQUIREMENT: High, shifting shade or north-side locations.

SOIL REQUIREMENT: Reasonably fertile, acid, moisture retentive yet well-drained soil is a requirement for success.

SALT TOLERANCE: Not tolerant.

AVAILABILITY: Nurseries offer small canned plants.

CULTURE: Plant in sterilized, fertile, slightly acid soil in a shady location, in a planter or on a north side; water faithfully; fertilize thrice annually.

PROPAGATION: Cuttage.

PESTS: Mites and mineral deficiency.

150 *Thunberg Spirea*

Spiraea (spy-REE-a): Greek for wreath.
thunbergii (thun-BERG-ee-eye): for C. Thunberg, Swedish botanist, 1743-1822.

FAMILY: Rosaceae. **RELATIVES:** Rose, firethorn, and loquat.

TYPE OF PLANT: Dwarf shrub. **HEIGHT:** 5'. **ZONE:** N

HOW TO IDENTIFY: Shrub of weeping habit bears half-evergreen alternate leaves 1½" long, with saw-tooth edges on fine, wire-like, arching stems. Tiny white flowers are produced in great quantity in late winter.

HABIT OF GROWTH: Arching, wire-like stems form compact plants.

FOLIAGE: Half-evergreen, alternate, of very fine texture and light green color.

FLOWERS: White, ⅓" across in 3- to 5-flowered groups along the arching stems.

FRUITS: Little pods when present.

SEASON OF MAXIMUM COLOR: January-February.

LANDSCAPE USES: For massing in naturalistic plantings where wintertime white is wanted, this spirea is excellent for northern Florida. To face taller shrubs, and for foundation plantings, it is highly acceptable, as well. Planting interval may be about 3' o.c.

This fine-scale plant has great usefulness that is not fully appreciated. It is recommended for use in northern Florida.

HABITAT: Eastern Asia; in Florida, superior soils of northern counties.

LIGHT REQUIREMENT: Shifting shade from high pines is excellent.

SOIL REQUIREMENT: Heavy, well-drained loamy or rocky soil is best.

SALT TOLERANCE: Not tolerant.

AVAILABILITY: Nurseries in northern Florida may offer Thunberg spirea.

CULTURE: Once plants become established on superior soil in northern Florida, culture is simple. Watering during very dry periods, pruning after flowering, and fertilization once each winter are all that is required.

PROPAGATION: Cuttage by long, hard, leafless cuttings in December.

PESTS: Aphids and mites.

151 Reeves Spirea

Spiraea (spy-REE-a): Greek for wreath.
cantoniensis (can-tone-ee-EN-sis): of Canton, China.

FAMILY: Rosaceae.   RELATIVES: Loquat, photinia, and rose.

TYPE OF PLANT: Shrub.   HEIGHT: 6'. ZONE: N

HOW TO IDENTIFY: A shrub of many branches that hold alternate, deciduous leaves which are rhombic-oblong in form and bluish-green in color. In springtime the white blossoms are notable.

HABIT OF GROWTH: Much-branched, ascending.

FOLIAGE: Deciduous, medium fine in texture, bluish-green in color.

FLOWERS: Conspicuous, white, ½" in diameter in dense corymbs.

FRUITS: Often not present in Florida.

SEASON OF MAXIMUM COLOR: Springtime, just at the end of azalea season.

LANDSCAPE USES: For glistening white foils with colored azaleas, spirea is superb. Plant 5-7 spireas together, allowing about 3' between plants. In front of all-green shrubbery these snow-white flowers are bright spring accents. Plant as above.
  Of the 80 species and many named clones of this group, Reeves spirea is best for Florida. On the panhandle, other kinds do well as garden shrubs.

HABITAT: China; in Florida, upper tier of counties.

LIGHT REQUIREMENT: Full sun or high, shifting, broken shade.

SOIL REQUIREMENT: Fertile soils of northern counties are best.

SALT TOLERANCE: Not tolerant.

AVAILABILITY: Some nurseries in northern Florida stock spireas.

CULTURE: Plant in moderately fertile land; water faithfully until well established; thereafter, prune after flowering for compact growth; fertilize once in late winter.

PROPAGATION: Cuttage, using long, hard, leafless cuttings in early winter.

PESTS: Aphids, mushroom root-rot.

152
Firethorn

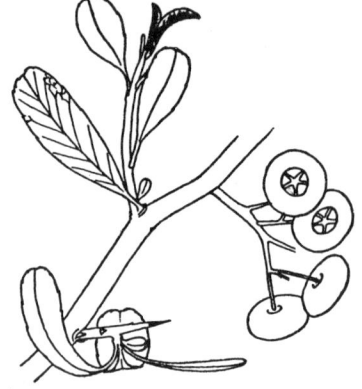

Pyracantha (pie-rah-CAN-tha): Greek for fire and thorn.
coccinea (cocks-SIN-ee-a): scarlet.

FAMILY: Rosaceae.   RELATIVES: Hawthorn, loquat, and photinia.
TYPE OF PLANT: Sprawling shrub.   HEIGHT: 20'. ZONE: N,C
HOW TO IDENTIFY: A sprawling shrub that has thorny branches that are gray-tomentose near the tips while young; evergreen, alternate, toothed leaves, about 1½" long and conspicuous fruits in fall and winter.
HABIT OF GROWTH: Awkwardly sprawling.
FOLIAGE: Evergreen, alternate, fine in texture, dark green in tone.
FLOWERS: White, showy, ⅓" in diameter, in corymbs on spurs of old wood.
FRUITS: Red or orange pomes ¼" in diameter, very showy in fall and winter.
SEASON OF MAXIMUM COLOR: April for blossoms, November-March for bright fruits.
LANDSCAPE USES: As freestanding specimens, firethorns have long been popular, as they are our best fruiting shrubs. For color interest in shrubbery enclosures, set 5' o.c. A single plant can be trained as an espalier against a masonry wall. Varieties of prostrate habit are used in planters because they will weep over the edges to soften the top line. Set these 3' o.c. There is great confusion in naming.
HABITAT: Southern Europe and Western Asia; in Florida, gardens of upper counties.
LIGHT REQUIREMENT: Full sun for best fruiting.
SOIL REQUIREMENT: Tolerant of many different types of soil.
SALT TOLERANCE: Not tolerant of dune conditions.
AVAILABILITY: Small plants in containers are widely offered in nurseries in northern and central Florida. This is the only class of planting stock that is recommended because of the difficulty of transplanting large plants.
CULTURE: Set small plants carefully from containers in well-prepared sites; water faithfully; mulch the roots; protect the foliage against lace bugs and mites. Fertilize twice each year and prune just after flowering, if needed.
PROPAGATION: Cuttage.
PESTS: Lace bugs, mites, scales, thrips, and fire blight.

153
Chinese Photinia

Photinia (foe-TIN-ee-a): Greek for shining, referring to the leaves.
serrulata (ser-you-LATE-a): saw-toothed.

FAMILY: Rosaceae.   RELATIVES: Loquat, India-hawthorn, and pear.
TYPE OF PLANT: Shrub, becoming tree-like with age.   HEIGHT: 15'.
ZONE: N

HOW TO IDENTIFY: Rank, upright growth, heavy twigs that bear sharply toothed, evergreen leaves to 7" long, in alternate arrangement.

HABIT OF GROWTH: Stiffly upright, usually bare beneath.

FOLIAGE: Evergreen, strap-shaped, saw-toothed, coarse, dark green.

FLOWERS: White, rose-like, ¼" across, in flat panicles about 6" in diameter.

FRUITS: Red, globose pomes ¼" across, if present.

SEASON OF MAXIMUM COLOR: Fall, when lower leaves turn red.

LANDSCAPE USES: For screens where large, upright, extremely coarse shrubs can be used, Chinese photinia could be indicated. Planting interval is 5' o.c.

Chinese photinia is a striking outsized shrub on superior soils in northern sections where winter chilling is experienced, but on the peninsula's sands where winters are mild, the plant leaves a lot to be desired. Here, Chinese photinia is not recommended for home-ground plantings.

HABITAT: China; in Florida, better soils of northern counties.

LIGHT REQUIREMENT: Full sun for compact growth.

SOIL REQUIREMENT: Better soils of northern Florida, only.

SALT TOLERANCE: Not tolerant.

AVAILABILITY: Nurseries in northern Florida offer Chinese photinia.

CULTURE: Plant in well-prepared site; water moderately until established; prune frequently to keep the plant compact and within bounds.

PROPAGATION: Cuttage.

PESTS: Caterpillars, mites, scales, and fire blight.

NOTE: There is an attractive hybrid between Chinese photinia and red-leaved *Photinia glabra* that displays desirable characteristics of both parents.

154
Red-Leaf Photinia

Photinia (foe-TIN-ee-a): Greek for shining, referring to the foliage.
glabra (GLAY-bra): not hairy.

FAMILY: Rosaceae.
RELATIVES: Loquat, quince, and pear.
TYPE OF PLANT: Shrub.
HEIGHT: 10′. **ZONE:** N
HOW TO IDENTIFY: Vivid red new leaves turn green at maturity. These are evergreen, alternate, 2″-3″ long and elliptic in form. The shrub is usually bare beneath.
HABIT OF GROWTH: Ungainly, open, bare below.
FOLIAGE: Evergreen, medium in texture, new leaves red, old leaves green.
FLOWERS: White, in compact clusters.
FRUITS: Red, berry-like pomes, hollow at the top, ¼″ across.
SEASON OF MAXIMUM COLOR: Spring, when new growth emerges.
LANDSCAPE USES: For color accent in a green shrubbery border, plant a group of 3 red-leaf photinia, with 3′ between plants. During seasons when all leaves are a dull green, the plant goes unnoticed.
HABITAT: Japan; in Florida, better soils of northern tier of counties.
LIGHT REQUIREMENT: Full sun for best growth and coloring.
SOIL REQUIREMENT: Better soils of northern Florida.
SALT TOLERANCE: Not tolerant.
AVAILABILITY: Red-leaf photinia and the hybrid are for sale in northern Florida.
CULTURE: Prepare rich sites in full sun; plant at the same level; attend to watering; prune regularly before flushes of growth to induce compact habit.
PROPAGATION: Cuttage.
PESTS: Mites, scales, and caterpillars.
NOTE: There is an attractive hybrid between red-leaf photinia and Chinese photinia, that displays desirable characteristics of both parents, that may extend the range of photinias down the peninsula slightly. Never a subtropical genus, *Photinia* behaves best where soil is good, winters are chill.

155
Loquat

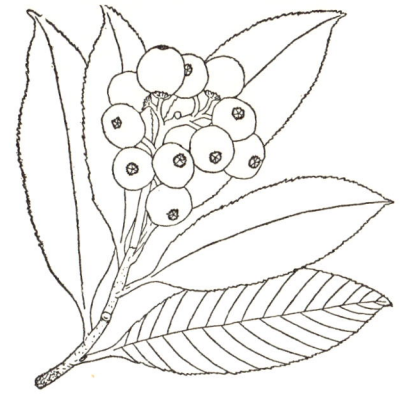

Eriobotrya (erry-oh-BOT-ree-a): Greek for woolly cluster, for the felty blossoms.
japonica (jap-ON-ee-ca): Japanese.

FAMILY: Rosaceae.   **RELATIVES:** India-hawthorn, photinia, and firethorn.
TYPE OF PLANT: Tree.   **HEIGHT:** 20'. **ZONE:** N,C,S

HOW TO IDENTIFY: Evergreen, alternate leaves, about 10" long, that are coarsely toothed, with sunken veins that go straight to the teeth. Fragrant little whitish blossoms appear in the fall to be followed by decorative and delicious yellow fruits in wintertime.

HABIT OF GROWTH: A neat little compact tree with upward-pointing branches.

FOLIAGE: Evergreen, alternate, very attractive, dark green above, fuzzy beneath.

FLOWERS: Fragrant ½" little white flowers in rusty-pubescent terminal panicles in the fall.

FRUITS: Yellow pomes with 1 or several large brown seeds.

SEASON OF MAXIMUM COLOR: Late winter when fruits ripen.

LANDSCAPE USES: Freestanding specimen for fruit and horticultural interest, as a part of an informal shrubbery border, as a shade tree for patio or terrace, loquat excels. This is unquestionably one of Florida's best trees. Its small size, complete hardiness, beautiful foliage, and delicious fruits endear the loquat to all.

HABITAT: China; in Florida, ubiquitous as a yard tree.

LIGHT REQUIREMENT: Full sun for best form, flowering, and fruiting.

SOIL REQUIREMENT: Tolerant of varying soil types.

SALT TOLERANCE: Tolerant of moderate salt air back of first-line dunes.

AVAILABILITY: Seedlings in containers appear in most nurseries.

CULTURE: Plant carefully; water moderately until established; thereafter just remember to fertilize once or twice a year. A mulch over the root zone is recommended.

PROPAGATION: Seedage, superior varieties by graftage are preferred.

PESTS: Scales, caterpillars, and fire blight.

156
India-Hawthorn

Rhaphiolepis (raf-ee-oh-LEP-us): Greek for needle scale.
indica (IN-dee-ca): of the Indies.

FAMILY: Rosaceae.   RELATIVES: Loquat, photinia, and quince.
TYPE OF PLANT: Dwarf shrub.   HEIGHT: 5'. ZONE: N
HOW TO IDENTIFY: Dwarfish shrub with evergreen, leathery, serrate leaves that are about 3" long; fragrant, white, ½" flowers that are followed by drupe-like purplish-black pomes.
HABIT OF GROWTH: Dwarf shrub, open beneath, with leaves clustered at twig tips.
FOLIAGE: Evergreen, sharply serrate, 3" long, of medium texture and dark green color.
FLOWERS: Rose-like, white tinged with pink, ½" in diameter, in loose clusters.
FRUITS: Drupe-like little pomes (⅓" in diameter) that are purplish-black in color.
SEASON OF MAXIMUM COLOR: Fall.
LANDSCAPE USES: As a dwarf seaside shrub, India-hawthorn is excellent. There, in lee-side foundation plantings or planter boxes, set at intervals of 2'. For low hedges, plant 18" o.c. North-side locations are highly suitable.
HABITAT: Southern China; in Florida, sparingly planted in northern counties.
LIGHT REQUIREMENT: Tolerant of shade.
SOIL REQUIREMENT: Soils of good quality grow the best-looking plants.
SALT TOLERANCE: Tolerant of salt drift.
AVAILABILITY: India-hawthorn is sparingly offered in nurseries as container and B & B stock.
CULTURE: Plant in good soil on lee sides of ocean-front homes, north-side locations are good. In improved, slightly acid soil, set 2' o.c.; water faithfully until well established; fertilize two or three times each year.
PROPAGATION: Cuttage or seedage.
PESTS: Scales, fire blight, and nematodes.
NOTE: Yeddo-hawthorn, *R. umbellata,* has thick leaves that are whitish-tomentose with revolute edges, white blossoms ¾" across that have calyx-lobes which are not red. This latter species is usually taller, more upright, than is *R. indica*.

157
Cherry-Laurel

Prunus (PRUNE-us): classical name of the plum.
caroliniana (car-oh-lin-ee-AY-na): Carolinian.

FAMILY: Rosaceae.   RELATIVES: Apple, peach, and pear.
TYPE OF PLANT: Tree, trained as a shrub in gardens.   HEIGHT: 40'.
ZONE: N,C

HOW TO IDENTIFY: Alternate, evergreen, glossy leaves with taste of bitter almond; white flowers in dense clusters that are followed by black fruits.

HABIT OF GROWTH: Tree in the wild; clipped shrub in gardens.

FOLIAGE: Evergreen, of medium texture, dark green color.

FLOWERS: White, fragrant flowers 1/8" across in axillary racemes.

FRUITS: Black, shining drupes 1/2" long.

SEASON OF MAXIMUM COLOR: Springtime when blossoms mature.

LANDSCAPE USES: As a clipped hedge, cherry-laurel has long been a southern favorite. Set the plants 18" o.c. As a part of an informal enclosing barrier, this native can be kept in shrub form by shearing. Set plants 5' apart.
  Cherry-laurel is not often planted and grown as a tree, but occasionally chance seedlings, that have grown to maturity, may be left when housing developments are put in hammock areas.

WARNING: Cherry-laurel foliage is poisonous.

HABITAT: Hammocks and rich woods of upper Florida.

LIGHT REQUIREMENT: Tolerant of shade.

SOIL REQUIREMENT: Rich soil makes the best looking specimens.

SALT TOLERANCE: Not tolerant.

AVAILABILITY: Some nurseries in northern Florida will have cherry-laurel plants in containers, bare root, or B & B during the winter.

CULTURE: No special cultural requirements need be met.

PROPAGATION: Seedage or by digging suckers around old plants.

PESTS: Mites, stem canker, and caterpillars.

Wisteria

Wisteria (wis-TEE-ree-a): for C. Wistar, an American professor.
sinensis (sin-EN-sis): Chinese.

FAMILY: Leguminosae.   RELATIVES: Mimosa-tree, royal poinciana, bean, and pea.

TYPE OF PLANT: Twining vine.   HEIGHT: Variable. ZONE: N,C

HOW TO IDENTIFY: Rampant vine of twining habit that bears deciduous, compound leaves that have horn-like stipules at the bases of the petioles; showy racemes of blue or white, pea-like blossoms in springtime.

HABIT OF GROWTH: Vigorous twining vine that grows to great heights.

FOLIAGE: Deciduous, compound, lacy in texture, medium green in color.

FLOWERS: Blue or white, pea-like, in drooping racemes before the leaves.

FRUITS: Conspicuous, velvety pods about 6" long.

SEASON OF MAXIMUM COLOR: Early spring.

LANDSCAPE USES: To cover a pergola or fence, wisteria has always been a favorite in northern Florida. Plants may be trained to tree-form by fastening to a vertical pipe until a trunk is developed. With this method, continual pinching is required to head in the rank shoots.

HABITAT: China; in Florida, often seen in the northern part.

LIGHT REQUIREMENT: Broken shade of woodlands is ideal.

SOIL REQUIREMENT: Tolerant of many soils.

SALT TOLERANCE: Not tolerant.

AVAILABILITY: Wisteria is ordinarily not a nursery item, but layers are usually given away by gardeners who have old, established vines.

CULTURE: Simply plant, water, and forget.

PROPAGATION: Simple layerage where stems touch the earth.

PESTS: Thrips, pecan twig girdler.

NOTE: White wisteria (*Wisteria sinensis*, 'Alba') is an interesting change from the usual blue-flowered type. It is especially useful when trained to tree-form in a naturalistic planting of colored azaleas. Reflected in water, white wisteria trees are very pleasing. The Japanese wisterias and the native American species are not widely cultured in Florida gardens.

159
Cockspur Coral-Tree

Erythrina (airy-THRINE-a): Greek for red, referring to the color of the flowers.
crista-gallii (KRIST-a GAUL-ee-eye): cock's comb, referring to the flowers.

FAMILY: Leguminosae.   **RELATIVES:** Orchid-tree, redbud, bean, and pea.

TYPE OF PLANT: Tree or shrub.   **HEIGHT:** 25'. **ZONE:** C,S

HOW TO IDENTIFY: Stems, petioles, and midribs armed with spines, alternate compound leaves; showy red flowers that have standards erect at full flowering; long pods constricted between seeds.

HABIT OF GROWTH: Upright-spreading, with or without distinct trunk.

FOLIAGE: Semievergreen, compound, medium in texture and medium green in color.

FLOWERS: Papilionaceous, brilliant crimson, appearing in late summer or fall.

FRUITS: Long pods, constricted between seeds, turn brown at maturity.

SEASON OF MAXIMUM COLOR: Late summer and early fall.

LANDSCAPE USES: As freestanding specimens, this, and other erythrinas, may be cultured for the interest of their reddish, butterfly-like flowers. There are half a hundred species in the genus. Some of the tree species are grown to shade coffee and cocoa in the tropics.

HABITAT: Brazil; in Florida, infrequently cultured as a garden tree in mild sections.

LIGHT REQUIREMENT: Full sun or partial shade.

SOIL REQUIREMENT: Tolerant of many soils, but fertile land is best.

SALT TOLERANCE: Not tolerant of dune conditions.

AVAILABILITY: Nurseries may have limited stocks of erythrina trees in containers.

CULTURE: Once established in nearly frostless districts, erythrina trees grow thriftily with a minimum of attention.

PROPAGATION: Seedage or cuttage.

PESTS: Nematodes, thrips, mites, and twig borers.

160
Cherokee-Bean

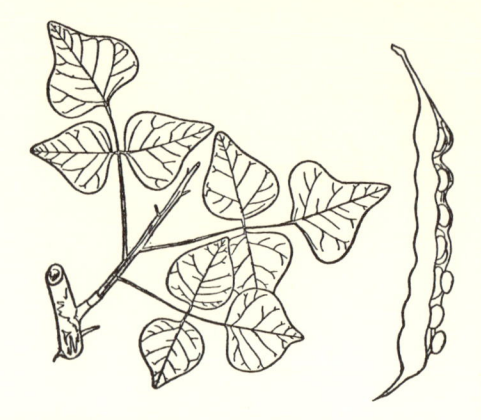

Erythrina (err-ee-THRINE-a): Greek for red, for the color of the flowers.
herbacea (er-BAY-see-a): herbaceous, not woody.

FAMILY: Leguminosae.   **RELATIVES:** Clover, orchid-tree, pea, and bean.

TYPE OF PLANT: Herbaceous perennial.   **HEIGHT:** 30′.   **ZONE:** N,C,S

HOW TO IDENTIFY: Deciduous, compound leaves composed of three spear-shaped leaflets, with prickles on midrib; showy scarlet, closed blossoms in spring followed by beans which split to reveal bright scarlet seeds.

HABIT OF GROWTH: Upright, unkempt, often close to trees, sometimes tree-like.

FOLIAGE: Deciduous, compound, of medium texture and medium green color.

FLOWERS: Bright scarlet, 2″ long, closed to form tubes, on 15″ spikes.

FRUITS: Drooping pods constricted between seeds, split to reveal red seeds.

SEASON OF MAXIMUM COLOR: May-June for flowers, autumn for bright seeds.

LANDSCAPE USES: For woodland plantings, Cherokee-bean is useful for bright high lights of red beside tree trunks. Conspicuous in unspoiled hammocks in springtime, Cherokee-bean is seldom planted in man-made gardens. Here is yet another indigene that warrants much wider planting. For those who want to have more maintenance-free plants in naturalistic arrangements, Cherokee-bean seems to be made to order. True, the effect is transitory, but this is not necessarily a disadvantage.

HABITAT: Hammocks of the state.

LIGHT REQUIREMENT: Broken shade of hammocks.

SOIL REQUIREMENT: Hammock soil.

SALT TOLERANCE: Not tolerant.

AVAILABILITY: Cherokee-bean is not an item of commerce.

CULTURE: Plant in prepared sites by tree trunks; water until established; fertilize in springtime; cut back dead tops in winter.

PROPAGATION: Seedage; cuttage.

PESTS: None of major consequence.

161
Orchid-Trees

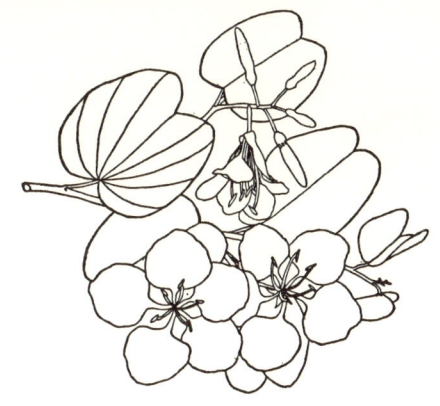

Bauhinia (bo-HIN-ee-a): for the brothers Bauhin, sixteenth-century herbalists. SPP.: several species are grown in Florida.

FAMILY: Leguminosae.   **RELATIVES:** Redbud, Jerusalem-thorn, and bean.
TYPE OF PLANT: Trees.   **HEIGHT:** 25'. **ZONE:** C,S
HOW TO IDENTIFY: Tree with 2-cleft deciduous leaves that resemble the print from an ox hoof; orchid-like flowers, followed by many long, brown pods.
HABIT OF GROWTH: Small head of many branches from a short, often crooked, trunk.
FOLIAGE: Deciduous, 2-cleft, coarse in texture, light green in color. Fall color, yellow.
FLOWERS: Orchid-like, 3"-4" across, colored in tones of purple, red, or white.
FRUITS: Flat pods 1' long, sharp-beaked, long-stalked.
SEASON OF MAXIMUM COLOR: Variable with the species.
LANDSCAPE USES: As freestanding specimens, or as framing for small houses, orchid-trees are highly acceptable. They may be fitted into shrubbery borders to give interest to the skyline and seasonal color.
  Bauhinia variegata, most popular, produces in winter and spring most nearly orchid-like blossoms of purplish casts or pure white in variety 'Candida.'
  Bauhinia purpurea, most variable, produces narrow-petaled flowers in the fall while leaves are on the trees.
  Bauhinia monandra, single-stamened, flowers in summer.
  Bauhinia blakeana, Hong Kong orchid-tree, most spectacular and most wanted bauhinia, bears orchid-like, 6" flowers of rich reddish or rose purple during the winter. This one is very tender to cold.
HABITAT: India to China; in Florida, popular in moderately warm sections.
LIGHT REQUIREMENT: Full sun or high, shifting pine shade.
SOIL REQUIREMENT: Tolerant of widely varying well-drained soils.
SALT TOLERANCE: Not tolerant.
AVAILABILITY: Offered in containers by most nurseries in central and southern Florida.
CULTURE: After establishment in made-up planting sites, no special care is needed.
PROPAGATION: Seedage; marcottage for rare types.
PESTS: Chewing larvae may despoil foliage.

162 Redbud

Cercis (sir-sis): ancient Greek name.
canadensis (can-a-DEN-sis): Canadian.

FAMILY: Leguminosae.   RELATIVES: Orchid-tree and Jerusalem-thorn.

TYPE OF PLANT: Tree.   HEIGHT: 40'. ZONE: N,C

HOW TO IDENTIFY: Alternate, heart-shaped deciduous leaves that are palmately veined; buds ovoid; pink, pea-like blossoms in very early springtime.

HABIT OF GROWTH: Spreading, broad, irregular head atop a branched or bending bole.

FOLIAGE: Deciduous, coarse in texture, medium green in color. Fall color: brown.

FLOWERS: Rosy-pink, ½" long, pea-like, in very early spring before the leaves.

FRUITS: Linear pods, 3½" long, acute at each end, brown and ugly.

SEASON OF MAXIMUM COLOR: January-February.

LANDSCAPE USES: As a street tree (plant 25'-35' apart), as a framing tree for small houses, as a shading device for terraces, as a part of an informal shrubbery border, redbud excels.
   A white-flowered form is occasionally seen.

HABITAT: Rich hammock areas of northern Florida.

LIGHT REQUIREMENT: Native to shaded hammocks.

SOIL REQUIREMENT: Rich, well-drained acid soils, high in organic matter.

SALT TOLERANCE: Not tolerant.

AVAILABILITY: Nurseries in northern counties sell redbud trees.

CULTURE: Plant in fertile soil that is well drained; wrap the trunk as protection against borers; water faithfully; place a mulch over the root zone; fertilize twice a year.

PROPAGATION: Graftage, using redbud seedlings as stocks.

PESTS: Borers, aphids followed by sooty-mold, root-rot disease.

NOTE: Chinese redbud (*Cercis chinensis*) has flowers that are larger and deeper in tone than those of the native species.

163
Cassia Shrubs

Cassia (cass-ee-a): ancient Greek name.
spp.: several shrub cassias are widely grown in Florida.

FAMILY: Leguminosae.   RELATIVES: Jerusalem-thorn, tamarind, and redbud.
TYPE OF PLANT: Shrubs.   HEIGHT: 15'. ZONE: N,C,S
HOW TO IDENTIFY: Upright shrubs that have compound leaves and fall and winter blossoms that resemble golden butterflies.
HABIT OF GROWTH: Upright, by means of several stems.
FOLIAGE: Evergreen, compound, of medium texture and light green color.
FLOWERS: Terminal spikes of golden yellow in the autumn.
FRUITS: Pods about half a foot long that turn brown at maturity.
SEASON OF MAXIMUM COLOR: Fall and winter.
LANDSCAPE USES: For bright yellow fall and winter color, group three cassias in front of green shrubbery. Frost will kill the best of the golden-flowered shrub cassias.
   Ringworm cassia (*C. alata*) has erect spikes that resemble fat candles before the individual blossoms open. This one should be planted only in nearly frostless locations, as the roots may not survive cold winters. In other sections, *Cassia bicapsularis* opens its yellow butterflies in October, to be killed to the ground in a month or so. The roots usually survive to sprout out again. (This species in sketch.)
HABITAT: Tropical America; in Florida, popular wherever the roots will survive.
LIGHT REQUIREMENT: Full sun for best growth and flowering.
SOIL REQUIREMENT: Tolerant of many varying soils.
SALT TOLERANCE: Not tolerant.
AVAILABILITY: Nurseries in southern Florida usually stock both shrub cassias; in northern sections, *Cassia bicapsularis* is widely offered in bloom in gallon cans in the fall.
CULTURE: After they become established, shrub cassias grow with little care. Protect the foliage and blossom buds from caterpillars in the fall; cut off at ground level as soon as frost kills back the stems.
PROPAGATION: Cuttage and seedage.
PESTS: Caterpillars consume leaves and flower buds in the autumn.

164
Golden-Shower

Cassia (CASS-ee-a): ancient Greek name.
fistula (FIS-tue-la): Latin for tube for the long, cylindrical pods.

FAMILY: Leguminosae.

RELATIVES: Jerusalem-thorn, redbud, bean, and pea.

TYPE OF PLANT: Tree.

HEIGHT: 40'. ZONE: S

HOW TO IDENTIFY: Tree with compound leaves with oval leaflets 8" long, pendent clusters of golden flowers in summertime, followed by numerous 2-foot, cylindrical brown pods.

HABIT OF GROWTH: Upright tree with open crown.

FOLIAGE: Evergreen, compound, lacy in appearance and medium green in color.

FLOWERS: Pale yellow, pea-like, in hanging racemes a foot in length.

FRUITS: Huge pods, 1" thick and 2' long, striking, but undecorative.

SEASON OF MAXIMUM COLOR: Summertime.

LANDSCAPE USES: Freestanding specimen for residential properties; on avenues set golden-shower trees 25'-35' o.c. This is one of southern Florida's favorite summer-flowering trees.

HABITAT: India; in Florida, around the tip of the peninsula.

LIGHT REQUIREMENT: Full sun or partial shade.

SOIL REQUIREMENT: Tolerant of many soil types.

SALT TOLERANCE: Tolerant of mild salt air back from the strand.

AVAILABILITY: Most retail nurseries in warm areas sell golden-shower trees in containers.

CULTURE: Once started, golden-shower grows freely in nearly frostless locations.

PROPAGATION: Seedage.

PESTS: Caterpillars.

NOTE: *Cassia* is a very large genus that contains some of the tropics' most colorful and beloved flowering trees. Among them the various pink-showers, pink-and-white-showers, and the spectacular hybrid rainbow-shower are standouts in hot countries.

165
Jerusalem-Thorn

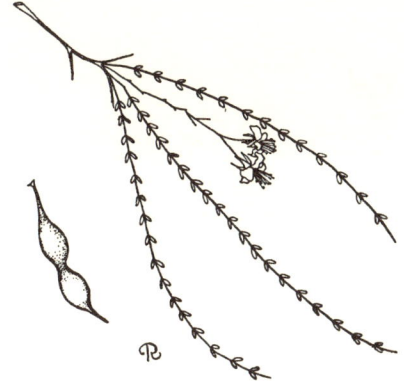

Parkinsonia (park-in-SONE-ee-a): for J. Parkinson, English apothecary.
aculeata (a-cule-lee-ATE-a): prickly.

FAMILY: Leguminosae.

RELATIVES: Powderpuff and royal poinciana.

TYPE OF PLANT: Small tree.

HEIGHT: 25'. ZONE: N,C,S

HOW TO IDENTIFY: Thorny, green branches hold deciduous leaves composed of flattened, twig-like stalks and many, small leaflets. Yellow, pea-like blossoms come out in springtime, to be followed later in the year by brown pods which are flattened between seeds.

HABIT OF GROWTH: Awkward, asymmetrical, open crowns assume picturesque shapes.

FOLIAGE: Deciduous, compound, very fine in texture, medium green in color.

FLOWERS: Yellow, fragrant, pea-like, very showy in spring and summer.

FRUITS: Pods 2"-6" long, constricted between the oblong seeds.

SEASON OF MAXIMUM COLOR: Spring and summer.

LANDSCAPE USES: As a freestanding specimen for warm-weather color, this splendid little tree is excellent in every section of Florida. To shade a part of a terrace, it serves well because of its small size and because the leaves fall to let the sun shine through in winter. Jerusalem-thorn may stand in a shrubbery border for sky line interest.

HABITAT: Tropical America; in Florida, it is common as a garden tree.

LIGHT REQUIREMENT: Full sun for best flowering.

SOIL REQUIREMENT: Tolerant of wide variation in soils.

SALT TOLERANCE: Tolerant of salt drift and saline earth.

AVAILABILITY: Many nurseries offer small seedlings in an assortment of containers.

CULTURE: After small trees from cans become established, no attention will be needed.

PROPAGATION: Seedage.

PESTS: Scales.

166 Royal Poinciana

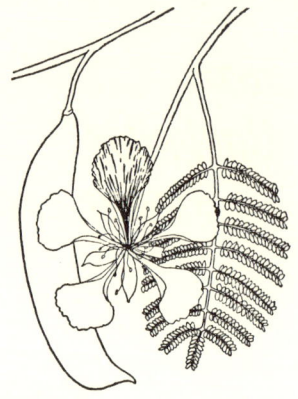

Delonix (de-LON-icks): Greek, referring to the long-clawed petals.
regia (REE-gee-a): royal.

FAMILY: Leguminosae.   **RELATIVES:** Tamarind, mimosa-tree, and cassia.

TYPE OF PLANT: Tree.   **HEIGHT:** 40'. **ZONE:** S

HOW TO IDENTIFY: Two-foot-long brown pods hang like razor strops; partially or wholly deciduous, compound foliage, and striking scarlet blossoms in early summer facilitate identification of this glory of the tropics.

HABIT OF GROWTH: Wide-spreading branches form a domed top above a stout trunk.

FOLIAGE: Deciduous, compound, fine in texture, medium green in color.

FLOWERS: Striking blossoms in tones of red, 4" across, with 1 striped petal.

FRUITS: Dark brown pods 2' long x 2" wide, resembling razor strops.

SEASON OF MAXIMUM COLOR: Early summer.

LANDSCAPE USES: As a freestanding specimen, as a shade tree, framing tree, or avenue tree, royal poinciana is world-famous because of its riotous summer color. This flamboyant (as it is often called in the tropics) the world's most colorful tree, is greatly admired in hot countries. Color varies slightly in individuals, but all are tender to cold.

HABITAT: Madagascar; in Florida, featured where frosts seldom occur.

LIGHT REQUIREMENT: Full sun for best habit and flowering.

SOIL REQUIREMENT: Tolerant of a wide range of soils.

SALT TOLERANCE: Tolerant of salt air at some distance from the strand.

AVAILABILITY: Nurseries in southern Florida have royal poinciana trees in containers.

CULTURE: Once it becomes established in nearly frostless districts, one annual fertilization and watering during dry times should keep the plant healthy and growing. Protection must be given on cold nights.

PROPAGATION: Seedage.

PESTS: None of major concern.

167
Barbados Flower-Fence

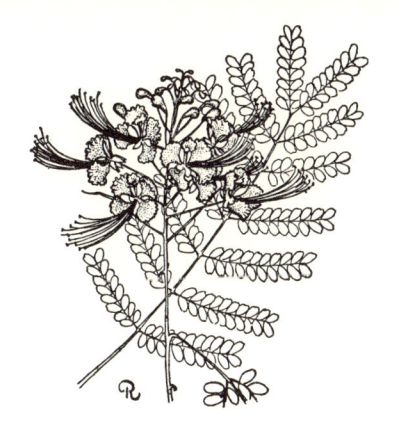

Poinciana (poin-see-AN-a): for M. de Poinci, a governor of the Antilles.
pulcherrima (pull-KARE-ee-ma): very handsome.

FAMILY: Leguminosae.   RELATIVES: Tamarind, cassia, bean, and pea.

TYPE OF PLANT: Shrub.   HEIGHT: 15'. ZONE: S

HOW TO IDENTIFY: Prickly branches bear fine, feathery foliage and brilliant scarlet and yellow flowers in erect clusters.

HABIT OF GROWTH: Ungainly, open-branched.

FOLIAGE: Evergreen, compound, very fine in texture, light green in color.

FLOWERS: Scarlet and yellow in erect, showy clusters.

FRUITS: Pods ¾" wide x 4" long; become unsightly when brown.

SEASON OF MAXIMUM COLOR: Much of the warm season.

LANDSCAPE USES: As a bright, informal division hedge, set plants 2' o.c. As an accent in front of green shrubbery, this bright legume serves, too.
  Barbados flower-fence is very popular in hot countries the world around, and it is widely planted in extreme southern Florida, as well.
  Sometimes this poinciana is grown as an annual or as a tender herbaceous perennial in sections where frost occurs regularly. The roots are quite tender, enduring but a few degrees below freezing for a very short period at best.
  Variety 'Flava' has yellow flowers.

HABITAT: Distribution general throughout the tropics.

LIGHT REQUIREMENT: Full sun for best flowering; tolerates some shade.

SOIL REQUIREMENT: Tolerant of varying soils in hot countries.

SALT TOLERANCE: Endures salt drift at some distance from the sea.

AVAILABILITY: Nurseries in southern Florida stock small plants in containers.

CULTURE: No special care after new plants become established.

PROPAGATION: Seedage.

PESTS: Scales, nematodes, and mushroom root-rot.

168
Paradise Poinciana

Poinciana (poin-see-AN-a): for M. de Poinci, a governor of the Antilles.
gilliesii (GILL-eze-ee-eye): for G. Gillies, Scottish traveler in South America.

FAMILY: Leguminosae.   RELATIVES: Royal poinciana, cassia, and tamarind.

TYPE OF PLANT: Shrub.   HEIGHT: 10'. ZONE: S

HOW TO IDENTIFY: Scraggly, open shrub with spineless branches that bear feathery foliage with black dots on the under sides of the leaflets. Showy yellow flowers with brilliant red stamens are in evidence during warm weather.

HABIT OF GROWTH: Scraggly, open.

FOLIAGE: Evergreen, compound, of finest texture and light green color.

FLOWERS: Flamboyant yellow, with contrasting red stamens.

FRUITS: Pods ¾" wide by 4" long, pea-like, brown and ugly.

SEASON OF MAXIMUM COLOR: Warm months when blossoms appear.

LANDSCAPE USES: As a bright, informal division hedge, set plants 2' o.c. For accent in front of dark green shrubbery use a group of 3 paradise poincianas set on 3' centers.

This poinciana is considered one of the choice shrubs of the tropics, and, like the preceding species it is very tender to cold. The roots will not endure conditions in northern Florida, usually.

HABITAT: Tropical America; in Florida, widely cultured in protected areas.

LIGHT REQUIREMENT: Full sun for best flowering and habit.

SOIL REQUIREMENT: Tolerant of many types.

SALT TOLERANCE: Not tolerant.

AVAILABILITY: Paradise poinciana, under several different names, is widely available in nurseries in southern Florida.

CULTURE: Plant in a reasonably fertile spot; water until well established, then during periods of drought; fertilize three times each year; keep lawn grasses back from the roots.

PROPAGATION: Seedage.

PESTS: Scales, mites, nematodes, and mushroom root-rot.

169
Powderpuff

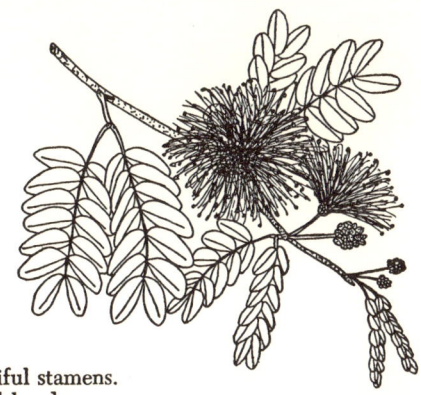

Calliandra (cal-ee-AN-dra): Greek for beautiful stamens.
haematocephala (he-mat-oh-SEFF-ah-la): red head.

FAMILY: Leguminosae.   RELATIVES: Mimosa-tree, cassia, and royal poinciana.

TYPE OF PLANT: Large shrub.   HEIGHT: 15'. ZONE: C,S

HOW TO IDENTIFY: Sprawling growth; compound evergreen leaves; red or pink pompons in terminal positions during warm months.

HABIT OF GROWTH: Sprawling to form huge mounds.

FOLIAGE: Evergreen, compound, of medium fine texture and dark green color.

FLOWERS: Globose heads formed by conspicuous red, pink, or white stamens.

FRUITS: Straight pods with thickened margins; unattractive.

SEASON OF MAXIMUM COLOR: Warm months.

LANDSCAPE USES: For enclosing barriers, set 5' o.c.; as a freestanding specimen, too.
   This is one of central Florida's most popular large flowering shrubs. Rainbow calliandra is similar, but the new growth is mottled with gold.

HABITAT: Brazil; in Florida, central and southern areas, on sandy soil.

LIGHT REQUIREMENT: Full sun for best flowering.

SOIL REQUIREMENT: Tolerant of varying types of sandy soil.

SALT TOLERANCE: Not tolerant.

AVAILABILITY: Small plants can be had at most nurseries in central and southern Florida.

CULTURE: After establishment with the aid of adequate water, no particular attention is needed other than regular pruning to keep the plant within bounds.

PROPAGATION: Marcottage or cuttage, using hardwood cuttings under mist.

PESTS: Caterpillars, mites, and thorn bugs.

NOTE: There are other calliandras, but these are usually less striking garden shrubs. Possibly selective breeding would bring to Florida gardens new powderpuffs of merit.

170
Womans-Tongue-Tree

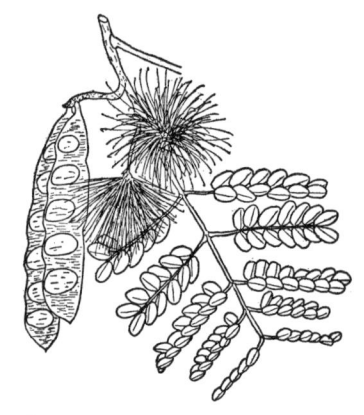

Albizia (al-BIZ-ee-a): for Sr. Albizzi, an Italian naturalist.
lebbeck (LEB-beck): an Arabic name.

FAMILY: Leguminosae.   RELATIVES: Powderpuff, mimosa-tree, and royal poinciana.

TYPE OF PLANT: Tree.   HEIGHT: 50'. ZONE: C,S

HOW TO IDENTIFY: A fast-growing, coarse tree that bears deciduous, pinnately compound foliage, globular greenish-yellow flowers and foot-long brown pods that hang for months.

HABIT OF GROWTH: Horizontal branching from a sturdy trunk.

FOLIAGE: Deciduous, fine in texture, light green in color, fall color, yellow.

FLOWERS: Globular heads of greenish-yellow tones.

FRUITS: Foot-long pods 1½" wide that contain many seeds that rattle in the breeze.

SEASON OF MAXIMUM COLOR: Spring.

LANDSCAPE USES: Where a specimen tree is needed in a very short time, womans-tongue-tree can be planted as a single specimen. It attains great size very rapidly, branches break in strong winds, the rattling pods are very annoying, and volunteer seedlings appear in great numbers. This tree is not recommended for home landscaping.

HABITAT: Tropical Asia; naturalized in warm parts of the Western Hemisphere.

LIGHT REQUIREMENT: Full sun.

SOIL REQUIREMENT: Widely tolerant.

SALT TOLERANCE: Somewhat salt tolerant, but not for dune planting.

AVAILABILITY: Nurseries in warmer parts stock womans-tongue-trees in containers.

CULTURE: Simply plant, water, and forget.

PROPAGATION: Seedage.

PESTS: Scales, mites, and mushroom root-rot.

171
Mimosa-Tree

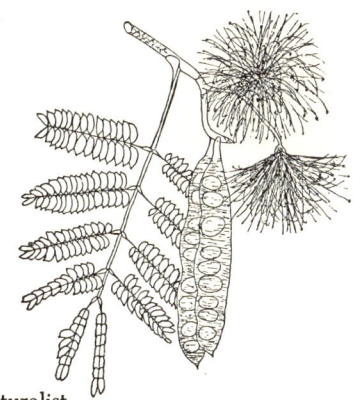

Albizia (al-BIZ-ee-a): for Sr. Albizzi, an Italian naturalist.
julibrissin (jew-lee-BRIS-in): Persian name.

FAMILY: Leguminosae.   RELATIVES: Powderpuff, cassia, bean, and pea.

TYPE OF PLANT: Tree.   HEIGHT: 40'. ZONE: N,C

HOW TO IDENTIFY: This tree has horizontal branching which makes it broader than tall, usually; deciduous, bipinnate foliage; pinkish pompons in May; unsightly brown pods thereafter.

HABIT OF GROWTH: Horizontal, bending branches from short, leaning trunks.

FOLIAGE: Deciduous, bipinnate, very fine in texture, light green in color.

FLOWERS: Globular heads in shades of pink.

FRUITS: Untidy brown pods that are produced in great numbers.

SEASON OF MAXIMUM COLOR: May.

LANDSCAPE USES: As a freestanding specimen and as a background tree, this well-adapted legume is extremely popular and highly recommended. As a terrace tree, it is good because the leaves fall to let the sun shine through all winter.

Most admired are seedlings that produce pompons of deep pink tones.

HABITAT: Old World; in Florida, very widely planted in central and northern parts.

LIGHT REQUIREMENT: Full sun for best flowering.

SOIL REQUIREMENT: Tolerant of many soils.

SALT TOLERANCE: Tolerant of conditions back of the front-line dunes.

AVAILABILITY: Mimosa-trees in containers are staple items in retail nurseries.

CULTURE: Under normal, back-yard conditions, mimosa-trees grow without attention.

PROPAGATION: Seedage; wilt-resistant types by cuttage.

PESTS: Mimosa wilt, cottony cushion scale, and mites.

NOTE: Wilt-resistant mimosa-trees, increased by root cuttings, are available in a few places.

172
Sissoo

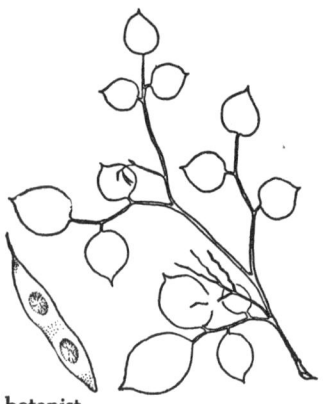

Dalbergia (dal-BURG-ee-a): for N. Dalberg, a Swedish botanist.
sissoo (SIS-oo):Indian name.

FAMILY: Leguminosae.   RELATIVES: Redbud and mimosa-tree.
TYPE OF PLANT: Tree.   HEIGHT: 45'. ZONE: C,S

HOW TO IDENTIFY: This shapely tree holds semievergreen, or deciduous, pinnate leaves of 3-5 roundish leaflets alternately arranged on a zigzag rachis. Inconspicuous blossoms are followed by slender brown pods about 4" long.

HABIT OF GROWTH: Spreading branches form a compact, symmetrical head.

FOLIAGE: Semievergreen or deciduous, compound, of medium texture and light green color.

FLOWERS: White, fragrant, inconspicuous, in very short, axillary panicles.

FRUITS: Slender, flat, brown pods 4" long, are 1- or 2-seeded in Florida.

SEASON OF MAXIMUM COLOR: Best color is summer green.

LANDSCAPE USES: As a framing tree, as a freestanding specimen, perhaps as an avenue tree, sissoo can be indicated for central and southern Florida. In Lake, Pinellas, and Lee counties, it thrives, and in several restricted areas there it has escaped from cultivation. In northern counties sissoo is defoliated by frost, killed by below-freezing temperatures. Apparently this tree is resistant to pests.

HABITAT: India; in Florida, sparingly cultured as a dooryard or campus tree.

LIGHT REQUIREMENT: Full sun, or broken, shifting high shade.

SOIL REQUIREMENT: Tolerant of widely varying soils, enduring drought and inundation.

SALT TOLERANCE: Not tolerant.

AVAILABILITY: Rarely will sissoo trees be found in nurseries.

CULTURE: Plant in nearly frostless site with reasonable care; water until well established; thereafter, no attention will be needed.

PROPAGATION: Seedage.

PESTS: None of major concern.

173
Ear-Tree

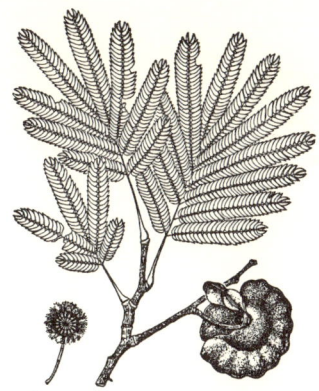

Enterolobium (enter-o-LOBE-ee-um): intestine-form, for the pods.
cyclocarpum (si-clo-CARP-um): circular fruit, for the pods.

FAMILY: Leguminosae.   RELATIVES: Orchid-tree and royal poinciana.

TYPE OF PLANT: Tree.   HEIGHT: 75′ ZONE: C,S

HOW TO IDENTIFY: A huge, fast-growing tree bears black pods that are shaped like ears of monkeys or humans, and graceful, bipinnate leaves.

HABIT OF GROWTH: Upright, symmetrical form above buttressed trunks.

FOLIAGE: Deciduous, compound, of very fine texture and light green color.

FLOWERS: Globose heads of small greenish-white flowers in springtime.

FRUITS: Black pods that are twisted so as to resemble anthropoid ears.

SEASON OF MAXIMUM COLOR: Springtime.

LANDSCAPE USES: As a single specimen on a campus, in a city park or botanical garden, ear-tree might be wanted for its interesting pods, but this monstrous legume is too large for home-ground plantings and it is not recommended for city lots, therefore. The brittle wood breaks in strong winds.

HABITAT: American tropics; in Florida, warm locations.

LIGHT REQUIREMENT: Full sun or high, shifting shade.

SOIL REQUIREMENT: Tolerant of various soils, including light sands.

SALT TOLERANCE: Not tolerant.

AVAILABILITY: Ear-trees are seen in nurseries in the warmer parts of the peninsula.

CULTURE: Very rapid growth without care is characteristic of ear-trees.

PROPAGATION: Seedage.

PESTS: None of major concern.

174
Pongam

Pongamia (pon-GAM-ee-a): native Malayan name.
pinnata (pin-NAY-ta): feather-formed.

FAMILY: Leguminosae.   RELATIVES: Redbud, wisteria, and orchid-tree.

TYPE OF PLANT: Tree.   HEIGHT: 40'. ZONE: S

HOW TO IDENTIFY: Close, dense head of odd-pinnate evergreen leaves with 5-7 leaflets that are broadly ovate and about 3" long. The short, thick, brown pods have incurving points and contain only 1 seed.

HABIT OF GROWTH: Heavily foliated drooping branches from a stout trunk.

FOLIAGE: Evergreen, odd-pinnate, of fine texture and dark green color.

FLOWERS: Pinkish to white, pea-like, in hanging, slender clusters.

FRUITS: Flat, brown pods about 1½" long, with incurving, beak-like points and single brown seeds within each pod. These seeds are poisonous to humans if taken internally.

SEASON OF MAXIMUM COLOR: Springtime when the trees are in flower.

LANDSCAPE USES: Because of its strength, pongam is recommended as a street tree, (set 45'-55' o.c.) and windbreak tree (set 25' in double, staggered row) for southern Florida. As a single shade tree for properties back from the dunes, pongam is excellent, as well.

HABITAT: Asian tropics; in Florida, a street tree in the southernmost part.

LIGHT REQUIREMENT: Full sun or partial shade; very resistant to wind.

SOIL REQUIREMENT: Tolerant of many different soils.

SALT TOLERANCE: Tolerant of salt air back of the first-line dunes.

AVAILABILITY: Nurseries in warm locations offer pongam trees in cans.

CULTURE: Set pongam trees in fertile soil; water well until well established; fertilize thrice annually while young; keep mulch over the root zone; hoe back grasses; protect the foliage against caterpillars.

PROPAGATION: Seedage.

PESTS: Caterpillars.

175
Lime-Berry

Triphasia (try-FASE-ee-a): Greek, triplex for the leaves.
trifolia (try-FO-lee-a): with three leaf(lets).

FAMILY: Rutaceae.   RELATIVES: Orange-jasmine, orange, and kumquat.
TYPE OF PLANT: Dwarf shrub.   HEIGHT: 6'. ZONE: S
HOW TO IDENTIFY: A shrub, usually low-growing, of weeping habit, with thorny branches that bear alternate, 3-foliate, evergreen leaves; little, white, fragrant flowers which are followed by red berries.
HABIT OF GROWTH: Dense, graceful, compact, weeping.
FOLIAGE: Evergreen, trifoliate, fine in texture, dark green in color.
FLOWERS: White, fragrant, ¾" in diameter, solitary, or several in axils.
FRUITS: Red berries ½" in diameter, decorative; sometimes used in jelly making.
SEASON OF MAXIMUM COLOR: During warm months when flowers or fruits are mature.
LANDSCAPE USES: Lime-berry is one of southern Florida's very best landscape shrubs. In foundation plantings, set 18" o.c.; for planters or for low hedges, use the same interval.

For use with diminutive structures lime-berry excels because of its fine texture, procumbent habit, and pleasing dark green color. The white flowers are pleasant accents and the bright red fruits are worthwhile high lights. As noted below, nematodes are troublesome pests and planting in sterilized soil is recommended most emphatically.
HABITAT: Malaya; in Florida, landscape plantings in most nearly frostless areas.
LIGHT REQUIREMENT: Sun or shade.
SOIL REQUIREMENT: Tolerant of varying soils, but very subject to attack by nematodes.
SALT TOLERANCE: Not tolerant.
AVAILABILITY: Lime-berry plants are offered in containers of sterilized soil by nurseries in southern Florida.
CULTURE: The soil should be enriched and sterilized before planting. Water faithfully until well established; place mulch over roots; fertilize 3 times each year.
PROPAGATION: Seedage or cuttage.
PESTS: Scales, nematodes, white-flies, and sooty-mold.

Boxthorn

Severinia (sev-er-IN-ee-a): for M. Severino, an Italian botanist.
buxifolia (bucks-i-FOL-ee-a): box-leaved.

FAMILY: Rutaceae.   **RELATIVES:** Orange, kumquat, and orange-jasmine.

TYPE OF PLANT: Dwarf shrub.   **HEIGHT:** 6'. **ZONE:** C,S

HOW TO IDENTIFY: A dwarf shrub with thorny branches that hold simple, oblong, evergreen leaves in alternate arrangement; white, orange-like blossoms; shining black fruits.

HABIT OF GROWTH: Very dense and compact, often with pendulous branches.

FOLIAGE: Evergreen, alternate, of fine texture and dark green color.

FLOWERS: White, small, orange-like, solitary or in small clusters in axils.

FRUITS: Globular black berries $\frac{1}{3}$" in diameter.

SEASON OF MAXIMUM COLOR: Cool months when fruits are colored.

LANDSCAPE USES: As a sheared hedge, plant 2' o.c.; as a foundation plant, use the same interval; as a transition plant for tall, leggy shrubs, set 3' apart.
   Boxthorn is one of the very best dwarf landscape shrubs for areas that are not subjected to hard freezes.

HABITAT: Southern China; in Florida, much planted as a garden hedge.

LIGHT REQUIREMENT: Full sun for compact habit, but shade is tolerated.

SOIL REQUIREMENT: Tolerant of most well-drained soils.

SALT TOLERANCE: Not tolerant.

AVAILABILITY: Seedlings in containers are displayed by most nurseries on the peninsula.

CULTURE: Plant in enriched holes; water until well established; thereafter prune annually; fertilize semiannually; protect the foliage against scale insects.

PROPAGATION: Seedage, selected forms by cuttage.

PESTS: Scales, white-flies, sooty-mold, thrips, mites, and nematodes.

NOTE: Spineless forms have been selected and increased vegetatively; but these are not yet widely available.

177
Orange-Jasmine

Murraya (MUR-ay-a): for J. Murray, a botanist of the eighteenth century.
paniculata (pan-ick-you-LATE-a): with flowers in a loose pyramid.

FAMILY: Rutaceae.   RELATIVES: Citrus, boxthorn, and lime-berry.
TYPE OF PLANT: Shrub or small tree.   HEIGHT: 20'. ZONE: C,S
HOW TO IDENTIFY: Attractive, compound, evergreen leaves that are made up of pear-shaped or rhombic leaflets; fragrant, white, orange-like blossoms which are followed by bright, decorative, red fruits.
HABIT OF GROWTH: Slender, upright, yet with dense head.
FOLIAGE: Compound, evergreen, of fine texture and dark green color.
FLOWERS: White, fragrant, citrus-like, ¾" long, with pointed petals.
FRUITS: Very attractive, pointed, red, ovoid berries, about a half-inch in length.
SEASON OF MAXIMUM COLOR: Much of the year as flowers or fruits mature.
LANDSCAPE USES: One of the tropic's most popular hedge plants comes into its own in southern Florida. Set plants 18" o.c. In foundation arrangements, allow 2'-3' between individuals, and if orange-jasmine is used as informal enclosure, employ a 5' interval. Grown to a single trunk, orange-jasmine can make an excellent small terrace or patio tree.
   Now, in Florida, there are clonal selections, propagated vegetatively and sold under name, that are most highly recommended for landscaping here.
HABITAT: Tropical Asia; in Florida, landscape plantings in warm locations.
LIGHT REQUIREMENT: Tolerant of moderate shade, but grows well in full sun, too.
SOIL REQUIREMENT: Moderately fertile, well-drained earth that is free of nematodes.
SALT TOLERANCE: Not tolerant of dune conditions.
AVAILABILITY: Most nurseries in warm locations sell small plants in containers. Named clones may be found in some establishments.
CULTURE: Like all members of the citrus family, orange-jasmine must be protected against scale insects and nematodes.
PROPAGATION: Seedage or cuttage.
PESTS: Scales, nematodes, and white-flies, followed by sooty-mold.

Citrus Trees

Citrus (SIT-russ): ancient classical name.
Fortunella (for-tune-ELL-a): for R. Fortune, English traveler.
SPP.: several species and many hybrids are widely grown in Florida.

FAMILY: Rutaceae. **RELATIVES:** Orange-jasmine and lime-berry.
TYPE OF PLANT: Tree or shrub. **HEIGHT:** Variable. **ZONE:** N,C,S
HOW TO IDENTIFY: Evergreen, spiny trees produce yellow, orange, or red fruits, many of which are deliciously edible.
HABIT OF GROWTH: Generally dense, much-branched, round-headed trees or large shrubs.
FOLIAGE: Evergreen, alternate, variable in size, texture, form, and color; aromatic when crushed.
FLOWERS: White, very fragrant, most abundant in springtime.
FRUITS: Yellow, orange, or reddish hesperidiums, among the world's most delectable fruits.
SEASON OF MAXIMUM COLOR: Wintertime when fruits color.
LANDSCAPE USES: Plants of the citrus tribe are widely used in landscape developments. For shade, framing, backgrounds, hedging, and for horticultural interest these beautiful plants excel. No fruits are more delicious, no blossoms more fragrant, no trees more beautiful than those of the citrus group. This is a very diverse group in which may be found kinds for many garden uses.
HABITAT: Eastern Asia; in Florida, much of the peninsula.
LIGHT REQUIREMENT: Full sun for best fruiting.
SOIL REQUIREMENT: Moderately fertile, well-drained soil that can be watered during periods of drought is best.
SALT TOLERANCE: Not tolerant.
AVAILABILITY: Trees of many named varieties are offered in containers in nurseries, garden centers, and chain stores.
CULTURE: Set carefully in made-up, fertile sites; water faithfully; prevent lawn grasses from invading the root zone; protect from pests; fertilize thrice annually.
PROPAGATION: Graftage and marcottage.
PESTS: Nematodes, scales, mites, caterpillars, virus, and fungus diseases.

179
Gumbo-Limbo

Bursera (burr-SER-a): For J. Burser, a European botanist.
simaruba (sim-a-RUBE-a): because of similarity to a tree in the genus *Simarouba*.

FAMILY: Burseraceae.   RELATIVES: This is the only genus in the family.

TYPE OF PLANT: Tree.   HEIGHT: 60'. ZONE: S

HOW TO IDENTIFY: Shining, oily-smooth brown bark which looks as though it had been freshly varnished; the compound leaves are deciduous, and mature trees bear angled pods.

HABIT OF GROWTH: Asymmetric, picturesque, with a few huge branches.

FOLIAGE: Deciduous, pinnate, of medium fine texture and dark green color.

FLOWERS: Inconspicuous, greenish, before, or with, the first leaves in late winter.

FRUITS: Three-parted pods, ½" long, dark red, ripening in summertime.

SEASON OF MAXIMUM COLOR: Possibly when fruits mature.

LANDSCAPE USES: For the curiosity of the distinctive, light-brown, peeling bark, gumbo-limbo may be used as a freestanding specimen, or as an avenue tree. Nothing quite like this native tree is to be found in Florida's plant life; growth is rapid, yet there is marked resistance to strong winds, drought, and neglect.

In tropical lands huge truncheons are driven into the earth close together to make living fences; as the gumbo-limbo trees grow, they are decapitated with machetes for firewood.

HABITAT: Southern Florida and the offshore islands.

LIGHT REQUIREMENT: Full sun or high, shifting shade.

SOIL REQUIREMENT: Tolerant of many soils, including basic ones.

SALT TOLERANCE: Tolerant of salt drift back from the shore.

AVAILABILITY: Nurseries in southern Florida offer small trees in containers.

CULTURE: Once established in a frostless location, little attention need be given.

PROPAGATION: Cuttage, using wood of any size.

PESTS: Caterpillars chew the leaves.

180
China-Berry

Melia (ME-lee-a): ancient Greek name.
azedarach (a-ZED-ar-ack): from the Arabic for noble.

FAMILY: Meliaceae. **RELATIVES:** Mahogany and Spanish-cedar.

TYPE OF PLANT: Tree. **HEIGHT:** 40'. **ZONE:** N,C,S

HOW TO IDENTIFY: Lacy, bipinnate, deciduous foliage with a characteristic odor; attractive blue blossoms in summertime, followed by sticky, yellow fruits.

HABIT OF GROWTH: Seedlings grow rangy and open; clones have tight, compact heads.

FOLIAGE: Deciduous, bipinnate, fine in texture, and dark green in color.

FLOWERS: Attractive, fragrant blue flowers are produced in 8" panicles in summer.

FRUITS: Yellow, sticky drupes ¾" in diameter, smooth and round at first, becoming wrinkled late in the season. These are toxic to humans.

SEASON OF MAXIMUM COLOR: Summer.

LANDSCAPE USES: Since the arrival of the white man, China-berry trees have been used in Florida to furnish shade, and while they helped to make life more comfortable for the pioneers, these fast-growing, weak trees are not in good repute today.

Texas umbrella-tree, known as the variety 'Umbraculiformis,' grows with a straight trunk and many, short, straight branches to give the effect of a giant umbrella. This one must be grown vegetatively.

HABITAT: Southwestern Asia; in Florida, ubiquitous.

LIGHT REQUIREMENT: Full sun or shade of hammocks.

SOIL REQUIREMENT: Any soil appears to be suitable.

SALT TOLERANCE: Not tolerant.

AVAILABILITY: Usually seedlings or cuttings are given away.

CULTURE: Once planted, soon forgotten, China-berry takes care of itself.

PROPAGATION: Seedage or cuttage.

PESTS: White flies followed by sooty-mold.

181
Mahogany

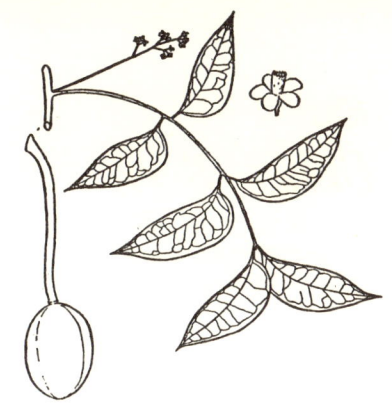

Swietenia (sweet-TEEN-ee-a): for G. von Swieten of the eighteenth century.
mahogani (ma-HOG-an-eye): an aboriginal American name.

FAMILY: Meliaceae.   RELATIVES: China-berry and Spanish-cedar.

TYPE OF PLANT: Tree.   HEIGHT: 40'. ZONE: S

HOW TO IDENTIFY: Large, high-headed tree bears even-pinnate deciduous leaves with petioled leaflets; conspicuous brown pods 5" long, by cords in wintertime.

HABIT OF GROWTH: Upright tree with broad, rounded, symmetrical crown.

FOLIAGE: Deciduous, compound, of medium texture and medium green color.

FLOWERS: Inconspicuous, greenish, on stalks in axils of current growth.

FRUITS: Ovoid, brown capsules about 5" long that hang downward from cords.

SEASON OF MAXIMUM COLOR: Possibly when new growth first emerges.

LANDSCAPE USES: As a street tree, 25'-35' apart, mahogany is in high favor in warm parts. As a framing tree, it serves, too, because it does not cast heavy shade to discourage the growth of grasses beneath, and, furthermore, it is notably storm-fast. Here is another native plant that is good for landscaping in Florida, and many thousands will be needed in future landscape developments.

HABITAT: Native in parts of Dade and Monroe counties; cultured there and in other warm areas.

LIGHT REQUIREMENT: Full sun or partial shade.

SOIL REQUIREMENT: Tolerant of many soils, acid or alkaline.

SALT TOLERANCE: Quite tolerant of salt drift.

AVAILABILITY: Small mahogany trees in containers are in nurseries in south Florida.

CULTURE: Plant with reasonable care in frost-free locations; water periodically; fertilize twice during each growing season.

PROPAGATION: Seedage.

PESTS: Tent caterpillars must be controlled.

Holly Malpighia

Malpighia (mal-PIG-ee-a): for M. Malpighi, Italian naturalist.
coccigera (cok-SIG-er-a): berry-bearing.

FAMILY: Malpighiaceae.   RELATIVES: Thryallis and stigmaphyllon.

TYPE OF PLANT: Dwarf shrub.   HEIGHT: 3'. ZONE: S

HOW TO IDENTIFY: Dwarf shrub furnished with evergreen, opposite, short-petioled, spiny-toothed leaves; open, pink flowers and red fruits.

HABIT OF GROWTH: Plants of the type grow upright by ascending branches; those of named clones are densely spreading or weeping in habit.

FOLIAGE: Opposite, evergreen, holly-like, of very fine texture and medium green color.

FLOWERS: Pink, flaring, wavy-petaled, ½" across, in axillary cymes.

FRUITS: Decorative, globose, red drupes ⅓" in diameter.

SEASON OF MAXIMUM COLOR: Much of the year when flowers or fruits mature.

LANDSCAPE USES: For foundation plantings, for planter bins, and as a transition plant, holly malpighia is one of southern Florida's very best dwarf shrubs. Set the plants 2' apart.
   Named clones of weeping habit are most popular, and as a striking accent, a clone with attractively variegated foliage may be chosen.

HABITAT: West Indies; in Florida, landscape plantings in warmest parts.

LIGHT REQUIREMENT: A partially shaded garden spot is highly suitable.

SOIL REQUIREMENT: A good, fertile soil, free of nematodes is requisite.

SALT TOLERANCE: Not tolerant of dune conditions.

AVAILABILITY: Nurseries in southern Florida market seedlings of the original type, and cutting-grown plants of the named varieties in containers of sterilized soil.

CULTURE: Plant in frost-free locations, in sterilized soil; water faithfully; fertilize twice during each growing season.

PROPAGATION: Seedage for the type, cuttage for the named clones.

PESTS: Nematodes, scales, and mites.

183
Thryallis

Thryallis (thry-AL-is): old Greek name.
glauca (GLAW-ka): for the dark red fuzz on the new growth.

FAMILY: Malpighiaceae.   **RELATIVES:** Malpighia and stigmaphyllon.

TYPE OF PLANT: Shrub.   **HEIGHT:** 9'.   **ZONE:** N,C,S

HOW TO IDENTIFY: Very fine twigs, reddish while young; evergreen opposite leaves almost, or quite, sessile; yellow flowers in terminal panicles.

HABIT OF GROWTH: Compact because of many fine close twigs, and abundant foliage.

FOLIAGE: Evergreen, opposite, medium in texture, light green in color.

FLOWERS: Showy yellow, in terminal panicles, abundant during much of the year.

FRUITS: Little capsules which split into 3 parts when brown and dry.

SEASON OF MAXIMUM COLOR: Late summer and fall.

LANDSCAPE USES: Foundation plantings, allow 3' between plants; for color in front of green shrubbery, use groups of 3 at 3' intervals between plants. Combine with blue plumbago or blue stokesia for a pleasing effect in complementary colors.
   Where winters are mild, thryallis is one of Florida's very best landscape shrubs. Plants may be injured by a temperature of 28° F.

HABITAT: Tropical America; in Florida, popular landscape shrub on the peninsula.

LIGHT REQUIREMENT: Full sun for best habit and free flowering.

SOIL REQUIREMENT: Dry, well-drained soils of many types are suitable.

SALT TOLERANCE: Tolerant of mild salt drift well away from the sea.

AVAILABILITY: Thryallis is widely available in containers.

CULTURE: No special culture is demanded within the climatic range of the plant.

PROPAGATION: Seedage, sow green fruits; cuttage, take cuttings in July.

PESTS: Caterpillars and mites.

184
African Milk-Bush

Synadenium (sin-a-DEAN-ee-um): Greek, referring to united floral parts.
grantii (GRANT-ee-eye): for a person named Grant.

FAMILY: Euphorbiaceae. RELATIVES: Castor-bean and poinsettia.
TYPE OF PLANT: Shrub. HEIGHT: 8′. ZONE: S

HOW TO IDENTIFY: Stiff, thick, sausage-like branches yield milky sap when wounded and hold thick, succulent, obovate, toothed leaves about 4″ long. These leaves may be more persistent than with some other cactus-like euphorbes. Clusters of red blossoms are produced terminally.

HABIT OF GROWTH: Scraggly, open, by thick, succulent stems.

FOLIAGE: Obovate, thick, succulent, toothed leaves with rounded midribs are perhaps more persistent than are those of other cactus-like euphorbes.

FLOWERS: Clusters of small red flowers are borne terminally.

FRUITS: Capsules, if present.

SEASON OF MAXIMUM COLOR: Warm months when red new growth or red flowers are present.

LANDSCAPE USES: African milk-bush, like other tropical euphorbes, is cultured for its bizarre, exotic effect. It can form striking compositions in frostless locations, and it thrives as an urn subject, too.

HABITAT: Tropical Africa.

LIGHT REQUIREMENT: Full sun or partial shade. 'Rubra' colors best in bright light.

SOIL REQUIREMENT: Any soil, including dune sand and bay-bottom marl.

SALT TOLERANCE: Excellent for ocean-front plantings.

AVAILABILITY: Many nurseries in warmer sections carry plants in containers.

CULTURE: Simply plant a piece of stem in a frostless site; water moderately until established; then forget.

PROPAGATION: Cuttage.

PESTS: None of major consequence.

NOTE: More attractive than the all-green type is its clone 'Rubra'. In this one the stems are reddish and the leaves have a reddish cast above and are a glowing wine-red beneath.

185
Crown-of-Thorns

Euphorbia (you-FOR-bee-a): old classical name.
milii (MILL-ee-eye): Baron Milius, once governor of Bourbon.

FAMILY: Euphorbiaceae. RELATIVES: Poinsettia and Mexican fire-plant.

TYPE OF PLANT: Dwarf shrub. HEIGHT: 3'. ZONE: C,S

HOW TO IDENTIFY: Milky sap from stems that are densely armed with 1" spines, leaves restricted to new growth; bright red bracts, ½" across, subtend the true flowers.

HABIT OF GROWTH: Sprawling.

FOLIAGE: Very sparse, restricted to tips of new growth, coarse in texture.

FLOWERS: Inconspicuous, subtended by bright red or pink bracts ½" across.

FRUITS: Not usually formed.

SEASON OF MAXIMUM COLOR: Warm months when red or pink bracts are expanded.

LANDSCAPE USES: For planters, and as a ground cover, crown-of-thorns is excellent because of its low, weeping habit and its ability to withstand adverse conditions. This is one of the many striking euphorbes that help to give Florida a tropical aspect. As noted above, bracts may be produced in tones of red or pink, some sorts having larger flowers than other varieties.

HABITAT: Madagascar; in Florida, well-drained situations protected from frost.

LIGHT REQUIREMENT: Intense light for best habit and flowering.

SOIL REQUIREMENT: Very well-drained soil of low fertility is sufficient.

SALT TOLERANCE: Excellent for ocean-front plantings.

AVAILABILITY: Most nurseries in warmer sections carry crown-of-thorns in containers.

CULTURE: Overwatering and overfertilization must be avoided.

PROPAGATION: Cuttage.

PESTS: None of great importance.

NOTE: Christ thorn hybrids, shown above left, are in great favor. These plants of slow growth and dwarf habit thrive under adverse conditions.

186
Milkstripe Euphorbia

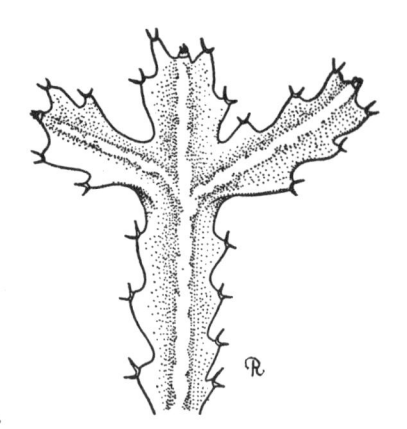

Euphorbia (you-FOR-bee-a): old classical name.
lactea (LACK-tee-a): milk-white.

FAMILY: Euphorbiaceae.　　RELATIVES: Poinsettia, crown-of-thorns, and pencil-tree.

TYPE OF PLANT: Cactus-like shrub.　　HEIGHT: 15'. ZONE: S

HOW TO IDENTIFY: A cactus-like plant with 3- or 4-angled stems that have brown spines and exude a milky sap when cut. The stems of this species have bands of yellow marbling toward their centers.

HABIT OF GROWTH: Candelabra-like, geometric branching of the angled stems.

FOLIAGE: Minute, ephemeral, very fine in texture, light green in color when present.

FLOWERS: Inconspicuous, cup-like, in terminal positions when present.

FRUITS: Usually not produced in Florida.

SEASON OF MAXIMUM COLOR: No seasonal color change.

LANDSCAPE USES: To enhance the tropical effect, milkstripe euphorbia is much used. It serves as an ocean-front, defensive hedge (set 18" o.c.), as a single specimen, and as an urn subject or planter material. This plant is very tender to cold.
　　Euphorbes can be distinguished from cacti by their milky sap.

HABITAT: East Indies; in Florida, much cultured in most nearly frost-free areas.

LIGHT REQUIREMENT: Full sun of dunes or shade of Florida rooms.

SOIL REQUIREMENT: Any soil, including dune sand and bay-bottom marl.

SALT TOLERANCE: Very tolerant of salt, recommended for ocean-front planting.

AVAILABILITY: Garden centers, and chain stores sell this, and other euphorbes.

CULTURE: Simply plant a piece of stem in a frostless location, water moderately until established, and forget.

PROPAGATION: Cuttage.

PESTS: None of major consequence.

NOTE: Crested milkstripe euphorbia has deformed, gnarled and crested, much-shortened branches.

187
Pencil-Tree

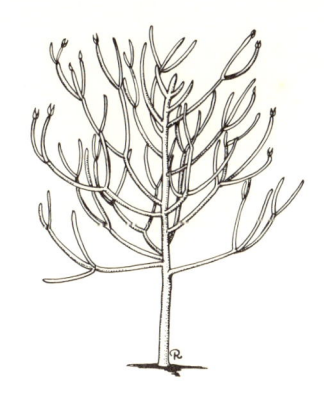

Euphorbia (you-FOR-bee-a): old classical name.
tirucalli (ter-oo-CALL-eye): native Indian name.

FAMILY: Euphorbiaceae.   RELATIVES: Poinsettia and crown-of-thorns.

TYPE OF PLANT: Cactus-like tree.   HEIGHT: 20'. ZONE: S

HOW TO IDENTIFY: A plant that has pencil-size, leafless branches that yield milky sap.

HABIT OF GROWTH: Candelabra-like branching of the upward-pointing pencil-form stems.

FOLIAGE: Minute, ephemeral, of very fine texture when present; medium green.

FLOWERS: Inconspicuous, cup-like, in sessile clusters at the tops of branches.

FRUITS: Capsules, which split at maturity, if present.

SEASON OF MAXIMUM COLOR: Little seasonal change.

LANDSCAPE USES: To enhance the tropical effect, pencil-tree is much used in frostless, ocean-front locations. As a defensive hedge (15" o.c.), especially on sand dunes, as a planter material, or as an urn subject for terrace or Florida room, this succulent is very popular.

HABITAT: Tropical Africa; in Florida, much cultured in most nearly frost-free areas.

LIGHT REQUIREMENT: Full sun of ocean dunes, or shade of porches or canopies.

SOIL REQUIREMENT: Any soil, including dune sand and bay-bottom marl.

SALT TOLERANCE: Very tolerant of salt, and recommended for dune planting.

AVAILABILITY: Widely available wherever plants are sold, pencil-tree is a favorite.

CULTURE: Simply plant a piece of stem in frostless location, water moderately until established, and forget.

PROPAGATION: Cuttage.

PESTS: None of major consequence.

188
Poinsettia

Euphorbia (you-FOR-bee-a): old classical name.
pulcherrima (pull-KARE-ee-ma): very handsome.

Family: Euphorbiaceae.   **Relatives:** Pencil-tree, crown-of-thorns, and copper-leaf.

Type of Plant: Large shrub.   **Height:** 12'.   **Zone:** N,C,S

How to Identify: Milky latex, huge alternating, simple leaves and red-bracted inflorescences at Christmas time.

Habit of Growth: Stiffly upright by long, unbranched canes.

Foliage: Evergreen, very coarse in texture, light green in color.

Flowers: Inconspicuous, cup-like, subtended by bright red floral leaves called bracts.

Fruits: Inconspicuous, lobed capsules.

Season of Maximum Color: Christmas time.

Landscape Uses: Because of huge size, coarse foliage, and susceptibility to frost injury, poinsettias should be planted in distant parts of shrubbery borders so that their great scale does not show to disadvantage, and so that, when they are killed to the ground, hardy shrubs growing nearby will maintain the form of the garden. Planting interval may be about 5' o.c.

Habitat: Central America; in Florida, ubiquitous in plantings about homes.

Light Requirement: Full sun for best flowering. Nights must be unbroken by light.

Soil Requirement: Any well-drained soil is adequate.

Salt Tolerance: Not tolerant.

Availability: Some nurseries offer poinsettias in containers.

Culture: No shrub is of easier culture. Fertilize 2 or 3 times in warm months, cut back in August to induce branching.

Propagation: Cuttage by long, hardwood cuttings stuck directly in the earth.

Pests: Poinsettia scab in southern Florida, scales, mites, and thrips.

Note: There are types with white bracts, others with pink floral leaves, some with many, closely packed red bracts to make heavy heads.

189
Pedilanthus

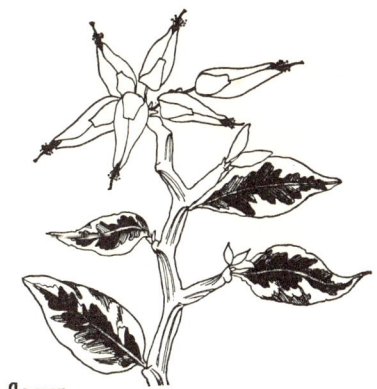

Pedilanthus (peddy-LAN-thus): Greek for slipper-flower.
tithymaloides (tithy-mal-OY-dez): like tithymalus, a euphorbe.

FAMILY: Euphorbiaceae.   RELATIVES: Poinsettia and pencil-tree.

TYPE OF PLANT: Herbaceous perennial.   HEIGHT: 6'. ZONE: C,S

HOW TO IDENTIFY: Zigzag, herbaceous, green stems exude milky sap when injured. Alternate, evergreen leaves, about 4" long, are often marbled with white, sometimes with pink, in popular varieties. Curious little blossoms are slipper-shaped as indicated by the generic name.

HABIT OF GROWTH: Stiffly upright by clustered, zigzag stems.

FOLIAGE: Evergreen or deciduous, clustered near tips of branches, medium in texture, often marbled with white, sometimes with pink.

FLOWERS: Inconspicuous, cup-like, in dense terminal cymes, the bright red bracts, about ½" long, are slipper-shaped.

FRUITS: Lobed capsules about ¼" long.

SEASON OF MAXIMUM COLOR: Warm months when blossoms appear.

LANDSCAPE USES: To enhance the tropical atmosphere, grown in the earth or in urns or planter bins, pedilanthus is widely approved. There are several popular forms, all of which are known as devils-backbone and slipper-flower. Like almost all euphorbes, pedilanthus is tender to cold.

HABITAT: Tropical America, warmest parts of Florida included.

LIGHT REQUIREMENT: Full sun or partial shade is satisfactory.

SOIL REQUIREMENT: Many kinds of soils are acceptable.

SALT TOLERANCE: Tolerant of conditions just back of the first dunes.

AVAILABILITY: Garden centers and chain stores offer plants in containers.

CULTURE: Like most euphorbes, pedilanthus is very easy to grow where frost is not a factor. Plant, water, and forget; but good growth will be the rule if a little fertilizer is thrown near the plant in springtime.

PROPAGATION: Cuttage.

PESTS: Mites and scales.

190
Snow-Bush

Breynia (BRAY-knee-a): for J. Breyn, German botanist of the seventeenth century.
nivosa (nye-VOE-sa): snowy.

FAMILY: Euphorbiaceae.　　RELATIVES: Poinsettia, slipper-flower, and copper-leaf.

TYPE OF PLANT: Shrub.　　HEIGHT: 10'. ZONE: C,S

HOW TO IDENTIFY: Dark red, zigzag branches, alternate leaves that are variously mottled with red, pink, and white.

HABIT OF GROWTH: Loose habit unless pruned frequently for compactness.

FOLIAGE: Evergreen, medium-fine in texture, brightly variegated in several colors.

FLOWERS: Inconspicuous, greenish, carried on long pedicels.

FRUITS: Berries that are ½" in diameter, or less.

SEASON OF MAXIMUM COLOR: The year around.

LANDSCAPE USES: Snow-bush is very popular for hedges because of its bright, multicolored leaves. Plants may be set 2' apart.

Because of the bright colors and somewhat loose, ungainly habit snow-bush is probably not best to use in foundation planting arrangements. As warm color accents, groups of 3 of a variety together, may highlight a bay in neutral green shrubbery. Plant 3' o.c. in this use.

There are many leaf-color arrangements. All are rather tender to cold.

HABITAT: South Sea Islands; in Florida, popular for hedges in warm locations.

LIGHT REQUIREMENT: Full sun for compact habit of growth.

SOIL REQUIREMENT: Light, sandy soils are adequate.

SALT TOLERANCE: Not tolerant.

AVAILABILITY: Most nurseries in central and southern Florida have plants for sale.

CULTURE: After planting in moderately fertile sites, no attention other than pruning for compactness, the usual watering, and fertilization is needed.

PROPAGATION: Cuttage.

PESTS: Mites and caterpillars.

191
Chenille-Plant

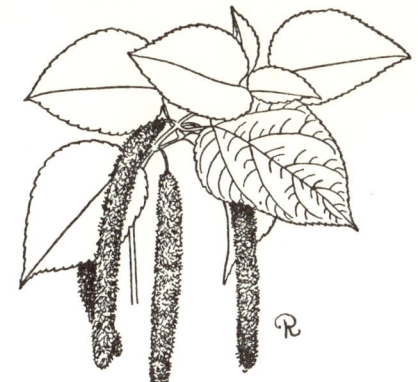

Acalypha (ack-a-LYE-fa): Greek for nettle.
hispida (HISS-pid-a): bristly, referring to the pistillate inflorescence.

FAMILY: Euphorbiaceae.   **RELATIVES:** Poinsettia, croton, and snow-bush.
TYPE OF PLANT: Shrub.   **HEIGHT:** 8′. **ZONE:** S

HOW TO IDENTIFY: A vigorous shrub that bears 8″ ovate, all-green leaves with pubescence on petioles and veins. Pistillate individuals produce spectacular red spikes of blossoms in cattail form.

HABIT OF GROWTH: Coarse, upright, from many, heavily foliated stems.

FOLIAGE: Evergreen, alternate, very coarse in texture, solid deep green in color.

FLOWERS: Showy red cattails up to 18″ long are borne by female plants.

FRUITS: Usually not seen in Florida.

SEASON OF MAXIMUM COLOR: Warm months when new growth produces red cattails.

LANDSCAPE USES: Chenille-plant attracts a great deal of attention because of its spectacular blossoms. Plant 3 bushes together, with 3′ between individuals, in front of all-green shrubbery, as a bright, warm-weather accent. While the red-flowered form is most popular, there is a clone that bears creamy-white cattails. Chenille-plant is tender to cold.

HABITAT: East Indies; in Florida, landscape plantings in warmest locations.

LIGHT REQUIREMENT: Full sun for best flowering.

SOIL REQUIREMENT: Grows well in many types of soil if drainage is adequate.

SALT TOLERANCE: Not tolerant.

AVAILABILITY: Specialty nurseries in southern Florida may have small plants in containers.

CULTURE: After reasonably careful planting in a frostless location, little maintenance is needed. After flowering, prune to keep plant within bounds.

PROPAGATION: Cuttage.

PESTS: Scales, mites, and aphids.

192 Copper-Leaf

Acalypha (ack-a-LYE-fa): Greek for nettle.
wilkesiana (wilkes-ee-ANE-a): for C. Wilkes, a nineteenth-century scientist.

FAMILY: Euphorbiaceae.   RELATIVES: Poinsettia, snow-bush, and croton.

TYPE OF PLANT: Shrub.   HEIGHT: 15'. ZONE: S

HOW TO IDENTIFY: A huge, coarse, sprawling shrub with outsize, evergreen, dentate leaves variously mottled in shades of red and purple, green and yellow. These run into many forms.

HABIT OF GROWTH: Huge, coarse, sprawling, many-stemmed shrub of vigorous growth.

FOLIAGE: Evergreen, alternate, dentate, variously mottled and variously shaped, but invariably very large in size.

FLOWERS: Axillary catkins, of no garden value.

FRUITS: Often absent in Florida.

SEASON OF MAXIMUM COLOR: Very colorful the year around.

LANDSCAPE USES: The only approved landscape use of this dazzling, huge shrub, is as a bright accent in an all-green shrubbery border. Set one group of 3 plants with 3'-5' intervals between them. There are numbers of clones that display varying leaf forms, but all are very tender to cold.

HABITAT: South Sea Islands; in Florida, ubiquitous in landscape plantings in warmest parts.

LIGHT REQUIREMENT: Full sun for best foliage color and compact growth.

SOIL REQUIREMENT: Grows well in many different soils.

SALT TOLERANCE: Not tolerant of dune conditions.

AVAILABILITY: All garden centers and retail nurseries in southern Florida market small copper-leafs (6 or 8 kinds) in containers.

CULTURE: These are among the easiest of all shrubs to grow, yet they are very sensitive to cold.

PROPAGATION: Cuttage, using any kind of wood at any season.

PESTS: Scales and mites.

193
Physic Nut

Jatropha (JAT-row-fah): Greek, referring to medicinal use.
curcas (CUR-cass): an aboriginal name.

FAMILY: Euphorbiaceae.   **RELATIVES:** Copper-leaf, poinsettia, and crown-of-thorns.

TYPE OF PLANT: Shrubby small tree.   **HEIGHT:** 15'. **ZONE:** S

HOW TO IDENTIFY: Milky sap, heart-shaped leaves that have 3-5 lobes; oval nuts 1" in diameter.

HABIT OF GROWTH: Upright, scraggly shrub.

FOLIAGE: Evergreen, of very coarse texture and deep green color.

FLOWERS: Inconspicuous, yellowish-green, in springtime.

FRUITS: Oval nuts 1½" long, 3-seeded, poisonous.

SEASON OF MAXIMUM COLOR: Not much seasonal variation.

LANDSCAPE USES: As a freestanding specimen, physic nut is sometimes seen for the curiosity of its fruits. The plant is very poisonous. The nuts are carried by some persons as lucky pocket pieces.
   This euphorbe is not recommended, but it must be known to all horticulturists.

HABITAT: Tropical America; in Florida, gardens in warmest parts.

LIGHT REQUIREMENT: Broken shade under tall trees.

SOIL REQUIREMENT: Any soil is suitable.

SALT TOLERANCE: Not tolerant.

AVAILABILITY: Nurseries in southern Florida carry jatrophas of several kinds.

CULTURE: Plant, water, and forget.

PROPAGATION: Cuttage or seedage.

PESTS: Mites, mushroom root-rot.

NOTE: Bellyache bush (*Jatropha gossypifolia*), with its purple, lobed, 6" leaves is grown for its tropical aspect. The little red flowers are attractive, yet the plant, like others in the genus, is extremely POISONOUS. All jatrophas are tender to frost.

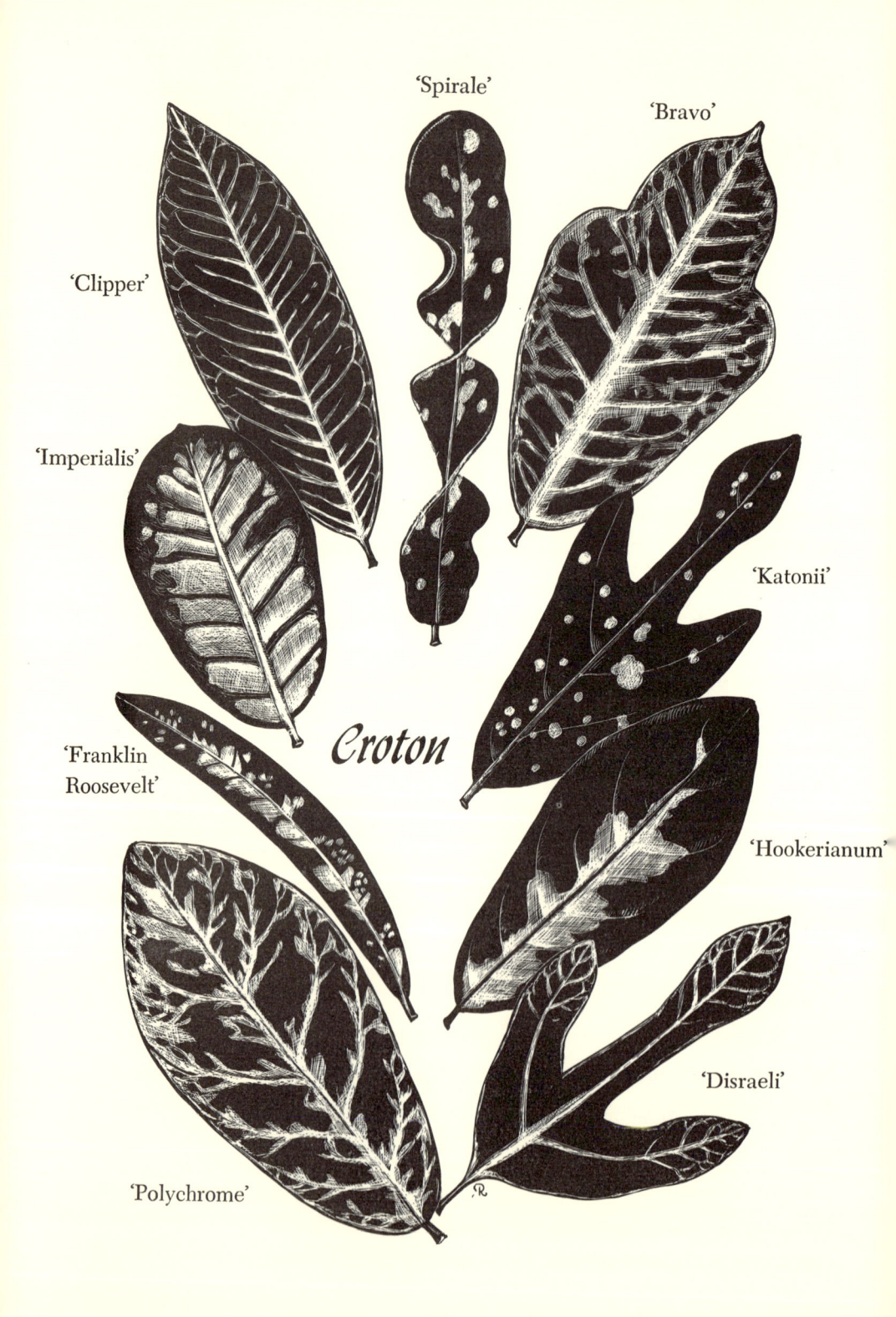

Croton

'Clipper' · 'Spirale' · 'Bravo' · 'Imperialis' · 'Katonii' · 'Franklin Roosevelt' · 'Hookerianum' · 'Polychrome' · 'Disraeli'

195
Croton

Codiaeum (co-dye-EE-um): Greek for head, referring to the use of croton leaves for wreaths.
variegatum (vare-ee-a-GAY-tum): variegated, referring to the mottled foliage.

FAMILY: Euphorbiaceae.   RELATIVES: Copper-leaf, poinsettia, and pencil-tree.

TYPE OF PLANT: Shrub.   HEIGHT: 10'. ZONE: C,S

HOW TO IDENTIFY: The world's most colorful and variable shrub.

HABIT OF GROWTH: Variable, there are dwarf forms and tree-like varieties.

FOLIAGE: Evergreen, highly variable, usually coarse in texture, brightly variegated in color.

FLOWERS: Inconspicuous, in racemes from leaf axils.

FRUITS: Globose capsules which break into lobes.

SEASON OF MAXIMUM COLOR: The year around!

LANDSCAPE USES: Accents in all-green compositions; use small groups of a single variety in front of neutral, all-green shrubs. Fine-leaved, all green varieties of dwarf habit may be used in planters upon occasion.
  Unquestionably, this is one of the most popular shrubs in hot countries the world around. The varieties are almost without end, but naming is confused.

HABITAT: Malaya; in Florida widely planted in frost-free sections.

LIGHT REQUIREMENT: Variable with variety, some thrive in sun, others in shade.

SOIL REQUIREMENT: Tolerant of many soil types if drainage is adequate.

SALT TOLERANCE: Tolerant of mild salt drift well back of the dunes.

AVAILABILITY: Small crotons in containers are offered by most nurseries on the peninsula.

CULTURE: After plants become established in protected locations, spraying for insect control and pruning for form are all that is needed.

PROPAGATION: Cuttage and marcottage.

PESTS: Scales of many species, thrips, mites, and root-rot diseases.

196
Coral Plant

Jatropha (JAT-row-fah): Greek, referring to medicinal use.
multifida (mul-TIFF-id-ah): much-cleft.

FAMILY: Euphorbiaceae.   RELATIVES: Copper-leaf, pencil-tree, and poinsettia.

TYPE OF PLANT: Shrub.   HEIGHT: 15'. ZONE: S

HOW TO IDENTIFY: Finely cut leaves grow out from the tip of a stout thorny trunk, whence emerge the clusters of bright, coral-red flowers. Milky sap is released if the bark is scored.

HABIT OF GROWTH: Erect, ungainly, from a single, stout, thorny trunk.

FOLIAGE: Evergreen, deeply cut to become almost fern-like, of fine texture.

FLOWERS: Bright, coral-red in very showy terminal clusters.

FRUITS: Three-cornered pods which turn from green to yellow at maturity.

SEASON OF MAXIMUM COLOR: Warm months when blossoms appear.

LANDSCAPE USES: For a note of bright coral color and the curiosity of its finely cut foliage, coral plant may stand alone in front of green shrubbery.

HABITAT: Tropical America; in Florida, rather popular in warmest parts.

LIGHT REQUIREMENT: Full sun or high, shifting, pine shade.

SOIL REQUIREMENT: Tolerant of many kinds of soils.

SALT TOLERANCE: Not tolerant.

AVAILABILITY: Retail nurseries in southern Florida offer small plants.

CULTURE: Plant in an enriched site; water a few times; and forget.

PROPAGATION: Cuttage or seedage.

PESTS: Mites and scales.

NOTE: Peregrina (*J. hastata*) is a large, compact shrub with evergreen fiddle-shaped leaves and conspicuous red flowers. All jatrophas are tender to frost, and are very toxic to human beings.

197
Toog

Bischofia (bis-CHOF-ee-a): for G. Bischoff, German botanist.
javanica (ja-VAN-i-ca): Javanese.

FAMILY: Euphorbiaceae.

RELATIVES: Croton, poinsettia, and crown-of-thorns.

TYPE OF PLANT: Tree.

HEIGHT: 40'. ZONE: C,S

HOW TO IDENTIFY: A fast-growing tree with milky sap; shiny, bronze-toned, trifoliate leaves. The bright, shining new growth is particularly striking.

HABIT OF GROWTH: Symmetrical, dense, round head from a huge trunk.

FOLIAGE: Evergreen, compound, of coarse texture and dark green color when mature.

FLOWERS: Inconspicuous.

FRUITS: Black, fleshy, ¼" in diameter.

SEASON OF MAXIMUM COLOR: Warm weather when bronze new growth appears.

LANDSCAPE USES: In southern Florida where quick, dense shade is needed, toog may serve. The tree grows very rapidly to large size, the dense crown discourages lawn grasses, and the brittle wood is very likely to break in high winds.

HABITAT: Old World Tropics; in Florida, sandy soils in most nearly frostless sections.

LIGHT REQUIREMENT: Full sun.

SOIL REQUIREMENT: Widely varying soils are tolerated, acidic or basic.

SALT TOLERANCE: Not tolerant of dune conditions.

AVAILABILITY: Toog is sometimes sold in retail nurseries.

CULTURE: Like most members of its family, toog grows with the greatest of ease in Florida.

PROPAGATION: Cuttage.

PESTS: None of major consequence.

Japanese Boxwood

Buxus (BUCKS-us): ancient Latin name.
microphylla (my-crow-PHIL-a): small-leaved.

FAMILY: Buxaceae.

RELATIVES: The genus stands alone.

TYPE OF PLANT: Dwarf shrub.

HEIGHT: 5'. ZONE: N,C

HOW TO IDENTIFY: Green, quadrangular, conspicuously winged branchlets bear little evergreen leaves in opposite arrangement.

HABIT OF GROWTH: Very compact.

FOLIAGE: Evergreen, opposite, very fine in texture, medium green in color.

FLOWERS: Inconspicuous.

FRUITS: Usually none are produced in Florida.

SEASON OF MAXIMUM COLOR: Winter, when leaves turn red-bronze.

LANDSCAPE USES: From Tampa northward, Japanese boxwood is one of Florida's very best all-green, dwarf shrubs. For shady, nematode-free soils, it is without superior. For foundation plantings, especially on north walls, set about 2' apart. For edging walks, plant in double, staggered rows at 1' intervals. In planters, with English ivy, use the same distance.

HABITAT: China and Japan; in Florida, upper central and northern areas.

LIGHT REQUIREMENT: Shade tolerant, north-side location is ideal.

SOIL REQUIREMENT: Fertile acid soil free of nematodes is recommended.

SALT TOLERANCE: Not tolerant.

AVAILABILITY: Nurseries in upper Florida sell boxwood in containers of various sizes.

CULTURE: On the peninsula, plant on a north-side location, in fertile soil that has been made free of nematodes. On superior soils of the panhandle, no special precautions are observed.

PROPAGATION: Cuttage.

PESTS: Nematodes, mites, and leaf-miners.

NOTE: Harland boxwood has narrower, darker foliage, is said to be somewhat resistant to nematodes.

199
Brazilian Pepper-Tree

Schinus (SKY-nus): Greek for the mastic tree.
terebinthifolius (terry-BIN-the-FOL-ee-us): for the turpentine odor of the foliage.

FAMILY: Anacardiaceae.   RELATIVES: Mango, sumac, and pistachio.

TYPE OF PLANT: Tree or shrub.   HEIGHT: 25'. ZONE: C,S

HOW TO IDENTIFY: Rough, odorous, evergreen, odd-pinnate leaves composed of 7 sessile leaflets complement the bright red fruits that are borne by pistillate individuals during the winter.

HABIT OF GROWTH: Stiffly upright by coarse, thick branches, densely clothed with foliage.

FOLIAGE: Evergreen, aromatic, coarse, dark green above, lighter beneath.

FLOWERS: Inconspicuous, unisexual, in dense, bracteate panicles.

FRUITS: Bright red drupes, 3/16" in diameter, in heavy clusters are produced by female plants.

SEASON OF MAXIMUM COLOR: The Christmas season.

LANDSCAPE USES: As a part of a barrier planting for large properties, set Brazilian pepper-trees 5' o.c. or use a single fruiting specimen as a shade tree for a terrace or patio.

HABITAT: Brazil; in Florida, widely planted in central and southern sections.

LIGHT REQUIREMENT: Full sun for best compact habit and full fruiting.

SOIL REQUIREMENT: Grows well in reasonably well-drained, moderately fertile sand.

SALT TOLERANCE: Tolerant of mild salt air back of the front-line dunes.

AVAILABILITY: Select fruiting individuals in containers at your garden center or retail nursery.

CULTURE: After careful planting, no special care is needed as this plant is very well adapted to conditions in central and southern Florida.

PROPAGATION: Seedage; cuttage for superior fruiting individuals.

PESTS: Foliage thrips, mites, scales, and nematodes.

NOTE: California pepper-tree (*Schinus molle*) is not widely planted in Florida.

American Holly

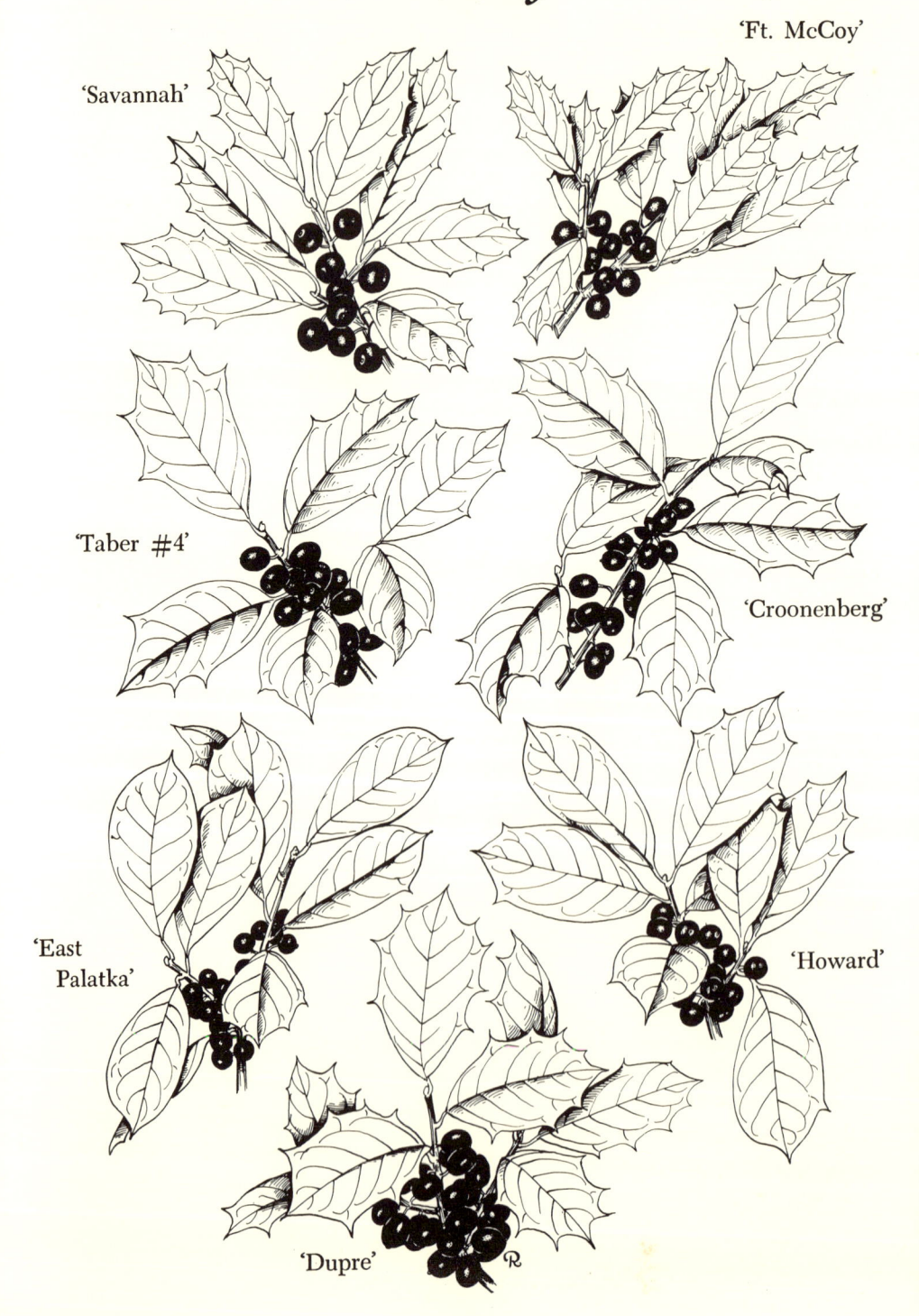

'Savannah'

'Ft. McCoy'

'Taber #4'

'Croonenberg'

'East Palatka'

'Howard'

'Dupre'

201 American Holly

Ilex (EYE-lecks): ancient Latin name for *Quercus ilex*.
opaca (oh-PAY-ka): shaded.

FAMILY: Aquifoliaceae.

RELATIVES: The hollies.

TYPE OF PLANT: Tree.

HEIGHT: 50'. **ZONE:** N,C

HOW TO IDENTIFY: Evergreen, alternate leaves, mostly with spines, growing from gray twigs, accompanied by red fruits on female trees during the winter.

HABIT OF GROWTH: Mostly pyramidal-upright with very dense, symmetrical head.

FOLIAGE: Evergreen, alternate, armed, fine to medium in texture, dull green in color.

FLOWERS: Unisexual, inconspicuous, in few-flowered axillary cymes.

FRUITS: Globose, berry-like drupes, usually red, and extremely decorative.

SEASON OF MAXIMUM COLOR: Winter.

LANDSCAPE USES: American holly is one of America's most beloved fruiting trees. Specimens have been used for avenue and yard plantings since the beginning of American history.
    There are scores of named clones that exhibit many diverse leaf forms, variation in fruiting habits, fruit color, and other characteristics.

HABITAT: Hammock areas in the upper half of the Florida peninsula.

LIGHT REQUIREMENT: Broken, shifting shade or full sun.

SOIL REQUIREMENT: Fertile, organic, slightly acid, well-drained soil.

SALT TOLERANCE: Tolerant of salt air back of the dunes.

AVAILABILITY: Nurseries in northern Florida offer holly trees in containers and B & B.

CULTURE: Plant in prepared sites at the same level the trees grew formerly; water faithfully; protect foliage from spittle bugs during hot weather; fertilize twice annually. A mulch over the roots is recommended.

PROPAGATION: Cuttage or graftage.

PESTS: Spittle bugs, scales, and leaf-miners.

202 Chinese Holly

Ilex (EYE-lecks): ancient Latin name for *Quercus ilex*.
cornuta (cor-NEW-ta): horned, referring to spines on the leaves.

FAMILY: Aquifoliaceae.
TYPE OF PLANT: Shrub or tree.
RELATIVES: The hollies.
HEIGHT: 20'. ZONE: N,C
HOW TO IDENTIFY: Shining, evergreen leaves, often with revolute edges and one or more sharp spines, are closely packed on stout twigs of compact large shrubs or small trees. Fruits are larger than those borne by any holly in Florida.
HABIT OF GROWTH: Shrubby in selected clones, yet seedlings become tree-like with age.
FOLIAGE: Evergreen, shining, armed, of medium texture and dark green color.
FLOWERS: Unisexual, inconspicuous.
FRUITS: Berry-like drupes, scarlet (yellow in one variety), ½" across.
SEASON OF MAXIMUM COLOR: Fall if fruits mature.
LANDSCAPE USES: Varieties must be listed with the most beautiful evergreen shrubs for upper Florida. In foundation plantings use a 3' interval between plants, for shrubbery borders, allow 5'. 'Burford,' the leading clone, is shrubby, with entire, revolute leaves with single, apical thorns. 'National' is quite similar in appearance. 'Hume' has narrower leaves, and 'Jungle Garden' has yellow fruits. On the Florida peninsula, Chinese holly may not fruit as heavily as it does farther to the north and west.
HABITAT: Eastern Asia; in Florida, gardens of central and northern counties.
LIGHT REQUIREMENT: Full sun or partial shade.
SOIL REQUIREMENT: Superior, well-drained soil that is slightly acid in reaction.
SALT TOLERANCE: Not tolerant.
AVAILABILITY: Container-grown plants of 'Burford' are commonly stocked by retail sales lots, other clones are not widely offered.
CULTURE: On superior soils of northern counties, plant carefully at former depth; water periodically; fertilize twice each growing season; and combat scales and spittle bugs.
PROPAGATION: Cuttage with the aid of root-inducing chemicals.
PESTS: Scales and spittle bugs.

203
Round Holly

Ilex (EYE-lecks): ancient Latin name for *Quercus ilex*.
rotunda (row-TUN-da): round, referring to the symmetrical head of the tree.

FAMILY: Aquifoliaceae.   RELATIVES: The hollies.
TYPE OF PLANT: Tree.   HEIGHT: 25'. ZONE: N,C,S
HOW TO IDENTIFY: Attractive small tree that often has gracefully drooping branches that bear alternate, evergreen, entire, shining green leaves; pistillate individuals produce heavy clusters of bright, shining red fruits from autumn until late spring.
HABIT OF GROWTH: Compact, central leader, and gracefully drooping branches.
FOLIAGE: Alternate, evergreen, unarmed, of medium texture and dark green color.
FLOWERS: Unisexual, inconspicuous, in heavy axillary cymes.
FRUITS: Small, berry-like drupes of glistening red, that are highly decorative.
SEASON OF MAXIMUM COLOR: October-April, when fruits are mature.
LANDSCAPE USES: Freestanding specimen for horticultural interest because this beautiful, heavy-fruiting, evergreen holly is one of the best fruiting trees from abroad. As a framing tree for small houses, and as a part of a shrubbery border, for sky-line interest, *Ilex rotunda* is very good, too.

Horticultural variety, 'Lord,' named for a former professor of horticulture at the University of Florida, has been selected, increased by graftage, and distributed in limited quantity by a nursery in northern Florida.
HABITAT: Japan; in Florida, a garden specimen in northern and central sections.
LIGHT REQUIREMENT: High, shifting, broken shade, or full sun.
SOIL REQUIREMENT: Fertile, organic, well-drained soil, with mulch, is best.
SALT TOLERANCE: Not tolerant.
AVAILABILITY: *Ilex rotunda* is rarely seen in nurseries, unfortunately.
CULTURE: Given reasonable fertility, good drainage, and moderate water supply, this beautiful holly needs no particular attention after it becomes established.
PROPAGATION: Cuttage, in May, treated with root-inducing chemicals, or graftage during late winter.
PESTS: Scales and possibly nematodes.

204
Dahoon

Ilex (EYE-lecks): ancient Latin name for *Quercus ilex*.
cassine (cass-SEEN-ee): American Indian name.

FAMILY: Aquifoliaceae.

TYPE OF PLANT: Tree.

RELATIVES: The hollies.

HEIGHT: 40'. ZONE: N,C,S

HOW TO IDENTIFY: A small tree growing in a wet location with conspicuous red fruits in winter. The evergreen leaves are alternate, about 4" long, shining above, pubescent beneath, with a few small teeth near the apex.

HABIT OF GROWTH: Small tree with a narrow, close head of upward-pointing branches.

FOLIAGE: Evergreen or partly deciduous of medium texture and of medium green color.

FLOWERS: Inconspicuous, unisexual, clustered on a common stalk.

FRUITS: Globose, berry-like drupes, usually red, occasionally yellow.

SEASON OF MAXIMUM COLOR: The Christmas season.

LANDSCAPE USES: For bright wintertime color in woodland plantings, an occasional pistillate tree of dahoon is very desirable. Homeowners near the peninsula's tip can have true hollies in this species.
    Myrtle dahoon is held by some botanists to be a variety of this.

HABITAT: Swamps and lake margins as far south as Biscayne Bay.

LIGHT REQUIREMENT: Reduced light of swamplands.

SOIL REQUIREMENT: Wet, boggy soil of swamps is dahoon's native environment.

SALT TOLERANCE: Tolerant of salt air back of the dunes.

AVAILABILITY: Dahoons are seldom offered for sale in nurseries.

CULTURE: Dig plants from land of a friend; plant in a moist location; after establishment, no further attention is needed.

PROPAGATION: Cuttage or graftage.

PESTS: Spittle bugs and scales.

205
Yaupon

Ilex (EYE-lecks): Latin name for *Quercus ilex*.
vomitoria (vom-i-TORE-ee-a): emetic, for the tea made from plant parts.

FAMILY: Aquifoliaceae.
RELATIVES: The hollies.
TYPE OF PLANT: Large shrub.
HEIGHT: 25'. ZONE: N,C

HOW TO IDENTIFY: A shrub with gray-green twigs that bears small, unarmed, scalloped, alternate, evergreen leaves and bright, little red fruits in clusters.

HABIT OF GROWTH: Dense, compact, spreading by stolons to form large cultures.

FOLIAGE: Evergreen, alternate, scalloped, unarmed, very fine in texture.

FLOWERS: Inconspicuous, unisexual, held in axillary cymes.

FRUITS: Glistening red, berry-like drupes, ¼" across, in axillary clusters.

SEASON OF MAXIMUM COLOR: Winter, when fruits assume full color.

LANDSCAPE USES: As a clipped hedge, yaupon cannot be excelled. Plant 18" apart. As a part of an enclosing barrier, this shrub is fine when set 5' o.c. Infusion made from young leaves and twig tips has served as a beverage since the beginning of history. Wild yaupons are protected by Florida statute.

Selection of types of dwarf habit, very fine texture, or special fruiting characteristics has begun, and should lead to even greater landscape usefulness of this sterling native plant.

HABITAT: Hammocks and stream banks in central and northern Florida.

LIGHT REQUIREMENT: Tolerant of shade.

SOIL REQUIREMENT: Tolerant of widely varying soils.

SALT TOLERANCE: Tolerant of salt, growing on the banks of tidal streams.

AVAILABILITY: Nurseries occasionally carry yaupons in containers or B&B. It is hoped that the selected forms will become more widely available.

CULTURE: Well-drained soil is essential; transplanting is extremely difficult; and spittle bugs must be controlled during warm months.

PROPAGATION: Cuttage, with root-inducing chemicals.

PESTS: Scales and spittle bugs.

Japanese Holly

Ilex (EYE-lecks): ancient Latin name for *Quercus ilex*.
crenata (cree-NAY-ta): crenate, referring to the leaf margins.

FAMILY: Aquifoliaceae.

RELATIVES: The hollies.

TYPE OF PLANT: Dwarf shrub.

HEIGHT: 5'. **ZONE:** N

HOW TO IDENTIFY: Alternate, evergreen, scalloped leaves 1½" or less in length, dull or shiny above, wedge-shaped at the bases. Black fruits are produced by pistillate individuals.

HABIT OF GROWTH: Compact, shrubby, leaves crowded on many small twigs.

FOLIAGE: Evergreen, fine in texture, medium green in color.

FLOWERS: Inconspicuous, unisexual.

FRUITS: Shining black globes, ¼" across, decorative if present in quantity.

SEASON OF MAXIMUM COLOR: Perhaps when fruits mature.

LANDSCAPE USES: For foundation plantings, north or east side, for the smallest structures, this oriental shrub serves well. Use 2' planting intervals. For planter bins in constant shade, it is recommended, as well.

Japanese holly is subject to pests (see below) and it is not always entirely satisfactory on landscape jobs, particularly when planted in poor soil in full sun.

There are a number of named clones that display differing leaf forms and growth habits.

HABITAT: Japan; in Florida, shady locations on superior soil.

LIGHT REQUIREMENT: Shade is essential.

SOIL REQUIREMENT: Superior soils for best performance.

SALT TOLERANCE: Not tolerant.

AVAILABILITY: Widely available under varietal name, in northern Florida.

CULTURE: Set carefully in fertile sites on the north or east sides, or under trees; water faithfully; mulch the roots, protect the foliage against pests.

PROPAGATION: Cuttage, with root-inducing chemicals.

PESTS: Nematodes, spittle bugs, mites, and scales.

207
Gallberry

Ilex (EYE-lecks): Latin name for *Quercus ilex*.
glabra (GLAY-bra): not hairy.

FAMILY: Aquifoliaceae. RELATIVES: The hollies.
TYPE OF PLANT: Clump-forming shrub. HEIGHT: 10'. ZONE: N,C,S
HOW TO IDENTIFY: Stoloniferous shrub, with evergreen, alternate leaves that are entire or with a few teeth near their apexes. Female plants bear black fruits.
HABIT OF GROWTH: Clump-forming to make huge cultures in the flatwoods.
FOLIAGE: Evergreen, or nearly so, of fine texture and varying tones of green.
FLOWERS: Inconspicuous, unisexual, on current growth; most desirable for honey.
FRUITS: Berry-like, black drupes, ¼" across, produced by pistillate individuals.
SEASON OF MAXIMUM COLOR: Winter, when fruits are colored.
LANDSCAPE USES: For barrier plantings in naturalistic arrangements, gallberry can be used to advantage on certain soils. Set wild clumps 3'-5' o.c. For semiformal, round-topped hedges, set wild clumps 18" o.c. and use the same interval if gallberry bushes are to be planted around the foundations of vacation cottages.
  There is a white-fruited gallberry, one with red fruits was once reported, and dwarf clones have been named from time to time.
HABITAT: Flatwoods over much of the state of Florida.
LIGHT REQUIREMENT: Full sun or shade of flatwoods.
SOIL REQUIREMENT: Acid, poorly drained, hardpan soils.
SALT TOLERANCE: Tolerant of light salt drift, well back from the dunes.
AVAILABILITY: Gallberries are not items of commerce.
CULTURE: Cut back stems; set clumps in acid soil; water periodically until well established.
PROPAGATION: Collect wild clumps, selected clones are increased by cuttage.
PESTS: Scales and spittle bugs.
NOTE: Large gallberry (*Ilex coriacea*) grows to a height of 12', but is quite similar to the well-known type.

208
Red Maple

Acer (AY-sir): classical Latin name.
rubrum (RUBE-rum): red.

FAMILY: Aceraceae.

RELATIVES: The maple trees.

TYPE OF PLANT: Tree.

HEIGHT: 75'. **ZONE:** N,C

HOW TO IDENTIFY: Deciduous, opposite, 3-lobed leaves that have V-shaped, shallow sinuses, regular teeth, and red petioles. Conspicuous red fruits are produced in January.

HABIT OF GROWTH: Narrow, upright.

FOLIAGE: Deciduous, 3-lobed, held by red petioles. The texture is medium fine, the color is medium green, the fall color is often a bright red.

FLOWERS: Red, in December-January.

FRUITS: Bright red keys in January are highly decorative.

SEASON OF MAXIMUM COLOR: January, keys mature; November, leaves turn red.

LANDSCAPE USES: For seasonal color in naturalistic plantings, set red maple trees 25'-35' apart. As a parking-lot tree in northern areas, set about 35' o.c. This excellent native tree is not widely used because of its short life in civilization, however, with good care, it makes an outstanding specimen.

HABITAT: Swamplands and bayheads.

LIGHT REQUIREMENT: Sun or broken shade of swamplands.

SOIL REQUIREMENT: Low, boggy soil, or rich upland earth that is kept wet.

SALT TOLERANCE: Not tolerant.

AVAILABILITY: Red maple is seldom offered for sale in nurseries in Florida.

CULTURE: Plant in rich soil; wrap the trunks as protection against borers; keep well-watered at all times; fertilize once in late winter.

PROPAGATION: Seedage; clonal selections must be increased vegetatively.

PESTS: Borers and mites.

209
Lychee

Litchi (LYE-chee): a Chinese name.
chinensis (chi-NEN-sis): Chinese.

FAMILY: Sapindaceae.   RELATIVES: Goldenrain-tree, soapberry, and akee.

TYPE OF PLANT: Tree.   HEIGHT: 40'. ZONE: C,S

HOW TO IDENTIFY: Glossy, evergreen leaves with 2-4 pairs of pinnae; bright red rough fruits, in hanging clusters, that are deliciously edible.

HABIT OF GROWTH: Compact, round-headed tree of attractive appearance.

FOLIAGE: Evergreen, 2-4 pairs of leaflets each of which is 3"-6" long.

FLOWERS: Small, greenish-white in foot-long drooping panicles.

FRUITS: Drupes, bright red in color, covered with angular, prominent tubercles, delicious to eat out of hand, highly decorative on the tree.

SEASON OF MAXIMUM COLOR: Late summer, when the fruits turn red.

LANDSCAPE USES: Freestanding specimens in home-ground arrangements, framing trees for small residences, shade tree for the back yard. Lychee is extremely popular, and rightly so, within its climatic zones, because its pleasing habit and beautiful, delicious fruits add interest to backyard landscape arrangements. Most outdoor living areas would have space for only one lychee tree, considering all the other woody trees and palms that might be wanted.

HABITAT: China; in Florida, warm locations on the peninsula.

LIGHT REQUIREMENT: Full sun for best habit, flowering, and fruiting.

SOIL REQUIREMENT: Sandy soil that has been improved with organic matter.

SALT TOLERANCE: Not tolerant.

AVAILABILITY: Nurseries offer small trees, from air layers, in cans.

CULTURE: With careful planting, in fertile, well-drained soil, regular watering, fertilizing, and spraying, lychee trees are not difficult to grow.

PROPAGATION: Marcottage.

PESTS: Scales.

210 Goldenrain-Tree

Koelreuteria (coal-roy-TEER-ee-a): for J. Koelreuter, a German professor.
formosana (for-mo-SAY-na): of Formosa.

FAMILY: Sapindaceae.   **RELATIVES:** Lychee, soapberry, and akee.

TYPE OF PLANT: Tree.   **HEIGHT:** 30′.   **ZONE:** N,C

HOW TO IDENTIFY: Deciduous leaves, 14″ long, composed of 7-15 lobed leaflets; yellow blossoms in autumn, followed one month later by showy, pinkish fruits.

HABIT OF GROWTH: Irregular from a bent, single trunk.

FOLIAGE: Deciduous, much-divided to give a lack effect. The color is medium green.

FLOWERS: Bright yellow, in 18″ panicles in the autumn.

FRUITS: Two-inch capsules with pinkish, papery walls, which gradually narrow to pointed apexes. These very decorative fruits mature one month after the yellow blossoms fade.

SEASON OF MAXIMUM COLOR: October-November.

LANDSCAPE USES: As a freestanding specimen or as a part of a shrubbery border, goldenrain-tree is rightly popular for its beautiful autumnal display.
  Because it is so well adapted to northern and central Florida, goldenrain-tree is highly commended to casual, part-time gardeners. As indicated below, seedlings usually are to be found under fruiting trees.

HABITAT: Eastern Asia; in Florida, widely planted in the upper parts.

LIGHT REQUIREMENT: Full sun for best flowering and fruiting.

SOIL REQUIREMENT: Tolerant of many soil types.

SALT TOLERANCE: Not tolerant.

AVAILABILITY: Easily found in nurseries in northern Florida.

CULTURE: Within its climatic range, goldenrain-tree requires little care.

PROPAGATION: Seedage. Volunteer seedlings usually grow under old trees.

PESTS: Scales, mushroom root-rot.

211
Grape-Ivy

Cissus (sis-us): Greek for ivy.
spp.: numerous kinds grow in Florida.

FAMILY: Vitaceae.

RELATIVES: Grape and wood-bine.

TYPE OF PLANT: Vine.

HEIGHT: Variable. **ZONE:** S

HOW TO IDENTIFY: Tendril-climbing, herbaceous vines, with pubescent new growth and decorative, waxy foliage, often compound.

HABIT OF GROWTH: Vining, to cover shady ground or trellis.

FOLIAGE: Evergreen, waxy, compound or simple, serrate or entire.

FLOWERS: Inconspicuous, of no decorative value.

FRUITS: Small, inedible berries, if present.

SEASON OF MAXIMUM COLOR: Little seasonal change.

LANDSCAPE USES: As a ground cover in densely shaded spots where frost does not occur; as hanging-basket or planter subjects, cissus vines are popular.

HABITAT: Warm parts of the globe.

LIGHT REQUIREMENT: Quite tolerant of reduced light, intolerant of direct sun.

SOIL REQUIREMENT: Tolerant of many soil conditions.

SALT TOLERANCE: Not tolerant.

AVAILABILITY: Most nurseries sell grape-ivies in containers.

CULTURE: Plant stem pieces; water with moderation; fertilize once each summer month.

PROPAGATION: Cuttage and simple layerage.

PESTS: Aphids, mites, and nematodes.

NOTE: Species may number a half dozen, perhaps, but nomenclature may be confused, as additional study in this group is badly needed.

212
Turks-Cap

Malvaviscus (mal-va-VIS-cus): sticky mallow, referring to the fruits.
arboreus (ar-BORE-ee-us): tree-like.

FAMILY: Malvaceae.

RELATIVES: Hibiscus, rose-of-Sharon, cotton, and okra.

TYPE OF PLANT: Shrub.

HEIGHT: 10'. ZONE: C,S

HOW TO IDENTIFY: Robust, branching shrub with green twigs, soft, hairy, evergreen leaves and nodding, closed, hibiscus-like flowers borne during much of the year.

HABIT OF GROWTH: Densely sprawling, but may assume vine-form if given support.

FOLIAGE: Alternate, evergreen, soft, long-heart-shaped, light green in color.

FLOWERS: Nodding, petals not flaring, produced in the axils of leaves during much of the year. The usual color is a bright red, but a variety with pink flowers, and one with white blossoms are often seen.

FRUITS: Fleshy, berry-like bodies; these may not form in Florida.

SEASON OF MAXIMUM COLOR: Much of the year, when blossoms are out.

LANDSCAPE USES: Much over-used as a clipped hedge and as a foundation plant because of its ease of propagation and culture, Turks-cap is seen in almost every community in central and southern Florida. The myriad blossoms give the plant a bright and cheerful aspect. Plants may stand 2' to 5' apart, depending upon the need.

HABITAT: Tropical America; in Florida, ubiquitous in warmer sections.

LIGHT REQUIREMENT: Full sun for compact habit and full-flowering.

SOIL REQUIREMENT: Any soil is acceptable.

SALT TOLERANCE: Not tolerant.

AVAILABILITY: Retail sales yards on the peninsula offer Turks-cap.

CULTURE: No exotic shrub is of easier culture.

PROPAGATION: Cuttage, employing wood of any size.

PESTS: Caterpillars may chew holes in the leaves.

213
Portia-Tree

Thespesia (thes-PEA-sea-a): Greek for divine.
populnea (poe-PUL-nee-a): poplar-like.

FAMILY: Malvaceae. RELATIVES: Mallow, hibiscus, cotton, and okra.
TYPE OF PLANT: Tree. HEIGHT: 35'. ZONE: S
HOW TO IDENTIFY: Poplar-like, sharp-pointed, evergreen leaves that are 1½ times longer than broad; rough trunk bark; faded flowers cling to twigs; leathery, flattened capsules. The leaves are the smallest in the tree-hibiscus group.
HABIT OF GROWTH: Very close-growing to form dense thickets by low branches.
FOLIAGE: Evergreen, sharp-pointed, medium coarse in texture, medium green in color.
FLOWERS: Hibiscus-like, 3" across, light yellow with purple-red center in the morning, turning to dark red in the afternoon. Old flowers hang on the tree for several days.
FRUITS: Flattened, leathery capsules, 1½" across, with 1 flat, and 2 rounded sides and persistent calyces.
SEASON OF MAXIMUM COLOR: Warm months.
LANDSCAPE USES: For seaside locations where rapid growth and land-holding ability is needed, portia-tree will serve. It is highly recommended for dune locations, yet it is not well thought of for inland locations because of its very rapid growth and dense head that prevents the growth of lawn grasses beneath.
   Portia-tree has escaped from cultivation on the Florida Keys.
HABITAT: Old World Tropics; in Florida, rather widely planted near the sea.
LIGHT REQUIREMENT: Full sun of tropical strands.
SOIL REQUIREMENT: Seaside sands, marl from bay-bottoms and rocks of the Keys.
SALT TOLERANCE: Very tolerant of salt, and highly recommended for dune planting.
AVAILABILITY: Nurseries will have small trees, but there may be confusion in naming.
CULTURE: No special care is needed for portia-tree.
PROPAGATION: Cuttage or layerage.
PESTS: None of major concern.

214
Sea Hibiscus

Hibiscus (hy-BIS-cus): ancient Greek and Latin name.
tileaceus (tilly-ACE-ee-us): tilia-like, referring to the foliage.

FAMILY: Malvaceae.   RELATIVES: Mallow, hibiscus, Turks-cap, and okra.

TYPE OF PLANT: Tree.   HEIGHT: 35'. ZONE: C,S

HOW TO IDENTIFY: Drooping branches, which may take root where they touch the earth, bear smooth-edged, evergreen leaves about 6" broad, and flowers which open yellow, turn pink the same evening. Velvety fruits with persistent calyces follow.

HABIT OF GROWTH: Very dense, close head, with branching to the ground.

FOLIAGE: Evergreen, heart-shaped, very coarse in texture, dark green.

FLOWERS: Mallow-like, yellow with maroon eye in morning, pink by evening.

FRUITS: Large, pointed, ovoid, tomentose capsules with persistent calyces ¾" long.

SEASON OF MAXIMUM COLOR: Warm months when blossoms are out.

LANDSCAPE USES: For quick, dense shade, sea hibiscus is planted by speculative builders. Its very rapid growth and dense head made it unpopular with many homeowners who have acquired it with new homes.
   Excepting for seaside locations where it is needed to help build land, this tree is not recommended.

HABITAT: Tropical shores of both hemispheres, in Florida, widely used.

LIGHT REQUIREMENT: Full sun.

SOIL REQUIREMENT: Tolerant of lightest sand of seaside conditions.

SALT TOLERANCE: Tolerant of dune-front locations.

AVAILABILITY: Ease of propagation makes sea hibiscus a popular tin can item.

CULTURE: After the tree becomes established, frequent pruning is needed to keep it in bounds.

PROPAGATION: Cuttage by huge truncheons.

PESTS: Scales, strap-leaf resulting from deficiency of molybdenum.

Fringed Hibiscus

Hibiscus (hy-BIS-cus): ancient Greek and Latin name.
schizopetalus (skiz-oh-PET-al-us): with cut petals.

FAMILY: Malvaceae.   RELATIVES: Hibiscus, mallow, and Turks-cap.
TYPE OF PLANT: Shrub.   HEIGHT: 12'.   ZONE: C,S
HOW TO IDENTIFY: Slim, drooping branches, slender evergreen leaves, small, fringed red flowers that hang downward from very long stems.
HABIT OF GROWTH: Scraggly, loose assemblage of many slender, drooping branches.
FOLIAGE: Evergreen, slender, serrate, of medium texture and medium green color.
FLOWERS: Attractive, much-cut red flowers with recurved petals, hanging from long, string-like peduncles.
FRUITS: Long, pointed capsules hanging on long strings.
SEASON OF MAXIMUM COLOR: Much of the warm season.
LANDSCAPE USES: As a point of interest in front of evergreen shrubs, use a clump of three fringed hibiscus, allowing about 3 feet between plants. This species is too open for foundation plantings.
   Fringed hibiscus has been much used in hybridization with the Chinese hibiscus, and its characteristics can be seen in many named hybrids.
HABITAT: Eastern tropical Africa; in Florida, planted where winters are not severe.
LIGHT REQUIREMENT: Full sun or shifting shade from high pines or palms.
SOIL REQUIREMENT: Tolerant of varying types, but moderate fertility is desirable.
SALT TOLERANCE: Not tolerant.
AVAILABILITY: Most nurseries on the peninsula sell plants of fringed hibiscus in containers.
CULTURE: Plant in fertile, slightly acid soil; use care in watering until the plant becomes well established; fertilize three times each year; protect the leaves and branches from scale insects by regular spraying.
PROPAGATION: Cuttage.
PESTS: Scales, nematodes, and deficiencies of minor elements upon occasion.

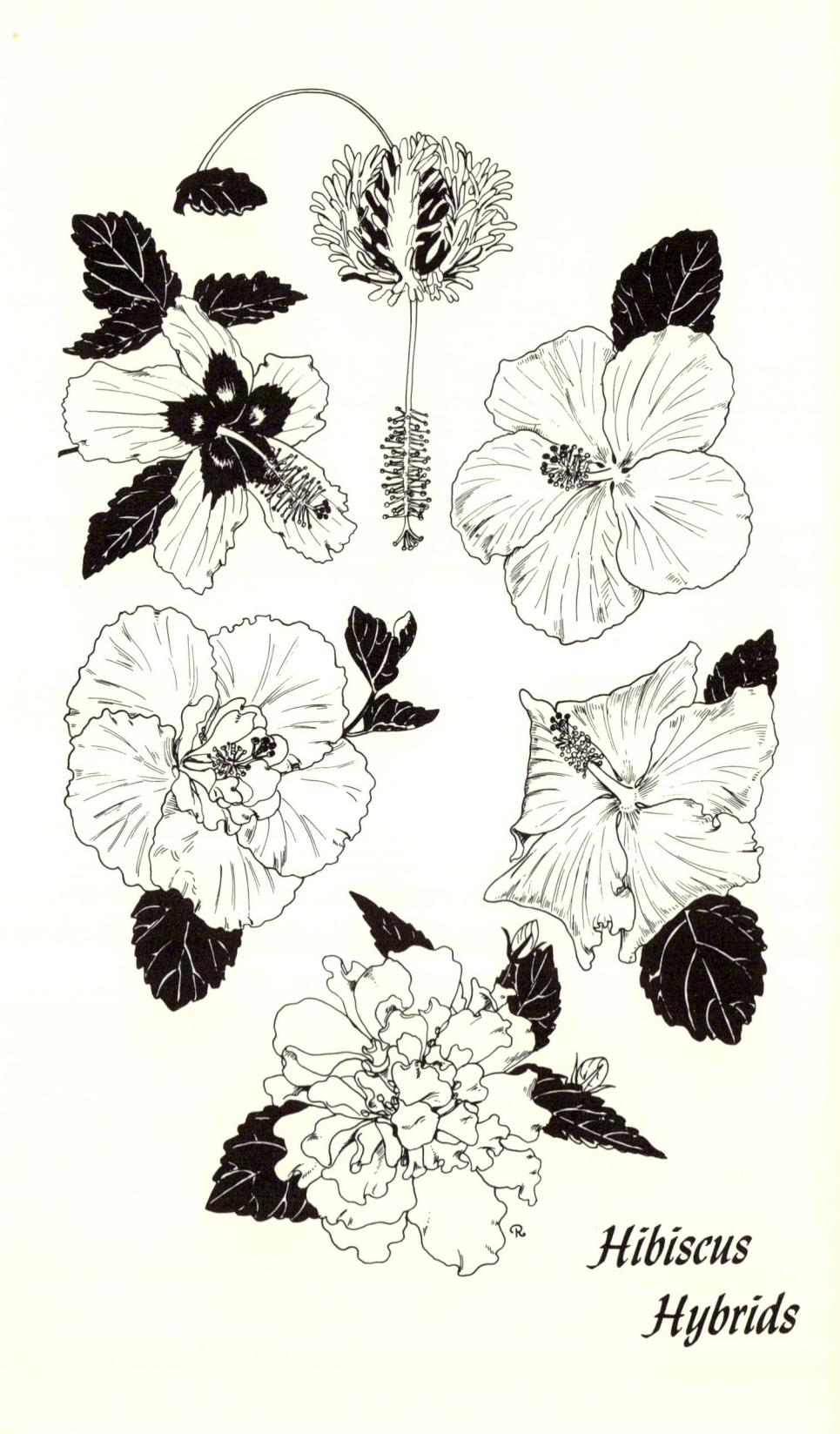

Hibiscus Hybrids

217
Hibiscus

Hibiscus (hy-BIS-cus): ancient Greek and Latin name.
rosa-sinensis (RO-sa sin-EN-sis): Chinese rose.

FAMILY: Malvaceae. RELATIVES: Mallow, cotton, and okra.
TYPE OF PLANT: Shrub. HEIGHT: 15'. ZONE: C,S

HOW TO IDENTIFY: Many-stemmed, robust shrubs hold large, variable, alternate, evergreen leaves and showy flowers almost all the year around.

HABIT OF GROWTH: Shrubby, often upright, often robust, usually many-stemmed.

FOLIAGE: Evergreen, alternate, assuming many forms, mostly dark green in color.

FLOWERS: Bisexual, 5-merous, highly variable, bell-shaped or flaring, very decorative.

FRUITS: Ovoid, beaked capsules, which split at maturity to release seeds.

SEASON OF MAXIMUM COLOR: Much of the year as new growth is made.

LANDSCAPE USES: Hibiscus, queen of shrubs, is used in every conceivable way; as screens, as informal shrubbery borders, as freestanding specimens, as foundation plantings for large buildings. A 5'-planting interval is usually satisfactory. Literally hundreds of named varieties, which bear beautiful blossoms in endless array, are grown by Florida homeowners. Here is, indeed, one of Florida's very best landscape plants.

HABITAT: Asia; in Florida, ubiquitous in gardens on the peninsula.

LIGHT REQUIREMENT: Full sun or broken, high shade for best flowering.

SOIL REQUIREMENT: Moderate moisture and fertility, and a slightly acid reaction make for satisfactory growth.

SALT TOLERANCE: Not tolerant of dune conditions.

AVAILABILITY: Nurseries on the peninsula offer hibiscus plants in containers.

CULTURE: Plant with reasonable care in well-drained, fairly rich earth; fertilize 2 or 3 times during the warm season; water during periods of drought. Some choice clones are not robust and need special care.

PROPAGATION: Cuttage for robust varieties, graftage for poor growers.

PESTS: Aphids, scales, nematodes, mites, and thrips.

218
Rose-of-Sharon

Hibiscus (hy-bis-cus): ancient Greek and Latin name.
syriacus (see-rye-a-cus): Syrian.

Family: Malvaceae. **Relatives:** Mallow, cotton, and okra.

Type of Plant: Shrub. **Height:** 20'. **Zone:** N

How to Identify: Deciduous, alternate leaves with palmate veining, that are usually lobed and toothed; usually ascending growth; beautiful mallow-like flowers in summertime.

Habit of Growth: Shrubby, usually ascending, but habit varies with the clone.

Foliage: Deciduous, alternate, medium coarse in texture, medium green in color.

Flowers: White to bluish, 3" in diameter, flaring, single or double in form.

Fruits: Capsules 1" long, abruptly short-beaked, split open lengthwise.

Season of Maximum Color: Summer.

Landscape Uses: As a part of a shrubbery border, include a clump of rose-of-Sharon, planted 5' o.c. In foundation arrangements for large buildings, use as north-side accents.

Scores of clones that bear beautiful blossoms in different forms and colors are available from nurseries north of Florida.

Habitat: Eastern Asia; in Florida, gardens in the northern part.

Light Requirement: High pine shade is beneficial.

Soil Requirement: Fertile, heavy, well-drained soils of northern counties.

Salt Tolerance: Not tolerant.

Availability: Rose-of-Sharon is not important in Florida's nursery industry.

Culture: In northernmost areas, rose-of-Sharon grows with a minimum of attention.

Propagation: Cuttage.

Pests: Nematodes, mites, and scales.

219
Ceiba

Ceiba (SAY-ba): an aboriginal name.
pentandra (pen-TAN-dra): with five stamens.

FAMILY: Bombacaceae.
RELATIVES: Shaving-brush-trees.
TYPE OF PLANT: Tree.
HEIGHT: 60'. ZONE: S

HOW TO IDENTIFY: Huge, buttressed trunks; branches with spines; deciduous, digitately compound leaves; flowers white or pinkish.

HABIT OF GROWTH: Majestic tree with conspicuously buttressed trunk.

FOLIAGE: Deciduous, digitately compound, 5-6 lobes, the central one, the largest.

FLOWERS: Remotely mallow-like, white or pinkish, while the tree is leafless.

FRUITS: Six-inch woody capsules filled with brown seeds and cotton-like fluff which is the kapok of commerce.

SEASON OF MAXIMUM COLOR: Early spring when the blossoms appear.

LANDSCAPE USES: Ceiba is recommended as a freestanding specimen for large public areas where there is plenty of room for full development. One of the tropic's most spectacular trees, this buttressed monarch is a standout in hot countries. In Florida, ceibas should be planted only in most nearly frostless locations, as these trees are easily damaged by cold.

HABITAT: Tropics of both hemispheres; in Florida, nearly frost-free sections.

LIGHT REQUIREMENT: Full sun or broken shade.

SOIL REQUIREMENT: Fertility above the usual Florida grade is required.

SALT TOLERANCE: Ceiba will grow several hundred yards back of the dunes.

AVAILABILITY: Some nurseries in extreme southern Florida stock ceiba trees.

CULTURE: Given reasonably good soil, moderate moisture, and freedom from frost, ceibas grow rapidly.

PROPAGATION: Seedage.

PESTS: None of major importance.

220
Shaving-Brush-Trees

Pachira (pack-EYE-ra): native name in South America.
SPP.: several species are seen in Florida.

FAMILY: Bombacaceae.
TYPE OF PLANT: Tree.
RELATIVES: Ceiba and bombax.
HEIGHT: 30'. ZONE: S

HOW TO IDENTIFY: Coarse trees bear deciduous, digitately compound leaves, with about 7 leaflets on branches that are *not* prickly. The striking shaving-brush-like flowers have purplish or reddish strap-shaped petals and many conspicuous reddish stamens forming the brushes. These appear in late winter.

HABIT OF GROWTH: Asymmetrical, spreading, from a stout trunk.

FOLIAGE: Deciduous, very coarse in texture, light green in color.

FLOWERS: Linear purplish petals curl back to reveal many red stamens to make the shaving brush.

FRUITS: Large woody capsules which contain edible seeds.

SEASON OF MAXIMUM COLOR: Late winter, when blossoms come out.

LANDSCAPE USES: For the curiosity of the shaving-brush blossoms, an occasional freestanding specimen might be wanted, but like most members of the family, pachiras are tropical trees that should be planted only in protected sites. These rare plants probably will never be widely used in Florida landscapes, but there is no gainsaying that the blossoms are attention-getters.

HABITAT: Tropical America; in Florida, very rare.

LIGHT REQUIREMENT: Full sun or broken shade.

SOIL REQUIREMENT: Fertile, moisture-retentive soils.

SALT TOLERANCE: Not tolerant of front-line dune locations.

AVAILABILITY: Small trees in gallon cans might be in specialty nurseries.

CULTURE: Plant in prepared sites in frostless locations with care; water periodically; keep lawn grasses back from the roots; fertilize in late winter, perhaps again in summer while the trees are young.

PROPAGATION: Seedage.

PESTS: Scales and mites.

221
Bombax

Bombax (BOM-backs): from Greek for silk, for contents of seed pods.
malabaricum (mal-a-BAR-ee-cum): from a district in India.

FAMILY: Bombacaeae. RELATIVES: Ceiba and shaving-brush-trees.

TYPE OF PLANT: Tree. HEIGHT: 75'. ZONE: S

HOW TO IDENTIFY: Flaming red blossoms in midwinter; buttressed prickly trunk; compound, deciduous leaves with 5 leaflets.

HABIT OF GROWTH: Stout, buttressed trunk, horizontal branching.

FOLIAGE: Deciduous, compound, of coarse texture and medium green color.

FLOWERS: Very conspicuous flaming red.

FRUITS: Capsules, 6" long, woolly within and with woolly seeds.

SEASON OF MAXIMUM COLOR: Winter, when red blossoms mature.

LANDSCAPE USES: Freestanding specimen for the brave show of the wintertime blossoms.

The bombax family contains numerous species that are characterized by spectacular flowers, heavy buttressed trunks, and prickly bark. These striking trees are great favorites with tourists, yet, as indicated on the preceding page, these are tropical species, rare in cultivation, that probably will never be very widely used in home landscapes. The red tulip-like flowers are crowd-stoppers when they appear in wintertime.

HABITAT: Tropics of the Eastern Hemisphere; in Florida, warmest locations.

LIGHT REQUIREMENT: Full sun for best flowering.

SOIL REQUIREMENT: Tolerant of varying soils.

SALT TOLERANCE: Tolerant of light salt drift well back from the strand.

AVAILABILITY: Nurseries stock small trees in cans; there might be confusion in naming.

CULTURE: Plant in well-prepared site in nearly frostless location; water faithfully; fertilize once or twice annually.

PROPAGATION: Seedage.

PESTS: None of major importance.

222
Pink-Ball

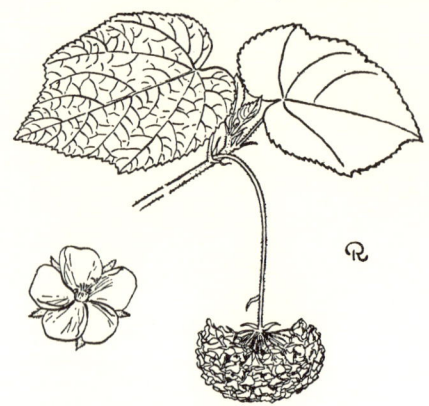

Dombeya (DOM-bay-a): for J. Dombey, French botanist of the eighteenth century.
wallichii (WALL-ick-ee-eye): for N. Wallich, a Danish botanist.

FAMILY: Sterculiaceae.   **RELATIVES:** Cocoa, cola, and bottle-tree.
TYPE OF PLANT: Tree, usually seen as a shrub in Florida.
HEIGHT: 30'. **ZONE:** C,S
HOW TO IDENTIFY: Scraggly, upright growth from unbranched canes; huge heart-shaped leaves that are densely tomentose beneath; bright, pink flowers on long, pendulous peduncles in winter.
HABIT OF GROWTH: Strongly upright, by vigorous unbranched canes.
FOLIAGE: Evergreen, very coarse in texture, medium green in color.
FLOWERS: Dense heads of little pink flowers hang from foot-long stems in winter.
FRUITS: Capsules which split into 5 parts at maturity.
SEASON OF MAXIMUM COLOR: Winter.
LANDSCAPE USES: As a freestanding specimen before hardy, evergreen shrubs, for the curiosity of the wintertime, corsage-like blossoms, pink-ball might be indicated. It is very tender to cold, grows to huge size and has such very coarse foliage that its use in little backyards should be carefully considered. Nonetheless people admire the wintertime pink balls and it is much planted despite these qualities.
HABITAT: Madagascar; in Florida, rather widely cultivated as a garden shrub.
LIGHT REQUIREMENT: Full sun or high, shifting shade.
SOIL REQUIREMENT: Tolerant of widely varying soils; sands are acceptable.
SALT TOLERANCE: Not tolerant.
AVAILABILITY: Pink-ball is occasionally found in nurseries in southern Florida.
CULTURE: Plant with reasonable care in frostless location; water until well established; and forget.
PROPAGATION: Cuttage.
PESTS: Aphids, soft scales, sooty-mold, and nematodes.

223
Tea

Thea (THE-ah): Latinized Chinese name for the tea plant.
sinensis (sin-EN-sis): Chinese.

FAMILY: Theaceae. RELATIVES: Camellia, eurya, and gordonia.

TYPE OF PLANT: Shrub. HEIGHT: 20'. ZONE: N,C

HOW TO IDENTIFY: Evergreen, alternate, serrate, short-petioled leaves 2"-5" long, acute or obtuse; white, nodding, fragrant flowers 1½" in diameter followed by woody capsules.

HABIT OF GROWTH: Compact, dense shrub in Florida.

FOLIAGE: Evergreen, of medium texture and dark green color.

FLOWERS: White, fragrant, nodding, 1½" across showing numerous stamens.

FRUITS: Woody capsules rather freely formed.

SEASON OF MAXIMUM COLOR: Wintertime.

LANDSCAPE USES: Tea may be planted as a horticultural curiosity in an informal shrubbery group, allow 5' of space for each plant.
 Landscape-wise, tea has many of the good qualities of camellia as a garden shrub, yet the latter is rightly preferred because of its gorgeous blossoms. Floridians are not likely to try to grow their own tea in their small back yards, but they may gain satisfaction from telling guests about their tea plants and demonstrating the kinds of leaves that are used in our table beverage.

HABITAT: China; in Florida, sparingly grown as a curiosity in northern and central counties.

LIGHT REQUIREMENT: Tolerant of shifting shade.

SOIL REQUIREMENT: Any reasonably fertile, well-drained soil is adequate.

SALT TOLERANCE: Not tolerant.

AVAILABILITY: Tea is occasionally sold in nurseries.

CULTURE: If given camellia culture, tea should thrive.

PROPAGATION: Seedage in Florida.

PESTS: Scales, twig die-back disease, mushroom root-rot.

'Amabilis'

'Lady Clare'

Camellia Hybrids

'Betsy Baker'

'C. M. Wilson'

'Pagoda'

'Sarah Frost'

225
Camellia

Camellia (kam-ELL-ee-a): for G. Kamel, a Jesuit of the seventeenth century.
japonica (jap-ON-i-ca): Japanese.

FAMILY: Theaceae.   RELATIVES: Tea, gordonia, eurya, and cleyera.
TYPE OF PLANT: Shrub.   HEIGHT: 40'. ZONE: N,C
HOW TO IDENTIFY: Alternate, shiny, bluntly serrate, evergreen leaves are held by green petioles from brown twigs; handsome flowers on current growth in midwinter.
HABIT OF GROWTH: Upright, dense, and compact.
FOLIAGE: Evergreen, alternate, of medium texture and dark green color.
FLOWERS: Handsome, variable, red, white, streaked, and blotched; during wintertime.
FRUITS: Globose capsules about an inch in diameter with 1-3 seeds within.
SEASON OF MAXIMUM COLOR: Midwinter.
LANDSCAPE USES: Camellia is the aristocrat of southern shrubs, and has been in favor for yard planting since ante-bellum days. As a freestanding specimen, as an accent in foundation plantings, as an informal hedge (plant 5' o.c.), camellia is very popular. Specimens for exhibition should stand 10' from other plants.
   Many volumes have been written about camellias, of which there are literally thousands of varieties.
HABITAT: Eastern Asia; in Florida, gardens of upper peninsula and panhandle.
LIGHT REQUIREMENT: Full sun in western Florida, broken shade on the upper peninsula.
SOIL REQUIREMENT: Superior, well-drained soils that are slightly acid in reaction.
SALT TOLERANCE: Not tolerant.
AVAILABILITY: All nurseries within the plant's range market camellias.
CULTURE: Plant carefully at exactly the same level that the plant grew formerly in sites made up with rich, acid compost; water faithfully; protect the foliage against insects and mites. A mulch is recommended.
PROPAGATION: Cuttage and graftage.
PESTS: Scales of many species, aphids, beetles, and camellia die-back diseases.

226
Sasanqua

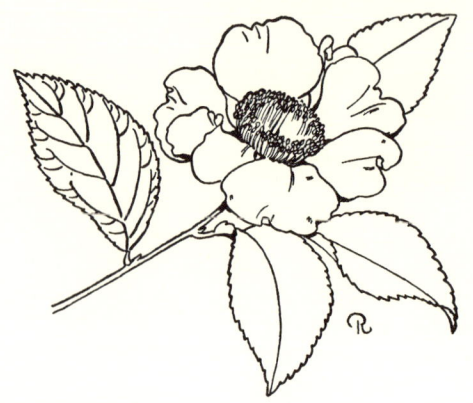

Camellia (kam-ELL-ee-a): for G. Kamel, a Jesuit of the seventeenth century.
sasanqua (sass-ANN-kwa): Japanese vernacular name.

FAMILY: Theaceae. **RELATIVES:** Tea, gordonia, eurya, and cleyera.

TYPE OF PLANT: Shrub. **HEIGHT:** 20'. **ZONE:** N,C

HOW TO IDENTIFY: An evergreen shrub that has downy branchlets that hold alternate leaves 1"-3" long. These are bluntly pointed, and hairy on the midrib above. Attractive blossoms appear in early autumn.

HABIT OF GROWTH: Variable with the clone, usually ascending.

FOLIAGE: Evergreen, fine in texture, dark green in color.

FLOWERS: White, pink or rose, 2" in diameter, with 5 petals or more, scented.

FRUITS: Globose capsules ½"-¾" in diameter, with 1-3 seeds within.

SEASON OF MAXIMUM COLOR: October-November.

LANDSCAPE USES: For screens, set plants 3' apart, as an accent in foundation plantings. Gardeners in northern Florida have shown much interest in this good, hardy shrub, and sasanquas are widely grown in gardens of the upper counties.

HABITAT: China, Japan; in Florida, well-distributed in gardens of the upper counties.

LIGHT REQUIREMENT: Full sun on good soils in western Florida, broken shade elsewhere.

SOIL REQUIREMENT: Sasanquas thrive on superior soils, but as a class, they endure less good drainage than do other camellias.

SALT TOLERANCE: Not tolerant.

AVAILABILITY: Sasanquas in cans are widely available.

CULTURE: Plant carefully in holes made up with rich, acid compost; water faithfully; protect the foliage against scales and mites.

PROPAGATION: Cuttage.

PESTS: Scales, mites, aphids, beetles, and camellia die-back disease.

227
Cleyera

Cleyera (CLAY-er-a): for A. Cleyer, a Dutch botanist.
japonica (jap-ON-i-ca): Japanese.

FAMILY: Theaceae.   **RELATIVES:** Tea, camellia, eurya, and gordonia.

TYPE OF PLANT: Shrub.   **HEIGHT:** 25'.   **ZONE:** N,C,S

HOW TO IDENTIFY: Upright habit, glossy, alternate, entire leaves sometimes with reddish midribs. Foliage often is clustered toward the ends of branches, leaving the plant somewhat open beneath.

HABIT OF GROWTH: Narrow, upright, many branches nearly erect in some specimens.

FOLIAGE: Evergreen, alternate, medium fine in texture, very deep green in color.

FLOWERS: White, fragrant, ½" across, clustered in axils.

FRUITS: Red, roundish berries, not of great decorative value.

SEASON OF MAXIMUM COLOR: When red fruits color.

LANDSCAPE USES: Cleyera can be used as a corner plant in foundation groupings, if there are no corner windows. In shrubbery borders, it may serve, too, when planted in groups with 3' between plants.
  Cleyera is hardy to cold and it is worthy of wider usage in northern areas of our state.

HABITAT: Asia; in Florida, on better soils, particularly, in the northern part.

LIGHT REQUIREMENT: Tolerant of shade, can endure north-side locations.

SOIL REQUIREMENT: Thrives on better soils of the upper peninsula and the panhandle.

SALT TOLERANCE: Not tolerant.

AVAILABILITY: Cleyera is generally on lists of nurseries in upper counties.

CULTURE: Plant in enriched, acid sites; water carefully; protect foliage from scale insects.

PROPAGATION: Seedage or cuttage.

PESTS: Scales.

228
Eurya

Eurya (YOU-ree-a): of uncertain derivation.
japonica (jap-ON-i-ca): Japanese.

FAMILY: Theaceae.

RELATIVES: Tea, camellia, cleyera, and gordonia.

TYPE OF PLANT: Dwarf shrub.

HEIGHT: 25'. ZONE: N,C

HOW TO IDENTIFY: Evergreen, serrate, short-petioled, alternate leaves about 1½" long; unisexual flowers ¼" across; branches upward-pointing.

HABIT OF GROWTH: Compact, with upward-pointing branches.

FOLIAGE: Evergreen, fine in texture, dark green in color.

FLOWERS: White, ¼" in diameter, unisexual, in small clusters.

FRUITS: Globose, black pods ⅛" across, seldom seen in Florida landscapes.

SEASON OF MAXIMUM COLOR: Little seasonal variation.

LANDSCAPE USES: Eurya is a useful shrub because of its small size, fine scale, and slow growth. In foundation arrangements, use a 3' interval. This is a good north-side plant, as it endures shade well and flowers and fruits are of no importance.

HABITAT: Coastal Asia; in Florida, superior soils of central and northern sections.

LIGHT REQUIREMENT: Broken shade of pine trees or full shade of north-side locations.

SOIL REQUIREMENT: Fertile soils free from nematodes, if possible.

SALT TOLERANCE: Not tolerant.

AVAILABILITY: Euryas in cans in nurseries are rather rare.

CULTURE: Excellent soil, partial or full shade, freedom from nematodes, and protection from scale insects are needed for success. Water and fertilizer must be applied regularly.

PROPAGATION: Cuttage.

PESTS: Many types of scale insects and nematodes.

229 Pitch-Apple

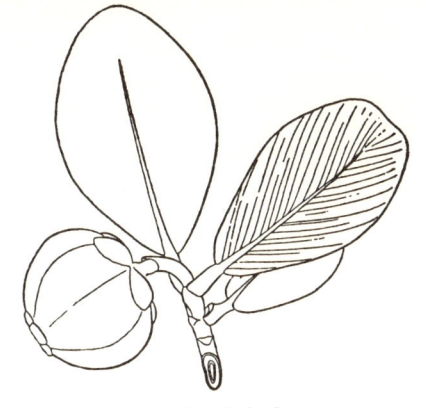

Clusia (CLEW-see-a): from an association of plants growing in flooded places.
rosea (ROSE-ee-a): rosy.

FAMILY: Guttiferae.   RELATIVES: Mangosteen and mamey.
TYPE OF PLANT: Tree, used as a shrub in landscaping.   HEIGHT: 30'.
ZONE: S

HOW TO IDENTIFY: Huge, evergreen leaves, 8" long x 4½" wide, leathery, and stiff. Attractive pink or white flowers 3" across are followed by prominent round fruits, 3" in diameter, with large pinkish calyces at their stem ends.

HABIT OF GROWTH: Wide-spreading, horizontal, irregular branching.

FOLIAGE: Evergreen, 8"x4½", bold in aspect, light green in color.

FLOWERS: Showy, pink or white, in terminal positions.

FRUITS: Prominent, fleshy fruits 3" across, which split at maturity to display seeds surrounded by black, resinous material.

SEASON OF MAXIMUM COLOR: Warm months when blossoms are out.

LANDSCAPE USES: To gain a tropical effect, pitch-apple is used as a shrub in informal borders and screens. It is really too large and too coarse to plant in bins, but it is used this way, nonetheless. The clone with the marbled leaves (*C. rosea* 'Variegata') is much in demand because of its unusual and very striking variegated foliage.

HABITAT: West Indian islands; in Florida, possibly the Keys. In gardens, frost-free locations only.

LIGHT REQUIREMENT: Full sun or broken shade from tall palms.

SOIL REQUIREMENT: Tolerant of light, open sands.

SALT TOLERANCE: Very resistant to salt air and salt spray.

AVAILABILITY: Small plants in containers may be found in some nurseries in south Florida.

CULTURE: Set in holes in fertile compost; water until well established; thereafter, keep lawn grasses back from the root zone.

PROPAGATION: Seedage or cuttage.

PESTS: Scales.

'President Carnot'

'Dew Drop'

'Baby Rainbow'

Rex Begonia

Seedling

'His Majesty'

'Her Majesty'

Seedling

Unidentified

231
Rex Begonia

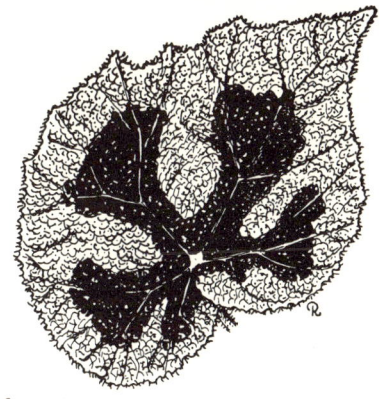

Begonia (be-GO-nee-a): for M. Begon, French botanist.
SPP.: probably several species are represented in Rex begonias.

FAMILY: Begoniaceae.   RELATIVES: The wonderful world of begonias.

TYPE OF PLANT: Herbaceous perennial.   HEIGHT: Variable. ZONE: S

HOW TO IDENTIFY: The fantastic leaves, in their multitudinous forms and colors, are the reasons why Rex begonias are among the world's most beloved house plants.

HABIT OF GROWTH: Compact, heavily foliated.

FOLIAGE: Universally appealing in its many forms.

FLOWERS: Attractive, yet incidental in this group of begonias.

FRUITS: Angled pods, often green with red markings.

SEASON OF MAXIMUM COLOR: Warm months when blossoms appear.

LANDSCAPE USES: Since the white man came to Florida, Rex begonias have figured prominently in porch and indoor decoration. In late years these beautiful plants have come into their own as urn subjects for Florida rooms and patios.

HABITAT: Warm parts of the world around.

LIGHT REQUIREMENT: Partial shade is best. Protection from wind is essential.

SOIL REQUIREMENT: Fibrous, organic, slightly acid soil, of moderately high fertility is recommended. Begonia soils must drain quickly.

SALT TOLERANCE: Not tolerant.

AVAILABILITY: Nurseries, chain stores, and garden centers sell Rex begonias in pots.

CULTURE: Water and feed as you do your other house plants; shift to larger containers when old plants become crowded.

PROPAGATION: Cuttage, using terminal shoots or whole leaves.

PESTS: Mealy-bugs, mites, and nematodes.

NOTE: On the facing page are diagrams of some Florida favorites, above is ever popular 'Iron Cross'.

232 Annatto

Bixa (BICK-sa): aboriginal name.
orellana (or-rel-AY-na): ancient name.

FAMILY: Bixaceae. RELATIVES: This plant stands alone in its family.

TYPE OF PLANT: Tree or large shrub. HEIGHT: 20′. ZONE: C,S

HOW TO IDENTIFY: Ovate, evergreen leaves, palmately veined, are about 7″ long; attractive pink flowers (sometimes white) in clusters are followed by spiny, brown fruits.

HABIT OF GROWTH: Usually a many-stemmed, bushy, small tree.

FOLIAGE: Evergreen, coarse in texture, and light green in color.

FLOWERS: Pink (sometimes white), 2″ across, in large clusters.

FRUITS: Conspicuous, spiny, brown capsules split open in winter to display many small seeds that are covered with a pulp that is used as a source of yellow dye.

SEASON OF MAXIMUM COLOR: Summer, when flowers open; winter, when pods split.

LANDSCAPE USES: For beautiful pink blossoms and unusual spiny fruits, annatto can be featured as a freestanding specimen. Advanced horticulturists might take pride in explaining to guests that the pulp has long been used as a natural dye for foodstuffs and as a body paint by aborigines. This tropical plant is injured by cold.

HABITAT: American tropics; in Florida, landscape plantings in warm locations.

LIGHT REQUIREMENT: Full sun for best flowering.

SOIL REQUIREMENT: Tolerant of many kinds of soil, from clay to sand.

SALT TOLERANCE: Endures salt air back of the first dunes.

AVAILABILITY: Small trees are in nurseries in southern Florida.

CULTURE: No special problems are encountered where frost is not a hazard.

PROPAGATION: Seedage.

PESTS: None of great importance.

233
Crab Cactus

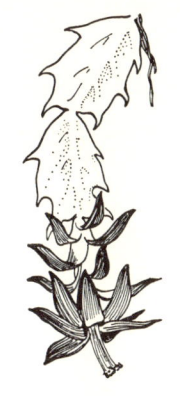

Schlumbergera (schlum-ber-GER-a): for F. Schlumberger, European horticulturist (left-hand sketch), and
Zygocactus (zy-go-CACK-tus): cactus with irregular flowers (right-hand drawing).
SPP.: several species in these 2 genera and their hybrids grow in Florida.

FAMILY: Cactaceae.   RELATIVES: Orchid cactus and prickly-pear.
TYPE OF PLANT: Epiphytic perennials.   HEIGHT: Variable. ZONE: S
HOW TO IDENTIFY: Flat, jointed, leafless stems resemble crabs' legs, and appear to have been clipped at their ends. Here, striking blossoms appear in their seasons.
HABIT OF GROWTH: Declinate, segmented stems fall over edges of their containers.
FOLIAGE: Absent.
STEMS: Flat, jointed, unarmed, in various tones of green, with ends that seem to have been sheared. *Schlumbergera* (left sketch) has slight indentations along stem margins. *Zygocactus* (right sketch) has stem joints about 2½" long by 1" broad, and the margins are furnished with 2 to 3 incurved horns. Bigeneric hybrids might violate these generalizations.
FLOWERS: Borne horizontally at stem ends, irregular, very beautiful, usually in tones of red or orange.
FRUITS: Red berries, if present.
SEASON OF MAXIMUM COLOR: Whenever blossoms mature.
LANDSCAPE USES: For generations, crab cacti have been front-porch favorites. Now they adorn Florida rooms and patios, yet still greater use could be made of these tropical epiphytes as accessories for lawn trees along with orchids and bromeliads.
HABITAT: Tropical America.
LIGHT REQUIREMENT: Partial shade in midsummer, but full sunlight is needed in late summer and autumn for flower-bud development.
SOIL REQUIREMENT: Although these are epiphytes, crab cacti are usually grown in fibrous compost by Floridians.
SALT TOLERANCE: Not tolerant.
AVAILABILITY: Nurseries and chain stores stock crab cacti in small pots.
CULTURE: Plant pieces of stems in small pots or baskets; water moderately during midsummer; and fertilize lightly each month. In late summer allow the substratum to be dry as you expose crab cacti to full sunlight to encourage flowering in season.
PROPAGATION: Cuttage or graftage.
PESTS: Mealy-bugs.

R. cappiliformis

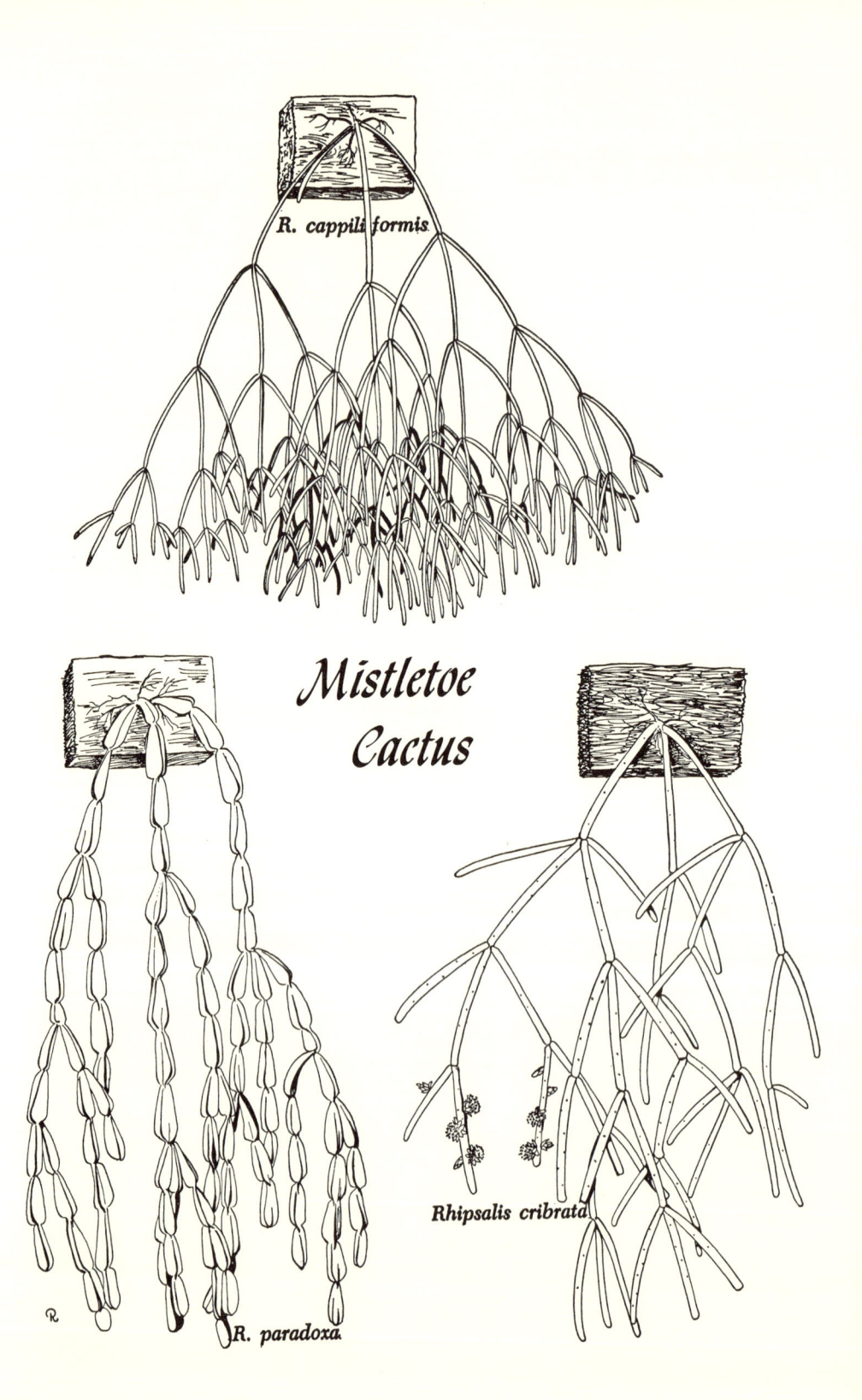

Mistletoe Cactus

R. paradoxa

Rhipsalis cribrata

235
Mistletoe Cactus

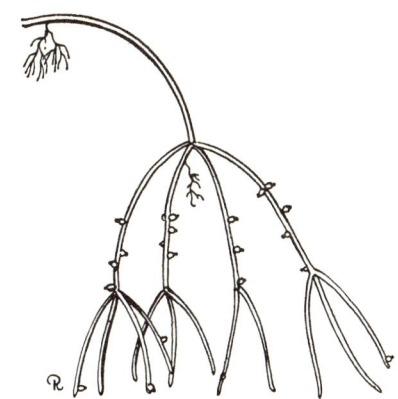

Rhipsalis (RIP-sal-is): from the Greek for wickerwork.
SPP.: a dozen species and their hybrids grow in our state.

FAMILY: Cactaceae. RELATIVES: Hedge cactus and organ cactus.
TYPE OF PLANT: Epiphytic perennial. HEIGHT: Variable. ZONE: S
HOW TO IDENTIFY: Spineless cacti hang from trees like Spanish-moss. Quite or nearly leafless plants divided into 3 general classes: (1) round-branched, those which hang like rawhide thongs; (2) angle-branched, those which have hanging, rooting, angled branches; (3) flat-branched, those with broad stems like orchid cacti.
HABIT OF GROWTH: Branching, leafless, green stems hang downward from the substratum.
FOLIAGE: Absent.
STEMS: Evergreen, functioning photosynthetically, rooting as they hang. Three arbitrary classes are noted above.
FLOWERS: Small, white, pink, red, or 2-toned.
FRUITS: Small, naked berries, some red, some white, others greenish.
SEASON OF MAXIMUM COLOR: Fall if fruits mature.
LANDSCAPE USES: To help cast the spell of the tropics, mistletoe cacti can be hung from trees, rafters, lanai or chickee posts, or other stable wooden objects in frostless locations. Very often these curious tropical exotics are kept in baskets and pots on porches, too. Many named mistletoe cacti, some of which are delineated across, are seen in the Sunshine State. The most widely grown, *Rhipsalis cassutha*, is illustrated above.
HABITAT: Tropical America.
LIGHT REQUIREMENT: Broken, high shade.
SOIL REQUIREMENT: Osmundine, driftwood, trees, palms, and tree fern planks serve as substrata for mistletoe cacti.
SALT TOLERANCE: Tolerant to salt drift well back of the frontline dunes.
AVAILABILITY: A few specialty nurseries offer different kinds of mistletoe cactus in pots.
CULTURE: Hang or tie with a bit of osmundine or tree fern plank where wanted; syringe frequently; and enjoy. Mistletoe cacti are among the least demanding of all tropical exotics.
PROPAGATION: Cuttage.
PESTS: Grasshoppers and roaches eat the succulent stems.

236
Orchid Cactus

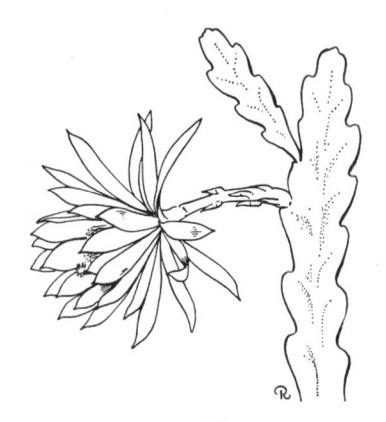

Epiphyllum (ep-i-FILL-um): Greek for on a leaf, alluding to position of flowers.
SPP.: 2 species and many hybrids bloom in Florida.

FAMILY: Cactaceae. RELATIVES: Crab cactus and night-blooming cereus.

TYPE OF PLANT: Epiphytic perennial.   HEIGHT: Variable. ZONE: S

HOW TO IDENTIFY: Yard-long, flat, leafless stems have crenatures in their margins, some of which produce the huge, glistening, orchid-like blossoms, held by some gardeners to be the most spectacular in the plant kingdom.

HABIT OF GROWTH: Declinate, flat stems hang downward.

FOLIAGE: Absent.

STEMS: Yard-long, unarmed, flat, with crenatures in the margins.

FLOWERS: Foot-broad, day- or night-blooming, white, red, pink, orange, or yellow, emerging from crenatures.

FRUITS: A red, bracted berry, if present.

SEASON OF MAXIMUM COLOR: Warm months when blossoms appear.

LANDSCAPE USES: Collectors' items, flowers of fanciers, these tropical, rain-forest cacti are usually cultured as pot specimens. Normally, they are not grown as garden plants. Occasionally, though, they may be set on branches of rough-barked trees.

HABITAT: Tropical America.

LIGHT REQUIREMENT: Partial shade, with more light in wintertime.

SOIL REQUIREMENT: Open, fibrous, leafy compost of slight acid reaction.

SALT TOLERANCE: Not tolerant.

AVAILABILITY: Plants of many varieties are in containers at Florida nurseries.

CULTURE: Plant stem pieces in pots of compost; water always with moderation; apply liquid fertilizer during warm months. When days become shorter, apply less water, but do not allow stems to shrivel.

PROPAGATION: Cuttage.

PESTS: Mealy-bugs, rot diseases if grown too wet.

237
Night-Blooming Cereus

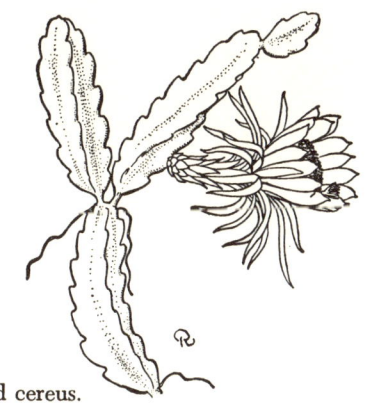

Hylocereus (hi-lo-SEAR-ee-us): Greek for wood and cereus.
undatus (un-DAY-tus): waved.

FAMILY: Cactaceae.
RELATIVES: The true cacti.
TYPE OF PLANT: Vine.
HEIGHT: 20'. ZONE: S

HOW TO IDENTIFY: Strong, climbing vine that clings to its support by many, twine-like, aerial roots, and produces, during summer nights, spectacular foot-broad white blossoms.

HABIT OF GROWTH: Vine-like, clinging by many strong roots.

FOLIAGE: Absent. The triangular stems, dark green in color, form interesting patterns.

FLOWERS: Noteworthy, foot-broad, white, funnel-form blossoms at night.

FRUITS: Red berries, 4½" long, that are highly decorative and edible as well.

SEASON OF MAXIMUM COLOR: Summer nights when blossoms unfurl; and fall, when fruits mature.

LANDSCAPE USES: For the tropical effect of the climbing stems and the much-talked-about nighttime blossoms, night-blooming cereus is widely cultured in warm countries. The cactus is planted by palms, walls, and masonry houses, where the tracery effect of its snake-like, clinging stems is much admired by tourists. Here is another tropical plant, very well-adapted to our state, that helps to enhance the feeling of the tropics in our southernmost counties.

HABITAT: Tropical America; in Florida, escaped from cultivation in the southern part.

LIGHT REQUIREMENT: Sun or shade.

SOIL REQUIREMENT: Any soil is suitable.

SALT TOLERANCE: Very tolerant of salt.

AVAILABILITY: From a friend, one may obtain a section of stem for planting.

CULTURE: Where frosts seldom occur, culture of night-blooming cereus is simplicity itself. Plant a section of stem and forget it.

PROPAGATION: Cuttage by pieces of mature stems.

PESTS: Scales.

Hedge Cactus

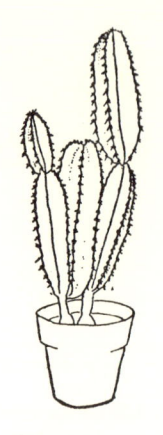

Cereus (SEA-ree-us): a Latin word of uncertain application here.
peruvianus (per-oo-vee-ANE-us): Peruvian.

FAMILY: Cactaceae.   RELATIVES: The true cacti.
TYPE OF PLANT: Succulent shrub in landscape use.   HEIGHT: 25'.
ZONE: N,C,S

HOW TO IDENTIFY: This is a hardy, upright-growing cactus, with ribbed stems about 8" in diameter.

HABIT OF GROWTH: Columnar growth with upright, leafless, flanged branches.

FOLIAGE: None.

FLOWERS: Spectacular, night-blooming, white, fragrant, almost a foot in diameter.

FRUITS: Red, oval, 3" or so in length. Often fruits do not mature on this species in Florida.

SEASON OF MAXIMUM COLOR: Summer nights, when blossoms unfurl.

LANDSCAPE USES: As a freestanding specimen to gain a tropical effect and as a part of the foundation planting of contemporary houses, hedge cactus is very popular.

    The type with the flanges in spiral arrangement is well liked.

    When blossom buds appear in May-June, specimen plants may be floodlighted after dark on nights when flowers open. Dramatic, night-time garden displays are possible when lighting is properly arranged.

HABITAT: South America; in Florida, widely used in landscape plantings.

LIGHT REQUIREMENT: Full sun or partial shade.

SOIL REQUIREMENT: Tolerant of widely varying soils.

SALT TOLERANCE: Tolerant of moderate salt drift.

AVAILABILITY: Nurseries frequently stock hedge cactus in gallon cans.

CULTURE: Plant in a well-drained site; fertilize at the beginning of the rainy season; protect from frost during the first winter or so until a heavy root system becomes established.

PROPAGATION: Simply cut a piece of stem and plant where a cactus is wanted.

PESTS: None of major consequence.

239
Silverthorn

Elaeagnus (ell-ee-AG-nus): ancient Greek name.
pungens (PUN-genz): sharp-pointed.

FAMILY: Elaeagnaceae. **RELATIVES:** Lingaro and oleaster.
TYPE OF PLANT: Shrub or vine. **HEIGHT:** 20'. **ZONE:** N,C

HOW TO IDENTIFY: Long, reaching, thorny canes with scurfy bark, often with sharp thorns; alternate, scurfy leaves, silvery beneath, with many brown dots; scurfy little brown flowers in winter, followed by scurfy brown fruits that are edible.

HABIT OF GROWTH: Sprawling, weeping, very amenable to shearing.

FOLIAGE: Evergreen, alternate, silvery beneath, with many brown dots. Variable with the clone. The texture is medium, the color variable with the clone. Many have leaves variously marbled with white or yellow.

FLOWERS: Tiny, brown, scurfy, fragrant in winter, clustered in leaf axils.

FRUITS: Little pinkish-brown, scurfy, drupe-like, acid fruits that are edible.

SEASON OF MAXIMUM COLOR: No seasonal changes.

LANDSCAPE USES: In foundation plantings, set 3' o.c.; for a hedge that is to be clipped, have the plants 18" apart; as a part of a large, enclosing shrubbery border, silverthorn plants can stand 5' o.c.
  This is one of Florida's very best broad-leaved evergreen shrubs because it grows well and survives all of Florida's minimum temperatures, yet it may develop deficiencies of minor elements on calcareous soils.

HABITAT: Eastern Asia; in Florida, ubiquitous as a garden shrub.

LIGHT REQUIREMENT: Full sun or light, shifting pine shade.

SOIL REQUIREMENT: Tolerant of varying soils.

SALT TOLERANCE: Very tolerant of salt.

AVAILABILITY: Retail nurseries stock silverthorn plants canned and B&B.

CULTURE: After careful planting and faithful watering for establishment, fertilize once a year; head in long canes by deep pruning; control mites during dry periods.

PROPAGATION: Cuttage. The small plants grow slowly at first.

PESTS: Mites, scales, cane die-back disease.

240
Lingaro

Elaeagnus (ell-ee-AG-nus): ancient Greek name.
philippensis (fill-ip-EN-sis): Philippine.

FAMILY: Elaeagnaceae.   RELATIVES: Silverthorn and oleaster.

TYPE OF PLANT: Shrub or vine.   HEIGHT: 20'. ZONE: C,S

HOW TO IDENTIFY: Long, arching canes with alternate, silvery-scurfy, evergreen leaves.

HABIT OF GROWTH: Sprawling, weeping, can be kept compact by shearing.

FOLIAGE: Texture, medium fine.

FLOWERS: Tiny, scurfy, brown, nodding, fragrant, clustered in leaf axils.

FRUITS: Little pinkish, drupe-like acid fruits that are edible.

SEASON OF MAXIMUM COLOR: No variation in color.

LANDSCAPE USES: In a foundation planting, set 3' o.c.; as a part of a large, enclosing shrubbery border, lingaro plants can stand 5' o.c. This is a useful shrub for nearly frostless sections of the lower peninsula, because of its weeping habit, medium-fine texture, silvery foliage, and fragrant little blossoms. There are annual crops of the little acid fruits, as extra dividends. For these, this plant was originally introduced.

HABITAT: South Sea Islands; in Florida, warmest locations.

LIGHT REQUIREMENT: Full sun for best color, habit, and fruiting.

SOIL REQUIREMENT: Adapted to various soils, except alkaline ones.

SALT TOLERANCE: Tolerant of salt drift.

AVAILABILITY: A few specialty nurseries offer this good shrub.

CULTURE: After careful planting in improved, slightly acid soil, pruning, fertilization, and protection against mites and scales are needed as with most other shrubs.

PROPAGATION: Seedage, cuttage, or marcottage.

PESTS: Mites, scales, cane die-back disease.

241
Crape-Myrtle

Lagerstroemia (lah-ger-STREAM-ee-a): for M. von Lagerstroem, Swedish botanist.
indica (IN-dee-ca): of the Indies, eastern tropics of Linnaeus' time.

FAMILY: Lythraceae. RELATIVES: Cuphea.
TYPE OF PLANT: Tree or shrub. HEIGHT: 20'. ZONE: N,C,S

HOW TO IDENTIFY: Deciduous, alternate, glabrous leaves with very short petioles; very smooth brown bark that sloughs off in large patches; showy spikes of beautiful blossoms in summertime.

HABIT OF GROWTH: Upright, suckering freely at the ground line.

FOLIAGE: Deciduous, alternate, smooth, medium fine in texture, light green in color. The fall color is yellow and red.

FLOWERS: Showy terminal or axillary panicles of white, pink, red, or purple flowers in summertime. These fringed and clawed blossoms are borne on current wood.

FRUITS: Brown, woody capsules that split from the top.

SEASON OF MAXIMUM COLOR: May, June, and July, when the blossoms are at their best.

LANDSCAPE USES: Crape-myrtle is an old garden favorite that has been a part of Florida home ground plantings for many generations. It may serve as a freestanding tree, a framing tree, or as a shrub to become a color high light in a shrubbery border. As a roadside plant, crape-myrtle also excels.

HABITAT: Asia; naturalized in Florida.

LIGHT REQUIREMENT: Full sun for best flowering and habit.

SOIL REQUIREMENT: Tolerant of many different kinds of soils.

SALT TOLERANCE: Not tolerant.

AVAILABILITY: Canned crape-myrtles in full bloom are frequently seen in nurseries.

CULTURE: No special culture is needed for success with crape-myrtle.

PROPAGATION: Cuttage, by long, leafless, hardwood cuttings in early winter.

PESTS: Aphids followed by sooty-mold, powdery mildew, mushroom root-rot.

242
Queen Crape-Myrtle

Lagerstroemia (lah-ger-STREAM-ee-a): for M. von Lagerstroem, Swedish botanist. *speciosa* (spee-see-OH-sa): showy.

FAMILY: Lythraceae. **RELATIVES:** Cuphea and common crape-myrtle.

TYPE OF PLANT: Tree. **HEIGHT:** 30'. **ZONE:** S

HOW TO IDENTIFY: Medium-sized tree with huge, simple deciduous leaves that resemble those of guava; very spectacular blossoms in summertime.

HABIT OF GROWTH: Undistinguished.

FOLIAGE: Deciduous, coarse in texture, dark green when fertilized. Fall color: red.

FLOWERS: 3 inches across, in large terminal panicles, are pink or mauve, produced in such numbers as to cause the stalks to bend.

FRUITS: Capsules 1" in diameter, sitting within the withered calyx.

SEASON OF MAXIMUM COLOR: July.

LANDSCAPE USES: As an avenue tree in warmest locations, or as a freestanding specimen in a garden development, queen crape-myrtle is one of the tropics' most spectacular summer bloomers. Additional species are offered by specialists in tropical trees.

HABITAT: Old World Tropics; in Florida, yard tree in warmest locations.

LIGHT REQUIREMENT: Full sun or broken, shifting, high shade.

SOIL REQUIREMENT: Tolerant of varying soils.

SALT TOLERANCE: Not tolerant.

AVAILABILITY: Queen crape-myrtle is for sale in cans in many nurseries.

CULTURE: Plant with reasonable care in fertile, acid soil; water faithfully; fertilize twice annually; keep lawn grasses back from root zone. Protection during cold nights is necessary.

PROPAGATION: Cuttage under mist or by sprouts from cut roots.

PESTS: Scales.

243
Cuphea

Cuphea (coo-fee-a): Greek for curved, for beak at base of the calyx tube.
hyssopifolia (hiss-op-ee-FOL-ee-a): with leaves like hyssop.

FAMILY: Lythraceae.   RELATIVES: Crape-myrtle, loosestrife, and henna.

TYPE OF PLANT: Dwarf shrub.   HEIGHT: 1'-2'. ZONE: C,S

HOW TO IDENTIFY: A tiny shrub with close, dense branching; leaves of finest scale; attractive little blossoms, colored or white, during much of the year.

HABIT OF GROWTH: Very close, tight, and compact; spreading branches.

FOLIAGE: Evergreen, opposite, of finest texture and medium green color.

FLOWERS: Tiny (¼"-½"), axillary, profuse much of the year.

FRUITS: Tiny oblong capsules enclosed by calyces.

SEASON OF MAXIMUM COLOR: Much of the year.

LANDSCAPE USES: For edgings (1' apart) cuphea is unexcelled in frost-free sections; for sunny planters (1' apart) it is favored, and as a foundation plant for the smallest buildings, cuphea is approved when set at 1½' intervals. The cheerful aspect produced by the many diminutive blossoms among the tiny leaves on the wiry stems is much appreciated. The various clones exhibit slightly differing growth habits, and bear flowers of white or in shades of lilac or red.

HABITAT: Highlands of Central America; in Florida, cold-protected areas.

LIGHT REQUIREMENT: Full sun or broken, shifting shade from high pines.

SOIL REQUIREMENT: Grows best in soils above average in fertility.

SALT TOLERANCE: Not tolerant.

AVAILABILITY: Cuphea is widely available in containers.

CULTURE: Nematode-free soil is recommended, an organic mulch is desirable; abundant watering during dry times and frequent, light fertilization are indicated.

PROPAGATION: Cuttage; the tips root readily almost any time of the year.

PESTS: Nematodes, occasional attacks by caterpillars.

244
Pomegranate

Punica (PEW-nick-a): from *Malum punicum,* early name for pomegranate.
granatum (gran-AY-tum): old name.

FAMILY: Puniceaceae.   RELATIVES: Pomegranate stands alone in its own family.
TYPE OF PLANT: Tree.   HEIGHT: 20'.   ZONE: N,C,S

HOW TO IDENTIFY: Spiny bush or small tree with square new growth; deciduous, simple leaves, that are red at first; bright red blossoms and hard brown fruits about the size of oranges.

HABIT OF GROWTH: Scraggly, much-branched shrub or small tree.

FOLIAGE: Deciduous, opposite, simple, of fine texture; and red color at first.

FLOWERS: Showy, orange-red or variegated with white, at tips of axillary shoots.

FRUITS: Berries with thick skin enclosing many seeds surrounded by juicy pulp; sepals persist on the blossom end.

SEASON OF MAXIMUM COLOR: Spring; new growth is red, blossoms are out.

LANDSCAPE USES: For the curiosity of the fruits which have been so important in history and mythology, and for the cheerful red blossoms, some gardeners like to have a pomegranate tree as a freestanding specimen in the out-of-door living area.

Through the ages the pomegranate has been prominent in art. The plant grows well here, but it does not flower and fruit here as freely as in drier, colder climates.

Several clones have been selected for various characters, increased vegetatively, and sold under name.

HABITAT: Southern Asia; in Florida, widely planted as a yard tree.

LIGHT REQUIREMENT: Full sun for best flowering.

SOIL REQUIREMENT: Tolerant of many different soil types.

SALT TOLERANCE: Not tolerant.

AVAILABILITY: Some nurseries in northern Florida propagate pomegranates.

CULTURE: Plant in reasonably fertile soil; water until well established, thereafter during dry spells; fertilize during late winter; keep mulch over the root area.

PROPAGATION: Cuttage by hardwood, leafless shoots in wintertime.

PESTS: Scales and a leaf-spotting disease.

Tropical-Almond

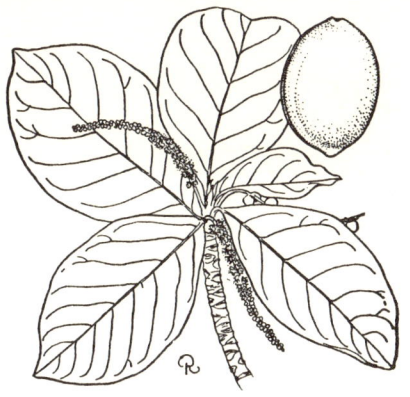

Terminalia (ter-min-ALE-ee-a): from the Latin *terminus*.
catappa (cah-TAP-a): East Indian name.

FAMILY: Combretaceae. RELATIVES: Combretum and Rangoon-creeper.
TYPE OF PLANT: Tree. HEIGHT: 30'. ZONE: S
HOW TO IDENTIFY: A large, symmetrical tree whose branches grow out horizontally in tiers from an erect central leader and bear foot-long, deciduous leaves at their very tips. The leaves, which turn red before falling, give seasonal color to the tree. There are green fruits about 2½" in length.
HABIT OF GROWTH: Striking, symmetrical, pagoda-like structure.
FOLIAGE: Huge, deciduous leaves, coarse in texture and medium green in color.
FLOWERS: Rat-tail spikes of tiny greenish-white flowers in springtime.
FRUITS: Drupes 2½" long with 2 angles that are winged.
SEASON OF MAXIMUM COLOR: Autumn when leaves turn red.
LANDSCAPE USES: As an avenue tree (planting distance 25') tropical-almond is without superior where wind-resistance and tolerance of salt are considerations. The tiered, pagoda-like effect is much to be desired.
   Terminalia trees are very tender to frost. Wild cultures have become established on Big Pine Key.
HABITAT: East Indian islands; in Florida, planted near salt water in frost-free sections.
LIGHT REQUIREMENT: Full sun of tropical beaches.
SOIL REQUIREMENT: Tolerant of sandy soil of acid or alkaline reaction.
SALT TOLERANCE: Very tolerant of the seaside, highly recommended.
AVAILABILITY: Nurseries in southern Florida offer almond trees.
CULTURE: Plant in holes that have been improved by the addition of organic matter; water until well established; place mulch over the root area; fertilize thrice annually while young, once a year as the tree grows older.
PROPAGATION: Seedage.
PESTS: None of major concern.
NOTE: *Terminalia arjuna* has smaller leaves (2" x 8") with 2 round glands at the base of the blade and 1" fruits with 5 vertical wings.
   Terminalia muelleri has 4" leaves, twigs growing out from the upper surfaces of the horizontal branches, and ovoid, dark blue fruits.

246
Rangoon-Creeper

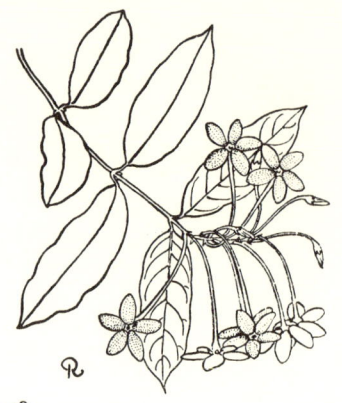

Quisqualis (kwiss-KWALE-is): Latin for who, what sort?
indica (IN-dee-ca): Indian.

FAMILY: Combretaceae.   **RELATIVES:** Combretum and tropical-almond.

TYPE OF PLANT: Vine.   **HEIGHT:** 30'. **ZONE:** S

HOW TO IDENTIFY: Opposite, deciduous leaves to 6" long; brown fuzz on new growth; terminal clusters of tubular blossoms that turn from white to red, or from pinkish to deep red. New leaves have a brownish cast.

HABIT OF GROWTH: Sprawling vine.

FOLIAGE: Deciduous, opposite, rough, coarse in texture, green in tone.

FLOWERS: Showy, tubular, 1" across, in loose, terminal clusters, white turning to pink, or pinkish turning to deep red.

FRUITS: Leathery pods, conspicuously 5-angled.

SEASON OF MAXIMUM COLOR: Warm months.

LANDSCAPE USES: For the beautiful blossoms that change color, Rangoon-creeper is planted to sprawl over fences, pergolas, or small buildings.
   Perhaps one vine of quisqualis would be sufficient within the out-of-door living area of a small home in southern Florida. In large public areas where tropical vines can be displayed adequately, Rangoon-creeper can be used in profusion to give a bright tropical effect, as its blossoms continually change color.

HABITAT: Old World tropics; in Florida, warm locations.

LIGHT REQUIREMENT: Full sun or partial shade.

SOIL REQUIREMENT: Tolerant of varying soils.

SALT TOLERANCE: Not tolerant.

AVAILABILITY: Nurseries in southern part display small vines in containers.

CULTURE: In nearly frostless locations, set vines in fertile soil near strong supports; water until well established; fertilize twice each year; prune after flowering to keep within bounds.

PROPAGATION: Seedage or marcottage.

PESTS: Scales and caterpillars.

247
Black-Olive

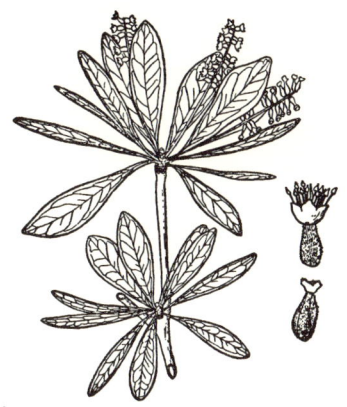

Bucida (bew-SIDE-a): crooked horn, alluding to the fruits.
buceras (bew-SER-as): ox-horned.

FAMILY: Combretaceae.   RELATIVES: Combretum and Rangoon-creeper.

TYPE OF PLANT: Tree.   HEIGHT: 40'. ZONE: S

HOW TO IDENTIFY: Evergreen, entire, leathery leaves clustered with thorns, at the ends of twigs; small black drupes clustered on long spikes.

HABIT OF GROWTH: Dense round head, very thick foliage, very slow growth.

FOLIAGE: Evergreen, of fine texture and medium green color.

FLOWERS: Inconspicuous, greenish-yellow, on long spikes.

FRUITS: Black drupes ⅓" long, clustered on long spikes.

SEASON OF MAXIMUM COLOR: Fruit color is about the only seasonal change.

LANDSCAPE USES: As a street tree, bucida is very fine because of its resistance to salt and wind, and because of its beautiful crown. Plant 25'-35' apart. As a shade tree for back yards it is without superior for the extreme southern part of the state. As a windbreak, when planted 10' o.c. in double staggered rows, it excels.

HABITAT: Extreme southern Florida.

LIGHT REQUIREMENT: Full sun or broken, high shade.

SOIL REQUIREMENT: Native on calcareous soils of the Florida Keys.

SALT TOLERANCE: Very resistant to salt and to wind.

AVAILABILITY: Some nurseries will have little black-olive trees in cans.

CULTURE: Plant in well-prepared sites; water faithfully; keep grasses back from the roots; fertilize twice each year.

PROPAGATION: Seedage and marcottage.

PESTS: None of major concern.

248
Combretum

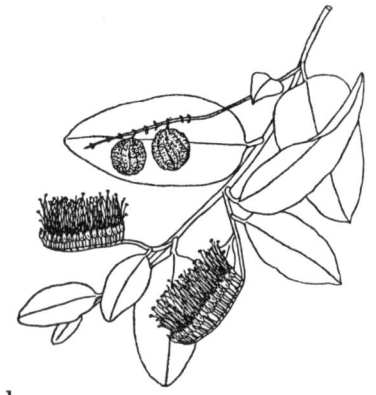

Combretum (com-BREET-um): old Latin name.
grandiflorum (gran-dee-FLOR-um): large-flowered.

FAMILY: Combretaceae.   RELATIVES: Rangoon-creeper and tropical-almond.

TYPE OF PLANT: Vine.   HEIGHT: Variable. ZONE: S

HOW TO IDENTIFY: Vine with slender, twining branches; slender leaves 6" long; showy red tubular flowers in one-sided clusters that resemble giant toothbrushes.

HABIT OF GROWTH: Rampant, twining vine.

FOLIAGE: Evergreen, alternate, rough, of medium texture and medium green color.

FLOWERS: Red, tubular, in large, one-sided clusters produced in summertime.

FRUITS: Papery, winged fruits in clusters.

SEASON OF MAXIMUM COLOR: Summer.

LANDSCAPE USES: To cover a fence, arbor, pergola, or small building, combretum is most desirable for southern Florida. It is a great attention-getter when the blossoms are out. Cut stems with either flowers or fruits are very much in favor for arrangements.

HABITAT: West Africa; in Florida, warm sections.

LIGHT REQUIREMENT: Full sun for dense habit and best flowering.

SOIL REQUIREMENT: Tolerant of many different soil types.

SALT TOLERANCE: Not tolerant.

AVAILABILITY: Combretum vines are in retail nurseries in southern Florida.

CULTURE: Plant in carefully prepared sites; water faithfully; keep lawn grasses back; fertilize twice each year.

PROPAGATION: Seedage and layerage.

PESTS: Scales and mites.

NOTE: There are several other species in this genus, some of which are native in our hemisphere.

249
Silver Button-Bush

Conocarpus (con-o-CAR-pus): an aggregate fruit.
erectus (ee-WRECK-tus): upright.

FAMILY: Combretaceae.   RELATIVES: Combretum and Rangoon-creeper.
TYPE OF PLANT: Tree, frequently seen and used as a shrub.
                                              HEIGHT: 60'. ZONE: S
HOW TO IDENTIFY: Silver leaves (made thus by silky down) that are persistent, alternate, and about 4" long; red-brown globular buttons in terminal position; habitat, brackish water or sandy shores.
HABIT OF GROWTH: Shrub-like, somewhat asymmetrical, becoming a tree with age.
FOLIAGE: Evergreen, alternate, medium in texture, silver, in the wanted form.
FLOWERS: Inconspicuous, greenish little flowers in dense heads on terminal panicles.
FRUITS: Reddish-brown, cone-like structures ½" in diameter.
SEASON OF MAXIMUM COLOR: No seasonal variation.
LANDSCAPE USES: For ocean-front landscaping in southern Florida, and the offshore islands, nothing surpasses silver button-bush. For screens, set wild plants about 5' apart.
    Not all plants of *Conocarpus erectus* have the bright silver foliage, normally one would seek those which do.
    All are very tolerant of lime soils.
HABITAT: Shores of tidal watercourses in southern Florida and offshore islands.
LIGHT REQUIREMENT: Full sun of beaches or broken shade of hammocks.
SOIL REQUIREMENT: Grows in brackish water and on sandy or rocky shores as well.
SALT TOLERANCE: Very tolerant of salt and highly recommended for seaside plantings.
AVAILABILITY: Silver button-bush may not be found in nurseries, but possibly one can obtain wild silver-leaved plants from a friend who has water-front property. Nurseries should grow bright specimens from cuttings.
CULTURE: Plant; water faithfully; fertilize once or twice a year.
PROPAGATION: Cuttage or marcottage.
PESTS: Sooty-mold.

250
Citrus-Leaved Bottle-Brush

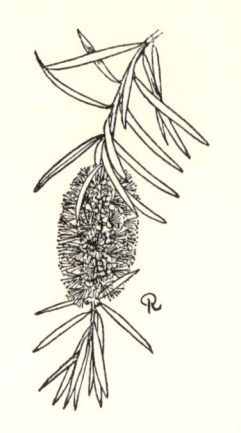

Callistemon (cal-is-STEAM-on): Greek for beautiful stamen.
citrinus (sit-RYE-nus): citrus-leaved.

FAMILY: Myrtaceae. **RELATIVES:** Feijoa, downy-myrtle, and guava.
TYPE OF PLANT: Small tree. **HEIGHT:** 20'. **ZONE:** C,S
HOW TO IDENTIFY: A tree bottle-brush with evergreen, pubescent leaves that have the odor of citrus when crushed. The bright red, 4" flower spikes are not very dense, the many little seed capsules that surround the older stems are ovoid, contracted at their summits.
HABIT OF GROWTH: Tree-like, dense, compact, or rangy and weeping.
FOLIAGE: Evergreen, pubescent, of fine texture and medium green color.
FLOWERS: Bright red spikes, about 4" long, in springtime.
FRUITS: Ovoid capsules, contracted at summits, surround twigs in 4" clusters.
SEASON OF MAXIMUM COLOR: Spring, when blossoms emerge on new growth.
LANDSCAPE USES: As a freestanding specimen, or as a bright accent in front of all-green shrubbery, bottle-brush is highly regarded. Unfortunately, there is confusion in naming, and the situation is complicated by the fact that many are hybrids.
HABITAT: Australia; in Florida, warmer parts of the peninsula.
LIGHT REQUIREMENT: Full sun for best flowering.
SOIL REQUIREMENT: Thrives in many different soils.
SALT TOLERANCE: Tolerant of mild salt drift, but not recommended for dune planting.
AVAILABILITY: Nurseries offer little bottle-brushes in containers.
CULTURE: Transplant only little trees from containers; plant very carefully; water faithfully until well established; keep back the grass; fertilize twice or thrice annually.
PROPAGATION: Seedage and marcottage.
PESTS: Mites and scales.
NOTE: Weeping bottle-brush, with willowy, pendulous branches and bright red brushes, might be *Callistemon speciosus*. Definitive study in the tree bottle-brushes is badly needed.

251
Bottle-Brush

Callistemon (cal-is-STEAM-on): Greek for beautiful stamen.
rigidus (RIDGE-id-us): rigid, possibly referring to the stiff foliage.

FAMILY: Myrtaceae.   RELATIVES: Cajeput-tree, guava, and feijoa.

TYPE OF PLANT: Large shrub.   HEIGHT: 15'. ZONE: N,C,S

HOW TO IDENTIFY: Aromatic, alternate, linear leaves with prominent lateral midveins. Hard capsules surround old stems at intervals following attractive springtime red bottle-brushes.

HABIT OF GROWTH: Stiffly upright.

FOLIAGE: Evergreen, aromatic, of fine texture and dark green color.

FLOWERS: Spectacular spikes resembling red bottle-brushes.

FRUITS: Capsules that surround old stems contain many dust-like seeds.

SEASON OF MAXIMUM COLOR: Late spring when flowers open.

LANDSCAPE USES: As a freestanding specimen for horticultural interest, or for a color note in an informal shrubbery border, this hardy, free-flowering plant is recommended.

HABITAT: Australia; in Florida, widely grown in gardens on light, sandy soils.

LIGHT REQUIREMENT: Full sun for best development.

SOIL REQUIREMENT: Tolerant of many well-drained soil types.

SALT TOLERANCE: Tolerant of moderate salt drift.

AVAILABILITY: Small seedlings are sometimes found in cans in retail nurseries.

CULTURE: Small plants from containers only are recommended, as bottle-brushes are notably intolerant of transplanting in larger sizes.

PROPAGATION: Seedage.

PESTS: Mites.

NOTE: Botanical status of bottle-brushes is unclear and confusion in naming is the rule in Florida.

252
Cajeput-Tree

Melaleuca (mel-a-LOO-ka): Greek for black and white.
leucadendra (loo-ka-DEN-dra): white tree.

FAMILY: Myrtaceae. RELATIVES: Bottle-brush, jaboticaba, and myrtle.

TYPE OF PLANT: Tree. HEIGHT: 50'. ZONE: C,S

HOW TO IDENTIFY: Paper bark tree is a popular name for this plant and it is very descriptive of the whitish, soft, many-layered bark that is positive identification. There are groups of hard, round seed capsules at intervals around stems and creamy-white flowers in bottle-brush-like clusters.

HABIT OF GROWTH: Ascending, narrow.

FOLIAGE: Evergreen, aromatic, fine in texture, light green in color.

FLOWERS: Showy, creamy-white, in close, terminal clusters.

FRUITS: Capsules ⅛" across surround stems where blossoms have been.

SEASON OF MAXIMUM COLOR: Springtime, when flowers are out.

LANDSCAPE USES: Its small size, tolerance of adverse growing conditions, and resistance to pests make this one of Florida's very best landscape trees. As a framing tree, cajeput is highly favored in warm parts of the state; as a hedge, it is popular there too (plant 3' o.c.). As a street tree, set individuals 25'-35' o.c.

For a striking effect, plant an allamanda vine by a paper bark tree so that the golden trumpets will be produced in the upper branches.

HABITAT: Australia; in Florida, very much grown as a yard tree in warm locations.

LIGHT REQUIREMENT: Full sun for compact growth and best flowering.

SOIL REQUIREMENT: Tolerant of differing soils, enduring inundation and salinity.

SALT TOLERANCE: Very tolerant of salt wind.

AVAILABILITY: Nurseries stock container-grown and B&B trees in all sizes.

CULTURE: This excellent tree is of easiest culture. Plant in prepared sites; water moderately during dry periods; keep lawn grasses back from the root zone. Freezing temperatures will injure paper bark trees.

PROPAGATION: Sow seeds on sterilized soil topped with sphagnum moss.

PESTS: None of major concern.

NOTE: Honey made from cajeput blossoms has an unpleasant flavor.

253
Feijoa

Feijoa (fay-JOE-ah): for J. Feijo, a Spanish naturalist.
sellowiana (sell-OH-ee-AY-na): for F. Sello, a German traveler in South America.

FAMILY: Myrtaceae. RELATIVES: Guava, cajeput-tree, and myrtle.
TYPE OF PLANT: Shrub. HEIGHT: 18'. ZONE: N,C,S

HOW TO IDENTIFY: Shrub that shows a white tomentum on new twigs and new leaves; bears attractive blossoms with many conspicuous red stamens in April.

HABIT OF GROWTH: Compact, shrubby, with many upward-pointing branches.

FOLIAGE: Evergreen, opposite, entire, of medium texture and of gray-green color.

FLOWERS: Solitary, axillary, with 4 fleshy white petals and many glistening red stamens.

FRUITS: Green berries, the size and shape of bantam eggs.

SEASON OF MAXIMUM COLOR: April, when blossoms are out.

LANDSCAPE USES: As a dependable, hardy, broad-leaved evergreen shrub, feijoa has proved its worth for Florida gardens. For informal barriers, use at remote boundary to help gain the illusion of distance brought about by the gray-green color of the foliage. Plant 5' apart in this use. For foundation planting groups allow 3' between plants. The sweet jelly inside that contains the seeds is enjoyed by youngsters and some adults.

HABITAT: Brazil; in Florida, ubiquitous as a garden shrub.

LIGHT REQUIREMENT: Tolerant of partial shade.

SOIL REQUIREMENT: Tolerant of varying soils.

SALT TOLERANCE: Tolerant of light salt drift back of the front-line dunes.

AVAILABILITY: Feijoas in containers are to be found in many retail nurseries.

CULTURE: Resistance to pests and complete adaptability to Florida's soils and climate make feijoa one of the best exotic shrubs for landscape use. No special care is needed.

PROPAGATION: Seedage.

PESTS: Wax scale upon occasion.

254
Cattley Guava

Psidium (SID-ee-um): Greek name for the pomegranate.
cattleianum (cat-lee-AY-num): for W. Cattley, English horticulturist.

FAMILY: Myrtaceae.   RELATIVES: Feijoa, myrtle, and cajeput-tree.

TYPE OF PLANT: Shrub or small tree.   HEIGHT: 25'. ZONE: C,S

HOW TO IDENTIFY: A much-branched shrub that bears evergreen, opposite leaves that are thick and leathery, about 4" in length; smooth brown bark that sloughs off in thin sheets; white flowers with many prominent stamens which are followed by showy, red fruits.

HABIT OF GROWTH: Compact, much-branched shrub with closely packed leaves.

FOLIAGE: Evergreen, opposite, medium in texture, very dark green in color.

FLOWERS: White, axillary, 1" in diameter, with many prominent stamens.

FRUITS: Round berries of bright red color, 1½" long, delicious to eat.

SEASON OF MAXIMUM COLOR: April, white flowers; midsummer, red fruits.

LANDSCAPE USES: As a part of an enclosing barrier, set at intervals of 5'. In foundation plantings for large buildings, use a 3' planting distance.

HABITAT: Brazil; in Florida, much planted in warm areas.

LIGHT REQUIREMENT: Full sun for best flowering and fruiting.

SOIL REQUIREMENT: Sandy soils are suitable, but fertility is reflected in good appearance, heavy flowering, and fruiting.

SALT TOLERANCE: Not tolerant.

AVAILABILITY: Nurseries in warmer parts offer small plants in containers.

CULTURE: Plant in enriched sites; water until well established; mulch the root zone; fertilize three times each year. Prune after fruiting, when necessary.

PROPAGATION: Seedage or marcottage.

PESTS: None of major consequence.

NOTE: Yellow Cattley guava, *P. cattleianum* 'Lucidum', has large yellow fruits of delightful, spicy flavor.

255
Downy-Myrtle

Rhodomyrtus (roe-doe-MUR-tus): Greek for rose and myrtle.
tomentosa (toe-men-TOE-sa): Greek for densely woolly.

FAMILY: Myrtaceae.   **RELATIVES:** Feijoa, callistemon, and guava.

TYPE OF PLANT: Shrub.   **HEIGHT:** 10'. **ZONE:** S

HOW TO IDENTIFY: All parts of the plant are downy. The attractive pink blossoms, with the many prominent stamens of the myrtle family, are followed by downy purple berries.

HABIT OF GROWTH: Bush-like, maintained in compact form by heading in terminals.

FOLIAGE: Evergreen, opposite, woolly, of medium fine texture and gray-green color.

FLOWERS: Showy, rose-pink, ¾" across with many prominent stamens.

FRUITS: Downy, purple berries, ½" across, esteemed in jellies and pies.

SEASON OF MAXIMUM COLOR: Warm months, when flowers or fruits mature.

LANDSCAPE USES: As a foundation plant for large buildings in southern Florida, downy-myrtle is highly acceptable. Set plants 5' o.c. As a part of an enclosing shrubbery border, use the same planting interval.
   Downy-myrtle attracts a great deal of attention because of its woolly foliage, beautiful pink flowers, and delectable fruits. It is one of the best shrubs for nearly frostless sites.

HABITAT: Eastern Asia; in Florida, warmest locations.

LIGHT REQUIREMENT: Full sun or partial shade.

SOIL REQUIREMENT: Tolerant of many soil types, but moderate fertility makes for best growth, flowering, and fruiting.

SALT TOLERANCE: Tolerant of salt air well back from the surf.

AVAILABILITY: Specialty nurseries in southern Florida will have downy-myrtle plants.

CULTURE: Plant in carefully prepared sites; water faithfully; keep lawn grasses back from the root zone; apply a mulch; fertilize twice each year.

PROPAGATION: Seedage and cuttage under mist.

PESTS: Scales, mites, and mushroom root-rot.

256
Surinam-Cherry

Eugenia (you-JEAN-ee-a): for Prince Eugene of Savoy, patron of botany.
uniflora (you-nee-FLOR-a): single-flowered.

FAMILY: Myrtaceae.　　RELATIVES: Brush-cherry, myrtle, and guava.

TYPE OF PLANT: Shrub.　　　　　　　　HEIGHT: 25'. ZONE: C,S

HOW TO IDENTIFY: Evergreen, sessile, shining leaves that are wine-colored while young; solitary white flowers that are followed by ribbed red or black fruits during much of the year.

HABIT OF GROWTH: Shrubby, very compact, with closely packed leaves.

FOLIAGE: Evergreen, of medium fine texture and a dark green color.

FLOWERS: Solitary, fragrant, with the many prominent stamens of the myrtle family.

FRUITS: Fluted or ribbed berries crowned by calyx lobes, about 1" in diameter. Many persons like the fruits for their sprightly, acid flavor; preserves are delicious.

SEASON OF MAXIMUM COLOR: Much of the year, when blossoms and/or fruits are out.

LANDSCAPE USES: For clipped hedges, Surinam-cherry is one of the very best materials within its climatic range. Set the plants 18" apart. As a part of an informal enclosing border, the plants can stand about 3'-5' o.c.

HABITAT: Brazil; in Florida, widely distributed where citrus is grown commercially.

LIGHT REQUIREMENT: Full sun for best habit, full bloom, and good fruiting.

SOIL REQUIREMENT: Tolerant of widely varying soils.

SALT TOLERANCE: Not tolerant.

AVAILABILITY: Most nurseries in central and southern Florida offer small seedlings.

CULTURE: Plant carefully in well-made sites; water moderately; clip frequently; cover the root zone with an organic mulch; apply fertilizer three times each year.

PROPAGATION: Seedage.

PESTS: Caterpillars and scales.

257
Australian Brush-Cherry

Eugenia (you-JEAN-ee-a): for Prince Eugene of Savoy, patron of botany.
paniculata (pan-ick-you-LAY-ta): with flowers in elongate spikes.

FAMILY: Myrtaceae.   RELATIVES: Surinam-cherry, myrtle, and guava.

TYPE OF PLANT: Shrub or tree, depending upon training.
                                                        HEIGHT: 25′. ZONE: S

HOW TO IDENTIFY: Slim, narrow, evergreen leaves to 3″ long, that are pinkish while young; compact, yet ascending habit; often seen in sheared forms.

HABIT OF GROWTH: Upright, with ascending branches, and closely packed foliage.

FOLIAGE: Evergreen, of medium texture and dark green color. New growth is pinkish.

FLOWERS: White, about 1″ across, with the many prominent stamens of the myrtle family.

FRUITS: Ovoid berries ¾″ in diameter, rose-purple, excellent in jellies.

SEASON OF MAXIMUM COLOR: Warm months, when flowers and fruits are present.

LANDSCAPE USES: As a sheared specimen for extreme southern Florida, brush-cherry is a favorite plant. As a clipped hedge, it is excellent when planted 18″ apart. As a part of an informal enclosure, brush-cherry is good when set 3′-5′ o.c.

HABITAT: Australia; in Florida, gardens in warmest parts of the peninsula.

LIGHT REQUIREMENT: Full sun for best form, flowering, and fruiting.

SOIL REQUIREMENT: Tolerant of varying soils, but grows best in good soil.

SALT TOLERANCE: Not tolerant.

AVAILABILITY: Brush-cherry is offered in nurseries in warmer parts.

CULTURE: Plant carefully in well-made sites; water moderately; clip frequently; cover the root zone with an organic mulch; apply fertilizer three times a year.

PROPAGATION: Seedage.

PESTS: Scales and mites.

Myrtle

Myrtus (MUR-tus): ancient Greek name.
communis (com-YOU-nis): growing in a community.

FAMILY: Myrtaceae.   RELATIVES: Bottle-brush, cajeput-tree, and guava.

TYPE OF PLANT: Shrub.   HEIGHT: 10'. ZONE: N,C

HOW TO IDENTIFY: Somewhat open shrub bearing simple, evergreen leaves closely packed near the branch-tips; white flowers in axillary cymes with many prominent stamens, followed by black berries.

HABIT OF GROWTH: Somewhat open below; on superior soils, growth may be compact.

FOLIAGE: Evergreen, simple, fine in texture, dark green in color.

FLOWERS: White, with 4-5 petals and the many prominent stamens of the myrtle family.

FRUITS: Bluish-black berries, sometimes borne in quantity on superior soil.

SEASON OF MAXIMUM COLOR: Springtime, when the blossoms unfurl.

LANDSCAPE USES: For foundation plantings, set plants 3' o.c.; as a facer shrub in front of larger, leggy plants space 3'-5' apart. Profuse flowering may be the rule for well-grown individuals.

The clone 'Microphylla' has little, closely packed, upward-pointing leaves, while 'Variegata' has mottled foliage. There are other selected clones, too.

HABITAT: Western Asia; in Florida, infrequently planted on better soils.

LIGHT REQUIREMENT: High, shifting pine shade is excellent.

SOIL REQUIREMENT: Superior soils of the upper counties.

SALT TOLERANCE: Not tolerant.

AVAILABILITY: Infrequently offered in retail sales yards.

CULTURE: On the panhandle, true myrtle grows with little care; on the peninsula, plant in well-made sites, water faithfully, and fertilize thrice annually.

PROPAGATION: Cuttage.

PESTS: Mites, scales, and mushroom root-rot.

259
Princess-Flower

Tibouchina (tib-oo-KINE-a): a native name in Guiana.
semidecandra (sem-ee-da-CAN-dra): with five stamens.

FAMILY: Melastomaceae.   **RELATIVES:** The melastomes.
TYPE OF PLANT: Large shrub.   **HEIGHT:** 15'. **ZONE:** C,S

HOW TO IDENTIFY: A rampant, sprawling shrub that has pubescent twigs that bear large, downy, evergreen leaves with 3-7 prominent nerves. The large, flaring, purple flowers are very showy during warm months.

HABIT OF GROWTH: Sprawling, ungainly, almost vine-like, needing support.

FOLIAGE: Evergreen, notably pubescent, coarse in texture, dark green above, lighter beneath.

FLOWERS: Purple, very showy, 5" across, near branch-ends, subtended by 2 circular bracts.

FRUITS: Five-valved capsules enclosed by persistent calyx-tubes.

SEASON OF MAXIMUM COLOR: Warm months, when flowers mature.

LANDSCAPE USES: For the glory of the purple blossoms to highlight the green of an enclosing shrubbery border, princess-flower is much liked. Plants may be set in clumps of three with 5' between the individuals. When in full bloom, a clump of princess-flowers is a sight long to be remembered. This is one of the most popular semitropical flowering shrubs at Florida's famous admission gardens.

HABITAT: Brazil; in Florida, popular as a yard shrub in warm areas.

LIGHT REQUIREMENT: Full sun for best flowering.

SOIL REQUIREMENT: Any well-drained soil appears to be suitable if slightly acid in reaction.

SALT TOLERANCE: Not tolerant.

AVAILABILITY: Plants in containers are in most nurseries in central and southern Florida.

CULTURE: Freedom from nematodes is desirable, but princess-flower will grow in almost any soil if it is well-watered and fertilized.

PROPAGATION: Cuttage.

PESTS: Nematodes and mushroom root-rot.

260
Aralia

Polyscias (pol-ISS-ee-us): Greek for many and shade, for the abundant foliage.
balfouriana (bal-four-ee-AY-na): for J. Balfour, English botanist.

FAMILY: Araliaceae.   RELATIVES: Ivy, rice-paper plant, and false aralia.

TYPE OF PLANT: Shrub.   HEIGHT: 25'.   ZONE: S

HOW TO IDENTIFY: Shrub with stiffly upright stems that show many prominent lenticels and large, circular leaf-scars; compound, evergreen leaves with rounded leaflets about 4" wide that are splotched with white.

HABIT OF GROWTH: Stiffly upright to make one of our narrowest shrubs.

FOLIAGE: Evergreen, coarse in texture, light green with white variegation.

FLOWERS: Inconspicuous, held on axillary sprays by older plants.

FRUITS: Smooth, round, drupe-like pods when present.

SEASON OF MAXIMUM COLOR: No variation.

LANDSCAPE USES: For a tall, narrow hedge for extreme southern Florida nothing surpasses aralia. Stick cuttings about 1' apart where the hedge is wanted. As an urn subject for terrace, patio, or Florida room, this upright shrub is also very popular. Aralias run into many forms, and botanical status is unclear.

HABITAT: Landscape plantings in the tropics around the globe.

LIGHT REQUIREMENT: Tolerant of shade, grows well in the sun too.

SOIL REQUIREMENT: Tolerant of many soils, including thin sands.

SALT TOLERANCE: Aralias grow well some distance back from the shore line.

AVAILABILITY: Nurseries in southern Florida display aralias in endless array.

CULTURE: No particular requirements are noted excepting to protect the foliage against mites and frost.

PROPAGATION: Cuttage, using any type of wood, at any season of the year.

PESTS: Mites, scales, and nematodes.

261
False Aralia

Dizygotheca (dizzy-go-THEE-ka): double receptable, for the 4-celled anthers.
kerchoveana (ker-chove-ee-AY-na): for O. de Kerchove, a Belgian horticulturist.

FAMILY: Araliaceae.　　　**RELATIVES:** True aralia, rice-paper plant, and ivy.

TYPE OF PLANT: Shrub.　　　**HEIGHT:** 10'. **ZONE:** S

HOW TO IDENTIFY: Finely cut, brownish leaves made up of 7-11 leaflets, about ½" broad. The stems have prominent lenticels like true aralia.

HABIT OF GROWTH: Narrowly upright like aralia.

FOLIAGE: Evergreen, digitate, coarse in texture of mottled brown tones.

FLOWERS: Inconspicuous when present.

FRUITS: Usually not formed.

SEASON OF MAXIMUM COLOR: No variation.

LANDSCAPE USES: For its tropical effect, false aralia may be used as a free-standing specimen or as an urn subject for patio, terrace, or Florida room. False aralia is usually labeled "Aralia elegantissima."

Interesting to most gardeners is the fact that large, mature plants of false aralia will develop two kinds of leaves. Some will be of the finely cut juvenile type that is characteristic of young plants, and then there will be heavier, broad-bladed adult foliage that is quite different from the juvenile.

HABITAT: Tropics; in Florida, warmest locations only.

LIGHT REQUIREMENT: Tolerant of shade.

SOIL REQUIREMENT: Very tolerant of varying soils.

SALT TOLERANCE: Not tolerant.

AVAILABILITY: Nurseries in southern Florida, many chain stores, offer false aralia in containers.

CULTURE: Partial shade, fertile, well-drained soil, moderate moisture, and freedom from frost are requirements for success.

PROPAGATION: Cuttage, marcottage, or graftage.

PESTS: Scales and nematodes.

262 Rice-Paper Plant

Tetrapanax (tet-TRAP-an-ax): Greek for four and panax, all healing.
papyriferus (pap-er-IFF-er-us): paper-bearing.

FAMILY: Araliaceae.   RELATIVES: Aralia, false aralia, and ivy.

TYPE OF PLANT: Shrub, sometimes becoming tree-like.   HEIGHT: 10′.
ZONE: N,C,S

HOW TO IDENTIFY: Great lobed leaves a foot or more across, felty beneath, felty new growth; large woolly panicles may appear in warm months.

HABIT OF GROWTH: Tall bush or small tree with huge felty leaves, and the tendency to send out suckers at great distances.

FOLIAGE: Evergreen, very bold in aspect, gray-green in color.

FLOWERS: Yellow-white in many globular umbels on large woolly panicles.

FRUITS: Small, globular.

SEASON OF MAXIMUM COLOR: Warm months when felty inflorescences appear.

LANDSCAPE USES: Rice-paper plant is useful in helping to create a tropical atmosphere, but it has a tendency to produce large numbers of suckers at great distances from the plant. These can become a real nuisance, and so many gardeners prefer not to grow this handsome tropical subject. These persons might consider having tetrapanax in decorative containers on the terrace.

Plants are killed to the ground level by temperatures below freezing.

HABITAT: Orient; in Florida, ubiquitous.

LIGHT REQUIREMENT: Full sun or partial shade.

SOIL REQUIREMENT: Any soil seems to meet the requirements of this plant.

SALT TOLERANCE: Not tolerant.

AVAILABILITY: Suckers which arise from roots are exchanged by neighbors.

CULTURE: No particular attention is needed for success with this frost-tender plant.

PROPAGATION: Transplant suckers.

PESTS: Mealy bugs.

263
Fatsia

Fatsia (FAT-see-a): from a Japanese name.
japonica (jap-ON-i-ca): Japanese.

FAMILY: Araliaceae.   RELATIVES: English ivy and rice-paper plant.
TYPE OF PLANT: Shrub.   HEIGHT: 4'. ZONE: N,C,S
HOW TO IDENTIFY: This is a shrub that bears foot-broad leaves, cut below the middle into 5-9 deep lobes. The petioles, about a foot in length, stand perpendicular to the stem to hold the leaves in attractive, horizontal array.
HABIT OF GROWTH: Stiffly upright by thick, green stems.
FOLIAGE: Evergreen, bold and handsome, foot-broad, deeply cleft.
FLOWERS: Terminal clusters of whitish little flowers that add nothing to the landscape effect.
FRUITS: Little black globes, if present.
SEASON OF MAXIMUM COLOR: No seasonal changes.
LANDSCAPE USES: As a Florida room urn subject, or as a north-side wall shrub, both fatsia and fatshedera are in high favor. For those who seek oriental effects in their gardens or Florida rooms, these Japanese shrubs are very useful.
HABITAT: Japan.
LIGHT REQUIREMENT: Reduced light of north-side or indoor locations; bright sunlight is unsuitable.
SOIL REQUIREMENT: Moderately fertile, slightly acid compost is best.
SALT TOLERANCE: Tolerant of moderate salt drift.
AVAILABILITY: Fatsia is found in cans in retail nurseries.
CULTURE: Plant in an urn or by a shaded patio wall; water with moderation, but do not allow the soil to become dry; fertilize once each month during warm weather. As stems elongate, they must be supported.
PROPAGATION: Cuttage.
PESTS: Mealy-bugs, scales, sooty-mold, and thrips.
NOTE: In addition to the type, there is a clone with white blotches near leaf-tips ('Variegata') and one of French origin of compact growth and broader, richer leaves known as 'Moseri'. Most popular of all, though, is the intergeneric hybrid *Fatshedera* which was man-made by crossing fatsia with ivy. This hybrid has smaller (6") lobed, fatsia-like leaves held by ivy-like stems. These branches, however, do not have aerial holdfasts, so they need to be tied to a support.

Ivy

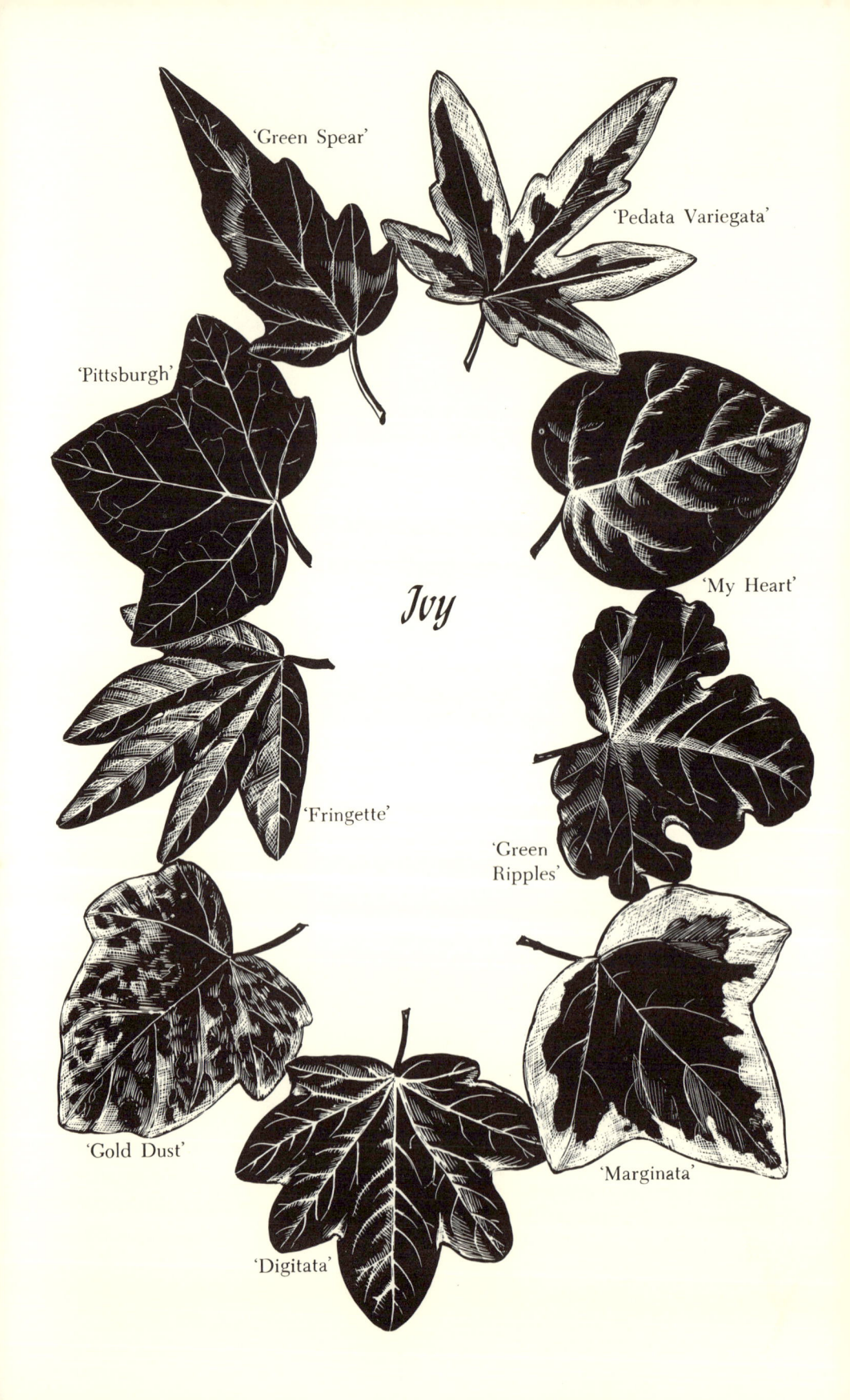

- 'Green Spear'
- 'Pedata Variegata'
- 'Pittsburgh'
- 'My Heart'
- 'Fringette'
- 'Green Ripples'
- 'Gold Dust'
- 'Marginata'
- 'Digitata'

Ivies

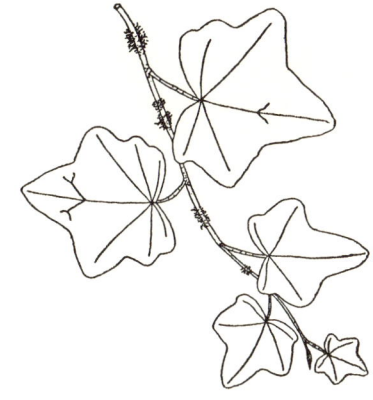

Hedera (HED-er-a): classical name for ivy.
SPP.: more than one species is grown in Florida.

FAMILY: Araliaceae. RELATIVES: Aralia, rice-paper plant, and fatsia.
TYPE OF PLANT: Vine. HEIGHT: 40′. ZONE: N,C,S
HOW TO IDENTIFY: Clinging vine with many aerial roots and leaves of varying sizes and patterns held alternately on smooth stems.
HABIT OF GROWTH: Clinging vine.
FOLIAGE: Evergreen, highly variable, usually medium or coarse in texture, usually dark green or variegated with white or cream.
FLOWERS: Inconspicuous in terminal umbels.
FRUITS: Black berries ¼″ across, when present.
SEASON OF MAXIMUM COLOR: No seasonal variation.
LANDSCAPE USES: As ground cover for shady locations, ivies excel; for planters and to soften north walls, they are without superiors.
   English ivy (*Hedera helix*) is known in more than 40 leaf forms.
   Algerian ivy (*Hedera canariensis*) is said to have twigs that are burgundy-red, few, remote aerial rootlets, juvenile leaves glossy and pale green. Botanical status is unclear, and great confusion in naming is the rule.
HABITAT: Southern Europe and northern Africa; in Florida, ubiquitous in shady gardens.
LIGHT REQUIREMENT: Tolerant of very deep shade.
SOIL REQUIREMENT: Tolerant of varying soils.
SALT TOLERANCE: Tolerant of light salt drift well back of the dunes.
AVAILABILITY: Canned or potted ivies are found in most garden centers and chain stores.
CULTURE: A shaded location that is well-drained, protection from scale insects, and occasional fertilization are the simple requirements of these excellent vines.
PROPAGATION: Cuttage.
PESTS: Scales, leaf-spots, on some varieties.
NOTE: Fatshedera is a foliage plant that resulted from crossing *Fatsia japonica* with the ivy. For north walls in northern Florida, this is a popular plant of tropical aspect. Fatshedera ordinarily requires careful support as there are no aerial rootlets.

Schefflera

Brassaia (brass-SAY-ee-a): for W. Brass, English botanist.
actinophylla (ac-tin-oh-FILL-a): with leaflets in radial arrangement.

FAMILY: Araliaceae.   RELATIVES: Aralia, ivy, and rice-paper plant.
TYPE OF PLANT: Tree.   HEIGHT: 40'. ZONE: C,S
HOW TO IDENTIFY: Huge, shiny, compound leaves held by 2' stalks from thick, straight trunks with broad leaf-scars. Mature specimens may send up showy, red inflorescences.
HABIT OF GROWTH: Upright, usually from a single trunk, leaves held gracefully.
FOLIAGE: Evergreen, digitate, of bold pattern, light green in color.
FLOWERS: Spectacular red inflorescences standing above the foliage to resemble the arms of an octopus.
FRUITS: Small, round, produced in great numbers by mature trees.
SEASON OF MAXIMUM COLOR: Summer, when in flower.
LANDSCAPE USES: Accent plant, urn subject for terrace, patio, or Florida room. Schefflera is very popular for landscaping in Florida, and tens of thousands of seedlings are shipped north each year.
  Schefflera is tender to cold, and use in permanent locations outdoors will be restricted, therefore, to warm areas on the peninsula. In other places, schefflera specimens can be grown in containers and moved in and out with the weather. Public acceptance is accounted for in part by the appearance of schefflera in so many color illustrations of interiors in home and garden magazines.
HABITAT: Australia; in Florida, warmer locations.
LIGHT REQUIREMENT: Tolerates shade, but will not flower well without sun.
SOIL REQUIREMENT: Sandy soils are acceptable.
SALT TOLERANCE: At some distance back of the beach, it grows well.
AVAILABILITY: Nurseries, garden centers, and chain stores sell schefflera.
CULTURE: After careful planting in fertile soil, little attention is required excepting for occasional irrigation and fertilization.
PROPAGATION: Seedage, cuttage, and marcottage.
PESTS: Scales followed by sooty-mold.

267
Trevesia

Trevesia (tree-VEE-see-a): for the Treves family, Italian patrons of botany.
palmata (pal-MAY-ta): palmate; lobed in a palm-like fashion.

FAMILY: Araliaceae.   RELATIVES: Aralia and false aralia.

TYPE OF PLANT: Tree.   HEIGHT: 20'. ZONE: S

HOW TO IDENTIFY: This small tree, usually grown as a pot plant in Florida, has handsome, large, deeply cut foliage from prickly stems.

HABIT OF GROWTH: Compact, prominent central leader with gracefully drooping branches.

FOLIAGE: Evergreen, 2' across, held by 2' petioles. There are 5-9 lobes to below the middle; young foliage is tomentose.

FLOWERS: Yellowish, showy flowers 1" across are borne in erect clusters.

FRUITS: Large, ovoid berries, if present.

SEASON OF MAXIMUM COLOR: Much of the warm season.

LANDSCAPE USES: This is yet another of the tropical exotics with king-size foliage of exotic aspect. As a pot plant, it resembles somewhat its commoner, plebeian cousin, rice-paper plant.

HABITAT: Eastern tropics.

LIGHT REQUIREMENT: Reduced light of terrace or patio.

SOIL REQUIREMENT: Moderately fertile, slightly acid compost is suggested.

SALT TOLERANCE: Tolerant of light salt drift back of the front-line dunes.

AVAILABILITY: Trevesias in containers are to be found in some retail nurseries in southern Florida.

CULTURE: After planting in fertile soil, little attention is required except for the usual watering and fertilization of pot plants.

PROPAGATION: Cuttage.

PESTS: Mealy-bugs, scales, and sooty-mold.

NOTE: *Trevesia sundaica* from Java has glossy-green leaves, lanceolate segments, and smooth, open, rounded sinuses.

Flowering Dogwood

Cornus (CORN-us): Latin for horn, for the toughness of the wood.
florida (FLO-ree-da): flowering.

FAMILY: Cornaceae.   RELATIVES: Other dogwoods and aucuba.
TYPE OF PLANT: Tree.   HEIGHT: 30'. ZONE: N,C

HOW TO IDENTIFY: Deciduous opposite leaves that often turn crimson in parts of Florida; symmetrical, whorled branching; showy white bracts surrounding flowers in springtime, followed by decorative red fruits in the autumn.

HABIT OF GROWTH: Regular, symmetrical branches in whorls from a central leader.

FOLIAGE: Deciduous, opposite, medium in texture. The color is medium green in spring and summer, red and gold in fall.

FLOWERS: Greenish, inconspicuous, clustered within 4 large white bracts.

FRUITS: Scarlet, ½" long, in terminal clusters in fall and winter.

SEASON OF MAXIMUM COLOR: Springtime, flowers; autumn, foliage and fruits.

LANDSCAPE USES: As a freestanding specimen, a background tree, framing tree, or avenue subject, nothing can surpass the dogwood. In northern Florida it is deeply appreciated for its many excellent qualities, and it is widely planted.

HABITAT: Hammocks with rich soil in northern and upper-central Florida.

LIGHT REQUIREMENT: Full sun or high, broken, shifting shade.

SOIL REQUIREMENT: Well-drained, fertile soil high in organic matter.

SALT TOLERANCE: Not tolerant.

AVAILABILITY: Field-grown dogwood trees are offered in retail sales lots during the winter dormant season.

CULTURE: Very careful planting in fertile, well-drained sites with protection of the trunks against borers is essential. Care in watering is needed at all times.

PROPAGATION: Seedage; graftage for superior types.

PESTS: Borers may invade the bark, thrips may destroy the bracts during hot, dry spring days, root-rot disease may cause death on poorly drained soils.

NOTE: Pink dogwoods, so very popular farther north, do not succeed in much of Florida because they do not experience sufficient chilling.

269
Aucuba

Aucuba (ow-coo-ba): Latin form of native Japanese name.
japonica (jap-on-ee-ca): Japanese.

FAMILY: Cornaceae.   RELATIVE: Dogwood.

TYPE OF PLANT: Shrub.   HEIGHT: 6'. ZONE: N,C

HOW TO IDENTIFY: Shrub with green stems; large, prominent leaf-scars; opposite, evergreen leaves that resemble those of a serrate-leaved croton. Leaves are crowded at branch-tips, and are green or variegated in various patterns.

HABIT OF GROWTH: Stiffly upright, leaves crowded near terminals.

FOLIAGE: Evergreen, opposite, serrate, pleasing in form, dark green in color.

FLOWERS: Small, purple, in terminal panicles, if present.

FRUITS: Berry-like drupes if present.

SEASON OF MAXIMUM COLOR: No variation.

LANDSCAPE USES: For use in shaded planters, particularly in outdoor sections of through-the-wall bins, aucuba may serve. Set about 14" o.c. On superior soils in shaded gardens on the panhandle, aucuba grows satisfactorily as a garden shrub. Full-sun locations are not recommended in Florida. A score of clones exhibit various leaf colors.

HABITAT: Eastern Asia; Florida, shaded sites on superior soils of the panhandle.

LIGHT REQUIREMENT: Shade, running to low light intensities in Florida.

SOIL REQUIREMENT: Superior, organic soil, free from nematodes is recommended.

SALT TOLERANCE: Not tolerant.

AVAILABILITY: Florida nurseries sometimes display aucuba plants.

CULTURE: Aucuba should be indicated with caution, lest it be unsatisfactory for your particular conditions.

PROPAGATION: Cuttage.

PESTS: Scales, nematodes, soil-borne diseases.

Native Azaleas

Rhododendron (roe-doe-DEN-dron): Greek for rose-tree.
SPP.: several species are native in Florida.

FAMILY: Ericaceae. RELATIVES: Mountain-laurel and blueberry.
TYPE OF PLANT: Shrubs. HEIGHT: 15'. ZONE: N,C
HOW TO IDENTIFY: Deciduous shrubs with alternate, pubescent leaves and beautiful, fragrant blossoms in early spring.
HABIT OF GROWTH: Upright, vase-shaped.
FOLIAGE: Deciduous, alternate, of medium texture and medium green color.
FLOWERS: Showy, fragrant, of funnel form, 1½" long with conspicuous stamens.
FRUITS: Little capsules that split from the top.
SEASON OF MAXIMUM COLOR: Early springtime.
LANDSCAPE USES: For massing in informal shrubbery borders, Florida's native azaleas are superb. Set native clumps about 5' apart. In woodland developments, these plants are almost indispensable.

Rhododendron canescens, wild honeysuckle, is the best known. It occurs in moist areas on acid soil in northern and central Florida. The pink or white flowers come in clusters of 6-15 before the leaves in March.

Rhododendron austrinum, Florida azalea, produces great masses of yellow to orange flowers, in groups of 19-21 before the leaves. This one grows in a restricted area in northwestern Florida.

Rhododendron calendulaceum, flame azalea, though not native in Florida, grows in superior soils of the panhandle, to delight all who see its gorgeous orange blossoms.

HABITAT: Moist areas with acid soil.
LIGHT REQUIREMENT: Broken shade of hammocks.
SOIL REQUIREMENT: Acid, fertile, well-drained, well-aerated soils are requisite.
SALT TOLERANCE: Not tolerant.
AVAILABILITY: Native deciduous azaleas are not usually sold by Florida nurseries.
CULTURE: Azaleas are very demanding in the matter of growing medium. It must be acid in reaction, well-drained, open, porous, yet able to retain water well. Water faithfully; fertilize once in late winter; prune in May to keep plants compact and well shaped.
PROPAGATION: Cuttage in May-June.
PESTS: Mushroom root-rot.

271
Kurume Azalea

Rhododendron (roe-doe-DEN-dron): Greek for rose-tree.
obtusum (ob-TOO-sum): obtuse, referring to the blunt ends of the leaves.

FAMILY: Ericaceae.   RELATIVES: Mountain-laurel, rose-bay, and blueberry.
TYPE OF PLANT: Dwarf shrub.   HEIGHT: 3'. ZONE: N
HOW TO IDENTIFY: A dwarf shrub bearing 1" leaves that are hairy, closely packed on thin, wire-like twigs that are usually upward-pointing. The bright blossoms are borne in such profusion that foliage is hidden.
HABIT OF GROWTH: Much branched, closely foliated, yet leggy on light soils.
FOLIAGE: Evergreen, alternate, of fine texture and dark green color.
FLOWERS: Very showy, extremely variable blossoms in spring. The petals may be white or in any shade of red. Some clones bear double flowers.
FRUITS: Little capsules which split downward from the top.
SEASON OF MAXIMUM COLOR: Late winter or very early spring.
LANDSCAPE USES: Foundation plantings, allow 2' between plants. To edge walks, plant about 18" apart. In front of green shrubbery, for color interest, Kurume azaleas may be planted 2' o.c. Varieties with colored flowers may be most effective when they are separated by generous drifts of white.
    There are many kinds of Kurume azaleas available to gardeners in northern Florida.
    There are, also, many hybrid azaleas that belong to other horticultural classes.
HABITAT: Kurume, Japan; in Florida, gardens in northern counties.
LIGHT REQUIREMENT: On the panhandle, full sun; elsewhere, plant in partial shade.
SOIL REQUIREMENT: Fertile, acid, porous, organic soils are requisite for success.
SALT TOLERANCE: Not tolerant.
AVAILABILITY: Most nurseries in northern Florida offer Kurume azaleas.
CULTURE: Set plants in carefully prepared sites; mulch the root area; keep lawn grasses back; water during periods of drought and syringe the foliage when watering to reduce infestation by insects and mites.
PROPAGATION: Cuttage.
PESTS: Thrips, mites, azalea defoliator, azalea flower-spot, and mineral deficiencies.

Indian Azalea

Rhododendron (roe-doe-DEN-dron): Greek for rose-tree.
simsii (SIMS-ee-eye): for J. Sims, an English botanist.

FAMILY: Ericaceae.   RELATIVES: Mountain-laurel, rose-bay, and blueberry.
TYPE OF PLANT: Shrub.   HEIGHT: 10'. ZONE: N,C
HOW TO IDENTIFY: A shrub of robust growth that bears evergreen, alternate, elliptic-lanceolate hairy leaves on hairy twigs. The blossoms that appear in late winter are justly famous.
HABIT OF GROWTH: Generally compact, well foliated to the ground.
FOLIAGE: Evergreen, alternate, of medium texture and dark green color.
FLOWERS: Very showy in 2- to 6-flowered clusters in early spring, in all shades of red, orange, pink. There are white varieties, too.
FRUITS: Capsules which split downward from the top.
SEASON OF MAXIMUM COLOR: Late winter or early spring.
LANDSCAPE USES: For enclosing devices, plant 5' apart, for foundation plantings for large public buildings, set at the same interval.
    There are many sterling varieties of Indian azaleas for gardeners in the upper part of Florida, where they appear in many garden arrangements. As a class, Indian azaleas are probably more tolerant of adverse growing conditions than any other group for Florida. Azaleas are most successful when set in large drifts of single colors separated by foils of white. These latter may be azaleas or other shrubs that flower coincidentally.
HABITAT: China; in Florida, very much planted as a garden shrub.
LIGHT REQUIREMENT: Full sun in western Florida; shade on the peninsula.
SOIL REQUIREMENT: Fertile, acid, porous, organic soils are requisite for success.
SALT TOLERANCE: Not tolerant.
AVAILABILITY: Most nurseries in upper Florida offer Indian azaleas in variety.
CULTURE: Set plants in carefully prepared sites; mulch the root area; keep lawn grasses back; water during periods of drought and syringe the foliage when watering to reduce infestation by insects and mites.
PROPAGATION: Cuttage.
PESTS: Thrips, mites, azalea defoliator, azalea flower-spot, and mineral deficiencies.

273
Coral Ardisia

Ardisia (ar-DIS-ee-a): Greek for point, referring to the corolla-lobes.
crenata (cree-NAY-ta): crenate, referring to the edges of the leaves.

FAMILY: Myrsinaceae.

RELATIVES: Myrsine and marlberry.

TYPE OF PLANT: Dwarf shrub.

HEIGHT: 6'. ZONE: N,C

HOW TO IDENTIFY: Straight, leggy stems hold evergreen leaves with crisped-undulate, glandular margins; coral-red fruits in decorative hanging clusters in the cool months.

HABIT OF GROWTH: Stiffly upright, from unbranching stems bare near the earth.

FOLIAGE: Evergreen, coarse in texture, very dark green in color.

FLOWERS: White or pink, ¼" across, on special lateral branches.

FRUITS: Coral-red (sometimes white), 1-seeded drupes, in decorative clusters.

SEASON OF MAXIMUM COLOR: Cool months when fruits color.

LANDSCAPE USES: On the north sides of oak or pine trunks, ardisias are very handsome. They serve well, also, in planters that are shaded, and in north-side foundation arrangements. This is one of several fruiting shrubs called "Christmas-berry" in Florida.
  An occasional plant of the white-fruited form planted in with the reds is good for contrast.

HABITAT: Japan and southeastern Asia; in Florida, deep shade of trees.

LIGHT REQUIREMENT: Full shade, north-side locations are recommended.

SOIL REQUIREMENT: Fertile, acid soil relatively free of nematodes is best.

SALT TOLERANCE: Not tolerant.

AVAILABILITY: Nurseries stock ardisias in containers.

CULTURE: Even though coral ardisia is very subject to attack by nematodes, it survives to form large cultures near the trunks of oaks and pines in wooded areas.

PROPAGATION: Seedage, volunteers abound under old plants in good locations.

PESTS: Nematodes, mites, and scales.

274
Marlberry

Ardisia (ar-DIS-ee-a): Greek for point, referring to the corolla-lobes.
paniculata (pan-ick-you-LATE-a): with flowers in pyramid-like clusters.

FAMILY: Myrsinaceae.   RELATIVES: Coral ardisia.

TYPE OF PLANT: Shrub or small tree.   HEIGHT: 20'. ZONE: S

HOW TO IDENTIFY: Shrub or small tree with evergreen, alternate, simple leaves that are held by branches that bend down under the weight of the showy, striped blossoms and shining black fruits.

HABIT OF GROWTH: A slender crown is supported by slender, branched stems.

FOLIAGE: Evergreen, alternate, simple; of coarse texture and dark green color.

FLOWERS: White with purple lines, ¼" in diameter, produced much of the year.

FRUITS: Smooth, shining, black drupes ¼" in diameter are much in evidence.

SEASON OF MAXIMUM COLOR: Springtime, flowers; summer, fruits.

LANDSCAPE USES: This native relative of popular coral ardisia has real merit for informal massing on seaside locations, in which use the plants may stand 5' o.c. Its complete adaptability to salt, marl, and shell should be carefully considered when beach dwellers are selecting their landscape plants.

HABITAT: Coastal hammocks of southern Florida.

LIGHT REQUIREMENT: Broken shade of hammocks or bright light of dunes.

SOIL REQUIREMENT: Marl, sand, or limestone soils are acceptable.

SALT TOLERANCE: Very tolerant of salt.

AVAILABILITY: Nurseries in southern counties can furnish marlberry plants.

CULTURE: After planting at its former level, water during periods of drought and fertilize annually.

PROPAGATION: Seedage, or collect from the wild, with permission of the owner.

PESTS: None of major consequence.

275
Plumbago

Plumbago (plum-BAY-go): Latin for lead, of doubtful application here.
capensis (cay-PEN-sis): of the Cape of Good Hope.

FAMILY: Plumbaginaceae. RELATIVES: Statice and thrift.
TYPE OF PLANT: Shrub or vine. HEIGHT: Variable. ZONE: C,S

HOW TO IDENTIFY: Clustered, evergreen, wavy, spiny-tipped leaves; long-tubed, bright blue, clustered flowers which are produced much of the year around.

HABIT OF GROWTH: Sprawling, compact, much-branched; may be trained as a vine.

FOLIAGE: Evergreen, fine in texture, light, yellow-green in color.

FLOWERS: Azure-blue, tubular, clustered, profuse during much of the year.

FRUITS: Elongate, bur-like capsules that cling by many curved spines.

SEASON OF MAXIMUM COLOR: Much of the year.

LANDSCAPE USES: As a foundation plant (2′ o.c.); as a transition plant, and as a hedge, plumbago is central Florida's most popular dwarf, flowering shrub. It serves well, also, as a light vine when planted by a metal support.
 For white flowers, choose variety 'Alba.'
 Plumbago is killed to the earth most winters in northern Florida.

HABITAT: South Africa; in Florida, ubiquitous in gardens on the peninsula.

LIGHT REQUIREMENT: Full sun for best growth and flowering.

SOIL REQUIREMENT: Adapted to widely varying soils, but may show mineral deficiency in presence of lime.

SALT TOLERANCE: Tolerant of light salt drift well back of the dunes.

AVAILABILITY: Both blue and white forms are offered by nurserymen.

CULTURE: Plant with reasonable care in enriched site; water periodically until well established; fertilize twice each year; prune heavily in late winter for fresh new growth.

PROPAGATION: Seedage and cuttage.

PESTS: Cottony cushion scale, mites, and mineral deficiency on calcareous earth.

Sapodilla

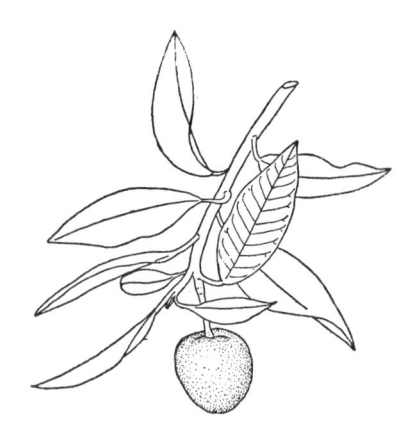

Achras (AK-ras): Greek for pear tree.
zapota (sap-OH-ta): aboriginal name.

FAMILY: Sapotaceae. RELATIVES: Egg-fruit, satin-leaf, and gutta-percha.

TYPE OF PLANT: Tree. HEIGHT: 35'. ZONE: S

HOW TO IDENTIFY: A symmetrical tree which holds its branches in even whorls, with entire, emarginate, evergreen leaves crowded near their tips, and rusty, brown, scurfy fruits.

HABIT OF GROWTH: Handsome form by a strong central leader and whorled branches.

FOLIAGE: Evergreen, coarse in texture, lustrous green in tone.

FLOWERS: White, ½" across, not showy.

FRUITS: Rusty, brown, globose berries 2"-5" in diameter, pleasant tasting to most.

SEASON OF MAXIMUM COLOR: Summer and fall, when rusty fruits mature.

LANDSCAPE USES: Storm-fast, salt-resistant sapodilla is most highly recommended for nearly frost-free sections of the state. This is a beautiful, useful tree that is fully appreciated for its many good points. For avenue planting, for shade, for framing, and for background it can be planted with confidence.

This tree is the source of chicle, from which chewing gum is made.

There are several named varieties which bear fruits of superior quality. These are increased by graftage.

HABITAT: Central American rain forests; in Florida, landscape plantings in warm areas.

LIGHT REQUIREMENT: Full sun for best form.

SOIL REQUIREMENT: Tolerant of many soils, including those of alkaline reaction.

SALT TOLERANCE: Very tolerant of salt.

AVAILABILITY: Seedlings and grafted trees under name are offered in cans by nurseries in southern Florida.

CULTURE: Once established in frostless locations, sapodilla trees require little attention.

PROPAGATION: Seedage; superior forms by graftage.

PESTS: Scales.

Satin-Leaf

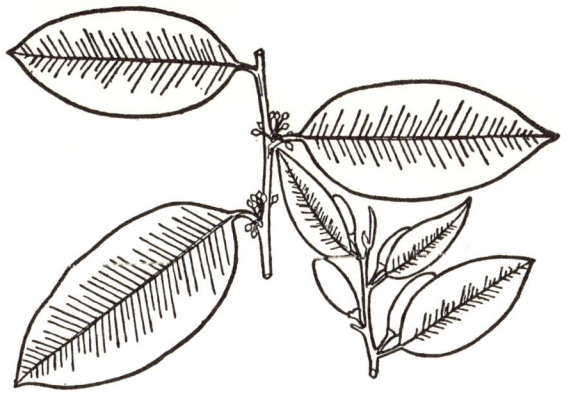

Chrysophyllum (cry-so-FILL-um): Greek for golden leaf.
oliviforme (ol-iv-ee-FORM-ee): olive-shaped.

FAMILY: Sapotaceae.   RELATIVES: Sapodilla, egg-fruit, and star-apple.

TYPE OF PLANT: Tree.   HEIGHT: 30'. ZONE: S

HOW TO IDENTIFY: Large, evergreen leaves that look as though the undersides are of burnished copper.

HABIT OF GROWTH: Somewhat irregular, open-topped small tree.

FOLIAGE: Evergreen, of coarse texture. The upper surfaces are green, the lower surfaces are of a glowing bright copper color.

FLOWERS: White, inconspicuous, on fuzzy brown stalks in leaf axils.

FRUITS: Fleshy berries, green to dark purple, ¾" long, ovate or nearly globose.

SEASON OF MAXIMUM COLOR: No variation.

LANDSCAPE USES: For a freestanding lawn specimen or in shrub borders in frost-free sections satin-leaf is desirable on account of the beauty of the lower leaf surfaces, which turn up attractively when the wind moves the foliage. This is truly a worth-while native plant that warrants wider landscape use.

HABITAT: Coastal hammocks of extreme southern Florida, especially on Cape Sable.

LIGHT REQUIREMENT: Broken shade of hammocks.

SOIL REQUIREMENT: Tolerant of varying soils, but fertile soil is best.

SALT TOLERANCE: Not tolerant of dune conditions.

AVAILABILITY: Nurseries in extreme southern Florida sell satin-leaf trees in containers.

CULTURE: Plant in fertile, slightly acid soil; water faithfully; mulch with leaves 6" deep; do not allow grass to grow over the root zone.

PROPAGATION: Seedage.

PESTS: Caterpillars chew the leaves.

NOTE: Star-apple (*C. cainito*), closely related, bears leaves of similar decorative quality and edible fruits that are sometimes as much as 4" long.

Osmanthus

Osmanthus (oz-MAN-thus): Greek for fragrant flower.
fragrans (FRAY-grans): fragrant.

FAMILY: Oleaceae. RELATIVES: Olive and native devilwood.

TYPE OF PLANT: Large shrub. HEIGHT: 20'. ZONE: N

HOW TO IDENTIFY: Opposite, evergreen leaves 2½" to 4" in length, finely and sharply toothed or entire on the same plant; most fragrant, inconspicuous, white blossoms in winter.

HABIT OF GROWTH: Open, bare stems below, foliage restricted to branch-tips.

FOLIAGE: Evergreen, opposite, medium in texture, dark green in color.

FLOWERS: Deliciously fragrant, small white flowers in winter.

FRUITS: Bluish, ovoid drupes ½" in diameter.

SEASON OF MAXIMUM COLOR: No seasonal variation, fragrance is the thing.

LANDSCAPE USES: For generations, osmanthus has been a favorite as a free-standing specimen for the delight of its wintertime blossoms. Plant a group of three (5' o.c.) in a shrubbery bay.

HABITAT: Eastern Asia; in Florida, superior soils of northern counties.

LIGHT REQUIREMENT: Full sun or broken, shifting shade from high pines.

SOIL REQUIREMENT: Superior soils of northern counties.

SALT TOLERANCE: Not tolerant.

AVAILABILITY: Nurseries in northern and western Florida sell canned plants.

CULTURE: On reasonably good soil, osmanthus is usually long-lived, in spite of neglect.

PROPAGATION: Cuttage.

PESTS: Scales, mushroom root-rot, and nematodes.

NOTE: Holly osmanthus (*O. ilicifolius*) has opposite 2½" leaves with 1-4 pairs of marginal spines and sweet flowers to distinguish it from true hollies. One clone has variegated foliage.
  A hybrid (*O. fragrans* x *O. ilicifolius*) is Fortune's osmanthus with 4" leaves that contain 8-10 teeth on each side.

279
Glossy Privet

Ligustrum (li-GUS-trum): ancient Latin name.
lucidum (LOU-sid-um): bright.

FAMILY: Oleaceae.   RELATIVES: Osmanthus, jasmine, fringe-tree, and olive.

TYPE OF PLANT: Tree.   HEIGHT: 40'. ZONE: N,C,S

HOW TO IDENTIFY: Fast-growing tree with huge, opposite, pear-like evergreen leaves that have 6-8 pairs of veins. Usually many of the drupe-like black fruits persist over much of the year.

HABIT OF GROWTH: Tree-like, with dense, compact head of bending branches.

FOLIAGE: Evergreen, opposite, pear-like, very coarse in texture, dark green.

FLOWERS: Little, white, odorous flowers in springtime, held up by terminal panicles.

FRUITS: Drupe-like berries, blue-black in color, with bloom, persist much of the year.

SEASON OF MAXIMUM COLOR: Fall, when blue-black fruits mature.

LANDSCAPE USES: Street tree at 40' intervals; as a very large shrub on very poor sandy soil, plant at 5' intervals, and attend to pruning frequently. There are numerous named varieties of glossy privet.

HABITAT: Eastern Asia; in Florida, ubiquitous, in landscape plantings.

LIGHT REQUIREMENT: Full sun or partial shade is suitable.

SOIL REQUIREMENT: Tolerant of widely varying soil types.

SALT TOLERANCE: Not tolerant.

AVAILABILITY: Usually sold as a shrub B&B or in containers by most nurseries.

CULTURE: If white flies are controlled, and the plant is pruned regularly, no additional attention is required.

PROPAGATION: Graftage on *L. quihoui*, as glossy privet is resistant to propagation by cuttage. Seedlings abound under old trees, and these may be used as they are or as grafting stocks.

PESTS: Scales, white-flies, and sooty-mold.

280
Japanese Privet

Ligustrum (li-GUS-trum): ancient Latin name.
japonicum (jap-ON-i-cum): Japanese.

FAMILY: Oleaceae. RELATIVES: Osmanthus, jasmine, and fringe-tree.
TYPE OF PLANT: Shrub. HEIGHT: 15′. ZONE: N,C,S

HOW TO IDENTIFY: A shrub with evergreen, opposite, entire leaves that are broad-ovate, nearly flat, with 4-5 pairs of veins and springtime panicles of small, white, odorous flowers.

HABIT OF GROWTH: Upright-spreading, strict, or low-spreading.

FOLIAGE: Evergreen, opposite, medium coarse in texture in most forms, yet some have fine texture, others coarse. The color is dark green in most all-green varieties, yet there are those that have leaves marbled with yellow.

FLOWERS: White, small, odorous, in terminal panicles in springtime.

FRUITS: Drupe-like berries that are blue-black and few on a panicle.

SEASON OF MAXIMUM COLOR: Early spring, when the blossoms are out.

LANDSCAPE USES: Florida's most over-used shrub is seen almost everywhere. As a foundation plant for large buildings, set plant 3′ apart; for informal enclosure, allow 5′ between plants; for sheared hedges, set the plants 2′ o.c.

HABITAT: Japan; Florida's most widely planted broad-leaved evergreen shrub.

LIGHT REQUIREMENT: Full sun or partial shade is suitable.

SOIL REQUIREMENT: Tolerant of widely varying soils.

SALT TOLERANCE: Not tolerant.

AVAILABILITY: All nurseries market Japanese privet, canned or B&B. There are a dozen or more named varieties from which to choose. Grafted plants are always to be preferred when available.

CULTURE: Grafted plants need little attention save for fertilization twice a year and irrigation during serious droughts.

PROPAGATION: Cuttage or by graftage on *L. quihoui* for protection against harmful nematodes.

PESTS: Nematodes, scales, white-flies, followed by sooty-mold and mushroom root-rot.

281
Primrose Jasmine

Jasminum (JAZZ-min-um): ancient name of Arabic origin.
mesnyi (MESS-nee-eye): for W. Mesny, its collector.

FAMILY: Oleaceae.   **RELATIVES:** Privet, osmanthus, olive, and fringe-tree.

TYPE OF PLANT: Shrub or vine depending upon culture.

HEIGHT: 10'.   **ZONE:** N,C

HOW TO IDENTIFY: A sprawling shrub that has smooth, 4-angled, green branchlets with opposite trifoliolate leaves and yellow flowers in late winter.

HABIT OF GROWTH: Strong vine or declinate shrub that can be clipped to bush form.

FOLIAGE: Evergreen, opposite, trifoliolate, of fine texture and light green color.

FLOWERS: Bright yellow, 2" in diameter, solitary, subtended by leaf-like bracts.

FRUITS: Usually not produced in Florida.

SEASON OF MAXIMUM COLOR: Late winter, best show following considerable cold.

LANDSCAPE USES: One of Florida's most over-used shrubs, this very common, yellow-flowered jasmine is seen everywhere over the upper part of the state. In foundation plantings, set 2' o.c.; as a hardy vine on a strong metal trellis plant at the same interval. Primrose jasmine can be planted to help prevent erosion on slopes and banks.

HABITAT: Western China; in Florida, ubiquitous in the upper part.

LIGHT REQUIREMENT: Full sun for compact growth.

SOIL REQUIREMENT: Completely tolerant of all soils.

SALT TOLERANCE: Not tolerant.

AVAILABILITY: This is usually not an item of commerce as there seems always to be an ample supply of planting of stock for free acquisition.

CULTURE: Simply plant, water, and forget. Flowering is best after cold winters.

PROPAGATION: Branches root where they touch the earth.

PESTS: Scales, mushroom root-rot.

282
Shining Jasmine

Jasminum (JAZZ-min-um): ancient name of Arabic origin.
nitidum (NIT-i-dum): shining.

FAMILY: Oleaceae.
RELATIVES: Privet and fringe-tree.
TYPE OF PLANT: Vine or shrub.
HEIGHT: Variable. ZONE: C,S
HOW TO IDENTIFY: A strong-growing vine with attractive 4" evergreen, opposite, glossy leaves; flower buds tinted pink, red calyx teeth *very* prominent, standing perpendicular to the corolla tube at anthesis. Blossoms are fragrant.
HABIT OF GROWTH: Strong, sprawling, twining vine, usually maintained as a shrub by careful, periodic pruning.
FOLIAGE: Evergreen, alternate, very waxy, medium *coarse* in texture.
FLOWERS: White, fragrant, 1½" in diameter, buds tinted pink outside, calyx and calyx teeth are red in cool weather.
FRUITS: 2-lobed berries, if present, frequently lacking in Florida.
SEASON OF MAXIMUM COLOR: Warm months.
LANDSCAPE USES: This, perhaps Florida's most popular landscape jasmine, is much planted in foundation groups, planters, and shrubbery borders in the most nearly frost-free sections. Planting intervals may be 3' o.c. This sterling landscape jasmine has been known as "*Jasminum ilicifolium*" and "*Jasminum amplexicaule.*"
HABITAT: Islands of the southern Pacific Ocean; in Florida, much planted in central and southern parts.
LIGHT REQUIREMENT: Full sun or broken shade; on north sides, plants will not bloom.
SOIL REQUIREMENT: Sandy soils, when reasonably well fertilized, are satisfactory.
SALT TOLERANCE: Not tolerant of dune conditions.
AVAILABILITY: This jasmine is widely offered for sale in central and southern Florida.
CULTURE: Set in well-prepared sites; water faithfully during all periods of drought; fertilize thrice annually; mulch and keep back lawn grasses.
PROPAGATION: Cuttage.
PESTS: Scales and mushroom root-rot.
NOTE: River jasmine (*Jasminum fluminense*) has trifoliate leaves, the center leaflet being the largest and held on a longer leaf stalk. This species fruits abundantly and volunteer seedlings are found in great numbers under old vines.

283
Downy Jasmine

Jasminum (JAZZ-min-um): ancient name of Arabic origin.
multiflorum (mul-tee-FLOR-um): many-flowered.

FAMILY: Oleaceae.   **RELATIVES:** Privet, olive, osmanthus, and fringe-tree.
TYPE OF PLANT: Vine, often trained as a shrub.   **HEIGHT:** Variable.
ZONE: C,S

HOW TO IDENTIFY: Densely pubescent, evergreen climber, that has opposite leaves about 2″ long that give a slightly gray-green effect; white flowers are very abundant in little axillary clusters. The blossoms are *not* strongly scented. The calyx teeth are densely covered with spreading yellow hairs.

HABIT OF GROWTH: Strong-growing, sprawling or clambering vine if supported.

FOLIAGE: Evergreen, opposite, downy, of medium fine texture and gray-green color.

FLOWERS: White, axillary, star-like, 1″ in diameter, with fuzzy calyx teeth.

FRUITS: Inconspicuous little capsules held within the calyx teeth.

SEASON OF MAXIMUM COLOR: Warm months.

LANDSCAPE USES: In central Florida, where it is known as star jasmine, this plant is very popular as a landscape shrub. For foundation plantings and as a part of shrubbery borders, 3′ is a satisfactory planting interval.

HABITAT: India; in Florida, much grown in the central section.

LIGHT REQUIREMENT: Full sun for best habit and profuse flowering.

SOIL REQUIREMENT: Sandy soil is adequate.

SALT TOLERANCE: Not tolerant.

AVAILABILITY: Widely available in retail nurseries in central and southern Florida.

CULTURE: Set plants in prepared sites; water periodically until well established, thereafter during dry spells; fertilize twice annually; prune as needed to keep within bounds.

PROPAGATION: Cuttage.

PESTS: Scales.

NOTE: *Jasminum gracillimum*, easily confused, has more dense *hanging* flower clusters; calyx teeth covered sparsely, with close, not spreading pubescence.

    Arabian jasmine (*Jasminum sambac*) has 2″, very fragrant, usually double flowers and very glossy, broad, prominently veined, dark green leaves.

284
Fringe-Tree

Chionanthus (kye-oh-NAN-thus): Greek for snowflower.
virginica (vir-GIN-ee-ca): Virginian.

FAMILY: Oleaceae. **RELATIVES:** Privet, jasmine, and osmanthus.

TYPE OF PLANT: Shrub-like tree. **HEIGHT:** 30'. **ZONE:** N,C

HOW TO IDENTIFY: Deciduous, entire, opposite leaves narrowing to both ends; brown twigs covered with scattered lenticels; showy clusters of white, narrow-petaled flowers before, or with, the first leaves.

HABIT OF GROWTH: Variable, round-topped or somewhat open and narrow.

FOLIAGE: Deciduous, opposite, coarse in texture, dark green above, paler beneath.

FLOWERS: White, in loose clusters, with four narrow, ribbon-like petals.

FRUITS: Black or dark blue one-seeded drupes ¾" long in summertime.

SEASON OF MAXIMUM COLOR: Late spring.

LANDSCAPE USES: As a freestanding specimen for late spring blooms and for the curiosity of the black fruits, this little native tree is recommended. Long popular as a front-lawn specimen, fringe-tree is appreciated for its beauty and adaptability.

HABITAT: Moist soils of northern and central Florida.

LIGHT REQUIREMENT: Broken shade of forests or full sun of gardens.

SOIL REQUIREMENT: Fertile moist earth or improved sand.

SALT TOLERANCE: Not tolerant.

AVAILABILITY: Small nurseries in northern Florida may have fringe-trees.

CULTURE: Plant in a moist, fertile spot; water faithfully until well established; thereafter, keep lawn grasses back; fertilize in late winter.

PROPAGATION: Seedage or cuttage.

PESTS: Scales and mites.

285
Carolina Yellow-Jasmine

Gelsemium (gel-SEM-ee-um): Italian *gelsomino* for true jasmine.
sempervirens (sem-per-VYE-rens): evergreen.

FAMILY: Loganiaceae.

RELATIVES: Butterfly-bush.

TYPE OF PLANT: Vine.

HEIGHT: Variable. **ZONE:** N,C

HOW TO IDENTIFY: Reddish stems which climb by twisting about supports; partially evergreen foliage; showy yellow blossoms in springtime.

HABIT OF GROWTH: Climbing vine by means of twisting stems.

FOLIAGE: Semievergreen, alternate, fine in texture, medium green in color.

FLOWERS: Funnel-form, five-lobed, bright yellow, fragrant, which make outstanding high lights in Florida hammocks during their season.

FRUITS: Ovoid capsules ½″ long split at maturity to release seeds.

SEASON OF MAXIMUM COLOR: January-February.

LANDSCAPE USES: For the beauty of the springtime gold, Carolina yellow-jasmine may be planted by trees, fences, or pergolas. This fine-scale native vine seldom gets out of hand to become a nuisance.

HABITAT: Hammocks of central and northern Florida.

LIGHT REQUIREMENT: Reduced light or full sun.

SOIL REQUIREMENT: Hammock soils support best growth and flowering.

SALT TOLERANCE: Not tolerant.

AVAILABILITY: Some nurseries might offer vines in containers; however, rooted layers are usually obtained from friends.

CULTURE: Plant near a support in moderately fertile earth; water periodically; place a mulch over the roots; fertilize once each winter.

PROPAGATION: Layerage, where branches touch the earth.

PESTS: Usually none of great importance.

286
Butterfly-Bush

Buddleja (bud-LEE-a): for A. Buddle, an English botanist.
officinalis (of-fis-in-ALE-is): medicinal.

FAMILY: Loganiaceae.   RELATIVES: Carolina yellow-jasmine and strychnine.
TYPE OF PLANT: Shrub, sometimes becoming tree-like.   HEIGHT: 20'.
ZONE: C,S
HOW TO IDENTIFY: All leaves, twigs, and flowers are densely pubescent; lilac flowers in midwinter are very fragrant.
HABIT OF GROWTH: Large, sprawling, almost tree-like if not frosted.
FOLIAGE: Evergreen, alternate, coarse in texture, light green above, white beneath.
FLOWERS: Tiny, but very fragrant, of lilac color in panicles 6" long in midwinter.
FRUITS: Inconspicuous capsules.
SEASON OF MAXIMUM COLOR: Midwinter.
LANDSCAPE USES: As a part of a tall shrubbery border to yield delicious fragrance in midwinter, butterfly-bush will serve. As the plant is frequently frosted to earth, it should stand near hardy evergreen shrubs that can maintain the form of the garden during the winter.
HABITAT: Asia; in Florida, warmer sections.
LIGHT REQUIREMENT: Full sun for compact habit and full-flowering.
SOIL REQUIREMENT: Tolerant of light sandy soils, but susceptible to nematode attack.
SALT TOLERANCE: Not tolerant.
AVAILABILITY: Small plants in containers are frequently found in nurseries.
CULTURE: Butterfly-bush grows rapidly, recovers after each freezing, usually.
PROPAGATION: Cuttage or marcottage.
PESTS: Nematodes, mites, and caterpillars.
NOTE: Several other buddlejas are sometimes seen in Florida. *B. madagascariensis*, with sprawling habit, white-tomentose branches, and yellow flowers grows in southern counties. *B. davidii,* the most famed of the genus, will grow fairly well in extreme western Florida. *B. asiatica,* of upright habit, and with white, fragrant flowers, grows fairly well in central Florida if it is protected against nematodes.

287
Lucky Nut

Thevetia (the-VEE-she-a): for A. Thevet, a French monk who traveled in Brazil.
peruviana (per-oo-vee-AY-na): Peruvian.

Family: Apocynaceae.   **Relatives:** Allamanda, frangipani, and oleander.

Type of Plant: Shrub or tree.   **Height:** 20′. **Zone:** N,C,S

How to Identify: Milky sap, evergreen, alternate, linear leaves to 6″ long; bell-like yellow flowers followed by angled fruits.

Habit of Growth: Dense, with upright branching.

Foliage: Evergreen, medium fine in texture, dark, shining green in tone.

Flowers: Bell-like, 2″-3″ long, yellow or peach-colored, attractive.

Fruits: Drupes, about an inch through, prominently angled, VERY POISONOUS.

Season of Maximum Color: Warm months, as flowers unfurl.

Landscape Uses: As a freestanding shrub for its attractive peach-colored flowers and curious angled fruits, lucky nut is rather widely planted. However, all parts of the plant are highly toxic.
   Frost will kill the plants back to the earth, and so garden use is restricted to warm sections if a permanent effect is desired. Roots tolerate cool soil fairly well and lucky nut plants frequently rally to develop new tops in springtime following cold injury.

Habitat: Tropical America; in Florida, rather widely planted in all areas.

Light Requirement: Full sun for best habit and flowering.

Soil Requirement: Any soil appears to be suitable for growth.

Salt Tolerance: Not especially salt-tolerant.

Availability: Frequently found in nurseries on the peninsula.

Culture: No special culture is called for, but every precaution must be observed so that children do not put parts of the plant in their mouths.

Propagation: Seedage.

Pests: Mushroom root-rot.

288
Frangipani

Plumeria (plume-ERE-ee-a): for C. Plumier, French botanist.
SPP.: several species are grown in Florida.

FAMILY: Apocynaceae.   RELATIVES: Heralds-trumpet, Confederate-jasmine, and oleander.

TYPE OF PLANT: Tree.   HEIGHT: 15'. ZONE: S

HOW TO IDENTIFY: Branches sausage-like, blunt, rough with crowded leaf-scars, and with deciduous leaves crowded at their tips. The blossoms are beautiful, waxy, and very fragrant.

HABIT OF GROWTH: Awkward, angular of sausage-like branches.

FOLIAGE: Deciduous, very large, very coarse in texture, of medium green color.

FLOWERS: Tubular, 2" across, waxy, fragrant, variable in color.

FRUITS: Foot-long twin pods that are brown and leathery.

SEASON OF MAXIMUM COLOR: Summertime.

LANDSCAPE USES: For the fragrance of the beautiful blossoms, frangipanis are among the most popular trees for hot countries. Plant as a free-standing specimen, as a patio tree, or as a part of a shrubbery border.

HABITAT: Tropical America; in Florida, warmest locations.

LIGHT REQUIREMENT: Full sun or high, shifting shade.

SOIL REQUIREMENT: Tolerant of many different soils.

SALT TOLERANCE: Will grow fairly close to salt water.

AVAILABILITY: Many kinds can be found in nurseries in southern Florida.

CULTURE: Set in soil that has been enriched. Water until well rooted in the earth.

PROPAGATION: Cuttage at any time using any kind of wood.

PESTS: Scales, frangipani caterpillar, and nematodes.

NOTE: *P. rubra* produces flowers in tones of red, and has the largest leaves in the genus (18" long), with conspicuous marginal veins.
P. alba has white flowers, narrow, lance-shaped leaves with revolute edges.
P. obtusa has spatula-like leaves with distinctly rounded apexes and white blooms centered in yellow. This one is variable in form and color to confuse the issue.

289
Allamanda

Allamanda (al-a-MAN-da): for F. Allamand, a Dutch professor.
cathartica (cath-AR-tee-ca): cathartic.

FAMILY: Apocynaceae.   RELATIVES: Oleander and Confederate-jasmine.

TYPE OF PLANT: Shrub or vine depending upon training.

HEIGHT: Variable.   ZONE: C,S

HOW TO IDENTIFY: Vining growth, milky sap; evergreen leaves in whorls; bright, yellow flaring trumpets during much of the year.

HABIT OF GROWTH: A vigorous vine that may be maintained as a shrub by pruning.

FOLIAGE: Evergreen, whorled, coarse in texture, light green in color.

FLOWERS: Handsome, large golden trumpets produced much of the year.

FRUITS: Prickly capsules, splitting to release winged seeds.

SEASON OF MAXIMUM COLOR: Much of the year, when flowers are produced.

LANDSCAPE USES: As a vine, as a hedge (set 18″ o.c.), as a freestanding, clipped specimen, allamanda is an all-time favorite. Planted by a cajeput tree to grow as a vine and to flower in the upper branches, allamanda is most effective.

The brown-bud variety is very popular with homeowners and nurserymen.

All allamandas are VERY POISONOUS, all are tender to cold.

HABITAT: Tropical parts of Brazil; in Florida, warm parts of the peninsula.

LIGHT REQUIREMENT: Full sun for best flowering.

SOIL REQUIREMENT: Tolerant of many soil types.

SALT TOLERANCE: Not tolerant.

AVAILABILITY: Allamandas are offered in most nurseries on the peninsula.

CULTURE: Excepting for their tenderness to frost, allamandas grow without major impediment.

PROPAGATION: Cuttage.

PESTS: Caterpillars and mites.

290
Purple Allamanda

Allamanda (al-a-MAN-da): for F. Allamand, a Dutch professor.
violacea (vye-oh-LAY-see-a): violet.

FAMILY: Apocynaceae.   RELATIVES: Confederate-jasmine and oleander.

TYPE OF PLANT: Vine or shrub depending upon training.
HEIGHT: Variable. ZONE: C,S

HOW TO IDENTIFY: Sprawling, declinate stems with milky sap; pubescent leaves in whorls and trumpet-shaped flowers of dull magenta.

HABIT OF GROWTH: Vining, maintained as a shrub by pruning.

FOLIAGE: Evergreen, pubescent, coarse in texture, and light green in color.

FLOWERS: Flaring trumpets of magenta-violet that fades to give a two-toned effect.

FRUITS: Prickly capsules that split to release winged seeds.

SEASON OF MAXIMUM COLOR: Warm months.

LANDSCAPE USES: As a vine for the curiosity of its violet-magenta flowers, purple allamanda is sometimes planted. It is not to be confused with *Cryptostegia*.

Like all allamandas, this species is tender to cold and plants will be killed back to the earth by frosts. Normally roots may survive many winters to produce new tops after the advent of warm weather.

HABITAT: Warm section of Brazil; in Florida, most nearly frostless regions.

LIGHT REQUIREMENT: Full sun for best flowering.

SOIL REQUIREMENT: Tolerant of widely varying soils.

SALT TOLERANCE: Not tolerant.

AVAILABILITY: Specialty nurseries may have purple allamandas.

CULTURE: Soil of reasonable fertility that is free of nematodes is best. Water faithfully until well established; prune to keep within bounds; offer protection on cold nights.

PROPAGATION: Cuttage.

PESTS: Mites and scales.

291
Heralds-Trumpet

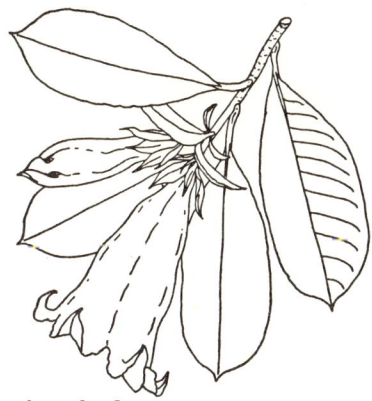

Beaumontia (bo-MONT-ee-a): for Lady Beaumont of England.
grandiflora (gran-dee-FLOR-a): large-flowered.

FAMILY: Apocynaceae.   **RELATIVES:** Frangipani, oleander, and Confederate-jasmine.

TYPE OF PLANT: Vine.   **HEIGHT:** Variable.   **ZONE:** C,S

HOW TO IDENTIFY: Huge, white, Easter-lily-like blossoms; opposite, evergreen leaves 8″ long; milky sap.

HABIT OF GROWTH: Rampant vine, that develops very heavy cover.

FOLIAGE: Evergreen, opposite, 8″ long, of very coarse texture and medium green color.

FLOWERS: Huge trumpets 8″ long, white, tipped with pink, veined with green, without scales at the throat. These trumpets, borne in warm weather, are very fragrant.

FRUITS: Long, woody pods which split lengthwise into two parts.

SEASON OF MAXIMUM COLOR: During the hot months.

LANDSCAPE USES: Heralds-trumpet is a breath-taking sight when it is in bloom, and the individual trumpets are good for indoor decoration, too. The vine will cover a pergola or old building, usually to exclude the supporting object from view. The growth is so heavy that strong supports are needed.

HABITAT: Himalayan region; in Florida, frost-protected areas.

LIGHT REQUIREMENT: Full sun or broken, high shade.

SOIL REQUIREMENT: Moderately fertile, well-drained soil is adequate.

SALT TOLERANCE: Not tolerant.

AVAILABILITY: Specialty nurseries will have vines.

CULTURE: Furnish a very strong support; plant in moderately fertile soil; water until well established; fertilize annually. Frost kills the vine to the ground, but recovery is the general rule.

PROPAGATION: Marcottage.

PESTS: Mites and scales.

Confederate-Jasmine

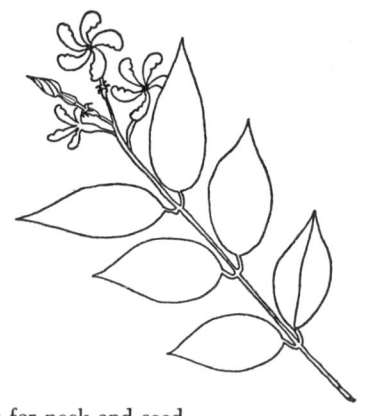

Trachelospermum (track-ell-oh-SPERM-um): Greek for neck and seed.
jasminoides (jazz-min-OY-dez): jasmine-like.

FAMILY: Apocynaceae.

RELATIVES: Natal-plum, periwinkle, and heralds-trumpet.

TYPE OF PLANT: Vine.

HEIGHT: Variable. ZONE: N,C,S

HOW TO IDENTIFY: A twining vine that has milky sap, opposite, thick, evergreen leaves and white, fragrant flowers with petals in pin-wheel arrangement in springtime.

HABIT OF GROWTH: Twining vine.

FOLIAGE: Opposite, evergreen, medium in texture, dark green in color.

FLOWERS: White, fragrant, 1" in diameter in axillary cymes that extend well beyond the leaves.

FRUITS: Two, slender long pods, if present.

SEASON OF MAXIMUM COLOR: April-May, when flowers mature.

LANDSCAPE USES: As a vine to train beside and across the top of a doorway, this hardy plant cannot be excelled. To cover pergolas, fences, and trellises and to add seasonal interest to pine trunks, Confederate-jasmine is much planted.

The little leaf variety 'Microphylla' is useful as a ground cover and for north-side planters.

There is at least one variety that produces leaves that are mottled.

HABITAT: China; in Florida, this cherished vine is in every community.

LIGHT REQUIREMENT: Sun or shade.

SOIL REQUIREMENT: Tolerant of many soils.

SALT TOLERANCE: Not tolerant.

AVAILABILITY: Widely available in gallon cans.

CULTURE: No special culture is required after well-planted vines become established.

PROPAGATION: Marcottage or cuttage with root-inducing powders under mist.

PESTS: Scales followed by sooty-mold.

293
Oleander

Nerium (NEE-ree-um): Greek name for oleander.
oleander (oh-lee-ANN-der): with leaves like olive.

FAMILY: Apocynaceae. RELATIVES: Allamanda, frangipani, and Natal-plum.
TYPE OF PLANT: Shrub. HEIGHT: 20′. ZONE: N,C,S

HOW TO IDENTIFY: Scraggly shrub of many stems bearing long, evergreen leaves mostly in whorls of 3 on heavy green twigs; an abundance of cheerful flowers in spring and summer in red, pink, white, or cream.

HABIT OF GROWTH: Stiffly upright by many ascending stems that are bare below.

FOLIAGE: Evergreen, lance-shaped, usually in whorls of 3.

FLOWERS: Showy, terminal, branching cymes during much of the warm season. The colors may be red, pink, cream, or white.

FRUITS: Hanging brown pods 7″ long, formed of 2 follicles together.

SEASON OF MAXIMUM COLOR: Warm months.

LANDSCAPE USES: As a heavy, informal screen at the rear of large properties, plant oleanders 5′ apart. For water-front plantings, oleander excels. It is too large and coarse for foundation plantings. All parts of the plant are VERY TOXIC.

There are varieties that have different growth habits and flowers of different sizes and colors. At least one clone is grown that has variegated foliage.

HABITAT: Mediterranean region; in Florida, ubiquitous.

LIGHT REQUIREMENT: Full sun for compact habit and free-flowering.

SOIL REQUIREMENT: Any soil seems to be suitable.

SALT TOLERANCE: Very tolerant of salt; excellent seaside shrub.

AVAILABILITY: Almost all nurseries grow oleanders in cans.

CULTURE: Of easiest culture, oleander nonetheless requires periodic pruning and protection against caterpillars.

PROPAGATION: Cuttage, at any season, using any kind of wood.

PESTS: Oleander caterpillar defoliates the plants upon occasion; scales, witches' broom, and mushroom root-rot.

294
Natal-Plum

Carissa (car-iss-a): African aboriginal name.
grandiflora (gran-di-flor-a): large-flowered.

Family: Apocynaceae.   **Relatives:** Crape-jasmine and Confederate-jasmine.

Type of Plant: Shrub.   **Height:** 10'.   **Zone:** C,S

How to Identify: Milky sap; stout, bifurcate thorns to 1½" long, at opposite evergreen leaves; beautiful, white, fragrant flowers followed by plum-like fruits.

Habit of Growth: Dense and compact because of much-branched, downward-growing limbs.

Foliage: Evergreen, of medium texture and dark green color.

Flowers: White, fragrant, 2" in diameter, petals overlapping to the left.

Fruits: Globose or elliptical berry 2" long, scarlet; very decorative. The reddish pulp is excellent in jellies. Fruits mature pretty much the year around.

Season of Maximum Color: Much of the year as fruits mature.

Landscape Uses: For ocean-front barriers, plant 5' o.c.; for foundation plantings for large buildings plant 4' apart. The reddish pulp is excellent in jellies. Fruits mature pretty much the year around.

Carissa is one of Florida's very best ocean-front plants. Ordinarily seedlings are used for these plantings. Outstanding dwarf clones 'Boxwood Beauty,' 'Linki,' and 'Dainty Princess' are available under name for special needs.

Habitat: South Africa; in Florida, widely planted on sandy soils in warm locations.

Light Requirement: Full sun for best fruiting.

Soil Requirement: Tolerant of sandy soils, even those which contain calcium in excessive amounts.

Salt Tolerance: Very tolerant of salt, one of Florida's best seaside plants.

Availability: Stocked by most nurseries in southern Florida.

Culture: Plant in enriched sites; water moderately; mulch with leaves; keep lawn grasses out of the root zone. Two or three applications of fertilizer each year are recommended.

Propagation: Seedage for the type, cuttage for named varieties.

Pests: Scales.

Note: Karanda (*C. carandas*), from India, is smaller in all respects, but serves in ocean-front landscaping in extreme southern Florida. The spines are unbranched; the fruits, but 1" long, turn a purple-black at maturity. Many nurseries will have seedlings in containers.

295
Ochrosia

Ochrosia (oak-ROSE-ee-a): from ochre, from the yellow color of the flowers.
elliptica (ee-LIP-tee-ca): of oval form, referring to the shape of the fruits.

FAMILY: Apocynaceae.   RELATIVES: Allamanda, periwinkle, and Natal-plum.

TYPE OF PLANT: Tree, used as a shrub in landscaping.   HEIGHT: 20'.
ZONE: S

HOW TO IDENTIFY: Large, leathery, evergreen leaves, opposite or whorled, with many transverse veins; scarlet fruits 2" long have violet odor when crushed.

HABIT OF GROWTH: Shrubby, becoming tree-like with age.

FOLIAGE: Evergreen, of striking pattern in medium green color.

FLOWERS: Fragrant, yellowish-white, in flat clusters.

FRUITS: Two scarlet drupes borne end-to-end, each about 2" long. These are POISONOUS.

SEASON OF MAXIMUM COLOR: Late summer, when fruits color.

LANDSCAPE USES: For seaside hedges ochrosia can be set 18" o.c. For planters, urn subjects, or as freestanding specimen trees for beach cottages, this plant may also serve.
   Erroneously known as "Kopsia arborea" in the Miami area, this salt-tolerant tree is in wide use. The fruits are poisonous.

HABITAT: Tropical islands of the Old World; in Florida, landscape plantings of the southern part.

LIGHT REQUIREMENT: Full sun of beaches or broken shade of palm trees.

SOIL REQUIREMENT: Tolerant of many kinds of soils.

SALT TOLERANCE: Very tolerant of salt, recommended for ocean-front plantings.

AVAILABILITY: Nurseries stock canned plants regularly.

CULTURE: Make sites with fertile, acid, organic mixture; plant at former level; water carefully; fertilize two or three times each year.

PROPAGATION: Seedage.

PESTS: Mites and scales.

296
Crape-Jasmine

Ervatamia (er-va-TAME-ee-a): from a vernacular name.
coronaria (core-oh-NARE-ee-a): used for garlands.

FAMILY: Apocynaceae. **RELATIVES:** Natal-plum, allamanda, and oleander.

TYPE OF PLANT: Shrub. **HEIGHT:** 10'. **ZONE:** C,S

HOW TO IDENTIFY: Green twigs with milky sap bear huge, shining, opposite, evergreen leaves; small, white, ruffled, fragrant flowers 1½"-2" across.

HABIT OF GROWTH: Symmetrical, spreading shrub of pleasing form.

FOLIAGE: Evergreen, opposite, of large size and shining dark green color.

FLOWERS: Waxy, white, fragrant, with wavy petals, often much doubled.

FRUITS: Orange-red pods, about 2" long, with recurved beaks.

SEASON OF MAXIMUM COLOR: Warm months, when in full bloom.

LANDSCAPE USES: As a part of an enclosing shrubbery border, plant 5' o.c. Thus the shining foliage and the fragrant flowers can be featured.
  Crape-jasmine is less hardy than gardenia; therefore it is less permanent in garden arrangements in cold locations. In northern Florida, *Ervatamia* seldom escapes cold damage.

HABITAT: India; in Florida, ubiquitous in gardens.

LIGHT REQUIREMENT: Tolerant of partial shade.

SOIL REQUIREMENT: Tolerant of many different kinds of soil.

SALT TOLERANCE: Not tolerant.

AVAILABILITY: Small plants in containers are offered in most nurseries.

CULTURE: After establishment, crape-jasmine grows with little attention. One or two applications of fertilizer each year, and the maintenance of a mulch over the root zone should keep plants healthy. Plants in exposed locations must be protected on cold nights.

PROPAGATION: Cuttage.

PESTS: Scales, sooty-mold, mites, and nematodes.

297
Palay Rubber-Vine

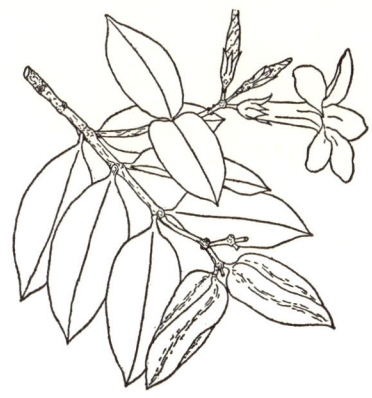

Cryptostegia (crip-to-STEEG-ee-a): Greek for conceal and cover.
grandiflora (grand-ee-FLOR-ah): large-flowered.

FAMILY: Asclepiadaceae.   RELATIVES: Milkweed, stephanotis, and stapelia.

TYPE OF PLANT: Vine.   HEIGHT: Variable. ZONE: S

HOW TO IDENTIFY: Milky-sap, evergreen leaves 4″ long, opposite, glabrous and shining; lilac-purple flowers 2″ across; long, pointed pods borne in pairs splitting to discharge "milkweed" parachutes.

HABIT OF GROWTH: Vining.

FOLIAGE: Evergreen, opposite, coarse in texture, dark green in color.

FLOWERS: Very showy, lilac-purple, bell-shaped 3″ in diameter, calyx leafy.

FRUITS: Pods 4″ long, sharply angled, produced in pairs.

SEASON OF MAXIMUM COLOR: Warm months, when flowers are out.

LANDSCAPE USES: As a cover for a fence or small building in southern Florida, this tropical vine may serve; as a freestanding, flowering shrub maintained by pruning, it is frequently seen, too.

HABITAT: Africa; in Florida, most nearly frost-free locations.

LIGHT REQUIREMENT: Full sun for dense habit and profuse flowering.

SOIL REQUIREMENT: Sandy, well-drained soils are adequate.

SALT TOLERANCE: Reasonably resistant to salt.

AVAILABILITY: Rubber-vines, sometimes erroneously called purple allamandas, are rather frequently seen in nurseries.

CULTURE: In nearly frostless locations, plant the vines in well-prepared sites, water, and forget, excepting for occasional pruning to keep within bounds.

PROPAGATION: Seedage, cuttage, and layerage.

PESTS: Scales and mites.

NOTE: Naming is in confusion: *Cryptostegia madagascariensis* has reddish-purple flowers, with smaller calyx about ¼″ long, and the scales of the crown are not divided.

298
Wax Plant

Hoya (HOY-a): for T. Hoy, English gardener.
carnosa (car-NO-sa): fleshy.

FAMILY: Asclepiadaceae.   RELATIVES: Carrion-flower and milkweed.
TYPE OF PLANT: Woody vine.   HEIGHT: Variable. ZONE: S
HOW TO IDENTIFY: This slow-growing vine with milky sap bears opposite, fleshy 4″ leaves. The profusion of tiny hairs makes these soft to the touch. Large, showy clusters of white and pink flowers, ½″ across, appear in spring and summer.
HABIT OF GROWTH: Sprawling little vine.
FOLIAGE: Evergreen, opposite, thick and fleshy, from short, thick petioles. Clones with marbled foliage are very attractive.
FLOWERS: Beautiful, waxy, long-lasting, star-shaped, pink-and-white. Blossoms come from old flower spurs, which must never be cut off.
FRUITS: Little pods, if present.
SEASON OF MAXIMUM COLOR: Spring and summer when new growth matures.
LANDSCAPE USES: Long a hanging-basket favorite, wax-plant can be grown to adorn a patio wall, if freedom from nematodes in the growing medium is assured.
HABITAT: Eastern tropics.
LIGHT REQUIREMENT: High, broken shade.
SOIL REQUIREMENT: Fibrous compost that has been made free of nematodes, or peat or sphagnum moss grow wax-plants.
SALT TOLERANCE: Tolerant of salt drift.
AVAILABILITY: Many nurseries offer small wax plants in an assortment of containers.
CULTURE: Water with moderation until after flowering, then during the cool months allow wax-plants to become dormant by reducing the amount of water. As days lengthen after winter, increase water and light; fertilize once each month. Since flowers come from old spurs, do not cut these structures if blossoms are gathered for arrangements.
PROPAGATION: Cuttage, layerage, and marcottage.
PESTS: Nematodes and mealy-bugs.
NOTE: Clones with foliage marbled with white are more popular than is the all-green species. Named hoyas have fantastically beautiful leaves that display shades of pink or red.

299
Christmas-Vine

Porana (poe-RAIN-a): native name.
paniculata (pan-ick-you-LATE-a): **with stalked flowers in clusters.**

FAMILY: Convolvulaceae.

RELATIVES: Cypress-vine and morning-glory.

TYPE OF PLANT: Vine.

HEIGHT: Variable. ZONE: S

HOW TO IDENTIFY: Evergreen, heart-shaped, entire, alternate leaves about 6" long; showers of wintertime fragrant, white blossoms in profuse axillary panicles.

HABIT OF GROWTH: Sprawling vine that may veil its support quickly.

FOLIAGE: Evergreen, heart-shaped, of coarse texture and gray-green color.

FLOWERS: Showy, axillary panicles of white flowers ⅓" across, in winter.

FRUITS: Hairy capsules about ⅕" across.

SEASON OF MAXIMUM COLOR: The Christmas season.

LANDSCAPE USES: To cover fences, tree trunks, small buildings, or pergolas, Christmas-vine is popular in warm sections of the lower peninsula.
   The slender stems may reach a length of as much as 30' and so pruning of vines growing under favorable conditions is needed to keep them within bounds. This cutting back should come just after flowering during the holiday season. During that time masses of blossoms might be cut for Christmas decorations.

HABITAT: India; in Florida, warmest locations.

LIGHT REQUIREMENT: Partial shade is acceptable.

SOIL REQUIREMENT: Tolerant of varying soils.

SALT TOLERANCE: Not tolerant.

AVAILABILITY: Some retail nurseries will have small vines in containers.

CULTURE: Plant in reasonably fertile soil; furnish a strong support; water until well established; fertilize once or twice each year.

PROPAGATION: Seedage or simple layerage.

PESTS: Mites and thrips.

300
Geiger-Tree

Cordia (CORE-dee-a): for V. Cordus, a sixteenth-century German botanist.
sebestena (seb-es-TANE-a): an Arabic name.

FAMILY: Boraginaceae. RELATIVES: Forget-me-not and heliotrope.
TYPE OF PLANT: Tree. HEIGHT: 30'. ZONE: S
HOW TO IDENTIFY: Showy orange-red flowers that resemble geraniums at a distance; 8" ovate, evergreen leaves with short-pointed tips, roughly downy on the upper surfaces.
HABIT OF GROWTH: Dense, round heads atop crooked trunks about 6" in diameter.
FOLIAGE: Evergreen, heart-shaped, fuzzy, of coarse texture and dark green color.
FLOWERS: Showy, orange-red or scarlet, 1"-2" long, in open clusters like geraniums.
FRUITS: White drupes ¾" long, enclosed in persistent calyces.
SEASON OF MAXIMUM COLOR: Summer, when orange-red blossoms appear.
LANDSCAPE USES: As a freestanding specimen or as a framing tree for a home in a tropical setting, this diminutive native is in high favor. Occasionally it is seen as an avenue tree standing at intervals of about 25'-35'. Geiger-tree is recommended for seaside use, but it will not endure frost.

The common name, according to legend, was bestowed by Audubon in commemoration of John Geiger, a pilot and Key West wrecker of the last century. Geiger-tree is quite universally used as the common name for this excellent native tree by Florida gardeners and nurserymen.
HABITAT: Florida Keys and West Indian Islands; on the mainland, warmest locations.
LIGHT REQUIREMENT: Full sun or partial shade.
SOIL REQUIREMENT: Tolerant of light, sandy, alkaline soils, rock, or marl.
SALT TOLERANCE: Tolerant of salt, recommended for seaside plantings.
AVAILABILITY: Geiger-trees will be found in nurseries in southern counties.
CULTURE: Plant with reasonable care; water with reasonable regularity; fertilize once or twice a year.
PROPAGATION: Seedage and marcottage.
PESTS: Mites, scales, and caterpillars.

301
Lantana

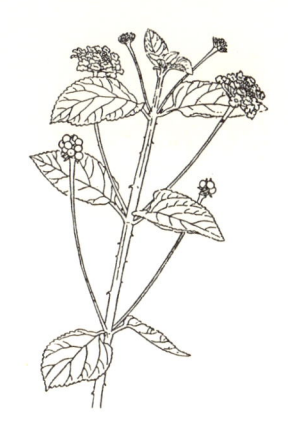

Lantana (lan-TAN-a): old name.
camara (cam-AIR-ah): South American name.

FAMILY: Verbenaceae.   **RELATIVES:** Verbena and chaste-tree.

TYPE OF PLANT: Shrub.   **HEIGHT:** 10'.   **ZONE:** N,C,S

HOW TO IDENTIFY: Square, prickly stems, strongly upward-growing; rough leaves that have an unpleasant odor when crushed; tiny flowers of many colors in terminal, flat nosegay arrangements, followed by prominent, shiny, blue-black fruits.

HABIT OF GROWTH: Stiffly upright from many-branched stems.

FOLIAGE: Evergreen, of medium texture and light green color.

FLOWERS: Showy, flat heads of tiny flowers, in tones of red and yellow.

FRUITS: Fleshy drupes, blue-black in color, ½" across, freely produced, toxic.

SEASON OF MAXIMUM COLOR: Summer months.

LANDSCAPE USES: For gay color in a sunny planter (set 18" o.c.) or against hardy evergreen shrubs, lantana may be used, especially near the ocean. Tender to frost, lantana will die to the ground every year excepting in warmest locations. Yellow-and-pink-flowered dwarf lantanas are favored by designers.

HABITAT: Tropical and subtropical America, including Florida.

LIGHT REQUIREMENT: Full sun for best habit and free-flowering.

SOIL REQUIREMENT: Any soil appears to be suitable.

SALT TOLERANCE: Quite salt-tolerant, recommended for seashore.

AVAILABILITY: Retail nurseries often sell lantanas in vessels.

CULTURE: Plant in moderately fertile soil; water until established; protect leaves from caterpillars in hot weather; cut back in late winter.

PROPAGATION: Seedage; cuttage for named varieties.

PESTS: Caterpillars chew the leaves, mites make them turn brown.

302
Weeping Lantana

Lantana (lan-TAN-a): old name.
montevidensis (mon-tay-vye-DEN-sis): from Montevideo.

FAMILY: Verbenaceae. RELATIVES: Verbena and chaste-tree.

TYPE OF PLANT: Dwarf shrub or vine. HEIGHT: Variable. ZONE: C,S

HOW TO IDENTIFY: Evergreen, opposite, dentate, rugose leaves with pungent odor when crushed; unarmed square twigs; lilac flowers borne through much of the year.

HABIT OF GROWTH: Sprawling, over the earth, vine-like if supported.

FOLIAGE: Evergreen, opposite, fine textured, and dark green in color.

FLOWERS: Dense heads at axils on long peduncles, of solid lilac color. There is a white-flowered form.

FRUITS: Usually not formed in Florida.

SEASON OF MAXIMUM COLOR: Much of the year, if there is no frost.

LANDSCAPE USES: Weeping lantana is an excellent ground cover and transition plant when set at 18" o.c. For sunny planters and to spill over a wall, this little shrub is without peer (plant 18" o.c.). It is rightfully very popular in sections of Florida where winters are mild. Frost will kill lantana to the earth.

HABITAT: South America; in Florida, ubiquitous in warmer parts.

LIGHT REQUIREMENT: Full sun for compact habit and heavy flowering.

SOIL REQUIREMENT: Tolerant of sandy soils.

SALT TOLERANCE: Not tolerant.

AVAILABILITY: Most retail sales lots display weeping lantanas in vessels.

CULTURE: Within its climatic range, this plant is undemanding in requirements for growth. Fertilize once each spring and water during drought.

PROPAGATION: Cuttage and simple layerage where stems touch the earth.

PESTS: Caterpillars and mites.

303
Chinese-Hat-Plant

Holmskioldia (holm-skee-OLD-ee-a): for T. Holmskiold, Danish scientist.
sanguinea (san-GWIN-ee-a): blood-red.

FAMILY: Verbenaceae.

RELATIVES: Lantana, chaste-tree, and verbena.

TYPE OF PLANT: Sprawling shrub. HEIGHT: Variable. ZONE: C,S

HOW TO IDENTIFY: Sprawling habit; evergreen, opposite leaves; and the outstanding feature of the plant is the showy, orange-red circular calyx subtending every flower.

HABIT OF GROWTH: Sprawling, becoming a vine with support.

FOLIAGE: Evergreen, opposite, of coarse texture and often, yellow-green color.

FLOWERS: Small dark red corollas, subtended by circular, orange-red calyces.

FRUITS: Ovoid, 4-lobed drupes about ⅓" long.

SEASON OF MAXIMUM COLOR: Springtime, when calyces color up.

LANDSCAPE USES: To sprawl over a white masonry wall (plant 10' o.c.) is the most effective use of Chinese-hat-plant. Thus, it resembles an orange bougainvillea. As a huge unkempt mound or trained beside and over doorways are other landscape uses. Chinese-hat-plant is very popular with Florida homeowners.

HABITAT: Himalayan region; in Florida, widely planted in protected gardens.

LIGHT REQUIREMENT: Full sun or light shade from tall trees.

SOIL REQUIREMENT: Any reasonably fertile soil.

SALT TOLERANCE: Not tolerant.

AVAILABILITY: Nurseries on the peninsula offer plants in containers.

CULTURE: Plant in reasonably fertile soil; water as needed; fertilize twice a year; prune to keep within bounds. If the plant is to be trained as a vine, offer strong support.

PROPAGATION: Cuttage or marcottage.

PESTS: Scales, mites, and nematodes.

304
Golden-Dewdrop

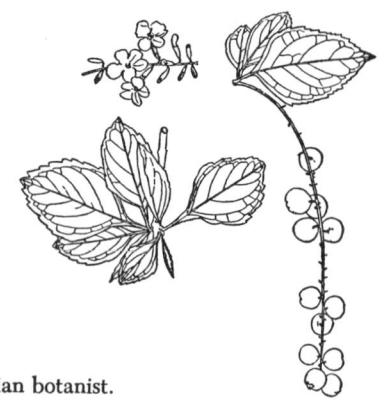

Duranta (dew-RAN-ta): for C. Durantes, an Italian botanist.
repens (REE-pens): creeping.

FAMILY: Verbenaceae.

RELATIVES: Verbena, lantana, and chaste-tree.

TYPE OF PLANT: Shrub.

HEIGHT: 18'. **ZONE:** C,S

HOW TO IDENTIFY: Evergreen, thin, scalloped opposite leaves, each with a sharp thorn; blue flowers in hanging clusters followed by bright yellow fruits.

HABIT OF GROWTH: Informal, ascending mound.

FOLIAGE: Evergreen, of medium fine texture and light green color.

FLOWERS: Blue flowers hang in loose axillary racemes about 6" long.

FRUITS: Conspicuous, yellow globose, about ½" in diameter, covered by calyx which is closed into a curved beak. The fruits are POISONOUS to humans.

SEASON OF MAXIMUM COLOR: Warm months, when flowers and/or fruits are present.

LANDSCAPE USES: For background and screening set plants 5' o.c. Golden-dewdrop is too large to use as a foundation plant and in much of the state it will be frosted back each winter. Occasionally a plant with white flowers is seen. There has been some selection for specimens that bear flowers larger than ordinary.

This beautiful plant is ubiquitous in the tropics where it is disseminated by birds.

HABITAT: Florida Keys, Caribbean Islands, Central America.

LIGHT REQUIREMENT: Full sun for best flowering, endures partial shade.

SOIL REQUIREMENT: Tolerant of varying soil types.

SALT TOLERANCE: Not tolerant.

AVAILABILITY: Golden-dewdrop is available in most nurseries in receptacles.

CULTURE: After establishment, golden-dewdrop requires no care.

PROPAGATION: Cuttage or seedage.

PESTS: Scales, caterpillars, nematodes; birds consume fruits.

Queens-Wreath

Petrea (pet-REE-a): for Baron Petre, English patron of botany.
volubilis (vol-oo-bill-is): twining.

FAMILY: Verbenaceae.

RELATIVES: Verbena, lantana, and chaste-tree.

TYPE OF PLANT: Vine.

HEIGHT: Variable. **ZONE:** S

HOW TO IDENTIFY: Twining vine with evergreen, opposite leaves that are so rough to the touch as to feel like sandpaper; conspicuous hanging clusters of purple (occasionally white) flowers.

HABIT OF GROWTH: Twining vine.

FOLIAGE: Evergreen, very rough, of coarse texture and gray-green color.

FLOWERS: Purple (sometimes white), 5-petaled, with 5-pointed calyx 1½" wide, in foot-long hanging clusters which resemble wisteria when viewed from a distance.

FRUITS: Drupes which include the dried calyces.

SEASON OF MAXIMUM COLOR: Late spring and early summer.

LANDSCAPE USES: To cover an arbor, fence, or small structure, queens-wreath is much planted in southern Florida, where it could be considered a substitute for wisteria.

HABITAT: Tropical America; in Florida, widely planted in warm areas.

LIGHT REQUIREMENT: Full sun or broken shade.

SOIL REQUIREMENT: Tolerant of soils of open texture and moderate fertility.

SALT TOLERANCE: Not tolerant.

AVAILABILITY: Nurseries in southern Florida offer queens-wreath in containers.

CULTURE: Enrich sandy soil by digging in organic matter; set the vine at its former level; water periodically; keep lawn grasses back from the root zone. Protect small vines when frost is forecast.

PROPAGATION: Cuttage or marcottage.

PESTS: None of great importance.

306
Chaste-Tree

Vitex (VYE-tex): ancient Latin name.
agnus-castus (AG-nus-CAST-us): ancient classical name.

FAMILY: Verbenaceae.   RELATIVES: Verbena, lantana, and golden-dewdrop.

TYPE OF PLANT: Tree.   HEIGHT: 20'. ZONE: N,C,S

HOW TO IDENTIFY: This little tree bears deciduous, opposite, digitate, pungent leaves, and summertime lilac flowers in terminal spikes.

HABIT OF GROWTH: Ungainly, open, small crown develops a picturesque form.

FOLIAGE: Deciduous, digitate, fine in texture, medium gray-green in color.

FLOWERS: Terminal spikes 5"-7" long produce lavender or white little fragrant flowers in summertime.

FRUITS: Little drupes with 4 stones enclosing pepper-like seeds.

SEASON OF MAXIMUM COLOR: Midsummer.

LANDSCAPE USES: As a summer-flowering tree for fragrance near a terrace, patio, or porch, chaste-tree is highly desirable. As a part of a shrubbery border, plant 5' apart in groups and prune to shrub habit.

Chaste-tree has long been a garden favorite because of its delightfully fragrant, lilac-like blossoms in summertime. There is a clone 'Alba' that bears white blossoms, another with variegated foliage, and 'Latifolia' has broad leaflets.

Seeds can be used for seasoning foods.

HABITAT: Southern Europe; in Florida, sparingly planted as a yard tree.

LIGHT REQUIREMENT: Sun or shade.

SOIL REQUIREMENT: Tolerant of various soils.

SALT TOLERANCE: Tolerant of salt drift back from the front dunes.

AVAILABILITY: Small chaste-trees are infrequently found in nurseries.

CULTURE: After establishment, this tree grows without attention excepting for the usual fertilization. Mulching is always helpful and watering during dry spells is expected.

PROPAGATION: Cuttage.

PESTS: Scales, mushroom root-rot, and nematodes.

307
Vitex

Vitex (vye-tex): ancient Latin name.
trifolia (try-FOL-ee-a): with three leaf(lets).
'Variegata' (vare-eye-ee-GAY-ta): variegated.

FAMILY: Verbenaceae. RELATIVES: Verbena, lantana, and golden-dewdrop.

TYPE OF PLANT: Shrub. HEIGHT: 12'. ZONE: C,S

HOW TO IDENTIFY: A vigorous shrub that has gayly variegated, trifoliolate leaves and little panicles of blue flowers in summertime.

HABIT OF GROWTH: Very dense and shrubby, but vigorous to become tree-like with neglect in warm locations.

FOLIAGE: Evergreen, fine in texture, gray-green to give a hazy tone.

FLOWERS: Tiny blue or lavender flowers with white spots in summertime.

FRUITS: Drupes with 4 stones.

SEASON OF MAXIMUM COLOR: Summer.

LANDSCAPE USES: In warm locations vitex hedge is extremely popular. Set plants 1½' o.c. In foundation plantings allow 3' between plants, but for informal enclosure set the plants 5' apart. Variegated plants are prone to revert to the all-green type, and these vigorous shoots must be pruned out lest the plant become all green.

Variegated vitex will be killed to the ground by frost.

HABITAT: Old World tropics; in Florida, much used as a hedge in warm locations.

LIGHT REQUIREMENT: Full sun for very compact hedge.

SOIL REQUIREMENT: Very tolerant of sandy soils.

SALT TOLERANCE: Tolerant of salt air at some distance back from the strand.

AVAILABILITY: Nurseries in southern Florida display small plants.

CULTURE: Plant in fairly fertile soil; water faithfully until well established. If the plants are in hedge arrangement, clip frequently for compact shape; if they are in foundation plantings, head in vigorous shoots to keep the plants in scale with the house.

PROPAGATION: Cuttage.

PESTS: Scales, mushroom root-rot.

308
Beauty-Berry

Callicarpa (cally-CAR-pa): Greek for beauty and fruit.
americana (a-mer-ee-CANE-a): American.

FAMILY: Verbenaceae.   RELATIVES: Verbena, golden-dewdrop, and chaste-tree.

TYPE OF PLANT: Shrub.   HEIGHT: 8'. ZONE: N,C

HOW TO IDENTIFY: A shrub with deciduous opposite foliage, held by fuzzy petioles. Unfurling buds and branchlets are quite tomentose. Lilac blossoms clustered around the stems in springtime are followed by purple fruits in autumn.

HABIT OF GROWTH: Compact, with outward-pointing branches.

FOLIAGE: Deciduous, opposite, coarse in texture, light green in color.

FLOWERS: Lilac, ⅛" long, in dense cymes around stems in springtime.

FRUITS: Subglobose, berry-like drupes in autumn, usually purple, rarely white.

SEASON OF MAXIMUM COLOR: Autumn, when the fruits color at maturity.

LANDSCAPE USES: For massing in woodland plantings, this native shrub is excellent, and should be more widely used.
  Birds are very fond of the ripe fruits and so beauty-berry will help attract and keep birds where it grows. As with coral ardisia, white-fruited individuals can be planted amongst the normal type as interesting contrast. Perhaps other colors will appear over the years.

HABITAT: Hammocks and rich woodlands in central and northern Florida.

LIGHT REQUIREMENT: The broken shade of hammocks is optimum.

SOIL REQUIREMENT: Fertile soil of hammocks is best, but tolerates lighter sands.

SALT TOLERANCE: Not tolerant.

AVAILABILITY: This is not a nursery item, but plants might be obtained from friends who have woodlots.

CULTURE: Cut back heavily after fruiting; move in from woodland; water carefully; after the root system has become established, no further attention is necessary.

PROPAGATION: Seedage.

PESTS: Caterpillars may chew leaves.

309
Bleeding-Heart Glory-Bower

Clerodendrum (cler-oh-DEN-drum): Greek for chance and tree, of no significance. *thomsoniae* (TOM-son-ee-ee): for Mrs. W. Thomson, wife of a missionary.

FAMILY: Verbenaceae.

RELATIVES: Beauty-berry, chaste-tree, and lantana.

TYPE OF PLANT: Vine.

HEIGHT: Variable. ZONE: N,C,S

HOW TO IDENTIFY: Vine-like growth; evergreen leaves to 6" long, that are opposite and prominently veined; flowers in showy racemes, calyces white, bag-like, with bright red corollas extending beyond their tips, stamens and styles extending well beyond both.

HABIT OF GROWTH: Vine-like, stems twining about supports.

FOLIAGE: Evergreen, of coarse texture and dark green color.

FLOWERS: Calyx white, bag-like, enclosing bright red corolla which extends beyond the bag, stamens and styles extending beyond both.

FRUITS: Drupes.

SEASON OF MAXIMUM COLOR: Summer, when blossoms are out.

LANDSCAPE USES: As a temporary, warm-weather vine for the curiosity of the flowers that remind northerners of *Dicentra,* this plant is popular. In warm locations, the vine persists all year around.

HABITAT: West Africa; in Florida, widely planted in all sections.

LIGHT REQUIREMENT: Partial shade seems to be satisfactory.

SOIL REQUIREMENT: Well-drained fertile soil is best and freedom from nematodes is most desirable.

SALT TOLERANCE: Not tolerant.

AVAILABILITY: Many retail sales lots offer small plants.

CULTURE: Set in a rich site that has been made free of nematodes by fumigation or drenching.

PROPAGATION: Cuttage, marcottage, or seedage.

PESTS: Nematodes, mites, and thrips.

NOTE: Turks-turban (*Clerodendrum indicum*) is a huge, upright-growing tender shrub that is well known for the showy black fruits with their bright red calyces. This one escapes from cultivation to become a real nuisance.

310 Woolly Congea

Congea (CON-ghe-a): East Indian vernacular name.
tomentosa (toe-men-TOE-sa): densely woolly.

FAMILY: Verbenaceae.

RELATIVES: Verbena, lantana, and golden-dewdrop.

TYPE OF PLANT: Vine.

HEIGHT: Variable. ZONE: S

HOW TO IDENTIFY: Fuzzy twigs hold fuzzy leaves and showy clusters of whitish bracts in winter or spring.

HABIT OF GROWTH: Sprawling, vine-like, may be trained as a vine or as a shrub.

FOLIAGE: Evergreen, opposite, rough, coarse in texture, and light green in color.

FLOWERS: Inconspicuous, in generous clusters, subtended by propeller-like bracts. These white appendages are the showy members as they change to lavender, then to lilac-mauve or dusky-gray over a period of many weeks.

FRUITS: Small drupes.

SEASON OF MAXIMUM COLOR: Late winter or early spring.

LANDSCAPE USES: To clamber over a fence or arbor, to veil a small building, congea is desirable for the wintertime show of the snowy bracts. Cut branches are popular for arrangements indoors, and after maximum flowering has passed, annual heading-in might be needed to keep mature vines from getting too large. As with queens-wreath, extended flowering comes from persistent bracts. These woolly appendages change through tints of pink over several weeks.

HABITAT: Burma; in Florida, warm locations.

LIGHT REQUIREMENT: Full sun for best performance.

SOIL REQUIREMENT: Tolerant of many, varying soil types.

SALT TOLERANCE: Not tolerant of dune conditions.

AVAILABILITY: Some retail sales lots will have small vines in gallon cans.

CULTURE: Plant with reasonable care, attend to watering, supply a strong support, fertilize two times a year, and prune after flowering to keep the vine within bounds.

PROPAGATION: Seedage.

PESTS: Mites and scales.

311
Potato Vines

Solanum (so-LAY-num): Latin, alluding to sedative qualities.
SPP.: several species are grown in Florida.

FAMILY: Solanaceae.   RELATIVES: Potato, tobacco, tomato, and eggplant.
TYPE OF PLANT: Vine.   HEIGHT: Variable. ZONE: S
HOW TO IDENTIFY: Herbaceous, tropical vines with evergreen, dissected leaves, and showy, potato-like flowers.
HABIT OF GROWTH: Vining, requires tying at first.
FOLIAGE: Evergreen, bold in form, dark green when well fertilized.
FLOWERS: Potato-like flowers, usually blue or blue-and-white in showy clusters.
FRUITS: Ovoid berries, variable in size and color with species.
SEASON OF MAXIMUM COLOR: Warm months, when flowers expand.
LANDSCAPE USES: For the beauty of the hanging blossoms, solanum vines are cultured in hot countries. They may add interest to palm trunks, hide fences, or veil small buildings.
  Brazilian nightshade (*S. seaforthianum*) has spineless stems and foliage, and blue, star-shaped, 1" flowers in small clusters.
  Wendland nightshade (*S. wendlandii*) has prickly stems, leaves both simple and pinnatifid, lilac-blue flowers 2½" across in foot-wide, forking clusters.
  Solanum jasminoides is spineless and bears attractive little star-shaped flowers that are white tinged with blue.
  All solanum vines are very tender to cold.
HABITAT: Tropical America; in Florida, warmest locations.
LIGHT REQUIREMENT: Partial shade.
SOIL REQUIREMENT: Tolerant of many soil types, but subject to attack by nematodes.
SALT TOLERANCE: Not tolerant.
AVAILABILITY: Nurseries in southern Florida offer vines in cans of sterilized soil.
CULTURE: Plant carefully in sterilized soil; water until well established; offer support and a heavy mulch over the roots; fertilize once in late winter.
PROPAGATION: Cuttage or layerage.
PESTS: Nematodes, mites, and scales.

Orange Cestrum

Cestrum (SES-trum): Greek name for some plant.
aurantiacum (are-an-TIE-a-cum): orange-colored.

FAMILY: Solanaceae.   RELATIVES: Tobacco, pepper, potato, and tomato.

TYPE OF PLANT: Sprawling shrub.   HEIGHT: 15'. ZONE: C,S

HOW TO IDENTIFY: Half-climbing shrub with simple, alternate leaves and tubular, orange-colored blossoms during warm months.

HABIT OF GROWTH: Sprawling, vine-like, by greenish succulent stems.

FOLIAGE: Evergreen, of medium texture and medium green color.

FLOWERS: Orange-yellow, tubular, 1" long, with lobes reflexed. The terminal panicles usually contain 2-5 blossoms.

FRUITS: Small, succulent berries.

SEASON OF MAXIMUM COLOR: Warm months.

LANDSCAPE USES: As a part of a shrubbery border, in warm locations, plant about 5' o.c.

HABITAT: Central America; in Florida, warmest sections.

LIGHT REQUIREMENT: Full sun for best habit and flowering.

SOIL REQUIREMENT: Light sandy soils are acceptable.

SALT TOLERANCE: Not tolerant.

AVAILABILITY: Cestrums are available in nurseries down the peninsula.

CULTURE: All cestrums seem to grow with the least possible care.

PROPAGATION: Cuttage.

PESTS: Mites, scales, and caterpillars.

NOTE: Purple cestrum (*Cestrum purpureum*) is also vine-like, and bears nodding clusters of urn-shaped, rose-purple flowers more than 1" long.
Members of this genus, like most members of their family, grow rapidly to attain maturity rather quickly. All must be pruned after flowering to keep within bounds. All are tender to cold, but usually will rally after having been frosted. Cestrums are leading beginners' plants because they are so easy to increase, so undemanding of the gardener.

313
Night Cestrum

Cestrum (SES-trum): Greek name for some plant.
nocturnum (nock-TURN-um): night-blooming.

FAMILY: Solanaceae.   RELATIVES: Tobacco, pepper, potato, and tomato.

TYPE OF PLANT: Sprawling shrub.   HEIGHT: 12'. ZONE: C,S

HOW TO IDENTIFY: Half-climbing shrub with green stems that bear simple, smooth leaves 4"-8" long with broad bases and distinct petioles. Greenish-white tubular blossoms with acute lobes erect or spreading are excessively fragrant at *night*. Fruits are *white*.

HABIT OF GROWTH: Sprawling with declinate stems, to make an untidy mound.

FOLIAGE: Evergreen, smooth, of medium texture and yellow-green color.

FLOWERS: Greenish-white with erect or flaring long-pointed lobes.

FRUITS: Shining white, succulent berries, freely produced.

SEASON OF MAXIMUM COLOR: No seasonal change in color.

LANDSCAPE USES: As a part of a shrubbery border in warm locations, plant about 5' apart. Nighttime fragrance is overpowering to some persons.

HABITAT: Tropical America; in Florida, much planted in warm locations.

LIGHT REQUIREMENT: Full sun for best habit and flowering, but light shade is tolerated.

SOIL REQUIREMENT: Tolerates light sandy soil.

SALT TOLERANCE: Not tolerant of dune conditions.

AVAILABILITY: Widely offered in cans at nurseries.

CULTURE: Like other cestrums these grow with but little care.

PROPAGATION: Cuttage and seedage.

PESTS: Mites, scales, and caterpillars.

NOTE: Day cestrum (*C. diurnum*) is somewhat more hardy, with thicker leaves, white blossoms with *rounded* lobes, day fragrance and *black* berries.
   These, and other cestrums, are favorite shrubs in dooryards in hot countries the world around.

314
Chalice-Vine

Solandra (so-LAND-dra): for D. Solander, Swedish naturalist.
guttata (gut-TAY-ta): spotted.

FAMILY: Solanaceae.   **RELATIVES:** Tobacco, pepper, and eggplant.

TYPE OF PLANT: Vine.   **HEIGHT:** Variable.   **ZONE:** C,S

HOW TO IDENTIFY: A rampant tropical vine which produces goblet-shaped flowers about 10″ long which turn to gold.

HABIT OF GROWTH: Vigorous vine that clings by tenacious aerial roots.

FOLIAGE: Evergreen, very bold in aspect, dark green when well fertilized.

FLOWERS: Very spectacular, goblet-formed blossoms that open white and turn golden before they fall. Purple lines decorate the interior, the pistil is prominent. Fragrance of coconut is released at night.

FRUITS: Round berries 2½″ wide, partially enclosed by the calyces.

SEASON OF MAXIMUM COLOR: Warm months, after good growth.

LANDSCAPE USES: For the tropical aspect of the huge gold cups, this vine is fancied. Strong metal and concrete trellises are needed to support the great weight.

HABITAT: Tropical America; in Florida, popular vine in warm areas.

LIGHT REQUIREMENT: Partial shade. Very tender to cold.

SOIL REQUIREMENT: Moderate fertility is recommended.

SALT TOLERANCE: Not tolerant.

AVAILABILITY: Small vines in cans are in some nurseries on the peninsula.

CULTURE: Once established near a strong steel and masonry trellis, chalice-vine will grow rampantly with little attention.

PROPAGATION: Layerage.

PESTS: Nematodes, mites, and caterpillars.

NOTE: There may be confusion in naming. *Solandra grandiflora* has the slender part of the flower tube not longer than the calyx. Other names are sometimes listed.

315
Angel's Trumpet

Datura (da-TOUR-a): Indian vernacular name.
arborea (are-BORE-ee-a): tree-like.

FAMILY: Solanaceae.   RELATIVES: Tobacco, potato, and tomato.
TYPE OF PLANT: Succulent shrub.   HEIGHT: 15'. ZONE: C,S
HOW TO IDENTIFY: Pubescent, evergreen leaves in pairs, one of which is a third shorter than the other; 9" nodding, fragrant white flowers in summer.
HABIT OF GROWTH: Upright, tree-like.
FOLIAGE: Evergreen, soft, tender, of huge size and medium color.
FLOWERS: Spectacular hanging trumpets of white that are very fragrant.
FRUITS: Smooth, broad-ovoid capsules about 2½" long.
SEASON OF MAXIMUM COLOR: Summer and autumn.
LANDSCAPE USES: For the tropical aspect of the plant and the monstrous, nodding trumpets, datura is planted as a freestanding specimen.
   ALL DATURAS ARE VERY POISONOUS. Nonetheless, they are widely grown in hot countries for their striking, fragrant blossoms.
HABITAT: Tropical America; in Florida, ubiquitous in all but coldest parts.
LIGHT REQUIREMENT: Full sun or partial shade.
SOIL REQUIREMENT: Tolerant of widely varying soils.
SALT TOLERANCE: Not tolerant.
AVAILABILITY: Small datura plants are sometimes seen in nurseries.
CULTURE: Plant with reasonable care; water until established; and forget. Protection on cold nights might save datura plants from being killed to the earth.
PROPAGATION: Cuttage and seedage.
PESTS: Nematodes, mites, and thrips.
NOTE: *D. sanguinea* has brilliant orange-red flowers with yellow nerves, without fragrance.
   D. suaveolens may be confused with *D. arborea*. Suaveolens has foot-long white trumpets on pedicels ¾"-1½" long and calyces that are inflated, angled, obscurely 5-toothed. Suaveolens capsules are unarmed, spindle-shaped, 5" long.

Coral-Plant

Russelia (russ-ELL-ee-a): for A. Russell, an English physician.
equisetiformis (eck-we-seat-i-FORM-is): horsetail-like.

FAMILY: Scrophulariaceae. RELATIVES: Angelonia and torenia.
TYPE OF PLANT: Dwarf shrub. HEIGHT: 4'. ZONE: C,S

HOW TO IDENTIFY: This tender shrub is of pendulous habit with rush-like stems that are ridged vertically. The leaves are reduced to bracts, yet the bright red, firecracker-like flowers make up for the paucity of foliage.

HABIT OF GROWTH: Weeping, fountain-like.

FOLIAGE: Usually lacking, the branches and bracts of fine texture and pleasing color.

FLOWERS: Bright red, cylindrical, 2-lipped, 5-cleft, hanging like little firecrackers during much of the year.

FRUITS: Little hanging capsules.

SEASON OF MAXIMUM COLOR: Summer, when flowers come out.

LANDSCAPE USES: For the cheerful aspect of the bright flowers, and the attractive weeping habit, coral-plant is much grown. In planters, foundation arrangements, and rock-'n'-sand gardens, it serves well. Use 18" planting intervals.

HABITAT: Tropical America.

LIGHT REQUIREMENT: Full sun; or broken, shifting, high shade.

SOIL REQUIREMENT: Tolerant of different soils, but thrives with moderate fertility and regular watering as needed.

SALT TOLERANCE: Not tolerant.

AVAILABILITY: Most nurseries in central and southern Florida offer coral-plants in cans.

CULTURE: When once established, coral-plants grow with little care. Protection from heavy competition and frost is suggested.

PROPAGATION: Simple layers where stems touch the earth.

PESTS: Chewing insects, nematodes, and mites.

317
Cat-Claw

Doxantha (docks-AN-tha): Greek for glory-flower.
unguis-cati (UN-guis CAT-eye): Latin for cat's claw.

FAMILY: Bignoniaceae.   RELATIVES: Trumpet-creeper, painted-trumpet, and flame-vine.

TYPE OF PLANT: Vine.   HEIGHT: Variable. ZONE: N,C,S

HOW TO IDENTIFY: Evergreen vine with 3-parted, claw-like tendrils for climbing and yellow trumpets in springtime.

HABIT OF GROWTH: Rampantly clambering by claw-like tendrils.

FOLIAGE: Evergreen, compound, of medium fine texture and light green color.

FLOWERS: Showy, trumpet-shaped, 2" long, clear, bright yellow with orange lines in throat.

FRUITS: Foot-long, bignonia-type pods about ½" wide.

SEASON OF MAXIMUM COLOR: April.

LANDSCAPE USES: To cover a metal fence, or to veil a small building, cat-claw will serve well.
 Stems root where they touch the earth, thus making the vine a nuisance under some conditions. At best, it is hard to control unless severe freezes cut canes to the earth.

HABITAT: American tropics; in Florida, ubiquitous excepting in coldest parts.

LIGHT REQUIREMENT: Full sun or broken shade.

SOIL REQUIREMENT: Tolerant of many varying soils.

SALT TOLERANCE: Not tolerant.

AVAILABILITY: This is usually not a nursery item; rather, simple layers are exchanged among neighbors.

CULTURE: Of easiest culture, cat-claw grows without attention.

PROPAGATION: Simple layerage where stems touch the earth.

PESTS: Mites and scales.

318
Painted-Trumpet

Clytostoma (cly-TOSS-to-ma): Greek for splendid mouth.
callistegioides (cal-lis-tee-gee-OY-dez): callistegia-like.

FAMILY: Bignoniaceae.   RELATIVES: Flame-vine, trumpet-creeper, and jacaranda.

TYPE OF PLANT: Vine.   HEIGHT: Variable. ZONE: N,C,S

HOW TO IDENTIFY: Evergreen leaves with 2 entire leaflets and a tendril that twines around support; showy, lavender trumpet-like flowers in springtime.

HABIT OF GROWTH: Rampant-growing, tendril-clinging vine.

FOLIAGE: Evergreen, of coarse texture and dark green color.

FLOWERS: Trumpets 3" long, of attractive lavender color produced during springtime.

FRUITS: Prickly capsules 3"-5" long, contain many flat, winged seeds.

SEASON OF MAXIMUM COLOR: Spring, when lavender trumpets open.

LANDSCAPE USES: As a permanent evergreen vine to soften a fence or to make shade beneath a pergola, painted-trumpet is very popular. This is one of the many bignonia-relatives that grow so well in Florida. For persons who live too far north in the state to grow pandorea and other tropical bignonia-relatives, painted-trumpet is suggested. Many homeowners in upper counties admire it for its excellent qualities.

HABITAT: South America; in Florida, ubiquitous as a garden vine.

LIGHT REQUIREMENT: Full sun or broken shade.

SOIL REQUIREMENT: Almost any well-drained soil seems to be adequate.

SALT TOLERANCE: Not tolerant of dune locations.

AVAILABILITY: Retail nurseries stock painted-trumpet vines.

CULTURE: Simply plant in reasonably fertile soil and water periodically until well established. This unusually dependable vine requires little attention.

PROPAGATION: Simple layerage where branches touch the earth.

PESTS: Scales and mites.

319
Pandorea

Podranea (poe-DRAIN-ee-a): anagram of pandorea.
ricasoliana (rick-a-sole-ee-ANE-a): for the Ricasoli gardens in Italy.

FAMILY: Bignoniaceae.   RELATIVES: Sausage-tree, trumpet-creeper, and painted-trumpet.
TYPE OF PLANT: Sprawling vine.   HEIGHT: Variable. ZONE: C,S
HOW TO IDENTIFY: Sprawling vine with pinnate, evergreen foliage and attractive pinkish, bell-form blossoms in springtime.
HABIT OF GROWTH: Sprawling vine, that needs to be tied until stems become established.
FOLIAGE: Evergreen, odd-pinnate, without tendrils, of medium texture and medium green color.
FLOWERS: Showy, pinkish, trumpet-like, about 2″ long, lined inside with red, borne in hanging, terminal panicles.
FRUITS: Foot-long bignonia pods which split into two segments.
SEASON OF MAXIMUM COLOR: Springtime.
LANDSCAPE USES: To add color-interest to a fence, pergola, small building, or palm trunk, this tropical vine is much planted where winter temperatures are mild.
   Of the many vines of the bignonia family, this is held to be the most delicately attractive by many experienced gardeners. The graceful foliage, delicate coloration of the attractive trumpets, and moderate growth-rate contribute to its excellence. It is highly commended to those who live within its climatic range.
HABITAT: South Africa; in Florida, in nearly frostless locations.
LIGHT REQUIREMENT: Light shade of high pines or palms is excellent.
SOIL REQUIREMENT: Reasonably fertile soil that is free of nematodes is recommended.
SALT TOLERANCE: Not tolerant.
AVAILABILITY: Nurseries in warm areas stock pandoreas in assorted vessels.
CULTURE: Nematodes are major parasites, so plant in sterilized, fertile soil if possible. Water frequently and train on a support. Frost will cut the vine to the ground.
PROPAGATION: Simple layerage where branches touch the earth.
PESTS: Nematodes, mites, scales, and caterpillars.

320
Flame-Vine

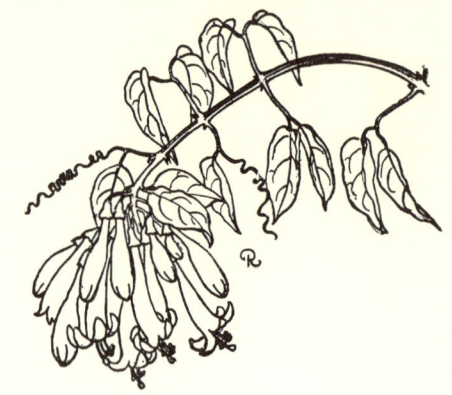

Pyrostegia (pie-roe-STEEG-ee-a): Greek for fire and roof.
ignea (IG-knee-a): fiery.

FAMILY: Bignoniaceae.

RELATIVES: Cape-honeysuckle and trumpet-creeper.

TYPE OF PLANT: Vine.

HEIGHT: Variable. **ZONE:** C,S

HOW TO IDENTIFY: Rampant vine, climbing by tendrils, evergreen leaves of 2-3 leaflets; terminal panicles of orange, tubular flowers in wintertime.

HABIT OF GROWTH: Clambering vine that clings tenaciously by tendrils.

FOLIAGE: Evergreen, compound, 2-3 leaflets and 3-parted tendrils, medium in texture, light-to-medium green in color.

FLOWERS: Conspicuous, bright orange tubular blossoms with 5 points curling back from the mouth. These are borne in panicles during the tourist season. The color does not combine well with red.

FRUITS: Foot-long pods in Brazil, sometimes not present in Florida.

SEASON OF MAXIMUM COLOR: Late winter and early spring.

LANDSCAPE USES: To cover a fence, pergola, small building, or unwanted tree, flame-vine is central Florida's most popular vine. Landscape use must be indicated with caution, because the vine grows so rampantly that it will soon cover every available support.

HABITAT: Brazil; in Florida, ubiquitous in the central section.

LIGHT REQUIREMENT: Full sun or partial shade.

SOIL REQUIREMENT: Light, sandy soil is quite acceptable.

SALT TOLERANCE: Not tolerant.

AVAILABILITY: Almost all retail nurseries market flame-vines.

CULTURE: Set in reasonably fertile soil; water periodically until established; furnish a strong support; fertilize once each winter; prune immediately after flowering to keep somewhat within bounds.

PROPAGATION: Simple layerage or cuttage.

PESTS: Scales, caterpillars, and mites.

321
Sausage-Tree

Kigelia (ki-GEE-lee-a): from an African native name.
pinnata (pin-ATE-a): feather-formed, referring to the foliage.

FAMILY: Bignoniaceae. RELATIVES: Jacaranda, African tulip-tree, and Cape-honeysuckle.

TYPE OF PLANT: Tree. HEIGHT: 30'. ZONE: S

HOW TO IDENTIFY: A medium sized tree that bears deciduous, odd pinnate leaves; claret-colored flowers on long stalks and huge, sausage-like fruits 2' long.

HABIT OF GROWTH: Spreading tree of generous size with somewhat open branching.

FOLIAGE: Deciduous, pinnate, of large size and light green color.

FLOWERS: Claret, bignonia-like, 3" flowers open at night to be pollinated by bats. In Florida, hand pollination by man is practiced to assure fruit setting.

FRUITS: Huge, gourd-like pods, 2' long hanging from long cords. Fruit shape and size varies with the individual that bears the fruits and with the pollen source as well.

SEASON OF MAXIMUM COLOR: Blossom-time.

LANDSCAPE USES: As a freestanding specimen in admission gardens, parks, campuses, and arboretums, sausage-tree is popular with all who view it. Moderate size does not preclude its use on large lawns in extreme southern Florida.

HABITAT: Tropical Africa; in Florida, a rarity in show gardens.

LIGHT REQUIREMENT: Full sun for best form, flowering, and fruiting.

SOIL REQUIREMENT: Moderate fertility in soils of many types.

SALT TOLERANCE: Not tolerant.

AVAILABILITY: Small sausage-trees are in specialty nurseries.

CULTURE: After careful planting in prepared site, water intermittently until well established. Keep mulch over the roots; hoe back grass; and fertilize when other plants are tended.

PROPAGATION: Seedage.

PESTS: Scales, mites, and nematodes.

322
Tabebuias

Tabebuia (tab-bay-BOO-ee-a): A Brazilian name.
SPP.: several species are grown in Florida.

FAMILY: Bignoniaceae.   **RELATIVES:** Jacaranda and flame-vine.
TYPE OF PLANT: Trees.   **HEIGHT:** Variable. **ZONE:** S

HOW TO IDENTIFY: Showy, flowering trees in the bignonia family, with typical trumpet-flowers, that are widely planted in tropical lands for their bright color.

HABIT OF GROWTH: Mostly awkward, asymmetrical trees or tall shrubs.

FOLIAGE: Mostly deciduous, usually bold in form, usually light green or gray-green in color.

FLOWERS: Usually very colorful and profuse, white, pink or yellow, typically trumpet-shaped, with spreading, irregular, lobed limbs. These may appear over a long period, perhaps more than once each year.

FRUITS: Long pods of the bignonia family.

SEASON OF MAXIMUM COLOR: Warm months; variable with the species.

LANDSCAPE USES: For the bright clusters of trumpets, tabebuia trees are popular as freestanding specimens and as avenue trees. As a patio tree, *Tabebuia argentea* excels because of its small size, and silvery-gray, contorted branches in picturesque arrangement. Protection overhead will be needed on cold nights. The brittle wood breaks in strong winds.

HABITAT: Tropical America; in Florida, gardens in warmest parts.

LIGHT REQUIREMENT: Full sun or partial shade.

SOIL REQUIREMENT: Tolerant of many soil types and conditions.

SALT TOLERANCE: Some species are quite salt-tolerant.

AVAILABILITY: Some specialty nurseries display small tabebuia trees.

CULTURE: Freedom from frost, reasonable fertility, and moderate moisture supply are requirements for success.

PROPAGATION: Seedage, marcottage, and graftage.

PESTS: None of major concern.

NOTE: Of the 100 species of *Tabebuia* known to science, less than half are grown in Florida, these by specialists.

323
African Tulip-Tree

Spathodea (spath-OH-dee-a): Greek for spathe-like, for the shape of the calyx. *campanulata* (cam-pan-you-LATE-a): bell-shaped, referring to the flowers.

FAMILY: Bignoniaceae. **RELATIVES:** Jacaranda and tabebuia.

TYPE OF PLANT: Large tree. **HEIGHT:** 50'. **ZONE:** S

HOW TO IDENTIFY: A tree that bears evergreen, compound leaves made up of 5" leaflets with 2-3 glands at the base; showy, tulip-like, orange-scarlet flowers are held above the foliage in late winter.

HABIT OF GROWTH: Large, ascending, heavy-headed tree.

FOLIAGE: Evergreen, compound, of medium texture and medium green color.

FLOWERS: Orange-scarlet, upward-looking, tulip-like, emerging from one-sided, recurved calyces.

FRUITS: Flattened pods about 8" long, when present.

SEASON OF MAXIMUM COLOR: Late winter when blossoms open.

LANDSCAPE USES: As an avenue tree (25'-35' o.c.) African tulip-tree is admired for the glory of its wintertime blossoms. As a shade tree or as a framing tree it excels in frostless locations, but it is very tender to cold and the brittle wood breaks in strong winds.

HABITAT: Tropical Africa; in Florida, gardens in warm locations.

LIGHT REQUIREMENT: Full sun for good flowering.

SOIL REQUIREMENT: Soil of moderate fertility is recommended.

SALT TOLERANCE: Tolerant of salt air back from the sea.

AVAILABILITY: Rather widely available in nurseries in southern Florida.

CULTURE: Plant in moderately fertile soil in frostless area; water faithfully until well established; thereafter, little attention is needed.

PROPAGATION: Cuttage.

PESTS: None of major concern.

324
Jacaranda

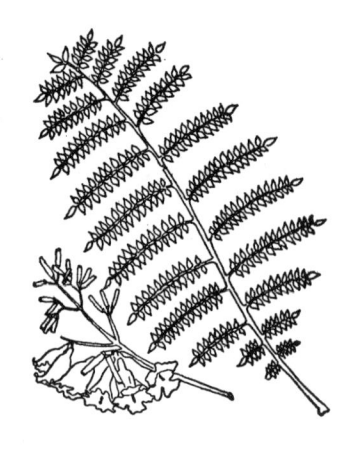

Jacaranda (jack-a-RAN-da): Brazilian name.
acutifolia (a-cute-ee-FO-lee-a): sharp-leaved.

FAMILY: Bignoniaceae.

RELATIVES: Cape-honeysuckle and flame-vine.

TYPE OF PLANT: Tree.

HEIGHT: 50'. ZONE: C,S

HOW TO IDENTIFY: Large, loose-branched, irregular tree with deciduous, 2-pinnate foliage and showy panicles of blue, bignonia-like flowers in late spring.

HABIT OF GROWTH: Awkward, asymmetrical, open head from a bending trunk.

FOLIAGE: Deciduous, very fine in texture, medium green in color.

FLOWERS: Showy, blue trumpets 1½" wide in terminal or axillary panicles.

FRUITS: Pods 2" across, more or less disk-shaped.

SEASON OF MAXIMUM COLOR: April-June.

LANDSCAPE USES: As a tree for summer shade (sun comes through in winter), framing tree, or avenue tree, jacaranda is cherished. It is widely planted in the central section of Florida, but it sometimes gets too large for its position in home landscapes.

HABITAT: Brazil; in Florida, much used in the citrus-producing areas.

LIGHT REQUIREMENT: Full sun for heavy flowering; small trees endure shade.

SOIL REQUIREMENT: Sandy soils, of reasonable fertility, are acceptable.

SALT TOLERANCE: Not tolerant of salt.

AVAILABILITY: Small jacaranda trees are for sale in most retail nurseries in central and southern Florida.

CULTURE: Plant in reasonably fertile soil of sandy nature; water periodically; keep lawn grasses back from the roots; fertilize along with the citrus trees.

PROPAGATION: Seedage.

PESTS: Mushroom root-rot.

NOTE: Several additional species of jacaranda may be seen upon occasion.

325
Cape-Honeysuckle

Tecomaria (teck-o-MARY-a): from Tecoma, an old genus name in the Bignoniaceae.
capensis (cape-EN-sis): of the Cape of Good Hope.

FAMILY: Bignoniaceae.   RELATIVES: Flame-vine, trumpet-creeper, and jacaranda.

TYPE OF PLANT: Vine or shrub, depending upon culture.

HEIGHT: Variable. ZONE: C,S

HOW TO IDENTIFY: This is a half-climbing shrub that may be made into a tree or a vine with training. It has flexible grayish branches, evergreen, compound leaves with 5-9 odd-pinnate serrate leaflets; dense terminal clusters of orange, trumpet-shaped flowers during much of the year, with heaviest flowering in autumn.

HABIT OF GROWTH: Sprawling shrub, vine, or tree, depending upon training.

FOLIAGE: Evergreen, compound, of fine texture and light green or yellow-green color.

FLOWERS: Orange, bignonia-like, in upright, terminal racemes much of the year. One variety has yellow flowers.

FRUITS: Small bignonia-type pods 2″ x ⅓″, rather freely produced.

SEASON OF MAXIMUM COLOR: Warm months, particularly the autumn.

LANDSCAPE USES: As a hedge, plant 3′ apart; as an informal shrubbery border, set 5′ o.c.; as a vine, or as a tree, Cape-honeysuckle is very popular in warm sections of the state because of its attractive foliage and very showy orange blossoms.

There is a clone with variegated foliage, one with yellow blossoms.

HABITAT: South Africa; in Florida, widely grown where citrus thrives.

LIGHT REQUIREMENT: Full sun for best habit and flowering.

SOIL REQUIREMENT: Tolerant of many soils, including open sands. Good drainage is a requirement for success.

SALT TOLERANCE: Tolerant of light salt drift, not recommended for dune planting.

AVAILABILITY: Widely available in gallon cans.

CULTURE: Once established, Cape-honeysuckle grows freely with little attention in areas that are not subject to sharp frosts.

PROPAGATION: Seedage, cuttage, and layerage.

PESTS: Scales, mites, and nematodes.

Episcia

'Dianthiflora'
'Lilacina'
'Viridis'
'Silver Sheen'
'Variegata'
'Chocolate Soldier'
'Reptans'
'Punctata'

327
Episcia

Episcia (ee-PIS-ee-a): Greek for shady, referring to the plant's habitat.
SPP.: more than 1 species and many cultivars grow in our state.

FAMILY: Gesneriaceae.   RELATIVES: Achimenes and gloxinia.

TYPE OF PLANT: Herbaceous perennial.   HEIGHT: 6". ZONE: S

HOW TO IDENTIFY: Shade-demanding, hairy-leaved, creeping tropical herbs that bear attractive, bright little blossoms are the hybrid episcias. The copper-toned, quilted leaves are variously marked and lined with silver.

HABIT OF GROWTH: Mat-forming by means of rooting stems.

FOLIAGE: Dark, copper shades, usually variegated with silver.

FLOWERS: Showy, red, purplish, or whitish, are borne during warm months.

FRUITS: Little pods, if present.

SEASON OF MAXIMUM COLOR: Summer, when flowers expand.

LANDSCAPE USES: As hanging basket and pot plants for very shady locations, episcias are very popular. They are also used today to soften the edges of Florida room planters.

HABITAT: Tropical America.

LIGHT REQUIREMENT: Fairly deep shade is requisite for success. Episcias are injured by sunlight, drafts, and low temperatures.

SOIL REQUIREMENT: Fibrous, fast-draining, slightly acid, moderately fertile compost that has been sterilized is recommended.

SALT TOLERANCE: Not tolerant.

AVAILABILITY: Episcias in small pots are to be found in some nurseries and chain stores.

CULTURE: Plant in containers that can be kept in shady, draft-free, warm (above 45°F) locations. Water with moderation and apply dilute liquid fertilizer once during each warm month.

PROPAGATION: Cuttage.

PESTS: Nematodes, mealy-bugs, and mites.

NOTE: Pictured above is a popular form of *Episcia cupreata*. On the facing page are drawings of other Florida favorites.

328 *Achimenes*

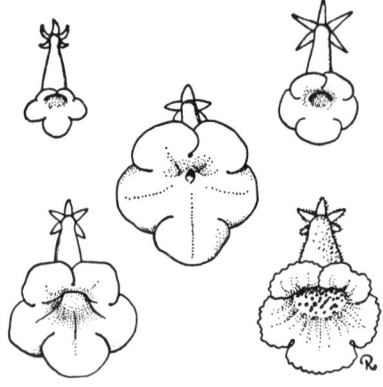

Achimenes (a-KIM-ee-nez): Greek, to suffer from cold.
SPP.: plants seen in collections are of hybrid origin.

FAMILY: Gesneriaceae.   RELATIVES: Cape-primrose and episcia.

TYPE OF PLANT: Rhizomatous perennial.   HEIGHT: 2'. ZONE: N,C,S

HOW TO IDENTIFY: Bushy, downy-leaved pot plants grow from little rhizomes during warm months, to produce many attractive, trumpet-shaped flowers in tones of red and violet. Depicted above are some of the flower shapes.

HABIT OF GROWTH: Compact, neat, little leafy mounds.

FOLIAGE: Variable, opposite or whorled, hairy.

FLOWERS: Variable, attractive, trumpet-shaped as depicted above. The colors are in tones of red or violet, seldom white.

FRUITS: Little capsules, if present.

SEASON OF MAXIMUM COLOR: Late summer when blossoms appear.

LANDSCAPE USES: Window box and porch plants par excellence, achimenes have been favorites with homeowners for centuries.

HABITAT: Tropical America.

LIGHT REQUIREMENT: Reduced light of porches or greenhouses. Drafts and cold must be avoided.

SOIL REQUIREMENT: Fibrous, well-drained, moderately fertile, sterilized compost is suggested. Prompt drainage and good aeration must be assured.

SALT TOLERANCE: Not tolerant.

AVAILABILITY: Dormant rhizomes appear in garden centers in season.

CULTURE: Start dormant rhizomes in pots of gritty, fibrous compost; water sparingly until growth is well along; then increase the amount of water daily; do not allow the soil to become dry. Apply liquid fertilizer once during each warm month. Store rhizomes in a dry place when growth matures in the autumn.

PROPAGATION: Division of underground or axillary rhizomes.

PESTS: Nematodes, soil-borne rots, mites, and mealy-bugs.

329
Crossandra

Crossandra (cross-AN-dra): Greek for fringed anthers.
infundibuliformis (in-fun-di-bull-i-FORM-is): funnel-form.

FAMILY: Acanthaceae.   RELATIVES: Bears-breech and clock-vine.

TYPE OF PLANT: Herbaceous perennial.   HEIGHT: 4'. ZONE: C,S

HOW TO IDENTIFY: This yard-high perennial may become shrub-like if not frosted to earth. The wavy-margined, smooth leaves are opposite, or whorled; above them appear the glowing, soft apricot spikes of bracted flowers during warm months.

HABIT OF GROWTH: Compact, shrub-like, by leafy, green stems.

FOLIAGE: Glossy, opposite, tender, and fragile.

FLOWERS: Showy spikes of bracted, funnel-form flowers of glowing, soft apricot are seen in warm months. No other flower displays this gorgeous tone.

FRUITS: Angled capsules.

SEASON OF MAXIMUM COLOR: Summer, when terminal flower spikes expand.

LANDSCAPE USES: In frostless locations, crossandra is grown with other herbaceous perennials or tender shrubs, usually with some shade here in Florida. As a pot plant, this exotic from India has long been in high favor.

HABITAT: India.

LIGHT REQUIREMENT: Reduced light is recommended in Florida.

SOIL REQUIREMENT: Sandy soil, of moderate fertility, that drains well is usually satisfactory.

SALT TOLERANCE: Not tolerant.

AVAILABILITY: Garden centers frequently offer canned crossandras.

CULTURE: In partially shaded, protected locations, plant with other tender exotics. If frosted, cut back to the earth; new shoots will appear with the advent of warm weather.

PROPAGATION: Cuttage.

PESTS: Mites and nematodes.

330
Aphelandra

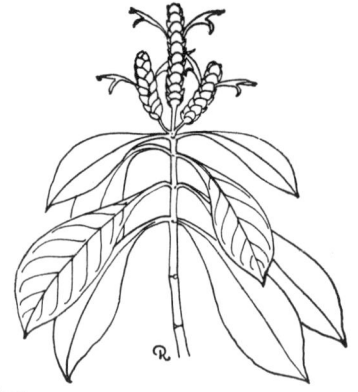

Aphelandra (a-fell-AN-dra): Greek for simple anther.
SPP.: numerous kinds grow in Florida.

FAMILY: Acanthaceae.   RELATIVES: Crossandra and sanchezia.

TYPE OF PLANT: Tender bush.   HEIGHT: 5'. ZONE: S

HOW TO IDENTIFY: The strikingly banded foliage is outstanding, yet spikes of orange or red flowers are attractive dividends. Easily confused with *Sanchezia*, differences in floral characters set the 2 genera apart.

HABIT OF GROWTH: Stiffly upright by herbaceous stems.

FOLIAGE: Opposite, bold, banded with contrasting colors.

FLOWERS: Showy spikes of bracted flowers, usually in tones of orange or red, are warm-weather highlights.

FRUITS: Oblong capsules.

SEASON OF MAXIMUM COLOR: Warm months when new growth produces colorful bracted spikes in terminal positions.

LANDSCAPE USES: For the gaiety of the banded or netted foliage, aphelandras may accent groups of all-green tender bushes.

HABITAT: Tropical America.

LIGHT REQUIREMENT: Broken shade is recommended for Florida.

SOIL REQUIREMENT: Sandy soil, of moderate fertility, that drains well is usually satisfactory.

SALT TOLERANCE: Not tolerant.

AVAILABILITY: Most nurseries and chain stores display small aphelandras in pots.

CULTURE: In partially shaded, protected locations, plant with other tender exotics. If frosted, cut back to the earth; new shoots will appear with the advent of warm weather.

PROPAGATION: Cuttage.

PESTS: Mites and nematodes.

331
Coromandel

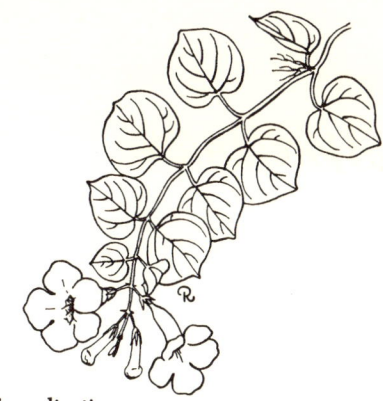

Asystasia (as-is-STAY-see-a): name of doubtful application.
gangetica (gan-JEE-ti-ca): of the Ganges.

FAMILY: Acanthaceae.   RELATIVES: Shrimp-plant and strobilanthes.

TYPE OF PLANT: Herbaceous perennial.   HEIGHT: Variable. ZONE: S

HOW TO IDENTIFY: Trailing, rooting stems bear thin-textured, light green opposite leaves, and bell-shaped flowers of white, pinkish, or lavender.

HABIT OF GROWTH: Densely sprawling, but may assume vine-form if given support.

FOLIAGE: Opposite, 2″, light-green leaves are held by long petioles.

FLOWERS: Tubular, white, pinkish, or purplish, appearing much of the year.

FRUITS: Little oblong capsules.

SEASON OF MAXIMUM COLOR: Summer when flowers come out.

LANDSCAPE USES: As a ground cover for partially shaded, narrow, or restricted spaces in frostless sections, this little tropical perennial is fully appreciated. Additional uses can be made of coromandel for planter bins and for covering the bases of tall, leggy, tropical shrubs.

HABITAT: Tropics of the Old World.

LIGHT REQUIREMENT: Partial shade is recommended.

SOIL REQUIREMENT: Moderately fertile, well-drained soil that can be watered as needed is suitable.

SALT TOLERANCE: Not tolerant.

AVAILABILITY: Easily found in nurseries in southern Florida.

CULTURE: Plant rooted cuttings about 1′ apart in the partially shaded area to be covered; water periodically, fertilize lightly 3 times during the summer. Heroic pruning will be needed when the mass becomes untidy.

PROPAGATION: Simple layerage, cuttage, and seedage.

PESTS: Nematodes, mites, and leaf-eating insects.

332
Strobilanthes

Strobilanthes (stro-bill-ANN-thez): Greek for cone flower.
dyerianus (die-er-ee-ANE-us): for W. Thiselton-Dyer, English horticulturist.

FAMILY: Acanthaceae.   RELATIVES: Coromandel and crossandra.

TYPE OF PLANT: Herbaceous perennial.   HEIGHT: 4'. ZONE: C,S

HOW TO IDENTIFY: The puckered, 8" leaves are bright purple beneath and variegated above in iridescent tints of blue and lilac.

HABIT OF GROWTH: Shrubby, upright, ungainly.

FOLIAGE: Opposite, bold in color, purple below, iridescent lilac and blue above, sessile, puckered, minutely toothed.

FLOWERS: Erect spikes of 1½" lilac, tubular flowers will appear on plants of some size, but small pot specimens may not bloom.

FRUITS: Little oblong capsules.

SEASON OF MAXIMUM COLOR: Very colorful the year around.

LANDSCAPE USES: Long popular as a pot plant for its colorful foliage, strobilanthes may also serve as a tall planter subject or, on occasion, as a tender shrub in protected spots.

HABITAT: Southeastern Asia.

LIGHT REQUIREMENT: Reduced light is recommended.

SOIL REQUIREMENT: Moderately fertile, well-drained soil is acceptable.

SALT TOLERANCE: Not tolerant.

AVAILABILITY: Retail sales yards on the peninsula offer strobilanthes in cans.

CULTURE: Care given to most popular pot plants should make for success with strobilanthes. Water with moderation and fertilize with a balanced mixture so as to maintain rich foliage tints.

PROPAGATION: Cuttage.

PESTS: Nematodes and mites.

333
Sanchezia

Sanchezia (san-CHEZ-ee-a): for J. Sanchez, early Spanish botanist.
nobilis (NOB-ill-is): renowned.

FAMILY: Acanthaceae.
RELATIVES: Acanthus and barleria.
TYPE OF PLANT: Shrub.
HEIGHT: 6'. ZONE: C,S

HOW TO IDENTIFY: Robust, upright-growing shrub with glabrous stems, and, in the types seen in Florida, foot-long, opposite leaves strongly marked with white or cream-colored veins. It is difficult for some gardeners to distinguish between *Aphelandra* and *Sanchezia,* differences being found in the flowers.

HABIT OF GROWTH: Shrubby, usually ascending, open, and coarse.

FOLIAGE: Bold and colorful by virtue of the strongly contrasting veins. Opposite leaves are foot-long, smooth, attached by very short petioles to smooth, squarish stems.

FLOWERS: Terminal spikes of yellow, tubular flowers, 2" long, are highlighted by bright red bracts.

FRUITS: Little pods.

SEASON OF MAXIMUM COLOR: The year around!

LANDSCAPE USES: Like many another acanthus-relative, sanchezia has long been popular as a pot plant. In tropical locations, it serves as an accent in a shaded shrubbery border.

HABITAT: Northwestern South America.

LIGHT REQUIREMENT: Partial shade is recommended; rather deep shade can be tolerated.

SOIL REQUIREMENT: Moderately fertile, well-drained soil is satisfactory.

SALT TOLERANCE: Not tolerant of dune conditions.

AVAILABILITY: Nurseries on the peninsula offer sanchezia plants in containers.

CULTURE: In partially shaded, protected locations, plant with other tender exotics. If frosted, cut back to earth; new shoots will appear with the advent of warm weather.

PROPAGATION: Cuttage.

PESTS: Mites and nematodes.

334
Eranthemum

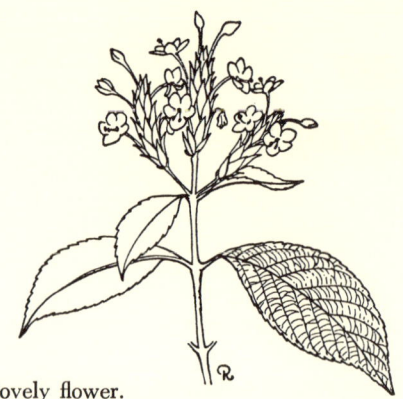

Eranthemum (er-ANN-the-mum): Greek for lovely flower.
nervosum (ner-vo-sum): nerved, referring to the puckered leaves.

FAMILY: Acanthaceae. RELATIVES: Bears-breech and shrimp-plant.
TYPE OF PLANT: Tender shrub. HEIGHT: 5'. ZONE: C,S
HOW TO IDENTIFY: Axillary *and* terminal spikes of bright blue flowers, ¾" across, subtended by typical acanthus bracts, strongly nerved, are produced during much of the warm season. The upright-growing shrubs are ungainly and not particularly striking in habit.
HABIT OF GROWTH: Strongly upright, open, and scraggly.
FOLIAGE: Opposite, 4" long, puckered, usually a deep-green on well-grown plants in partially shaded situations.
FLOWERS: Celestial blue, ¾" across, in axillary *and* terminal spikes, above prominently nerved bracts.
FRUITS: Little capsules.
SEASON OF MAXIMUM COLOR: Winter, when terminal spikes of blue appear.
LANDSCAPE USES: For its flowers of deepest blue, eranthemum has long been prized. To provide blue in front of other tropical shrubs in shade, this oriental plant may be massed.
HABITAT: India.
LIGHT REQUIREMENT: Partial shade is recommended.
SOIL REQUIREMENT: Sandy soil, of moderate fertility, that drains readily is usually satisfactory.
SALT TOLERANCE: Not tolerant of dune conditions.
AVAILABILITY: Nurseries in southern Florida sell container-grown eranthemums.
CULTURE: In partially shaded, protected locations, plant with other tender exotics. If frosted, cut back to the earth; new shoots will appear with the advent of warm weather.
PROPAGATION: Cuttage.
PESTS: Mites and nematodes.
NOTE: *Daedalacanthus* is the old generic name, now held to be invalid, and "blue-sage" is the most popular common designation.

335
Firespike

Odontonema (oh-dont-oh-NEE-ma): Greek, referring to toothed filaments.
strictum (STRICT-um): upright.

FAMILY: Acanthaceae.   RELATIVES: Barleria and sanchezia.
TYPE OF PLANT: Herbaceous perennial.   HEIGHT: 6'. ZONE: N,C,S
HOW TO IDENTIFY: Straight, smooth, green, herbaceous stems bear opposite, shiny, undulate leaves, and, in autumn, spikes of fire red, tubular flowers for a period of several weeks. These are among Florida's most showy red flowers of the fall season.
HABIT OF GROWTH: Usually a many-stemmed, compact mound of shining green.
FOLIAGE: Evergreen, opposite, smooth and shining, wavy-margined. Nodes somewhat enlarged, and marked by 2 series of whitish dots.
FLOWERS: Tubular blossoms of fire-red are borne in terminal and axillary spikes in the fall. Those in a given spike do not all open at one time, thus to extend anthesis.
FRUITS: Little pods.
SEASON OF MAXIMUM COLOR: Late summer or autumn, when red spikes appear.
LANDSCAPE USES: For notes of bright red in the fall, firespike is very widely grown throughout our state. Very tender to cold, plants die to earth following first frosts; therefore, firespike should be planted near hardy shrubs. Hummingbirds and butterflies frequent *Odontonema* blossoms.
HABITAT: Central America.
LIGHT REQUIREMENT: Full sun for best habit and heavy flowering.
SOIL REQUIREMENT: Moderately fertile, sandy soil is adequate.
SALT TOLERANCE: Not tolerant.
AVAILABILITY: Nurseries occasionally carry firespike plants in cans.
CULTURE: Plant divisions or rooted cuttings in moderately rich earth near woody shrubs; water; and forget. After frost blackens stems, cut them back to the ground line.
PROPAGATION: Cuttage and division.
PESTS: None of major consequence.

336
Pseuderanthemum

Pseuderanthemum (sue-der-ANN-the-mum): false eranthemum.
atropurpureum (at-roe-purr-PURE-ee-um): dark purple.

FAMILY: Acanthaceae. RELATIVES: Eranthemum and mackaya.
TYPE OF PLANT: Shrub. HEIGHT: 4'. ZONE: C,S

HOW TO IDENTIFY: This glabrous shrub has herbaceous, purple twigs that hold opposite, shining leaves 6" long. These leaves are glowing wine-purple with shaded blotches of lighter tones that may run out to the margins. There may be shallow notches near the apical ends.

HABIT OF GROWTH: Upright, many-stemmed, heavily foliated.

FOLIAGE: Evergreen, opposite, wine-purple with irregular blotches of different tones.

FLOWERS: Short spikes of white or purple flowers completely dotted with darker tones.

FRUITS: Capsules.

SEASON OF MAXIMUM COLOR: Warm months when new leaves come out.

LANDSCAPE USES: As a gay urn subject, pseuderanthemum (we should have a valid common name!) is a change from red-leaved crotons and acalyphas. In very warm spots that are free from nematodes, this acanthus-relative may grow as a shrub.

HABITAT: Polynesia.

LIGHT REQUIREMENT: Tolerant of reduced light of greenhouses, porches, and patios.

SOIL REQUIREMENT: Fertile, moist soils, free from nematodes, are suggested.

SALT TOLERANCE: Endures salt air back of the first dunes.

AVAILABILITY: Small plants are in nurseries in southern Florida.

CULTURE: Growing techniques that are successful for other pot plants will be good for this tropical exotic.

PROPAGATION: Cuttage.

PESTS: Nematodes, mites, scales, and thrips.

NOTE: Sister species, *Pseuderanthemum reticulatum,* has light, yellow-green foliage strikingly netted with golden veins. Young leaves unfurl orange-yellow; as they mature they shade through chartreuse to become a solid green finally. The white flowers of this species are dotted with purple.

Caricature Plant

Graptophyllum (grap-toe-FILL-um): Greek for write and leaf, referring to the variegated foliage.
pictum (PICK-tum): painted.

FAMILY: Acanthaceae.

RELATIVES: Shrimp-plant, thunbergia, and strobilanthes.

TYPE OF PLANT: Shrub.

HEIGHT: 8'. ZONE: S

HOW TO IDENTIFY: Glabrous shrub with opposite, shining leaves 6" long, blotched with cream along the midrib. Purplish-red, tubular flowers appear in compact clusters.

HABIT OF GROWTH: Compact, well-foliated, tender shrub.

FOLIAGE: Evergreen, opposite, blotched with cream around the midrib, of coarse texture and cream-and-green color.

FLOWERS: Purplish-red, tubular, 1½" long borne in short clusters.

FRUITS: Capsules.

SEASON OF MAXIMUM COLOR: No seasonal variation.

LANDSCAPE USES: As a gay urn subject, caricature plant evokes favorable comment. In frostless gardens it may serve as a warm accent in front of green shrubs. Set in groups 3' o.c.

As a change from croton and gold-dust-tree, both of which it resembles superficially, caricature plant may interest some homeowners in extreme southern Florida. The pattern of variegation about the midribs varies in size and color in several selections. In Latin-American gardens this plant is very popular and may be known as *cafe con leche*.

HABITAT: New Guinea; in Florida, warmest locations.

LIGHT REQUIREMENT: Tolerant of reduced light of greenhouses, porches, and patios.

SOIL REQUIREMENT: Fertile, moist, organic soils, free of nematodes.

SALT TOLERANCE: Not tolerant.

AVAILABILITY: Some nurseries in southern Florida will have small plants in receptacles.

CULTURE: Nematode-free, rich, moist soil is suggested for planting; therefore, container- or bin-culture might be best for caricature plant.

PROPAGATION: Cuttage.

PESTS: Mites, nematodes, thrips, and scales.

338
Cardinals Guard

Pachystachys (pack-is-tack-eez): Greek for thick spike.
coccinea (cock-sin-ee-a): scarlet.

FAMILY: Acanthaceae. RELATIVES: Acanthus and crossandra.

TYPE OF PLANT: Herbaceous perennial. HEIGHT: 7'. ZONE: C,S

HOW TO IDENTIFY: Shade-loving, coarse, spindly perennials bear thick red plumes in terminal positions. These are made up of 2" scarlet, tubular corollas, split nearly to their middles, subtended by conspicuous green bracts.

HABIT OF GROWTH: Upright, many-stemmed.

FOLIAGE: Evergreen, opposite, 8" long, pointed both ends.

FLOWERS: Thick spikes of scarlet; curved, split corollas held within broad, green, entire bracts.

FRUITS: Little pods.

SEASON OF MAXIMUM COLOR: Late summer when flowers mature.

LANDSCAPE USES: For a dash of red in a shaded corner, cardinals guard can stand with other tender tropical exotics.

HABITAT: Caribbean region.

LIGHT REQUIREMENT: Shade is a requirement.

SOIL REQUIREMENT: Moderately fertile, well-drained earth seems to suffice.

SALT TOLERANCE: Not tolerant.

AVAILABILITY: Small plants in cans appear in some nurseries and garden centers.

CULTURE: Plant rooted cuttings in protected, shady spots; water moderately; fertilize lightly thrice annually; cut back hard after blooming.

PROPAGATION: Cuttage.

PESTS: Mites and nematodes.

339
Jacobinia

Jacobinia (jake-oh-BIN-ee-a): probably a personal name.
SPP.: different species and their hybrids grow in Florida.

FAMILY: Acanthaceae. RELATIVES: Red justicia and shrimp-plant.

TYPE OF PLANT: Herbs or shrubs. HEIGHT: 7'. ZONE: C,S

HOW TO IDENTIFY: Thick spikes of curved flowers in tones of red, yellow-apricot, rose-purple, or orange are produced in terminal positions by coarse, tender herbaceous perennials or shrubs with large, opposite, wavy leaves.

HABIT OF GROWTH: Upright, by heavily foliated green stems.

FOLIAGE: Evergreen, large, wavy, opposite, usually light-green in color.

FLOWERS: Decorative thick spikes of curving corollas in tones of red, yellow, apricot, rose-purple, or orange are well liked by gardeners.

FRUITS: Little pods.

SEASON OF MAXIMUM COLOR: Late summer when flower spikes expand.

LANDSCAPE USES: For the handsome spikes, these tender, tropical exotics are cultivated in frostless locations.

HABITAT: Tropical America.

LIGHT REQUIREMENT: Shade is a requirement.

SOIL REQUIREMENT: Moderately fertile, well-drained earth seems to suffice.

SALT TOLERANCE: Not tolerant.

AVAILABILITY: Some nurseries carry canned jacobinias.

CULTURE: Plant rooted cuttings in protected, shady locations with other tender tropical exotics; water moderately; fertilize thrice annually; cut back hard after blooming to maintain compact habit.

PROPAGATION: Cuttage.

PESTS: Mites and nematodes.

340
Shrimp-Plant

Beloperone (bell-oh-PER-oh-nee): Greek for the arrow-shaped anthers.
guttata (goo-TAH-tah): spotted, referring to the spotted throats of the flowers.

FAMILY: Acanthaceae.   RELATIVES: Cardinals guard and coromandel.

TYPE OF PLANT: Herbaceous perennial.   HEIGHT: 8'.   ZONE: N,C,S

HOW TO IDENTIFY: Terete stems bear 2½" fuzzy leaves; blossom spikes with showy brownish bracts resemble shrimps.

HABIT OF GROWTH: Clusters of slender, terete, herbaceous stems.

FOLIAGE: Evergreen, hairy, of medium texture and light green color.

FLOWERS: Spikes some 3½" long made showy by the reddish-brown, heart-shaped, hairy bracts which surround the true flowers.

FRUITS: Long-stalked capsules.

SEASON OF MAXIMUM COLOR: Springtime and much of the summer.

LANDSCAPE USES: Shrimp-plant is much used for mass plantings in front of shrubbery, and around palms and woody trees; planting interval, 18". For planters and urns, shrimp-plant also is popular. Here is another herbaceous perennial that is a favorite with beginning or casual part-time gardeners because it is so easy to propagate, so undemanding of its owner. Shrimp-plant has many good qualities that make it worthy of the esteem with which it is regarded in Florida.
Frost cuts the stems back to the earth.

HABITAT: Mexico; in Florida, ubiquitous in gardens all over the state.

LIGHT REQUIREMENT: Full sun or high, broken pine shade.

SOIL REQUIREMENT: Tolerant of widely varying soils.

SALT TOLERANCE: Not tolerant.

AVAILABILITY: Every retail sales yard offers shrimp-plants in assorted vessels.

CULTRE: Plant in fairly fertile soil; water until established; furnish a mulch; cut back to the ground after the first frost injures the succulent herbaceous stems.

PROPAGATION: Cuttage or division of old, matted clumps.

PESTS: Caterpillars.

341
Ixora

Ixora (icks-OH-ra): a Malabar diety.
coccinea (cox-IN-ee-a): scarlet.

FAMILY: Rubiaceae.
TYPE OF PLANT: Shrub.
RELATIVES: Gardenia, coffee, and serissa.
HEIGHT: 15'. ZONE: C,S

HOW TO IDENTIFY: Opposite, evergreen leaves with cordate, amplexicaul bases, often showing chlorosis; tubular flowers of red, yellow, or tones of red during much of the year.

HABIT OF GROWTH: Very compact, much-branched, amenable to shearing.

FOLIAGE: Evergreen, opposite, of medium texture and medium green color; frequently chlorotic.

FLOWERS: Showy, red, yellow or orange, 1½" long, in dense axillary corymbs.

FRUITS: Berries.

SEASON OF MAXIMUM COLOR: Much of the warm season.

LANDSCAPE USES: As a hedge for southern Florida, ixora is a great favorite; set plants 18" apart. In foundation arrangements it is used as a sheared accent and as filler material, too. In the garden, as a part of an enclosing shrubbery border, set ixoras 3' o.c. for bright color notes.

HABITAT: Southern Asia; in Florida, warmest parts.

LIGHT REQUIREMENT: Full sun for best habit and profuse flowering.

SOIL REQUIREMENT: Slightly acid soil of high fertility and good drainage.

SALT TOLERANCE: Endures mild salt air, back of the front-line dunes.

AVAILABILITY: Ixoras are widely available in containers of all sizes.

CULTURE: In protected locations, plant in rich, acid soil that is free of nematodes; water faithfully; spray to control insects; fertilize twice or thrice annually.

PROPAGATION: Cuttage.

PESTS: Nematodes, scales, mushroom root-rot, deficiencies of trace elements.

NOTE: One of southern Florida's leading flowering shrubs is available in many colors and forms now that hybrids have been introduced. Most spectacular is Malay ixora (*Ixora macrothyrsa*), a species which bears flowers in showy clusters 10" across.

Ixoras are very sensitive to cold.

Serissa

Serissa (ser-iss-a): from the Indian name.
foetida (fet-id-a): bad-smelling.

Family: Rubiaceae. **Relatives:** Coffee, ixora, and pentas.
Type of Plant: Tiny shrub. **Height:** 2'. **Zone:** N,C,S

How to Identify: Tiny shrub with ½" leaves that have fetid odor when crushed; tiny white flowers in axillary position much of the year.

Habit of Growth: Dwarf shrub of several stems with upward-pointing branches.

Foliage: Evergreen, fine texture, dark green or margined with yellow in the clone 'Variegata.'

Flowers: Tiny, white, single or double flowers. The unexpanded buds are pink.

Fruits: Tiny, subglobose drupes.

Season of Maximum Color: When flowers are out, which is much of the year.

Landscape Uses: As an edging (set 1' o.c.) serissa is excellent; for planters it is widely accepted, and for foundation plantings, it has come into its own with contemporary architecture. In this latter use set 2' o.c.

'Variegata' has leaves margined with yellow, and a variety with double flowers has little all-green leaves that are crowded to give a compact appearance to the plants.

Habitat: Japan; in Florida, rather widely grown as a garden shrub.

Light Requirement: Partial shade is desirable in much of Florida.

Soil Requirement: A fertile, moisture-retentive soil is recommended.

Salt Tolerance: Not tolerant.

Availability: Nurseries propagate quantities of this diminutive shrub.

Culture: Plant in fertile soil that is free of nematodes, if possible. Water faithfully; keep a mulch over the roots; do not allow grasses to encroach; fertilize once late in the winter.

Propagation: Cuttage.

Pests: Nematodes, mites, and scales.

343
Pentas

Pentas (PEN-tass): Greek five, referring to the flower parts.
lanceolata (lan-see-oh-LATE-a): lance-shaped.

FAMILY: Rubiaceae.
RELATIVES: Coffee and gardenia.
TYPE OF PLANT: Herbaceous perennial.
HEIGHT: 4'. ZONE: N,C,S
How TO IDENTIFY: Here is Florida's most popular herbaceous member of the famed madder family, that great group of plants that contains so many species important in the tropics. Pentas is a tender, but vigorous perennial with fuzzy, deeply veined, opposite leaves and terminal heads of star-like flowers in tones of red, in lilac, or in white during much of the warm season.
HABIT OF GROWTH: Sprawling, leafy mounds usually crowned by bright blossoms.
FOLIAGE: Opposite, hairy, deeply veined, 6" long.
FLOWERS: Bright, attractive terminal clusters of star-like flowers, in many shades, are produced much of the year.
FRUITS: Little capsules bear many small seeds.
SEASON OF MAXIMUM COLOR: Much of the year, when blossoms are out.
LANDSCAPE USES: For splashes of bright color in front of green shrubs, pentas is unexcelled. Although some gardeners like to mix plants of different shades, best usage suggests that pentas be set in drifts of separate colors with generous foils of the white-flowered clone to divide these groups.
HABITAT: Tropical Africa.
LIGHT RQUIREMENT: Full sun for best habit and full flowering, though light shade from high-headed pines or palms is good.
SOIL REQUIREMENT: Moderately fertile, well-drained earth is adequate.
SALT TOLERANCE: Not tolerant.
AVAILABILITY: Most nurseries have plants in cans for sale.
CULTURE: Plant rooted cuttings in generous drifts by separate colors; water moderately; fertilize lightly once each summer month; and remove seed heads to keep plants in production for long periods.
PROPAGATION: Cuttage or seedage.
PESTS: Mites.

344
Scarlet-Bush

Hamelia (ham-ALE-ee-a): for H. Duhamel, early French botanist.
patens (PAY-tens): spreading.

FAMILY: Rubiaceae.   RELATIVES: Ixora, gardenia, and coffee.

TYPE OF PLANT: Shrub.   HEIGHT: 12'. ZONE: S

HOW TO IDENTIFY: Bush with reddish hairs on all young parts; evergreen leaves to 6" long in whorls of 3; bright red tubular flowers with red stalks, followed by black berries ¼" in diameter which are edible.

HABIT OF GROWTH: Bushy, from several branching stems.

FOLIAGE: Evergreen, whorled, of bold aspect. The young leaves are reddish from tomentum, the old ones are dark green or tinted with red or purple.

FLOWERS: Tubular, red, very showy, in terminal forking cymes.

FRUITS: Black berries ¼" in diameter, almost sessile, edible.

SEASON OF MAXIMUM COLOR: Warm months, when blossoms emerge.

LANDSCAPE USES: As a part of an enclosing barrier, in extreme southern Florida, set scarlet-bush 5' o.c. Residents of Dade, Monroe, and Lee counties would do well to consider the use of this calcium-tolerant native in enclosing shrubbery borders. True, the large leaves and considerable height rule out scarlet-bush for foundation plantings, but in barrier plantings it can serve well.

HABITAT: Tropical America, including southern Florida.

LIGHT REQUIREMENT: Reduced light of hammocks.

SOIL REQUIREMENT: Tolerant of lime-bearing soils of southern Florida.

SALT TOLERANCE: Tolerant of salt drift back from the ocean-front.

AVAILABILITY: Some nurseries might have small scarlet-bushes in cans.

CULTURE: In prepared sites, plant carefully; water faithfully; fertilize twice or thrice each year. Do not allow lawn grasses to encroach upon the root zone.

PROPAGATION: Seedage, cuttage, or marcottage.

PESTS: Scales and mites.

345
Gardenia

Gardenia (gar-DEAN-ee-a): for A. Garden, a physician of Charleston.
jasminoides (jas-min-OI-dez): jasmine-like.

FAMILY: Rubiaceae.
RELATIVES: Coffee and ixora.
TYPE OF PLANT: Shrub.
HEIGHT: 8'. ZONE: N,C,S

HOW TO IDENTIFY: Evergreen, opposite leaves with interpetiolar stipules, and in springtime, the famed, beloved gardenias.

HABIT OF GROWTH: Compact, shrubby by many stems, and closely packed twigs.

FOLIAGE: Evergreen, of medium texture and dark green color when properly fertilized.

FLOWERS: White, fragrant, solitary in axils in springtime.

FRUITS: Fleshy, orange-colored, sessile, ribbed capsules, about 1½" long.

SEASON OF MAXIMUM COLOR: April-May.

LANDSCAPE USES: Gardenias have been favorites as freestanding specimens with generations of southerners. As a part of an informal shrubbery border, set groups of gardenias with about 5' between plants. Sometimes they are used as urn subjects on terraces.

There are many varieties which display slightly varying characters in the flowers. One clone has variegated foliage, but it is not very widely grown.

HABITAT: China; in Florida, ubiquitous in gardens.

LIGHT REQUIREMENT: Light, shifting, high pine shade is excellent.

SOIL REQUIREMENT: Acid, fertile soils that are free from nematodes are wanted.

SALT TOLERANCE: Not tolerant.

AVAILABILITY: Most retail nurseries sell gardenia plants. In northern Florida, they are own root, B&B, or canned; in southern Florida, canned specimens grafted on stocks of *Gardenia thunbergia* are offered.

CULTURE: Plant in rich, acid, nematode-free soil; water faithfully; spray frequently to control white-flies.

PROPAGATION: Cuttage in northern Florida; graftage on stocks of nematode-resistant *Gardenia thunbergia* in southern Florida.

PESTS: White-flies, sooty-mold, cottony cushion scale, mealy bugs, and nematodes.

346
Sandankwa Viburnum

Viburnum (vye-bur-num): ancient Latin name.
suspensum (sus-pen-sum): hung.

Family: Caprifoliaceae.   **Relatives:** Honeysuckle, abelia, and elder.
Type of Plant: Shrub.   **Height:** 12'.   **Zone:** N,C,S

How to Identify: Brown twigs that are warty and quite rough to the touch because of prominent lenticels; evergreen, opposite, dark green leaves that have densely crenate-serrate margins.

Habit of Growth: Shrubby, compact, dense from many stems.

Foliage: Evergreen, opposite, coarse in texture, dark green in color.

Flowers: Little white flowers produced in winter and early spring.

Fruits: Red, subglobose drupes, very sparingly produced in Florida.

Season of Maximum Color: Little variation excepting when tiny white blossoms show in January-February.

Landscape Uses: As a part of an enclosing barrier, plant 3' o.c.; as a part of a foundation planting, use the same interval. Sandankwa viburnum is the best of the genus for much of Florida and it is fully appreciated by landscape architects and advanced hobby gardeners here.

Habitat: Asiatic islands; in Florida, all areas.

Light Requirement: Tolerant of shade.

Soil Requirement: Fertile soil that is free of nematodes is recommended.

Salt Tolerance: Not tolerant.

Availability: Most retail sales lots offer sandankwa viburnum in cans.

Culture: Plant carefully in well-made sites; water diligently; supply with a deep organic mulch. Regular pruning is needed to remove the long, upward-growing shoots.

Propagation: Cuttage.

Pests: Aphids, white-flies, sooty-mold, thrips, mites, nematodes, and stem canker.

Note: There are several native species here that could be used in landscape plantings, notably rusty blackhaw (*V. rufidulum*).

347
Laurestinus

Viburnum (vye-BUR-num): ancient Latin name.
tinus (TYE-nus): ancient name for this plant.

FAMILY: Caprifoliaceae.   RELATIVES: Abelia and honeysuckle.
TYPE OF PLANT: Shrub.   HEIGHT: 12'. ZONE: N

HOW TO IDENTIFY: Evergreen, opposite, dark green leaves, 3" long are entire and have revolute edges; the twigs are somewhat hairy; the growth habit is symmetrical and compact.

HABIT OF GROWTH: Attractive, upright, dense, and compact.

FOLIAGE: Evergreen, opposite, medium in texture, dark green in color.

FLOWERS: White or pinkish flowers are produced in convex cymes in late winter or early spring.

FRUITS: Bright blue drupes in early winter.

SEASON OF MAXIMUM COLOR: Spring, when blossoms are open.

LANDSCAPE USES: Foundation plant for large buildings, set 3'-5' o.c. Informal enclosure, allow 5' between plants.
   This is the most beautiful evergreen viburnum for Florida, but it is successful only on superior soils of the panhandle and is not recommended for the peninsula generally.
   In states north of the Florida line laurestinus may look even better than it does in our state. Planters in other areas utilize this excellent shrub more fully than do we Floridians.

HABITAT: Mediterranean region; in Florida, gardens of the panhandle.

LIGHT REQUIREMENT: Full sun on superior soils, high shade on sands.

SOIL REQUIREMENT: Fertile soils that are free from nematodes.

SALT TOLERANCE: Not tolerant.

AVAILABILITY: Small canned plants may be in nurseries in northern counties.

CULTURE: In western Florida, no special care is needed after establishment. Mulching is a good practice, of course, and pruning may be needed to keep laurestinus shapely.

PROPAGATION: Cuttage.

PESTS: Aphids, thrips, mites, and nematodes.

348 Sweet Viburnum

Viburnum (vye-BUR-num): ancient Latin name.
odoratissimum (o-dor-a-TIS-a-mum): most fragrant.

FAMILY: Caprifoliaceae. RELATIVES: Honeysuckle, abelia, and elder.

TYPE OF PLANT: Large shrub.   HEIGHT: 25'. ZONE: N,C,S

HOW TO IDENTIFY: Evergreen, opposite, bright green leaves, 6" long, remotely serrate toward the apex, tufts of brown hairs in axils of veins beneath; twigs green and smooth.

HABIT OF GROWTH: Very robust, dense, thick, becoming tree-like with age.

FOLIAGE: Evergreen, opposite, coarse in texture, bright green in color.

FLOWERS: Little, white, fragrant flowers in panicles in springtime.

FRUITS: Drupes, changing from red to black at maturity, very sparingly produced in Florida.

SEASON OF MAXIMUM COLOR: None.

LANDSCAPE USES: As an enclosing device, or as a screen, set sweet viburnum plants 5' o.c. Use the same interval if this shrub is planted by large, multistoried buildings. Very often sweet viburnum is allowed to become too big in landscape plantings if regular semi-annual pruning is not practiced. Indeed this heading-in twice each year can be quite severe. It is always a good plan to prune frequently so that comparatively small branches can be cut to leave small wounds. When large limbs are removed and big cuts are made, disease organisms may enter and cause decline, possibly death, of the plant.

HABITAT: Asia; in Florida, every community in the state.

LIGHT REQUIREMENT: Full sun or high, shifting shade from tall trees.

SOIL REQUIREMENT: Tolerant of many, varying soil types.

SALT TOLERANCE: Not tolerant.

AVAILABILITY: Practically every Florida nursery markets sweet viburnum in cans.

CULTURE: No special attention is needed after establishment, except for regular pruning to keep the plant within bounds.

PROPAGATION: Cuttage and simple layerage.

PESTS: Aphids, white-flies, sooty-mold, thrips, mites, and stem canker.

349
Japanese Honeysuckle

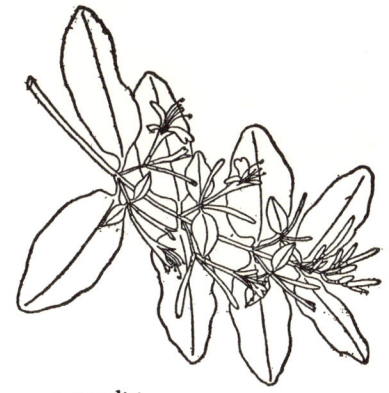

Lonicera (lon-is-er-a): for A. Lonicer, early German naturalist.
japonica (jap-on-i-ca): Japanese.

FAMILY: Caprifoliaceae.

RELATIVES: Viburnum and abelia.

TYPE OF PLANT: Vine.

HEIGHT: Variable. ZONE: N,C

HOW TO IDENTIFY: A vigorous, twining, evergreen vine with opposite, simple leaves of dark green color, and fragrant flowers that open white and turn yellow in the clone 'Halliana,' which is the one most often seen in Florida.

HABIT OF GROWTH: Vigorously twining.

FOLIAGE: Evergreen, opposite, of medium texture and dark green color.

FLOWERS: Showy, tubular, pubescent, very fragrant, produced in pairs in summer. In 'Halliana,' as noted above, the flowers are white at first, aging to yellow.

FRUITS: Showy, black berries are borne in clusters around stems.

SEASON OF MAXIMUM COLOR: Summer, when flowers are out.

LANDSCAPE USES: To veil a fence and add fragrance to the evening air, plant 10' o.c. To prevent erosion on steep slopes, plant 1'-2' o.c. There is always the possibility that Japanese honeysuckle will get out of hand and become a nuisance, especially on rich soil.

HABITAT: Eastern Asia; in Florida, naturalized in some places.

LIGHT REQUIREMENT: Full sun or reduced light of woodlands.

SOIL REQUIREMENT: Tolerant of many soil types, except lightest sands.

SALT TOLERANCE: Not tolerant of conditions near the strand.

AVAILABILITY: This is usually not an item of commerce, but rooted layers may be acquired from friends.

CULTURE: Plant, water, and forget.

PROPAGATION: Simple layerage where stems meet the earth.

PESTS: None of major concern.

NOTE: Trumpet honeysuckle (*Lonicera sempervirens*), with upper leaves joined at their bases, and red trumpets, is native in much of Florida. This one is not as likely to become a nuisance as is the exotic species.

350
Glossy Abelia

Abelia (a-BEE-lee-a): for C. Abel, physician and author.
grandiflora (grand-ee-FLOR-a): large-flowered.

FAMILY: Caprifoliaceae.

RELATIVES: Honeysuckle, viburnum, and elder.

TYPE OF PLANT: Shrub.

HEIGHT: 10′. **ZONE:** N

HOW TO IDENTIFY: White, tubular blossoms subtended by reddish calyces which persist for much of the year; opposite, shining leaves on reddish twigs; shredding bark on old stems.

HABIT OF GROWTH: Spreading, tending to become leggy and open below.

FOLIAGE: Evergreen, opposite, shining, of deep green color and finest texture.

FLOWERS: White, tubular, subtended by persistent reddish calyces.

FRUITS: Usually none.

SEASON OF MAXIMUM COLOR: Summer, white blossoms; later, red calyces.

LANDSCAPE USES: Clipped hedge, set 18″ o.c.; informal screen, plant 3′ apart; foundation plant, arrange at 2′ intervals. Abelia is very useful in northern counties because of its fine texture, attractive foliage, and flowers, but it is not recommended for use south of Gainesville. As one proceeds down the peninsula, abelia becomes less good as a garden shrub.

HABITAT: Gardens of warmer United States; in Florida, western part.

LIGHT REQUIREMENT: Full sun or high, light, shifting shade.

SOIL REQUIREMENT: Fertile, moisture-retaining clay-loams.

SALT TOLERANCE: Not tolerant.

AVAILABILITY: Abelia is offered by nurseries in the northern part.

CULTURE: Plant on fertile, clay-loam soil in western Florida; pinch succulent canes as soon as they appear in springtime; fertilize once each winter.

PROPAGATION: Cuttage by long, leafless, hardwood stems in December-January.

PESTS: Usually none of major concern.

351 Mexican Flame-Vine

Senecio (sen-EE-see-o): Latin *senex* for old man.
confusus (con-FUSE-us): uncertain.

FAMILY: Compositae.   RELATIVES: Daisy, calendula, and marigold.

TYPE OF PLANT: Herbaceous vine.   HEIGHT: Variable. ZONE: C,S

HOW TO IDENTIFY: A smooth-stemmed vine that bears alternate, evergreen leaves 4" long with coarse teeth and sharp points. Daisy-like, orange flowers are produced during warm months.

HABIT OF GROWTH: Sprawling vine by herbaceous, green stems.

FOLIAGE: Evergreen, medium in texture, dark green in color.

FLOWERS: Orange daisies about 1" across with 15 ray flowers that deepen to red with age.

FRUITS: Little, bristled achenes like dandelion fruits.

SEASON OF MAXIMUM COLOR: Warm months, then heavy-flowered.

LANDSCAPE USES: To add interest to palm trunks, to soften fences, or to veil small buildings, Mexican flame-vine is popular in warm sections of the state. This is primarily a home-gardener's vine because of its very easy culture. Variation in flower color may be noted upon occasion, but no named clones have been isolated and increased vegetatively.

HABITAT: Mexico; in Florida, widely grown in warm locations.

LIGHT REQUIREMENT: Full sun or shade from high-headed trees.

SOIL REQUIREMENT: Tolerant of widely varying soils.

SALT TOLERANCE: Not tolerant.

AVAILABILITY: Most nurseries on the peninsula offer Mexican flame-vines.

CULTURE: Of easiest culture, this vine grows without attention. First frosts will usually cut stems to the earth.

PROPAGATION: Seedage, layerage, and cuttage.

PESTS: Nematodes, mites, scales, and caterpillars.

352
Wedelia

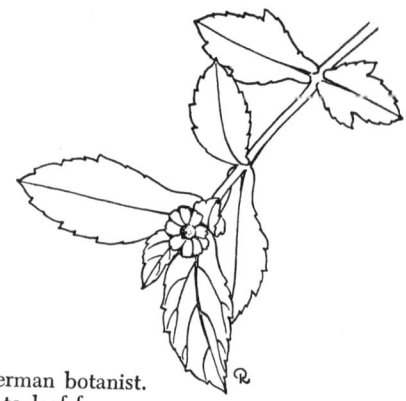

Wedelia (we-DELL-ee-a): for G. Wedel, a German botanist.
trilobata (try-low-BAIT-a): 3-lobed, referring to leaf-form.

FAMILY: Compositae. RELATIVES: Aster, cosmos, and daisy.
TYPE OF PLANT: Creeping herbaceous perennial. HEIGHT: 18". ZONE: C,S
HOW TO IDENTIFY: Creeping, horizontal stems bear fleshy, toothed, or lobed, hairy leaves, and yellow, daisy-like flowers.
HABIT OF GROWTH: Mat-forming by horizontal rooting stems.
FOLIAGE: Fleshy, toothed or lobed, closely packed when plants grow in the sun.
FLOWERS: Yellow, daisy-like, 10-12-rayed, each ray pleated and tipped with 3 lobes. It is hoped that additional colors will appear in the future.
FRUITS: Seed heads typical of the daisy family.
SEASON OF MAXIMUM COLOR: Blossoms open much of the year around.
LANDSCAPE USES: As a ground cover for sunny expanses, even near the sea, wedelia is in high favor in frostless locations. For sunny planters, it excels as the trailing habit softens the top line and relates the planters and their contents to the earth beneath. Plants may be set 18" apart.
HABITAT: Tropical America; escaped from cultivation in Florida.
LIGHT REQUIREMENT: Intense light of open, sandy expanses is optimum, yet partial shade from high-headed trees is tolerated.
SOIL REQUIREMENT: Sandy soil of moderate fertility is adequate; yet good soil and plentiful moisture produce beautiful, lush plants of deep-green color.
SALT TOLERANCE: Very tolerant of salt, dune locations are acceptable.
AVAILABILITY: Wedelia is a standard nursery item in central and southern Florida.
CULTURE: After establishment, light fertilization and regular watering will make for good growth. When plantings become thick and heavy, prune drastically with hedge shears or a sharp hoe. Frost kills wedelia to the earth.
PROPAGATION: Simple layerage; stems root where they touch the earth. Unrooted tip cuttings are set where new plants are wanted.
PESTS: Chewing insects and mites.

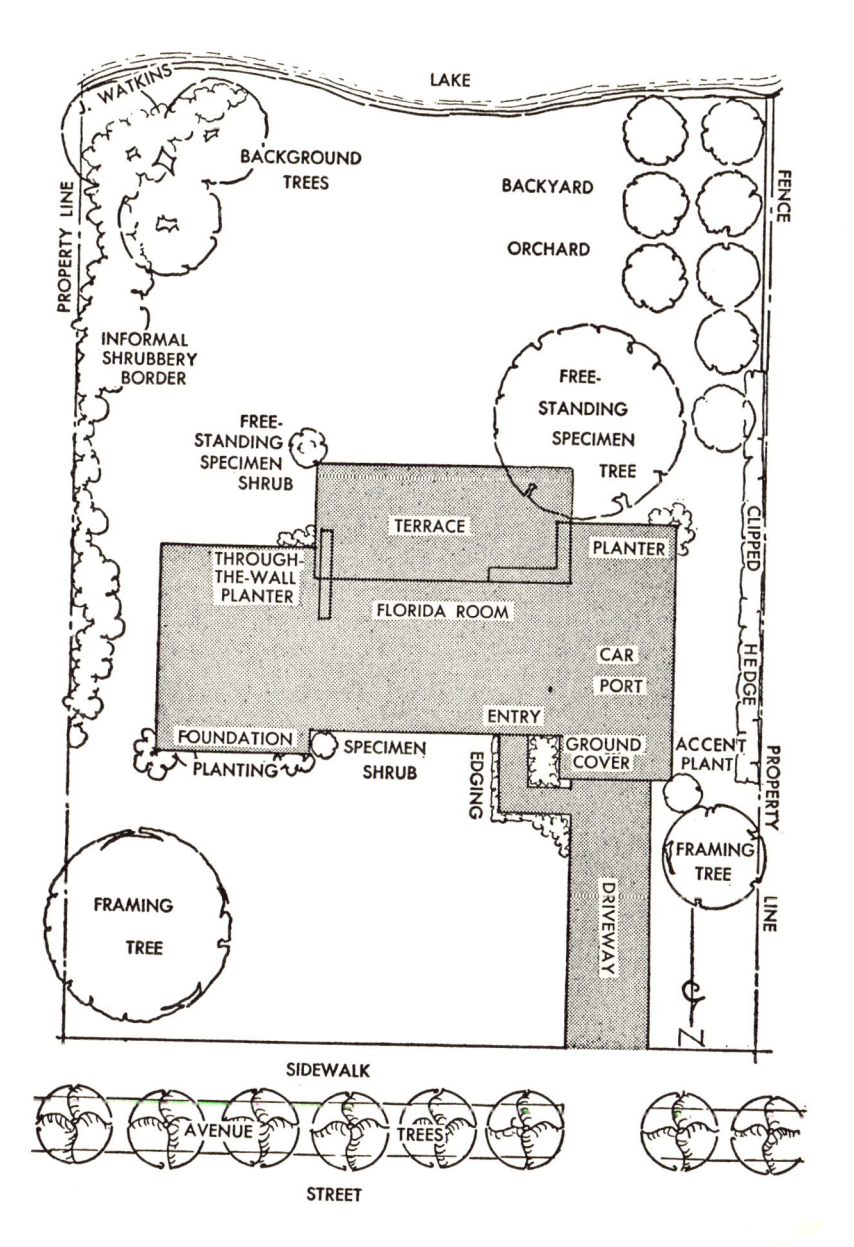

Model plan illustrating uses of landscape plants.

Pest Control Guide

Pest	Suggested Control
Algal leaf-spot	Usually not controlled.
Ants	Chlordane dust.*
Aphids	Lindane, malathion, nicotine sulphate, or Cygon.
Azalea defoliators	Malathion, or Sevin.
Azalea leaf-miners	Lindane, malathion, or Cygon.
Azalea petal blight	Dithane combination spray; Acti-dione RZ or Zineb.
Bagworms	Sevin or chlordane.
Borers	Wrap trunks of newly transplanted trees.
Caterpillars	Sevin or chlordane.
Chlorosis	Correct growing medium, supply minor elements.
Cottony cushion scales	Malathion, Cygon or Diazinon.
Crickets	Poison bran bait.
Earthworms	Chlordane.
Fire blight	Deep pruning with sterilized shears.
Florida red scales	White summer oil emulsion.
Grasshoppers	Chlordane dust.
Lace bugs	Malathion or Lindane.
Leaf-miners	Lindane, malathion, or Diazinon.
Leaf-gall fungi	Pick malformed leaves and destroy.
Leaf-spot fungi	Captan, ferbam, Phaltan, or copper compounds.
Mealy-bugs	Malathion, Cygon or Diazinon.
Mildew	Acti-dione PM, sulfur dust, or Karathane.
Mites	Kelthane, Trithion, or Tedion.
Mole-crickets	Prepared bran bait containing chlordane, kepone or Dylox.
Moles	Steel mole trap.
Mushroom root-rot	Dispose of plant, drench area with formalin.
Nematodes	Fumigate soil, keep organic mulch over roots; VC13 or Nemagon.
Oleander moth larvae	Chlordane or Sevin, repeat often.
Orange-dogs	Sevin or chlordane.
Palm leaf skeletonizer	Sevin or chlordane.
Palm weevil	There is no feasible control.
Pith borer	There is no feasible control.
Pocket gophers	Steel gopher trap.
Red spiders	Kelthane or Trithion.
Roaches	Chlordane or Diazinon.
Scales	White summer oil emulsion, Cygon, Diazinon.
Sooty-mold	White summer oil emulsion.
Spittlebugs	Lindane or malathion.
Squirrels	Protective bags of open-mesh cloth.
Tea scales	White summer oil emulsion or Cygon.
Thornbugs	Malathion or Lindane.
Thrips	Lindane, malathion, Cygon, or Meta-Systox-R.
White-flies	Malathion, or white summer oil.*

Consult your garden center manager; use only by directions printed on labels.

Glossary

ACAULESCENT (aye-call-ES-cent). Stemless, or apparently stemless; sometimes the stem is subterranean or protrudes only slightly.
ACID. Having an excess of free hydrogen ions. Acid solutions taste "sour" and turn litmus red.
ACUMINATE (a-KEW-min-ate). Tapering to a slender point.
ACUTE. Sharp, ending in a point, the sides of the tapered apex essentially straight or slightly convex.
ADNATE (AD-nate). Grown to, organically united with another part; as stamens with the corolla tube or an anther in its whole length with the filament.
ADVENTITIOUS (ad-ven-TISH-us). Arising by chance, or unpredictably, out of the usual place.
AERIAL (AIR-ree-al). In the air; borne above the surface.
AIR-LAYERING. A method of vegetative propagation in which a rooting medium is placed in aerial position. Now commonly done with sphagnum moss and plastic film or aluminum foil.
ALKALINE (AL-ku-line). Having an excess of free hydroxyl ions, and so a deficiency of free hydrogen ions; basic. Lacking any sour taste, alkaline or basic soils are often called "sweet."
ALTERNATE (OL-ter-nat). Any arrangement of leaves not opposite or whorled; placed singly at different heights on the axis, stem or rachis.
AMPLEXICAUL (am-PLECKS-e-call). Encircling a stem.
ANTHER (AN-ther). The enlarged tip of the stamen in which pollen is developed.
ANTHESIS (AN-the-sis). Flowering.
APETALOUS (ay-PET-al-us). No petals.
APICAL (A-pick-al). At the apex or tip of a plant organ.
AROID (AIR-oid). A member of the family Araceae.
APPRESSED. Closely and flatly pressed against a surface.
ARMATURE. Any covering or occurrence of spines, barbs, or hooks.
ARIL (A-rill). A special appendage growing from the point of attachment of the seed.
ARMED. Provided with any kind of strong and sharp defense, as of thorns, spines, prickles, or barbs.
ASCENDING. Rising up; produced somewhat obliquely or indirectly upward.
ASEXUAL. Sexless; without sex.
AXIL (ACKS-ill). The angle formed by a petiole with the trunk.
AXIS (ACKS-is). The main or central line of development of any plant or organ; the main stem.
B & B. Balled and burlapped.
BARBED. With bristles that are hooked.
BASAL. At the base of a plant or plant organ.
BASIC. See Alkaline.
BERRY. Pulpy fruit that does not split open.
BIFID (BI-fid). Two-cleft, as in apices of some leaves.
BIFURCATE (bye-FUR-cate). Forked, as some Y-shaped hairs or thorns.
BIGENERIC (bi-gen-ERR-ic). Resulting from crossing two genera of plants.

GLOSSARY

BLADE. The expanded part of a leaf.

BLOOM. The thin waxy coating, easily rubbed off, on some fruits and on some palm foliage.

BOLE. A strong unbranched stem; the trunk.

BRACT. A modified leaf intermediate between the sepals and vegetative leaves.

CALCAREOUS (cal-CARE-e-us). Having a high content of lime or limestone.

CALYX (KAY-licks). The sepals collectively; the outer of the two series of modified leaves in most flowers.

CAPSULE. Compound pod; a fruit of more than one carpel, usually splitting at maturity along lines.

CATERPILLAR. A worm-like larva of a butterfly or moth that may despoil foliage.

CAUDEX (CAW-decks). Stem.

CAULESCENT (caw-LESS-cent). Having an evident stem above ground.

CHELATE (KEY-late). An organic compound which combines with iron or other heavy metals to release them slowly in the soil for plant use and yet prevents their being tied up in unavailable form by other soil chemicals.

CHLOROSIS (klor-o-sis). Loss of the green color from leaves, leaving them yellowish-green. It may be due to lack of needed nutrient elements, to inability to absorb those elements because of excess water or root disease, or to the direct action of insects or fungi on the leaves.

CILIATE (SILL-ee-ate). Fringed with hairs; bearing hairs on the margin.

CLASPING. Leaf partly or wholly surrounding stem.

CLAY. Mineral matter of exceedingly fine particle size in the soil, colloidal in character and often holding water tenaciously.

CLONE. A group of plants, increased vegetatively, from a single bud; a horticultural variety.

COLLOID (KOLL-oid). Composed of particles too small to be seen with the naked eye, and, by reason of its tremendous surface area, holding water and mineral elements with very great force.

COMA. The leafy crown or head, as of many palm trees.

COMPOST. Partially decomposed plant residues.

CORDATE (CORE-date). Heart-shaped in outline.

COSTAPALMATE (cost-a-PAL-mate). Said of a palmate palm leaf whose petiole continues through the blade as a distinct midrib, as in the cabbage palm.

CROWN. The head of foliage.

CROWNSHAFT. A trunk-like extension of the bole formed by the long broad overlapping petiole bases of some palms.

CULTIGEN (CULT-e-jen). Plants known only in cultivation; presumably originating under domestication; contrast with indigen.

CUTICLE (CUTE-e-cal). A waxy coating developed by the epidermis of some plants which reduces somewhat the loss of water through the epidermis. Unlike bloom, it cannot be rubbed off.

CYMBA (SIM-ba). A woody, durable, boat-like spathe that incloses the inflorescence, opens and persists, as in many palms; see Manubrium.

DECIDUOUS (dee-SID-you-us). Shedding its leaves periodically.

DIOECIOUS (dye-E-shus). Staminate and pistillate flowers on different plants; a term properly applied to plants, not to flowers.

DISTAL (DIS-tal). Farthest from the point of attachment or reference.

DISTICHOUS (DIS-tick-us). Arranged in two vertical rows.

DIVISION. Cutting, tearing, or breaking a plant into two or more independent units.

DRUPE (DROOP). A fleshy, one-seeded fruit.

ELLIPTIC (e-LIP-tick). A flat object that is oval and narrowed to rounded ends and widest near the middle.

EPIDERMIS (ep-e-DER-mis). The skin or outermost layer of cells of a plant.

FIBROUS. Composed of, or resembling fibers; a root system, as in palms, consisting chiefly of long, slender roots.

FILAMENT. Thread, particularly here, threads on some leaves.

358 GLOSSARY

FLATWOODS. Low, level land covered by forest, often under water during some of the rainy season. Flatwoods occupy much of the coastal areas and the north-central part of Florida, and have the saw palmetto and cabbage palm as important species.

FLORIDA ROOM. A room for informal living, usually with glass walls, overlooking the garden.

FOLIAGE. Leaves taken collectively.

FOLLICLE (FALL-ick-al). A dry fruit which splits open only along a single line.

FOUNDATION PLANTING. The shrubs, vines, and trees placed close around a building to soften the abrupt transition from the horizontal ground to the vertical wall.

FREEZE. A condition where plant temperatures below 32°F. result from the inflow of masses of air below this temperature, so that the air is colder than plants or ground.

FROST. A condition where plant temperatures below 32°F. result from radiation of heat from plants and ground, occurring only on still, cloudless nights. The air is coldest next to the ground and may be several degrees above 32° at a few feet above the ground.

FUNGICIDE (FUN-gee-side). A chemical which kills fungi.

FUNGUS. A leafless plant that may parasitize plants. Mildews, rusts, and molds are fungi.

GENUS (JEAN-us). A closely related group of species; the first and always capitalized word in the scientific name of a plant. The plural form is *genera* (JEN-er-a).

GLABROUS (GLAY-brus). Smooth, without hairs or scaly outgrowth.

GLAUCOUS (GLAU-cuss). Covered with a bloom or a whitish substance that rubs off.

GROUND COVER. A plant, other than a grass, used to cover the earth.

HABIT. The general appearance of a plant.

HABITAT (HAB-e-tat). The particular location in which a plant grows, as along stream bank, on the seashore, or in a hammock.

HAMMOCK. A slightly elevated island of hardwoods in a sea of pines or marsh grass.

HERB. A non-woody plant, naturally dying back to ground on the completion of its (usually) brief season of active growth.

HERMAPHRODITE (her-MAF-roe-dite). A plant which has perfect flowers, each one having stamens and pistils.

HUMIDITY. Water vapor in the air. Of interest is the relative humidity expressed as percentage of what would saturate the air at a given temperature.

HUMUS. Decomposed remnants of organic matter in the soil, which undergoes further decomposition only very slowly and so exercises a rather lasting effect on soil properties.

HYBRID. A plant obtained by using pollen of one species on the stigma of another; or, more loosely, the product of crossing any two dissimilar plants.

INDIGENOUS (in-DIDGE-en-us). Native to a given area; not introduced.

INFLORESCENCE (in-flor-ESS-ence). Specialized leafless, flowering shoots.

INSECT. A six-legged organism that may attack and despoil plants.

INSECTICIDE. A chemical which kills insects.

LEAFLET. One part of a compound leaf.

LITTORAL (LIT-o-ral). Growing along the shore of a sea or lake.

LOAM. A very desirable soil for plants, composed of a mixture of clay, silt, sand, and organic matter.

MANUBRIUM (man-oo-bry-um). The long thin, more or less cylindrical base, of certain cymbas or palm spathes.

MARCOTTAGE (mar-cot-TAZH). The same as air-layering.

MARL. A gray soil of claylike particle size, consisting of calicum carbonate plus a little sand and organic matter, which is built of shells and ograsnisms of microscopic size in shallow seas.

MEDIUM. The material in which seeds, cuttings, or plants are placed.

MIDRIB. The main rib of a leaf, a continuation of the petiole.

MINOR ELEMENT. A mineral element needed by plants only in very small amounts, although no less essential than those needed in large amounts. Copper, zinc, iron, manganese, boron, molybdenum, chlorine, and perhaps sodium for some plants, are in this group.

GLOSSARY

MITE. An eight-legged organism that sucks plant juices from leaves.

MONOECIOUS (mon-EE-shus). Having separate male and female flowers on the same plant.

MULCH. A porous material covering the ground. Usually an organic mulch is meant, such as a layer of leaves, straw, pine needles or sawdust.

NEUTRAL. Of soil or water, being neither acid nor alkaline in reaction.

NODE. The part of a stem from which arises a leaf or branch.

NUTRIENT (NOO-tree-ent). A material supplying a chemical element needed by plants.

OBOVATE (OB-o-vate). The reverse of ovate; the terminal half broader than the basal.

o.c. On center.

OOLITE (o-o-lite). A very porous limestone composed of shells of small marine organisms cemented together; found in southern Florida and some adjacent islands.

ORGAN. One of the parts of a plant which has a definite function, as stem, root, or flower.

ORGANIC. As used to describe fertilizers and mulches, this means material derived from the bodies of plants or animals.

OVATE. Egg-shaped in outline; broadened in the basal half.

PALMAN (PAL-man). Undivided part of a palmate leaf between the petiole and segments of the blade.

PALMATE (PAL-mate). With leaf lobes, leaflets, or veins radiating from a common origin.

PANICLE (PAN-i-cal). A branched inflorescence, with flowers being developed toward the tips of the branches as they elongate.

PATIO (PAH-te-o). A courtyard or outdoor living room with enclosing walls.

PEDICELLATE (ped-DIS-sell-ate). Having a flower stalk or pedicel.

PEDUNCLE (PEA-dunk-cal). Stem of a flower-cluster or of a solitary flower when that flower is the remaining member of an inflorescence.

PEST. An organism which is injurious to plants, including bacteria, insects, mites, fungi, and rodents.

PESTICIDE. A chemical which kills pests.

PETAL (PET-al). One of the separate parts of the corolla.

PETIOLE (PET-ee-ole). The stalk of a leaf.

pH. (pee-aitch). A number expressing the degree of acidity or alkalinity of a soil or solution. 7.0 is the neutral point. Numbers decreasing from 7 indicate acidity; numbers higher than 7 indicate alkalinity.

PITH. The soft spongy central cylinder of a stem.

PINNA (PIN-a). A primary division or leaflet of a pinnate leaf.

PINNATE. Featherlike; a leaf which has leaflets arranged on both sides of a rachis.

PISTIL. The female organ of the flower, consisting of ovary, style, and stigma.

PISTILLATE (PIS-till-ate). Having a pistil but no stamens; thus a female flower or plant.

PLANTER OR PLANTER-BIN. A masonry box, raised above the grade, used for growing plants.

PLICATE (PLY-cate). Folded, as in a fan, or approaching this condition.

PLUMOSE (PLUME-ose). Plumy; feather-like.

POLLEN. The yellow dust contained in the anthers which must be deposited on stigmas for fertilization to take place. Pollen grains germinate on stigmas, producing tubes which carry male sex cells (sperms) down to unite with egg cells (female) in the ovule.

POLYGAMOUS (poll-IG-a-mus). Bearing unisexual and hermaphrodite flowers on the same plant.

PROXIMAL. Nearest to the point of attachment or reference.

PUBESCENT (pew-BESS-ent). Covered with hairs or fuzz.

RACEME (ray-SEAM). An elongated, indeterminate inflorescence with stalked flowers.

RACHIS (RAY-kiss). The main axis of a palm frond.

RECLINATE (WRECK-lin-ate). Reclining; bent down from the perpendicular.

RECURVED. Bent or curved downward or backward.

RHIZOME (RYE-zome). An underground stem, distinguished from a true root by the presence of nodes, buds, or scale-like leaves.

SALTDRIFT. Air laden with salt water vapor, coming ashore from ocean or gulf.
SCALE. An insect which, in its usual adult form, resembles a tiny bump or excrescence. The insect sucks juice from plant tissues.
SCALECIDE (SCALE-i-side). A chemical which kills scale insects.
SCANDENT (SKAN-dent). Climbing or scrambling without the use of tendrils.
SCAPE. A flower stem, usually leafless, but sometimes furnished with bracts.
SEEDLING. A plant which has been grown from seed.
SEGMENT. One of the parts of a leaf, that is divided but not truly compound.
SEPAL (SEE-pal). One of the parts of the calyx.
SERRATE (SER-ate). Saw-toothed; said of leaf margins.
SESSILE (SES-ill). Without a stalk or stem.
SPADIX (SPAY-dicks). A thick flower spike, subtended by a spathe.
SPATHE. A bract subtending a flower cluster.
SPATULATE (SPAT-you-late). Like a spatula blade in outline.
SPECIES (SPEE-shees). A kind of plant distinct from other kinds and reproducing its characteristics when self-pollinated. The second (usually uncapitalized) word in the scientific name of a plant.
SPHAGNUM (SFAG-numb). A type of moss growing in acid bogs and widely used in marcottage and in seed sowing because of its combination of good moisture holding, good aeration, and freedom from disease.
SPICULES (SPIC-yewls). Minute needle-like crystals.
SPIKE. As used here, a generalized term for an elongate flower cluster.
SPRAY. To apply a pesticide in water under pressure, to emerge as a spray.
STACHYS (STAY-kiss). In Greek compounds, signifying a spike.
STAMEN (STAY-men). The male organ in the flower, consisting of anther (containing pollen) and filament.
STAMINATE (STAM-in-ate). Flowers or plants having stamens but no pistils; male.
STIGMA. The tip of the pistil which receives pollen.
STOLON. A horizontal stem, at or below surface of the ground, that gives rise to a new plant at the tip.
STOMATA (STOH-mat-ta). Openings through the epidermal layer of leaves which allow internal air cavities to communicate with outside air.
STRAND. A shore, especially of the sea.
SUCCULENT (SUCK-you-lent). Juicy; used for plants characterized by the water-conserving and storing capacity of their stems, branches, and leaves.
SYRINGE (SEER-inge). To water plant foliage with a fine, misty spray.
TAXONOMY (tacks-ON-omy). The study of plant classification and relationship.
TERETE (tee-REET). Cylindrical and tapering; round in cross section.
TERMINAL. At the tip or apex.
TERRACE. A raised platform of earth, preferably paved with masonry.
TERRESTRIAL (ter-ES-tree-al). Earth-dwelling; growing in the ground as opposed to aerial or aquatic.
THRIPS. A tiny insect that may injure plants by sucking juices.
TOMENTOSE (TOE-men-tose). Densely wooly or pubescent; with matted soft hairs.
TRIGENERIC (tri-gen-ER-ic). A plant resulting from crosses involving three genera.
UBIQUITOUS (you-BICK-wit-us). Found everywhere; growing in a wide variety of habitats.
UNISEXUAL. Of one sex; staminate only or pistillate only.
VARIEGATED (VERY-e-gay-ted). Irregularly colored in patches; blotched.
VARIETY. A plant differing in minor characters from the type species.
VEGETATIVE. The portions of a plant other than the flowers and fruits, i.e., stem, leaves, and roots. Vegetative reproduction must involve plant parts other than seeds.
VIABLE. Alive; said of seeds capable of germinating.
VILLOUS (VIL-us). Provided with long and soft, not matted hairs; shaggy.
WHORL. The arrangement of three or more leaves, branches, or flowers at one node.
XEROPHYTE (ZARE-o-fite). A plant adapted to living under conditions of very little moisture, as a desert plant.

Index

Abelia grandiflora, 350
Acalypha spp., 191-92
Acer rubrum, 208
Achimenes spp., 328
Achras zapota, 276
Acrocomia spp., 28
Acti-dione, 355
Adam's needle, 91
adonidia palm, 42
Aechmea spp., 74
African milk-bush, 184
African tulip-tree, 323
Agave spp., 87
Aglaonema spp., 58-59
Albizia spp., 170-71
Alexandra palm, 43
algal leaf spot, 355
Allamanda spp., 289-90
almond, 245
Alocasia spp., 66-67
Aloe spp., 80-81
Alpinia spp., 103
Alsophila spp., 6
aluminum-plant, 117
American holly, 200-201
Amomum spp., 102

angel's trumpet, 315
anise-tree, 140
annatto, 232
Anthurium spp., 62-63
Antigonon leptopus, 126
ants, 355
Aphelandra spp., 330
aphids, 355
Arabian jasmine, 283
aralia, 260
Araucaria spp., 13-14
arbor-vitae, 20
Archontophoenix spp., 43
Ardisia spp., 273-74
areca palm, 40
Arecastrum romanzoffianum, 49
aroids, 52-69
Aspidistra elatior, 85
Asystasia gangetica, 331
Aucuba japonica, 269
Australian brush-cherry, 257
Australian-pine, 111
azalea defoliator, 355
azalea leaf-miner, 355
azalea petal blight, 355
azaleas, 270-72

bamboo palm, 40
banana, 97
banana-shrub, 139
Banks grevillea, 125
banyan tree, 121
Barbados flower-fence, 167
Bauhinia spp., 161
bear-grass, 91
Beaucarnea recurvata, 82
Beaumontia grandiflora, 291
beauty-berry, 308
Begonia spp., 230-31
bellyache bush, 193
Beloperone guttata, 340
benjamin fig, 122
Berberis spp., 133
BHC, 355
big-leaf sea-grape, 129
Billbergia spp., 72-73
bird-of-paradise flower, 100
Bischofia javanica, 197
Bixa orellana, 232
black-olive, 247
bleeding-heart glory-bower, 309
blood-leaf, 130
Bombax spp., 221
borers, 355
bo tree, 121
bottle-brush, 250-51
bottle palm, 50
Bougainvillea spp., 131
bowstring-hemp, 88-89
boxthorn, 176
boxwood, Japanese, 198
Brassaia actinophylla, 266
Brazilian pepper-tree, 199
Breynia nivosa, 190
bromeliads, 71-75
Bromelia pinguin, 75
bromels, 71-75
brush-cherry, 257
Bucida buceras, 247
Buddleja spp., 286
bugs, 355
bunya-bunya, 13
Bursera simaruba, 179
Butia capitata, 46
butterfly-bush, 286
Buxus microphylla, 198

cabbage palm, 34
cacti, 233-38
cajeput-tree, 252
Caladium spp., 65
calamondin. See *Citrus*

Calathea spp., 106-7
California pepper-tree, 199
Calliandra spp., 169
Callicarpa americana, 308
Callitris robusta, 15
Camellia spp., 224-26
camphor-tree, 141
Canary Island date palm, 36
candle-bush, 163
cane palm, 40
Cape-honeysuckle, 325
Cape-jasmine, 345
Cape Sable palm, 27
captan, 355
cardinals guard, 338
caricature plant, 337
Carissa spp., 294
Carolina yellow-jasmine, 285
Carpobrotus edulis, 132
Caryota spp., 39
Cassia spp., 163-64
cast-iron plant, 85
Casuarina spp., 111
cat-claw vine, 317
caterpillars, 355
Cattleya spp., 109
Cattley guava, 254
Cecropia spp., 123
Ceiba pentandra, 219
century plant, 86-87
Cephalotaxus harringtonia, 12
Cercis spp., 162
Cereus peruvianus, 238
Cestrum spp., 312-13
chalice-vine, 314
Chamaecyparis thyoides, 19
Chamaedorea spp., 47
Chamaerops humilis, 31
chaste-tree, 306
chenille-plant, 191
Cherokee-bean, 160
cherry-laurel, 157
China-berry, 180
China-fir, 16
Chinese elm, 118
Chinese evergreen, 59
Chinese fan palm, 33
Chinese fountain palm, 33
Chinese-hat-plant, 303
Chinese hibiscus, 217
Chinese holly, 202
Chinese photinia, 153
Chinese redbud, 162
Chionanthus virginica, 284
chlordane, 355

INDEX

chlorosis, 355
Christmas cactus, 233
Christmas-vine, 299
Christ thorn hybrids, 185
Chrysalidocarpus lutescens, 40
Chrysophyllum spp., 277
Cibotium spp., 6
Cinnamomum camphora, 141
Cissus spp., 211
citrus-leaved bottle-brush, 250
Citrus spp., 178
Clerodendrum spp., 309
Cleyera japonica, 227
cliff date palm, 37
climatic zones of Florida, viii
Clusia spp., 229
Clytostoma callistegioides, 318
Coccoloba spp., 128-29
Cocculus laurifolius, 135
cockspur coral-tree, 159
coconut palm, 45
Cocos australis, 46; *nucifera*, 45; *plumosa*, 49
Codiaeum variegatum, 195
Colocasia spp., 67
Combretum grandiflorum, 248
Confederate-jasmine, 292
Congea tomentosa, 310
Conocarpus erectus, 249
coontie, 8
copper fungicides, 355
copper-leaf, 192
coral ardisia, 273
coral-plant, 316
coral-tree, 159
coral-vine, 126
Cordia sebestena, 300
Cordyline terminalis, 96
Cornus florida, 268
coromandel, 331
Costus spp., 105
cottony cushion scales, 355
crab cactus, 233
crape-jasmine, 296
crape-myrtle, 241
Crassula spp., 143
creeping fig, 119
crickets, 355
Crossandra infundibuliformis, 329
croton, 194-95
crown-of-thorns, 185
Cryptanthus spp., 70-71
Cryptostegia spp., 297
Cuban-laurel, 122
Cuban royal palm, 41

Cunninghamia lanceolata, 16
Cuphea hyssopifolia, 243
Cupressus spp., 17-18
Cyathea spp., 6
Cycas spp., 7
Cygon, 355
Cyperus spp., 51
Cyrtomium falcatum, 4

dahoon, 204
Dalbergia sissoo, 172
date palms, 36-38
Datura spp., 315
day cestrum, 313
DDT, 355
Delonix regia, 166
Dendrobium spp., 109
devils-backbone, 189
Diazinon, 355
Dicksonia spp., 6
Dieffenbachia spp., 56
Dieldrin, 355
Dithane, 355
Dizygotheca kerchoveana, 261
dogwood, 268
Dombeya wallichii, 222
downy jasmine, 283
downy-myrtle, 255
Doxantha unguis-cati, 317
Dracaena spp., 95
dracena, 94-95
Duranta repens, 304
dwarf century plant, 86
dwarf elm, 118
dwarf lily-turf, 84

earthworms, 355
ear-tree, 173
Elaeagnus spp., 239-40
elephant-ear, 66-67
elm, 118
Enterolobium cyclocarpum, 173
Epidendrum spp., 109
Epiphyllum spp., 236
Episcia spp., 326-27
Eranthemum nervosum, 334
Eriobotrya japonica, 155
Ervatamia coronaria, 296
Erythrina spp., 159-60
Eugenia spp., 256-57
Euphorbia spp., 185-88
European fan palm, 31
Eurya japonica, 228
everglade palm, 27

364 INDEX

false aralia, 261
fancy-leaved caladium, 65
Fatshedera, 263, 265
Fatsia japonica, 263
Feijoa sellowiana, 253
ferbam, 355
fern podocarpus, 9
ferns, 2-6
Ficus spp., 119-22
fiddle-leaf fig, 121
fig: benjamin, 122; creeping, 119; Cuban-laurel, 122; fiddle-leaf, 121; laurel, 122; lofty, 121
Fiji fan palm, 35
fire blight, 355
firespike, 335
firethorn, 152
fishtail palm, 39
flame-vine, 320; Mexican, 351
Florida anise-tree, 140
Floridian royal palm, 41
flowering-banana, 99
flowering dogwood, 268
formalin, 355
Fortunella spp., 178
frangipani, 288
fringed hibiscus, 215
fringe-tree, 284
fungicides, 355

galingale, 51
gallberry, 207
Gardenia spp., 345
garden pests, 355
garden plan, 353
Geiger-tree, 300
Gelsemium sempervirens, 285
ginger, variegated, 101
ginger-lily, 104
gingerworts, 101-5
glory-bower, 309
glory-bush, 259
glossary, 356-60
glossy abelia, 350
glossy privet, 279
golden-dewdrop, 304
goldenrain-tree, 210
golden-shower, 164
gopher trap, 355
grapefruit. See *Citrus*
grape-ivy, 211
Graptophyllum pictum, 337
grasshoppers, 355
Grevillea spp., 124-25
gru-gru palm, 28

guava, 254
gumbo-limbo, 179

Hamelia patens, 344
Harland boxwood, 198
Hedera spp., 265
hedge cactus, 238
Hedychium spp., 104
Heliconia spp., 99
heralds-trumpet, 291
Hibiscus spp., 214-18
holly: American, 201; Chinese, 202; da-hoon, 204; gallberry, 207; Japanese, 206; round, 203; yaupon, 205
holly malpighia, 182
holly osmanthus, 278
Holmskioldia sanguinea, 303
Homalocladium platycladum, 127
honeysuckle: Japanese, 349; trumpet, 349
Hong Kong orchid-tree, 161
Hottentot-fig, 132
household palms, 47
house holly-fern, 4
Howeia spp., 48
Hoya carnosa, 298
Hydrangea spp., 146-47
Hylocereus undatus, 237

Ilex spp., 201-7
Illicium spp., 140
India-hawthorn, 156
Indian azalea, 272
insecticides, 355
insects, 355
Iresine lindenii, 130
Italian cypress, 18
ivies, 264-65
ivy-arum, 61
Ixora spp., 341

Jacaranda acutifolia, 324
Jacobinia spp., 339
jade-plant, 142-43
Japanese barberry, 133
Japanese boxwood, 198
Japanese holly, 206
Japanese honeysuckle, 349
Japanese juniper, 22
Japanese plum-yew, 12
Japanese privet, 280
japonica, 225
jasmine: Arabian, 283; cape, 345; Carolina yellow-, 285; Confederate-, 292; crape-, 296; downy, 283; orange-, 177; primrose, 281; river, 282; star, 283

Jasminum spp., 281-83
Jatropha spp., 193, 196
jelly palm, 46
Jerusalem-thorn, 165
juniper: Japanese, 22; Pfitzer, 24; shore, 23; southern red, 21
Juniperus spp., 21-24

Kalanchoë spp., 144-45
karanda, 294
Karathane, 355
Kelthane, 355
kentia. See *Howeia*
Kigelia pinnata, 321
Koelreuteria formosana, 210
kopsia. See *Ochrosia*
kumquat. See *Citrus*
Kurume azalea, 271

lace bugs, 355
lady palm, 29
Lagerstroemia spp., 241-42
landscape plan, 353
lantana: common, 301; weeping, 302
Lantana spp., 301-2
large-leaf ficus, 121
laurel oak, 115
laurestinus, 347
leaf-gall fungi, 355
leaf-miners, 355
leaf-spot fungi, 355
leather-leaf fern, 5
lemon. See *Citrus*
Licuala grandis, 26
Ligustrum spp., 279-80
lily-turf, 83
lime. See *Citrus*
lime-berry, 175
lindane, 355
lingaro, 240
Liriope spp., 83
Litchi chinensis, 209
live oak, 116
Livistona chinensis, 33
lobster-claw, 99
lofty fig, 121
Lonicera spp., 349
loquat, 155
Loropetalum chinense, 149
lucky nut, 287
lychee, 209

MacArthur palm, 44
Madagascar palm, 40
magnolia, 138; Oriental, 137; saucer, 137; starry, 136

Magnolia spp., 136-38
mahogany, 181
malathion, 355
Malay ixora, 341
Malpighia coccigera, 182
Malvaviscus arboreus, 212
Manila palm, 42
maple, red, 208
marlberry, 274
Mascarena spp., 50
mealy-bugs, 355
Melaleuca leucadendra, 252
Melia azedarach, 180
Merrill palm, 42
Mexican flame-vine, 351
Michelia fuscata, 139
mildew, 355
milkstripe euphorbia, 186
mimosa-tree, 171
mistletoe cactus, 234-35
mites, 355
model plan, 353
mole-crickets, 355
moles, 355
mole trap, 355
Monstera spp., 57
mountain-ebony, 161
Murraya paniculata, 177
Musa spp., 97
mushroom root-rot, 355
Myrica cerifera, 114
myrtle, 258
Myrtus communis, 258

nagi, 10
Nandina domestica, 134
Natal-plum, 294
native azaleas, 270
Neanthe bella. See *Chamaedorea*
Nemagon, 355
nematodes, 355
Nerium oleander, 293
New Zealand flax, 90
nicotine sulphate, 355
night-blooming cereus, 237
night cestrum, 313
nightshade: Brazilian, 311; Costa Rican, 311; jasmine, 311
Norfolk-Island-pine, 14

oak: laurel, 115; live, 116
oak-leaf hydrangea, 146
Ochrosia elliptica, 295
Odontonema strictum, 335
oil, summer spray, 355

oleander, 293
oleander moth larvae, 355
Oncidium spp., 109
Ophiopogon spp., 84
orange cestrum, 312
orange dogs, 355
orange-jasmine, 177
orange trees. See *Citrus*
orchid cactus, 236
orchids, 108-10
orchid-trees, 161
Oriental arbor-vitae, 20
Osmanthus spp., 278
oyster-plant, 78

Pachira spp., 220
Pachystachys coccinea, 338
painted-trumpet, 318
Palay rubber-vine, 297
palm: adonidia, 42; Alexandra, 43; bottle, 50; cabbage, 34; Canary Island date, 36; cane, 40; Cape Sable, 27; Chinese fan, 33; Chinese fountain, 33; cliff date, 37; coconut, 45; European fan, 31; Fiji fan, 35; fishtail, 39; gru-gru, 28; household, 47; kentia, 48; lady, 29; MacArthur, 44; Madagascar, 40; Manila, 42; paurotis, 27; pests of, 355; pindo, 46; pygmy date, 38; queen, 49; royal, 41; Seaforthia, 44; Senegal date, 37; sentry, 48; Thurston fan, 35; Washington, 32; windmill, 30; wine, 39
palmetto, cabbage, 34
palm leaf skeletonizer, 355
palm weevil, 355
Pandanus spp., 25
pandorea, 319
paper bark tree, 252
papyrus, 51
paradise poinciana, 168
Parkinsonia aculeata, 165
Paurotis wrightii, 27
Pedilanthus tithymaloides, 189
pencil-tree, 187
Pentas lanceolata, 343
Peperomia spp., 112-13
pest control guide, 355
pesticides, 355
petal blight, azalea, 355
Petrea volubilis, 305
Pfitzer juniper, 24
Phaeomeria speciosa, 102
Phaius spp., 110
Phalaenopsis spp., 109
Phaltan, 355

Philodendron spp., 52-55
Phoenix spp., 36-38
Phormium tenax, 90
Photinia spp., 153-54
physic nut, 193
pigeon-plum, 128
Pilea cadierei, 117
pindo palm, 46
pine cone-lily, 101
pinguin, 75
pink-ball, 222
pink-shower, 164
pitanga, 256
pitch-apple, 229
pith borer, 355
Pittosporum spp., 148
Platycerium spp., 3
Plumbago capensis, 275
Plumeria spp., 288
plum-yew, 12
pocket gophers, 355
Podocarpus spp., 9-11
Podranea ricasoliana, 319
Poinciana spp., 167-68
poinsettia, 188
poison bran bait, 355
Polyscias balfouriana, 260
Polystichum spp., 5
pomegranate, 244
pongam, 174
Pongamia pinnata, 174
pony-tail, 82
Porana paniculata, 299
portia-tree, 213
Portuguese cypress, 17
potato vines, 311
powderpuff, 169
primrose jasmine, 281
princess-flower, 259
Pritchardia spp., 35
privets, 279-80
Prunus caroliniana, 157
Pseuderanthemum spp., 336
Psidium cattleianum, 254
Ptychosperma spp., 44
Punica granatum, 244
purple allamanda, 290
purple cestrum, 312
pygmy date palm, 38
Pyracantha coccinea, 152
Pyrostegia ignea, 320

queen crape-myrtle, 242
queen palm, 49
queen sago, 7

INDEX

queens-wreath, 305
Quercus spp., 115-16
Quisqualis indica, 246

Rangoon-creeper, 246
Ravenala madagascariensis, 98
red bauhinia, 161
redbud, 162
red-cedar, 21
red-cotton-tree, 221
red-hot cattail, 191
red-leaf photinia, 154
red maple, 208
red spiders, 355
Reeves spirea, 151
Rex begonia, 230-31
Rhaphiolepis spp., 156
Rhapis spp., 29
Rhipsalis spp., 235
Rhododendron spp., 270-72
Rhodomyrtus tomentosa, 255
Rhoeo discolor, 78
ribbon-bush, 127
rice-paper plant, 262
ringworm cassia, 163
roaches, 355
rose-of-Sharon, 218
round holly, 203
royal palm, 41
royal poinciana, 166
Roystonea spp., 41
rubber-plant, 121; -tree, 121
rubber-vine, 297
Russelia equisetiformis, 316
rusty blackhaw, 346

Sabal spp., 34
sago "palm," 7
Sanchezia nobilis, 333
sandankwa viburnum, 346
Sansevieria spp., 89
sapodilla, 276
sasanqua camellia, 226
satin-leaf, 277
satsuma. See *Citrus*
saucer magnolia, 137
sausage-tree, 321
scale insects, 355
scarlet-bush, 344
schefflera, 266
Schinus spp., 100
Schismatoglottis picta, 60
Schlumbergera spp., 233
Scindapsus spp., 61

screw-pine, 25
Seaforthia palm, 44
sea-grape, 128
sea hibiscus, 214
self-heading philodendron, 54-55
Senecio confusus, 351
Senegal date palm, 37
sentry palms, 48
Serissa foetida, 342
Setcreasea spp., 77
Severinia buxifolia, 176
Sevin, 355
shaving-brush-trees, 220
shell-flower, 103
shining jasmine, 282
shore juniper, 23
shower-of-gold tree, 164
shrimp-plant, 340
Siberian elm, 118
silk-oak, 124
silver button-bush, 249
silverthorn, 239
sissoo, 172
slipper-flower, 189
snow-bush, 190
Solandra spp., 314
Solanum spp., 311
sooty-mold, 355
Soulange magnolia, 137
southern red-cedar, 21
southern wax-myrtle, 114
Spanish bayonet, 92
Spathiphyllum spp., 64
Spathodea campanulata, 323
spindle palm, 50
spineless yucca, 93
Spiraea spp., 150-51
spiral-flag, 105
spirea, 150-51
Spironema fragrans, 79
spittlebugs, 355
squirrels, 355
staghorn-fern, 2-3
star-apple, 277
starry magnolia, 136
Strelitzia spp., 100
Strobilanthes dyerianus, 332
sulfur, 355
Surinam-cherry, 256
sweet-olive, 278
sweet viburnum, 348
Swietenia mahogani, 181
Swiss-cheese plant, 57
Synadenium grantii, 184
Syngonium spp., 68-69

Tabebuia spp., 322
tangelo. See *Citrus*
tangerine. See *Citrus*
tea, 223
tea-olive, 278
tea scales, 355
Tecomaria capensis, 325
Tedion, 355
Terminalia spp., 245
Tetrapanax papyriferus, 262
Thea sinensis, 223
Thespesia populnea, 213
Thevetia peruviana, 287
thornbugs, 355
thrips, 355
Thryallis glauca, 183
Thuja orientalis, 20
Thunberg spirea, 150
ti, 96
Tibouchina semidecandra, 259
toog, 197
torch-ginger, 102
toxaphene, 355
Trachelospermum jasminoides, 292
Trachycarpus fortunei, 30
Tradescantia spp., 76
travelers-tree, 98
tree fern, 6
Trevesia spp., 267
Triphasia trifolia, 175
trithion, 355
tropical-almond, 245
trumpet honeysuckle, 349
Turks-cap, 212
Turks-turban, 309
twin live oak, 116

Ulmus spp., 118
umbrella-plant, 51

Vanda spp., 110
VC 13, 355
Veitchia merrillii, 42
Viburnum spp., 346-48
vining philodendron, 52-53
Vitex spp., 306-7

wandering-Jew, 76
Washingtonia spp., 32
wax-myrtle, 114
wax-plant, 298
wax privet, 280
Wedelia trilobata, 352
weeping bottle-brush, 250
weeping lantana, 302
white-cedar, 19
white-flies, 355
wild plantain, 99
windmill palm, 30
wine palm, 39
wintergreen barberry, 133
Wisteria sinensis, 158
womans-tongue-tree, 170
woolly congea, 310

Xanthosoma spp., 67

yaupon, 205
Yeddo-hawthorn, 156
yellow palm, 40
yew podocarpus, 11
Yucca spp., 91-93

Zamia floridana, 8
Zebrina spp., 76
Zingiber zerumbet, 101
zones, Florida gardeners', viii
Zygocactus spp., 233

Bud
Leaf Blade
Petiole
Stipule
Stem

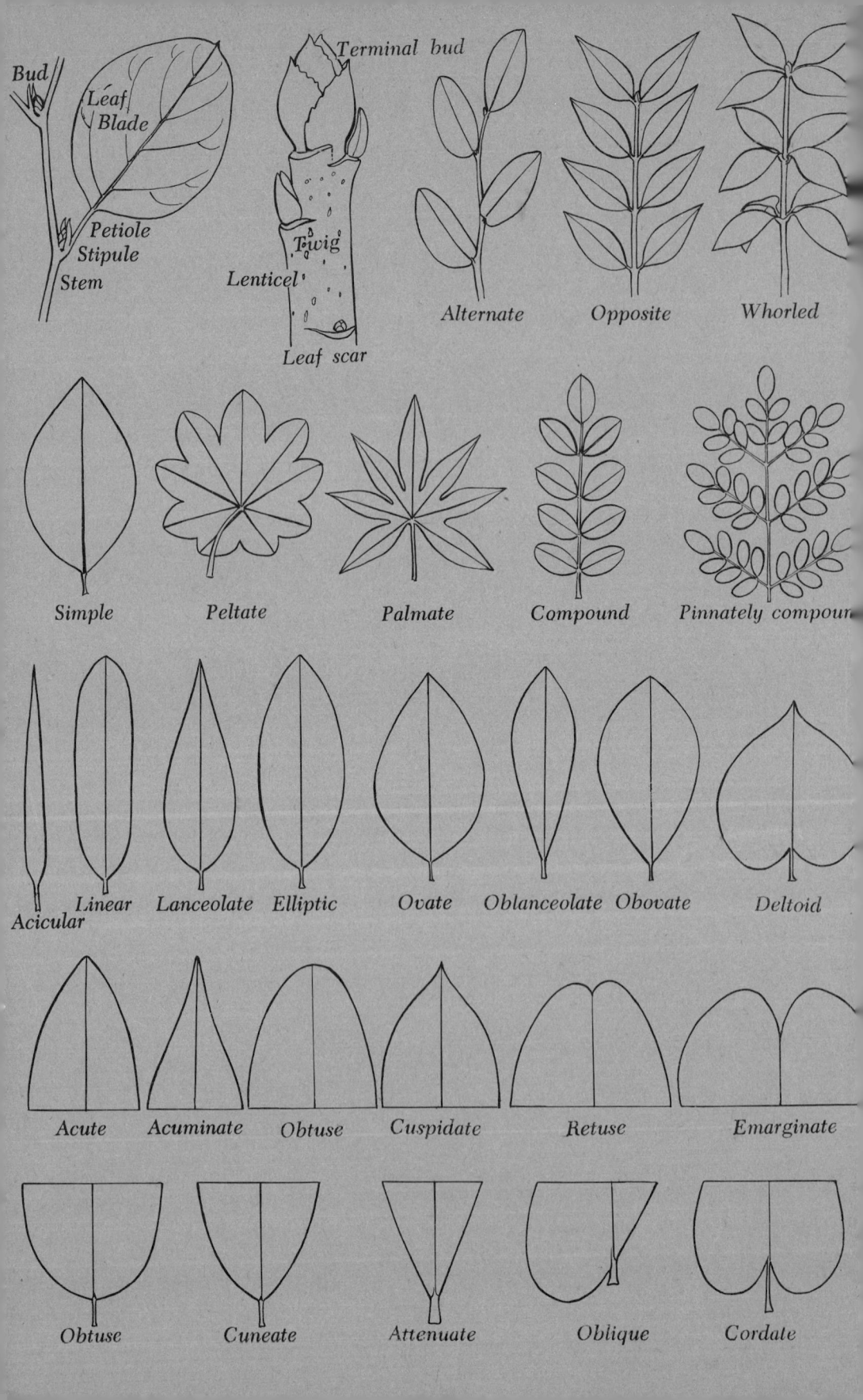

Terminal bud
Twig
Lenticel
Leaf scar

Alternate *Opposite* *Whorled*

Simple *Peltate* *Palmate* *Compound* *Pinnately compound*

Acicular *Linear* *Lanceolate* *Elliptic* *Ovate* *Oblanceolate* *Obovate* *Deltoid*

Acute *Acuminate* *Obtuse* *Cuspidate* *Retuse* *Emarginate*

Obtuse *Cuneate* *Attenuate* *Oblique* *Cordate*